TOWARD A *Female Genealogy* OF *Transcendentalism*

TOWARD A *Female Genealogy* OF *Transcendentalism*

EDITED BY
Jana L. Argersinger
AND *Phyllis Cole*

The University of Georgia Press
ATHENS AND LONDON

Athens, Georgia 30602
www.ugapress.org

Designed by Kaelin Chappell Broaddus
Set in 10/13 Dante Std by Graphic Composition, Inc.
Manufactured by Thomson-Shore
The paper in this book meets the guidelines for permanence and durability of the Committee on Production Guidelines for Book Longevity of the Council on Library Resources.

Most University of Georgia Press titles are available from popular e-book vendors.

Printed in the United States of America
14 15 16 17 18 P 5 4 3 2 1

Library of Congress Cataloging-in-Publication Data
Toward a female genealogy of transcendentalism / edited by Jana L. Argersinger and Phyllis Cole.
pages cm
Includes bibliographical references and index.
ISBN 978-0-8203-4339-6 (hardcover : alk. paper) —
ISBN 0-8203-4339-0 (hardcover : alk. paper) —
ISBN 978-0-8203-4677-9 (pbk. : alk. paper) —
ISBN 0-8203-4677-2 (pbk. : alk. paper)
1. American literature—19th century—History and criticism.
2. American essays—Women authors—History and criticism.
3. Transcendentalism in literature. 4. Women and literature—United States—History—19th century. 5. Transcendentalism (New England)
I. Argersinger, Jana L., 1957– editor of compilation.
II. Cole, Phyllis, editor of compilation.
PS217.T7.T69 2014
810.9'384—dc23
2014001808

British Library Cataloging-in-Publication Data available

ALL CONTRIBUTORS
JOIN IN DEDICATING
THIS COLLECTION
TO THE MEMORY OF
Charlie Argersinger
1951–2013.

Contents

Primary Interludes

Acknowledgments

This project celebrates a web of genealogical relations across years and miles, and it comes to birth through an extraordinary community of present-day scholars. We would like to thank all who proposed papers, the specialist readers we enlisted to provide constructive criticism of work-in-progress, and the authors whose insights and dedicated labors led to chapters in this collection. At the University of Georgia Press, Nancy Grayson sought out this work and joined the editors in imagining its reality, and since her retirement Sydney Dupre and Walter Biggins have sustained that commitment without hesitation. Kay Kodner's copyediting in the last phase made the text tighter and more consistent. Our gratitude to them all, as well as to the press's three anonymous readers who saw the potential of this enterprise and helped bring it to fruition.

We appreciate the knowledge and generosity of those who offered newly discovered and little-known texts for "Primary Interludes"—not only our authors but also Bruce Mills with Lydia Maria Child, Elizabeth Stockton and Jennifer Putzi with Elizabeth Stoddard, Jennifer Gurley with Ellen Sturgis Hooper, and Albert von Frank with Margaret Fuller (in the *Liberty Bell*). We thank the libraries and librarians whose care for rare books and manuscripts—as well as the scholars seeking them out—have made this collective work of recovery and interpretation possible.

Importantly, *ESQ: A Journal of the American Renaissance* granted permission to include extended versions of four essays that appeared in the 2011 special issue "Exaltadas: A Female Genealogy of Transcendentalism"—those by Katherine Adams, Noelle Baker, Dorri Beam, and Laura Dassow Walls—a generative courtesy at the core of this volume. As the special issue developed, the efforts of Tanya Gonzales, Amber LaPiana, Aaron Moe, and James Trout were invaluable.

Phyllis Cole would like to acknowledge the extraordinary setting and community of the University of Connecticut Humanities Institute, where she completed a major portion of her work for this project while an External Fellow during the 2011–12 academic year. For their support both before and after that, thanks are especially due to the people and resources of Penn State Brandywine—indefatigable reference librarians, administrators who support sabbatical ventures, and colleagues and students with kindred passion for research.

Abbreviations for Frequently Cited Texts

PRIMARY SOURCES

CW	*The Collected Works of Ralph Waldo Emerson*, ed. Alfred R. Ferguson and Joseph Slater et al., 10 vols. (Cambridge, Mass.: Harvard Univ. Press, Belknap Press, 1971–2013).
EMF	*The Essential Margaret Fuller*, ed. Jeffrey Steele (New Brunswick, N.J.: Rutgers Univ. Press, 1992).
"GL"	Margaret Fuller, "The Great Lawsuit. Man *versus* Men. Woman *versus* Women," *Dial* 4 (1843–44): 1–47.
JMN	*The Journals and Miscellaneous Notebooks of Ralph Waldo Emerson*, ed. William H. Gilman and Ralph H. Orth et al., 16 vols. (Cambridge, Mass.: Harvard Univ. Press, Belknap Press, 1960–82).
LE	*The Letters of Ralph Waldo Emerson*, ed. Ralph L. Rusk and Eleanor Tilton, 10 vols. (New York: Columbia Univ. Press, 1939–96).
LEPP	*Letters of Elizabeth Palmer Peabody: American Renaissance Woman*, ed. Bruce Ronda (Middletown, Conn.: Wesleyan Univ. Press, 1984).
LMF	*The Letters of Margaret Fuller*, ed. Robert Hudspeth, 6 vols. (Ithaca, N.Y.: Cornell Univ. Press, 1983–94).
MFC	*Margaret Fuller, Critic: Writings from the "New-York Tribune," 1844–1846*, ed. Judith Mattson Bean and Joel Myerson (New York: Columbia Univ. Press, 2000).
MMFO	*Memoirs of Margaret Fuller Ossoli*, ed. James Freeman Clarke, Ralph Waldo Emerson, and W. H. Channing, 2 vols. (Boston: Phillips, Sampson, 1852).
SL	Margaret Fuller, *Summer on the Lakes, in 1843*, ed. Susan Belasco Smith (Urbana: Univ. of Illinois Press, 1991).
WHT	*The Writings of Henry D. Thoreau*, 22 vols. to date (Princeton: Princeton Univ. Press, 1971–2013).
WNC	Margaret Fuller, *Woman in the Nineteenth Century: An Authoritative Text, Backgrounds, Criticism*, ed. Larry Reynolds (New York: Norton, 1998).

ARCHIVES

MHi	Massachusetts Historical Society.
MH-H	Houghton Library, Harvard University.

SECONDARY SOURCES

Capper 1	Charles Capper, *Margaret Fuller: An American Romantic Life*, vol. 1, *The Private Years* (New York: Oxford Univ. Press, 1992).
Capper 2	Charles Capper, *Margaret Fuller: An American Romantic Life*, vol. 2, *The Public Years* (New York: Oxford Univ. Press, 2007).
Capper and Wright	*Transient and Permanent: The Transcendentalist Movement and Its Contexts*, ed. Charles Capper and Conrad Edick Wright (Boston: Massachusetts Historical Society, 1999).
Elbert, Hall, and Rodier	*Reinventing the Peabody Sisters*, ed. Monika M. Elbert, Julie E. Hall, and Katharine Rodier (Iowa City: Univ. of Iowa Press, 2006).
Gura	Philip Gura, *American Transcendentalism: A History* (New York: Hill & Wang, 2007).
Marshall	Megan Marshall, *The Peabody Sisters: Three Women Who Ignited American Romanticism* (Boston: Houghton Mifflin, 2005).
OxH	*The Oxford Handbook of Transcendentalism*, ed. Joel Myerson, Sandra Harbert Petrulionis, and Laura Dassow Walls (New York: Oxford Univ. Press, 2010).
Ronda	*Elizabeth Palmer Peabody: A Reformer on Her Own Terms*, ed. Bruce Ronda (Cambridge, Mass.: Harvard Univ. Press, 1999).
Wayne	Tiffany K. Wayne, *Woman Thinking: Feminism and Transcendentalism in Nineteenth-Century America* (Lanham, Md.: Lexington Books, 2005).
Zwarg	Christina Zwarg, *Feminist Conversations: Fuller, Emerson, and the Play of Reading* (Ithaca, N.Y.: Cornell Univ. Press, 1995).

TOWARD A

Female Genealogy

OF *Transcendentalism*

PRELUDE

Lydia Maria Child, from Letter 13, in *Letters from New York, Second Series* (New York: C. S. Francis, 1845), 125–30.

April 24th, 1844.

You ask me what *is* transcendentalism, and what do transcendentalists believe? It is a question difficult, nay, impossible, to answer; for the minds so classified are incongruous individuals, without any creed. The name is in fact applied to everything new, strange, and unaccountable. If a man is a nonconformist to established creeds and opinions, and expresses his dissent in a manner ever so slightly peculiar, he is called a transcendentalist. It is indeed amusing to see how easily one may acquire this title. A southern lady lately said to a friend of mine, "I knew you were a transcendentalist the first half hour I heard you talk." "How so?" inquired my friend. "Oh, it is easy enough to be seen by your peculiar phrases." "Indeed! I had thought my language was very plain and natural. Pray what transcendental phrase have I used?" "The first time I ever saw you, you spoke of a person at the North as unusually *gifted*; and I have often since heard you use other transcendental expressions."

If you wish to know the origin of the word transcendentalism, I will explain it, briefly and simply, as I understand it.

All, who know anything of the different schools of metaphysics, are aware that the philosophy of John Locke was based on the proposition that *all* knowledge is received into the soul through the medium of the senses; and thence passes to be judged of and analyzed by the understanding.

The German school of metaphysics, with the celebrated Kant at its head, rejects this proposition as false; it denies that all knowledge is received through the senses, and maintains that the highest, and therefore most universal truths, are revealed within the soul, to a faculty *transcending* the understanding. This faculty they call pure Reason; it being peculiar to them to use that word in contradistinction to the Understanding. To this pure Reason, which some of their writers call "The God within," they believe that all perceptions of the Good, the True, and the Beautiful, are revealed, in its unconscious quietude; and that the province of the Understanding, with its five handmaids, the Senses, is confined merely to external things, such as facts, scientific laws, &c. This idea of an inwardly revealing faculty, *transcending* mere intellectual perception, will naturally remind many of the "inward voice," believed in by the Society of Friends. . . .

[But] there is slight resemblance between Quakers and Transcendentalists. The former abjure imagination and the Arts, and love to enclose everything within prescribed rules and regulations. The latter luxuriate in the beautiful, and their theories are so expansive and indefinite, that they remind one of the old story of transmigration, in which a philosopher, being asked what form he would like to have his disembodied soul enter, answered, "Form in general; no form in particular."

But the doctrine of perpetual revelation, heard in the quietude of the soul, produces one similar result in both. Neither of them favour the activity of reforms. The Quaker wishes "Israel to remain in his tents;" his cure for evils is to "keep in the quiet." The transcendentalist phrases it otherwise; he advises "to lie still in the spiritual sunshine, and grow." Neither are fond of the maxim, that "action strikes fiery *light* from the rocks it has to hew through." . . .

New-York is in too much of a hurry scurry all the time, to "lie still in the sunshine" and ripen such fruit as either transcendental philosophy, or its poverty-stricken imitations. It never enters into the head of a Wall-street merchant, that he is, as a friend of ours asserts, "personally responsible for the obliquity of the earth's axis."

"Transcendental muslins" I have often seen advertised in the Bowery; but I have rarely met with transcendentalism in any other form, in this city. I did once, out of pure mischief, send a politician and an active man of business to a house, where I knew they would encounter three or four of these disciples, who occasionally ride a pretty high horse. When they came back, I asked with a sober face, what they had talked about. They said they did not know; but being unmercifully urged to tell something that was said, the politician at last answered: "One of them divided man into three states; the disconscious, the conscious, and the unconscious. The *dis*conscious is the state of a pig; the conscious is the baptism by water; and the *un*conscious is the baptism by fire." "How did the conversation impress your mind?" said I, restraining a smile. "Why, after I had heard them talk a few minutes," replied he, "I'll be hanged if I knew whether I *had* any mind." . . .

I am sometimes called a transcendentalist myself, perhaps because I sometimes use the phrase "highly gifted." But I acknowledged considerable sympathy with the perplexed politician and man of business. For there are people, very intellectual ones too, who mystify me in the strangest fashion. After talking with them, my spirit always has to bite its finger, to know whether it exists or not; and even then, the question arises whether a sensation *is* a sensation. As for the received axiom that "a thing cannot *be* and *not* be, at the same time," they always set it twirling.

If asked to explain themselves, they answer with Jean Paul, "probably God knows what I meant, but I have forgotten."

Introduction

PHYLLIS COLE, WITH JANA ARGERSINGER

Lydia Maria Child's gently satiric portrait of the transcendentalists, first written for the *National Anti-Slavery Standard*, shows her capacity to think both inside and outside their domain. As she acknowledged, she could identify with people who derived their powers from the "God within," who valued beauty and spiritual growth, and she certainly understood the intellectual origins of their movement. But in the spring of 1844 this daughter of Boston also spoke as a commonsense New York journalist whose spirit wanted to "bite its finger" at such mysticism. Indeed her thoughts had been prompted by conversation with a skeptical "southern lady"; her cultural world had widened. But even more, readers knew that her column in the *Standard* spoke regularly against slavery and urban injustice. With a commitment beyond this whimsical humor, she regularly affirmed the value of action that "strikes fiery *light* from the rocks it has to hew through," and she did not see such action resulting from the transcendentalists' passive attunement to the spirit.

Child's portrait aptly introduces our collective study of women and transcendentalism, all the more for its complexity of allegiance. Yet before the end of 1844 her description of the movement would be surpassed by her colleague Margaret Fuller. Migrating like Child from Boston to New York to pursue a journalistic career, Fuller first completed her feminist manifesto, *Woman in the Nineteenth Century*, for publication as a book.[1] In it she articulated the power of inward transcendence with passion rather than whimsy, and she went beyond evoking women's conversation about the God within to redefining their history and future possibility on its strength. Fuller named male and female exemplars of the coming era "Los Exaltados, Las Exaltadas," constructing from the masculine title of a Spanish political party a term to describe utopian womanhood. Most of all, she saw no barrier between spirit and action, but rather an imperative moving from one to the other in response to immediate political crisis. "Last week" had brought news of James Polk's election as president, along with the ominous prospect that the people's choice would "rivet the chains of slavery and the leprosy of sin permanently on this nation" by annexing Texas. It was in the face of such apostasy by the voting public that Fuller addressed *her* readers as bearers of moral force:

> Women of my country!—Exaltadas! if such there be, . . . have you nothing to do with this? You see the men, how they are willing to sell shamelessly, the happiness of countless generations of fellow-creatures, the honor of their country, and their immortal souls, for a money market and political power. Do you not feel within you that which can reprove them, which can check, which can convince them? You would not speak in vain; whether each in her own home, or banded in unison.[2]

Instead of a meditation on the transcendentalist movement, Fuller offered a rhetorical enactment and transformation within it. The need of a slaveholding nation called forth women's power of prophetic speech and action.

Child's and Fuller's respective thoughts, however, grow in significance when seen in dialogue, both with each other and amid a network of friends. In the spring of 1844 Fuller had written to Louisa Loring, an abolitionist and participant in her Boston Conversations, resisting the plea to speak out on Texas and slavery. "I don't feel ready," she commented in her journal. Six months later her readiness had grown through continued listening to surrounding voices. And Child recognized the resulting power of *Woman in the Nineteenth Century*: "It is a *bold* book," she wrote to Loring after its publication. Fuller's antislavery appeal had proved a "noble testimony," and even more her probing of women's condition and potential was "brave," beyond any daring Child herself could muster.[3] Also a onetime participant in Fuller's Conversations, she recognized a pronouncement of shared and ongoing influence.

Exaltadas

Fuller's call to her readers as "Exaltadas" has multiple resonances within the larger history of transcendentalism: she offers a cosmopolitan allusion with American application, directs utopian imagination into the present political moment, and appeals urgently to readers to change themselves and the world. In all these respects, "Exaltadas" represents a claim *for women* as possessors of a high, quasi-divine consciousness and truth-telling power "within." It was a claim that intervened powerfully in the larger histories both of the transcendentalist movement and of women as thinkers and actors.

Our aim is to discover, within those longer historical lines, more voices and dialogues of the sort that Child and Fuller exemplify. The seventeen essays gathered here extend through a range of female predecessors, contemporaries, and heirs of transcendentalism who contributed to it singly or in relationship, with or without Fuller's mediation. One disciple, Ednah Dow Cheney, testified of Fuller in 1895, "She planted in my life the seeds of thought, principle, and purpose which have grown with my growth, and strengthened with my strength." Yet Cheney insisted on the contributions of others in a generation of burgeoning intellectual life, naming Child as well as Elizabeth Palmer Peabody, Catharine Sedgwick, Sophia Ripley, Eliza Farnham, and Eliza Cabot Follen among the "fellow-workers."[4] To these we might add women of the previous generation like Mary Moody Emerson and Sarah Bradford Ripley; contemporaries like Sophia Peabody, Caroline and Ellen Sturgis, Sarah Clarke, Marianne Dwight, and Elizabeth Oakes Smith; as well as a host of heirs including Caroline Dall, Julia Ward Howe, Charlotte Forten, Edmonia Highgate, Louisa May Alcott, Margaret Sweat, and Cheney herself. In parallel with other scholars who have recently extended the timeline of the movement from core moments in the 1830s and 1840s, we open this study of transcendentalism to a full century—reaching not only through the end of Elizabeth Peabody's movement-spanning life but, more unexpectedly, into the heart of Mary Wilkins Freeman's and Pauline Hopkins's era.[5]

This is a project in archaeology and reinterpretation. Well over half of the authors engage with newly recovered or rarely consulted manuscripts and printed texts, and all advance fresh perspectives on understudied subjects. In addition, the primary interludes between essays offer textual moments, like Child's essay, not represented in recent editions or anthologies. Though online sources and means of searching them have vastly expanded our access to archives, there is still value in highlighting new finds, and in turn archival expansion serves the goal of advancing a collective history. The project charts such directions while integrating work already accomplished. For over thirty years, a veritable scholarly industry has been widening the base for understanding transcendentalism, even as the women's studies movement has overturned the canon with its body of recovery work. At times these currents of scholarship apparently stood in opposition, discovering antagonistic nineteenth-century cultures. We hope to move beyond such a standoff. Starting in the late 1970s with Margaret Fuller, scholars attuned to both kinds of work have recognized individual women participating in the transcendentalist movement or influenced by it; our bibliography attempts to acknowledge and make more widely available the resources they provide.[6]

Inquiry into the larger contribution of women to the movement has moved more slowly. In 1981 Joel Myerson drew several women into his study of authorship in the *Dial* magazine, and a year later Anne C. Rose focused her path-breaking study of transcendental reform on a field of six writers including two women, Fuller and Elizabeth Peabody.[7] More recently, literary histories and anthologies of transcendentalism have all set Fuller alongside Ralph Waldo Emerson and Henry David Thoreau among the movement's canonical figures, and all include promising vignettes of other women. Barbara Packer discovers irony and artistry in Elizabeth Peabody's record of Bronson Alcott interacting with his young pupils at the Temple School, and Philip Gura presents the little-known Eliza Thayer Clapp as a representative "engine" of the movement. Myerson's anthology includes Sophia Ripley in the *Dial* and Caroline Dall's woman-centered history, while Lawrence Buell's anthology starts with the letters of Mary Moody Emerson and compares the "compressed intensity" of Ellen Sturgis Hooper's poems to those of Emily Dickinson.[8] The landmark *Oxford Handbook of Transcendentalism* (2010) signals a new moment in this evolution, with a substantial majority of its fifty authors considering women as well as men within broad and innovative categories of study. Together these works offer material toward an account of the movement's female genealogy, and Cole's essay on "Woman's Rights and Feminism" offers an abbreviated version of that account.[9]

Over the same decades, even fewer interpreters have asked what transcendentalist women contributed to a broader women's history. Again, there were some remarkable early insights. In 1976 Susan Phinney Conrad included several major women of the movement, as well as the transcendentally inflected journal *The Una*, in mapping a "country of the mind" for antebellum women; and four years later Marie Mitchell Olesen Urbanski positioned Fuller's *Woman in the Nineteenth Century* between preceding and subsequent feminist declarations. A strong and controversial line of division instead characterized Ann Douglas's *Feminization of American Culture* (1977), where Fuller stood as the sole heroic figure who avoided the debilitating habits of sentimentalism in a religious and literary culture of women assuming ministerial authority. Peabody, Child, and Elizabeth Oakes Smith, on the other hand, stood along with Harriet Beecher Stowe among the feminizers. But as Jane Tompkins and others responded to Douglas with a strong defense of Stowe and sentimentalism, very little corollary attention returned to the transcendentalists.[10] It took over a decade before Judith Mattson Bean and Cole wrote respectively of Fuller's impact on the wider traditions of women's oral culture and feminist activism. In 2005 Tiffany K. Wayne offered the first book-length study of Fuller and her disciples in their cross-generational pursuit of "self-culture," arguing for a collective contribution to the nineteenth-century women's rights and transcendentalist movements in so doing. More recently Judith Strong Albert has published a study gestating ever since the seventies, which compares the lives and texts of Fuller, Child, Peabody, and Dall and claims their strong legacy for second-wave feminism.[11]

In the meantime, however, so much new material and perspective has emerged that the challenge of integrating it grows at an increasing rate. The past decade has seen freshly researched biographies of Fuller, the Peabody sisters, and the Alcotts; new editions and interpretations of Caroline Sturgis, Julia Ward Howe, and Caroline Dall; and recast histories of the transcendentalists' utopian communities, Brook Farm and Fruitlands. Work is ongoing by both contributors to this volume and others.[12] Meanwhile two of our authors, Eric Gardner and Katherine Adams, begin considering the relevance of transcendental authors and ideas to nineteenth-century black women writers and activists—a different matter from these white liberals' own antislavery idealism. The door has at least opened between African American literary studies—that other major field of scholarly recovery since the seventies—and what Gardner calls "the seemingly 'whitest' of spaces" (279), American transcendentalism. Without aiming at any final closure, we represent a changing field and aspire to perspectives that draw it together.

Woman Reading

The functional and emblematic center of this "female genealogy" was Elizabeth Peabody's bookstore at 13 West Street, Boston, where European authors could be discovered and Fuller's conversations for women took place, from the store's opening in 1840 through Fuller's departure for New York City in 1844. Whether by direct access or secondary impact, the women discussed in our collection benefited from both Peabody's books and Fuller's frontal questions: "What were we born to do? How shall we do it?"[13] If the Emersons' house in Concord provided the country setting for the transcendentalists' meetings, both private and public, 13 West Street was the urban gathering point; here the Transcendental Club held its last meeting, Brook Farm planning took place, and much of the *Dial* magazine was published.[14] For our purposes, however, the bookstore looms large because it was run by and uniquely open to women and their freelance self-culture.

Fuller evoked one sighting of women at West Street in a brief report of November 1840 to Ralph Waldo Emerson: "The other day I was sitting there and two young ladies coming in asked first for Bettina and then for Les Sept Chordes &c." In the present collection, Carol Strauss Sotiropoulos details Fuller's own reading and translation that year of the German writer Bettina Brentano, while Gary Williams examines Fuller's concurrent engagement with French novelist George Sand, including her *Les Sept Cordes de la Lyre*. Both European authors offered Fuller powerful models for independent religious consciousness based on God's immanence in the female self—Bettina's "Schwebereligion" (92), Sand's "psychotheism" (111)—integral to the "great changes" of mind she had reported that very week to her Conversations group. It is striking, though, that neither of the young seekers of Bettina and Sand at the bookstore was apparently part of that group or even known to Fuller. Peabody's door stood open to these venturesome readers, as well as to teenaged Caroline Healey (later Dall) and aging Mary Moody Emerson.[15]

The bookstore becomes emblematic because, in unfolding the divinely human faculties of the self, reading had a fundamentally different significance for women than for men. Traditional histories of both the transcendentalist movement and Ralph Waldo Emerson as its initiator begin with crises in the authority of the Unitarian clergy and Harvard College. Emerson called these institutions to account in the name of "Man Thinking" and his natural perceptions. Given the soul's spontaneous power, as he famously declared to Harvard students, "Books are for the scholar's idle times. When he can read God directly, the hour is too precious to be wasted in other men's transcripts of their readings."[16] Of course he took as a given the male authority granted by college and pulpit even as he exited from them. But by cultural prescription women had access to neither. Counting on natural perception, these lay scholars with domestic obligations hungered for prime-time reading. For many, books offered a transforming alternative to silent attendance at Sunday sermons. In the American and European romanticism thereby made available, they found a new validation of individual intuition, as well as the alternative communities of literacy, spiritual seeking, and ethical commitment based upon it.

Through the nineteenth century, the authority of women rose enormously, including access to college and entry by at least a few into the Protestant ministry. But the initiating and continuing scene of action was a woman reading, responding, and taking part in conversation, whether directly or through exchange of letters and journals.[17] Noelle Baker provides the context not only for Mary Moody Emerson's circulation of journal manuscripts but also for the longer tradition in describing patterns of "dialogic self-cultivation" (36) that followed the tradition of European *salonnières*. Intellectually aspiring women met both with each other and with men signing off from institutional authority in the social circles central to transcendentalism. Starting from Peabody's bookstore not only brings into focus an understudied aspect of the transcendentalist movement itself but also provides an important case of "scribbling women" on the larger scale. In multiple locations and through a wide variety of means, female readers became writers, first in private and then for the press. Perhaps the women of transcendentalism took part in metaphysical inquiry beyond the norm for their sex, pursuing a "culture of truth," as Baker notes (52).[18] But they did so while also participating in an expanding women's culture of literacy and authorship.

The four groups of essays in this book extend through time and space from the Peabody-Fuller scenes of reading, talking, and writing. Early voices and originating moments come first in studies of Mary Moody Emerson, Sophia Peabody, Margaret Fuller, and Elizabeth Peabody, which collectively survey the first four decades of the century. The last of these also anticipates a longer development through Elizabeth's ongoing activity and retrospective vision. Post–Civil War voices, including engagements with the legacy, conclude the collection with studies of Caroline Dall, Mary Wilkins Freeman, Pauline Hopkins, and Louisa May Alcott. Between these two periods of time lie the primary years of the movement. But here we divide spatially. The first consideration is its Boston-Concord circle, in essays focusing variously on Fuller, Caroline Sturgis, Sarah Clarke, Julia Ward Howe, Lydia Maria Child, and the women of Brook Farm. We follow with expanding circles of impact, taking up the conservationism of Fuller and her contemporaries outside New England, the "African American transcendentalism" of Edmonia Highgate, the social science activism of Dall, and the explorations of spirit and sexuality of Margaret Sweat. The late fiction of Freeman and Hopkins also represents such expansion into wider American culture of transcendental influence.

Baker's Mary Moody Emerson was clearly a generational precursor, but Sophia and Elizabeth Peabody, as presented by Ivonne García and Phyllis Cole respectively, read early and deeply in the English romantics as well. Sophia cited them amid the rhapsodic nature descriptions of her *Cuba Journal* (1833–35), while on their authority Elizabeth sought to publish (as early as 1826) in the periodicals of controversial theology. In such forms Mary Emerson and the Peabody sisters either anticipated or influenced major themes of the transcendentalist movement, as Waldo Emerson and Margaret Fuller would later pronounce them. These women were formative, not derivative. But the movement must be defined in large enough terms to include all their ideas and enactments, rather than only evaluating them as they fit into later structures of thought.

A corollary principle is that writing originally intended for private audiences merits consideration equally with published writing, indeed that private and public expression were intimately joined.[19] Fuller's innovative encounters with Bettina and Sand in 1840 were expressed first in letters and journals, but, as Sotiropoulos and Williams show, they evolved into projects of translation, interpretation, and fictional imagination in the *Dial*. As its new editor that year, while also leading the Conversations, Fuller opened paths for women by offering its pages to female friends as well as using them for her own work. Poems by Ellen and Caroline Sturgis, for instance, began as privately circulated manuscripts but reached wider audiences through this protected form of publication, without authorial signature or even the gender marking of a pseudonym. The *Dial* has often been called a voice of the male-dominated Transcendental Club, but it was also the first outlet for a significantly different circle of women.

Nor was verbal form the only expression of these women's reading and consciousness. As Sarah Wider shows, Sarah Clarke and Caroline Sturgis recorded in writing their "attention" to the inward movements of soul and luminous qualities of the external landscape, but both women also sought to give form to perception in visual art. Sketching might begin as a woman's avocation, the equivalent of "scribbling"; it also, however, aspired to professional accomplishment. Clarke was coached toward a career by Boston painter Washington Allston. García's Sophia Peabody sketched Cuban scenes in the pages of her journal, then returned to Boston and painted in a studio upstairs from her sister's bookstore. Marianne Dwight, as described by Sterling Delano, pursued her gift for painting the local flora and fauna of Brook Farm to a rather different end: sale of her work in Boston for much-needed community income as well as, in her own words, "the elevation of woman to independence, and an acknowledged equality to man" (197). Discovering a critical mass of visual artists has been among the highlights of our collective work on these women.[20]

Such forms of expression and vocation are tracked by our contributors across a geographical terrain wider than eastern Massachusetts. As a Bostonian, Child had written the transcendental novel *Philothea* and published her essay on "Beauty" in the *Dial*, as well as led the city's Female Anti-Slavery Society.[21] But by the time she published her first volume of *Letters from New-York* (1843), she had lived in that larger metropolis for two years. As Jeffrey Steele argues, she responded with a new affective language of sympathy, a "sentimental transcendentalism" in the service of political reform, that Fuller's New York journalism in turn would develop. Julia Ward Howe offers an opposite path from childhood in New York to consultation about her poetry with Fuller, visits to the Conversations, and subsequent leadership in Bostonian arts and reforms for the rest of the century. Monika Elbert takes up Howe's constricted life as a wife and mother and its exploration in the fictional guise of a male-identified hermaphrodite—following Fuller's endorsement of the sexes' "great radical dualism" to tragic consequence. But Elbert also positions this novel amid Howe's later, nationally influential feminist writing and reform, where male and female aspirations are seen as open to reconciliation through social change.

The line of development past 1850 leaves Boston's originating scenes behind, as the bookstore had dwindled and Brook Farm closed even before Fuller's death that year. But direct continuities still emerge within the individual lives of participants in the earlier awakening. Cole finds Elizabeth Peabody expanding her career of educational reform in later years of simultaneous autobiographical reflection and interchange with younger women. Caroline Dall, as Helen Deese writes, was the "most self-conscious and the most direct early inheritor of Margaret Fuller's feminism" (303). Carrying that message forward, however, she valued "sympathy for commonplace persons" in institutional forms distinct from the sentiment of Fuller and Child, leading in formation of the new Social Science Association and working to ensure women's leadership within it. Yet both private and public writing also belonged in her arsenal of weapons, as Mary De Jong shows in studying Dall's notebook of responses to Julian Hawthorne's attack on Fuller's character in 1884. Mobilizing members of the old movement by personal letter, Dall appealed to the press both in her own voice and through others. Then and through the nineties, she sustained the force of transcendentalism in both active memorializing and new vocational urgency. Meanwhile, in an even younger cultural generation, Louisa May Alcott drew deeply on the transcendentalism of her parents and their friends. Laura Dassow Walls finds that continuity on the broader scale in a study of Alcott's fiction, discovering her childhood formation in transcendental ideology, her later representation of the elders, and her German romantic reach in evoking a "peaceful global domesticity" of women (426).

In addition to such personal inheritance of antebellum transcendentalism by later nineteenth-century writers, a proliferation of influence took place through new print media and cultural institutions. Out of myriad individual women readers, a feminist reading public grew. From 1853 to 1855 the nation's first women's rights newspaper, *The Una: A Paper for the Elevation of Women*, gathered women in a quest for ideal truth and social transformation; and in 1870, the American Woman's Suffrage Association founded its weekly *Woman's Journal*, which incorporated the *Una*'s idealism in more eclectic form and continued for forty-seven years. Both of these Boston periodicals were led by editors and columnists of transcendental affiliation—the *Una* by Fuller disciples Dall and Paulina Wright Davis, the *Woman's Journal* by Howe and Thomas Wentworth Higginson. Meanwhile the New England Women's Club, founded in 1868 by Cheney, Howe, and their friends, offered a social and intellectual forum that, through subsequent decades, honored both Fuller's memory and Peabody's ongoing life.[22]

Two studies in our collection suggest some of the ways that these cultural settings brought latter day transcendentalism to bear on new writing careers that have previously been considered in other contexts. Susan Stone describes Mary Wilkins Freeman in terms of her proximity to Boston and acquaintance with representatives of its postbellum feminist culture. Most important, however, is Stone's resulting interpretation of Freeman's fiction of the 1890s as "transcendental realism," with heroines—seemingly apart from the cultural hub in their villages—charting Fuller-like independence and authority in relation to men. Katherine Adams presents Pauline Hopkins amid a black Boston culture that maintained significant contact with white reform institutions—her *Woman's Era* journal and club with the organizations and media that Cheney and Howe represented. In this context Adams emphasizes Fuller's *absence* as a significant reference point in Hopkins's journalism and fiction, suggesting the limitations of Fuller's racially white vision of an ideally directed progress. Nonetheless, as Adams sees, the linkage of Fuller and Hopkins in cultural "DNA" and "common contexts" (402) opens the possibility of reading them in juxtaposition.

So indeed the DNA extended directly through the literary marketplace so that, before and after the Civil War, the transcendentalism of women as well as men became part of the national discourse. Daniel Malachuk presents Fuller as an environmental writer in *Summer on the Lakes* not only in comparison with neighboring transcendentalists Emerson and Thoreau but also among contemporary women writers of more diverse location, such as Caroline Kirkland, Susan Fenimore Cooper, and Eliza Farnham. The double context allows for new recognition of Fuller's observational realism and affirmation of spirit in commentary on the West. Spirit likewise provides a key to the quite different enactments of Margaret Sweat's heroine Ethel. Dorri Beam claims affinity rather than influence between Fuller and Maine writer Sweat, whose 1859 novel *Ethel's Love-Life* traces the fluid dynamics of male and female identity. Locating the bond of these authors in their new feminist politics of "spirit, ecstasy, and passion" (345), Beam evokes a larger cultural provision from the movement as well. Likewise the transcendental discourse of spirit could in some instances cross the nation's racial divide. Eric Gardner finds young black journalist Edmonia Highgate, a New Yorker in Louisiana in the immediate aftermath of the Civil War, leading with Fuller's words as she affirms a "personal truth" issuing from nature with power to "save this nation, and the world" (290).

The women of transcendentalism would continue to invite dismissal for their aestheticism and disengagement from the world, as one of our interludes dramatically attests: in 1890 Elizabeth Cady Stanton, who herself had attended Fuller's Conversations and subsequently developed her own romantic language of self-reliance, still recalled Theodore Parker's words about "the stuff that Margaret Fuller used to twaddle forth" on the arts.[23] Our essayists implicitly respond to such caricature of the aesthetic, whether through García's reading of Sophia Peabody's rhapsodies in Cuba, Wider's sense of "attention" expanding from beauty to self-possession, or Malachuk's visual and political reading of the Western landscape. Whether for Fuller or her contemporaries and protégées, the sequels to transforming experiences of beauty remained open.

Exalted moments of insight provide these women's widest common ground and starting point. Ralph Waldo Emerson's account of becoming a "transparent eyeball" in nature is the most famous touchstone for such a core experience of transcendentalism. But our collective archaeology discovers an abundance of such moments, included among our interludes as well as essays. In 1842 Fuller translated a stunning "Apocalyptical Fragment" by Bettina's friend Karoline von Günderode, set on a Mediterranean outcropping rather than Emerson's bare New England commons (79–80). And a year later, amid Peabody's work as bookstore owner, publisher of Fuller's *Günderode*, and transcriber of the Conversations, she offered her own quintessential transcendental expression in "A Vision" (129–30).

Most significantly for our argument as a whole, Peabody presents her vision as it arises from reading rather than nature, and it grants her authority amid a celebration of multiple art forms from the world's cultures. While "sitting in deep reflection over a pamphlet that contains a new definition of life," the narrator is lifted off her feet and allowed to witness "all Time," with ancient music and visual forms palpable to her senses. What follows is an ecstatic first-person report of religious knowledge. Her essay both revises Emerson and parallels Fuller, who in 1843 was ransacking ancient mythologies for archetypes of woman in "The Great Lawsuit," the first version of her feminist book. In the essay's longer argument, Peabody witnesses the arts and mythologies of India and Greece, imagines a dialogue with Plato and Socrates, and finally reconciles the splendors and limits of ancient religions with "the way, the truth, and the life" of Christian scripture. Her account offers no Fulleresque plea for women, but it enacts a woman's priestly power and celebrates, as she later explained to Mary Moody Emerson, "the individual visible church, to which I belong." Even in solitary reflection, her thoughts proceed by conversation. And in Peabody's own life they lead to further conversation: decades afterward she republished the piece because friends had found it "suggestive and heart awakening." As Diane Brown Jones has commented, Peabody's "Vision" deserves consideration as not just a private utterance but a "manifesto" of the larger transcendentalist movement.[24]

Genealogy

Mapping these reading women through time and space in turn invites reflection and theorization about patterns of relationship among them. Received genealogical models come under strain, as female transcendentalism travels across intricate webs and disperses into the more general culture—but they do not snap. Instead we are prompted, as we hope future students of women's transcendentalism will be, to complicate how we see modes of transmission and fields of influence. More pointedly, we would ask whether, in those modes and fields, new topographies become visible by distinct virtue of a study that constitutes itself in gender. Do diverging ideas of the energies that flow from person to person, between minds and bodies, inflect what we can conceive of as *female* transcendentalism? Gary Williams quotes Moncure Conway's dictum of 1904: "All the aspiring and discontented women known to me in America,—poets, orators, reformers,—were the offspring of George Sand, endeavouring to build in the

New World a palace for Women" (105). Not all the American women we trace are palace-builders, though the metaphor surely resonates with Fuller's utopian energies. But Conway's tracing of "offspring" from Sand surely unsettles any neat derivation of the lineage from Fuller alone (or Elizabeth Peabody or Mary Moody Emerson).

A rich field of investigation opens in the relationship of generations. Literary mothers and daughters significantly formed each other: in the sequence from Elizabeth Peabody to Caroline Dall to Louisa Alcott, for instance, each woman directly mentored the next, guaranteeing a powerful (if not untroubled) transmission of the legacy.[25] Women's relationships with parents and precursors has little in common with the Oedipal struggles that Harold Bloom has described between literary fathers and sons. As Sandra Gilbert and Susan Gubar wrote in response to Bloom in their founding feminist study *The Madwoman in the Attic*, women writers were pioneers rather than belated followers, and their "anxiety of authorship" found assurance in the discovery of models for innovation and rebellion. Surface and subterranean conflict also arose, but it was almost always overcome in favor of tribute, whether Elizabeth Peabody's recognition of Mary Moody Emerson or the celebrations of Fuller for fifty years after her premature death.[26] In addition, early and late, we find women inspired and provoked not only by female but also by male texts and authority figures—as well as men and their traditions by women, nephews by aunts, fathers by daughters, husbands by wives. Ralph Waldo Emerson plays a particularly important role in this history as both heir to Mary Moody Emerson's thought and interlocutor to Peabody, Fuller, Clarke, and Alcott; indeed we find him both quoted and contested to the century's end.[27]

A larger reading of history is at stake in the particular American generations that we are tracing. Scholars of transcendentalism once assumed that after the Civil War the movement lapsed into nostalgia or irrelevance amid a new "Gilded Age" of capitalist expansion and philosophical pragmatism. Accordingly, late nineteenth-century reminiscences and histories of earlier generations have not been valued as exercises of mind or sources of information. More recent reassessment even of the male tradition discovers engagement and continuity across time. A particular case, however, must be made for women: any change of eras after the Civil War was particularly offset by renewed urgency by individuals and organizations in pursuing suffrage, educational access, and literary achievement. The antebellum generation provided vital models, even while some lives continued to old age in authorship and advocacy. Perception of present need, rather than nostalgia for the past, often motivated memory. As Cheney told her national audience of clubwomen in 1895, "I owe it to [Margaret Fuller] to speak in her name, and try to make her life again fruitful in others."[28]

But we need not think only in terms of vertical genealogy, whether grateful or resistant, through cultural generations; a second kind of connection also becomes apparent on the map of women as generators and receivers of transcendental thought. Creativity flowered in dialogue among contemporaries, fostered by the conversation, manuscript exchange, and acts of reading already described here. Relationality, in some scenarios, might become a term more apropos than influence or lineage. Susan Manning's work promises fertile ground for a gendered look into models of literary relation that turn hierarchies of influence on their side, while pushing the beautiful abstraction of Deleuze and Guattari's organic metaphors to greater specificity of analysis: as opposed to the vertical and linear development of a tree, texts and voices multiply laterally like underground root systems or "rhizomes."[29]

Manning's sense of lateral proliferation applies with illuminating power to the responses of transcendental women to European contemporaries such as Bettina, Sand, and the new translators of Asian scripture. So might it apply to the communities of reading and writing that grew from the *Dial* and eventually the *Una* and *Woman's Journal* in the United States and across the Atlantic. But it becomes personal in the group of contemporary women assembled at Peabody's bookstore for Fuller's Conversations. Common experiences of friendship, school, church, and region—as well as of gender—bound these women into a sisterhood.

In fact that feminist metaphor was grounded in literal relationship, for two biological sets of sisters were prominent among them, the Peabodys and the Sturgises. Much more has been written about the former than the latter, though ongoing work by Kathleen Lawrence and Jennifer Gurley promises a new visibility to Caroline Sturgis Tappan and Ellen Sturgis Hooper, respectively.[30] The Sturgises offer a compelling case of lateral dialogue both in person and in print since, as already noted, their poems appeared in the *Dial* from its earliest issues. Despite anonymous publication, other women in the circle of conversations would have known the authors of Caroline's "Life" and Ellen's "Poem I" and recognized their substantially different perspectives as women of vision. "Greatly to Be / Is enough for me," Caroline declared, then asked a quintessential question on behalf of the transcendentalist movement:

> Why for work art thou striving
> Why seek'st thou for aught?
> To the soul that is living
> All things shall be brought.

Ellen, on the other hand, tempered and deferred self-fulfillment in accordance with a countering realism:

I slept, and dreamed that life was Beauty;
I woke, and found that life was Duty.
Was that dream then a shadowy lie?
Toil on, sad heart, courageously,
And thou shalt find thy dream to be
A noonday light and truth to thee.

In print form, with or without knowledge of authorship and gender, readers made both poems well known. Ironically, Christopher Cranch assumed a male speaker when he drew a caricature of Caroline's transcendentalist as a reclining husband expecting "all things" to be brought by a wife; of course the poem is much more disruptive as a woman's declaration. But Ellen's somber pairing of Beauty and Duty apparently won even more response: lateral influence yielded to vertical repetition as Moncure Conway reprinted the poem in his 1860 resurrection of the *Dial*, and by the early twentieth century it was included in *Bartlett's Familiar Quotations*.[31]

Such pairings and networks might be pursued for many members of the Conversations group. Expanding from the Sturgis sisters, we would like to present the case of a lesser-known participant who illustrates with particular clarity the interweaving of lateral relationship and vertical genealogy among the Exaltadas. Commentators have identified Elizabeth Bancroft only by marriage—in Capper's terms, as the "witty second wife of historian and Democratic party leader George Bancroft."[32] What can be known of her? Elizabeth Peabody's written transcription of the fall 1839 Conversations offers only a single remark by Bancroft, as she resisted the leader's urging of a wider sphere for women's Genius and defended its exercise in the domestic sphere. Yet Fuller herself found Bancroft neither resistant nor marginal, but exemplary of the experiment's success. "Mrs. Bancroft came out in a way that surprised me," Fuller wrote to a friend the same month. "She seems to have shaken off a wonderful number of films. She showed pure vision, sweet sincerity, and much talent."[33] If face-to-face conversation provoked such coming out, letters also conveyed the news (rhizome-like) beyond that moment and scene.

Seven years later, Bancroft's own correspondence crossed not with but around Fuller, both personally and thematically. Her *Letters from England, 1846–49* (excerpted in an interlude) (301–2) reveal ongoing family preoccupation and considerably more of her wit. But the setting has changed dramatically to London society, after George Bancroft's 1846 appointment as American ambassador to the Court of St. James, under the same Democratic President Polk whose election Fuller had deplored. Though this is the very year Fuller sailed for England and the Continent, Bancroft's printed record of letters makes no reference to her. Instead they tell of social and political learning beyond Fuller's reach, as

Bancroft compares the conversation of British and American women, protests her lack of "cosmopolitan" knowledge, and meets England's leaders—even, "with tall feathers and long train, making curtsies to a queen." She emerges as a critic of her hosts, however, in defending republican values amid the rising revolutions of 1848; conversation with the British political elite provides "a world of light" about their opposition to the new order in France. No Fuller-like radical, she could still have sustained further conversation with her old leader and admirer at this point. Apparently Bancroft did not do so literally, but her summary of European lessons is instead addressed to fellow Bostonian Emelyn Story, about to emigrate to Rome with her husband and there, amid revolution, become Fuller's closest confidante.[34] The network of lateral communication expands.

But now take a vertical as well as a lateral step. Two acts of reminiscence, recorded decades later by descendants of fellow Conversationalists, best illuminate Elizabeth Bancroft's longer life story. In the 1890s Ellen Tucker Emerson wrote the life of her mother, Fuller Conversationalist and transcendentalist wife Lidian Jackson Emerson. In it she recounted memories of memories, reaching back through decades of mother-daughter talk to Lidian's youth in Plymouth. There, growing up as Lydia Jackson, the young woman found her best friend in Betsey Davis, the same individual who two marriages later became Mrs. Elizabeth Bancroft. Betsey declared to Lydia that they were "twin souls," and both belonged to a reading society of young, boarding-school-educated women who published their thoughts in a newspaper called "The Wisdom of the Nine." Through the years Lydia and Betsey shared learning, writing, and mutual affection. As Ellen tells the story, when Betsey heard the news of her friend's engagement to Waldo Emerson, she "walked the room unable to . . . do anything but keep saying 'My Lydia!' 'My dear Lydia!'" The friends even cowrote a letter to Lydia's sister shortly before the wedding, reporting how Betsey's "witch-work" was preparing Lydia for the event by providing a close-fitting lavender silk dress, to make her appear, in Betsey's words, "externally as well as internally transcendental." Clearly Bancroft valued marriage and elegant clothing. But Ellen Emerson adds that Elizabeth Davis Bliss Bancroft gave her parents their one wedding present, a bronze double inkstand.[35] Material objects are also texts open to interpretation: What better gift could Betsey have given Lydia than this tool for *two* lives of writing at the Emerson house?

One more step takes us again to Ellen and Caroline Sturgis, who befriended Lydia Jackson in 1835 when Betsey (their second cousin) gave a grand Boston party in her honor. Clearly many of Fuller's Conversationalists were already well acquainted when they gathered four years later. Through Sturgis genealogy, moreover, we have a powerful final glimpse of Elizabeth Bancroft in old age. In 1884 Clover Hooper Adams, daughter of Ellen Sturgis Hooper, was living in Washington, D.C., with her husband Henry Adams and pursuing the art of photography; and there at forty-one she created a portrait of her close neighbor, cousin, and fellow historian-wife, eighty-one-year-old Bancroft. The photograph, described by Adams's recent biographer as a "compelling chiaroscuro," presents its subject with strong light and shadow on her alert features, lace shawl, and notepaper in hand. Adams also captures Bancroft's character in a contemporary letter to her father: "Mrs. Bancroft looks very frail and has been in her room for six months but reads & discusses everything from Henry's history to the Supreme Court decisions. . . . Her will bids fair to keep her alive as long as she chooses unless death catches her in a nap, and that I believe she is on her guard against by dozing with one eye open."[36]

In both visual and verbal forms, this is a veritable icon of the reading, talking, death-defying woman of transcendentalism. It arguably meant more than individual portraiture to the photographer and letter-writer. From early childhood Clover had grown up without her mother, who had died of tuberculosis at thirty-six. But she was bound to the Sturgis legacy in multiple ways. Genetic inheritance made her suffer acutely from depression, like her grandmother and aunt Susan, so that she committed suicide only a year after taking the Bancroft photograph. Beyond that genealogical burden, however, lay a shared passion for the visual arts with her aunt Caroline and, even more, pride in her mother's accomplishment. Ellen Sturgis Hooper had left two small daughters the whole of her papers and also spoken to Clover directly in verse: "I give thee all, my darling, darling child, / All I can give—the record of good things." As adults the Hooper children arranged to publish a private edition of the poems. Clover had the means of traveling back to Fuller's Conversations and the *Dial*, then, through both Bancroft's talk and the written record of her mother, whom she described as "our lady of Emersonian thought and sentiment."[37] She may have been memorializing a surrogate transcendental mother in her portrait of Bancroft, even drawing personally upon the vitality she represented.

We trace these evocations of Elizabeth Bancroft to discover not so much a new American author as an example of energy flow and a figure in the larger topography of women's engagement with transcendentalism. Copious life-writing and experimentation in the arts constitute the largest text of these women's lives. Memoirs, portraiture, and private editions reveal lives and perceptions otherwise unknown, in detailed and evocative recollection that cuts more deeply than nostalgia. Ellen Emerson's *Life of Lidian Jackson Emerson* might be called a "compelling chiaroscuro" as much as Clover Adams's photograph. Bancroft's description of the lavender dress as "transcendental" suggests her skeptical humor; she seems always to have preferred observation and irony to the epiphanies of solitary genius. She shared her cousin Ellen Sturgis's realism in a more comic vein. Yet the luminous figure Adams made of Bancroft through the photographic medium suggests that a common celebration of women's consciousness also endured into the 1880s.

Prospects

In what directions do these collected essays move the fields of scholarship on transcendentalism and women writers? The editors would like to recognize some of the questions and interventions that our authors offer. Several conceptual binaries are either complicated or discarded. Aesthetic and ethical awareness are claimed as coexistent. Body and spirit, as Beam sees, commingle through the force-fields of magnetism common to transcendentalist and mesmeric belief, so that the spirit has senses. (We might add that Child's spirit is able even to bite its finger.) Cosmopolitan consciousness, whether through reading or travel, enlarges and enhances American possibility without denying it, in many of these studies of women's transcendentalism, and García adds the complexity of a colonial space in Cuba where Sophia Peabody can, through the mediation of European romanticism, express aesthetic visions more readily than at home.

The double dynamics of selfhood and group identification characterize all the Exaltadas. The transcendentalist movement, Philip F. Gura maintains, was divided between individualist and collectivist wings, exemplified especially by Emerson on one hand and Brook Farm on the other.[38] Among women this distinction still proves useful: Fuller and her Miranda represent the fully cultivated self, sometimes seen by her detractors as a "mountainous ME," while Peabody always envisioned a movement based on the "social principle" of mutual obligation and fellowship.[39] Yet our gendered study of transcendentalism finds these possibly contrasting dimensions in both women's work. Peabody had strong moments of independent vision, though idealizing community over self, while Fuller gathered others around her and moved from individual accomplishment to collective action.

One of our greatest hopes is to interrogate the various lines between transcendental spirit and the "sentiment" of a broader women's culture. Too often transcendentalism is seen by feminist critics as only a discourse of male egotism and privilege. Mere allusion to Louisa May Alcott's satire of her father's utopia in "Transcendental Wild Oats," with its discovery of the community's "one beast of burden" in the founder's wife, can dispatch the idealist's dream. Such satiric observation, to be sure, is integral to women's experience of the movement, and its positive corollaries are cooperative work and women's sentimental feeling.[40] But the lines of division refuse to stay fixed. Walls follows out the dynamics of Alcott's Sylvia, the heroine of *Moods*, who aspires beyond marriage, finds keen pleasures of soul and senses in nature, but enters problematically into domestic partnership under the influence of "moods" that are the negative incarnation of emotion. Cole finds a positive relational ethic in Elizabeth Peabody's early essays; Steele follows its political transformation and application in the New York journalism of Child and Fuller, positioning this form of transcendentalism in the vibrant context of current "affect" theory. Whether in consonance or conflict, demands of heart and soul are both imperative in these lives and texts, as they surely are for the very different heroines of Sweat, Freeman, and Hopkins as well. Such complexity endures well into the nineteenth-century era confidently distinguished as "realism" from antebellum romanticism of either transcendental or sentimental variety. As Susan Stone demonstrates in the case of Mary Wilkins Freeman's stories, our interpretation of texts would benefit from working across such rigid compartmentalization of periods and fields.

Our authors follow out multiple disruptions of the gender binary in their subjects' pursuit of transcendental self-development. "I long to be a man," Walls quotes from Alcott, but she has Fuller complete the thought: "I wish I were a man, and then there would be one" (436, 437). As Stone points out, Freeman's heroine Esther becomes the protector of her intended and he, shaded by her umbrella, a "literal *homme covert*" (384). The legal designation of women's identities as "covered" by their male partners might indeed be reversible. Two essays in the collection address Fuller's "great radical dualism" of male and female in its implications for same-sex love. Howe's "hermaphrodite" protagonist Laurence finds little pleasure in desire as either man or woman, instead retreating to ascetic asexuality that Elbert associates with a wider pattern of transcendental self-denial. Margaret Sweat's heroine Ethel, on the contrary, embraces her own "spherical," bisexual nature in multiple partnerships; as Beam argues, Sweat discovers this fluidity of homo / heterosexual love in possibilities of embodied spirit that sexuality studies have not previously engaged.

Our opening juxtaposition of Child and Fuller promises further consideration of the Exaltadas as reformers, and here our authors have delivered abundant and varied new study. Malachuk makes a broad claim for the "motive force" that transcendentalism lent to American reform, adding environmentalism to the short list of its key movements; his argument about Fuller's Western women also defends the environmentalist value of "middle landscapes" of habitation rather than only untrammeled wildness. Delano offers a window on the experience of women in Brook Farm's period of Fourierist socialism by inquiring into the community's gendered patterns of labor; able to choose work according to personal "passion," they could also, in the words of feminist historian Carol Kolmerten, "enjoy the best advantages that American culture had to offer" (180). Delano's emphasis on the success of Brook Farm's school, with women the backbone of its faculty, also complements claims for Peabody's leadership in educational reform.[41] Women could teach when prevented from preaching, and their rising access to secondary education opened the door to such vocations on a massive scale. Or women could turn, following Lydia Maria Child or Caroline Dall as presented here by Steele and Deese, to improving conditions for the laboring and immigrant poor; the Progressive Era's "social gospel" had origins in earlier generations.[42]

All of these reform traditions, furthermore, drew upon and contributed to cultural and political feminism in the nineteenth century. Often women were moderators and mediators, voices of domestic feminism. De Jong makes the valuable point that Fuller's disciples of the 1880s, while defending her against Julian Hawthorne's attack, were the opposite of "radical" in their insistence on Fuller's domestic values, as demonstrated by her devotion to family needs and her firmly wedded relationship with the Marquis d'Ossoli, recalled without significant interest in their Italian revolution. Nor did Cheney or Peabody celebrate the earlier, unmarried autonomy of Fuller and her alter ego Miranda, let alone her opening of women's identity to crossings of the "great radical dualism" between male and female identification. And while Elbert explores Howe's decidedly radical, unpublished *Hermaphrodite* of the 1840s precisely in terms of such crossings, apparently as Howe the later political feminist became optimistic about women's potential, she also saw "The Halfness of Nature" to be resolved within successful marriage rather than androgynous womanhood or manhood. But more subversive thematics could also be revived by younger generations. Walls's Alcott imagined the cross-dressing heroine Sylvia, and Stone's Freeman the eloquent, unfeminine, decisively unmarried Juliza. In the 1880s, as Caroline Dall was mounting her public relations blitz to defend Fuller, Mary Wilkins Freeman could perhaps refract Fuller into the more radical critique of marriage, deploying humorous irony and village vernacular as disarming tactics in such stories as "A Conflict Ended." Even so, she withheld the more extreme "Juliza" from publication.

Walls evokes the earliest impetus to other reforms by newly tracing the abolitionist convictions of Louisa May Alcott's family, around her fictional characterization of Charles and Eliza Follen. However, the abolitionist sentiments of white transcendentalism, while providing context, cannot predict content for the adjacent African American calls of liberation that Katherine Adams and Eric Gardner explore. Though the two authors reach quite different conclusions about historically separate moments in nineteenth-century history, together they point to possibilities for ongoing work on the intersections of black and transcendental writing. Adams focuses on Pauline Hopkins's heroine Dianthe in *Of One Blood* (1905), who stages a "spectacular" appearance at Boston's Tremont Temple comparable to Fuller's earlier public example. But Dianthe shares no exaltation with her audience, instead remembering more than half a century of ongoing oppression since the Emancipation Proclamation. Invoking the ideas of modernist philosopher Walter Benjamin, Adams locates Fuller within a model of historical memory that self-propels into the utopian future without pausing over dark counter-realities; in Fuller's case, this means "finessing" American slavery—and blackness itself—in favor of a racially white progressive idealism. By contrast, Hopkins's memory loops from "now time" to old wreckage; along with the Fisk Jubilee Singers, she is still singing "Let My People Go." Gardner's Highgate, on the other hand, participates in teaching freedmen and writing for periodicals shortly after Emancipation (1865–67). The denominational *Christian Recorder* in which she publishes, while radically espousing racial liberation, also quotes and critiques Emerson and Thoreau. Thus Gardner makes cultural sense of Highgate's calling in Fuller's terms for at once "sounding one's soul depths" and "forgetting self, losing personal identity, and becoming atomic parts of personified principle" (285).

The textual studies of Adams and Gardner are both enriched by evocation of broader cross-racial networks of lives and writing. Adams's discovery that Howe, Cheney, and Lucy Stone were regularly referenced in the African American *Woman's Era* surely deserves further investigation, as Gardner's sense of Highgate recalling Thoreau and Fuller in a setting of black racial danger may point to more such discovery. Both Adams and Gardner provide contexts in which we might revisit Charlotte Forten Grimké, a black writer who has been deemed somewhat anomalous in her privileged education of the 1850s as the only nonwhite student at her school in Salem, Massachusetts. By the age of twenty-one, as our interlude from her journal attests, she had read hundreds of books, including both Fuller's *Woman in the Nineteenth Century* and Child's *Philothea*, and like any other Exaltada aspired to knowledge of European languages and scenes. But in close proximity to these influences, her highest moments were of direct contact with Child and Follen through shared abolitionist work. Most of all, this work took her directly, like Highgate, to teaching freedmen; and by the time of Emancipation she was, like Hopkins, quoting slave spirituals rather than the transcendentalists.[43] As Gardner writes, we "do not know the shape and extent of black engagement with transcendentalism. . . . [But] it *is* essential that we look" (278).

We also might continue looking for Margaret Fuller. Courtesy of Albert von Frank, we include among the interludes his recent discovery of an 1846 essay by Fuller advancing the abolitionist idealism of her call to "Exaltadas" within the abolitionists' own publication, *The Liberty Bell* (203–5). It surely continues the conversation with which we began, between Fuller and her friends Child and Loring. In this imagined scenario, legendary German knights, hearing the chime of a sacred bell, ride forth on white steeds to support the cause of liberty wherever it is violated. Fuller tells their story in calling for an "Order of Liberators" at the present moment who will not allow the national legacy to descend to heirs with coins bearing "the name of Texas [and] stamped on the reverse with slavery" (205). This essay might well be considered in support of Adams's thesis that Fuller is advancing a campaign for ideal, white-identified justice rather than engaging with the actual plight of slaves. Yet it takes a major step in commitment and affiliation, with greater imaginative strength than her often-quoted proclamation from Europe a year later, "How it pleases me here to think of the Abolitionists!" By then she had joined the "Order of Liberators" for European revolution as well; as Larry Reynolds argues, she was rapidly becoming the exemplar of "righteous violence" who—after her own death—would inspire supporters of John Brown's antislavery insurrection in the United States a decade later.[44] Here indeed is a radical Fuller.

We first proposed this project in 2010, the auspicious year of Fuller's bicentennial, calling for expansion from her single example to the longer legacy of private and public writers, artists and reformers, acknowledged leaders and newly recovered contributors among women who experienced the "newness" of American transcendentalism. Now Brigitte Bailey, introducing essays presented at the bicentennial conference, declares Fuller "less exceptional yet more substantial" than previous scholars had perceived, her influence expanding through "circles" of engagement with others. We concur as we pursue such engagements. Indeed, as powerful as Fuller's leadership proved, we find that all the circles need not radiate from her alone. In 2011, responding to public advocacy, the Boston Landmarks Commission officially designated Elizabeth Peabody's bookstore as a historic site; thus they guaranteed survival and preservation of the place best representing multiple lives and directions within the female genealogy of transcendentalism.[45] We offer this collection as a further effort to consolidate such a history. But like our subjects we are futurists, hoping that readers will extend the conversation begun here.

NOTES

1. See Bruce Mills, *Cultural Reformations: Lydia Maria Child and the Literature of Reform* (Athens: Univ. of Georgia Press, 1994), 98–104, for Child's response to Fuller. Mills's edition of Child's *Letters from New-York* (Athens: Univ. of Georgia Press, 1998) draws only from *Letters from New York* (New York: C. S. Francis, 1843) and not the *Second Series* (New York: C. S. Francis, 1845), which includes the essay on transcendentalism (125–30). Our thanks to him for recommending this text.
2. *EMF*, 334, 341. See Capper 2, 173, on James K. Polk's victory in the election of November 1844.
3. Fuller and Child, quoted in Capper 2, 173, 186–87.
4. Ednah Dow Cheney, "Lecture Given at the Congress of American Advancement of Women—New Orleans—November, 1895: Sarah Margaret Fuller," in *Reminiscences of Ednah Dow Cheney* (Boston: Lee & Shepard, 1902), 193, 192.

5. Barbara L. Packer ends her history with the "Antislavery Years" of the 1850s; Philip F. Gura extends past the Civil War to Caroline Dall, the Free Religious Association, and the "Genteel Tradition"; Tiffany K. Wayne emphasizes the heritage of transcendentalism for Dall, Cheney, and Howe, as well as the presence of women as speakers and audience at the Concord School of Philosophy from 1879 to 1888; the *Oxford Handbook of Transcendentalism* concludes with a section explicitly titled "Transcendental Afterlives." See Packer, *The Transcendentalists* (1995; Athens: Univ. of Georgia Press, 2007); Gura, *American Transcendentalism: A History* (New York: Hill & Wang, 2007); Wayne, *Feminism and Transcendentalism in Nineteenth-Century America* (Lanham, Md.: Lexington Books, 2005); and *OxH*.
6. Joyce W. Warren, even while engaging with Fuller, represents a wider inclination to dismiss transcendental individualism as male privilege in *The American Narcissus: Individualism and Women in Nineteenth-Century American Fiction* (New Brunswick, N.J.: Rutgers Univ. Press, 1984). It is worth noting that *Legacy*, since 1984 the flagship journal for recovery of American women writers, has consistently included Fuller in its purview.
7. Joel Myerson, *The New England Transcendentalists and the "Dial": A History of the Magazine and Its Contributors* (Rutherford, N.J.: Fairleigh Dickinson Univ. Press, 1980); Anne C. Rose, *Transcendentalism as a Social Movement, 1830–50* (New Haven: Yale Univ. Press, 1981).
8. Packer, *Transcendentalists*, 58; Gura, 181, 188–93; Joel Myerson, ed., *Transcendentalism: A Reader* (New York: Oxford Univ. Press, 2000), 314–18, 674–81; and Lawrence Buell, ed., *The American Transcendentalists: Essential Writings* (New York: Modern Library, 2006), 3–8, 476. Reference books also increase the visibility of women in the movement: Wesley T. Mott, ed., *Encyclopedia of Transcendentalism* and *Biographical Dictionary of Transcendentalism* (Westport, Conn.: Greenwood, 1996); and, aiming consciously for more inclusive coverage, Tiffany K. Wayne, *Encyclopedia of Transcendentalism: The Essential Guide to the Lives and Works of Transcendentalist Writers* (New York: Facts on File, 2006).
9. Phyllis Cole, "Woman's Rights and Feminism," *OxH*, 222–40. Among other *OxH* essays considering female figures, see Barbara L. Packer, "Romanticism," 84–101; Albert J. von Frank, "Religion," 117–35; Noelle A. Baker, "Conversations," 348–60; Todd H. Richardson, "Transcendentalist Periodicals," 361–72; Susan Belasco, "The *Dial*," 373–83; and Elizabeth Addison, "Families and Friendships," 524–36.
10. See Susan Phinney Conrad, *Perish the Thought: Intellectual Women in Romantic America, 1830–1860* (New York: Oxford Univ. Press, 1976); Marie Mitchell Olesen Urbanski, *Margaret Fuller's "Woman in the Nineteenth Century": A Literary Study of Form and Content, of Sources and Influence* (Westport, Conn.: Greenwood Press, 1980); Ann Douglas, "Margaret Fuller and the Disavowal of Fiction," chap. 8 in *The Feminization of American Culture* (New York: Alfred A. Knopf, 1977); and Jane Tompkins, *Sensational Designs: The Cultural Work of American Fiction, 1790–1860* (New York: Oxford Univ. Press, 1985).
11. Judith Mattson Bean, "A Presence among Us: Fuller's Place in Nineteenth-Century Oral Culture"; Phyllis Cole, "The Nineteenth-Century Women's Rights Movement and the Canonization of Margaret Fuller," in *ESQ: A Journal of the American Renaissance* 44 (1998): 79–123 and 1–33; Wayne, 5; Judith Strong Albert, *Minerva's Circle: Margaret Fuller's Women* (Novato, Calif.: Paper Mill Press, 2010).
12. Since 2004, biographies of Fuller include Charles Capper, *Margaret Fuller: The Public Years* (2007); Meg McGavran Murray, *Margaret Fuller: Wandering Pilgrim* (2008); John Matteson, *The Lives of Margaret Fuller* (2012); and Megan Marshall, *Margaret Fuller: A New American Life* (2013). Biographies of other transcendentalist women include Megan Marshall, *The Peabody Sisters* (2005); and (on the Alcott family) John Matteson, *Eden's Outcasts* (2007) and

Eve LaPlante, *Marmee and Louisa* (2012).On Caroline Sturgis, see Kathleen Lawrence, "The 'Dry-Lighted Soul' Ignites" (2005). For new editions, see Howe, *The Hermaphrodite* (2004); Dall, *Daughter of Boston* (2005); and Dall, *Selected Journals* (2006, 2013). On the two utopian communities, see Sterling Delano, *Brook Farm* (2004) and Richard Francis, *Fruitlands* (2010). (See Bibliography for full publication information on these works.) Editorial projects currently underway include an edition of Mary Moody Emerson's Almanacks by Noelle A. Baker and Sandra Harbert Petrulionis (project prototype at http://marymoodyemerson.net/), more of Caroline Dall's Journals by Helen Deese, and the letters of Caroline Sturgis by Ronald Bosco and Sarah Wider. Kathleen Lawrence is working on a biography of Caroline Sturgis Tappan, and Jennifer Gurley on a study of the poetry of Ellen Sturgis Hooper, while Derek Pacheco is surveying children's literature by transcendentalist authors including Tappan, Child, Alcott, and Mary Peabody Mann.

13. *LMF*, 2:87.

14. On the transcendentalists' meetings and publications at the bookstore, see Marshall, *Peabody Sisters*, 396–97, 415, 424–25. Leslie Perrin Wilson details the history and booklist of the store in "'No Worthless Books': Elizabeth Peabody's Foreign Library, 1840–52," *The Papers of the Bibliographical Society of America* 99 (2005): 113–52.

15. *LMF*, 2:182, 183. For Mary Moody Emerson's visit, see Phyllis Cole, *Mary Moody Emerson and the Origins of Transcendentalism: A Family History* (New York: Oxford Univ. Press, 1998), 260; for Dall's, Helen R. Deese, ed., *Selected Journals of Caroline Healey Dall* (Boston: Massachusetts Historical Society, 2006), 1:46.

16. Ralph Waldo Emerson, "The American Scholar," in *CW*, 1:53.

17. Barbara Sicherman finds "near literacy parity" between men and women by 1850, even though higher education and professional roles were still largely male-exclusive (*Well-Read Lives: How Books Inspired a Generation of American Women* [Chapel Hill: Univ. of North Carolina Press, 2010], 38). Mary Wilkins Freeman's one year at Mount Holyoke is the closest to college experience of the writers discussed here, though many were students at secondary female seminaries.

18. Baker's term, as she acknowledges, is adopted from Laura Dassow Walls's title *Emerson's Life in Science: The Culture of Truth* (Ithaca, N.Y.: Cornell Univ. Press, 2003).

19. Without emphasizing the particular role of journals and letters for women, Packer claims that such informal genres offer "some of the liveliest" writing of the transcendentalist movement (*Transcendentalists*, 94).

20. See also Kathleen Lawrence, "Soul Sisters and the Sister Arts: Margaret Fuller, Caroline Sturgis, and Their Private World of Love and Art," in "Exaltadas: A Female Genealogy of Transcendentalism," special issue of *ESQ: A Journal of the American Renaissance* 57 (2011): 79–104.

21. On *Philothea* within Child's larger career, see Caroline L. Karcher, *The First Woman of the Republic: A Cultural Biography of Lydia Maria Child* (Durham, N.C.: Duke Univ. Press, 1994), 233–37. The only specialized study of this novel, Robert E. Street's "Mrs. Child's 'Philothea': A Transcendentalist Novel?" (*New England Quarterly* 16, no. 4 [1943]: 648–54) deserves a drastic update.

22. For an overview of these developments, see Cole, "Canonization of Margaret Fuller," 5–8, 13–19; and Rita K. Gollin, *Annie Adams Fields: Woman of Letters* (Amherst: Univ. of Massachusetts Press, 2002).

23. Stanton recalled Fuller and Parker in "Reminiscences" (*Woman's Tribune*, 21 June 1890), but in editing this periodical series for book publication as *Eighty Years and More: Rem-*

iniscences 1815–1897 (1898; New York: Schocken Books, 1971), she left out the critical anecdote.

24. *LEPP*, 265–66; "Dedication," *Last Evening with Allston* (Boston: D. Lothrop, 1886), which also includes the essay (62–72); Diane Brown Jones, "Elizabeth Palmer Peabody's Transcendental Manifesto," *Studies in the American Renaissance 1992*, ed. Joel Myerson (Charlottesville: Univ. Press of Virginia, 1992), 197. Though never anthologized or reprinted, this essay has garnered several other commentaries as well: see Ronda, 213–16; Marshall, *The Peabody Sisters*, 444–45; and Charlene Avallone, "Elizabeth Palmer Peabody and the 'Art' of Conversation," in Elbert, Hall, and Rodier, 36–37.
25. On moments of friendship and antagonism between Peabody and Dall, see Ronda, 192–94 and 259–60; on Dall's sponsorship of Alcott's early writing career, see Helen Deese, "Louisa May Alcott's *Moods*: A New Archival Discovery," *New England Quarterly* 76 (2003): 439–55.
26. Harold Bloom, *The Anxiety of Influence: A Theory of Poetry* (New York: Oxford Univ. Press, 1973); Sandra M. Gilbert and Susan Gubar, *The Madwoman in the Attic: The Woman Writer and the Nineteenth-Century Literary Imagination* (New Haven: Yale Univ. Press, 1979), 47, 49. See Elizabeth Palmer Peabody, "Tribute to Mary Moody Emerson," first published in the *Boston Evening Transcript* and reprinted in *Notes on the History of Waterford, Maine*, ed. Thomas Hovey Gage (Worcester, Mass.: privately printed, 1913), 54–57; and on the tradition of memorializing Fuller, see Cole, "Canonization of Margaret Fuller," 1–33.
27. See also Sarah Ann Wider's sense of women in late nineteenth-century Emerson Clubs and colleges, finding "life-altering power" in self-reliance (*The Critical Reception of Emerson* [Rochester, N.Y.: Camden House, 2000], 73, 93–94).
28. Ednah Dow Cheney, "Lecture: Sarah Margaret Fuller," in *Reminiscences*, 193.
29. This volume's editors first encountered Manning's innovative ideas in "Literary Friendship and Lateral Thinking," a plenary conference presentation at "Transatlanticism in American Literature: Emerson, Hawthorne, Poe," St. Catherine's College, Oxford, U.K., 15 July 2006. For an evolution of her argument in which Fuller's "thinking across" with Wordsworth and Carlyle features prominently, though without the gendered slant that interests us, see Manning, "'Grounds for Comparison': The Place of Style in Transatlantic Romanticism," in *Wordsworth in American Literary Culture*, ed. Joel Pace and Matthew Scott (New York: Palgrave Macmillan, 2005). See also Gilles Deleuze and Félix Guattari, *A Thousand Plateaus*, trans. Brian Massumi (London and New York: Continuum, 2004; originally published in French in 1980).
30. See n. 12.
31. [Caroline Sturgis], "Life," *Dial* 1, no. 2 (October 1840): 195; [Ellen Sturgis], "Poem I," *Dial* 1, no. 1 (July 1840): 123. For Cranch's drawing, see Frederick De Wolfe Miller, *Christopher Cranch and His Caricatures of New England Transcendentalism* (Cambridge, Mass.: Harvard Univ. Press, 1951), fig. 17, titled "Moral Influence of the *Dial*." Conway reprinted Ellen Sturgis's poem in his later publication that appropriated the *Dial* as title (1, no. 4 [April 1860]: 236). Also see *Bartlett's Familiar Quotations*, 10th ed. (Boston: Little, Brown, 1919), searchable on www.bartleby.com. The routes by which Ellen's poem became "familiar" have not been explored.
32. Capper 1, 292.
33. Nancy Craig Simmons, "Margaret Fuller's Boston Conversations: The 1839–1840 Series," in *Studies in the American Renaissance 1994*, ed. Joel Myerson (Charlottesville: Univ. Press of Virginia, 1994), 205; *LMF*, 2:101. Lilian Handlin, in *George Bancroft: The Intellectual as*

Democrat (New York: Harper & Row, 1984), reveals more about the Bancrofts' blended family and ambivalent relation to the transcendentalists; they later referred to the daughter born to them in 1839 as their "transcendental baby" (169, 201, 153–57). Two years later, as Sterling Delano tells the editors, the couple had their two Bancroft sons "Johnny and Geordie" boarding at the Brook Farm school (see Georgiana Bruce Kirby, *Years of Experience* [New York: G. P. Putnam's Sons, 1887], 94).

34. Bancroft's manuscript letters and diary are in the Bancroft-Bliss Families Papers at the Library of Congress. See *MMFO*, 2:281–93, for Story's narrative of Fuller's "Private Marriage" and childbirth in Italy.

35. Ellen Tucker Emerson, *The Life of Lidian Jackson Emerson*, ed. Delores Bird Carpenter (Boston: Twayne, 1980), 92, 29–30, 48, 56; *Letters of Lidian Jackson Emerson*, ed. Delores Bird Carpenter (Columbia: Univ. of Missouri Press, 1987), 23–25. Ellen adds that the inkstand is "good and whole as ever" as she writes sixty years later, and today one very much like it remains in the parlor of the Emerson house.

36. Natalie Dykstra, *Clover Adams: A Gilded and Heartbreaking Life* (Boston: Houghton Mifflin, 2012), 177–78; the portrait is reproduced in "Clover's Photographs," after 206.

37. Poem quoted in Dykstra, *Clover Adams*, 1; Clover on Ellen Hooper, quoted in Eugenia Kaledin, *The Education of Mrs. Henry Adams* (Philadelphia: Temple Univ. Press, 1981), 21. For a thoughtful assessment of Clover's and Ellen's relation to transcendentalism, see Kaledin, 20–24; she notes that the Boston Public Library's copy of Ellen Sturgis's *Poems*, originally owned by Elizabeth Peabody, was donated by Ednah Cheney.

38. Gura, xiv.

39. For the Fuller description, see *MMFO*, 1:236; on Peabody, see Megan Marshall, "Elizabeth Palmer Peabody: The First Transcendentalist?" *Massachusetts Quarterly Review* 8 (2006): 4–6.

40. The value of Alcott's satire to Boston-based, transcendentally influenced advocates of women's rights is directly attested to by its publication in their *Woman's Journal*, 21 February 1874. For one among many recent editions of this piece, see *Alternative Alcott: Louisa May Alcott*, ed. Elaine Showalter (New Brunswick, N.J.: Rutgers Univ. Press, 1988), 364–79.

41. Carol Kolmerten, *Women in Utopia: The Ideology of Gender in the American Owenite Communities* (Bloomington: Indiana Univ. Press, 1990); quoted in Delano, *Brook Farm*, 175. See Wesley T. Mott's claim for transcendentalism as an educational as well as a religious "demonstration" over the decades of its influence (*OxH*, 153, 155). He expands such thinking and gives evidence of women's advocacy in "'America's intellectual morning': or, How the Transcendentalists Founded Boston University," in *Resources for American Literary Study* (New York: AMS Press, 2012), 95–138.

42. See Bruce Ronda, "Elizabeth Peabody and the Fate of Transcendentalism," in Elbert, Hall, and Rodier, 240–41; and Cole in *OxH*, 236–37.

43. Forten published her observations of the freedmen in "Life on the Sea Islands," *Atlantic Monthly* (May and June 1864), reprinted in *Two Black Teachers during the Civil War* (New York: Arno, 1969), 65–89.

44. Von Frank located this text after completing his essay on Fuller's reading of the slavery issue, "Margaret Fuller and Anti-Slavery: 'A Cause Identical,'" in *Margaret Fuller and Her Circles*, ed. Brigitte Bailey, Katheryn P. Viens, and Conrad Edick Wright (Durham, N.C.: Univ. of New Hampshire Press, 2013), 128–47. For Fuller's later declaration about the abolitionists, see *These Sad But Glorious Days: Dispatches from Europe, 1846–1850*, ed. Larry J. Reynolds and Susan Belasco Smith (New Haven and London: Yale Univ. Press, 1991), 166; and for Fuller's evolving radicalism, see Larry J. Reynolds, *Righteous Violence: Revolution,*

Slavery, and the American Renaissance (Athens: Univ. of Georgia Press, 2011), 41, 53–55. Reynolds also points to seven antislavery pieces that Fuller wrote for the *New-York Tribune* in 1845.

45. Brigitte Bailey, "Introduction: Fuller at Two Hundred," in *Margaret Fuller and Her Circles*, 10, 3. For documentation supporting the successful bookstore petition, see "13–15 West Street: Elizabeth Peabody Bookstore and Circulating Library Boston Landmarks Commission Study," http://www.cityofboston.gov/Images_Documents/13-15_West_Street_Study_Report_tcm3-31148.pdf, 24 July 2013.

SECTION I
Early Voices, Origins, Influences

INTERLUDE

Eliza Clapp, from "Spirit," in *Studies in Religion* (New York: C. Shepard, 1845), 9–10.

We meet together, a band of learners; every thing invites us to study: every thing seems to us in possession of a secret, and allures us by the promise of unfolding it. We are at home in our world, and yet not at home in it. We are full of questions. The overhead sky, with its floating islands of condensed light, the broad earth, the regal domain of flowers, the shy birds, the serious animals, the busy insects,—to all we say, Tell unto us, whence come and whither go you? They move around in dignified possession. We are all askers of them. We importune them in their haunts, follow them to their recesses; but they say nothing: they are dumb, alas! for them and us. A subject still more interesting than this world without, invites us. We question about ourselves: we become unto ourselves a study. Whence and why came we hither, with these curiously fashioned eyes and ears, these impish fingers, this irresistible vigor that burst forth in the leap and shout of infancy, these visions of future might, that wove their fantastic shapes so early in the hidden life of the child, that "wheel within a wheel," those sudden wailings of affection, that weakness, that thoughtlessness and yet unconscious consciousness of thoughts, far back in itself, and yet not belonging to it: a possessed creature? Whence this wondrous childhood,—this questioning youth?

"Let me do nothing smale"

Mary Moody Emerson and Women's "Talking" Manuscripts

NOELLE A. BAKER

I am not on the whole sure, that it would not be a very excellent mode of keeping up correspondence, if friends would transmit to one another the pages of their common place books . . . & thus give one another faithful & unaffected representations of the intellectual life. . . . You will see that a scrap from your day-book must always have the worth & the effect of a letter; for it is as much like conversation, *in the true sense of the term, if it is not so much like* How do you do *&c.*

—Edward Bliss Emerson to Mary Moody Emerson, 29 June 1830

A few single grand ideas, which become objects, pursuits, & all in all!!

—Mary Moody Emerson, 1830 Almanack

If not superficial chitchat, such as the polite "*How do you do* &c," what was "*conversation*, in the true sense of the term," for Mary Moody Emerson and her several literary circles? In June 1830 nephew Edward Emerson suggests that the circulating leaves from her commonplace books converse with their readers. For him, these "faithful & unaffected" "scraps" communicate more effectively than a letter, seemingly because they embody Mary Emerson's intellectual endeavors with the authenticity of verbal discourse. Contemporaries such as Henry James Sr., Henry Thoreau, and Elizabeth Palmer Peabody similarly acknowledge Mary Emerson's striking intellectual force and pursuit of a "few single grand ideas" as the "object" of life. It is Edward, however, who astutely finds a vital connection, characterizing his aunt's "representations of the intellectual life" as "talk" nearly a decade before Margaret Fuller advocated vocational self-culture in her Boston Conversations.[1]

Edward's observation invites further inquiry into the "talking" manuscripts of Mary Moody Emerson and genre's role in these conversations.[2] A brilliant single woman and intellectual mentor to nephew Ralph Waldo Emerson, Mary Moody Emerson (1774–1863) published epistolary and occasional essays early and late in life, but she dedicated her intellectual maturity to a series of unpublished fascicles that she called her "Almanacks" (ca. 1804–55), as well as her "pole star," "*home*," and "the only images" of self-existence.[3] The product of fifty years and running to over one thousand pages, Emerson's handmade booklets are constructed of letter paper bound with thread, and they combine the features of commonplace books, spiritual journals, letters, critical reviews, and original compositions. As Edward Emerson implies, the Almanacks are thoroughly dialogic; they display actual conversations with readers and include direct addresses to the authors of Emerson's own reading. Moreover, in these manuscripts and in advance of Fuller's practice of orchestrating "pacquet" writings as an "intertextual conversation" among intimates,[4] Emerson actively juxtaposes genres, as when she begins a letter on a partially completed Almanack leaf. Begun as reflections on her eclectic reading, these material forms of discourse fostered self-cultivation for Emerson as well as for her fortunate interlocutors.[5]

Though Emerson was not a *salonnière*, an apt subject for a pious memoir, or a transcendentalist, she nonetheless eagerly surveyed these diverse conversational cultures in her Almanacks. Commenting on these wide-ranging intellectual investigations, Thoreau observes rightly in 1851 that "in spite of her own biases [Emerson] can entertain a large thought with hospitality."[6] This broad-minded desire to acquire and disperse knowledge uniquely enabled Emerson to influence different communities, connecting the cultures of eighteenth-century transatlantic women's coteries, salons, and generic conventions with nineteenth-century feminist and transcendentalist pursuits. Acting as a bridge between generations and in advance of the more feminist Fuller, Emerson experimented with diverse conversational media in order to achieve mutual self-cultivation, enlightened truth, and even professional opportunity.[7]

In this essay, I first examine the flourishing manuscript culture of Emerson from the perspective of book history, focusing on the commonplace book. Next, I consider her commonplace writing within a circle of women in the early nineteenth century. The interaction between coterie writing, print publication, and conversation, standard to transatlantic eighteenth- and nineteenth-century women's salons, was significant for these early American women writers. Finally, I explore the scope and variety of dialogic self-cultivation in the papers of Mary Emerson and investigate the ways in which her earlier focus on genre and coterie writing intersects with and differs from transcendentalist and feminist cultures of conversation. A pivotal figure between two generations and multiple conversational cultures, Emerson borrows from each as she chases her own evolving truth within the leaves of her commonplace books.

"I . . . get scraps & write them down, as the buzzing fly sips from the rich floweret": Commonplace Book Writing

Such experimental *salonnières* as Germaine de Staël and Rahel Varnhagen offered first-generation transcendentalists stimulating examples of the mind-expanding potential of reading, writing, and talking in groups, but older traditions provided Mary Emerson with similar inspiration. Prized by Renaissance humanists and grounded in classical Greek and Roman "philosophical and rhetorical theories," the commonplace book replicates the ancients' practice of collecting "*sententiae*, or wise sayings," to buttress arguments,[8] a practice that Emerson also employed. She likewise experimented with another eighteenth-century intellectual convention, coterie writing, nearly a decade prior to the publication of de Staël's provocative chapter on French and German styles of conversation in her groundbreaking romantic text *Germany* (1813). Notably, Ralph Waldo Emerson compares Fuller's Conversations and Mary Emerson's Almanacks to this formative work, where dialogue also figures as a "lively exercise, in which subjects are played with like a ball, which in its turn comes back to the hand of the thrower."[9] In their own commonplace books, eighteenth-century Americans transcribed, arranged, and commented upon extracts from their reading. As Susan Stabile notes, this "intertextual format resembles" the conversational "reciprocity" of eighteenth-century women's salons as well as de Staël's verbal sport.[10] Assembling commonplace transcriptions in this way made it possible for Emerson and her fellow writers and readers to orchestrate conversations with the writings of poets, novelists, and divines in their journals. Emerson's interest in manuscript and print forms of publication derived in part from her early engagement with such transatlantic genres as pious and secular memoirs in addition to commonplace books, each of which documents or facilitates self-culture through "social" or group authorship and the circulation of manuscripts. As Margaret Ezell reminds us, the culture of social authorship enabled early modern women readers to become writers and expand the scope of their audience.[11]

Nineteenth-century women were encouraged to keep commonplace books for conventionally feminine purposes—in such forms as personalized versions of conduct books, collections of verse, and exercises to enhance memory. However, as Catherine Kerrison suggests, female commonplace book writers understood that writing enables "acquisitive self-development" and, moreover, that commonplace extracts represent "literary property" that can be "as revelatory of their thinking" as letters or diaries.[12] Much like the commonplace books of such eighteenth-century Philadelphia-area writers and salon leaders as Annis Boudinot Stockton and Milcah Martha Moore, Emerson's Almanacks witness an ongoing participation in a "third sphere" of public discourse, a "social" realm that mediates "private" and "public" spheres for eighteenth-century coterie, commonplace book, and coffeehouse talkers, regardless of gender.[13] Within this stimulating dialogic zone, Emerson engages in the scientific, theological, political, and philosophical debates that animated influential transatlantic periodicals such as the *Edinburgh Review*, the *North American Review*, and the *Christian Examiner*, whose male reviewers and essayists—Thomas Carlyle, Frederic Henry Hedge, Victor Cousin, Samuel Taylor Coleridge—Emerson read and to whom she responds, sometimes acerbically. Commenting on David Hume in an 1826 fascicle, for example, she grumbles resignedly, "I feel that I shall war with the old Sophist as long as I exist" (385:8).

Coincidentally, Emerson's very next Almanack entry aptly summarizes the ambitious nature of this and her countless other spirited intellectual engagements. Claiming that her previous life has "consisted of noughts," Emerson charts a new course, insisting, "I touch eternity—let me do nothing smale." While piously asserting a need to hide an ostensibly zero-sum existence within the enveloping "omnipotence" of a Christian deity, Emerson nonetheless admits an aspiration to reflect divine power; her identity and its intellectual achievements must persist into a limitless future. "Oh Father of the universe!" she proposes, "Absorb me in thyself—let my consciousness remain—& it will!" As is typical of her flexible intellect, in this passage Emerson extends her religious framework for identity formulation to include Wordsworth's romantic notion of a divinity "who didst wrap the cloak of infancy around us" (385:8). In *The Excursion*, the spiritual gifts of childhood uplift Wordsworth's autobiographical speaker to a visionary intensity of perception. Emerson quibbles characteristically with Wordsworth's idealism here, but both romantic and Protestant thinking inform her sense of the infinite range of her soul. This fascicle offers a glimpse into the ways in which the relationship between self-construction and the activity of literary "commonplacing"—transcribing, arranging, and commenting upon extracts from her reading—plays out in the Almanacks.

Emerson relates her excitement at this process in March 1835 with the explicit classical trope for commonplace pursuits:[14] "This holiday of soul I beginn the 1st vol. of Cousin: get scraps & write them down, as the buzzing fly sips from the rich floweret. The very preface disturbs with delight" (385:18; 1280H:149; 579:18). In gathering "scraps" of knowledge from French eclectic philosopher Victor Cousin and sharing them in an expansive third sphere, Emerson might seem to aspire to the actions of male public figures from Thomas Jefferson to Waldo Emerson, for whom commonplace books stored the extracted knowledge that would invigorate their published commentary. However, although the Almanacks occasionally yielded print publications and frequently circulated in manuscript, significantly, with this metaphor, Emerson underscores the festive leisure spirit of the emotions attendant upon her daily reading and writing.

Her "holiday of soul" draws inspiration and pleasure not only from Cousin's stimulating ideas but from commonplacing itself; her terms for the act of reading, transcribing, and sharing new ideas underscore the "disturbing" and almost sensuous enchantment of intellectual fertilization. Delighting in its generic liberty, in this fascicle Emerson culls the intellectual sweets of Cousin—along with Coleridge, Herder, Channing, Adam Smith, Harriet Martineau, Socrates, and Spinoza. As the classical trope for commonplacing proposes, in the manner of the honeybee Emerson sips from scented and varied blossoms. Reading and commentary enrich her soul and signal her artistry, and like the communal bee, she shares this self-cultivation with other members of her coterie by dispersing Almanack leaves for them to read and comment on in turn.

"We antisapate new powers in eternity . . . but they will be in unison . . . to those we exercise now": Pious and Secular Memoirs

Although Emerson embarked upon her earliest coterie experiments with female collaborators and continued this tradition in the nineteenth century with Elizabeth Hoar, Peabody, Sarah Alden Bradford Ripley, and younger female kin, male voices dominate the Almanacks' extracts. In the 1835 Almanack, for instance, Harriet Martineau is a lonely figure amid the primarily male authors that Emerson excerpts. In this respect, the Almanacks differ from Milcah Martha Moore's unpublished commonplace books, whose pages are replete with women's writings.[15] Emerson also does not appear to reflect Fuller's feminist self-consciousness about what it might mean to write for and about gender.

Because of their relative scarcity, however, Emerson's transcriptions of and commentary about women are particularly noteworthy. Some of the most enthusiastic examples record her excitement at discovering the manuscript writings, eminent piety, and reformist actions of earlier and contemporary women, the most interesting of which do begin to approach Fuller's feminist self-consciousness. Such memoirs as Mary Hays's *Female Biography* (1803) and Elizabeth Smith's *Fragments in Prose and Verse* (1810)—both of which Emerson read—highlight transatlantic women, from Sappho and Aspasia to Margaret Cavendish, Aphra Behn, and Marie-Jeanne Roland, who exert intellectual ambition and spiritual authority in glowing language. Further, since editors printed their subjects' manuscript letters, commonplace books, and spiritual diaries with such memoirs, they fostered a culture of manuscript preservation and circulation as either a precursor or a viable alternative to print publication.[16] As Joanna Bowen Gillespie suggests, pious memoirs proclaim "the right of an everyday human being to write, think, dream, and be published."[17]

This inspirational promise suggests that eighteenth-century memoirs provide an important reference point for Emerson's multigenerational discourse. Transcendentalists associated the spontaneous power of "talk" with Jesus of Nazareth, magnetism, and electricity. In parlor conversations and "literature of the portfolio"—packets of unpublished writings dispersed among intimates—they attempted to recapture and conduct conversation's vital truth through the effervescent language of the "living Word." Anticipating these conversations and the transcendentalist belief, as Bronson Alcott expresses it, that the "living Word" embodies fluid power and the promise of a professional outlet,[18] Mary Emerson also reflects the conventions of pious memoirs, in which circulating manuscripts act as "witnesses" within communities.

Within this early, evangelical context, Emerson disperses her Almanacks in order to promote a higher truth. However, her pursuit of this spiritual and intellectual truth also figures as vocation, in Alcott's transcendentalist sense of conversation's power. "The xian is engaged in a career the most grand & important," Emerson exults in an 1806–7 Almanack. "As long as identity exists," she theorizes, "so long the prerogative of a happy ima^{n} [imagination] will remain: the peculiar gifts, the indefinable combinations of genius will never be the portion of vulgar souls. . . . We antisapate new powers in eternity—true, but they will be in unison . . . to those we exercise now" (385:2). In such a "career," piety harmonizes with the "genius" that was standard to pious memoirs. Moreover, the work begun in life is imperishable, and such vocational acts of self-cultivation will redouble with "new powers in eternity."

At the turn of the nineteenth century, Emerson experimented in such "combinations of genius" with a group of unmarried eastern Massachusetts women, led by Mary Van Schalkwyck (1778–1811) of Concord. In their conversations, letters, and journals, coterie members exchanged books and ideas, after the manner of the young Abigail Smith, Mercy Otis Warren, and their circle. As Abigail Adams's biographer Woody Holton suggests, these young women circulated their writings "with the explicit purpose of furthering each other's education," and this process also brought forth an incipient feminism in Adams and prompted publication in Warren's case.[19]

A similarly collaborative spirit encouraged Emerson and Van Schalkwyck to publish seven letters—as "Constance" and "Cornelia"—between 1804 and 1805 in the *Monthly Anthology*, a periodical edited by Emerson's brother William.[20] The interaction between coterie writing, print publication, and Emerson's dialogic experimentation in keeping commonplace books proved significant for her as an aspiring writer. In another piece, she published an extract from her reading of British philosopher and theologian Richard Price in the *Monthly Anthology*; and in both her published *Anthology* epistolary essays and the unpublished Almanack pages, she responded to two other pseudonymous *Anthology* authors—"The Botanist" and "Sylva." As these publications amply document, pious and intellectual labors, recorded in commonplace books and circulated among fellow readers and writers, could lead to further conversation and the publication of epistolary essays. In fact, in the first of the seven letters published by Emerson and Van Schalkwyck, the latter begins her essay by contemplating Emerson's "private" commentary on the learned piety of an unnamed woman.[21]

But these public dialogues also flow back into the social realm, as suggested by the interaction between Van Schalkwyck's essay, published in July 1804, and an Almanack entry conjecturally dated 18 November of the same year. In their respective pieces, Van Schalkwyck and Emerson discuss the possibility, in Van Schalkwyck's words, that "intelligent beings" converse productively in the afterlife, an expectation that each woman bolsters by quoting selectively from a specific verse in the book of John: "In my Father's house are many mansions; if it were not so, I would have told you. I go to prepare a place for you."[22] Van Schalkwyck speculates that the stars represent these storied mansions, where her "Saviour assure[s]" his disciples of a "reception," along with other "congenial spirits," who will "thence pass to more glorious orbs, as they acquire greater purity and perfection."[23]

Likely stimulated by verbal and epistolary conversations in addition to this published letter, Emerson expands on Van Schalkwyck's commentary in greater detail. Notably, however, while agreeing with her friend's faith in mutual-cultivation, she also hints at the vocational aspiration that links her to Bronson Alcott and echoes throughout these manuscripts. Despite a pointed reminder that "*humility . . . clothes* the soul for mansions w'h Jesus prepares," Emerson cannot rest with Van Schalkwyck's expectation that these conversations will yield mutual-culture's "greater purity and perfection." She unabashedly and equally longs to "be distinguished" among her nebular communicants. "Would we when coasting the riegions of other worlds behold new orders of intelligences," Emerson enthuses hopefully, "with advantages . . . arrest their attention and invite their interest" (385:1)—much as Fuller herself would later draw out or "magnetize" her fellow Conversationalists. But in the end and like Van Schalkwyck, Emerson emphasizes the importance of combined voices to attain higher laws—the significance of other talkers' "distinguished laurels of wisdom & penetration" and "inlightening vision" to self-culture. "How nameless the importance of our society then!" she declares gratefully (385:1; 385:1, 1280H:147).

As the foregoing exchanges imply, like the young Abigail Adams and her set, Mary Emerson's early coterie benefited from these published and private epistolary conversations. Unfortunately, however, little of Emerson's correspondence from this period survives. The primary evidence that she circulated her manuscripts and that Van Schalkwyck extracted that writing for other coterie members subsists in a few letters from Van Schalkwyck's published memoirs. In a December 1805 epistle to Emerson, for example, Van Schalkwyck responds to a recent Almanack gift, Emerson's critique of the popular work by British Methodist Samuel Drew, *An Original Essay on the Immateriality and Immortality of the Human Soul* (1802). In her reply, Van Schalkwyck offers a bemused commentary that any reader of Emerson's passionate writing style can appreciate. "To a mind but little accustomed to the abstraction of metaphysical disquisition," she gently reminds her friend, "a minute attention to the finest links that unite the chain of reasoning is essential. When to this observation, I add—my dear Mary writes too much like other great people, to be always legible, she will not be surprised when I acknowledge I have not enjoyed the whole of her valuable manuscript."[24] As Van Schalkwyck allows, Emerson's intellectual enthusiasm occasionally renders her "metaphysical disquisitions" more challenging than their original subject matter.

Importantly, however, constructive criticism only increases the inherent "value" in coterie writing; as Emerson's manuscripts circulate, both reader and writer gain in self-cultivation. Moreover, coterie members understand that they can articulate such moments of expanding knowledge in the third sphere of public discourse. Denied her father's, brother's, and nephews' Harvard pedigree, autodidact Mary Emerson achieves this productive and communal life of the mind both *despite* and *because of* her gender—for an eighteenth-century woman's tradition of generic, social, and literary conventions informs her writings, their dialogic style, and their vocational role in her life.

"To Talk of Time—to Make Epochs—to Write Histories": Transcendentalist Conversations

As her nineteenth-century contemporaries might have recommended, Mary Emerson should be considered along with professional talkers such as Fuller and Alcott in assessments of the role of transcendentalist conversation and literature of the portfolio in promoting mutual-culture. Thoreau claims in 1851, for instance, that Emerson's open mind and insatiable hunger for knowledge "provoke" her interlocutor to "his best thought" or higher truth. "She relates herself surely to the intellectual where she goes," he observes of Emerson, then age seventy-seven. "It is perhaps her greatest praise & peculiarity that she more surely than any other woman gives her companion occasion to utter his best thought."[25] Thoreau emphasizes here the breadth of Emerson's intellectual generosity, and although he also commends Fuller in this regard, he names Mary Emerson the greatest converser. As the century unfolded, the scope of her conversations extended to transcendentalists and related intellectuals, including Thoreau, nephews Waldo and Charles, Elizabeth Hoar, Elizabeth Palmer Peabody, Sarah Alden Bradford Ripley, Lydia Maria Child, Orville Dewey, and Frederic Henry Hedge. Complaining of a "dearth of books" and metaphysical conversationalists in December 1838, Emerson peppers Hedge with questions to goad him to talk. "Now my dear Sir," she warns, "dont answer me as if I were a timid old woman & would boast of your sayings or be alarmed" (*SLE*, 401). Prepared by her immersion in transatlantic eighteenth-century cultures of discourse, Emerson challenges a younger generation to converse.

This foreground also enabled Emerson to connect with the female transcendentalists who would ultimately benefit from the gendered and feminist self-consciousness of Fuller's more prominent conversational experiments—for Emerson began practicing self-cultivation and sharing it with others over thirty years before Fuller established these practices as central pedagogical tools in her Boston Conversations in 1839. Emerson's lifelong devotion to this vocation directly influenced another great talker, Elizabeth Palmer Peabody, who as an intellect and educator in turn fostered second-generation transcendentalist Caroline Healey Dall's more radical self-cultivation as activist, critic, and theological writer.[26] A longtime friend of Emerson, Peabody depicts her as a rebel spirit engaged in a perpetual flirtation with life, both social and intellectual. You "do not exhibit any of this death-in-life which I complain of," Peabody wrote to her in 1845, "but coquette with life like a girl of fifteen, who knows herself sovereign and can afford to play with *All*." Claiming that she and other Unitarian children are burdened with an "excessive fear of doing wrong" and thereby robbed of "something within us—which is vital," Peabody admires the lithe and stimulating ways in which her friend playfully interrogates universals without regard to rules, an estimation shared by others (quoted in Ronda, 217; emphasis original). "Here is M.M.E.," comments Waldo Emerson in June 1835, "always fighting in conversation against the very principles which have governed & govern her" (*JMN*, 5:64). Waldo and Peabody recognize that "M.M.E." was willing to turn on a dime in order to "coquette" with other engaged talkers. In fact, these transcendentalists saw in Mary Emerson and her circulating manuscripts a powerful and inventive conversationalist, a precursor of Fuller's professional and feminist modeling of that role.

In early and late circles, Emerson routinely circulated her manuscripts, and in the nineteenth century, she formally dedicated specific fascicles as gifts. More frequently, however, she dispatched Almanack leaves as letters, one of them, for example, in March 1830 to Charles Chauncy Emerson. Noting that she herself had been enjoying "much good talk with my learned Cousin," and hoping to extend that same experience to her nephew, Mary Emerson requests: "Do do write. I have nothing else to say—so send an old page to make up talk." Her "good talk" with Cousin is in fact commonplacing—extracts and commentary—so here she both conceives of commonplace writing as discourse and self-consciously proposes, as does Edward Emerson in 1830, that circulating manuscripts represent actual talk. The "old page" that Emerson encloses with her letter is an Almanack leaf from a few months earlier, an imaginative framing of an intellectual debate, "were Plato & Shakespear to meet!" She imagines "old Shakes. holding a pencil there—and Plato etherealizing the images—more—sketching the eternal forms of beauty" and concludes, "Ah what an education awaits the hungry & thirsty who sojourn in this dreamy waste" (*SLE*, 285–86).

When she circulates this Almanack leaf to Charles, Emerson importantly reiterates the extent to which, for her, and in advance of the transcendentalists, conversation flows freely, like electricity, from one communicant to another; moreover, it offers a higher truth. Here, she compares Plato's "eternal forms of beauty" with Shakespeare's "gross" focus on "human actions & high wrought passion." Shakespeare, whom she admires as the "bard of nature," nonetheless cannot ascend to Plato's "loftiest sta[r]" and is in sad need of the higher laws comprehended in the philosopher's idealism. So too, potentially, is Charles Emerson, as the recipient of this Almanack leaf. But manuscript "talk" replenishes its recipient: with each circulating leaf, Emerson promotes yet another conversation about "the education" that "awaits the hungry and thirsty" (*SLE*, 286). Again reflecting the honeybee as trope, commonplacing enriches its author and feeds her correspondents.

These wandering Almanacks also evidence numerous textual discussions between aunt and nephews and thus shed significant light on manuscript culture within the Emerson family and its role in shaping transcendentalist literature of the portfolio.[27] At its best, this practice fostered a vibrant exchange of ideas: a "living leaping Logos"—as Waldo Emerson wrote in another context—that inspired both parties (*LE*, 1:402). Although it is unclear who initiated it, the Emersons shared a metaphor, suggested by the biblical parable of the ten wise and foolish virgins, for Mary's manuscript dialogues. According to the book of Matthew, five enlightened virgins filled their lamps with oil in expectation of Christ the bridegroom's approach; the other five virgins procrastinated, purchasing oil at the twelfth hour and thus recklessly squandering their prospects for divine union.[28] In an 1807 Almanack, Emerson invokes this allusion, as conventionally understood, to the Christian who is singularly prepared to receive the illuminating presence of divinity: "In League with God," she proclaims. "Henceforth the picture I'll image shall be girded loins a bright lamp fervent devotions" (385:3). Phyllis Cole argues convincingly, and relevantly, that after refusing several proposals of marriage at this time, Emerson consecrated her life to a solitary and vocational commitment to God.[29]

In 1807 and throughout her writings, Emerson reiterates what is perhaps the most common theme of these evolving manuscripts: that spiritual and intellectual wisdom enrich one another, and that the pursuit of both is her vocation. Returning to her personal image of the virgin's lamp in an 1826 Almanack, Emerson exclaims: "A few lamps held out in the firmament enable us to talk of time—to make epochs—to write histories—to do more—to date the revelations of God to man—But these lamps are held to measure out some of the moments of eternity. . . . & we measure duration by the number of our thoughts—by the activity of reason—the discovery of truths—the acquirement of virtue—the approach to God!" (385:8). In this passage, Emerson boldly raises her "lamp" to light her own spiritual and intellectual "firmament" and enable "the discovery of truths." Pointedly and in words that evoke William Ellery Channing's prototranscendentalist Unitarianism, she measures her "approach to God" in a way similar to her calculation of eternity itself: through the fertile acts of her self-cultivating mind.

Emerson again refines her thinking on the lamp metaphor in 1829, when she recognizes new terminology for old ideas in Coleridge's *The Friend* and *Aids to Reflection*, a recognition further illustrated, and with a Platonic inflection, in a letter conjecturally dated 17 December 1837 to Elizabeth Hoar. Emerson observes that physics, science, mathematics, and "of late transcendentalism" were repackaging (somewhat unsuccessfully, in her view) a metaphysical truth that she had recognized in her earliest Almanacks: "That there is a pure domaine of reason is our shield of faith in God & that He has given a spark of it to all . . . it is an holier inspiration—intuition itself w'h places the mind in communion with Reason w'h may be said 'to be identical with God.'" Recognizing in Coleridge's "pure domaine of reason" her long-cherished faith in a divinely endowed "spark" of "intuition," Emerson offers Hoar a glimpse of her own Almanack description of these glories, much as she had dispersed countless other manuscript leaves to Charles, Waldo, and their associates. "Is my dear Elisabeth willing to enter my cave where the 'obscura' is so very dim?—then a page for the Almanack shall go. Had I your capasity for metaph.s [metaphysics] I need not 'roam' but with that internal 'lamp' . . . get into high places" (*SLE*, 384). Despite her self-deprecating tone in regard to Hoar's greater "capasity," in this letter Emerson associates her manuscripts and their circulation with the lamplight of "a pure domaine of reason" granted by divinity, and she implicitly allies herself with the Platonic explorer who "get[s] into high places" or "roams" above the shadows of the cave's camera obscura. The Emerson family frequently recounted and even parodied Mary Emerson's insatiable roaming after metaphysics, but in this case individual leaves quite literally travel from Almanack fascicle to new readers. Indeed, in another letter to Hoar of the following year, Emerson playfully describes her circulating manuscripts as "my Almanak scraps w'h love to wander" (*SLE*, 390). And with such routinely extensive flights of textual wanderlust she initiates yet another conversation about Reason, truth, and intellectual "capasity."

As these wandering scraps suggest, vocational activities find rich expression within communal intellectual circles—lamps are "held out" to "enable us to talk of time," and Emerson's nephews echo the multiple valences of this key metaphor in their manuscript discourse with her. In January 1828, Charles implores his aunt for an Almanack leaf, adding, "I want the light of a gifted intellect fed by the oil of knowledge, to illuminate for me the dark passages of human nature, history, & philosophy."[30] Likewise, in June 1830 Edward Emerson acknowledges that the value of Emerson's Almanack gifts resides in their "representations of the intellectual life" and their function as true "*conversation.*" Nonetheless, he begs to forgo the manuscript dialogue she has proposed: "It does seem to me more reasonable that I should take posture as a scholar, & ask to be favored with interpretations, of the pages of nature and philosophy which you have had a most happy leisure . . . for inspecting." "Is it not rather more prudent for me to be 'prosed with,'" he continues persuasively, "if I can only prevail on you to give me of your oil.—Do not say that the parable directs you to answer—'not so.'"[31]

Although they interpret the biblical allegory differently, both nephews associate their aunt's "oil of knowledge" with Almanack circulation. Edward, who argued with Mary Emerson at this time about his profession, begs off a mutual exchange of manuscripts; moreover, and unlike Charles, he asks for intuition, genius, or the oil that *inspires* knowledge, rather than (Mary's) commonplace wisdom itself. Charles's request, however, emphasizes the Almanacks' method of enacting a circulating economy of production and consumption vitalized by the "living Word," processes that would soon fundamentally inform transcendentalist parlor conversations and literature of the portfolio. Unlike the parable's instruction that the precious oil cannot be shared, in the economy of conversation, oil passes freely from one reader to another. Further, one member's unreadiness can be compensated for by another's largesse, a gesture of mutual-cultivation that Mary Emerson had established years earlier with fellow coterie members.

An 1829–30 Almanack, while offering a fascinatingly interactive example of this mutual-cultivation, illustrates the ways in which genre, "large ideas," and women's rhetorical traditions guide Emerson's eclectic search for truth. After extracting extensively from the third volume of Samuel Taylor Coleridge's revised and enlarged republication of the periodical *The Friend* (1818), Emerson abruptly interrogates her objectives. "Truth, which I hunt, may be found. . . . The *simple truth* w'h amusement has tempted me to injure is the only chart of my life—leads *nessecarily* to the Center of all truth & being. . . . Oh dear as these things are I do wish that I could spare a daily writing of them. . . . —let the revelation go—& Coleridge whose topsy turvy pharseology I *suspect* had conjured away my real strenght" (385:12; 1280H:147). Throughout this fascicle Emerson fluctuates between exhilaration and skepticism regarding Coleridge's "topsy turvy" terminology, for it seductively echoes and challenges—and often renames—aspects of her own long-held ideas about intuition, the soul, truth, and religion itself. Days of transcribing and challenging Coleridge, Emerson suddenly realizes, have distracted her from her true objective and "real strenght"—the hunt for a higher truth. Yet ironically, after reaching this decision, Emerson immediately resumes her elusive search for books, people, and ideas in this Almanack, since as she well knows, the "disturbing delight" of the "hunt" compels her to "daily writing."

Fascination with commonplace writing also induces Emerson to an elaborate dramatization in this fascicle of her quest for "the Center of all truth"—and its social manifestations. Herein, she conjures a poignant scene that shifts from traditional monologue to complicated exhortation between Almanack writer and the autobiographical persona of a "book scavanger." Her self-description reminds us that, denied a college education and lacking a scholar's library, Mary Emerson in her commonplace quest for truth had to "scavange" books from male relatives and the homes in which she boarded in rural Maine and Massachusetts for over thirty years, frequently selecting a specific city because of the reputation of its minister. In her Almanack dramatization, this defiant figure is stranded ashore, stymied in her attempt to hasten toward a "vast ocean." Because her "bark" is both "unrigged" and "unoared," the book scavenger relies for guidance on "the pole star." "Discourged at defeat in knowledge" from childhood to old age "& not quiting pursuit," Emerson explains in her own voice, "I somtimes feel as tho' an illusive demon was spiriting me on." Apparently regarding her spirit daemon as whimsical, she draws strength from her true intellectual and spiritual Polaris—her Almanacks, both "*home*" and representation of self. Despite momentary distractions and frustrations, Mary Emerson will never quit her "pursuit" of "knowledge": "Courage and go on to the mistifying work of years—transcribing," Emerson exhorts her persona, explicitly honoring three decades of toil within her commonplace book genre. "But to thy task slave—boatwoman—cabin rotter—book scavanger! Waldo lives & praises thy lines—there was no Waldo—no idea of society when thou wert up early & late to copy a sermon or a scrap lent thee by a rustic. Too it, to it!" (385:12; 579:12; 1280H:147).

"No idea of society" gives way, at the end of the 1829–30 fascicle, to a complexly layered conversation between Emerson, her "book scavanger" persona, French author and Girondist Marie-Jeanne Roland, and a female correspondent—imaging and realizing the kind of interactive network of readers and writers, relationships and manuscripts, that will later constitute transcendentalists' dialogic self-culture. This Almanack is one of several fascicles in which a recipient converses with Emerson directly on its pages: Ellen Ward Blake Blood (1807–99), a sister of Thoreau's disciple H. G. O. Blake and wife of Waldo's Harvard classmate Oliver Hunter Blood, initiates a commonplace conversation with Emerson after reading it. The fascicle's stirring challenge to Coleridge, quickly followed by Emerson's "book scavanger" composition and extracts from the prison memoirs of Roland, display the "large ideas" and sovereign flirtation with "*All*" that charmed Thoreau, Peabody, and other transcendentalists. Prompted by Emerson's "oil of knowledge," Ellen Blood answers its intertextual record of dialogic self-culture with her own aspirational offering.

Blood and Emerson's "talking" manuscript offers a particular boon to scholarship given the ephemeral nature of transcendentalist conversation as an art form. Unlike the scribal transcriptions of public, formalized conversations recorded by Elizabeth Peabody, Caroline Healey Dall, Ednah Cheney, and other female participants in the parlor conversations of Alcott and Fuller, the unmediated discourse that Emerson and Blood produce situates itself on a social platform between "private" and "public" spheres. Their conversation in manuscript also adds a provocative context to a women's genealogy of transcendentalism as it anticipates questions central to Fuller's 1839 Boston Conversation series: "What were we born to do? How shall we do it?" (*LMF*, 2:87).

Departing from her more common neglect of gender, in this Almanack dedicated to genre, vocation, and truth, Emerson overtly models herself on another woman—and, moreover, the secular Roland, a courageous writer and *salonnière* who battled political injustice during the Reign of Terror. Emerson begins her transcriptions from Roland's *An Appeal to Impartial Posterity* with a statement astonishing for one so attuned to her unique identity. "I should rather be Madame Roland than myself," she admits. "Yet at this moment her fortitude rather humbles than raises me." Having declined a marriage proposal from the man she would ultimately marry, Roland dedicated her life to solitary intellectual study—choices and pursuits with which Mary Emerson certainly identified. Roland commemorates as "treasures" the strength of her mind, her virtue, and the habitual practices of reading and writing. "I fortify my heart against adversity by deserving happiness," Emerson transcribes from *An Appeal*, "& thus I avenge myself on that fortune that refuses to grant it. . . . & if I was not happy I had within my own bosom all that was nessecary to make me so" (385:12).[32]

Appropriately for a fascicle that tentatively explores gender and culture, after recording this expression of intellectual conviction in the face of literal incarceration, Emerson reinforces her identification with Roland by describing her own detainment—caught in a "painfull lodging," a boarding situation that exacerbates her "imprisoned health" (385:12). Emerson's likening of her physical complaint to Roland's internment while awaiting execution may feel strained, but the comparison bears directly on the "hunt for truth" in this fascicle. As Nancy Simmons observes, "mental, like physical, wandering had a tonic effect [on Emerson]; her quest for excitement was a means of keeping the soul open to new influences." Considered from this perspective, Emerson the autodidact keenly suffered "painfull lodging" when health or affordable lodging restricted movement to a place where she "could learn instead of living with ignorance."

In fact, Emerson exchanged boarding locations in part to slake her desire for "intelligent & worthy objects," and throughout 1830 she chose to reside in varied Massachusetts and Connecticut towns rather than in her own home in Maine (*SLE*, 281; quoted in 279, 280; 274, 276). Emerson, as did her "Almanak scraps," "love[d] to wander," and those journeys enabled mutual-cultivation.

Moreover, and as Almanack reader Ellen Blood surely recognized, Roland also echoes Emerson's autobiographical "book scavanger" in her determination to hold fast to her intellectual Polaris. Roland confronts "adversity" by seeking comfort in the personal fortress of her mind. The pursuit of "virtue," and "that delicate taste of a sound understanding w'h finds in the sentiment of existence, & in the idea of it's own value, indemnification unknown to the vulgar," Roland insists in her memoir, "such were my treasures!" Sorrowfully, and likely also aligning her book scavenger's victories and "discourage[ments] at defeat in knowledge" with her French heroine's defiant incarceration, Emerson directly addresses Roland as she copies these lines, a familiar practice in the Almanacks, whose pages are punctuated with fond apostrophes to "Dear sainted Plotinus!" "dear Plato," "Dear transcendentalist," or even "dear Mrs Blood," as in this fascicle. "Ah Roland thou wert not happy," she mourns—"how idle to possess a treasure we cannot use. But thou wert well—in health. What could prevent thee? If this most most painfull lodging—& this imprisoned health were away—one single hour would find me blest" (385:32; 385:12; 385:22; 579:17; 385:12; 385:12).

In this ambiguous conversation with Roland, Emerson appears to suggest that Roland (and by virtue of her pronoun use, Emerson also) "possess a treasure we cannot use," a broad and potentially gendered analysis that may underscore Emerson's tentative but self-conscious exploration in this fascicle of the cultural and intellectual challenges that early modern women faced on either side of the Atlantic. Roland in fact rose to prominence and was executed for her political writings and activist defiance, but the brilliant daughter and granddaughter of Harvard-trained ministers undoubtedly realized that she would pursue theology, literature, science, and philosophy primarily in the pages of her Almanacks and in conversation with other like-minded souls.

Paradoxically, however, and in quick succession, Emerson appears to reverse her previous position. Roland can "possess" her intellectual "treasure" and use it to foster her "idea of [her mind's] own value," the "indemnification unknown to the vulgar." "What could prevent thee?" Emerson insists. In contradicting her initial assessment of women's cultural restrictions, Emerson appears to reconfirm her faith that commonplace activities insure against loss and endorse intellectual and moral worth. Evidently, the ill Emerson longed to turn more of her book scavenger's hard-fought "defeats" in self-education into successes, and her current boarding house may have lacked an adequate library or sitting area in which to read and write, had she the good health to pursue the hallowed activities through which a mere sixty minutes could "find me blest." More than ever (and again like her book scavenger), she requires the Almanacks' intellectual compensation at a time of weakness. And, intriguingly, her fellow Almanack reader supplies this renewal. As in the honeybee trope, within the economy of manuscript exchange, one member's abundance feeds another's hunger; in transcendentalist terminology, Blood and Emerson magnetize each other with the "living Word."

Responding to the stimulating textual catalyst of this conversation about books and their blessings, Blood joins Emerson's social sphere debate with Roland by writing on the reverse of this Almanack leaf. Dating and signing her epistolary offering as "Brookfield. Feb. 29th 1830" and "E. W. B.," Blood also proffers a commonplace excerpt, a passage from William Ellery Channing's discourses that complements the fascicle's multilayered discussions.[33] "The *mind* is the seat of happiness or of misery," she transcribes, directly contradicting Emerson's assessment of Roland's emotional state. Reiterating Emerson's previous exhortations to her "book scavanger" persona and perhaps remembering that Roland has "within [her] own bosom" all things needful, Blood argues, "*outward* circumstances are comparitively inconsequential." In her own words, she adds admiringly, "I have never been so fully convinced of this as since I have known the author of these fragments, her faith is fixed, her business is improvement of her mental & moral powers. . . . What then shall I wish for her whose felicity is within herself? Only that . . . the stream of her days glide peacefully on to the 'vast ocean of Eternity.'" Admittedly, the "vast ocean of Eternity" is a common nineteenth-century allusion to the afterlife, but the phrase also resonates with Emerson's imaginary composition, in which the clear-eyed author reminds her "book scavanger," who hastens to the water's edge: "In earth's ocean is many a treasure & when the fires prevail they will come forth in preservation" (385:12). Roland's self-professed "treasures" offer identical forms of defense.

Blood's spirited vindication of shared intellectual riches may have assuaged any lingering doubts in the Almanack writer, for Emerson concludes this dialogue by reflecting Roland's promise that reading and writing practices awaken the "sound understanding" to the glorious "idea of it's own value." Blood champions mutual-cultivation and self-reliance in her Channing extract and gloss, and then beneath Blood's signature an invigorated Emerson mischievously answers her correspondent: "dear Mrs Blood," she retorts, "you stole my MMS tho' you did not steal any reading" (385:12). As Emerson acknowledges, Almanack leaves may stray, but each speaker holds fast to her interpretation or "reading" of these intertextual exchanges. Reciprocated commonplace writing offers true "indemnification" by promoting talkers' awareness of the intrinsic "value" of their intellect, so Blood's culling of the sweets, to return again to the honeybee trope, ultimately nourishes both conversers and ensures that the light emanating from the virgin's lamp resides within. Importantly for a fascicle conversation that self-consciously examines, in Blood's words, the "business" of intellectual vocation, Emerson—like the noble Roland—has achieved that exalted state in which "felicity is within herself."[34]

In *Woman in the Nineteenth Century*, Fuller similarly honors Roland's felicitous "self-sufficingness" and in words that resemble the praise Blood showers on Emerson. "[Roland] is an antetype of a class to which the coming time will afford a field," Fuller suggests, "the Spartan matron, brought by the culture of the age of Books to intellectual consciousness and expansion" (*WNC*, 43). Being neither "matron" nor political revolutionary, however, the proudly single Mary Emerson also differs from her role model Roland. Moreover, Emerson and Fuller, despite their shared awareness of dialogic power, proved incompatible. Their disastrous 1841 meeting in Newburyport, during which Fuller "catechised" the older woman while reclining on a sofa,[35] suggests that Emerson's vocational pursuit of commonplacing and ethics collided with Fuller's aesthetic approach to self-reform and transatlantic idealism at that time, before she commenced her revolutionary career as a journalist in the United States and Rome. "This hasty attempt at skimming from the deeps of theosophy," Fuller afterward complained of Emerson to Elizabeth Hoar, "is as unpleasant as the rude vanity of reformers. Dear Beauty where where amid these morasses . . . shall we make thee a temple[?]" In her view, Emerson radiates a few lingering "sparkles" from buried "gems"—perhaps an allusion to what Charles Capper characterizes as Fuller's "key symbol" for "energizing and revelatory knowledge," the German romantics' carbuncle—but in the end Fuller could only muster lukewarm praise: Emerson "is still valuable as a disturbing force to the lazy."[36]

While also acknowledging their conflict, Emerson openly admired the younger woman's brilliance—and yet, intriguingly, she uses related language. Emerson criticizes Fuller for "want of beauty" (a comment that, coming from a woman who scorned adornment and prized Plato's "eternal forms of beauty," likely does not refer to physical features) and for cruelly withholding from her eager interlocutor even "one sparkel of her fine wit" or "one argument . . . from her fine mind" (*SLE*, 523). Ironically, neither of these emblematic female conversationalists could recognize and respond to scintillating "sparkles" of "beauty" in the other; the alchemic and erotically charged carbuncle and the ascetic virgin's lamp failed to produce a "living Word" in this meeting.[37]

Reflecting her fondness for "large ideas," however, these jarring notes did not impede Emerson's interest in Fuller's estimable talk. Further, although she did not attend them, Emerson contributed to the circulation of Fuller's 1839–40 Conversations. Knowing her fascination with dialogic performance, Elizabeth Hoar transcribed portions of these formal discussions and sent them to Emerson, who then shared them with her niece Hannah Haskins. Thanking Hoar,

Emerson excitedly emphasizes the value of conversation over "pasteboard" or book enlightenment: "the pictures of beauty & elegance are *very* welcome—for they inspire Hannah whose rays of genius have been more awakned than by any thing I tell her w'h is contained between pasteboard." Nancy Simmons speculates that Hoar deliberately copied Fuller's Conversations 16–18 in this series, a discussion of "woman," in part because Emerson had requested to "hear *practical* questions discussed among these *young* ladies."[38] In keeping with her own search for a higher truth, Emerson preferred to read conversations on reform, self-cultivation, or metaphysics rather than on Fuller's previous subjects, Greek mythology, art, and "poesy."

This truth-seeking quest likewise informs a late (probably 1857) letter to Waldo, in which the fervent abolitionist commends her nephew for his antislavery efforts in behalf of Free Kansas by offering him a rare late example of a circulating Almanack leaf. In this fragment, dating from 1853, Emerson discusses William Hannah's *Memoirs of the Life and Writings of Thomas Chalmers* in the context of her late eighteenth- and early nineteenth-century Almanacks, fascicles that, to her, represent uniquely pure expressions of piety. In light of her lifelong interests in memoirs, manuscript circulation, and enlightened truth, one could argue that in dispersing this leaf to Waldo, Mary Emerson allies his attempts to speak truth to power with memories of her own youthful expressions of divine truth, captured in her much earlier, and now lost, Almanacks.[39]

This 1850s attempt to encourage Waldo in his abolitionist efforts by offering him yet another "talking" manuscript exemplifies the powerful ways in which the Almanacks of Mary Emerson could prompt the members of her early and late circles to grasp a higher truth—whether political, intellectual, or spiritual. Phyllis Cole and Sandra Harbert Petrulionis have demonstrated that Emerson and other Concord women "prod[ded] Waldo toward antislavery," and this kind of truth-seeking social activism would especially inform the dialogic writings of later nineteenth-century "Exaltadas."[40] Nearly thirty years later, in an article titled "Note upon a Conversation at the Radical Club," Elizabeth Peabody highlights collaborative discourse as the means to pursue an ever-elusive quarry, a process that she notably associates with John Brown. "Every mind has the possibility of seeing something the others do not see," she remarks, "whence the absolute necessity for a wide intercommunion of minds, in order to the evolution of truth."[41] As Laura Walls has observed, for Waldo Emerson, Peabody, and others in their circle, moral and natural laws—in dialogue with science—generated a "culture of truth," in which "words and actions converted principles of belief" into instruments of sacred power.[42]

This search for a "higher law" achieved through informed yet spontaneous conversation and its "intercommunion of minds" is often considered a uniquely transcendentalist—or an abolitionist—impulse, but as the foregoing discussion suggests, Mary Emerson from earlier years pursued an eclectic path toward truth with the aid of such underappreciated genres as memoirs and commonplace books. Above all, she voices the intrepid assumption that her words should reach—and even transform—the lives of other known and unknown pilgrims. In fact, and as Emerson imagined, the audience for her circulating manuscripts is humanity itself, and certainly future generations of readers: In a gesture at once poignant and ambitious, on a faded blue leaf enclosing an 1850s Almanack, an elderly Emerson scrawled the prophetic words, "For any body" (385:30).

NOTES

I wish to express my thanks to Sandra Harbert Petrulionis, who generously commented on earlier versions of this essay.

1. See Edward Bliss Emerson to Mary Moody Emerson, 29 June 1830, in Emerson Family Correspondence, MS Am 1280.226 (179), and Ralph Waldo Emerson Journals and Notebooks, MS Am 1280H:147, one of three notebooks recording extracts from Mary Emerson's Almanacks. Emerson's Almanacks reside with the Emerson Family Papers, MS Am 1280.235:385 (1–47), along with Almanack transcriptions by Ralph Waldo Emerson, MS Am 1280H:147–49, and by George Tolman, MS Am 1280.235:579 (1–50). These materials are part of the Ralph Waldo Emerson Memorial Association deposit, MH-H. Not to be reproduced in whole or in part without permission. Hereafter, Almanack references and Tolman and Ralph Waldo Emerson transcriptions are cited parenthetically and in notes by call numbers as "385," "579," and "1280H," respectively, and by folder number. They derive from a recent transcription of the complete text, in preparation for an edition now in progress, *The Almanacks of Mary Moody Emerson: A Scholarly Digital Edition*, edited by Noelle A. Baker and Sandra Harbert Petrulionis, currently being published in Women Writers Online, in collaboration with the Women Writers Project and supported by the National Endowment for the Humanities and the Ralph Waldo Emerson Fund, MH-H.
2. I am extending Phyllis Cole's groundbreaking treatment of Mary Emerson's intellectual conversations with Waldo Emerson in *Mary Moody Emerson and the Origins of Transcendentalism: A Family History* (New York: Oxford Univ. Press, 1998).
3. Emerson describes her Almanacks as her "pole star" in an 1829–30 fascicle (385:12). She characterizes them as her "*home*" and "images" in *The Selected Letters of Mary Moody Emerson*, ed. Nancy Craig Simmons (Athens: Univ. of Georgia Press, 1993), 287; hereafter cited parenthetically and in notes as *SLE*.
4. Larry J. Reynolds, "From *Dial* Essay to New York Book: The Making of *Woman in the Nineteenth Century*," in *Periodical Literature in Nineteenth-Century America*, ed. Kenneth M. Price and Susan Belasco Smith (Charlottesville: Univ. Press of Virginia, 1995), 20–21.
5. For a fuller discussion of Emerson's dialogic use of genre and the material culture of manuscripts, see Noelle A. Baker, "'Somthing more than material': Nonverbal Conversation in Mary Moody Emerson's Almanacks," *Resources for American Literary Study* 35 (2010): 29–67.
6. Henry David Thoreau, *Journals*, ed. John C. Broderick et al., 8 vols. to date, in *WHT*, 4:184.
7. Explorations of the influence of Fuller's Conversations on transcendentalist thought and the emerging woman's movement include Zwarg; Judith Mattson Bean, "'A *Pres-*

ence among Us': Fuller's Place in Nineteenth-Century Oral Culture," *ESQ: A Journal of the American Renaissance* 44 (1998): 79–123; Phyllis Cole, "Woman Questions: Emerson, Fuller, and New England Reform," in Capper and Wright, 410–20, 425; Cole, "Stanton, Fuller, and the Grammar of Romanticism," *NEQ* 73 (2000): 533–39; and Wayne, 18–26.

8. Scholarship on women's rhetorical traditions and the European salon influence includes Jane Donawerth, "Nineteenth-Century United States Conduct Book Rhetoric by Women," *Rhetoric Review* 21, no. 1 (2002): 5–21; Charlene Avallone, "Catharine Sedgwick and the 'Art' of Conversation," in *Catharine Maria Sedgwick: Critical Perspectives*, ed. Lucinda Damon-Bach and Victoria Clements (Boston: Northeastern Univ. Press, 2003), 192–208; and Avallone, "Elizabeth Palmer Peabody and the 'Art' of Conversation," in Elbert, Hall, and Rodier, 23–44. Earle Havens examines commonplace books historically in *Commonplace Books: A History of Manuscripts and Printed Books from Antiquity to the Twentieth Century* (New Haven: Beinecke Rare Book and Manuscript Library, distributed by Univ. Press of New England, 2001), 8.
9. *JMN* 16:259; Germaine de Staël, "Of the Spirit of Conversation," in *Germany*, 2 vols. (1814; reprint, New York: Derby and Jackson, 1859), 1:77–89, 70.
10. Susan M. Stabile, "Introduction: Elizabeth Fergusson and British-American Literary History," in *The Most Learned Woman in America: A Life of Elizabeth Graeme Fergusson*, by Anne M. Ousterhout (University Park: Pennsylvania State Univ. Press, 2003), 20.
11. Margaret J. M. Ezell, *Social Authorship and the Advent of Print* (Baltimore: Johns Hopkins Univ. Press, 1999), 40.
12. Catherine Kerrison, *Claiming the Pen: Women and Intellectual Life in the Early American South* (Ithaca, N.Y.: Cornell Univ. Press, 2006), 163.
13. Scholarship on this social sphere includes Carla Mulford, introduction to *Only for the Eye of a Friend: The Poems of Annis Boudinot Stockton*, ed. and intro. Mulford (Charlottesville: Univ. Press of Virginia, 1995), 1–57; David S. Shields, *Civil Tongues & Polite Letters in British America* (Chapel Hill: Univ. of North Carolina Press, 1997); and Susan M. Stabile, *Memory's Daughters: The Material Culture of Remembrance in Eighteenth-Century America* (Ithaca, N.Y.: Cornell Univ. Press, 2004).
14. In *Commonplace Books*, Havens traces this persistent trope to Seneca the Younger's *Epistulae morales* (14–15).
15. Karin A. Wulf, "Milcah Martha Moore's Book: Documenting Culture and Connection in the Revolutionary Era," in *Milcah Martha Moore's Book: A Commonplace Book from Revolutionary America*, ed. Catherine La Courreye Blecki and Karin A. Wulf (University Park: Pennsylvania State Univ. Press, 1997), 56.
16. Scholarship on the effect of such memoirs on early American women includes Laurel Thatcher Ulrich, "Vertuous Women Found: New England Ministerial Literature, 1668–1735," *American Quarterly* 28, no. 1 (1976): 20–40; and Lonna M. Malmsheiner, "Daughters of Zion: New England Roots of American Feminism," *New England Quarterly* 50 (1977): 484–504.
17. Joanna Bowen Gillespie, "'The Clear Leadings of Providence': Pious Memoirs and the Problems of Self-Realization for Women in the Early Nineteenth Century," *Journal of the Early Republic* 5, no. 2 (1985): 213.
18. "Bronson Alcott's 'Journal for 1837' (Part Two)," ed. Larry Carlson, in *Studies in the American Renaissance*, ed. Joel Myerson (Charlottesville: Univ. Press of Virginia, 1982), 71–72. For transcendentalist conversation, see Lawrence Buell, *Literary Transcendentalism: Style and Vision in the American Renaissance* (Ithaca, N.Y.: Cornell Univ. Press, 1973), 75–139; for

cultural contexts, see Peter Gibian, *Oliver Wendell Holmes and the Culture of Conversation* (New York: Cambridge Univ. Press, 2001).

19. Woody Holton, *Abigail Adams* (New York: Free Press, 2009), 8, 50–52, 56. Mary Kelley similarly describes the self-conscious goal of women's reading circles in *Learning to Stand and Speak: Women, Education, and Public Life in America's Republic* (Chapel Hill: Univ. of North Carolina Press, 2006), 114–17.
20. Cole, *Mary Moody Emerson*, 107–8, 112–18.
21. Cornelia, "To Constance," *Monthly Anthology* 1, no. 9 (1804): 394.
22. John 14:2.
23. Cornelia, "To Constance," 394.
24. Mary Van Schalkwyck, quoted in Elizabeth Amelia Dwight, *Memorials of Mary Wilder White: A Century Ago in New England*, ed. Mary Wilder Tileston (Boston: Everett Press, 1903), 223.
25. Thoreau, *Journals*, in *WHT*, 4:183–84.
26. Helen R. Deese, "A New England Women's Network: Elizabeth Palmer Peabody, Caroline Healey Dall, and Delia S. Bacon," *Legacy* 8, no. 2 (1991): 80, 81.
27. For Waldo Emerson's discussion of "literature of the portfolio," see "The Editors to the Reader," *Dial* 1, no. 1 (1840): 4; and "New Poetry," *Dial* 1, no. 2 (1840): 220–32.
28. Matthew 25:1–13.
29. Cole, *Mary Moody Emerson*, 101.
30. Charles Emerson, quoted in Ronald A. Bosco and Joel Myerson, *The Emerson Brothers: A Fraternal Biography in Letters* (New York: Oxford Univ. Press, 2006), 256.
31. Edward Bliss Emerson to Mary Moody Emerson, 29 June 1830, MS Am 1280.226 (179).
32. Emerson may have read *An Appeal* (first American edition, corrected, 1798) directly, but this appears to be a loose transcription of a passage from Roland's memoir included in Mary Hays's *Female Biography; or Memoirs of Illustrious and Celebrated Women, of All Ages and Countries* (Philadelphia: Printed for Byrch and Small, 1807), 3:362–63. In a letter conjecturally dated 1806, Emerson writes sister-in-law Ruth Haskins Emerson, requesting a list of books, including "female biography," the British edition of which appeared in 1803 (*SLE*, 37).
33. I have not been able to identify Blood's transcription in Channing's works.
34. Kelley offers an alternative reading of Roland's modeling of a woman writer in *Learning to Stand and Speak*, 202–10.
35. Mary Moody Emerson to Ralph Waldo Emerson, in *SLE*, 523; Cole fully describes the meeting (*Mary Moody Emerson*, 260).
36. *LMF*, 2:246; Capper 2, 21.
37. Capper 2, 21.
38. See *SLE*, 426; and Nancy Craig Simmons, "Margaret Fuller's Boston Conversations: The 1839–1840 Series," quoting Mary Moody Emerson, in *Studies in the American Renaissance*, ed. Joel Myerson (Charlottesville: Univ. Press of Virginia, 1994), 197.
39. See *SLE*, 582. Simmons transcribes Emerson's letter to Ralph Waldo Emerson (speculatively dating it 6 January 1857) but does not include the earlier Almanack leaf upon which the letter is written. The leaf is in the Emerson Family Correspondence, 6 January 1857, MS Am 1280.226 (949), Ralph Waldo Emerson Memorial Association deposit, MH-H.
40. Phyllis Cole, "Pain and Protest in the Emerson Family," in *The Emerson Dilemma: Essays on Emerson and Social Reform*, ed. T. Gregory Garvey (Athens: Univ. of Georgia Press, 2001), 67–92; Sandra Harbert Petrulionis, *To Set This World Right: The Antislavery Movement in Thoreau's Concord* (Ithaca, N.Y.: Cornell Univ. Press, 2006), 15, and esp. 7–35.

41. Elizabeth Palmer Peabody, "Note upon a Conversation at the Radical Club," *Radical* 6 (1869): 318, 316.

42. Laura Dassow Walls, *Emerson's Life in Science: The Culture of Truth* (Ithaca, N.Y.: Cornell Univ. Press, 2003), 15–16. Charles Capper discusses the European romantic notion, shared by Alcott, that conversation uniquely enabled participants to reveal an ever-expanding truth ("Margaret Fuller as Cultural Reformer: The Conversations in Boston," *American Quarterly* 39 [1987]: 515, 526n20).

INTERLUDE

Sophia Peabody, from "Letters from Cuba" (*Cuba Journal*), 3:10–11, journal MS in 3 volumes, Sophia Peabody Hawthorne papers, Berg Collection of English and American Literature, New York Public Library, Astor, Lenox, and Tilden Foundations.

Such a morning! What a blessing to have been out in it—Should I live to be an old woman grown grey—I am very sure that from the ashes of this past/paradox/my memory will spring a phoenix till the last breath is breathed through these organs—& I rise a Phoenix from the ashes of this body—It is not a slight thing to see a newborn world every day—& to become daily a *living soul* as I seem to—for the breath of life is breathed into my nostrils as if for the first time whenever I am early enough in the Temple not hewn by hand—Magnificent & still. GOD dedicated it with the glance of his eye for man to worship in. I passed a deep pit this morning—perhaps forty feet deep—& from the edges to the bottom the [vines?] had trailed & entirely covered the sides—Vines are the tapestry of this island temple—When I came home I took Herder's beautiful book & with the Bible, read his illuminating thoughts—till we were summoned to the little church—& Madame read a sermon of Dr Channing—but I had been up so long & had read so much that I was completely overwhelmed with drowsiness before she finished & had to go & lie down!

"With the Eyes That Are Given Me"

Early Transcendentalism and Feminist Colonial Poetics in Sophia Peabody's *Cuba Journal*

IVONNE M. GARCÍA

> *Ah me! even above the roar of the blue Atlantic—about the time when this letter is being read by some of my friends at home—I expect to hear a shout of "Oh was there any thing so unfathomable—so incorrigible as that child's extravagance!" Infeliz de mi —! I see with the eyes that are given me. What would ye else?*
>
> —Sophia Peabody, *Cuba Journal* (1833–35)

This sorrowful passage appears in a long letter Sophia Peabody began in late March 1835 as her eighteen months in Cuba came to a close. To describe her feelings, Peabody uses a Spanish phrase (Infeliz de mi—!), loosely translated as "woe is me"; followed by a statement that seems self-evident (I see with the eyes that are given me); and then a question that could be interpreted as an apology (What would ye else?). I suggest, however, that this question also functions as a challenge to readers. Peabody asserts that what she has "seen," referring to how she represented herself and her environs in the highly literary letters she wrote from Cuba, is the inevitable product of a unique perspective. Her self-description as a "child" and use of an archaic "ye" signal deference to her audience—mostly family, but also the larger circle of friends and even strangers whom she knew read the letters.

But the statement also challenges those who might judge her negatively for the highly exalted tone of her metaphorical descriptions.[1] This attempt at self-justification requires her critics to acknowledge that she could not have described anything other than what her aesthetic sensibilities allowed her to "see." There is an interesting tension in the passage between Peabody's protestation that she could have done nothing differently—suggesting a lack of agency—and her defense of the individuality of her gaze. The seeming contradiction between lacking agency and exerting her individuality, a common theme throughout the letters, conveys the duality of Peabody's experience in Cuba. This focus on her gaze and its literary effects plays an integral part in Peabody's early transcendentalist self-fashioning.[2]

Peabody's transcendentalism goes well beyond an aesthetic engagement with Cuban nature and its mediation between her and "the divine," which other scholars have noted.[3] Through a highly descriptive style—what I have termed a "colonial poetics"—Peabody reflects a woman-centered gaze that I categorize as feminist because of its consistently transgressive assertions of female power. Her "seeing" is also colonialist because of its appropriation of Cuba as the foreign space that enables her empowerment. Peabody's early transcendentalism connected aesthetic and sensual pleasure in nature, the woman as individual spectator and actor, and her relation to the divine within a colonial context—all of which coalesced in her expressions of female agency. I refer to this perspective as woman-centered because, unlike other women writing in colonial contexts, Peabody did not ventriloquize or subjugate herself to a masculinist gaze but rather transgressed gender expectations, identifying herself with such figures of female power as queens and the biblical Eve.[4] While the feminism we find in Peabody's letters from Cuba is different from Margaret Fuller's more theorized and activist engagement, it articulates—and enacts—similar desires for influence and authority.

At the same time, in constructing her colonial poetics, Peabody refashioned the male British romantic poets—especially those not then fully included in the canon, such as Percy Bysshe Shelley and John Keats—using frequent literary allusions to bolster her representations of Cuba.[5] Peabody's boldly individualistic gaze transformed these poets into supporting actors on the stage of her life in the Caribbean. She was among those transatlantic readers who recognized the literary impact of these poets before their poems became almost obligatory reading in the late nineteenth century. In this way, Peabody transmitted a deeply romantic aesthetic, which she simultaneously appropriated and transformed to buttress her own literary descriptions of Cuba. What her audience considered "unfathomable," even exaggerated or untruthful, may have been a perceived romantic excess in her accounts. That Peabody recurred to the British romantics, especially in later stretches of her journal, suggests the ways in which she was receptive to and helped disseminate the literary discourse that would be so influential in developing the transcendentalist ethos. As an early transcendentalist, Peabody filtered romantic sensibilities through her lens as an American woman in Cuba, triangulating important literary influences in vitally transnational ways. More to the point, as a woman writer, Peabody borrowed from a British male literary tradition and put it in the service of her own designs on Cuba. Unlike the romantics, Peabody did not privilege imagination in her colonial poetics; instead, she used their lens to describe what she actually saw and felt in Cuba.

Peabody's poetics were enabled and incited by the place in which they developed: the Spanish Caribbean island of Cuba, where she lived between 1833 and 1835 to recuperate her health. Megan Marshall, in her foundational study of the Peabody sisters, quotes relatives who described Sophia as a "'very willful, obstinate child'" who was "born with a 'rebellious spirit.'" Sickly in childhood, Peabody was made worse by the treatments her physician father attempted, including doses of mercury. She eventually developed into a chronic invalid who took meals in her room because she found "the clatter of knives and forks" at the family table an "excruciating torture." When a renowned physician recommended a "rest cure in a warm climate," the family began to consider sending her to South America or Cuba, and after a particularly debilitating bout of illness that left her weighing only eighty pounds, the rest cure materialized.[6] Older sister Mary took a job as governess for a prosperous U.S. doctor named Morrell, who owned coffee and sugar plantations in Cuba and also accepted paying guests for lengthy visits.[7] Sophia accompanied Mary, and her letters from Cuba became a nearly eight-hundred-page-long, three-volume, homemade book, which circulated so widely among the intellectual elite of New England that, by the time of her return, Sophia was generally known as its author. Her husband-to-be, Nathaniel Hawthorne, was so impressed with Peabody's text that he copied more than a dozen entries into his own journal between 1837 and 1841.[8] Although Elizabeth prepared the letters for publication in the *American Monthly*, Sophia opposed their publication; however, the *Cuba Journal* continued to circulate for almost twenty years after her return to the United States.[9]

Peabody's contribution to transcendentalism, as biographer Patricia Dunlavy Valenti and other scholars have noted, may have predated or, at the very least, developed concurrently with the individual-in-relation-to-nature philosophy formulated by Ralph Waldo Emerson, as well as the socially minded feminism elaborated by Fuller.[10] Marshall has argued that had Peabody's *Cuba Journal* been formally published at its time of composition, Peabody would be recognized as one of the earliest transcendentalists. Phyllis Cole, in her important work on feminist transcendentalists, has also located Peabody within that movement's "antinomian tradition of joy," which included Mary Moody Emerson, Ralph Waldo's famous aunt.[11] Here, I focus not on how Peabody predated the more canonical figures of the movement but on how her particular transcendentalist gaze, by appropriating British literary influences in a specifically colonial location and through a uniquely feminist lens, establishes her as one of the most significant early American romantics.

In the passage quoted at the head of this chapter, we feel Peabody's frustration and even sadness at her inability to persuade readers that what she described of her Cuba experience was grounded in fact. She anticipates the kind of objection that had become common by the time she ended the *Cuba Journal*. This seems to have been the case especially with her mother and sisters, including Mary, who persuaded Sophia to put down her pen for three months out of fear that writing the journal was "possessing" her younger sister.[12] The tension between the incredibility of Peabody's outsized representations of life in Cuba and her desire to make the experience translatable through words, whether describing a Cuban sunset or waltzing for the first time, suffuses the *Cuba Journal* from start to finish. This frustration at both rhetorical ends—on the writer's part because she felt unequal to the task of making her audience share in (or believe) what she saw and felt, and on her readers' part because they mistrusted her exaltation—is one of the text's most salient characteristics.

Although Peabody's stay in Cuba yielded the hoped-for result of nearly curing her ailments, relatives in New England were troubled by the ever-increasing "Exaltada" tone of many of her letters.[13] Relatives also expressed concern that Peabody did not seem inordinately troubled that the life of luxury she reveled in was enabled by the island's slave economy. For her part, Peabody claimed that avoiding slavery (whether as cause or concern) was crucial to her bodily cure, allowing her untroubled aesthetic immersion in the Cuban landscape. Valenti has observed that Peabody felt a keen unhappiness at her impending departure not only because she was losing the unprecedented freedom she enjoyed in Cuba but also because she was leaving behind those who had become her "Paradisaical people."[14] Peabody knew she would be deprived of the exaltation constantly inspired in her by the Cuban landscape and by the social engagements of plantation society. What Valenti has described as the nearly orgasmic rapture expressed in some letters reveals not only Peabody's uninhibited sensuousness while in Cuba, especially in her descriptions of nature, but also her determination to articulate a perspective that often privileged the colonial zone above her native country, despite repeated remonstrations against such exaltation.[15] In the opening quotation above, Peabody's focus on the contextual frame of her gaze in Cuba points to how her transcendentalist sensibilities were deeply individualistic at the same time that they depended on the colonial space that enabled her perspective.

Pamela Lee, another scholar who has identified Peabody's "nascent transcendentalism," situates the *Cuba Journal* in recent scholarship on the relationship between transcendentalism and U.S. "imperial tendencies." Lee rightly argues that Peabody's text contributes to U.S. discourses on colonialism developing during the time the letters were written. However, Lee ultimately finds that Peabody's representations of Cuba cannot be read simply as expressions of an "imperial" gaze because her visual mastery over the landscape is disrupted by a "colonial ambivalence."[16] While I agree that the *Cuba Journal* is firmly rooted in the colonial discourses of its time, I find that Peabody's imperial gaze upon a colonial object (Cuba) is distinctly unambiguous (if occasionally ambivalent) and even functions as the creative engine for her transcendentalist poetics. In my opening quotation, Peabody acknowledges the transatlantic or transnational nature of her writings, which she knew contributed to her relatives' perception of her as an unreliable narrator, yet she still asserts the interpretive power of her gaze. Her regret arises not from a sense of fault—after all, she *sees* "with the eyes that are given" her—but rather from her inability to persuade her readers.

Like the final letter in the *Cuba Journal*, which closes the thematic arc of her work, Peabody's first letter of 20 December 1833, written "40 miles from land," demonstrates the self-consciousness of her gaze and her identification with figures of female power, as well as her ability to connect physical pleasure with sublimity and nature with a greater principle. Peabody writes: "I look upon the compass and meditate upon the sublimity of the eternal principals [*sic*] of nature; upon the ship, and admire the inexhaustible invention and power of man; as to the motion of it, it is the constantly felt presence of beauty, soft as a plume, bending and falling away to the wind and wave with the same pliancy and ease" (3–4). In this lyrical description of the ship's motion, she notices how "the power of man" and nature are inextricably linked in the creation of beauty. She also links her gaze to an emotional response, which allows her to appreciate more fully what is beautiful. In addition, the passage begins to articulate the tension that informs the *Cuba Journal*—between the agency of her gaze and interpretive abilities and the powerful feelings that come unbidden (and provoke her readers' mistrust) in response to what she experiences. This conflict, which goes unresolved in the text, points us to the synthesis of opposites—of unfettered appreciation and constricting regulation—that characterizes Peabody's transcendentalist vision.

The painstaking attention to metaphorical language in this first letter exemplifies Peabody's emerging literary style and her desire to translate experience effectively for her audience. As her time in Cuba progressed, Peabody's letters became incrementally more aware of her readers, with increasingly frequent use of literary quotations and allusions and with strikingly metaphorical prose as her stylistic trademark. Later in that same passage, Peabody remarks on her first Caribbean sunset, a time of day that would later acquire great significance for transcendentalists: "We had a most beautiful sun set the evening before the last I was particularly struck with the pale & dark green clouds. Can you imagine how they would look? pale peagreen and the brightest grassy tint upon a faint topaz sky, melting into blue above, and deepening into dazzling gold beneath, and round the northern horizon the clouds were saffron colour, purple and white upon deeper blue" (4). The appeal to her intended reader (primarily her mother) that she try to "imagine" what Peabody is describing reveals the concern over translatability woven throughout the *Cuba Journal*.

Later, in his own writings, Emerson will observe that the transcendentalist looks at nature with "a distinct but most poetical sense in the mind" and focuses on "the integrity of impression made by manifold natural objects" (*CW*, 1:9). While Emerson sees the poet "whose eye can integrate all the parts" of the landscape as male (ibid.), Peabody in her descriptions of Cuba displays a gaze that is not only poetical and integrative but also female. She anticipates Emerson's poet in her writings but does so upon seeing "the first Palm tree wave through the glass," largely thanks to the "strange consciousness" that she is "approaching a foreign land" and must translate this foreignness for her readers (10). Thus, Peabody's early transcendentalism firmly grounds itself in the experience produced within the colonial context of Cuba, one that engenders self-awareness, a poetical instinct, and the nearly obsessive need for self-expression.

In that first letter, Peabody also begins to celebrate the freedom and agency she feels even before touching land, repeatedly casting herself as royalty. As other scholars have noted, Peabody's trip to Cuba allows her to fashion herself as a pampered "queen," an identity impossible in her financially straitened and stress-filled home in Salem.[17] This self-representation as a queen, attended to by cavaliers and knights, recurs throughout the journal and is in keeping with a trope frequently used by other women writers before and after Peabody's time, from Anne Bradstreet's identification with Queen Elizabeth to Emily Dickinson's self-fashioning as a queen. As she sets off on this journey of personal revivification, Peabody styles herself "queen of the atlantic [*sic*], perched upon that high place, ploughing so gracefully and majestically through the deep, deep blue sea," embarking on her own colonial mission for her own benefit (3).

Casting herself as a queen entitled to claim all she surveys, Peabody constructs a colonial poetics that allows her to express her wants freely—especially the physical ones. The constant state of excitement and the appropriative power of her female gaze are as much in evidence aboard the ship as they are later in Cuba. In the first letter, Peabody states, "It is very interesting to watch the sailors, especially one, which is a splendid looking creature, with as much grace as strength, fine features and large blue eyes, which he has a way of casting down quite bewitchingly" (4). Her admission of "watching" the sailors on the ship, whether proper to her own account or (perhaps less plausibly) added by her mother, who copied many of the letters, begins to craft a colonial gaze openly appreciative of sensual stimulation. Simultaneously dehumanizing the sailor as a "creature" and feminizing him despite his physical strength—he casts down his eyes under her gaze—Peabody shifts traditionally gendered power relations. Her ability to transgress and subvert gender roles in this new atmosphere of freedom starts even before she sets foot on the island.

At the same time that Peabody displays her fledgling literary style in that first letter, she reveals a colonizing gaze that deploys a woman-centered authority to sexualize and to possess. The colonial gaze has traditionally been categorized as male centered and the colonized body sexualized as female. But Peabody's sexualization of both female and male bodies in the *Cuba Journal* subverts the asymmetries of traditional gender representations.[18] Unlike the passive female gaze, as conventionally theorized, Peabody's appropriation of the Cuban landscape and lifestyle reveals a sexual agency fueled by the colonial location she inhabits. As Indira Ghose has argued in her study of British colonial women writers, "concepts of gender are bound with colonialist ideology," and women writing in colonial contexts have been both instrumental to and complicit with "the politics of imperialism." For Ghose, the "autonomous female gaze" falls somewhere between "objectification," or mimicking the male colonial gaze, and "identification," or taking on the role of the woman "as a sex object of the male gaze." In promoting the notion of an "erotics of difference," Ghose argues for "a more active mode of spectatorship for women," one that explores the relations of power within which the gaze is wielded and recognizes the drive of the female gaze to control what it gazes upon. We can read Peabody's *Cuba Journal* as an erotics of difference, given that her gaze is no less possessive because it is woman centered.[19]

One way in which Peabody claimed dominion over Cuba was through the notion that the island was her personal paradise, which becomes a key theme in her colonial poetics. In the new Eden Peabody crafts, she casts herself as an American Eve, boldly rewriting the Fall of Man. This striking rumination on Eden comes after another "lovely ride round the plantation," during which the Morrells' son plucks a "Guava from a tree, arrived at its most delicious state for eating." Peabody eats the luscious fruit and writes, "had there been an Adam near, I am afraid that with Eve I should have said, 'Take thou & eat like wise'" (42). In her re-creation of the biblical story, Peabody transforms the serpent into a Cuban youth and the apple of seduction into a native fruit. More significantly, while Peabody admits to momentary fear and hesitation about what she would do if recast as Eve in her Cuban Eden, she almost defiantly acknowledges that she "should have" tempted Adam all over again. Firmly rooted in an antinomian tradition, Peabody eschews the story that ends in eternal doom, privileging instead an Eve-centered paradise made possible by the Cuban landscape she so willingly "takes" and so willingly "gives away" to her imagined Adam. In this scenario, Peabody reimagines herself not as a repentant, sinful woman but as a fully empowered "Exaltada," sensuously consumed by a desire I have elsewhere argued is clearly colonial.[20]

In the context of U.S. imperial expansion and the long-standing desire for Cuba, Peabody's colonial poetics can be located among the rhetorical approaches of U.S. women writing in her time. While Annette Kolodny does not consider Peabody in her generative study on this topic, Peabody's colonial visions add important nuances to Kolodny's theorization of how U.S. women writers using their own literary strategies discursively contributed to the claiming of new territories. Principally, Kolodny finds that these women diverged from the gendered representations of their male counterparts, who saw the colonial landscape as feminine and sexually conquerable. Instead, the women Kolodny studies "radically reshap[ed] the wilderness" into domestic gardens and appropriated the frontier by recasting this newly created garden space as home. For Kolodny, this "American Eve had at last found her proper garden," in which women also "reveal themselves healed, renewed, revitalized—and even psychically reborn."[21] By moving the American frontier outside U.S. continental borders, in keeping with her contemporaries, Peabody envisions Cuba as her personal Garden of Eden, a space of empowerment and renewal. However, instead of establishing the domestic garden that other women writers sought, Peabody's American Eve appropriates the Cuban colonial zone to enable her own artistic and sensual agency.

Peabody's transcendentalist individualism in the colonial zone also deviates from the "manifest domesticity" identified by Amy Kaplan in American women writers between the 1830s and 1850s. In her study, Kaplan finds that women's writings engaged with imperial expansionism, especially in relation to Texas and Mexico, in ways that show how the discourses of domesticity and Manifest Destiny were "intimately intertwined" and how the "'empire of the mother'" became a cultural ideal "at a time when the United States was violently and massively expanding its national domain across the continent." Kaplan adds that these women participated in the project of Manifest Destiny by transforming "conquered foreign lands into the domestic sphere of the family and nation."[22] Even though Peabody's poetics contribute to colonial discourses in her time, which coincides with the period studied by Kaplan, Peabody does not follow her American "sisters" in their domestically colonial focus. Instead, Peabody's poetics claim Cuba for her own personal and aesthetic purposes, creating an "empire of the woman," one who need not be a mother to exert power.

Manifesting her individualistic gaze in representations of Cuba from earliest contact with the island, Peabody relates the landscape to her own project of physical and emotional restoration. After being a near-invalid during most of her adolescence, plagued by headaches and "visions" that made even the slightest noise painful, Peabody found in Cuba a previously unimagined energy that spurred her to race the Morrells' children, ride her horse for long periods of time even on moonlit nights, experience heights of joy she had never imagined, and sleep better than ever before. As she reports in a 3 February 1834 letter: "I am *drowsy* very often, which is an entirely new condition of being to me, & proves beyond doubt that Nature is beginning to rest herself after such a desperate action & wakefulness of years. I have as much hope from this inclination to sleep as from any thing else. I always felt in a perfectly unnatural state of existence in the north. I can compare it to nothing but being suspended between heaven and earth like Mahomet's tomb" (25). Surprised at her own improvement, Peabody began to hope that Cuba would exert the curative influence that everyone in her family wished for. Cuba in the 1830s was a location to which many Americans traveled for medical reasons, especially to recover from such illnesses as tuberculosis. Many travelers perceived it as a variety of sanatorium primarily because of its climate. Like others who saw Cuba as a place to heal, Peabody began to feel a kind of magic at work so that in her letters she associates herself with a "Nature" that is finally "beginning to rest" (25).

By revealing herself as having felt "unnatural" in her native New England and by deploying the Orientalist metaphor of "Mahomet's tomb," Peabody establishes a binary opposition between Cuba and New England that becomes a primary theme in the *Cuba Journal*. This conflict, however, privileges Cuba, not New England, setting up the colonial and Orientalized landscape as the cause for finally feeling "natural." Emerson also recognized the importance of bodily well-being in *Nature* (1836), published the year after Peabody returned from Cuba, asserting that to "the body and mind which have been cramped by noxious work or company, nature is medicinal and restores their tone," and that in the "eternal calm" of sky and woods, the beleaguered man "finds himself" anew (*CW*, 1:13). But Peabody goes further, not only anticipating this idea of nature's medicinal power, but privileging her aesthetic engagement with Cuba as her "natural" state. Unlike Emerson's "beleaguered" man who regains his misplaced sense of self in nature, Peabody discovers her actual self in Cuba. Instead of "being suspended between heaven and earth," or between spirit and flesh, Peabody is enabled to become whole. The importance of maintaining this physical and emotional balance is the reason she later gives for not "dwell[ing]" too much on the issue of slavery in Cuba's plantation system.

Although sometimes sympathetic, Peabody typically represents the slaves—just as she does the rest of what Cuba offered—in light of her own gratification in landscape and experience. But that self-centeredness does not mean she was unfeeling about slavery's effects. In an early letter, dated 16 March 1834, Peabody tells of becoming "heart sick" while watching slaves work at the sugar mill, producing the hot liquid expressed from sugar cane. She notices one in particular with "fierce eye and brow" who "look[s] like the very spirit of evil": "Yet even *he* was courteous, and when I attempted to get a crust of the sugar, moved away the impediments with a promptitude that wrung my heart a great deal more than if he had flung the burning fluid in my face." The slave, Peabody says, looks like "the untamable *obliged* to *appear* tame" while he is "furious for revenge"

(61; emphasis in original). This repeated mention of eyes and of gazing in the *Cuba Journal* highlights a concern with perspective. Peabody's empathy for this slave, whom she realizes must pretend to be "tame" even though he is rebelling inwardly, reminds us of her own continual appeasements of her mother even as she insists on living—and describing—her life in Cuba in her own terms. Arguably, it is her sympathy for the "untamable," not necessarily for the slaves themselves, that makes this a key moment in Peabody's account: it suggests that this slave functions as a kind of mirror that reflects back a struggle with which she can identify.[23]

Lee reads this passage as exemplifying Peabody's colonial ambiguity because she shows herself torn between fear of and sympathy for the slaves.[24] However, Peabody immediately follows up with a detailed explanation of why she—unlike Mary, who would later write an antislavery novel based on her own experience in Cuba[25]—does "not allow [herself] to dwell upon slavery." For this, she gives two reasons: "One is, it would certainly counter the beneficent influences, which I have left home and country to court, and another is, that my faith in GOD makes me sure that he makes up to every being the measure of happiness which he loses thro' the instrumentality of others. I try to realize how much shorter time is, than eternity & then endeavour to lose myself in other subjects of thought" (61). Dwelling on slavery, Peabody explains, would be not only counterproductive to her personal project of recovery but also pointless, given her faith in a divine plan. Instead of belaboring the issue, which her sister Elizabeth also warned her against, Peabody chooses to devote her mental energies to subjects that focus on her empowerment and on the relationship she sees between Cuban nature and her spirit as well as body.[26] The fate of the slaves, Peabody suggests, is best left to this "divine plan," which divests her of responsibility or agency to change their lot. But when it comes to her own actions in Cuba, there is no such constraint on her will.

Although Peabody's argument for not dwelling on slavery rationalizes her lack of interest in the cause of abolition, it also articulates her own notion of transcendence, which differs from that of Emerson and other later transcendentalists. Unlike those who took up social causes as part of their spiritual calling, Emerson and Fuller among them, Peabody predicates her sense of transcendence on her project of bodily revivification. While her culture had long established bodily sensations in a woman as dangerous and suspect, Peabody unifies the spirit and the senses, representing them as inseparable. In fact, she suggests that the spirit is able to transcend *because* of the body's sensual experience. This articulation of the joined transcendence of spirit and flesh was daringly feminist in an unmarried woman of her time. If for Emerson Nature (or the material) "is made to serve" the Spirit and Reason, and these are positioned over the "despotism of the senses" (*CW*, 1:25, 30), in Peabody's feminist poetics, the soul, the intellect, and the body are in balance. In that communion, Peabody achieves transcendence through a vibrant and sensually embodied spirit. Because Peabody puts forward this idea as a woman within the context of a colonial slave economy, any perceived ambiguity in her representation of the rebellious slave must be juxtaposed with her explanation of why she chooses to ignore the plight of slaves by asserting her own will and determination to do what is in her own best interest.

Like scenes of slavery that brought Peabody back to herself, the Cuban landscape led her to physical exaltation that reached nearly religious raptures, the descriptions of which vividly evoke those moments in the mind's eye of her reader. Sunrises and sunsets, which were not only romantic tropes but also times of liminality, inspire some of her most transcendental representations. In her 16 March 1834 letter, Peabody integrates these two moments of time through their luminosity and connects them to a higher intelligence:

> There is no way to give you an idea of the *diffused goldeness* [*sic*] of the atmosphere in this country. The glory does not seem confined to sunset land; but is all around you. It is in your eye and breath. . . . Long before sunrise, was I mounted this morning, in the light of a dawn almost unparalleled in my experience for its beauty and freshness. While under the young Palms I lifted up my eyes in uncontrollable worship of the Omnipresent Divinity of which I seemed to be especially conscious just at that moment. (56–57)

Peabody's "eye," like Emerson's famous "transparent eyeball," which makes him "part or parcel of God" (*CW*, 1:11), conveys to her readers how landscape produces a physical reaction that can heighten spiritual experience. The "uncontrollable worship" Peabody describes anticipates Emerson's notion that the "intellect searches out the absolute order of things as they stand in the mind of God" (*CW*, 1:16). But unlike Emerson with his disembodied eyeball, Peabody holistically receives the effects of the landscape through her vision, through the air she breathes, and through the horse she is riding, so that her gaze incorporates the spirit as an extension of the body itself. Finding in the glorious sights of Cuba a transcendent reciprocity with divine presence, she prefigures some parts of Emerson's philosophy but at the same time causes his floating "eyeball," by contrast, to appear less substantial in its ability to transmit nature's physical effects and their relationship to a larger spiritual consciousness.

Predicating her transcendentalism on this spiritual and physical affinity to the Cuban landscape—her "newly made" Eden—Peabody's *Cuba Journal* evokes colonial discourses of possession, especially those related to a fledgling American empire. The paradise of this self-fashioned Eve is a "treasure-laden" place whose wealth she is appointed to "collect." As she writes later in the 16 March 1834 letter:

> My dearest Mother, a brilliant dawn attracted me out of bed and to a very early ride this morning, and the singing of the birds in the orangery were the only audible sounds of thanksgiving; the only sound that broke the sabbeth [*sic*] stillness of nature. The dews are so heavy here that the world seems just made every morning. At the tip of every leaf hangs a jewel, which if value were to be measured by beauty should not be mentioned with the diamond, and every green thing looks polished and new, & the inexpressibly [*sic*] claritude of the atmosphere allows you to penetrate further into the infinite above and around than it is possible to do in our climate. (58)

These ideas of "thanksgiving" and of the Sabbath's "stillness of nature" build on the representation of a spiritual, even religious, experience. This, in turn, links to the "value" of beauty in Cuba inasmuch as it allows Peabody's gaze to go farther into the "infinite above" than is possible in her native land. "Penetrat[ing] further into the infinite above and around," Peabody exerts her agency, using sexually allusive language, as she achieves greater spiritual understanding through her contact with nature in Cuba.

Here, Peabody contributes to writing "the plot" of American empire, as Kris Fresonke has suggested about Emerson's *Nature*. According to Fresonke, if we assume that "American" is "a sort of philosophical given, a question always posed rhetorically and formally for Emerson by nature—then we may find in *Nature* a peculiar but vivid set of proofs for American exceptionalism."[27] This claim of exceptionalism is a foundational tenet of Manifest Destiny—the idea that the United States was uniquely called upon by God to spread its civilizing light across the world. In partial contrast, Peabody's colonizing gaze appropriates the Cuban landscape to represent it as *more* desirable than her native New England—where she cannot achieve the same level of communion with nature. Through a transcendentalist ethos, Peabody naturalizes both her ability and her God-given right to take possession of Cuba and benefit from this world "just made every morning" for her.

The comparisons between Cuba and New England become much more marked in the third volume, when a tone of nostalgia, along with an awareness of the transitory nature of her life in Cuba, begins to tinge her letters as the moment of departure draws nearer. Her aesthetic appreciation of the tropical landscape remains strong as she continually sets her Cuban environment in opposition to her native New England. But Peabody does not privilege her U.S. home, as sister Mary will in *Juanita: A Romance of Real Life in Cuba Fifty Years*

Ago, her 1887 novel of the sisters' time in Cuba. Instead, Peabody anticipates that the remembered beauty of her Cuban environs will become a balm when she is confronted with the gray, cold vistas of New England. In a letter dated 16 November 1834, she writes, "Whenever I am tired of straight lines & square houses & chimnies [*sic*] hereafter, I shall shut my eyes to the outward & open them to the inner world where vines will forever hang in circles & curves of eternal beauty round the realm of Memory" (426). The juxtaposition of the straightness, squareness, and tallness of her New England life—all patterns of regularity and order—against the graceful, vine-like nature of her romantic psyche suggests that Peabody's time in Cuba afforded her a life of artistic affinity that she feared would not be available to her in New England. Also in this respect, Peabody's transcendentalism is different because it is not grounded in a U.S. landscape: hers takes possession of the Cuban scenery and aims to retain such ownership through the medium of memory.

While her literary representations are meant to preserve and share her remembrances of Cuba, Peabody expresses self-conscious concerns about the quasi-public nature of her journal: "There are a great many little bursts & enthusiasms & notions in it which I do not relish having exposed" (471). She goes so far as to say of its wide dissemination by oldest sister Elizabeth that it is "as if every body had got the key of my private cabinet & without leave of the owner—are appropriating whatever they please" (471). Notwithstanding these feelings of invaded privacy, Peabody's more lyrical and sophisticated literary craft in the third volume suggests a heightened sense of audience. Perhaps Peabody did mind that her first two volumes had been so widely circulated, but that same awareness may have inspired her to strive for a higher literary standard. She makes more evident allusions to the established and rising classics of British literature, and her literary ecstasies over the tropical sunsets in Cuba are even more transcendentally poetic. In a 15 December 1834 letter, Peabody describes the "excessive splendor" of Cuban nature and the "enchanted grounds" of the plantation she was visiting, again giving evidence of her integrative gaze: "Returning to the house we mounted to a terrace on the top of a projecting hall—from which we had an extensive view—of the estate & of a sunset that mocks description. It was like the wing of the flamingo, the plumes of the bird of Paradise—The throat of a humming bird—& 'the neck of a dove'—all blended together in dulcet harmony" (493). In this lovely passage, the colors of the exotic, of the Caribbean flamingo and the African bird of paradise, harmoniously blend with those of birds more common to New England, the hummingbird and the dove. This combination of colors in Peabody's "extensive view" of the Cuban sunset calls to mind the clash as well as the syncretic unity of cultures in the colonial zone, where the colonizing power that turns the native birds into captives displays them for its own enjoyment.

At the same time, Peabody's colonial poetics in the final volume take on a yet more defiant antinomian attitude toward any fetters on her sensuous pleasure. Drawing from Milton's *Paradise Lost*, an originative text for British romanticism, Peabody exalts a Cuban sunset by quoting from arguably the best-known literary representation of Lucifer. In a 21 January 1835 letter, Peabody compares the "glories unfolding over the western heaven" to "the arch fiend's 'emperial [*sic*] ensign'—mighty standard which Arzazel held, that 'cherub tall'—shining 'like a meteor streaming to the wind, / With gems & golden lustre rich emblazoned, / Seraphic arms & trophies—.'" "My exclamations," Peabody recalls, "brought all forth upon the gallery—What king or angel ever unfurled such a banner as that with which the Sun is preceded & followed in his triumphal march through the blue fields of space?" (568). As she did in the journal's first volume, Peabody rewrites a biblical story: here she can think of no better metaphor for the sunset than the colors of Lucifer's imperial banner.

But unlike sister Mary, who in her novel describes Cuba as a hellish place because of slavery, Peabody admires the power and abandon of Lucifer's colors.[28] Peabody is evidently seduced by the sheer sensuality of the tropical sky. But the fact that she draws on images of kings, empires, and military triumphs and, specifically, that she quotes *Paradise Lost* suggests that at some level Peabody acknowledges the moral costs of her colonial desire.[29] Nonetheless, both in her recasting of the Fall and in this passage, where she recalls Lucifer's attempt against Heaven, Peabody does not ally herself with those who ostensibly defend goodness and purity. Her colonial poetics breaks with contemporary women writers on the frontier, not only by focusing on individual pleasure and power rather than on domestic felicity but also by defiantly siding with two of the most reviled outcasts of Christian religion: Eve and Lucifer. In so doing, Peabody again firmly establishes herself within the antinomian tradition of early feminist transcendentalists, as identified by Phyllis Cole.

Further articulating her sensuous colonial desire in the last volume of the *Cuba Journal*, Peabody analogizes it with a pleasant dream contingent on location, not on sleep. After describing in detail the luxuries and amenities of a nearby plantation, which she visits for the island's social season, Peabody tells of a supper table spread in an open-air gallery where the "gales from the tea roses—& *Verbena trees*—& other aromatic shrubs—and the frescos by astral lamp-light—lull one into a dream that can only be dreamed no where but under the tropics" (551; emphasis in original). This connection between pleasurable dreams and bodily experience recurs in a later description. After the conclusion of a social event, Peabody reports, she and a male friend "fled into the garden—into the heavenly moonlight—& ran a *gentle* race round that low parapet—." Then, addressing her readers, she asks: "Would you realize all your dreams of classic lands & oriental luxury? Come & stand on that parapet within reach of the perfume of the tea rose—the Verbena & the spicey [*sic*] flowers of a tropical clime—when the dew melts & diffuses their sweetness—& within sight of those gleaming columns lost in a hanging cloud of waving green—under a January Cuba moon—the brightest of the year—& you will ask no more for the *senses*—" (565–66). That Peabody describes her race in the garden with a male escort as "gentle" sounds like an attempt to appease her strict, remonstrative mother. But posing the question of whether her New England audience (her mother or other readers) would like to fulfill dreams of "oriental luxury" seems almost a provocation, especially this late in her Cuban sojourn.[30]

Even the modern reader can see why Mrs. Peabody expressed sustained concern for her daughter. These last letters reflect Sophia Peabody's comfortable acceptance of a life in which "the *senses*" are continually exercised, and in which she perceives no tension between the intellect and the heart. Peabody goes on to note: "[Cuba] is not ground consecrated by all that was beautiful & glorious & heroic in past time—The heart & the intellect are not kindled by any burning memories—But it is pure, single Nature, alone in her power & loveliness, that touches subdues and exalts the soul—We do not remember the godlike here—but we think of GOD himself" (566). Unlike Peabody's native New England, the Cuban landscape is not invested with a personal history that produces both feeling and understanding in her because of its sociohistorical meaning. Instead of being reminded by acculturation of what she should find significant, Peabody connects with the divine itself and is led into an exalted state in Cuba through her encounter with "pure" nature. Here, Peabody's association of a masculinized "God" with an equally powerful and feminized Nature borrows from the British romantics to articulate a gendered balance distinct from the highly individuated Nature that Emerson and later transcendentalists espoused.[31]

As her language becomes more self-conscious in volume 3 of the journal, Peabody's deployment of the romantic poets becomes more prominent. Struggling with her own credibility back home, she increasingly quotes longer passages, especially from Shelley. But she also draws on Keats and Wordsworth, as well as Shakespeare and Milton. In just the first four letters of the volume, according to the footnotes provided by *Cuba Journal* editor Claire Badaracco, Peabody quotes Shelley at least thirteen times; Keats four times; Shakespeare, Wordsworth, and Frances Cowper at least once each; and Milton at least twice (670). This is persuasive evidence that she found in the romantic poets, and in their literary forefather Milton, voices that would lend credence to her own descriptions of Cuba. It is possible that many of her readers would not have been able to identify her sources, especially Shelley and Keats, who were not then widely available in print.[32] Because she did not footnote or identify the texts she was quoting, her letters assume a high degree of literariness for readers.

Weaving these literary allusions into the *Cuba Journal* alongside her own highly poetical descriptions, Peabody not only borrows from the romantics but also adapts them in her own manner to tell of her unique experiences in another land and culture. Peabody here is not simply having the poems speak for themselves. She inserts them in her letters to explicate—in specific ways—her own transcendental experience as an American woman in Cuba. Further, she uses the poems to bolster her insistence that there is no transcendence without bodily exaltation, without "delicious pain." Describing one of her rides on horseback on a "superb morning," Peabody quotes a long passage from Shelley's "Epipsychidion" to capture her experience:

> "And all the place was peopled with sweet airs:
> The light clear element which the isle wears
> Was heavy with the scent of orange flowers—
> Which floats like mist laden with unseen showers
> And falls upon the eyelids like faint sleep!
> And from the moss, violets & jonquils peep
> And dart their arrowy odor thro' the brain
> Till you might faint with the delicious pain!" (393)

The title of Shelley's 1821 poem, published a year before his death, is a Greek word that means "concerning a little soul," and the poem represents an "isle" of exotic nature, a retreat where the narrator and his love can find bliss in their physical and emotional union.[33] Imagine Peabody reading with delight and recognition Shelley's descriptions of the "scent of orange flowers" and reveling in the idea that the odors of an isle could be like arrows through the brain, causing "delicious pain." If we were only able to read Shelley as Peabody did we might be persuaded to think he was also writing about Cuba. Peabody transforms Shelley's imagination into description to show how her spirit transcends not because of what it invents but because of what it actually experiences. Describing an earlier dawn in a 31 October 1834 letter, she says: "Such a morning! What a blessing to have been out in it—. . . . It is not a slight thing to see a new born world every day—& to become daily a *living soul* as I seem to—for the breath of life is breathed into my nostrils as if for the first time whenever I am early enough in the Temple not hewn by hands—when Magnificent & still—GOD dedicates it with the glance of his eye for man to worship in—" (394–95). The glance of "GOD" allows "man" to worship in this natural temple, but it is Peabody who, by gazing upon nature like the "God" she mentions, translates its magnificence and philosophical significance for her readers, bridging geographical and cultural divides.

In quoting Shelley's description of a shower as "rainbow-winged armies" in "Epipsychidion,"[34] Peabody suggests that her own account of what she feels upon gazing at the Cuban sky cannot be so far-fetched: "It was indeed a time to be out under the free heaven—The air was full of sparkling Hebes presenting the immortal elixir—My spirit drank & lived again—I begin to have an entirely new perception of the Beauty of Nature!—"(399). Freedom and transformation are central themes in this passage, which show Peabody experiencing renewal by virtue of what she perceives and feels. Peabody's "Exaltada" tones may not have been directed to social causes, but her desire to transcend spiritually is certainly apparent when she is representing the effects of Cuba's nature on her whole being. For Peabody, the transcendentalist ideal does not only convey itself through the physical gaze. Through its bodily effects, it frees, resuscitates, and immortalizes the spirit. In Peabody's poetics, the senses, the emotions, and the spirit are interdependent and inseparable.

One of Peabody's most significant contributions to early transcendentalism is precisely this weaving together of gaze, affect, and physical exaltation. In other words, gazing is not enough to achieve a special intercourse between nature and spirit. There have to be powerful physiological effects involved as well so that feeling is represented as both physical and emotional. Quoting another passage from "Epipsychidion" to describe the Morrells' youngest son, Peabody writes: "Carlito . . . had been comforting himself in my arms, & now we went out together to walk & talk—Oh this child—He is 'sweet as stops of planetary music heard in trance—.'" The child, Peabody continues, "has more true—genuine, exquisite sentiment than I ever saw in a child—or often in older persons—It is something too delicate to describe. It can only be *felt*" (391; emphasis in original). Perhaps this is her way of explaining to herself and readers why they cannot make sense of what she describes: they lack the affective stimulus and are unable to feel as she does, not just emotionally but also physically. Her focus on the body as an extension of the gaze, and her reveling in the body as a site of sensory pleasure and knowledge, are further ways in which Peabody's poetics are distinctly woman centered and feminist. Her colonial poetics openly challenge her culture's distrust and repression of a woman's bodily pleasure.

What resounds repeatedly in Peabody's colonial poetics is the woman-centered value she places on being sensuously stimulated and socially unfettered. Of the continual pleasure she derives from her surroundings, Peabody says in the 21 January 1835 letter: "We who enjoy it, not in proportion to the revenue of gold it yields to our coffers, but in the infinite proportion of unappropriating & immaterial pleasure it pours into our hearts with all the holy & immeasurable influences it brings with it—we it is who possess the earth. It was mine that morning—I was the queen of all—" (566–67). In this passage, Peabody connects her ability to enjoy the Cuban "earth," not with material gain—it is, she insists, not about a physical appropriation—but with the aesthetic pleasure that comes to those who own the earth. Once again fashioning herself "queen of all," Peabody unifies her desire for possession and the power of her gaze to effect that possession.[35]

As an American woman living in Cuba in the waning years of the Spanish Empire, and as a writer who acculturated enough to be able to use Spanish, and who regularly sketched native flora in her letters, Peabody moved across national, racial, gendered, cultural, and linguistic borders. Her literary and aesthetic appropriation of the Cuban landscape coincided with the rising influence of the United States over Cuba, a desired colonial site since before the American Revolution, which culminated in the emergence of a U.S. empire in the Spanish Caribbean in 1898. At the crossroads of empires, Peabody defiantly claimed Cuba as a space where she could break with patriarchal restrictions and express a vibrant poetics that was at the same time colonial, feminist, and transcendentalist. Examining her *Cuba Journal* as an early transcendentalist text not only helps trace the female genealogies of the transcendentalist movement but also further connects the journal's inception to the imperialist desire for possessions outside of U.S. continental borders—and not just in terms of westward expansion.

In her comparison of a vivid Cuban landscape with a drab New England scene, her refashioning of the biblical story of Eve, her appropriation of Milton's Lucifer, and her deployment of the romantic poets to support her own representations of Cuba, Peabody contributes a distinct vision to canonically recognized strains of transcendentalism. Peabody would eventually marry Nathaniel Hawthorne and become a mother, and although she never authorized publication of the *Cuba Journal*, the text stands as persuasive testimony that she exulted in the intertwined relationship between nature and the individual's body and spirit—especially a woman's—before Emerson and Fuller published their transcendentalist manifestos. Indeed, Peabody's profoundly romantic poetics might entitle her to be recognized as the most "Exaltada" of the women who helped inaugurate this quintessentially American movement.

NOTES

1. Dorri Beam argues that style branded as "excessive" in American women writers "embodies an account of gendered power relations in the literary field and is itself an instance of women taking a position as writers of the florid and gorgeous." See her *Style, Gender, and Fantasy in Nineteenth-Century American Women's Writing* (New York: Cambridge Univ. Press, 2010), 29.
2. For more ways in which women transcendentalists gave "form" to their focus or "attention," see Sarah Ann Wider, "'How It All Lies before Me To-day': Transcendentalist Women's Journeys into Attention," in this volume.
3. As I discuss later, scholars who have pointed to Peabody's early transcendentalism include Patricia Dunlavy Valenti, Megan Marshall, and Phyllis Cole.

4. See Ivonne M. García, "Transnational Crossings: Sophia Hawthorne's Authorial Persona from the 'Cuba Journal' to *Notes in England and Italy*," *Nathaniel Hawthorne Review* 37, no. 2 (2011): 97–120.
5. I wish to thank my friend and colleague James P. Carson, Professor of Romantic Studies and Eighteenth-Century Literature at Kenyon College, for reading and commenting on this aspect of my argument in an earlier draft.
6. Marshall, 72, 190, 198.
7. Marshall, 214–15, 268. There seems to be disagreement as to the nationality of the Morrells. While Marshall describes Dr. Morrell as "a French doctor," Pamela Lee refers to the Morrells as "a well-to-do Creole family." Claire M. Badaracco states that the Morrells were "prosperous Americans." I have chosen Badaracco's identification since she has extensively researched the Peabody sisters' stay in Cuba. See Lee, "'Queen of All I Surveyed': Sophia Peabody Hawthorne's 'Cuba Journal' and the Imperial Gaze," in Elbert, Hall, and Rodier, 164; and Badaracco, "Sophia Peabody Hawthorne's Cuba Journal: Volume Three, 31 October 1834–15 March 1835," *Essex Institute: Historical Collections* 118 (1982): 280.
8. See Claire Badaracco, ed., introduction to *The Cuba Journal, 1833–35, by Sophia Peabody Hawthorne* (Washington, D.C.: Library of Congress, 1981), xxci. See also Anna Brickhouse, *Transamerican Literary Relations and the Nineteenth-Century Public Sphere* (Cambridge, U.K.: Cambridge Univ. Press, 2004), 199.
9. See Patricia Dunlavy Valenti, *Sophia Peabody Hawthorne: A Life, Vol. 1, 1809–1847* (Columbia: Univ. of Missouri Press, 2004), 82, 84, 89.
10. See Valenti, *Sophia Peabody Hawthorne*, 66.
11. Marshall, 278; Phyllis Cole, "Woman's Rights and Feminism," in *OxH*, 227.
12. At the end of a 21 January 1835 letter, Mary observes that Sophia "writes as if she were possessed with a writing demon the first thing in the morning" (*The Cuba Journal, 1833–35, by Sophia Peabody Hawthorne*, ed. Claire M. Badaracco [Washington, D.C.: Library of Congress, 1981], 575). All *Cuba Journal* citations are to this edition.
13. "Exaltada" was Margaret Fuller's term and her feminist call to action to American women. See *WNC*, 92.
14. See Valenti, *Sophia Peabody Hawthorne*, 64. According to Sophia, "Paradisaical people" was the term Elizabeth used to describe her younger sister's social circle in Cuba. See *Cuba Journal*, 355.
15. See Valenti, *Sophia Peabody Hawthorne*, 66.
16. See Lee, "'Queen of All I Surveyed,'" 169, 163.
17. See Valenti, *Sophia Peabody Hawthorne*, 30. Sophia had given indications of this desire to represent herself as a queen, along with a capacity for unbridled excitement, in her visit to Dedham, Massachusetts, during the summer of 1830, when in a letter she pronounced herself "Queen of all I survey when I am riding" and described riding as "an exhilaration" she "never dreamed of elsewhere."
18. Laura Mulvey famously discusses "woman as image, man as bearer of the look" ("Visual Pleasure and Narrative Cinema," in *Feminisms: An Anthology of Literary Theory and Criticism*, ed. Robyn R. Warhol and Diane Price Herndl [New Brunswick, N.J.: Rutgers Univ. Press, 1997], 442). Indira Ghose, writing about female travelers in colonial India, notes, "What it was possible to *see* as a woman was determined by the discourses of femininity in circulation at a specific moment in history" (*Women Travellers in Colonial India: The Power of the Female Gaze* [Oxford: Oxford Univ. Press, 1998], 10).

19. Ghose, *Women Travellers*, 4, 53, 59–60.
20. See Ivonne M. García, "Anticipating Colonialism: U.S. Letters on Puerto Rico and Cuba, 1831–1835," in *U.S. Letters and Cultural Transformations, 1760–1860*, ed. Theresa Gaul and Sharon Harris (New York: Ashgate, 2009), 73.
21. Annette Kolodny, *The Land before Her: Fantasy and Experience of the American Frontiers, 1630–1860* (Chapel Hill: Univ. of North Carolina Press, 1984), 6, 8.
22. Amy Kaplan, "Manifest Domesticity," in Kaplan, *The Anarchy of Empire in the Making of U.S. Culture* (Cambridge, Mass.: Harvard Univ. Press, 2002), 25.
23. Diane G. Scholl has observed, "In some sense the power of the enslaved is a force Sophia too wields, exercised by her pen, her vantage point that of a foreigner, a woman, and an invalid." See Scholl, "Fallen Angels: Sophia Hawthorne's *Cuba Journal* as Pièce de Résistance," *Nathaniel Hawthorne Review* 35, no. 1 (2009): 39.
24. Lee, "'Queen of All I Surveyed,'" 175.
25. See Mary Peabody Mann, *Juanita: A Romance of Real Life in Cuba Fifty Years Ago*, ed. Patricia Ard (1887; Charlottesville: Univ. of Virginia Press, 2000).
26. Teresa A. Goddu notes that Elizabeth Peabody cautioned her younger sister "to 'drive slavery from [her] thoughts.'" Goddu also argues that Sophia Peabody "detaches the labor of slavery . . . from its political and economic meanings by transforming it into a picturesque backdrop." See her "Letters Turned to Gold: Hawthorne, Authorship, and Slavery," *Studies in American Fiction* 29, no. 1 (2001): 49.
27. See Kris Fresonke, "Emerson's *Nature*: West of Ecstasy," in Fresonke, *West of Emerson: The Design of Manifest Destiny* (Berkeley and Los Angeles: Univ. of California Press, 2003), 114.
28. In *Juanita*, Mann's protagonist Helen Wentworth describes the "wretched" slaves in Cuba as looking "more like demons than like human beings" and establishes her New England home as "the very vestibule of heaven" in opposition to Cuba (131).
29. See Martin J. Evans, *Milton's Imperial Epic: "Paradise Lost" and the Discourse of Colonialism* (Ithaca, N.Y.: Cornell Univ. Press, 1996), 1–9.
30. Valenti argues that early in life Peabody developed a pattern with her mother whereby she professed verbal affection but failed to meet her mother's demands—a way of resisting maternal influence (*Sophia Peabody Hawthorne*, 36).
31. During her first year of marriage to Hawthorne, Sophia painted *Endymion*, based on Keats's poem. Valenti suggests that the painting represented "her appreciation for the union of the spiritual and the physical" (*Sophia Peabody Hawthorne*, 199).
32. William St. Clair notes that Keats was "scarcely read in the first half of the [nineteenth] century." Shelley was also among the romantic poets who were "rediscovered" and anthologized after midcentury. See *The Reading Nation in the Romantic Period* (Cambridge, U.K.: Cambridge Univ. Press, 2004), 422.
33. See Donald H. Reiman and Neil Fraistat, eds., *Shelley's Poetry and Prose*, 2nd ed. (New York: Norton, 2002), 392.
34. See Badaracco, endnotes to *Cuba Journal*, 670–75.
35. On taking possession of a landscape through an imperial gaze, see Mary Louise Pratt, *Imperial Eyes: Travel Writing and Transculturation* (London: Routledge, 1993).

INTERLUDE

Karoline von Günderode, "Apocalyptical Fragment," from *Die Günderode*, by Bettina von Arnim, trans. Margaret Fuller (Boston: E. P. Peabody, 1842), 14–16.

1. I stood on a high rock in the Mediterranean sea; before me, the East; behind me, the West; and the wind lay still upon the sea.
2. The sun sank; scarcely was it hid from sight, than the dawn of morning began to rise. Morning, noon, evening, and night chased one another in giddy haste across the dome of heaven.
3. Astonished, I saw them circle round; my blood, my thoughts, moved not more swiftly. Time, while it without me conformed to new laws, went on within me at its wonted pace.
4. I would have rushed into the morning-red, or have bathed myself in the shadows of night, hastily, with her, flowing on, away from this slow life; but sunk in contemplation, I grew weary and fell asleep.
5. Then saw I before me a sea, girt in by no shore, neither to the East, the South, the West, or the North. No breeze swelled the waves, but from its depths was moved, as if excited by inward fermentation, the immeasurable sea.
6. And many forms rose from the depths of the sea, and mists arose, and were lost in the clouds, and again, in sudden lightnings, saluted the parent waves.
7. And always more manifold arose these forms from the deep. I was seized with giddiness and dread; my thoughts were driven hither and thither, like a torch by the stormwind, till my memory was extinguished.
8. As I again awoke, and began to know of myself, then I could not tell

whether I had slept ages or minutes; for, in the dull, confused dream, there had been nothing to remind me of time.

9. It was dark within me, as if I had rested in the bosom of the sea, and risen from it like the other forms; to myself I seemed a drop of dew; I moved merrily to and fro in the air, and rejoiced, and my life was that the sun mirrored himself in me, and the stars looked upon me.

10. I let myself be borne upon the breezes, I joined myself with the evening-red, to the ocean-colored drops; I ranged myself with my playfellows round the moon, when she would hide herself, and accompanied her path.

11. The past was entirely past; I belonged to the present solely; a longing was in me, which knew not its aim. I sought ever, and what I found was not what I sought; and with still more ardent longing was I drawn forth into the Infinite.

12. Once was I aware that all the forms, which had ascended from the sea, returned to it and were again produced in changing forms. This apparition surprised me, for I had known of no end. But now, I thought, my desire is also to return to the source of life.

13. And, as I thought of this, and felt more life than in all my past conscious being, was suddenly my mind embraced as by overwhelming mists; but they vanished soon. I seemed no more myself; my limits I could no longer find; my consciousness I had transcended; it was greater, different, and yet I felt myself in it.

14. I was released from the narrow limits of my being, and no single drop more; I was restored to the all, and the all belonged to me. I thought and felt, flowed as waves in the sea, shone in the sun, circled with the stars; I felt myself in all, and enjoyed all in myself.

15. Therefore, who has ears to hear, let him hear. It is not two, nor three, nor a thousand, but one and all; it is not body and spirit separately, one belonging to time, the other to eternity, but one, belongs to itself, and is at once, time and eternity, visible and invisible, constant in change, an infinite life.

Fuller, Goethe, Bettine

Cultural Transfer and Imagined German Womanhood

CAROL STRAUSS SOTIROPOULOS

Scholarly studies of Margaret Fuller and her celebrated "German connection" have centered primarily on her passion for Johann Wolfgang von Goethe and the male German romanticists.[1] Fewer have addressed her *Dial* essay "Bettine Brentano and Her Friend Günderode," which discusses the friendship of Bettina Brentano von Arnim (1785–1858) and Karoline von Günderode (1780–1806) as portrayed in von Arnim's epistolary novel *Die Günderode* (1840).[2] I suggest that Fuller drew creatively on historical legends, on "ideal" female figures in Goethe's fiction, and on von Arnim's literary presentation of an extraordinary female friendship to build an inspirational myth of German women's intellectual development and community.

As the foremost promoter of German literature and a mediator of German culture in her day, Fuller capitalized on her construct of German female identity to draw attention to American cultural deficiencies she perceived as especially pernicious for women. While current popular application of the term "cultural transfer" evokes fluidity across and through permeable national cultural borders, a certain fixity was earlier ascribed to such constructed categories as "German" or "American."[3] This essentializing of national cultures informs the German setting that Fuller imagined.

In this essay I question whether Fuller's perception held true. Further, I seek to contextualize her (mis)perception as an intrinsic dimension of the human yearning for an imagined ideal elsewhere, in an otherness that transcends a lack, or sense of displacement, in our own world. I suggest that Fuller's imagined German womanhood speaks more to her aspiration for personal and societal transformation than to concern over substantive evidence. Yet we are invited to interrogate Fuller's perception, if only to better understand how her romantic vision affected her writerly development.

Goethe and His Female Characters

From legends and ballads, Fuller inferred an exceptionally principled German tradition of respect for women. "Germany did not need to *learn* a high view of woman; it was inborn in that race. Woman was to the Teuton warrior his priestess, his friend, his sister, in truth, a wife. . . . The idea of woman in their literature is expressed both to a greater height and depth than elsewhere" (*WNC*, 33). Fuller wove this perception of German womanhood through her discussions of Goethe's female literary characters, hailing Goethe as woman's champion.

Everything by and about Goethe fascinated Fuller, and her multidimensional appreciation spills easily from his works onto his person: "Goethe, proceeding on his own track, elevating the human being, in the most imperfect states of society, by continual efforts at self-culture, takes as good care of women as of men." The women Fuller cites are both real (Goethe's mother, his sister, "Duchess Amelia," "Lili")[4] and fictional (characters in his *Iphigenia in Taurus*, *Faust*, *Wilhelm Meister*) (*WNC*, 74–77). Fuller's assessment of Goethe's high regard for women can be attributed in part to her (mis)perception of his character, which in turn helps us to understand her (mis)imagined Germany. Had she been able to conduct onsite research in Germany for the Goethe biography she had once commenced writing, she might have encountered discomfiting aspects of Goethe's stance on civic and women's rights.[5] Further, if she had had access to his review of novels by three women writers, she might have been disturbed by his condescending dismissal of women writers as dilettantes.

Yet Fuller was not entirely unaware that Goethe at times disparaged women. In the preface to her translation of Johann Eckermann's *Gespräche mit Goethe in den letzten Jahren seines Lebens* (Conversations with Goethe in the Last Years of His Life), she declares that she has not omitted anything "which would cast either light or shade on his character."[6] And truly, Fuller omitted very little from Eckermann's work—itself a constructed journal that has prompted disputes concerning fact versus fiction. What *is* omitted, however, invites us to question her imagined ideal of a Goethe who "takes as good care of women as of men."

In her rendering of a passage about Goethe's sister Cornelia, Fuller refrained from completing his remarks. Fuller's translation: "What relates to her . . . will be read with interest by accomplished women, of whom many, like her, do not combine the advantage of personal beauty with their intellectual and moral endowments" (*CG*, 394). The original continues: "She was a remarkable being. . . . [S]he stood morally very high, and had not a trace of sensuousness about her. The thought of resigning herself to a man was repulsive to her, and we may imagine that this peculiarity caused many unpleasant hours in marriage. Women who have a similar aversion, or do not love their husbands, will feel the force of this. On this account I could never look upon my sister as married; she would have been much more in her place as an abbess in a convent."[7] Fuller, sensitive to the subject of her own physical self-image,[8] would understandably have chosen to omit the denigrating lines as an instinctive reaction to the conjoining of intellectual prowess, physical plainness, and sexual frigidity.

The offensive content of another omission, embedded in a discussion of Lord Byron, suggests Goethe's disrespect for basic female intelligence. Fuller's translation: "But when he [Byron] would create, he always succeeds; inspiration supplies the place of reflection. He never fails when he speaks out his own feelings as a man" (*CG*, 138). The original continues: "He [Byron] produced his best things as women do pretty children, without thinking about it or knowing how it was done."[9] Clearly this analogy provoked some measure of cognitive dissonance, most easily resolved by its omission. But rather than slighting Fuller for eliding, consciously or not, indications of Goethe's patronizing stance toward women, we can observe the ambivalence in her sustained construct of Goethe as a prime representative of the imagined German culture that so inspired her.

Turning this discussion from Fuller's veneration of Goethe to her admiration of his female characters allows us to question further her imagined ideal of autonomous German women. Interpretations of Goethe's female characters among feminist critics tend to swing between binary opposites, particularly in treatments of his Bildungsroman, *Wilhelm Meister*. Several argue that Goethe's view of women is chauvinistic, patriarchal, and thoroughly in line with the dominant prejudices of his day. Countering this interpretation are those who credit Goethe with producing protofeminist characters equal to their male counterparts.[10] While Fuller's views situate her in the latter camp, she confronted cultural obstacles in applying to herself the central Goethean tenet of *Bildung*—of self-cultivation, self-development, self-culture, and education.

Imagining *Bildung*

Fuller enthusiastically adopted the project of *Bildung*. While conceptual discourse proved intellectually empowering, gendered obstructions to implementing power required a crucial intervention. On the one hand, *Bildung* through reading, listening, discussion, and observation goes toward integrating knowledge and culture into a self-philosophy.[11] On the other, the discourse of *Bildung* also embraces active engagement with the world to fulfill one's potential. Fuller looked to the male heroes of several German romantic writers as models of *Bildung* and then to Goethe's female characters as corollaries. "Goethe always represents the highest principle in the feminine form," she asserted in her forty-one-page *Dial* essay, "Goethe."[12] Characters' embodiment of high principles does not, however, necessitate active engagement with the world. Fuller reads the female characters in their chronological appearance in *Wilhelm Meister* as a progression toward perfection. The last to appear is Makaria, a figure of wisdom who withdraws from society and seeks solace in personal correspondence and astronomy. Fuller lauds her as "the soul of a star, *i.e.*, a pure and perfected intelligence embodied in feminine form" (*WNC*, 75–76): "Consulted by her connexions and acquaintance as an unerring judge in all their affairs . . . she knows all, governs all, but never goes forth from herself. . . . [S]he is 'divine Philosophy.'"[13] Thus Fuller recognized that Goethe's female characters could work toward individual fullness only in a limited domain, operating less in the external world of experience than as imparters of knowledge and insight for the development of the male hero.[14]

Palpably frustrated that experience toward self-cultivation within the Goethean frame was ultimately gendered male, Fuller wrote a friend: "Experience! Why cannot I value thee and make thee my peculiar household deity, as did our Master, Goethe? I suppose I could, if I had the same reproducing power."[15] Here Fuller assigns the term "reproduce," in other contexts so redolent of female fertility, to the expression of ideas grounded in passively received knowledge.[16] Such expression before an audience she then ascribes to the realm of active experience: "So it seems the mind must reveal its secret; must reproduce" (*MMFO*, 1:265–66).[17] To provide women the experience of "reproducing"—of critical expression and response in a semipublic forum—Fuller designed her Conversation series (1839–44). In her central role as organizer, purveyor of knowledge, and discussion facilitator, Fuller created her own experiential arena as agent and mediator.

The Conversation Series and Imagined Germany

In conceiving the Conversation series Fuller was indebted not only to the educational power of the Lyceum movement and the promotion of "Conversations" by Unitarian leaders but also to the European "salon" movement.[18] Here, where women organized and presided over mixed-sex intellectual gatherings—"salons" in France, "open houses" or "gatherings" in Germany[19]—space opened for intellectual women to "reproduce." Fuller extolled Rahel Levin Varnhagen (1771–1833),[20] founder of one of the earliest weekly gatherings in Berlin (1790–1806), as the "intellectual Queen" of her city.[21] Familiar with Varnhagen's activities and renown as early as 1834, through her letters (published posthumously in 1833) and through Thomas Carlyle's lengthy review of her husband's memoirs (1838), Fuller appreciated Varnhagen as a kindred spirit. Aside from their equally staunch defense and praise of Goethe, both contended with women's marginalization, overcame obstacles to creating loci for intellectual exchange, advanced literary criticism as a genre, and struggled to adapt to patriarchically endorsed writing modes. Foremost, however, was their common belief in the transformative power of self-expression and dialogue. Fuller drew on her imagined experience of Varnhagen's gatherings to create her own intellectual setting in which a community of women would feel comfortable engaging in the experiential imperative of *Bildung*.

Based on her reading of Goethe's female characters, on von Arnim's *Günderode*, and on her perception of the German gatherings, Fuller imagined German women had access to deeper learning. And she believed in the power of such learning, in tandem with active participation in conversation forums, to effect reform. In actuality, female institutional education in German lands was far more limited than in the United States.[22] A small minority of girls received a substantive home education, particularly if instructed by their brothers' tutors or, like Fuller, by erudite fathers. Even the most progressive school of this era, Betty Gleim's Institute for Girls (Lehranstalt für Mädchen) in Hamburg, offered a narrower curriculum than that of progressive American women's and coeducational academies—in fact, coeducational secondary institutions were nonexistent. German girls' schools expanded in Fuller's era but directorships were almost exclusively male, and the curricula of most attended to the conventional female "accomplishments" and training for domesticity. Until the late nineteenth century, the termination age was generally fourteen, the age of confirmation and the age at which girls were expected to focus on domestic arts in the home. The opportunity to present public speeches and recitations, a requisite in young men's schools, was denied young women. In terms reminiscent of conduct books, girls' school directors censured public presentations as the "strongest stimulus to ambition and thus the greatest danger to humility and modesty" and, therefore, "repugnant to the essence of femininity."[23] In contrast, the concurrent expansion of American coed and female academies (where public exhibition was promoted), as well as female literary societies and reading circles, attests to a broader base for self-improvement than in German lands.[24]

Bettina Brentano von Arnim

The Ursuline convent school where Bettina resided from age seven to eleven, between the deaths of her mother and father, undoubtedly followed conduct-book precepts. She was then taken into the home and under the haphazard tutelage of her elderly grandmother Sophie von La Roche, the celebrated novelist, founder of a women's educational periodical, and friend of the Goethe family. There Bettina encountered the circle of European literati whom La Roche hosted. As La Roche's granddaughter, the sister of romantic writer Clemens Brentano and the wife of another, Achim von Arnim, Bettina embodies, for devotees of German romanticism, the enviable good fortune to have come of age amid the constellation of late eighteenth- and early nineteenth-century German romantic writers. The brilliant and accomplished grandmother La Roche, though rigorously tutored in childhood by her own father, accommodated the mentality of her day by cautioning against women's public display of learnedness.[25]

Bettina rebelled, not by intellectual ostentation but by adopting the persona of a "child of nature" quick to announce her stance against socially prescribed dicta for women. She sought counsel and comfort in Goethe's mother, who in 1807 encouraged Bettina, then twenty-two, to correspond with her already renowned son, then fifty-eight. *Goethes Briefwechsel mit einem Kinde* (Goethe's Correspondence with a Child), the epistolary novel Bettina published twenty-eight years later, attracted a wide popular audience. Because letters—by women as well as men—were a site of the public as well as the private, shared and read aloud, it was expected that the writer shape and embellish for a presumed wider audience than the recipient. When von Arnim transformed her letters into a literary incarnation, however, critics accused her of exploiting and misrepresenting Goethe by falsifying the correspondence.[26] Von Arnim, unperturbed, produced several subsequent conversational and epistolary novels, including *Die Günderode*, in which letters from historical figures serve as the medium for self-exploration. From the standpoint of current theoretical inquiry into self-writings, narratology, and memory, the work has been studied as an exploration of self and of the multifaceted nature of love.[27]

Fuller was naturally among the first Americans to read *Goethe's Correspondence with a Child*, which appeared at the height of her immersion in Goethe's life and works, an English translation appearing in 1837.[28] Her response contrasted starkly with the positive reception the work received among the broader transcendental circle: Fuller did not appreciate it.[29] She may well have viewed the character Bettine's flirtatiousness and public display of private relationship as demeaning to Goethe. As she wrote one friend: "More properly it should be named 'A Child's Correspondence with Herself'"; and to another: "I am astonished to see how much Bettine's book is to all these people. . . . The men wish they had been loved by Bettine; the girls wish to write down the thoughts that come, and see if just such a book does not grow up."[30] Envy of von Arnim / Bettine's relationship with Goethe likely fueled Fuller's criticism, as to be befriended and mentored by him had been her own fervent wish. In 1833 she had written her cousin James Clarke: "How often I have thought, if I could see Goethe, and tell him my state of mind, he would support and guide me! He would be able to understand; he would show me how to rule circumstances, instead of being ruled by them."[31] Lastly, returning to the topic of female characters in *Wilhelm Meister*, Fuller would surely have been inflamed by Bettine's derogatory and self-aggrandizing commentary: "In *William Meister* . . . all the women are disgusting to me. . . . I could 'drive them all out of the temple,' and I had built too upon it, that you have loved me as soon as you knew me, because I am better and more amiable than the whole female assemblage in your novel."[32]

The lone female figure von Arnim exempted from her critique of the female figures in *Wilhelm Meister* is one with whom both she and Fuller felt a particular affinity: Mignon, the ethereal, androgynous, child-woman actor, singer, musician, and poet, who embodies romantic attributes of incessant yearning—for her homeland (Italy) and for love—and who fades into a melancholic death. In Fuller's public writing she calls Mignon "a prophetic form, expressive of the longing for a state of perfect freedom, pure love" (*WNC*, 37). Viewed less abstractly, Mignon suffers from profound displacement. Tellingly Fuller quotes a particular statement by Mignon, ostensibly for her reading audience, yet devoid of English translation. Mignon, dressed in angelic garb for a theatrical performance, declares: "Jene himmlische Gestalten, sie fragen nicht nach Mann und Weib" (*WNC*, 37). By resisting translation, Fuller assigns to the German language exclusive properties for conveying this particularly painful truth: that only in death can the wish for a genderless space be delivered, because only in the afterlife does one meet "heavenly figures [who] ask not who is man or woman" (author's translation). Privately Fuller identifies with Mignon's suffering, casting herself in her 1840 journal as "poor Mignon" and instructing herself, as Mignon, to "fear not the transition through death," as "no penal fires can have in store worse torments than thou art familiar with already" (*MMFO*, 1:260).[33] Thus Fuller extends the shared sense of displacement to include all the ills and suffering that ensue from gender difference, past, present, and future.

Von Arnim read *Wilhelm Meister* at the age of sixteen and immediately called herself Mignon, as reported in the diary of Henry Crabb Robinson upon his first visit to the La Roche home in 1801: "[Bettina] was always considered a wayward, unmanageable creature. . . . I recollect also hearing her speak in terms of extravagant admiration of the Mignon of Goethe's 'Wilhelm Meister.' Clasping her hands over her bosom, she said, 'I always lie thus when in bed, in imitation of Mignon.'"[34] This imitation of Mignon's repose in death highlights Bettina's empathic response to Mignon's displacement, as does the character Bettine's comment, in *Goethe's Correspondence with a Child*, that Wilhelm should have enabled Mignon to return home to Italy and accompanied her there.[35] Only by coexperiencing displacement, Bettine intimates, can one empathize with the suffering it engenders.

Die Günderode

Given Fuller's initial aversion to the character / narrator Bettine, it may be surprising that she elected to read von Arnim's *Günderode*, a work over 600 pages long that, unlike *Goethe's Correspondence with a Child*, had not been translated and was not to be found in the American literary marketplace. Most likely Fuller requested that friends bring the volume back from Europe, as it did not appear in the catalogues of Elizabeth Peabody's Foreign Library.[36] No extant evidence suggests that Fuller knew of Karoline von Günderode's poetry or of the historical person, aside from Günderode's suicide as reported by Bettine in *Goethe's Correspondence with a Child*.[37] Regardless of how Fuller was able to obtain *Die Günderode*, von Arnim seems to be the only female German writer she read aside from one novel by Ida Hahn-Hahn.[38] Although works by German women writers were not as easily obtained as, for example, those by Madame de Staël and George Sand, we are invited to ask why Fuller did not vigorously investigate the several popular German women writers who produced contemporaneously with the male German romantic writers who so inspired her.[39]

The correspondence between von Arnim and Günderode took place between 1804 and 1806, commencing when von Arnim was nineteen and Günderode twenty-four, thus thirty-four years before von Arnim's 1840 publication. The title of the epistolary novel is somewhat misleading, as the letters from Bettine far outnumber those from Karoline: thirty-seven from Bettine, twenty-three from Karoline. Thus Bettine is very much a subject and object of her own book, along with Karoline.[40] Critics who questioned von Arnim's absolute adherence to the wording of the original letters—and placed a premium on such "veracity" as the value standard—dominated much of the negative reception. Was the work to be understood as a historical document or as fictionalized history, as historically inauthentic or fictional truth? As Patricia Simpson notes, scholarship on *Die Günderode* points to two trends: "one emphatically distinguishes between the 'fact' and the 'fiction'; the second celebrates the suspension of such rigid definitions." Notably, the first trend is dominated by male critics, the second by female.[41] As mentioned, von Arnim was not deterred by the same questions concerning her prior epistolary novels. Fuller's forty-three-page *Dial* essay "Bettine Brentano and Her Friend Günderode" was one of the first critiques on either side of the Atlantic to celebrate the creativity and literary value of von Arnim's *Die Günderode* over its factuality. Anticipating twentieth- and twenty-first-century theorists of self-writings and memory construction, Fuller defended von Arnim's "embellishings," writing that her "poetical growth" over the years since the correspondence "makes what really happened seem an inadequate expression of what really was."[42]

With respect to the power of an imagined German womanhood, *Die Günderode* seized Fuller as no other work did. A critic of American materialism and cultural vacuity, Fuller directs readers to find in the letters not only "the interior of German life, and of an ideal relation realized, but the high state of culture in Germany which presented to the thoughts of those women themes of poesy and philosophy as readily, as to the English or American girl come the choice of a dress, the last concert or assembly" ("BB," 320). Fuller (mis)represents the work as a signpost of widespread female engagement with literature and philosophy or, at the least, as a demonstration of German women's greater capacity, via cultural permeation, for sophisticated intellectual thought: "Many of Günderode's poetical fragments would not have been written, had she not been the contemporary of Schelling and Fichte, yet are they native and original, the atmosphere of thought *reproduced* in the brilliant and delicate hues of a peculiar plant" (ibid.; emphasis added). From this endorsement of female creativity, drawn in romantically inspired organicist terms, Fuller urges readers to esteem the work's genre hybridity as well as its rich intellectual (and intertextual) content. "This transfusion of such energies as are manifested in Goethe, Kant, and Schelling into these private lives is a creation not less worthy our admiration, than the forms which the muse has given them to bestow on the world" (ibid.).

Because chronology is important to situating cultural transfer in Fuller's embrace of *Die Günderode*, I now turn to those life events that propelled her to conceive German culture and womanhood as empowering alternatives to challenging circumstances. At age twenty-five, upon her father's death (1835), Fuller shouldered heavy responsibility for her mother and five younger siblings. As Jeffrey Steele observes, this left her scant opportunity to mourn the death of this central intellectual figure who had home schooled her to age eleven according to a curriculum designed for male prodigies (*EMF*, xiv–xvi). With the exception of female characters in the works of Goethe, de Staël, and George Sand, Fuller's literary heroes had been male—a natural consequence of her "male" education and the phenomenon of female identification with male values.[43] For a short period in her teens, Fuller was one of a few girls permitted to attend a small school for classical instruction that prepared boys for Harvard. Naturally these conditions of being "educated male," only to realize the limited prospects for future application, would result in severe disappointment.

Along with mourning and contemplating her father some five years later, Fuller was jolted into recognizing that his educational approach had obstructed her creative production as a writer.[44] She characterized the fall and winter of 1840–41 as "the era of illumination in [her] mental life."[45] Until then her public writing, primarily literary criticism and translations, had centered on male writers and masculine genius. Her reading of *Die Günderode* between January and March 1841 coincided with the realization that "her psychological dependence upon the image of her dead father recapitulated the dependence of women in general upon patriarchal values" (*EMF*, xv). This literary and life trajectory may resonate with readers today, as it anticipates twentieth-century feminism's "first wave" focus on analysis and critique of male values and practices, followed by the "second wave" difference-based studies of women writers.

Fuller began to translate *Die Günderode* in the months following her reading,[46] and she wrote a brother that she was in better health than at any time since their father's death.[47] I suggest that Fuller's revaluation of female agency, abetted by her reading of *Die Günderode*, liberated her to promote publicly the transformational potential of intimate female friendships to nurture intellectual growth (*Bildung*) as well as to provide emotional sustenance.

This major psychological turning point also induced Fuller to reassess significant male figures aside from her father. In the opening pages of the *Dial* essay on the Bettine-Karoline friendship, Fuller dethrones Goethe as male hero. Here, though she slips between the historical figures and their literary presentations, Fuller reverses her earlier disapproval of the flighty and flirtatious Bettine in von Arnim's *Goethe's Correspondence with a Child* and castigates Goethe for his exploitation of a trusting young devotee: "Goethe is so cold, so repulsive, diplomatic, and courteously determined not to compromise himself. . . . [T]here is an air as of an elderly guardian flirting cautiously with a giddy, inexperienced ward, or a Father Confessor, who . . . uses it [the thoughts of his devotee] to gratify his curiosity" ("BB," 316). Fuller's transformation pertained not only to breaking through values imposed by patriarchy but also to revaluing the importance of female friendship in the process of deconstructing her ideal male hero. As a reader of the dynamics of the Bettine-Karoline friendship, as presented by von Arnim, Fuller encountered Karoline as the deeply learned figure who attempts to discipline Bettine into reading and engaging with philosophers and historians.[48] Bettine, alternatively positioned as the "child of nature," quickly loses patience and insists that personal experience in nature and in human interaction provides keener insights into the mysteries of life. Readers of Fuller easily understand her sympathetic reading of both figures—or, to borrow from Christina Zwarg, her "oscillating identification" with each (Zwarg, 94). This point cannot be underestimated, and it returns us again to events in Fuller's life that converged with her reading of *Die Günderode*.

Friendship, Self-Reliance, and Gender

Beginning in 1838, friendship had been a topic of animated discussion and correspondence among Fuller, Ralph Waldo Emerson, and other close friends. Emerson's reputed distance, coldness, and insularity aligned smoothly with his philosophy of friendship and of self-reliance at this time. He could easily classify the relation between the two: self-reliance was not to suffer in deference to friendship. Joyce Warren succinctly encapsulates Emerson's view of the individual's positioning toward others: "The individual should insulate himself from others as much as possible. . . . [A]ll acquaintances, even friends, are principally valuable for the way in which they can serve the self."[49] For Fuller, the transformational potential inhering in female friendship complicated the principle of self-reliance inculcated by her father, manifested in her male literary and historical heroes, and formulated into a philosophy by Emerson. At face value, to question the terms of self-reliance would risk acceptance of the patriarchal view of female weakness: dependence on others for self-worth (as well as material support), sacrifice of individuality, and selflessness to the obliteration of selfhood.[50]

Between August and October 1840, this discussion developed into an intense debate between Fuller and Emerson. In fact, Emerson incorporated segments of his letters into his 1841 "Friendship" essay, including the following: "We are armed all over with subtle antagonisms, which, as soon as we meet, begin to play, and translate all poetry into stale prose. Almost all people descend to meet. All association must be a compromise, and, what is worst, the very flower and aroma of the flower of each of the beautiful natures disappears as they approach each other. What a perpetual disappointment is actual society, even of the virtuous and gifted!" (*LE*, 2:168). Thus according to the creed of individualism and self-reliance, friendship becomes "weakness," "a perpetual disappointment," "a descend[ing] into society," "a compromise." Those familiar with Emerson's essay would recognize Fuller's response in her discussion of the Bettine-Günderode friendship: "Theirs was a true friendship. They needed not 'descend to meet'" ("BB," 322).[51]

Fuller's imagined German ideal is operative in this discussion of friendship. While male friendship had been thematized in German literature since the eighteenth century, often represented by pairs from antiquity and medieval literature, there emerged no literary tradition of women's friendship as an intellectual-spiritual relationship between equal, autonomous women.[52] In her "Bettine-Günderode" essay Fuller offers a corrective in her discussion of a work by British contemporary Walter Landor. In the friendship between Aspasia and Cleone in Landor's *Pericles and Aspasia* (1836), Fuller found a model that, while "marble-cold compared with the one before us" (that is, Bettine and Günderode), exemplified a similar "intimacy," showing the "influences of the two [female] characters upon one another" ("BB," 349). The timing of Fuller's assessment of von Arnim's *Günderode* as a poetic "breathing life" intersects with the friendship debate, which resurfaced in October 1841, nine months after Fuller's reading of *Günderode* and the formulation of her essay: "You go upon the idea that we must love the most beauteous," Fuller wrote Emerson, "but this is not so." When her friends did not live up to their fullest potential, she felt "a deeper tenderness and even a higher hope than did these forms in the greatest perfection they ever attained" (*LMF*, 2:235). As Dorothy Berkson illustrates, Fuller's promotion of potential, grounded in romantic ideology, is "formative and generative, finding promise in the process of discovery rather than in the finished, perfect object or condition."[53] Thus, as Fuller wrote to William Channing, she accepted "the possibility of failure to achieve perfection and the suffering and anguish that may accompany defeat" (*LMF*, 2:214). Her reading of the rare works that depict female friendship—Landor's and especially the German *Die Günderode*, whose comprehensive, sympathetic, and intellectually satisfying women's friendship she extended to her imagined German womanhood—granted the affirmation of all that friendship should and could be. As iterated in the *Dial* essay: "No friendship can subsist . . . without generosity, without unwearied sympathy, and the modesty that permits, when suffering, to receive this balm. . . . There must be faith in one another, action upon one another, love, patiently to wait for one another" ("BB," 349–50). Studies on the relational model of women's psychological development by present-day feminist psychologists and social theorists, such as Carol Gilligan, Nancy Chodorow, Nell Noddings, and Jane Roland Martin, resonate to Fuller's celebration of female friendship—as well as of *Bildung*—and should provide students of Fuller further possibilities for scholarly inquiry.

Though it is beyond the scope of this essay to examine fully Fuller's sympathetic reading of *Die Günderode*, Bettine's invention of a religion serves as an example of one arena in which the playful, intimate aspect of female friendship melds with the development of self-philosophy intrinsic to *Bildung*. In a letter to Karoline, Bettine presents her idea for a new religion, her "Schwebereligion [Hovering Religion],"[54] for Karoline's approval and codevelopment. Fuller, creatively invoking readers' "unmingled pleasure" in the friendship ideal, situates the two together, first seated by the stove in Günderode's room and then walking in Madame La Roche's garden, where they *"founded a religion"* ("BB," 323). The Schwebereligion, grounded in the pantheistic immanence of God in (wo)man and nature, in action and courage, and in the fusing of art (poesy) and religion, would have meshed comfortably with Fuller's own philosophical outlook.[55]

Returning to Fuller's Conversation series, though she encouraged her attendees to think beyond conventional presumptions, this did not in itself translate into liberal religious ideology. As Phyllis Cole points out, "Emerson and Fuller had brought an unsettling reading of German and English romanticism to bear on the liberal religious question of self-culture, for they argued that all traditional scriptures, doctrines, and preachers fell short of the individual's inner potential for spiritual and intellectual unfolding."[56] According to Elizabeth Peabody's account of one Conversation, several women objected to what they perceived as Fuller's heretical venerating of Greek pagan culture over Christian doctrine; for example, "Mrs. Quincy . . . expressed wonder & some horror at the thought of *Christians* enjoying *Heathen* Greeks."[57] A young woman attending a later series wrote to a friend, "My . . . objections to these conversations is that I sometimes feel as if I would rather not have doubts and difficulties suggested to me which I have not yet met with in my experience of life; and as if a simple faith in the words of Jesus were better than, even *better without*, all philosophy and reasoning of mortal men."[58] When we contrast this with the image of Bettine and Karoline animatedly discussing their self-created religion and briefly consider the romantic philosophical underpinnings of the Schwebereligion, we can understand Fuller's sense of displacement, afflicting both gender and cultural identity, and thus her fervor for imagined German womanhood.

In Bettine and Karoline's Schwebereligion, religion became aesthetisized, an expression for art. Bettine writes: "God is poesy, and nothing else. . . . The medium between God and the soul is Music; thought is the blossom of omnipresent Spirit, as melody is the blossom of harmony. All that is revealed to the human mind is melody, borne by the omnipresence of Spirit: it is God's poesy."[59] If God is poesy, then (wo)man, created in God's image, is a born poet. Fuller is unlikely to have broached "God as poesy" to her Conversation participants. Nonetheless, she emphasized the centrality of poetry to the soul: "We should always keep in mind that poetry of life was not something aside,—a path that might or might not be trod,—it was the only path of the true soul. . . . We might not always be poetic in life, but we might and should be poetic in our thought and intention."[60] Fuller's literary encounter with *Die Günderode* enabled her to envision women empowered to discourse subversively against religious orthodoxy. The striking contrast with her interactions even among Conversation participants could only enhance the impulse to idealize German womanhood.

Fuller's reading of the provocative philosophical and personal conversation presented in *Die Günderode* not only affirmed the value of female friendship but imparted a liberating effect to her writing as well. In *Die Günderode*'s hybridity—the correspondence includes dramatic dialogues, poems, and imaginary travel narratives, in addition to literary discussions and philosophical explorations—Fuller discovered relief from the vexing struggle to perform according to the requisites of male-defined genre categories, a frustration she expressed succinctly and poignantly in a letter: "For all the tides of life that flow within me, I am dumb and ineffectual, when it comes to casting my thought into a form. No old one suits me" (*LMF*, 6:143).[61] While *Die Günderode*'s mixing of genres provided another target for the disparagement of male reviewers, for Fuller this hybridity helped mitigate anxiety over producing narratives that did not conform to prescriptive norms of literary patriarchy.[62] *Summer on the Lakes* (1844), her travel narrative that incorporates landscape writing, poetry, letters, reports, and stories, was not surprisingly critiqued as unstructured, fragmented, digressive, disunified, slipshod, and random. Fortunately, in light of feminist scholarship and challenges to masculine determinants of literary value, *Summer on the Lakes* is enjoying renewed scholarly attention.[63]

Questions and Conjectures

As mentioned, Fuller did not read or seek to acquaint herself with works by German women romanticists writing concurrently with the male authors whom she revered. Given Fuller's reception of *Die Günderode*, one might assume that she would have obtained subsequent works by von Arnim, two of which were published in quick succession to *Die Günderode*. No evidence has surfaced to indicate that she did. We can assume she was aware of von Arnim's 1843 *Dies Buch gehört dem König* (The King's Book),[64] a conversational novel that boldly criticized the religious-political establishment and presented von Arnim's vision of an ideal government. Shortly after Fuller turned editorship of the *Dial* over to Emerson, he published his translation of a lengthy review of this book, which originally appeared in the immigrant newspaper *Deutsche Schnellpost*.[65]

This "discontinued connection" is magnified by Fuller's and von Arnim's chronologically parallel turn to social justice issues in the 1840s. Those familiar with Fuller know of her increasing activism, first in New York and then in Italy. Those familiar with von Arnim know of her courageous activism in bringing visibility to the politically and economically oppressed, defending victims in letters to the king of Prussia, publicizing the plight of the underclass in her writings, and undertaking humanitarian missions in the most deprived districts of Berlin. Among her essays in social criticism for the *Tribune*, Fuller wrote about the need for prison reform; she surely would have been receptive to von Arnim's challenge, in *The King's Book*, to reduce criminality by tackling the causes of poverty. Even prior to her overtly political writings, von Arnim had dedicated *Die Günderode* "to the students [den Studenten gewidmet]," specifically to the revolutionary Young Hegelians to whom she lent moral support. Fuller did not include the dedication in her translation, and one wonders whether she noticed it or knew that, in response, the students staged a torchlight parade in von Arnim's honor.[66]

Several tantalizing points at which Fuller and von Arnim link and diverge lie beyond the scope of this essay and will, it is hoped, be pursued by others in future scholarly investigations.[67] Fuller devotees agree that her astounding life trajectory assumes a compelling and unforgettable narrative arc of its own. This is true of von Arnim as well, and, as Marjanne Goozé aptly remarks, the "cult of personality" surrounding her caused literary historians to see her "more as a poetic subject than a producer of art."[68] One likes to imagine that Fuller would have delighted in knowing that von Arnim's notoriety as social activist and romantic figure inspired immigrant German Freethinkers in Texas to name a community for her in 1847.

Was there the chance that Fuller's and von Arnim's lives might have intersected in person? Fuller had written von Arnim a friendly laudatory letter and sent a packet of readings in 1840 (*LMF*, 6:328–29), and von Arnim remembered Fuller when prodded by Theodore Parker on his visit to von Arnim in 1844.[69] When Fuller was financially enabled by friends to voyage to Europe in 1846, she was tentatively prepared to include Hamburg in her plans in order to visit a friend. This did not happen.[70] Whether she considered traveling from Hamburg to Berlin to pay a visit to von Arnim one can only conjecture. Taking the trajectory of this essay into account, however, I would argue that she avoided Germany on other grounds.

We need only look again to the romantic image of Germany that Fuller evoked in her *Dial* essay on the Bettine-Günderode friendship to be reminded of the power of cultural transfer, essentialized as it was in Fuller's day: "Let him who has seated himself beneath the great German oak, and gazed upon the growth of poesy, of philosophy, of criticism, of historic painting, of the drama, till the life of the last fifty years seems well worth man's living, pick up these little acorns which are dropping gracefully on the earth, and carry them away to be planted in his own home, for in each fairy form may be read the story of the national tree, the promise of future growths as noble" ("BB," 321). Fuller's mythologizing of Germany as a perfect cultural habitat filled a personal desire that would have been severely diminished, if not eradicated, when confronted by the painful exigencies of the actual German social and political landscape. Perhaps most important to any discussion of Fuller is that the yearning fulfilled by medieval legends, Goethe's *Wilhelm Meister*, and von Arnim's *Die Günderode* reached far beyond the personal. Applying her imagined ahistorical German female community to advocate for the elevation of educational standards and the diminishment of materialism for American girls and women was but one piece in the Fuller legacy of appropriating private need to serve public betterment.

NOTES

1. See especially Christel-Maria Maas, *Margaret Fuller's transnationales Projekt* (Göttingen: Univ-drücke, 2006); Sigrid Bauschinger, *The Trumpet of Reform: German Literature in Nineteenth-Century New England* (Columbia, S.C.: Camden, 1998), 71–136; Renate Delphendahl, "Margaret Fuller: Interpreter and Translator of German Literature," in *Margaret Fuller: Visionary of the New Age* (Orono, Me.: Northern Lights, 1994), 54–100; Arthur R. Schultz, "Margaret Fuller—Transcendentalist Interpreter of German Literature," in *Critical Essays on Margaret Fuller*, ed. Joel Myerson (Boston: G. K. Hall, 1980), 195–208; and Henry Pochmann, "Margaret Fuller and Germany," in *German Culture in America* (Madison: Univ. of Wisconsin Press, 1957), 440–47, 760–68.
2. Maas, *Margaret Fullers transnationales Projekt*, 214–24; Anke Finger, "Bettine in Boston: Margaret Fuller and the Reception of *Die Guenderode* in Transcendental America," MA thesis, Brandeis Univ., 1995; Zwarg, 88–96; Konstanze Bäumer, "Margaret Fuller (1810–1850) and Bettina von Arnim: An Encounter between American Transcendentalism and German Romanticism," *Internationales Jahrbuch der Bettina-von-Arnim-Gesellschaft* 4 (1990): 47–69; Edith Toegel, "Margaret Fuller, Bettina von Arnim, Karoline von Günderrode: A Kinship of Souls," *Yearbook of German-American Studies* 23 (1988): 141–51. Von Arnim differentiated herself as author / person and literary persona as "Bettina" and "Bettine"; some critics also use "Karolina" and "Karoline" as author / character markers. Potential confusion in these slight variations is compounded by slippery questions of truth to

fiction in the letters themselves and of author and narrator more broadly. In this essay, von Arnim and Günderode are the historical persons, Bettine and Karoline the literary personae. Occasional reference to von Arnim in childhood will be "Bettina."

3. Lynne Tatlock and Matt Erlin, *German Culture in Nineteenth-Century America: Reception, Adaptation, Transformation* (Rochester, N.Y.: Camden House, 2005), xii–xiii.
4. The latter two figures are Duchess Anna Amalia of Saxe-Weimar, in whose court Goethe served as privy counselor in the period 1795–1805, and Lilie Schönemann, to whom Goethe dedicated several poems.
5. For example, he approved of the death penalty in the controversial infanticide case of Anna Höhne. See W. Daniel Wilson, "Goethe, His Duke and Infanticide," *German Life and Letters* 61, no. 1 (2008): 8–32. Wilson details a number of Goethe's harsh judgments in his *Das Goethe-Tabu: Protest und Menschenrechte im Klassischen Weimar* (Munich: Deutscher Taschenbuch, 1999).
6. *Conversations with Goethe in the Last Years of His Life, Translated from the German of Eckermann, by S. M. Fuller* (Boston: Hillard, Gray, 1839), xxv–xxvi; hereafter cited parenthetically as *CG*. The original appeared in 1836; Fuller's was the first English translation. Fuller states earlier in the preface (xxiv–xxv) that she has deliberately left out certain passages in order not to exceed one volume: those on Goethe's theory of colors, on his visit to Italy, and on a novel that had not yet been translated.
7. Translations of the gaps in the Fuller translation are here filled by John Oxenford, trans., *Conversations of Goethe with Johann Peter Eckermann* (1850; reprint Cambridge, Mass.: Da Capo Press, 1998), here 405. Though Oxenford based his translation on Fuller's, his is the one that received multiple publications.
8. See Capper 1, 265–66.
9. *Conversations of Goethe*, trans. Oxenford, 89.
10. For views on Goethe as patriarchal, see Jill Anne Kowalik, "Feminine Identity Formation in *Wilhelm Meisters Lehrjahre*," *Modern Language Quarterly* 53, no. 2 (1992): 149–72; Anneliese Dick, *Weiblichkeit als natürliche Dienstbarkeit. Eine Studie zum klassischen Frauenbild in Goethes "Wilhelm Meister"* (Bern: Peter Lang, 1986), esp. 17–26; and Susanne Zantop, "The Beautiful Soul Writes Herself: Friederike Helene Unger and the 'Große Goethe,'" in *In the Shadow of Olympus*, ed. Katherine Goodman and Edith Waldstein (Albany: State Univ. of New York Press, 1992), 29–52. For views on Goethe's characters as protofeminist, see Diane Buse, "Die Symbolik der Frauengestalten in Goethes Roman *Wilhelm Meisters Lehrjahre*," *Zeitschrift der Germanisten Rumäniens* 7, nos. 1 and 2 (1998): 53–61; and Amanda Ritchie, "Margaret Fuller's First Conversation Series: A Discovery in the Archives," *Legacy* 18, no. 2 (2001): 216–31, esp. 233.
11. On transcendentalists and *Bildung*, see Lawrence Buell, *Literary Transcendentalism* (Ithaca, N.Y.: Cornell Univ. Press, 1973), 90–93.
12. Margaret Fuller, "Goethe," *Dial* 2, no. 1 (July 1841): 26.
13. Fuller, "Goethe," 26–27.
14. A useful source for interrogating concepts of female *Bildung* is the landmark volume *The Voyage In: Fictions of Female Development*, ed. Elizabeth Abel, Marianne Hirsch, and Elizabeth Langland (Hanover, N.H.: Dartmouth Univ. Press, 1983); also see Lorna Ellis, *Appearing to Diminish: Female Development and the British Bildungsroman, 1750–1850* (Cranbury, N.J.: Associated Univ. Presses, 1999).
15. Margaret Fuller to Almira Barlow, 6 October 1834, in *LMF*, 1:210.
16. For discussion of Fuller's use of the term "reproducing" contextualized in the framework of gender, see Ingrid Fry, "Elective Androgyny: Bettine Brentano-von Arnim and Margaret Fuller's Reception of Goethe," *Goethe Yearbook* 10 (2001): 246–62, esp. 251.

17. I refer to *Memoirs* only when there is no other extant source. This quotation appears in Emerson's segment.
18. Capper provides more in-depth background (1:296–97); for a broader discussion of conversation in the transcendentalist tradition, see Buell, *Literary Transcendentalism*, 77–101. Also see Noelle Baker, "'Let me do nothing smale': Mary Moody Emerson and Women's 'Talking' Manuscripts," in the present volume.
19. Because the term "salon" has become an easy referent for discussion of such gatherings transnationally, I emphasize that hostesses and participants in German lands did not relate their activity to the French tradition. Instead, they used a variety of terms associated with convivial social gatherings (Tee-, Tisch-, or Lesegesellschaften; gesellige Abende; "unsere Gesellschaft / unser Kreis"; soirée). On falsely perpetuated notions about the Berlin "salons," see Ulrike Weckel, "A Lost Paradise of a Female Culture? Some Critical Questions Regarding the Scholarship on Late Eighteenth- and Early Nineteenth-Century German Salons," *German History* 18, no. 3 (2000): 310–36; and Barbara Hahn, "Der Mythos vom Salon: 'Rahels Dachstube' als historische Fiktion," in *Salons der Romantik*, ed. Hartwig Schultz (Berlin: Walter de Gruyter, 1997), 213–34.
20. See Liana Borghi, "Margaret Fuller: Maps and Patterns of a Transgressive Journey," Università di Roma, http://dev.dsmc.uniroma1.it/dprs/sites/default/files/333.html, accessed 3 March 2011. Also see Karl Varnhagen von Ense, *Rahel: Ein Buch des Andenkens für ihre Freunde* (Berlin: n.p., 1833); and Thomas Carlyle, "Varnhagen von Ense's Memoirs," *London and Westminster Review* 42 (December 1838): 32–44. Fuller also quoted (and translated) Varnhagen's comments about Goethe in the *Dial* "Goethe" essay, 28. For an excellent biography of Varnhagen in English, see Heidi Tewarson, *Rahel Levin Varnhagen: The Life and Work of a German Jewish Intellectual* (Lincoln: Univ. of Nebraska Press, 1998).
21. Margaret Fuller, "The Modern Jews," *New York Daily Tribune*, 21 April 1845.
22. See James Albisetti, "Europeans and the American Model of Girls' Secondary Education," in *Girls' Secondary Education in the Western World*, ed. J. Albisetti, Joyce Goodman, and Rebecca Rogers (New York: Palgrave-Macmillan, 2010), 181–90; and Carol Strauss Sotiropoulos, *Early Feminists and the Education Debates* (Madison, N.J.: Fairleigh Dickinson Univ. Press), 2007.
23. Quoted in James Albisetti, *Schooling German Girls and Women* (Princeton: Princeton Univ. Press, 1988), 45–46. Only the small minority seeking formal teachers' training had access to further education.
24. See Mary Kelley, *Learning to Stand and Speak: Women, Education, and Public Life in America's Republic* (Chapel Hill: Univ. of North Carolina Press, 2006); and Margaret Nash, *Women's Education in the U.S., 1780–1840* (New York: Palgrave-Macmillan, 2005).
25. See Carol Strauss Sotiropoulos, "*Pomona für Teutschlands Töchter*: Sophie von La Roche as Editor, Educator, and Narrator," *Colloquia Germanica* 33, no. 3 (2000): 213–38.
26. Marjanne Goozé, "The Reception of Bettina Brentano-von Arnim as Author and Historical Figure," in *Bettina Brentano-von Arnim: Gender and Politics*, ed. Elke Frederiksen and Katherine Goodman (Detroit: Wayne State Univ. Press, 1995), 349–420, esp. 366–67.
27. See Edith Waldstein, *Bettine von Arnim and the Politics of Romantic Conversation* (Columbia, S.C.: Camden House, 1988), 33–58.
28. Von Arnim translated it herself, studying English for this express purpose.
29. For example, Emerson (*LE*, 1:210, 31 July 1839); Lydia Maria Child (*Lydia Maria Child: Selected Letters, 1817–1880*, ed. Milton Meltzer and Patricia G. Holland [Amherst: Univ. of Massachusetts Press, 1982], 212); and Bronson Alcott (cited from his Diary of 2 August 1939, in Thomas Wentworth Higginson, *Margaret Fuller Ossoli* [Boston: Houghton Mifflin, 1890], 191).

30. Fuller to Georgiana Bruce, December 1844, and Fuller to William H. Channing, 25 October 1840 (*LMF*, 3:250, 2:172). On the manifold interpretations of Bettine's child voice, see Mary McAlpin, "Goethe's Number-One Fan: A Neo-Feminist Reading of Bettina Brentano-von Arnim," *Comparative Literature* 57, no. 4 (2005): 294–311; and Ruth-Ellen Joeres, *Respectability and Deviance: Nineteenth-Century German Women Writers and the Ambiguity of Representation* (Chicago: Univ. of Chicago Press, 1999), 104–10.
31. Fuller to James Clarke, 17 August 1833, in Capper 1, 130; letter held in the Massachusetts Historical Society (also see *MMFO*, 1:107).
32. Letter of 26 September 1809, in *Goethe's Correspondence with a Child*, 2 vols. (London: Longman, Orme, Brown, and Longmans, 1837), 2:32.
33. Capper quotes one variant from Emerson's "Notebook Margaret Fuller Ossoli": "No hell" in place of "No penal fires" (Capper 1, 287, note on 396).
34. *Diary, Reminiscences, and Correspondence of Henry Crabb Robinson*, ed. Thomas Sadler, 3rd ed., 2 vols. (London: Macmillan, 1872), 1:108.
35. Letter of 20 March 1809, in *Goethe's Correspondence with a Child*, 2:11.
36. *Die Günderode* is in neither the 1840 nor the 1842 catalogues; though the catalogues are not complete, other evidence strongly suggests that it was not in the Foreign Library at the time Fuller obtained it.
37. In any case, neither of Günderode's two publications (under the pseudonym "Tian")—*Gedichte und Phantasien* (1803) and *Poetische Fragmente* (1805)—was available in the United States.
38. Fuller wrote a very brief review of Ida Hahn-Hahn's *Countess Faustina* for the *New York Daily Tribune*, 12 March 1845. Hahn-Hahn was a contemporary of Fuller and one of a few German women writers to be translated.
39. Aside from Goethe, Fuller appreciated Schiller, Tieck, Novalis, Jean Paul, and the earlier Lessing. If she were even aware of popular romantic German women writers, she would have had to order their works or ask traveling friends to obtain them for her in Europe.
40. See Patricia Simpson, "Letters in Sufferance and Deliverance: The Correspondence of Bettina Brentano-von Arnim and Karoline von Günderode," in *Bettina Brentano-von Arnim: Gender and Politics*, 247–77, esp. 251. See also Carola Hilmes, "'Lieber Widerhall,' Bettine von Arnim: Die Günderode—Eine dialogische Autobiographie," *Germanisch-Romanische Monatsschrift* 46 (1996): 424–38.
41. Simpson, "Letters in Sufferance and Deliverance," 250.
42. Margaret Fuller, "Bettine Brentano and Her Friend Günderode," *Dial* 2, no. 3 (January 1842): 352; hereafter cited parenthetically as "BB."
43. Judith Fetterley applies the term "immasculation" to this phenomenon in *The Resisting Reader: A Feminist Approach to American Fiction* (Bloomington: Indiana Univ. Press, 1978), xx.
44. Steele draws on the work of Neal Tolchin to interpret Fuller's case as one of "'disordered mourning'": "a process in which 'grief becomes *frozen*, or blocked' until 'the mourner works through the conflicts he or she feels toward the deceased.'" Steele continues this line of thought: she "returned to the ghost of her unmourned father, measuring the hidden powers that had been repressed by his influence and then frozen by her failure to mourn" (*EMF*, xiv–xv). For details of Fuller's suffering in this period, see Capper 2, 18–22.
45. Fuller to Elizabeth Hoar, 20 March 1842, in *LMF*, 3:55.
46. Fuller translated the first quarter of the text, brought out by Elizabeth Peabody in 1842, and Minna Wesselhoeft completed the translation in 1861, eleven years after Fuller's

death. A letter in the "Literary Intelligence" column of the *Dial*, from an unnamed American intellectual in Germany, indicates that Fuller's translation was circulating (*Dial* 3, no. 3 [January 1943]: 393). Emerson was the editor of the *Dial* at this point.

47. In a 2 February 1841 letter to William H. Channing, she wrote that she would send him extracts from her translation (*LMF*, 2:201–2). Regarding Fuller's communication with her brother Richard, see Joan von Mehren, *Minerva and the Muse: A Life of Margaret Fuller* (Amherst: Univ. of Massachusetts Press, 1995), 143.

48. After receiving a thorough home education, Günderode continued an autodidactic regimen at a Protestant residence for women, studying chemistry, geography, physiognomy, Latin, and both ancient and contemporary philosophy. For more about Günderode, see Barbara Becker-Cantarino, *Schriftstellerinnen der Romantik* (Munich: C. H. Beck, 2000), 199–225; on her education, esp. 206–8.

49. Joyce Warren, *The American Narcissus: Individualism and Women in Nineteenth-Century American Fiction* (New Brunswick, N.J.: Rutgers Univ. Press, 1984), 30.

50. To her cousin James Clarke in 1832: "The time is probably near when I must live alone . . . take care of my ideas without aid,—except from the illustrious dead,—answer my questions, correct my own feelings, and do all that hard work for myself. How tiresome 't is to find out all one's self-delusion! I thought myself so very independent . . . And I am not independent, nor never shall be, while I can get anybody to minister to me. But I shall go where there is never a spirit to come, if I call ever so loudly" (*LMF*, 1:178).

51. This also appears at the end of Fuller's preface to her *Günderode* translation (Boston: E. P. Peabody, 1842), xii.

52. On the friendship in *Günderode*, see Becker-Cantarino, *Schriftstellerinnen der Romantik*, 248–50. Fuller would also have assimilated Varnhagen's discussion regarding reliance on friends from von Ense's 1833 publication of her letters.

53. Dorothy Berkson, "'Born and Bred in Different Nations': Margaret Fuller and Ralph Waldo Emerson," in *Patrons and Protégées*, ed. Shirley Marchalonis (New Brunswick, N.J.: Rutgers Univ. Press, 1988), 3–30, here 15.

54. "Schwebereligion" poses a translation challenge. The term does not appear in the first quarter of the work, that is, in the segment Fuller translated; however, she translates the "Schwebereligion" segment specifically for the *Dial* essay. Wesselhoeft keeps to this translation. In critical treatments it has been variously rendered. For the translation "Floating Religion," see Simpson, "Letters in Sufferance and Deliverance," 257; and Jan van Heurck's translation of Christa Wolf's 1979 essay "Nun Ja! Das nächste Leben geht aber heute an!" (Your Next Life Begins Today: A Letter about Bettine), in *Bettina Brentano von-Arnim: Gender and Politics*," 61. Kari Lokke also suggests "Soaring" in "Beyond Impossibility: Bettine von Arnim's *Die Günderode*, 'An Ideal Relation Realized,'" in her *Tracing Women's Romanticism: Gender, History, and Transcendence* (London: Routledge, 2004), 106. Lokke refers to an essay by Elisabeth Moltmann-Wendel ("Bettina von Arnim und Schleiermacher," *Evangelische Theologie* 31 [1971]: 395–414) to suggest that the name "Schwebereligion" was inspired by Schleiermacher's visions, as recounted in his *Reden über die Religion* (Talks on Religion, 1799), of "floating in the infinite between the self and the universal" (107).

55. See Lokke, "Beyond Impossibility," 106–9; Simpson, "Letters in Sufferance and Deliverance," 257–62; and Becker-Cantarino, *Schriftstellerinnin der Romantik*, 254–56. Becker-Cantarino details von Arnim's and Günderode's indebtedness to Schleiermacher, a close friend of von Arnim, with respect to the melding of art and religion.

56. Phyllis Cole, "Stanton, Fuller, and the Grammar of Romanticism," *New England Quarterly* 73 (2000): 533–59, esp. 538.

57. Quoted from Elizabeth Palmer Peabody's journal, American Antiquarian Society, Papers, Mss Box P. The remark also appears in Nancy Craig Simmons, "Margaret Fuller's Boston Conversations: The 1839–40 Series," in *Studies in the American Renaissance 1994*, ed. Joel Myerson (Charlottesville: Univ. Press of Virginia, 1994), 195–226, esp. 204.
58. Letter to Sarah Hodges, 16 December 1842 [?], vol. 10 of Fuller Manuscripts and Works, Box A, Houghton Library, Harvard University; as quoted in Charles Capper, "Margaret Fuller as Cultural Reformer: The Conversations in Boston," *American Quarterly* 39 (1987): 509–28, esp. 519.
59. *Correspondence of Fräulein Günderode and Bettine von Arnim*, trans. Margaret Fuller and Minna Wesselhoeft (Boston: T. Burnham, 1861), 203.
60. As recorded by Elizabeth Peabody, in an Emerson segment of *Memoirs* (*MMFO*, 1:302–3).
61. Bell Gale Chevigny elucidates Fuller's struggles as a writer in *The Woman and the Myth: Margaret Fuller's Life and Writings* (New York: Feminist Press, 1973), 26–27.
62. From *MMFO*, 1:296–97: "For all the tides of life that flow within me, I am dumb and ineffectual, when it comes to casting my thought into a form. No old one suits me. If I could invent one, it seems to me the pleasure of creation would make it possible for me to write. What shall I do, dear friend? I want force to be either a genius or a character. One should be either private or public. I love best to be a woman; but womanhood is at present too straitly-bounded to give me scope. At hours, I live truly as a woman; at others, I should stifle; as, on the other hand, I should palsy, when I would play the artist."
63. See especially Stephen Adams, "'That Tidiness We Always Look for in Woman': Fuller's *Summer on the Lakes* and Romantic Aesthetics," in *Studies in the American Renaissance*, ed. Joel Myerson (Charlottesville: Univ. Press of Virginia, 1987), 247–64; and Daniel Malachuk, "Green Exaltadas: Margaret Fuller, Transcendentalist Conservationism, and Antebellum Women's Nature Writing," in the present volume. Further, Annette Kolodny argues with compelling evidence that Fuller adapted specific approaches to persuasion with the aim of creating a conversation-based discursive mode in *Woman in the Nineteenth Century*—a treatise long recognized for its content value but disparaged for its structure. See "Inventing a Feminist Discourse: Rhetoric and Resistance in Margaret Fuller's *Woman in the Nineteenth Century*," *New Literary History* 25 (1994): 355–82.
64. The other work of von Arnim's is *Clemens Brentanos Frühlingskranz* (The Spring Wreath, 1844), and additional works followed just before and after Fuller's death in 1850. Fuller may have heard about some of these during her years in Italy (1847–50), when she was befriended by the Viennese-born Marchioness Costanza Arconati, an acquaintance of von Arnim who shared Fuller's fascination with German intellectual history.
65. Ralph Waldo Emerson, trans., review of *Dies Buch gehört dem König*, by Bettine von Arnim, *Dial* 4, no. 2 (October 1843): 267–70.
66. Studies in English on von Arnim's political engagement include Kathleen Hallihan, "Envisioning an Ideal State: The Literary Politics of Bettina von Arnim from 1830–1852," PhD diss., Ohio State Univ., 2005, https://etd.ohiolink.edu/ap:10:0::NO:10:P10_ACCESSION_NUM:osu1116600876, accessed 20 May 2011; Heinz Härtl, "Bettina Brentano-von Arnim's Relations to the Young Hegelians," trans. Dorothee Krahn, in *Bettina Brentano-von Arnim: Gender and Politics*, 145–84; Lorely French, "Strategies of Female Persuasion: The Political Letters of Bettina Brentano-von Arnim," in *Bettina Brentano-von Arnim: Gender and Politics*, 71–94; and Waldstein, *Politics of Romantic Conversation*, 59–93.
67. For example: How has each been discussed and dismissed by patriarchal arbiters of literary value? On Fuller and this question, see especially Charlene Avallone, "What American Renaissance? The Gendered Genealogy of a Critical Discourse," *PMLA* 112 (1997):

1102–20. On von Arnim, see Goozé, "Reception of Bettina Brentano-von Arnim." And how did each appropriate and validate androgyny? On both Fuller and von Arnim, see Fry, "Elective Androgyny." On von Arnim, see Catherine Grimm, "'*Wie ist Natur so hold und gut, die mich am Busen hält*': Nature Philosophy and Feminine Subjectivity in the Epistolary Memoirs of Bettine von Arnim," in *Schwellenüberschreitungen: Politik in der Literatur von Frauen, 1780–1918*, ed. Elisa Müller-Adams and Caroline Bland (Bielefeld: Aisthesis, 2007), 151–68; Elizabeth Krimmer, "Bettina and Louise: Gender Constructions in Bettina Brentano-von Arnim's *Clemens Brentanos Frühlingskranz*," in *Conquering Women: Women and War in the German Cultural Imagination*, ed. Hillary Sy-Quia and Susanne Baackmann (Berkeley and Los Angeles: Univ. of California Press, 2000), 156–76; Waldstein, *Politics of Romantic Conversation*, 67–72; and Konstanze Bäumer, *"Bettine, Psyche, Mignon": Bettina von Arnim und Goethe* (Stuttgart: Heinz, 1986).

68. Goozé, "Reception of Bettina Brentano-von Arnim," 366. Several solid German biographies and renewed scholarship attest to this, as well as more creative works such as Wolf's "Nun Ja!" At the time of this writing, the most accessible biography in English is dated, loosely constructed, and reliant on questionable perpetuated anecdotes; see Arthur Helps and Elizabeth Howard, *Bettina: A Portrait* (London: Chatto & Windus, 1957). Milan Kundera's 1990 novel *Immortality* relies on von Arnim's *Goethe's Correspondence with a Child* to explore von Arnim's relationship with Goethe creatively (see McAlpin, "Goethe's Number-One Fan").

69. Theodore Parker, European travel diary, MHi, series 1, vol. 1. Parker was a Unitarian minister, social reformer, Germanist, essayist, and member of the transcendentalist circle.

70. Evidence suggests that Fuller might have gone to Hamburg to meet James Nathan, a German Jew whom she had known in New York, but learned while in London that he had become engaged. See Capper 2, 272; and Katherine Anthony, *Margaret Fuller: A Psychological Biography* (New York: Harcourt, Brace, 1920), 115.

INTERLUDE

George Sand, from *Spiridion* (London: Charles Fox, 1842), 225–26.

On the side of the perpendicular bank which commands the coast, I had contrived an opening in my bower, and, through a frame of flowers and verdure, I could admire, at leisure, the sublime spectacle of the sea breaking over the rocks, and becoming tinged, towards the horizon, with the radiance of sunset or sunrise. There, lost in endless reveries, I seemed to become sensible of harmonies inappreciable to the gross senses of other men, some plaintive chaunt, breathed on the dark coast, and borne over the waters by the southern winds, or the song of some dervise, or unknown saint, lost in the rugged solitudes of Atlas, and happier, with faith, in his ascetic misery, than I, with doubt, in the midst of my monastic opulence.

By degrees I discovered a deep meaning in the slightest phenomena of nature. In abandoning myself to the charm of my impressions, with the singleness of purpose which despondency produces, I insensibly extended the narrow bounds of the *certain* as far as those of the *possible*; and soon the possible, beheld with a certain emotion of the heart, opened around me horizons more vast than my reason had dared to foresee. I seemed to find motives of mysterious foresight in all which had appeared to me delivered up to a blind fatality. I recovered the sense of happiness which I had so deplorably lost. I sought out the joys incident to all beings, as I had sought the sufferings, and I was astonished to find them so justly distributed. Every creature took a new form and voice, to reveal to me faculties unknown to the cold and superficial observation which I had taken for the purposes of science. Infinite mysteries unfolded themselves around me, contradicting all the decisions of an incomplete knowledge and precipitate judgment. In a word, life assumed in my eyes a sacred character, and a vast aim, of which I had not had a glimpse, either in religion or in science, and which my heart taught anew to my erring intellect.

One evening I was listening, abstractedly, to the noise of the calm sea breaking on the sand: I was seeking the meaning of the three waves, which, stronger than the rest, always came together, and at regular intervals, like a measure in the eternal harmony; I heard a fisherman, who, extended on his back in his boat, was singing to the stars. Undoubtedly I had very often heard the songs of the fishermen of the coast, and this one, perhaps, as often as the others. My ears had always been shut to music, as my brain to poetry. I had seen in the singing of the people, only the expression of gross passions, and I had turned my attention from it with contempt. This evening, as on other evenings, I was, at first, offended with the sound of the voice, which drowned that of the waves and disturbed my hearing. But, in a few moments, I remarked that the song of the fisherman followed instinctively the measure of the sea; and I thought that this was, perhaps, one of those great and true artists whom nature herself takes care to instruct, and who, for the most part die, as they have lived, unknown. This thought responding to the habits of conjecture in which I had formerly delighted, I listened without impatience to the half savage chaunting of this man, half savage also, who was celebrating with a slow and melancholy voice, the mysteries of night, and the gentleness of the breeze. His verses had little rhyme and little measure, his words still less meaning and poetry; but the charm of his voice, the simple skill of his rhyme, and the wonderful beauty of his melody, sad, free, and monotonous, like that of the waves, struck me so forcibly, that all at once the charm of music was revealed to me. It seemed to me that music, independent of any words and any written poetry, must be the true poetical language of man, subject to a logic of its own, and able to express ideas of the most elevated order; ideas too vast even to be well rendered in any other language.

What Did Margaret Think of George?

GARY WILLIAMS

All the aspiring and discontented women known to me in America,—poets, orators, reformers,—were the offspring of George Sand, endeavouring to build in the New World a palace for Women.

—Moncure Daniel Conway,
Autobiography, Memories and Experiences (1904)

Reading French literature in the 1830s, if you were English or American, could get you in real trouble. It could, for example, unmoor your mind from the secure haven of faith and virtue. French culture might look decorous from a distance, but the France of Louis Philippe housed (in the view of a writer for *Blackwood's* in 1833) a "mass of licentiousness probably unprecedented in any modern state." *Blackwood's* put the blame for this sewer of a culture squarely on French novelists, whose books focused almost exclusively on adultery "or other guilty and extravagant sensual passion." Worst of the lot, by most accounts, was George Sand, "a monster, a Byronic woman," whose 1833 work *Lélia*, to cite one instance, trapped readers in a "mire of blood and dirt, over which, by a strange perversity of feeling, the talent of the writer, and that writer a woman! has contrived to throw a lurid, fearful, and unhallowed light."[1]

The American press, except for reprinting British indictments, officially ignored Sand until 1841, when the first full-length American-produced essay on her work appeared in the *North American Review*. In reviewer Francis Bowen's view, Sand's imagination is "morbid," her spirit "gloomy," her mind and heart "thoroughly diseased"; she is an instance of "a noble nature . . . gone astray." Her androgynous persona is invoked specifically to invite the reader's repugnance: it is a "desire to ape the manly character," the function of her having "chos[en] to set at defiance the laws of morality and the opinions of the world."[2]

One would like to know how Bowen's characterization of Sand struck Margaret Fuller, since Fuller's image in her friends' eyes bore some resemblance to the Frenchwoman's persona. Emerson reported in the *Memoirs* that Fuller "had a feeling that she ought to have been a man, and said of herself, 'A man's ambition with a woman's heart, is an evil lot'"—not precisely Sand's own sentiment about her conditions during the early 1830s, but certainly descriptive of the way she was perceived in England and the United States. Further, Emerson noted, Fuller "found something of true portraiture" in Balzac's character Séraphîta, a Swedenborgian androgynous figure from his 1834 novel of that name, who offers instruction on how to move beyond materiality to a sexually undifferentiated plane of spiritual existence (*MMFO*, 1:229).[3]

Emerson's sense of Fuller as hermaphroditic (and therefore Sand-like) would have found substantiation in her 1839 notes on *la jeune France*,[4] which Emerson excerpted for the *Memoirs*, but which have never been printed in full. These notes—Charles Capper calls them her "first extensive writings on recent contemporary literature"—are an indispensable starting point for understanding Fuller's response to George Sand, far more important than her reflections on Sand in *Woman in the Nineteenth Century* or in several short pieces for the *New York Tribune*. The *la jeune France* commentary shows Fuller's particular interest in *Spiridion* (1839) and *Les Sept Cordes de la Lyre* (1839), not the more scandalous novels of Sand's first prominence. These works were a source, as Capper notes, for "one extraordinarily important idea—that it was possible to write in a literary genre that combined the emotional, private, and 'feminine' with the intellectual, public, and 'masculine'" (Capper 1, 260, 262). The idea emerges in this passage:

> These books have made me for the first time think I might write into such shapes what I know of human nature. I have always thought that I would not, that I would keep all that behind the curtain, that I would not write, like a woman, of love and hope and disappointment, but like a man of the world of intellect and action. But now I am tempted, and if I can but do well my present work and show that I can write like a man, and if but the wild gnomes will keep from me with their shackles of care for bread in all its shapes of factitious life, I think I will try whether I have the hand to paint, as well as the eye to see. For I cannot but feel that I have seen from the mouth of my damp cave, stars as fair, almost as many, as this person from the Flèche of the Cathedral [Hélène in *Les Sept Cordes de la Lyre*] where she has ascended at such peril. But I dare boast no more, only please fate be just and send me an angel out of this golden cloud that comes after the pelting showers I have borne so long.

Capper observes that Fuller did indeed try to "paint" in a Sandian mode, in "a few tales," unspecified, written a few years after this time, but emphasizes her eventual choice of the genre of "intellect and action" over the "ethereal" one of romantic fiction as the appropriate and salutary route for her. We can agree that Fuller's signature medium was eventually quite distinct from Sand's and still feel that we have somewhat underappreciated the deliberateness and seriousness of Fuller's efforts, on certain occasions, to emulate Sand's mode.[5] I suggest that a more systematic reading of Fuller's commentary on Sand provides a useful matrix for reexamining one of Fuller's least characteristic and most intriguing texts, "The Magnolia of Lake Pontchartrain."

When Fuller first visited the Emersons in 1836, she was, according to her host, already well read in French literature: "she knew Molière, and Rousseau, and any quantity of French letters, memoirs, and novels." She had also a far-reaching stock of information about French socialism, "especially as it concerned woman" (*MMFO*, 1:204, 218). But although Sand's frequent appearances in the *Revue des Deux Mondes* during the 1830s surely must have caught Fuller's attention, her significant encounter with Sand began in the spring or summer of 1839. Her early reactions are recorded in letters to Emerson, in a journal she kept while visiting the DeWolfes in Bristol, Rhode Island, and in the reading notes on *la jeune France*.

Why at this moment did Fuller turn her attention to Sand? She had been much occupied with Goethe, Novalis, and German thought generally, and aside from George Ripley's publication of Cousin, Constant, and Jouffroy in his *Specimens of Foreign Standard Literature* series, there was little impetus in Fuller's immediate circle to regard French writers and thinkers as contributing significantly to the development of transcendental ideas. The impact of Charles Fourier was yet to be felt. Although no specific reference in Fuller's writings supports this claim, I posit that she was prompted to read Sand systematically by two articles appearing in British periodicals in April and July of 1839.[6]

The first, a piece in the *British and Foreign Review* by Henry F. Chorley, addresses five works published by Sand between 1835 and 1839 and thus begins to chronicle a quite different writer from the one who had become infamous after John Wilson Croker's savage attack in the April 1836 *Quarterly Review* three years earlier. Among the works Chorley discusses are two that Fuller found deeply absorbing (*Lettres d'un Voyageur* and *Spiridion*) and a third that she also urged on Emerson, though without the same avidity (*Mauprat*). Chorley's attitude toward Sand cannot be characterized as balanced or objective, but he does make it clear that he intends to modify somewhat the cartoonish image promulgated by the

British press. He invokes a widely reproduced drawing of Sand by Luigi Calamatta, depicting her "half-sibylline, half-animal countenance," in order to suggest that readers need to look beyond this mask: "To any one who derives from the study of contemporary imaginative literature some aids to his knowledge of the progress of belief and intelligence, a certain acquaintance with the works of Madame Dudevant is almost essential" (361). Chorley's theme is Sand's movement "from advocating the sensualism of the body to that of the mind—from the passionate extravagances of Lelia and Jacques to the mystical rhapsodies of Spiridion—from pleading for a social revolution in which law and opinion should offer no civil barrier to man's wildest appetites, to preaching the doctrine of a universal church in which there shall be as many divinities as man's most grasping imagination may covet" (362–63). Many particulars in Chorley's commentary on the excerpts he includes would presumably have piqued Fuller's interest—especially, perhaps, his highlighting of similarities between *Lettres d'un Voyageur* and Bettina Brentano von Arnim's *Goethes Briefwechsel mit einem Kinde* (1835), for which Emerson and Fuller shared an enthusiasm. Chorley names *Spiridion* "the most remarkable" of Sand's works (385), noting however that, in order for an English reader to appreciate the work, he must "throw himself loose of his insular tastes and habits of judgement as regards works of fiction," and concluding that it contains "some episodical gleams of what is true and lofty, some breathings of imperfect faith uttered in the most elevated language of poetry" (386, 390).

The second article appeared in the *Monthly Chronicle* in July, its author a person later to play a vital role in Fuller's life: Giuseppe Mazzini. This essay is—as Mazzini himself points out—the first published in England to demand a "fresh and more considerate examination" of Sand's work; it responds explicitly to both Chorley and Croker. Whereas Chorley's approach had been to invite attention to Sand on the grounds that her more recent works abjured sensuality and the depiction of immoral behavior, Mazzini urges a reconsideration of the earlier works, the very ones Chorley dismissed as a "catalogue of monstrosities" (364), by suggesting that the morality of a literary performance consists not in the topics presented but in "the final effect" produced by the book. Mazzini's defense of Sand is rational and rhetorically sophisticated. It rests on a sense of shared political sympathies and indirectly expresses his own (republican) sentiments, to which Fuller would have resonated. It also finds evidence of discrimination on the basis of gender, both in the vitriol critics had spewed regarding Sand's life circumstances and in the differential treatment her characters and plots had received in comparisons with those of Sue, Janin, Balzac, and Goethe. Most notably, it is suffused with a spirit of great sympathy and admiration for Sand's achievement—and, it would seem, for her plurally gendered persona, as in this climactic paragraph:

> Such is George Sand, his life, his labours. *She* has suffered—she revolted,—she has struggled—she has sought, hoped, found; and she has told us *all*. The long series of her compositions form a grand confession. Spirits young, pure, and innocent, not worn by unhappiness, whom contact with the world has not yet endowed with the knowledge of evil, may well—perhaps, should—abstain from reading it; but let the rest, numerous as they are, boldly go through the whole; they cannot, we say it with profound conviction, but rise the better. (27; italics in original)

Mazzini's comments on specific works focus on *Indiana*, *Jacques*, and *Lélia*. *Spiridion*, which he also regards as one of Sand's most significant novels, gets only a footnote due to space limitation.

Whether these essays were influential in increasing Fuller's interest in Sand is unprovable. What is known is that she had read her first Sand work, *Les Sept Cordes de la Lyre*—published in April and May 1839 in *Revue des Deux Mondes*—as well as *Spiridion*, twice, by 31 July when she traveled to Bristol, Rhode Island, for a ten-day stay with the DeWolfe family.[7] The months preceding this departure were a period of high intellectual and emotional intensity: Fuller's first book-length publication, a translation of Johann Eckermann's *Gespräche mit Goethe*, appeared in May; she quarreled with Caroline Sturgis; she had begun to conceive the idea of her Conversations (which would begin that fall); and she was beginning to sense that her hopes regarding Samuel Gray Ward, a man she had regarded as a potential suitor, would be disappointed. This moment in which matters of head and heart concentrated, it could be argued, was a fertile field into which the seed of George Sand dropped.

Incipient fertility is, in fact, the dominant motif in the opening lines of Fuller's Bristol journal: "I have never been so near the fountain of inspiration, yet I have not attained to drink. The divinity flits before me, a glittering phantom on the mead, her eyes divine look up to me from the depths of still waters, yet I can never lay hold on her robe or dive to the door of her grotto. . . . It seems as if I drew nearer to my aim, and as if much was accumulating which a moment might cast into a state of crystallization. . . . One who feels like me must either be or write a poem." Immediately following is a note about *Spiridion*, which she had finished rereading earlier in the day: "Never was a nobler conception of the lot of the Seeker. The Maker is not so easily portrayed, yet this writer could do it—Many chords vibrated in my bosom, especially where the monk resigned himself at last to the influences of external Nature and was almost reclaimed. This work is less divine than La Lyre, but manly and masterful."[8] The "Seeker" in *Spiridion* to whom Fuller refers is presumably Father Alexis, an elderly monk sequestered from his associates to keep them from the pollution of his alleged impiety. It could equally well be Angel, the initial narrator of the work and its nominal protagonist, a novice who runs afoul of the hypocritical hierarchy in the Franciscan monastery and finds common ground with Alexis through shared visions of the monastery's founder, Spiridion. The novel is a series of embedded narratives contained by Angel's efforts to articulate his own beliefs. It has trappings of the gothic novel, but like an earlier Sand work, *Lélia*, it is what Sand describes as a "non-visible novel"—not intended to "amuse and entertain readers with an idle imagination . . . appeal[ing] little to the eye [but] constantly to the soul." The texture of the work is that of a philosophical dialogue, which near the end gives way to a melodramatic climax. Angel and Alexis open Spiridion's tomb to retrieve the founder's manuscript credo; the monastery is destroyed and Alexis murdered by soldiers of the revolution; and the novel ends abruptly ("And he died. Then a radiant form appeared beside him, and I fainted" [320]).[9]

Les Sept Cordes de la Lyre, Sand's response to Goethe's *Faust*, is a philosophical drama that additionally reflects Sand's involvement with Chopin and Liszt. George Kennedy, the work's twentieth-century translator / editor, notes that Sand attempted a difficult task: "to cast into words the effect of music and to give dramatic interest to philosophical abstractions" (2). The complicated plot is structured around the relationship between Albertus, a philosophy teacher, and his ward Hélène, who is the inheritor of a magic lyre. Albertus is besieged by Mephistopheles, who can win Albertus's soul only by destroying the lyre and capturing the spirit that lives in it. Albertus has tried to teach philosophy to Hélène, but her sensibility is an unfertile field for rational thought: she responds to nature and music, and eventually evokes the love of the Spirit of the Lyre. This love allows the Spirit to escape Mephistopheles's designs and thereby saves Albertus, too, from his sterile rationalism.

When Hélène first makes the lyre sing, Sand's stage directions indicate that the Spirit's words "are not heard by men, and only the melody of the lyre, of which the words are the expression, strikes their ears" (87). Sand's efforts to render the Spirit's meaning produce rapturous, mystical "speeches," probably what Fuller had in mind in describing the work as "divine." Eventually, Hélène, too—or rather, the "Spirit of Hélène"—speaks in a mystical idiom. Hers and the Lyre's discourse is not the antisensual, nonvisual language Sand intended in *Lélia* and *Spiridion*, but rather a lush, poetic mode intended to make the natural world palpable. Yet in the work's climactic scene, Hélène ascends to the spire of the cathedral and, in dialogue with the Spirit of the Lyre, rejects its vision of the world's beauty: what she sees of "the empire of man" is a devastating view of "immeasurable depths of despair . . . the howlings of grief without resource and without end" (146).

Fuller's impressionistic commentary on these two works, incorporating a number of comparisons with other texts, first records a disappointment that *Spiridion* does not contain the same "lyric effusion" that she values in *Les Sept Cordes* and that has seemed increasingly beautiful on reflection. She notes, however, that the religious sentiment in both is the same, and on a second reading of *Spiridion* she is as enthusiastic about the "different mould." The question of how to incorporate religious and philosophical speculation within a narrative frame absorbs Fuller: "A piece of character-painting does not seem to be the place for a statement of these high and wide subjects. For here the philosophy is not merely implied in the poetry and religion, but assumes to show a face of its own. And, as none should meddle with these matters who are not in earnest, so, such will prefer to find the thought of a teacher or fellow-disciple expressed as directly and as bare of ornament as possible" (*MMFO*, 1:245). Capper finds in this passage a sense that the novel form is "dilettantish" and suggests that Fuller's admiration in general is aroused rather by the works' "unabashed intellectuality" than by their aesthetics (Capper 1, 261). It is true that later in the passage Fuller expresses astonishment at Sand's "insight into the life of thought" and, further, a conviction that she must have known "it" through a man, specifically a philosopher. She seems to find the whole idea of George Sand improbable, so entirely do these books exhibit a sensibility that Fuller has no experience of in a woman (save perhaps herself). Yet Fuller's praise is for *both* the thought and the art of the two works.

Spiridion has also piqued her interest in Hugues-Félicité Robert de Lamennais (the French Catholic republican humanist whose spiritual quest is reflected in Father Alexis), and she asks Emerson to send her Lamennais's *Les Paroles d'un Croyant* (1834). Here is Fuller's reflection on the evidence that "the Dudevant has loved a philosopher":

> I am more curious than ever. I had supposed the view taken by these persons in France, to be the same with that of Novalis and the German Catholics, in which I have been deeply interested. But from this book [*Spiridion*], it would seem to approach the faith of some of my friends here, which has been styled Psychotheism. And the gap in the theoretical fabric is the same as with them. I read with unutterable interest the despair of Alexis in his Eclectic course, his return to the teachings of external nature, his new birth, and consequent appreciation of poetry and music. But the question of Free Will,—how to reconcile its workings with necessity and compensation,—how to reconcile the life of the heart with that of the intellect,—how to listen to the whispering breeze of Spirit, while breasting, as a man should, the surges of the world,—these enigmas Sand and her friends seem to have solved no better than M.F. and her friends. The practical optimism is much the

> same as ours, except that there is more hope for the masses—soon. (*MMFO*, 1:246)

Obviously, Sand's skill in integrating such questions into an imaginative work draws Fuller to contemplate the issues themselves.

But Fuller's interest goes beyond a pondering of the "enigmas," and in fact even in her reflections on Alexis's spiritual course, she seems to be thinking aesthetically. She goes on to address the novel's literary qualities directly:

> This work is written with great vigor, scarce any faltering on the wing. The horrors are disgusting, as are those of every writer except Dante. Every genius should content itself in dipping the pencil in cloud and mist. The apparitions of Spiridion are managed with great beauty. As in Hélène, as in Novalis, I recognized, with delight, the eye that gazed, the ear that listened, till the specters came, as they do to the highlander on his rocky couch, to the German peasant on his mountain. How different from the vulgar eye which looks, but never sees! Here the beautiful apparition advances from the solar ray, or returns to the fountain of light and truth, as it should, when eagle eyes are gazing. (*MMFO*, 1:246–47)

I will return to several particulars of these notes, but I want here to reproduce comments on *Les Sept Cordes* from the second set of Fuller's notes, dated "1839." Here again, Fuller's perceptions focus on the successful fusion of thought and art. As Chorley had done in the *British and Foreign Review* essay, and as Emerson was repeatedly to do in his exchanges with Fuller about Sand, Fuller juxtaposes Sand's work to Bettina von Arnim's highly stylized correspondence with Goethe:

> When I first knew George Sand, I thought I found tried the experiment I wanted. I did not value Bettine so much; she had not pride enough for me; only now when I am sure of myself, would I pour out my soul at the feet of another. In the assured soul it is kingly prodigality; in one which cannot forbear, it is mere babyhood. I love *abandon* only when natures are capable of the extreme reverse. I knew Bettine would end in nothing, when I read her book. I knew she could not outlive her love.
>
> But in *Les Sept Cordes de la Lyre*, which I read first, I saw the knowledge of the passions, and of social institutions, with the celestial choice which rose above them. I loved Hélène, who could so well hear the terrene voices, yet keep her eye fixed on the stars. That would be my wish, also, to know all, then choose; I ever revered her, for I was not

> sure that I could have resisted the call of the Now, could have left the spirit, and gone to God. And, at a more ambitious age, I could not have refused the philosopher. But I hoped from her steadfastness, and I thought I heard the last tones of a purified life:—Gretchen, in the golden cloud, raised above all past delusions, worthy to redeem and upbear the wise man, who stumbled into the pit of error while searching for truth. (*MMFO*, 1:248)

Fuller's mode here is less analytical, more personal. Both works have inspired an identification with the female protagonist; Fuller does not distinguish between the fictional Hélène and the real Bettina in their impact on her—surely a testament to Sand's success in embodying Hélène. I do not read the phrase "the experiment I wanted" as referring to a literary experiment but rather to a way of being, specifically a model for how, as a woman, to pursue a "purified life." The character of Hélène manifests what Fuller sees as Sand's own experiential achievement: "the knowledge of the passions, and of social institutions, with the celestial choice which rose above them." Yet the means through which Fuller grasps the person George Sand is a *literary* work, and although the notes go on to chronicle Fuller's disappointment in the personal George Sand when she reads *Lettres d'un Voyageur*, the novels themselves remain powerful in her imagination.

André and *Jacques*, earlier works that Fuller would read after those just discussed, also evoke her admiration (qualified by her distaste for their claims on behalf of "passion"). *Jacques*, in particular, captures her interest, the title character and his female soulmate Sylvia representing for her an "ideal—the soul that, capable of the most delicate and strongest emotions, can yet look upon the world as it is with a free and eagle gaze, and, without any vain optimism or weak hope of a peculiar lot, can . . . *accept life*."[10] "That is the true stoicism," Fuller reflects, "not to be insensible but superior to pain. How noble to rush to battle like the Spartan youth without a buckler." Thought of this nobility leads Fuller again to the question of "painting"—whether it "is impossible to paint the heroic woman." Consideration of other fictional women—the Countess St. Leon in William Godwin's *St. Leon*, Constantia in Charles Brockden Brown's *Ormond*, unspecified characters in Byron and Scott—puts Sand's Sylvia in a class of her own: "These are more superficial, and you feel rather how they affected the observers than what they were. Sylvia speaks more directly to us than any of them." Ultimately, in Fuller's estimation, Sylvia's state of mind is more palpably realized than Jacques's:

> Such persons [as Jacques] should be given with "large, sharp strokes." He could not have described himself, and the attempt to lay bare the

> springs of his being is vain. The expectation he excited is so great that he cannot fulfill it. . . . I say like Sylvia how could you live for the heart alone; and his answer is not satisfactory. He ought to have respected himself too much to die that persons like Fernand and Octave might be happy. Shall Prometheus refuse chains and torture because the flies and fishes are happier than he. It is natural enough that he should feel this world not worth his stay, much less fit for his abode, but so strong a mind should have felt that much earlier and as strongly as it ever could feel it. The truth is he could not find any way to live nobly at last and so he dies.

This train of thought takes her somewhat away from the book: Jacques's attitude reminds her of Byron, of Bulwer, of the irritating conceit that intellectual men, men of experience, cannot be properly loved by "soft and exigeantes [demanding]" women. "My experience of women is very different," she observes: "women of any imagination wish to make ideals of the men they love and it is not possible for their heroes to have too many advantages over them." The role Sand performs in Fuller's developing perspective on how women can and should live (despite Fuller's reservations arising from the close-up view provided by *Lettres d'un Voyageur*) is clear from such passages—more clear, certainly, than what emerges from her brief remarks in *Woman in the Nineteenth Century*.

The most significant note in these reflections, however, is the passage that closes them, what Capper designates as "one extraordinarily important idea" (reproduced in full earlier): "These books have made me for the first time think I might write into such shapes what I know of human nature." The writing Fuller imagines would cross a gender divide: she would write "like a man[,] of the world of intellect and action," and not "like a woman, of love and hope and disappointment." But this writing would also *integrate the perspective of both genders*. I believe Fuller's language here is extremely precise and at the same time susceptible to misreading. She does not seem to bar inclusion of the characteristic female themes of love, hope, and disappointment—she seems willing to pull aside the "curtain" behind which she has vowed to keep such emotions—but in taking up these topics she will do so the way a man would, as she sees George Sand to have brilliantly done. "If I can but do well my present work and show that I can write like a man": such an effort will determine whether she has "the hand to paint, as well as the eye to see." Fuller will in fact trump Sand's achievement, since the "insight into the life of thought" that she praises in Sand will come not "from a man," as she suspects it has in Sand's case, but from Fuller alone. It is specifically Hélène's vision in Act 4, Scene 1, of *Les Sept Cordes* that inspires this sense of possibility: "I cannot but feel that I have seen from the mouth of my damp cave, stars as fair, almost as many, as this person from the Flèche of the Cathedral where she has ascended at such peril."

These notes on *la jeune France* initiated Fuller's exchange with Emerson about Sand, but Emerson at this moment had become smitten with Bettina von Arnim. At first dubious, he wrote to Fuller on 9 July 1839, "[Bettina] is a wonderful genius & yet these creatures all wing & without any reserve make genius cheap & offend our cold Saxon constitution"; but by the end of the month, just before Fuller left for Bristol (and in the same letter that requested her notes on French writers), Emerson amended this "faint praise." Bettina's book "now that I have read [it] moves all my admiration": "What can be richer and nobler than that woman's nature. What life more pure and poetic amid the prose and derision of our own time." Bettina was, moreover, "the only formidable test that was applied to Goethe's genius . . . genius purer than his own," and Emerson found it "cowardly" that Goethe never directly acknowledged "the transcendant superiority of this woman's aims and affections in the presence of which all his Art must have struck sail." His next letter to Fuller records his urging of the book on several friends (*LE*, 2:208–9, 210, 211–12, 223).

Fuller's regard for von Arnim's work, always more restrained than Emerson's, had diminished as she read *Les Sept Cordes* and *Spiridion*. Next to these, the effusions of a "Lolita-like ingenue" (Caleb Crain's epithet) struck Fuller as "mere babyhood" (*MMFO*, 1:248).[11] In the fall of 1839, as she tried repeatedly to bring Emerson to understand Sand's merit, he was unmoved; his sense of Bettina's excellences impeded his ability to catch the seriousness in Fuller's praise for Sand. On 14 August, responding probably to her first flush of excitement, he wrote teasingly: "And pray who & what is the spectacle you so oracularly announce? Is it book or is it woman? . . . I have with my eyes transpierced so many goodly reputations & found them paper, that when the wind is east I make a covenant with my ears never to hearken to a new report. And yet to such a herald all faith is due, and at all events I will sit with meek expectation" (*LE*, 2:216). Three days later Fuller sent Emerson her notes and the Bristol journal, which he answered on 9 September with praise for her comments on Alfred de Vigny—and with complete silence on her reflections on Sand (*LMF*, 2:99; *LE*, 2:223). In early November he noted in his journal that he had read "Linnaeus's Tour in Lapland, & two French novels," adding a note of appreciation for the Linnaeus work but dismissing the novels as "lamp smoke & indigestion" (*JMN*, 7:293–94). These novels, which he names in a letter to Fuller on 14 November, were by Sand (*André* and *Leone Léoni*; he also bought *Indiana* about this time). Although he acknowledges not having followed Fuller's directions about which

Sand works to read first, he nevertheless pronounces largely on her value as a writer in terms that make his standard of comparison clear:

> A fervid eloquence certainly this woman has, & makes sometimes authentic revelations of what passes in man & in woman. There are a few wonderful things in the book but she is not superior to her story, I fancy, but is herself sick with the sickness of the French intellect & has not surmounted this taste for the morgue & the hells. Pity too that with so much narrative eloquence she cannot clear her plot of such ridiculous improbabilities. With all the manifest strength & steadiness of this woman, I will not compare her to Bettina a moment on such evidence as I have. She is but a Parisian Corinna, Bettina a sublime original. (*LE*, 2:235–36)

Emerson modified this judgment somewhat after reading *Spiridion* in late December, but even in his praise remained cool. The book "discovers wonderful opulence of mind—it is all brilliant, inventive, never poor," but he finds it too long: "after the first conversation, we wish the doctrine less voluminous, that is, we wish it had more profoundness." Perhaps remembering that Fuller has absorbed this work "with unutterable interest," Emerson seems to cast about for something positive to say—"A marvelous variety of accomplishment this writer has, who knows nature & society & books so well and takes in one book such scholastic and in another such Parisian glances"—but what dominates is a tone of reserve. He ends with a cursory word of enthusiasm for one passage near the end ("Beautiful account of the fisher's music in Spiridion p 334 I believe!") (*LE*, 2:245–47).[12] He kept reading Sand, but the next novel he tried, *Mauprat*, served only as a distraction from his grief over the untimely death of Charles Follen in the sinking of the steamer *Lexington*, and the impetus to continue faded. His letters and journals record no thoughts of Sand until almost three years later, when in a letter to John Heath, again praising von Arnim, he notes: "She is a finer genius than George Sand or Mme de Stael, more real than either, more witty, as profound, & greatly more readable. And where shall we find another woman to compare her with" (*LE*, 3:77).

Fuller, I speculate, was disappointed, most sharply on receiving Emerson's 23 December 1839 letter with its ho-hum response to *Spiridion*. Her letter to him three days later alludes to a grim emotional state, from which she has determined to extricate herself by reading Plato. The ploy is partly successful, but her description of the work she has put aside in order to right herself suggests the influence of Sand: "Last Sunday, I wrote a long letter, describing it [her mood] in prose and verse, and I had twenty minds to send it to you as a literary curiosity; then I thought, this might destroy relations, and I might not be able to be calm and chip marble with you any more, if I talked to you in magnetism and music;

so I sealed and sent it in the due direction." What she describes is an exorcism, followed by an embrace of the rationalist Plato, with a hope "to be tuned up thereby." She observes, "with gladness, a keener insight in [her]self, day by day," but sees the cost: "after all, could not make a good statement this morning on the subject of beauty" (*LMF*, 2:104–5).

The work of Margaret Fuller's that most clearly reflects her complex encounter with Sand's 1830s oeuvre, I propose, is "The Magnolia of Lake Pontchartrain," written in October–November 1840 and published in the *Dial*'s third issue in January 1841. Two other *Dial* pieces are usually linked with "Magnolia": "Leila," in the fourth issue, and "Yuca Filamentosa," in the seventh. All three bear the impress of Fuller's reading of Sand, but I focus here on "Magnolia" because its structure derives from narrative and thus is generically closest to Sand's work. But it is important to reemphasize that Fuller's goal was never to reproduce the precise kinds of texts that Sand published. In Fuller's imagination, George Sand appears to stand for a fusion of mystic exaltation, intellectual venture, a perspective uniquely available to women, and an ability to write (as a woman) like a man.

It is also important to distinguish between what Fuller wrote as a result of her first reading of the 1830s works and what she later wrote about Sand for publication. This distinction embodies an obstacle Samuel Ward, Julia Ward Howe's brother, had noted in an 1839 letter to Longfellow: "I wish [Sand] might be criticized here—but a Reviewer would be forced to endure a censorious and moral [grimace?] and she is excessively heterodox."[13] Sand's "genius" deserves the attention, but a reviewer would be fatally constrained in the praise s/he could extend. Fuller's published comments on Sand—in the *Dial* ("The Great Lawsuit," expanded into *Woman in the Nineteenth Century*) and in three articles for the *New York Tribune*—span a three-year period and bridge the moment when the appearance of *Consuelo* and *The Countess of Rudolstadt* gave prudish readers a reason to "forgive" the earlier radical outlaw. Careful examination of the evolving perspective of these four (really, five) pieces is a subset of this current study. But I would argue, briefly, that the various rhetorical positionings Fuller adopts in these remarks are in part the result of her sense of what the public could be induced to listen to rather than statements to be comprehended as Fuller's full opinion. I do not mean to suggest duplicity, yet the private and public remarks are strikingly different.

In "The Great Lawsuit" (*Dial*, July 1843), Fuller expresses a sympathetic understanding of the circumstances that led to Sand's rebellion, but she is harsh on her nonetheless, reproducing the standard inflammatory description of the novelist smoking and wearing male clothes and chastising her for speaking "in the heat of wild impulse" out of "passionate error." Society, Fuller says, is right to outlaw such women: they are perhaps the prophets, but not the parents, of a new era. The revision for *Woman in the Nineteenth Century* (February 1845) does not soften the criticism, although Fuller's inclusion of Elizabeth Barrett's two poems about Sand interestingly intensifies both the sympathy and the dismissal: Barrett has "precisely the qualities that the author of Simon and Indiana lacks" and is the kind of person "unblemished in character . . . pure in soul" who offers a helping hand to women "noble in nature, but clouded by error" (*EMF*, 284). The first *Tribune* piece (1 February 1845), however, although it also includes the Barrett poems and Fuller's praise for Barrett at Sand's expense, is distinctly gentler: Sand is "a person of strong passions, but of original nobleness and a love of right sufficient to guide them all to the service of aims." And there is direct focus on her work, as opposed to her life. Fuller praises Sand's ability to transcribe her mind so exactly: her "nature glows beneath the words, like fire beneath the ashes, deep;—deep!" Seven months later (19 September 1845), Francis Shaw's translation of *Consuelo* had begun appearing in the *Harbinger*; Fuller writes to call attention to it and to revisit the sentiments of her earlier published comments. Now, "let no man confound the bold unreserve of Sand with that of those who have lost the feeling of beauty and the love of good." Readers are asked to recognize the "upward tendency and growing light [in] all her works for several years past." And when Shaw's translation was complete, Fuller wrote (24 June 1846) that Sand was "the best living French writer, and in some respects the best living prose writer." Those who would demur on the basis of the author's stained life are admonished: "There is in her a soul so capable of goodness and honor as to depict them most successfully in her ideal forms.—It is her works and not her private life that we are considering."[14]

Of course, even in Fuller's 1839 journal notes, as described above, there are reservations. Sand's "horrors" are disgusting, as is the "sophistry of passion," and *Lettres d'un Voyageur* has annoyed her with its pictures of an "unfortunate woman wailing her loneliness, wailing her mistakes, writing for money." Sand's genius and "manly grasp of mind" are offset, Fuller complains, by her lack of a "manly heart," and Fuller grumbles about not consistently finding in Sand "a being to combine a man's mind and a woman's heart . . . who yet finds life too rich to weep over."[15] Yet these failings are not those conventional ones bemoaned in statements intended for wide consumption. And in any case they pale in the context of Fuller's initial and constant enthusiasm for the novels—inspiration, I believe, for the clearest proof of her admiration of Sand: imitation.

As Fuller relates in a letter of 19 October 1840 to William H. Channing, the stories of the magnolia and the yucca came to her from a family friend, Dr. William

Eustis, who described his gardening one evening to Fuller's mother while Fuller herself lay resting on the couch. Fuller transcribes a brief version of "Yuca" in the letter and notes also that Eustis's "interview" with the magnolia was "most romantic." Jeffrey Steele's reading of these two works in *Transfiguring America* enlarges the context by associating their origins with the sentiments of Fuller's remarkable letter to Caroline Sturgis on 22 October 1839 and with her reaction to Anna Barker's feeling "kindled" during the first Conversation on 4 November 1839, but neither he nor Capper references Fuller's reactions to Sand, which invoke most of the themes Steele finds in these *Dial* works.[16]

"One who feels like me must either be or write a poem," Fuller writes just after reading *Spiridion*. The third section of the 1839 notes on Sand, ending with the remark that this reading has encouraged her to try to write in Sand's mode, is preserved among her manuscripts in a transcribed version. Steele's chapter "Lunar Flowers" begins with an analysis of two fragments, "Moonlight" and "Moonlights," the second of which immediately follows the notes on Sand in this transcription. Although Steele does not address it, this same fragment includes a long untitled poem beginning "These pallid blooms thou wilt not disdain," which anticipates the images and themes of "Magnolia" and is perhaps Fuller's first effort to "paint" in a mode inspired by Sand. The "pallid blooms" (columbines, we learn midway through) are not the kind of flowers that "tell the Soul," nor do they attract crowds of admirers. Like the elusive Magnolia, they are "self-nurtured, self-sustaining, self-approved." The lesson they impart is "to live alone / To deck whatever spot the fates provide / with graces worthy of the garden's pride," a version of the story the Magnolia tells about her own coming-into-being. In lines that might allude to the sources of the untitled poem and that recall Fuller's notes especially on *Les Sept Cordes* and *Spiridion*, the speaker says these musings are "faint shadows of some beauteous hand / When to the soul the highest thoughts have spoken / And brightest hopes from pregnant twilight broken." If this poem is indeed related to Fuller's earliest reflections on the impact of Sand, it is plausible to read "Magnolia" as the development of this impact—and much about the Rider's encounter with the mystical Magnolia evokes particulars of Fuller's reaction to Sand's "lyric effusions."[17]

In general, the work's dramatized encounter between sharply distinguished modes of perception and understanding echoes the central tension of *Les Sept Cordes de la Lyre*. Albertus's determined rationalism has its analogue in the Rider's preoccupation with the expression "He was fulfilled of all nobleness" (*EMF*, 44). Perhaps there *is* a difference "wide as from heaven to earth," as the Rider claims, between nobleness and the fulfillment of nobleness, but I suspect the purpose of the second paragraph is to establish the Rider's "before" character—before he meets the Magnolia, before the extraordinary sensual experience of the Magnolia's fragrance interrupts his dry (and very male) "meditation."

The first paragraph serves as a précis of the whole work; it is the wisdom the narrator has gleaned from the experience he is about to relate, a truth about finding the answer to all wishes at one's feet once one learns of the connection between stars and flowers. Prior to learning that truth, the Rider was the abstraction-loving youth who fixed his eyes on "distant worlds of light." As in *Les Sept Cordes*, there is synesthetic blending: the Magnolia's scent is a poetic "voice" that the Rider both smells and hears, and it is musical as well—like "the full peal of an organ" (*EMF*, 44–45).

Although Albertus in *Les Sept Cordes* acknowledges that he has too much emphasized thought at the expense of sensual experience, he at first can conceptualize Hélène only negatively, as a "pretty face" whose perceptions are "limited" and who is wearied by metaphysical subtleties (39). Hélène's first appearance illustrates that she has hitherto taken her self-image from Albertus's conception of her, a psychological state like the Magnolia's in her earlier incarnation as an orange blossom. But as soon as Hélène picks up the lyre, she is transformed: a halo surrounds her and her language becomes "sublime" (85). Albertus's philosophy students immediately perceive this sea change: "[Hanz:] There is some marvel at work here. The ribbons of her hair break and fall at her feet. . . . Yes, see how her hair billows out in free and lusty rings, like those of a young child that runs in the morning wind. It glistens, it flares, it streams over her beautiful body, like a cascade seized with fire from the sun. O Helen, how beautiful you are now!" (86). In this altered state Hélène retreats to the natural world ("I shall go to see the rising of the moon over the lake. . . . [and] neither hear nor see anyone" [91]) in a sequence that is reproduced both stylistically and imagistically in Fuller's floral translation from social orange blossom to queenly, private Magnolia. In both works the transformed being is limned in language inaccessible to unreconstructed ears; the Magnolia cannot speak to the Rider of the queen / guardian of the flowers, a spirit "which cannot be known until thou art it" (*EMF*, 48). And after her rhapsodic narrative concludes, the Magnolia retreats from communication with "alien spirit[s]," not wishing again to tell the tale of her being "in words that divide it from itself" (*EMF*, 49).

It is in the specific nature and effect of the transformation, however, that the works most closely resemble one another and in which Sand's influence on Fuller is clearest. Sand's heroic being in *Les Sept Cordes* is female, yet male in her impulse to rise above "finite things" and be devoured by "love of the infinite" (176). In dying, she enacts the lyre's plea to her: "if you dare to take me and enclose me in your intelligence, I agree to lose myself there, to assimilate myself to it forever" (170). Thereafter, she speaks as a dual being, promising Albertus that "we" will always be with him. Hélène's significance for Fuller, her notes testify, is both that she is a purified Gretchen-like being *and* that she is "worthy to redeem and upbear the wise man, who stumbled into the pit of error while searching for truth." Further, Hélène reconciles "the life of the heart with that of the intellect"; she can listen simultaneously to the "whispering breeze of the Spirit, while breasting, as a man should, the surges of the world."

Fuller's Magnolia, as Steele suggests, is an instance of a female voice defining masculine values that she learns to resist. In that sense she is the newly awakened Hélène. But as Steele also notes, the male Rider seems to "switch gender."[18] He incorporates aspects of the Magnolia's perspective into an enlarged view: his masculine self endorses the Magnolia's redefined female essence that replaces the conventional femininity of the orange blossom. The Rider, then, is able to comprehend the Magnolia. He repeats the ritual she has earlier enacted, taking "a step inward," forgetting a voice, losing a power, signified by his not leaving the Magnolia but rather "abid[ing] forever in the thought to which the clue was found in the margin of that lake" (*EMF*, 49). Again, the framing first paragraph affords insight into this reconstructed male-female narrator; s / he knows and can reproduce the language of the queen of the flowers because s / he has become "it."

Certain facets of Fuller's experience of *Spiridion* are also echoed in "Magnolia." In terms of form, the novel's extended first-person account of spiritual questing perhaps provided a model for incorporating the Magnolia's tale within a framing narrative. This aspect prompted comment from both Fuller and Emerson; she noted the difference (from *Les Sept Cordes*) of the "mould" into which the development of the religious sentiment is poured, and he was put off by the length of the discourse. Fuller also resonated to the pivotal role played by the natural world in Father Alexis's "new birth," responding to a passage in which Alexis, soul-sick, lies on a grassy mound between the monastery and the sea and loses himself in attentiveness to nature: "There, lost in endless reveries, I seemed to become sensible of harmonies inappreciable to the gross sense of other men, some plaintive chaunt, breathed on the dark coast, and borne over the waters by the southern winds" (224). This experience is life transforming; Alexis, through discovering "deep meaning in the slightest phenomena of nature," recovers a sense of happiness and a more just view of the balance of human joy and suffering:

> Every creature took a new form and voice, to reveal to me faculties unknown to the cold and superficial observation which I had taken for the purposes of science. Infinite mysteries unfolded themselves around me, contradicting all the decisions of an incomplete knowledge and precipitate judgment. In a word, life assumed in my eyes a sacred character, and a vast aim, of which I had not had a glimpse, either in religion or in science, and which my heart taught anew to my erring intellect. (225)

Immediately following this passage is the section in which Emerson (in a postscript to his 23 December letter) remarked on Alexis's description of hearing a fisherman "singing to the stars." The fisherman's song instinctively follows the measure of the waves, so that the singer strikes Alexis as "one of those great and true artists whom nature herself takes care to instruct" and leads him to feel that music "must be the true poetical language of man" (226). This portrait of the quester determined to develop his sensual apparatus so that it becomes a *gradus ad Parnassum* is another of the important impressions *Spiridion* made on Fuller: "I recognized, with delight, the eye that gazed, the ear that listened, till the specters came, as they do to the highlander on his rocky couch, to the German peasant on his mountain. How different from the vulgar eye which looks, but never sees!" (*MMFO*, 1:247). These elements of Sand's novel seem clearly to reverberate in the Rider's experience.

Fuller kept her authorship of "Magnolia" private from Emerson; when he read it in January 1841, he did not guess she had written it. After she claimed it as her work, Emerson wrote, cryptically: "I read it with gladness & good will: Depart ye profane this is of me & mine! . . . The Magnolia is a new Corinna with a fervid Southern eloquence that makes me wonder as often before how you fell into the Massachusetts. It is rich and sad—sad it should not be—if one could only show why not!—but the piece will have a permanent value" (*LE*, 2:376, 378). Possibly the reference to "a new Corinna" suggests his sense of the work's derivation from Sand—in a letter of 14 November 1839 he had scorned Sand as "but a Parisian Corinna" (inferior to Bettina, the "sublime original")—but whether he consciously associated Fuller and Sand or not, and despite his seeming praise, the prevailing tone is less than enthusiastic for this new direction. Why would "good will" be needed to read the piece? Why would he view it as sad? Why, if it is, should it *not* be sad? Why can he not explain why it should not be? Why the act of appropriation ("this is of me & mine"), when "Magnolia" feels quite distant from anything Emersonian?

Steele's reading of "Magnolia" emphasizes its role in a patient effort on Fuller's part to make her otherness comprehensible to her admired friend and mentor, and such a reading is supported by their letters during this time. When he was first reading Sand, Emerson noted the following in his journal (17 November 1839): "*Eyes*. Women see better than men. Men see lazily if they do not expect to act. Women see quite without any wish to act. Men of genius are said to partake of the masculine & feminine traits. They have this feminine eye, a function so rich that it contents itself without asking any aid of the hand" (*JMN*, 7:310).

We can, if we wish, dream the French novelist's agency, and Fuller's, in moving Emerson toward a perception of women more subtle (and more modern, or at least more self-conscious) than that of most men of his historical moment. But this note, beginning with a statement of women's superiority, slides into appreciation for the putative androgynous vision of *men* of genius. And we remember his preference for Bettina over either Sand or de Staël—or, perhaps, over Margaret Fuller, although in the year after her death, trying to strike the right tone for *Memoirs*, he wrote to Samuel Gray Ward that the work had to come across "tête exaltée, and in the tone of Spiridion, or even Bettine, with the coolest ignoring of Mr. Willis, Mr. Carlyle and Boston and London" (*LE*, 4:222). To Caroline Sturgis, similarly: the book "must be written in the bravest mood of Spiridion, or of Bettine, better yet of Dante,—mystically in Novalis' sense, that is, as if the world were one pair of lovers" (*LE*, 8:257). We might have hoped that he would eventually distinguish more sharply between *Spiridion* and *Goethe's Correspondence with a Child*.[19]

Nonetheless, though he shared Fuller's interest in Sand (and in what Sand represented for her) only to a degree, Emerson seemed genuinely glad to hear, in 1847, that Fuller had met the celebrated lady. "It was high time, dear friend, that you should run out of the coop of our bigoted societies full of fire damp & azote, and find some members of your own expansive fellowship," he wrote at the end of April (*LE*, 3:394).[20] Fuller had approached the meeting feeling disadvantaged by her inability to speak French fluently, and then she suffered other small impediments before the two were finally face to face. But when Sand entered the room, Fuller was deeply struck by the "almost ludicrous" contrast between the dignified, "lady-like" woman before her and the "vulgar caricature idea" that most Americans, herself included, had so readily embraced.

> What fixed my attention was the expression of *goodness*, nobleness, and power, that pervaded the whole,—the truly human heart and nature that shone in the eyes. As our eyes met, she said, "*C'est vous*" and held out her hand. I took it, and went into her little study; we sat down a moment, then I said, "*Il me fait de bien de vous voir*" and I am sure I said it with my whole heart, for it made me very happy to see such a woman, so large and so developed a character, and everything that *is* good in it so *really* good. I loved, shall always love her.

Fuller stayed most of the day. She provided few details of their conversation, but the view of Sand that emerges from her narrative confirms Emerson's sense of the value to her of entering this fellowship. Fuller felt that she and Sand had "always known one another" and observed that Sand's position as "an intellectual woman and good friend" was "the same as [her] own in the circle of [her] acquaintance." Certain aspects of the mythic Sand persona faded. She lacked an "independent, interior life," and she was not "a Helena" (by which Fuller apparently meant the kind of woman "whose mistakes are the fault of the present state of society"—not quite the way she had earlier described the heroine of *Les Sept Cordes*). The actual Sand was better: "I heartily enjoyed the sense of so rich, so prolific, so ardent a genius. I liked the woman in her, too, very much; I never liked a woman better." In fact, Fuller continued, "she needs no defence, but only to be understood, for she has bravely acted out her nature, and always with good intentions":

> She might have loved one man permanently, if she could have found one contemporary with her who could interest and command her throughout her range; but there was hardly a possibility of that, for such a person. Thus she has naturally changed the objects of her affection, and several times. Also, there may have been something of the Bacchante in her life, and of the love of night and storm, and the free raptures amid which roamed on the mountain-tops the followers of Cybele, the great goddess, the great mother. But she was never coarse, never gross, and I am sure her generous heart has not failed to draw some rich drops from every kind of wine-press.

Eight years earlier, Fuller's substantial delight in the work had been reduced by her disappointment in Sand's public plaints about her life circumstances. In 1847, although Sand in Fuller's view "[held] her place in the literary and social world of France like a man, and seem[ed] full of energy and courage in it," it was not the work that Fuller emphasized. The recently published *Teverino* and *La Mare au Diable* were "as original, as masterly in truth, and as free in invention" as anything Sand had done earlier, but the real joy Fuller took was from the life, the grace with which it was lived, the reasons for it, the passion of it. Fuller's narrative concludes with a retailing of gossip regarding Sand's relationships with Chopin and Liszt, with admiration for and possibly even envy of this womanly and manly person who redefined boundaries and provided maps for those interested in staking a claim in this new terrain.

NOTES

This essay is dedicated to Albert von Frank, in gratitude for his friendship over many years and in tribute to a career's worth of indispensable contributions to the study of mid-nineteenth-century American literature.

1. "France in 1833; No. II," *Blackwood's Edinburgh Magazine* 34 (December 1833): 919, 922; "Leila: a Novel," *Athenaeum*, September 1833, 646, 647.
2. Francis Bowen, review of Sand, *North American Review* 53 (July 1841): 103–39. For more on Bowen and this essay, see Albert L. Rabinovitz, "Criticism of French Novels in Boston Magazines, 1830–1860," *New England Quarterly* 14 (1941): 488–504. The vicissitudes and nuances of early Anglo-American reaction to Sand's fiction are a study unto themselves,

as are those of the twentieth-century scholarly work on this topic. The most recent such study is Catherine Masson, "George Sand, le 'génie devenu fou' et sa conquête de l'Amérique," *Oeuvres et Critiques* 28 (2003): 157–87. Masson includes a reliable list of references to Sand in American books, newspapers, and periodicals between 1837 and 1876, as well as brief accounts of the histories and political slants of the periodicals.

3. Fuller's reaction to Sand has been a focus of scholarly attention on several (but surprisingly few) occasions, most extensively in Lucy Gregory's "The Influence of George Sand on Margaret Fuller," MA thesis, Columbia Univ., May 1918. Complex analysis of the impact Sand made on Fuller begins with Julie Ellison's and Christina Zwarg's close readings of Fuller's comments in "The Great Lawsuit" (Ellison, *Delicate Subjects: Romanticism, Gender, and the Ethics of Understanding* [Ithaca, N.Y.: Cornell Univ. Press, 1990], 264–66); Zwarg, 170–74). But by far the fullest and most useful consideration to date is Charles Capper's *Margaret Fuller: An American Romantic Life, the Private Years*, 259 ff., which extensively comments on Fuller's 1839 reading notes on *la jeune France* as prologue to her published comments in the *Dial* and the *Tribune*. See also Capper's occasional references to Sand in *Margaret Fuller: An American Romantic Life, the Public Years*.
4. The phrase *la jeune France* designated a group of French writers, led by Victor Hugo, who in the 1830s began to agitate for rejection of classical forms in favor of freer literary structures.
5. Although Emerson, in a letter dated 31[?] July 1839 (*LE*, 2:211–12), asked for Fuller's reading notes on *la jeune France*, not all the fragments we now recognize under that rubric had yet been written. The notes themselves are not dated, and I include no discussion here of those focused on Béranger, Lamennais, Vigny, or Balzac. Further, these notes must be read in juxtaposition with a journal Fuller kept during a ten-day stay in Bristol, Rhode Island, published by Robert N. Hudspeth ("Margaret Fuller's 1839 Journal: Trip to Bristol," *Harvard Library Bulletin* 27 [1979]: 445–70). Within the *la jeune France* reading notes, the first section concerning Sand is headed "Thursday evening" and begins with the information that Fuller is about to go away for a period; I thus speculate that this Thursday was 25 July 1839, six days before she left for Bristol. (On the other hand, these reading notes and the opening of the Bristol journal are not quite in accord about when exactly Fuller finished *Spiridion* a second time.) In this section there is reference only to *Les Sept Cordes* and *Spiridion*. Another section dated "1839," clearly written later in the fall, discusses *Les Sept Cordes*, *André*, *Jacques*, *Lettres d'un Voyageur*, and *Leone Léoni*. These two sections are substantially reproduced in *MMFO*, 1:245–50. A third section headed "Wednesday" returns to the letters exchanged between Jacques and Sylvia in *Jacques* and includes the passage in which Fuller explicitly declares Sand's influence: "These books have made me for the first time think I might write into such shapes what I know of human nature." Capper reproduces portions of this section within his account of Sand's influence, but otherwise it has not appeared in print. My quotations are transcribed from Margaret Fuller, *Works*, 3:297–309 (MS Am 1086, MH-H).
6. Henry F. Chorley, "The Works of George Sand," *British and Foreign Review* 8 (April 1839): 360–90; Giuseppe Mazzini, "George Sand," *Monthly Chronicle* 4 (July 1839): 23–40. Both are hereafter cited parenthetically.
7. Fuller's reading of *Spiridion* is described in her journal, edited by Hudspeth. Her only access to *Spiridion* and *Les Sept Cordes de la Lyre* in the summer of 1839 would have been through their publication in the *Revue des Deux Mondes*. *Spiridion* has appeared in English translation in book form only once, published in London in 1842 by Charles Fox. My quotations are from this regrettably hard-to-find edition. *Spiridion* was also translated

by Caroline Healey Dall in 1854 and published serially in two journals; see *Daughter of Boston: The Extraordinary Diary of a Nineteenth-century Woman / Caroline Healey Dall*, ed. Helen Deese (Boston: Beacon Press, 2005). *Les Sept Cordes* is available in a modern English translation with introduction and notes by George A. Kennedy: *A Woman's Version of the Faust Legend: "The Seven Strings of the Lyre" by George Sand* (Chapel Hill: Univ. of North Carolina Press, 1989); in-text citations are to this edition.

8. "Fuller's 1839 Journal," 454–55. The close association of the two works in Fuller's mind reflects their composition: Sand wrote on 8 August 1838 to her publisher's wife that she was having difficulty finishing the last twenty pages of *Spiridion* and so had plunged into "a little fantastic drama"—*Les Sept Cordes* ("La Lyre")—completed a month later. The two thus were born of a single aesthetic impulse, despite their generic differences, and Fuller's comments repeatedly juxtapose them.
9. Sand's remark about the "non-visible novel" is from an 1833 essay titled "Obermann," quoted in David A. Powell, *George Sand* (Boston: Twayne, 1990), 33. Two informative English-language studies of *Spiridion*, which provide additional perspective on its style and its indebtedness to the writings of Pierre Leroux (to whom the book is dedicated), are chap. 6 of Isabelle Hoog Naginski's *George Sand: Writing for Her Life* (New Brunswick, N.J.: Rutgers Univ. Press, 1991), 138–67; and Ted Underwood's "Historical Difference As Immortality in the Mid-Nineteenth-Century Novel," *Modern Language Quarterly* 63 (2002): 441–69.
10. This and the following several quotations discussing *Jacques*, previously unpublished, appear in Fuller, *Works*, 3:297–309.
11. Fuller's essay "Bettine Brentano and Her Friend Günderode" (*Dial* 2 [January 1842]: 313–57) provides a broader perspective on her attitude toward von Arnim's work. Fuller admired the 1840 publication, Bettina's exchanges with the Canoness Günderode, more than the correspondence with Goethe, but reserve is still the primary note (Caleb Crain, *American Sympathy: Men, Friendship, and Literature in the New Nation* [New Haven: Yale Univ. Press, 2001], 198).
12. This passage and one just preceding, 222 and following in the English edition, make an appearance in my argument, below, for the thematic influence of *Spiridion* on Fuller's writing.
13. Samuel Ward to Henry Wadsworth Longfellow, 25 April 1839, bMS Am 1340.2 (5820), MH-H.
14. The three *Tribune* pieces are reproduced in *MFC*: "French Novelists of the Day: Balzac . . . George Sand . . . Eugene Sue," 1 February 1845, 54–64; "Jenny Lind . . . The Consuelo of George Sand," 19 September 1845, 227–32; and "[Review of George Sand, *Consuelo*]," 24 June 1846, 457–63.
15. Quoted material in this paragraph, transcribed from a manuscript, varies slightly from Emerson's reproduction in *Memoirs*.
16. *LMF*, 2:164–66 (see also 2:166–68 and 183–84); Jeffrey Steele, *Transfiguring America: Myth, Ideology, and Mourning in Margaret Fuller's Writing* (Columbia: Univ. of Missouri Press, 2001), 66. See as well Capper's reading of these works, which emphasizes their associations with Neoplatonic writings, Paracelsus, Böhme, Novalis, *Kunstmärchen*, and the "mothers" in *Faust* (Capper 2, 44–46).
17. Steele, "Lunar Flowers," in *Transfiguring America*, 64–82; Fuller, *Works*, 3:297–309.
18. Steele, *Transfiguring America*, 74.
19. Emerson's August 1842 letter to John Heath remarks of Bettina von Arnim: "I have seen two or three travellers who have seen her and who did not much distinguish her in their

memories, but we are indebted to her for the most remarkable book ever written by a woman" (*LE*, 3:77). For the use of de Staël's Corinne and Sand's Consuelo by nineteenth-century women writers as iconic references, see Linda M. Lewis, *Germaine de Staël, George Sand, and the Victorian Woman Artist* (Columbia: Univ. of Missouri Press, 2003).

20. Fuller had written the first installment of details of the meeting to Elizabeth Hoar on 18 January 1847 and sent the rest to Emerson on 17 March. He printed her accounts as a single narrative in *MMFO*, 2:193–99, the source of the quotations that follow here. See also *LMF*, 4:256–58.

INTERLUDE

Elizabeth Palmer Peabody, from "A Vision," *Pioneer* 1 (March 1843): 97.

A few evenings since, while sitting in deep reflection over a pamphlet that contains a new definition of life, and seeming to catch a gleam of light upon that mysterious *death-in-life* which so extensively characterizes modern genius, suddenly I found myself taken off my feet, and realized before my eyes at once all Time. And not only the real personages of history, but the fictitious beings of poetry and romance—equally palpable—were present, and all the creations of the masters of art. The pictures of which Pausanius gives an account, and which I supposed lost long ago, were before me, not only in all their original coloring, but even alive as they were not on the canvass. The lost statuary reappeared; and temples, whose decayed remnants alone have been seen since the period of recorded history, were fresh to my sense as the Gothic churches of the middle ages, and the mixed architecture of the present.

What was more remarkable still, the air seemed pervaded with music:—nay, music seemed the substance of the atmosphere. Now the Doric, now the Lydian, and even the lost Olympian measure, obeyed, as it were, my thought; and I heard Arion's and Orpheus's songs, no less plainly than the later music of modern times.

Vainly should I attempt to describe the ancient music. Its effect was not—like the modern—to plunge the soul into dreams and prophecies and vain longings. It acted on my senses, and whirled me into an intoxication of delight. I understood at once all the wild forms on the Etruscan terra cotta; the stories of the Bacchanalian fervor; the martial deeds of high antiquity; the taming of monsters; the conquest of the infernal regions; the rising of the walls of Thebes, and the following of Orpheus by the rocks and trees. The fables of antiquity seemed to me no longer fables, but inevitable facts. I did not pretend to ask about probabilities; I did not question my perceptions; I saw, and believed my senses. Not more easily does the eye integrate with the distant horizon the various objects of the landscape, and even, in proportion to the sweep of vision, give the mind a sense of deeper repose, than, with the same calming effect, appeared in the world of time "one day as a thousand years, and a thousand years as one day." In this music life, Forms unfolded to me their meanings,—I mean more especially those forms which owe their existence to the plastic genius of men. I saw Architecture was solid harmony, and Painting liquid harmony; every statue a single chord, every picture a melody.

Elizabeth Peabody in the Nineteenth Century

Autobiographical Perspectives

PHYLLIS COLE

At age sixty-six in 1870, Elizabeth Peabody outlined her plan for a book to be called "Memoirs of Myself." However, she described such an autobiography as the means of revealing not self, but "all the people with whom [she had] come into relation, and in whose communion this happy life has grown." The ways of self-examination in spiritual narratives of the past did not appeal; instead she sought to affirm the "Divine Ideal which we are at the center"—and to discover that center precisely through communion with others. "God creates mankind as a whole," she pronounced. "An individual requires therefore the supplement of all other men to bring out the full circle of the image of God."[1]

Peabody never wrote the socially inclusive narrative she proposed, but this preamble encapsulates the idealism and collective ethic that together lay at the heart of her transcendental conviction.[2] Such principles motivated both activism and authorship. She did not complete an autobiography because, as her sixties turned to seventies and eighties, she worked instead to reform American society, traversing the nation to campaign first for the establishment of kindergartens and then for Native American rights. When she wrote for publication, moreover, the overt subject usually lay outside herself; among other projects, her *Reminiscences of William Ellery Channing, D. D.* (1880) honored the father of Unitarianism upon the centennial of his birth. But if "Memoirs of Myself" would have focused on relationship with others, the converse also held true. Peabody could give an account of her mentor, she wrote, only by offering the "impression Dr. Channing made on [her] mind."[3] This too was an account of relationship and "communion," to such an extent that it became, in effect, the book-length autobiography she never wrote otherwise. One contemporary reader certainly took *Reminiscences* as such. "I have been more interested in Miss Peabody than in Channing," pioneering scientist Maria Mitchell commented. "How many of Channing's sermons were instigated by her questions! . . . Miss

Peabody must have been very remarkable as a young woman to ask the questions which she asked."[4]

I propose to read Peabody's *Reminiscences* in Mitchell's spirit, for its female autobiography as well as its extensive interpersonal history.[5] Lawrence Buell initially identified self-representation as a crucial element of "literary transcendentalism,"[6] but his chapter on four first-person male authors left many more autobiographical texts to consider: not only women's narratives, journals, and letters but also the proliferation from midcentury onward of memoirs and reminiscences about figures of both sexes. Memoirs often enter the subject's mind and life process by quoting letters and journals, framed retrospectively by either the older subject or an acquaintance. In this subgenre, a significant middle ground may lie between biography and autobiography. Yet Peabody's *Reminiscences* stands out among kindred texts for openly dialogic construction of the oral and written record between herself and Channing.[7] Seen in the context of her larger body of writing, moreover, this narrative has particular value. As Monika M. Elbert points out, the lively first-person presence in Peabody's letters is barely audible amid the abstraction of her published essays on theology and world history.[8] *Reminiscences* mediates private and public voices, revealing a personal quest against the richly documented unfolding of Unitarian and transcendentalist history.

Indeed this narrative might be imagined as the stem of a more complex plant, a line in relation to which both Peabody's essays and her journals, letters, and other autobiographical sketches gain in significance. While focusing on the self-revelations in her Channing book, I also discover connections and comparisons to both formal essays and other first-person texts. In addition to her published work, Peabody left behind a vast store of letters and journals. Many letters survive today as manuscripts, and a selection has been ably edited by Bruce A. Ronda.[9] Still, a significant number of letters and virtually all journals are accessible only as transcribed after Peabody's death by Mary Van Wyck Church, the colleague in education who undertook to write Peabody's memoirs for the centennial of her birth in 1904. These manuscript transcriptions add vital new branches to our plant. Unpublished at the time and never consulted except by Megan Marshall for her biography of the Peabody sisters, Church's memoir amounts to a second partial fulfillment, through the letters and journals it tracks, of Peabody's promise to write her own life.[10] The 1870 letter outlining "Memoirs of Myself," for example, survives only in Church's transcription.

Peabody's composite autobiography has special import because it evokes a woman's experience of transcendentalism through the longest life span of all the movement's founding members. Peabody lived as a "woman in the nineteenth century" far longer than Margaret Fuller, from 1804 to 1894 rather than from 1810 to 1850, and she enjoyed the opportunity for retrospection denied her colleague. Peabody's *Reminiscences of William Ellery Channing*—especially with Church's memoir as a supplement—harvests her record of the movement from its early days of emergence through post–Civil War legacies. Even more, her devout, socially oriented values express a significantly different genealogical line from the self-affirming and iconoclastic feminism of Fuller. Charles Capper distinguishes Fuller from Peabody by calling the latter a "Romantic Channingite" rather than a transcendentalist (Capper 1, 317). Peabody's own account would embrace that title but also locate both romanticism and affiliation with Channing in the narrative of transcendentalism. So also would it bring new life and value to the terms Henry James used in *The Bostonians* (1886) to caricature the aged Peabody as "Miss Birdseye," a woman so "consumed by the passion of sympathy" that she herself is blurred beyond recognition.[11] Over the decades, "sympathy" lies at the heart of her articulate transcendentalist legacy, making possible the larger social self of her ideal.

Coming of Age

Peabody's *Reminiscences of William Ellery Channing* demonstrates the strength Theodore Parker saw in her—that of "a Boswell," able "to inquire and answer, 'What did they say?' 'What are the facts?'"[12] Just as she later recorded Bronson Alcott's classes and Fuller's Conversations, so Peabody took detailed notes on Channing's sermons and conversations of the mid-1820s. Kept for fifty years, these papers provide fresh material for retrospective tribute. But objective reporting is not her central project. She also claims the power of memory to reconstruct her side in conversations without notes (52), and she risks the "charge of egotism" through extensive self-revelation. *Reminiscences* portrays "that portion of [her] own life which was most subjective, [when] Dr. Channing was a prevailing influence in all [her] intellectual and religious experience" (iii, 12). Such subjectivity is consciously romantic, recalled as the joint faith of mentor and disciple. In giving the world "*my* Channing," she likens herself not to Boswell writing of Johnson, but to Eckermann giving the world "*my* Goethe," one possible portrait of the romantic master (1).

Subjectivity determines both shape and content of the book. Rather than plotting a well-proportioned narrative of Channing, she devotes two-thirds of its 450 pages to fewer than five years, the period of most intense conversation with him beginning in 1825 (52). After that—under pressure from her publisher to abbreviate and complete the project—she offers a hundred-page history of transcendentalism, based on conversations before Channing's death in 1842. And as introduction, the book's first fifty pages explain in effect how she, a twenty-one-year-old female teacher of children, managed in the first place to gain the ear of this eminent cleric. Indeed nurture of young souls is a theme resounding across decades. The grandmothers of 1880 protest that Friedrich Froebel, German founder of the kindergarten movement, offers "nothing new": "more than fifty years ago Dr. Channing taught us to live with our children, and to look upon them as capable of the life of Christ. . . . Indeed he . . . declared the child to be the original man, on whom, as Wordsworth says, 'those truths do rest, that we are toiling all our lives to find'" (66, 84–85, 93). Peabody's personal narrative—from her own childhood to Channing and Wordsworth to educational reform—claims such affirmations even more centrally as her own.

Early memory begins with her "devout, unconventional mother" (14), but Peabody turns quickly from home in Salem to a larger world of religious and intellectual power where her precocity flourishes. Mother Eliza's chief role is to take eight-year-old Elizabeth to hear the visiting preacher from Boston because, as she explains, "it takes genius to reach children." Peabody always remembers these words, but even more the thrill of Channing himself, his eyes lifted up and voice in prayer, "communing with God, face to face" as she has never before seen (12–13). Several years later, a woman from Boston invites the thirteen-year-old to come speak with Channing. Elizabeth flies into the minister's parlor and eagerly answers his questions. Only years later does she hear his comment about their meeting: "I have had a genuine pleasure and surprise to-day; a child ran into my arms and poured out her heart in utter confidence of my sympathy" (31, 36–38). Such sympathy is among Channing's central theological principles. Eventually Channing will argue for its exercise as more than "mere emotion," but instead an "*intentional*" and reflective effort to cooperate with God's benevolence, recalling the "boundless flood of joy" he felt at fifteen in discovering it through the moral-sense philosopher Francis Hutcheson (5, 83).[13]

Possibly sympathy and divine love even arose as topics within Peabody's first conversation with Channing; in any case, she portrays herself at thirteen as ready for such discussion. She had already found her intellectual calling within the Unitarian-Calvinist controversy, which "raged in old Salem" even among schoolchildren. One eleven-year-old argued that "all unsaved souls necessarily hated God," and Elizabeth with equal precocity responded that Jesus' youthful growth in wisdom was a model others could follow (30). As she entered adolescence and young adulthood, Elizabeth became "something of a Unitarian *doctrinaire*," following in detail the arguments of sermons and the controversial press. She consumed Channing's work, finding the heart of his creed in "the moral sentiment"—in "Jesus' manifestation of character in his human relations" rather than his divinity or atoning power (39–40, 25). Elizabeth took up her teaching vocation at seventeen in direct response, coming to Boston and feeling "consecrated" by Channing's blessing (42).

This portrait of a child's growth within liberal religious culture deserves attention alongside Peabody's more often discussed portraits of herself as "prenatally educated" by her mother for a teacher's role. She wrote such autobiographical vignettes for women teachers in the 1880s, evoking mother Eliza as the semimythic source of her vocation. Peabody's maternal portraits have their own truth. As her daughter's first teacher, Eliza upheld models of learned women and aspiring authors, like Elizabeth Montague and Germaine de Staël. Even earlier she had told inspiring stories, including one of Pilgrim "ancestors" whom Elizabeth creatively misunderstood as "a procession of fair women in white robes," "*sisters* . . . who all strangely enough were named *Ann*," streaming past Plymouth Rock and building schoolhouses in service to God.[14] But these images oversimplify a life that early on had also engaged directly with the church, and variant memories of inspiration by her mother and Channing surely complement each other. Religious and intellectual vocation begins at home and is always gendered female, but searching after a "face to face" meeting with Channing and God registers ambition in the larger culture. Nina Baym presents the narrative of "Ann sisters" as evidence that Peabody is more than a "great man groupie."[15] The narrative of Channing, however, tells of a personal coming of age in which this great man (like the mother) is instrumental rather than absolute.

More of Peabody's agency and agony in such development emerges when, alongside both of these idealized narratives, we read two life accounts written closer in time to the events they evoke. Available only in Church's transcription, they show her autobiographical preoccupation beginning in young adulthood. The earlier journal, written about 1822, idealizes no family or clerical elder and makes the story very much Peabody's own. "My early life was full of faults and uneasiness," she begins. Though both parents are religious seekers, Elizabeth vows to resolve on her own the question of Christ's relation to God, and at thirteen she crosses into heresy by reading "Lardener on the Logos," a "Socinian book" that seems "like taking hold of hot coals to touch." Immediately this presentation of Christ as human rather than divine offers "a feeling of strength in [her] mind, a sense of clearness in [her] ideas." Instructed by alarmed parents to read only the Bible for a year, she reads it thirty times in identification with Jesus' human character, and when Channing's sermon "Unitarian Christianity" reaches publication, her delight in it mixes with dissent from his claim of Jesus' preexistent divinity. "Now that I had found my own mind and its powers," Peabody recalls, "the testimony of men was of comparatively little consequence to me."[16]

If this early journal reveals a strong and combative self, by August 1825 Peabody is also expressing new personal beatitude in relation to others. As a child, she reflects, she had feared the judgments of both God and other children; the latter showed her either ridicule or roughness, so that "study was [her] refuge." Only more recently has "heart" come alive in the double lessons of self-love and sympathy for others, both within a supportive relationship with God. As the daily journal surrounding this recollection reveals, just six weeks later she encounters Channing in Boston Common after church and accepts an invitation to his home.[17] Peabody's questions will now have a new respondent, but both of the journals reveal her first raising them independently.

That meeting with Channing returns us to *Reminiscences*, for only in long retrospect can she articulate the importance of their conversation, along with her boldness in pursuing it. Finishing a year of teaching in Maine, Peabody sent him an eleven-page letter, telling of the morally destructive impact of Calvinist revivalism there and making a proposal. Why not require second-year students at Harvard Divinity School to do "missionary work" in response? (50). They meet for a discussion whose terms she has proposed. Hearing his skepticism about the role untrained ministers might play, she ventures that, as "a student of controversial divinity, like them," she believes they would at least benefit by learning to preach a "positive original generosity" in the face of beliefs in original depravity (57–59). Not only identifying with her male peers at Harvard, she is taking the direction of their training upon herself. But Channing responds in curiosity rather than offense. Where has she gotten her idea of intrinsic generosity? That question most of all launches subsequent conversation, for she claims it as the fruit of childhood experience, and Channing responds by recounting his own early life (60–63). A tone of intimacy and confidence is set between them as well as a mutual fascination with the child's potential for religious insight.

Peabody's narrative of sequels to this conversation claims an encounter with British romanticism as the heart of her new learning through Channing. While she comes to the meeting from a year in Calvinist Maine, he offers, with far less caution than in the pulpit, convictions gained from recent months in Europe. "He was so delighted to get a patient open ear for his cherished thoughts," Peabody recalls, "that he poured them out in a flood on all subjects," from the division in New England religious life to "the transcendental philosophy" rising in England (76). "'In the poetry of Coleridge and Wordsworth,'" he ventures, "'I find a theology more spiritual than in the controversial writings of either Unitarians or Trinitarians. . . . A new moral world [is] coming on, of which the Lake poets of England are the still persecuted prophets'" (69, 72, 80). Peabody recalls that such words "made an era" in her life (74).

If her account reads powerfully as autobiography as well as memoir of Channing, the details also provide new contours in the history of transcendentalism. Almost five years before Ralph Waldo Emerson and his friends will encounter Coleridge's affirmations of intuitive "reason" from James Marsh's American edition of *Aids to Reflection*, Peabody finds Coleridge through the tutelage of Channing.[18] He lends her Coleridge's *Friend*, with its description of a "telescope of Reason" allowing the human mind its highest powers, and follows with tutorials on Coleridgean "Method" (72, 75, 143–44). Such privileged friendship—across gender, generation, and professional status—allows the earliest and most direct access of any future transcendentalist to this writing.

Their reading of Wordsworth is even more fully dramatized in the narrative, and his significance owned as a foundation of Peabody's subsequent thought and teaching practice. Most vividly, they experience Wordsworth's "Immortality Ode" in counterpoint: amid conversation he unexpectedly asks her to read it, as she writes, "with his great eyes gazing on me as if he would have read my inmost soul while this flood of poetry was pouring over me for the first time." When she identifies with Wordsworth's sense of "fallings from us," losses of the child's primal knowledge, he urges her to move beyond such sorrow, then himself finishes reading the poem, "seeming to enjoy [her] rapturous delight in it." "Those stanzas," she concludes, "ever ring in my soul with his voice" (81, 127–30). The Hutchesonian affirmation of sympathy and divine benevolence that she and Channing have already shared now opens into "more spiritual" and transformative possibilities, for self and humanity alike. By the following year she is composing letters to Wordsworth "from an American girl of twenty two."[19]

Out of her experience of teaching children and reading the romantics, Peabody rises quickly to authorship during 1825 and 1826. She begins composing a meditation on the creative "word" of St. John's gospel (to be discussed later in this essay). In *Reminiscences* she recounts the experience of composing another biblical essay, ostensibly in answer to the needs of female students who ask for help understanding scripture after the death of a devout adviser. Writing in her journal, as she recalls in *Reminiscences*, "I first expressed thoughts of my own" (144). But the thoughts in the resulting six-part treatise, "Spirit of the Hebrew Scriptures," are far more theoretical and systematic than either journal reflection or teaching notes require. Despite protestations to the contrary, she surely intended this work for publication in a theological journal of the sort she had been reading for years. In the essay, influenced by Coleridge's essay on "Method" as well as higher criticism of the Bible, she reads the Genesis stories of creation and fall as poetry, "in the spirit of wonder," putting aside narrow doctrine in favor of "the light of [Jesus'] *unfallen* mind" (144–45). In effect she is restoring the potentially unfallen mind of all humanity, fulfilling her previous year's agenda of asserting a positive human nature in the face of Calvinist insistence on depravity. Man and woman, her essay argues, were set in Eden equally to enjoy "likeness to God," and despite their mutual fall, it is still possible to "induct" the soul into divine communion. Her argument is both poetic and practical. Quoting Wordsworth's "Immortality Ode," she admits, "there has passed away a glory from the earth." But glory once perceived can be recalled, and she argues for the teaching of such potential through the human bond of "sympathy, the social principle."[20] This homiletic lesson from biblical history expresses both an early culmination of Peabody's development and a credo for her long career.

Silent Ladies and Beyond

The 1826 essays did not, however, reach publication that year. After reading Peabody's manuscript, as she recounts in *Reminiscences*, Channing amicably dismissed the project, commenting that her "great truths" held less interest for him since they were based on Old Testament origins rather than present experience. In this book honoring Channing, Peabody displaced her disappointment to another target, noting that eight years later she managed to publish three of her six essays in the *Christian Examiner*, at which point one of its editors cut off her series without courtesy of reading, "because, as he said, [she] must needs be incompetent to the subject from want of learning" (145). Her urgency to publish is in fact evident outside *Reminiscences*, since she still later solicited Orestes Brownson to publish the series' second half. Her letter to him in 1840 identifies the dismissive editor as Andrews Norton, adds that her fourth essay spoke of "transcendentalism," and comments on her missed opportunity: the series "would have recorded quite a little historic fact, there in the bosom of Unitarianism, [that] an unlearned girl, with only the help of those principles of philosophizing she gathered from the perusal of Coleridge's [F]riend, & . . . relying only on her own poetical apprehension as a principle of exegesis, should have seen what is here expressed, concerning the *socialism* of true religion & the divinity of Christ."[21]

Peabody ironically names herself in Norton's terms, as an "unlearned girl," but disappointed desire for authority is rarely as explicit as in this account of her essays and their historic significance. The autobiographical subtext in her memoir of Channing, as well as letters and journals, concerns a woman's approach to authorship, through the channels and despite the obstructions of religious opinion-making in Massachusetts. We can read through silence, moreover, to see Channing as the authority figure in "the bosom of Unitarianism" whose lack of support originally derailed the project. His negative view of women's publication is clear. Even in *Reminiscences*, Peabody quotes his advice in 1826 that her older friend Hannah Adams should not seek public scrutiny by publishing memoirs: "[Having] your sex . . . send out their own histories while living would, I think, do the female character no good" (305). Channing implies an equally negative judgment of publishing the theology and history that Peabody and Adams shared as an intellectual vocation. In an 1838 letter to her friend Eliza Guild, recorded in the Church memoir, Peabody explicitly recalls his advice in response to her innovative interpretation of St. John's gospel: praising her "genius," he warned her not to use it "to make [her]self distinguished." Instead, he advised, "devote your powers to the service of others."[22]

She clearly hoped for more from the minister who had listened to her views as "a student of controversial divinity" like the men of Harvard. As *Reminiscences* reveals, Channing himself held the door half open. Emphasizing the "intrinsic disadvantages of the marked distinction between clergy and laity," he advised, "you in your school-room, can . . . preach Christ more effectually, perhaps, than the minister in his pulpit!" (201, 126). Blessing women's teaching as an opportunity to "preach," however, did not in Channing's view lead to other pulpits, either at his own church or on the printed page.

Peabody's personal narrative and her recollection of Channing both nonetheless explore an important opening toward women's religious authority. Both the minister and the female laity value women's character in its capacity for "sentiment," a term closely akin to the sympathy that Channing defined as "sensibilities of heart," "feeling penetrated with thought" (154). In the recently burgeoning scholarship on nineteenth-century sentimentalism, focusing primarily on women's fiction, the origin of the term in eighteenth-century moral-sense philosophy is sometimes acknowledged, but without substantial focus on church culture as a conveyor of it to women. Ann Douglas, founder of this body of work in the 1970s, saw most clearly the religious dimension of the "feminization of American culture," though she presented sentimentalism only as a vitiation of religious discourse accompanying women's assumption of clerical or authorial status; sarcastically, she called their ambition "pulpit envy." In fact Douglas drew on Peabody's *Reminiscences* for an important "parable" in this negative argument about the emotional interdependence of clergy and female laity: two aged and paranoiac women in Channing's flock, she recounted, took food only from the hand of their minister, and he in turn depended on their needing him.[23] However, Douglas lifted the incident out of Peabody's context, which was Channing's delegation of visits to the poor (including these two parishioners) to young women in his congregation. The parable does not address such commissioning of women any more than it details Peabody's relationship with Channing. Surely there is mutual dependence, even exploitation, in either version of his relation to female laity, but there is also incremental change. Activities like teaching, visiting the poor, and acting upon the emotional bonds labeled "sentiment" had implications whose result Channing could not ordain.[24]

Peabody—our indirectly assertive narrator of this memoir—offers the major case of dependence and autonomy in Channing's feminized church. The prefatory chapter frames her history as response to the "calumnious report" that he took advantage of her unpaid secretarial labor. In fact, as she readily admits, she transcribed fifty of his sermons for publication in their early years of conversation. When she proposed such tasks, however, he refused without reciprocal benefit to her. So, in an act of prodigious double concentration, she began copying while he read to her from Cousin's translation of Plato (8–10). Later he offered four years of work transcribing, editing, and serving as agent in the publication of his sermons, but only if such work could be financially profitable to her (392, 400). In Peabody's account, its totality fell considerably short of the defining role as Channing's "amanuensis" that even some modern scholars assign her.

Their dialogue as teacher and preacher lies closer to the heart of vocational purpose on both sides. While consistently claiming that he gave her "liberty to grow," she also reveals influence upon him. When she walks into Boston from Brookline to talk with Channing after Saturday conversations with the older schoolgirls, her topic often reappears in his Sunday sermon. Eventually he asks if she, acting as a mole amid the laity, might reflect on their religious conversation when he is not present to alter its tone: "Will you think over these questions and give me your thoughts? I wish to preach on these topics" (148–49, 280–81). Key phrases from her "Hebrew Scriptures" essays—that series whose publication he did not support—even reappear in his ministerial discourse. He explains in 1826 that religious growth depends on "the social principle" and two years later entitles his prototranscendental sermon "Likeness to God," a phrase also employed in her earlier text (227, 364). If this is not overt theft of language, at least it reveals common sources, vocabulary, and generation of ideas under circumstances of unequal status and authority.

Meanwhile, other women are also evoked throughout Peabody's *Reminiscences*. When Peabody first visited Federal Street Church at thirteen, she found that the female laity could not rise to questions he posed at a meeting especially for them. The adolescent also held her tongue: "Though I was not afraid of Dr. Channing, I was so of the silent ladies" (34–36). Still, out of the silence grew women leaders during the years when Peabody knew his church best. One of them, Eliza Lee Cabot, arranged for her to move her school from Brookline to Boston (204). Cabot was also among the eight laywomen and laymen whom Channing chose to teach children and young adults in a new Unitarian institution, the Sunday School. Peabody joined the weekly meeting of teachers with Channing to discuss the next Sunday's gospel text. But men still dominated these discussions, especially as they grew into a "conversation-party" and diverged from teaching to social issues (205, 213–17, 336).

Another level of women's conversation, however, took place outside the church with less constraint. In addition to recording notes about Channing in her journal, Peabody regularly reported by letter to two women who were mothers of her students in Brookline, Eliza Guild and Sarah Russell Sullivan. A new chapter of *Reminiscences* begins in excitement with recovery of these letters, which she recalls as growing "'like the grass' out of [their] own daily life." Common womanly experience shapes their religious interpretations, as when they confirm Wordsworth's idea of the child as "original man" on the strength of personal experience nurturing children (78, 92–93, 213).

For Peabody, reflecting on the women of Channing's church after fifty years shifts that feminized world to feminist significance. She recalls Nancy Lowell, mentor to both Guild and Sullivan, who "foreclosed in Boston society the question of the equality of women to men," as well as Quaker Mary Newhall, from nearby Lynn, whose independent prophecy proved her "a brilliant and free intellect as well as a spiritual seer" (307–8, 310–11). In more worldly terms, she quotes Ruth Gibbs Channing, the minister's wife, who appears sporadically as a third partner in their conversation. William claims to have loved her from childhood and therefore idealizes the power of women, for "men are what women make them." "Why then," Ruth shoots back, "are the mass of women treated as inferiors? . . . Are you not rather singular even in believing that they should have their own property, and all the responsibility for it?" (81–85).

Even short of such confrontations, the undercurrents of feeling among Channing's laity unsettle traditional gender roles. Her recollection of the minister is suffused with sublimated Eros on both sides, as he metaphorically embraces a pubescent "child," and she recalls her fluttering heart, his penetrating eyes, and the flood of language between them. Moreover, emotional release is widely shared in this congregation through the safe medium of tears. According to Peabody's 1825 journal, both men and women sometimes begin weeping at Channing's mere presence.[25] In *Reminiscences*, Peabody describes Sullivan's "soft blue eyes . . . full of tears of devout joy" as she sees the impact of Channing's sermon on Daniel Webster, sitting near her in church (153). Tears are the sign of both inspiration and commiseration. Douglas rightly calls the *Reminiscences* a "sentimentalized" memoir; even more, however, it is a knowing history *of* moral sentiment as, in Peabody's terms, "the true Emmanuel, the *God with us*" (154).[26] Channing's sermons and their affective power bring these ideas from the British Enlightenment to the laity, and Peabody extends them into an "excited state of sensibility" and a calling to work for others' welfare (19, 40).

However, such permission of feeling is hardly an unmixed blessing. In her recollections, barely manageable storms of grief and conflict coexist with positive exercise of sentiment. Fleeting references in *Reminiscences* show the extent to which she has already, by the time she meets Channing, internalized self-doubt; his sympathy offers healing after three years of "painful moral experience," especially when a valued friend declared her "the fool of mere ambition and vanity" (74, 132). The contemporary journal provides more details of such humiliation, which she admits has caused her to "fall into egotism";[27] this key term of self-reproach is always defensive, a response to attack and a source of sorrow. There are all too many tears in Peabody's life. When she is not defending her own ego, she feels a paralyzing heartsickness for others; the death of Sarah Sullivan and all her daughters in the mid-1830s leaves her grieving with the widower, "as much a prey to the Furies as poor Orestes" (386).

Though Peabody always sustains a capacity for sympathetic feeling, she also affirms the balance to be gained for women by cultivating intellect. *Reminiscences* testifies to this process in her own case, but the resulting work with other women is recorded in "My Experience as a Teacher," written just two years afterward. Teaching children was only half of her career; in addition she pioneered the education of adult women by teaching "Historical Conferences" for decades. She names no dates, but letters show her offering such classes as early as 1830—very much in times of personal flux and grief.[28] Possibly such courses offered the teacher a means of personal control in these years. More widely, as her retrospective account emphasizes, such learning had valuable rigor for the students; history might "take the place that law, medicine, or theology takes in the liberal education of men." Surely it provided the rubric within which Peabody and her students could engage in theology outside the church and university, for as her classes evolved they drew upon the best European scholarship to investigate ancient China, India, Persia, Babylon, Egypt, Ethiopia, Greece, and Rome in comparison with Israel "as so many experiments of mankind for self-recovery from a fall from primeval civilization." Freelancing as a professor, she enlarged through cross-cultural comparison the redemptive search first evoked in her "Hebrew Scriptures" essay; by 1832 she published three volumes in a *Key to History* that moved from "First Steps" to the Hebrews and Greeks. In these classes there could be no "silent ladies." Each student was asked to read independently on one country, providing Peabody with written questions for "bringing out from her what proved a lecture to the rest."[29]

The Historical Conferences succeeded as both an intellectual platform and a means of developing community among women. Building personal authority, Peabody published such essays about ancient civilization as "A Vision" and "The Dorian Measure," and she spelled out the value of such learning to women in *The Una*, Boston's transcendentally inflected women's rights newspaper.[30] Meanwhile, as she recounts in "My Experience," former students heard her presentations and asked for more. The children of former times had grown up, "always writing to [her] as a confessor, to get [her] moral and spiritual advice." Without ordination, she was playing a ministerial role as both scholar and counselor. The Church memoir emerged directly from this Peabodian culture. Among the letters it quotes is Mary Peabody Mann's testimony that Elizabeth has influenced three generations of Boston women—as pupils, as adults in her classes, and as mothers entrusting their children to her kindergartens. And an 1868 letter to Peabody, as she travels in Europe, reports the first organization of the New

England Women's Club (NEWC); younger friends and students (Ednah Cheney, Julia Ward Howe, Anna Q. T. Parsons) have voted that she should serve as their "vice president abroad," communicating to the club "all that can raise us up to our duties, give us knowledge, and entertain us."[31] The NEWC's long post–Civil War history acted out an agenda that she had significantly pioneered, promoting women's intellectual development, interpersonal bonding, and social service.

Peabody never joined the women's rights movement, though some of her club friends, especially Howe and Cheney, took leadership in it.[32] As she wrote to Caroline Dall in 1859, she disliked the "personal ambition and display" of public speech; her origins in the Channing era remained in her preference for a "high ideal of woman" based upon faith that "the *inward* scope is the *highest* scope of human action." The collective action of others also informed her ultimate judgment, however. She recalled in "My Experience" that, after first preferring "Women's Duties" to "Women's Rights," she had "ever since been learning that the Woman's Rights party was an inevitable protest . . . against laws, customs, and growing sentiments that operated to degrade woman and make her secondary to man in the serious work of life, which ought to include *noble politics*."[33] Starting with fledgling efforts of the 1820s, "noble politics" had always been her aim, and she drew others after her.

The Apocalypse of Our Transcendental Era

As part of its romantic affirmation, Peabody's *Reminiscences* charts a theologically sophisticated history of transcendentalism and her life amid the movement. First hearing from Channing in the mid-twenties about the "moral revolution" of Wordsworth and Coleridge, she proceeds to the movement of the 1830s and 1840s, surveys its "picturesque assembly" from her bookstore on West Street in Boston, and assesses its heritage in 1880 (364, 413, 447). There is "no name older than Dr. Channing's" in its history, she asserts, and apprenticeship with him has allowed her to receive a "peculiar blessing" from Emerson (364, 367). Her boldest claims about the movement, however, must be discovered outside the pages of her memoir of Channing. She completed the book under pressure, without expanding often to the "subjective" and dialogic quality of earlier pages. It shows constraint, furthermore, in expressing the extent of her turn from him to Emerson, let alone the quality of her collaboration and competition with Fuller for leadership among women. Again the journals and letters that were potential source material for her memoir deserve new and comparative attention.

Even in the public voice of *Reminiscences*, Peabody has no difficulty expressing the multiple ironies of her relationship with fellow educator Amos Bronson Alcott. While respecting his insight into children, she notes that he had just read Coleridge and Plato when first setting out to organize the Temple School in

1834, whereas her narrative has already claimed such an encounter for herself in 1825.[34] "I happened then to be at leisure," she notes casually, so she volunteered to teach the Latin needed for boys' academic advancement, "Mr. Alcott confining himself to teaching the English language" with his signature aims of spiritual development (355). Her own intellectual precedence, by standards of the male academy, cannot be missed. She also takes responsibility for the volume that gave Alcott's school its positive fame, noting her preface as well as provision of classroom transcripts for the *Record of a School* (1835). From the perspective of 1880, she clearly prefers Friedrich Froebel's pedagogy over Alcott's: half a century's experience allows her to affirm that children must begin by *"doing something* to be thought about" rather than merely thinking (356).[35]

No self-vindication accompanies the laudatory account of Emerson, however. His lecture career signals a shift for the women as well as the men of Unitarian Boston, a displacement of Channing's authority as their shepherd. As Peabody recalls of herself in 1836, "this terrible Idealist did more to correct my morbid moral sensibility than Dr. Channing had been able to do." Even Channing salutes the change, coming just after the dark years that she has confided in him (365–66).

What soul cure is there in a "terrible Idealist"? Peabody does not fill out the thought in *Reminiscences*, but three extraordinary journals of her visits to the Emersons in 1836 through 1838, available through the Church memoir, bring her responses to life. Emerson "seems to have given me the freedom of my own reason," she writes. Already familiar with Coleridgean "reason," she now internalizes it differently: "I must learn to remember that this phenomenon of myself envelopes the Infinite also. . . . I have warred against personal pride disproportionately I think."[36] Elbert, noting the failures of self-affirmation in Peabody's writing, finds a cause in Emerson's flawed, male-exclusive ideology of self-reliance. I would argue that these journals enact a woman's successful adaptation of Emersonian individualism to her own life. "He puts forth the society around him from his own being," she reflects. "So can I . . . sometimes arrange all whom I know around me as my 'leaves & fruit.'"[37] She can both affirm self and keep the "social principle," her ongoing value.

Indeed the same journals articulating this correction of "morbid moral sensibility" also affirm positive, woman-identified bonds of feeling. At the Emerson house, Peabody alternates reading Waldo's manuscripts and sharing the women's work of sewing and baby-care, thereby hearing mother Ruth's memories and Lidian's "theosophy of her marriage."[38] The male Idealist of the household, furthermore, is hardly without emotion. The three years of these journals extend from the death of Waldo's brother Charles to the illness and death of two Peabody brothers, so mourning and condolence often arise in conversation. When Waldo surprises Elizabeth by telling her not to blame herself for feeling "overpowered," she exclaims, "Give me the friend who divines my needs. This is the true heart." But then comes the journal's most uncanny moment, spoken and recorded without prescience. Explaining why he cannot write about the death of Charles, the father lifts his toddler son on one shoulder and asks, "Waldo! Why do people die? Will you die Waldo—say no papa, I will not die—nothing is farther from my thoughts than dying!"[39]

At the core of her reflections on Emerson, from contemporary journals to late public addresses, Peabody follows out the theological heresy she has embraced since adolescence. Previous experience of reading the Bible figuratively, as well as long-held belief in a Christ of human example, come together in her exhilaration over Emerson's 1838 "Divinity School Address." In her later lecture on Emerson at the Concord School of Philosophy, Peabody looks back on this moment as "the apocalypse of our Transcendental era in Boston."[40] Even such reference to God's last disclosure in the book of Revelation suggests the way she has long interpreted scripture as figuration of possibility in human culture and consciousness. Yet Emerson's 1838 pronouncement also arouses anxiety in her. In *Reminiscences* Peabody tells how the controversy drives her from Salem to Boston to query Channing's ideas of Christ. Having left behind the concept of a preexistent Christ from which Peabody had once dissented, Channing declares that, unlike conservative Unitarians, he can accept the impersonal godhead of Emerson's manifesto (374–75, 377–79).

Peabody's own investment in such a theology of divine principle—even her precedence over Emerson in it—is best expressed in private writing. A letter of 1838 to Eliza Guild rises to personal history from Andrews Norton's "insane attack" on Emerson. "As to his doctrine, it was my creed before I knew it was his," she recalls. In 1825 she wrote about the creative "word" of John's gospel as an emergence from divine origins to the "moral truth" of humanity; seven years after Channing advised her against publishing, her friend Mary Moody Emerson took the manuscript to Waldo, and he asked for both a copy and a chance to converse. "It is pretty plain therefore," Peabody concludes, "that this heresy does not belong to his mind alone and it is not strange, is it, that I am interested deeply in his having a chance to promulgate views so dear to my soul, being the theory of its life and resurrection from my long previous miseries of mind." Declaring loyalty to Emerson, she is even more staking her own claim as a theologian and biblical interpreter who has foreseen this change.[41]

Peabody is rightly known as a Christian transcendentalist, but both the Guild letter and Channing book nuance that position. Even as she internalized creation and revelation as human possibilities, she wished not to forget the Bible's self-renunciatory example of Christ. As Emerson edited the "Divinity School Address" for publication, she urged him to restore a line from the original manuscript warning against the "puppyism . . . of looking down on the head of all human culture; setting up against Jesus Christ every little self magnified." He declined, but Peabody felt that such a warning might have saved "many a weak brother and sister Transcendentalist from going into the extreme of *ego-theism*" (380, 372–73; emphasis in original). In 1858 she built a full essay from this term, labeling "Egotheism" the subtle, spiritual "Atheism of Today." As others have argued, it is her most explicit critique of transcendentalism.[42] But the critique arises from within the movement, finding both grandeur and danger in giving individual spirit free rein and distinguishing interpretations of a human Christ. *Reminiscences*, moreover, spells out her many engagements with other transcendentalists' thinking about Christ, as she endorses both Theodore Parker's iconoclasm and James Freeman Clark's organization of a free Christian "Church of the Disciples" (423, 445–46). Reacting against Parker, Channing's defense of Christ becomes increasingly conservative, and he declares he can get "no light from the 'new views'" (430). Peabody, on the other hand, deploys her characteristic theology in the *Dial*, in "A Glimpse of Christ's Idea of Society," to advocate for George Ripley's utopian Brook Farm: "There are men and women . . . who have dared to say to one another; why not have our daily life organized on Christ's own idea? . . . Let us communicate with each other, and live."[43]

Such words also epitomize Peabody's vision of men and women responsive to each other in daring change. However, silence and evasion in the autobiographical record suggest strain in her relationship with Fuller, the more overt leader of transcendental women. In *Reminiscences* we hear of the central moment joining their fortunes, the opening of Fuller's Conversations in 1839, as Peabody travels weekly from Salem for Fuller in the morning, Emerson's lecture in the evening, and dinner with Channing in between. Never more assiduous in note taking, she gives Channing detailed reports on Fuller's discourse of genius and wisdom as represented by Greek gods and goddesses. But Peabody is here a minimal presence in her own record, merely commenting: "Margaret's Conversations were full of interest to me also. I had been studying Greece for several years in its historians, poets, and philosophers" (402–4). This understatement leaves silent her own pioneering of Conversations about ancient history for women, including an entire textbook on Greece. If she intends any irony, she does not (as in the case of Alcott) provide the context needed to discern it.[44]

Under the surface lay fundamental difference. It was the younger woman who refused the older. "I admit that I have never done you justice," Fuller wrote upon leaving Boston for New York in 1844. "There is so much in you that is hostile to my wishes, as to character, and especially as to the character of woman." Admitting no antagonism in return, Peabody also held no illusion: later sending Emerson recollections for the *Memoirs*, she admitted that she could not presume to stand "among [Fuller's] intimate friends, as she decidedly wished I should not." When the two women met in 1828, Peabody recalls, "Margaret said almost nothing, but I thought she was laughing at me, for which there seemed good cause" (*LMF*, 3:253–54; *JMN*, 11:482). To Peabody, renunciation of ego was both psychologically necessary and a key to Christian community, whereas to Fuller such accommodation obstructed the development of women's character. The women's joint mentors both showed distress at the resulting strain; as Emerson recorded in his journal, "Dr. W. E. Channing said to [Fuller], . . . when I consider that you are all that Miss P—— wished to be, and that you despise her, and that she loves and honors you, I think her place in Heaven must be very high" (*JMN*, 11:259). In the long run, however, Peabody found use for Emerson's famous charge that Fuller projected a "mountainous ME." An 1870 reminiscence invoked the phrase only to provide counterevidence of Fuller's devotion to family, friends, and causes, but in earlier correspondence with Caroline Dall she recalled it to support core convictions: "If like great Margaret *your Me* is *'mountainous'*—it may become for you . . . the Mt of Transfiguration—He that would *gain* his life must *lose* it."[45] Surely Peabody considered Fuller among those in danger of "ego-theism."

Yet these two women, in their respective paths to influence, frequently collaborated as well as competed. Peabody began as the more experienced provider of contacts, helping the younger woman to find publishers and meet Emerson. Fuller's deferential letter of 1836, as transcribed by Church, refers to Peabody's recent visit in Concord and declares Emerson's ministry "more beneficent than that of any American mind though," she allows, "I do not know him in private." Soon she would, thanks to Peabody's urging on top of others'. The 1870 reminiscence tells this story. When Eliza Farrar admitted that in Fuller's self-styled "intense times" she was "obliged to let herself out in sonnets," Emerson balked at ladies with "intense times" and doubted that Fuller had uttered "one striking sentence." In return Peabody declared that even their first conversation had left her feeling, "I had seen the Universe." "'Seen the Universe!' Emerson exclaimed to his wife; 'now that is something definite. . . . Queenie, let us invite her here.'" From the distance of thirty-four years Peabody accepts a mediator's role in arranging this "fine war of the Olympians." But in 1836, as her journal indicates, she seems instead to have taken satisfaction in Emerson's measure of the new visitor's limitations: Fuller, he said, knew European literature but not English, declined to let "the moral . . . lead the intellectual," and talked too much about her father and uncles.[46]

Even among the "Olympians," Peabody knew her own mind. In August 1840, three months after the first season of Conversations ended, Peabody wrote to Channing from her new Boston bookstore, commenting on Fuller in the course of so wide a survey that she called her letter a "newspaper." Fuller has begun editing the *Dial* in July, but rather than commenting on this success, Peabody questions her colleague's discernment in the first issue's criticism of

Washington Allston's paintings. From her viewpoint, the religious mystery in one painting is powerful, and "Miss Fuller cannot argue me out of it"; clearly Peabody has not acquiesced to the other woman's rising authority. Indeed the letter goes on to tell Channing of Fuller's trials rather than accomplishments: instead of suffering the "heroism of daily self sacrifice" for her brothers' entry into life, she "needs to break away from all apparent duties and go to Europe really to follow out her own fancies." In an interesting exercise of her own sympathy, Peabody wishes Fuller not to sacrifice self for others when a true calling is at stake.[47]

These personal glimpses of Fuller grow in significance, moreover, alongside Peabody's portrait of herself in the "newspaper" letter as owner of Boston's first bookstore and library to specialize in European books. Omitted from her *Reminiscences of William Ellery Channing* and available only through Church, the letter allows us to hear Peabody's voice in direct response to his. *Reminiscences* recalls that, just when "commerce seemed about to be reformed out" by the transcendentalists, she returned to Boston to take up commerce, and Channing expressed both sanction and skepticism. The man who once disapproved of women as writers now finds nothing in bookselling "inconsistent with your sex." He merely comments, "the ladies want a literary lounge," not imagining that her operation will serve both sexes or unsettle women's sphere. But he seriously questions Peabody's "business talent": "You must be a machine, so far as this consists in going through a set of regular motions" (408–9). Her letter recites successes in reply: a hundred dollars in sales the first month, a one-week self-education in bookkeeping, and a stock safe from all risks but fire and earthquake. "Now do you not think this proves quite a business talent?"[48]

From this new position, Peabody's intellectualism also soars. "I have had a great many orders on Europe and already begin to dream of the time when I shall go thither myself for direct transactions with the French and German book stores. . . . I already see the advantages I possess in knowing something of the interior of books."[49] She has never before enjoyed Fuller's luxury of even planning a trip to Europe, always working to support an impecunious family; now trading in books might take her to the source of the intellectual traditions she has long been studying.

If there is an "annus mirabilis" for women in the transcendentalist movement, it is not 1836 but 1840, with Fuller editor of the *Dial* and Peabody proprietor of her bookstore the same summer.[50] A season later the bookstore will house Fuller's Conversations. The frustrated progress of these two as intellectual women, the ultimate source of competitive tension, has reached a momentary place of resolution, with each able to accomplish genuine work and influence.

The moment also suggests new recognition of the balance of power between Peabody and her longtime mentor. Channing responds to Peabody's letter with delight in its survey of "what is stirring." The transcendentalist movement is converging on West Street, and Peabody has found her base. In their last conversation before his death in October 1842, Channing asks, "Will you . . . make me partner of your new thoughts?" (449). Always tacitly acknowledging the value of her thoughts, he has reached a moment of explicit dependence on his conversational partner. The thoughts he seeks out will continue to evolve beyond his death in active dialogue with the transcendentalists. As her *Reminiscences of William Ellery Channing* and kindred autobiographical utterances reveal, Peabody has participated in leading the movement from its earliest moments and will continue to shape its influence on the larger century.

NOTES

1. Elizabeth Palmer Peabody to Benjamin Pickman Mann, 17 May 1870, in Mary Van Wyck Church, "Biography of Elizabeth Palmer Peabody," 1869–1921, 492 (3) addendum (1), ms. MHi (abbreviated subsequently as MVWC). Quotation from this manuscript is with permission from MHi. I would like to thank Megan Marshall and Reed Gochberg, her research assistant, for sharing their partial transcription of Church's manuscript, and I dedicate this essay to Megan as my conversational partner since the 1980s.
2. On the "social principle" in Peabody's transcendentalism, see Megan Marshall, *Peabody Sisters*, 165, and "Elizabeth Palmer Peabody: The First Transcendentalist?" *Massachusetts Historical Review* 8 (2006): 13.
3. Elizabeth Palmer Peabody, *Reminiscences of William Ellery Channing, D.D.* (Boston: Roberts Brothers, 1880), iii; hereafter cited parenthetically by page number.
4. Maria Mitchell, *Life, Letters, and Journals*, ed. Phebe Mitchell Kendall (Boston: Lee & Shepard, 1896), 248. My thanks to Wesley Mott for this reference.
5. Susan Phinney Conrad first made critical claims for *Reminiscences* in *Perish the Thought: Intellectual Women in Romantic America, 1830–60* (New York: Oxford Univ. Press, 1976), 207–10.
6. Lawrence Buell, "The First Person," pt. 4 of *Literary Transcendentalism: Style and Vision in the American Renaissance* (Ithaca, N.Y.: Cornell Univ. Press, 1974). See also Buell, "Autobiography in the American Renaissance," in *American Autobiography: Retrospect and Prospect*, ed. Paul John Eakin (Madison: Univ. of Wisconsin Press, 1991), 47–69.
7. Cf. William Henry Channing, *Memoir of William Ellery Channing*, 3 vols. (Boston: Crosby & Nichols, 1848), which actively sought to "disengage" from a nephew's memories (vii). On the varieties of life writing, see chap. 1 of Sidonie Smith and Julia Watson, *Reading Autobiography: A Guide for Interpreting Life Narratives*, 2nd ed. (Minneapolis: Univ. of Minnesota Press, 2010); on transcendentalist memoirs, Robert Habich, "Biography, Memoir, and Reminiscence," in *OxH*, 426–37; on a relational model of women's autobiography, see Carol Holly, "Nineteenth-Century Autobiographies of Affiliation: The Case of Catharine Sedgwick and Lucy Larcom," in *American Autobiography*, ed. Eakin, 216–34.
8. Monika M. Elbert, "Elizabeth Palmer Peabody's Problematic Feminism and the Feminization of Transcendentalism," in *Reinventing the Peabody Sisters*, ed. Monika M. Elbert, Julie E. Hall, and Katharine Rodier (Iowa City: Univ. of Iowa Press, 2006), 199–200.

9. Ronda collects these letters in *LEPP* and cites an even wider range in his biography, *Elizabeth Palmer Peabody: A Reformer in Her Own Terms* (Cambridge, Mass.: Harvard Univ. Press, 1999).
10. Church aimed for publication but lost the backing of Peabody's executor, her nephew Benjamin Pickman Mann.
11. Henry James, *The Bostonians: A Novel* (London: Macmillan, 1886), 37. See Kristin Boudreau's sense of this character in *Sympathy in American Literature: American Sentiments from Jefferson to the Jameses* (Gainesville: Univ. Press of Florida, 2002), 148.
12. Theodore Parker, quoted in Franklin B. Sanborn, *Recollections of Seventy Years* (Boston: Badger, 1909), 548.
13. Hutcheson's role as the earliest theorist of sympathy is specified in Boudreau, *Sympathy in American Literature*, 5; and explored at length in Michael L. Frazer, *The Enlightenment of Sympathy: Justice and the Moral Sentiments in the Eighteenth Century and Today* (New York: Oxford Univ. Press, 2010).
14. Elizabeth Palmer Peabody, "My Experience as a Teacher: Principles and Methods of Education," *American Journal of Education* 32 (1882): 740, 741; *Lectures in the Training Schools for Kindergartners* (Boston: D. C. Heath, 1886), 102–3.
15. Nina Baym, "The Ann Sisters: Elizabeth Peabody's Millennial Historicism," *American Literary History* 3 (1991): 27.
16. Peabody, Diary [1822], in MVWC, 18, 32–37.
17. Peabody, Diary, 25 August 1825, 12 October 1825, in MVWC, 92–97, 121–22.
18. See Barbara L. Packer, *The Transcendentalists* (Athens: Univ. of Georgia Press, 2007), 23–27, for the men's encounter with Coleridge; and Capper 1, 105, for Fuller's.
19. Margaret Neussendorfer, ed., "Elizabeth Palmer Peabody to William Wordsworth: Eight Letters, 1825–1845," in *Studies in the American Renaissance 1984* (Charlottesville: Univ. Press of Virginia, 1984), 183–84.
20. Elizabeth Palmer Peabody, "The Spirit of the Hebrew Scriptures," *Christian Examiner* 16–17 (1834): 185, 310–12, 320, 188.
21. *LEPP*, 248. Also see Marshall, *Peabody Sisters*, 316, 425, and "EPP," 2–4.
22. Peabody to Eliza [Mrs. Benjamin] Guild, [1838], in MVWC, 340–41. On Adams's career, see Elizabeth Curtiss, "Hannah Adams," in *Dictionary of Unitarian and Universalist Biography*, http://www25.uua.org/uuhs/duub/articles/hannahadams.html, 10 October 2011.
23. Ann Douglas, *The Feminization of American Culture* (New York: Alfred A. Knopf, 1977), 102–3. Among the most helpful recent studies of sentiment, in addition to Boudreau's, is Glenn Hendler, *Public Sentiment: Structures of Feeling in Nineteenth-Century American Literature* (Chapel Hill: Univ. of North Carolina Press, 2001).
24. See Jeffrey Steele's reading in this collection of a more secularized and politicized "sentiment" short years later in the work of Lydia Maria Child and Margaret Fuller.
25. Peabody, Diary, 12 October 1825, in MVWC, 120–21.
26. Douglas, *Feminization of American Culture*, 102.
27. Peabody, Diary, 12 May 1826, in MVWC, 148; see Marshall, *Peabody Sisters*, 116, 141–43, 157, 167–68 for such episodes, the memory of which could leave her "crying uncontrollably."
28. Marshall, *Peabody Sisters*, 215 on 1830; Ronda, 89–93 on classes and textbooks of the 1830s, 202 and 294 on continuation in the 1840s through 1860s. Wesley Mott portrays Peabody among other transcendentalist teachers in "Education," *OxH*, 153–71.
29. Peabody, "My Experience," 736–38.
30. Elizabeth Palmer Peabody, "A Vision," *Pioneer* 1 (March 1843): 97–100; "The Dorian Measure, with a Modern Application," *Aesthetic Papers*, ed. Elizabeth Palmer Peabody (Boston: self-published by the editor; New York: G. P. Putnam, 1849), 64–111; "The Place of

History in the Education of Republican Men and Women," as well as four sequels, in *The Una: A Paper Devoted to the Elevation of Woman* 3 (February, March, April, June, August 1855). On Peabody's historical vision, see Baym, "Ann Sisters"; on the *Una* essays, Conrad, *Perish the Thought*, 213–17.

31. Elizabeth Palmer Peabody, "My Experience," 738, 731; Mary Peabody Mann to Mary Van Wyck Church, 1 February 188?, in MVWC, 582; Fanny McDaniel to Peabody, [20 October? 1868], in MVWC, 492 [1–2].
32. See Monika M. Elbert's essay in this collection on the growth of Howe's commitment to organized feminism.
33. *LEPP*, 296–98; Peabody, "My Experience," 741.
34. Alcott himself recorded first reading Coleridge and Wordsworth in 1832. See *Journals of Bronson Alcott*, ed. Odell Shepard (Boston: Little, Brown, 1938), 32.
35. See Joel Myerson, *Transcendentalism: A Reader*, ed. Myerson (Oxford: Oxford Univ. Press, 2000), 97–120, for Peabody's "Explanatory Preface" to *Record of a School*.
36. Peabody, Diary, 22 September 1837, August 1838, in MVWC, 320, 385.
37. Elbert, "Peabody's Problematic Feminism," 208–9; Peabody, Diary, August 1838, in MVWC, 388.
38. Peabody, Diary, 24 November 1836, September 1837, in MVWC, 272–73, 315.
39. Peabody, Diary, 10 August 1838, in MVWC, 381–82.
40. Elizabeth Palmer Peabody, "Emerson as Preacher," in *The Genius and Character of Emerson: Lectures at the Concord School of Philosophy*, ed. F. B. Sanborn (1885; Port Washington, N.Y.: Kennikat Press, 1971), 158.
41. Peabody to Eliza Guild, in MVWC, 340–41. See Peabody, "Emerson as Preacher," 151, for a second account of Emerson's interest in her essay on John's gospel; Marshall quotes and comments on the letter to Guild in *Peabody Sisters*, 164, 559–60.
42. Elizabeth Palmer Peabody, "Egotheism, the Atheism of To-day," in *Last Evening with Allston* (Boston: D. Lothrop, 1886), 240–52. Also see Susan H. Irons, "Channing's Influence on Peabody: Self-Culture and the Danger of Egoism," in *Studies in the American Renaissance 1992* (Charlottesville: Univ. Press of Virginia, 1992), 121–35; and Gura, 215–16. My reading of Peabody's romantic millennialism differs from Baym's assertion that she was not a transcendentalist at all but affirmed an orthodox belief in Christ's future return ("Ann Sisters," 27).
43. Elizabeth Palmer Peabody, "A Glimpse of Christ's Idea of Society," *Dial* 2 (October 1841): 222.
44. Peabody's journal of notes on the Conversations shows her participating without challenging Fuller's leadership. See "Margaret Fuller's Boston Conversations: The 1839–40 Series," ed. Nancy Simmons, in *Studies in the American Renaissance 1994* (Charlottesville: Univ. Press of Virginia, 1994), 195–226.
45. "Miss Peabody's Reminiscences of Margaret's Married Life," *Boston Evening Transcript*, 10 June 1885 (thanks to Mary De Jong for this reference); *LEPP*, 302. For Emerson's judgment of Fuller, see *MMFO*, 1:236.
46. Margaret Fuller to Peabody, 3 February 1836, in MVWC, 297; "Miss Peabody's Reminiscences"; Journal, November 1836, in MVWC, 82.
47. Peabody to William Ellery Channing, August 1840, in MVWC, 405 [6–8].
48. Peabody to Channing, August 1840, in MVWC, 405.
49. Ibid.
50. See Perry Miller's use of this classic phrase in his role as editor of *The Transcendentalists: An Anthology* (Cambridge, Mass.: Harvard Univ. Press, 1967), 106–56.

SECTION 2
Transcendentalist Circles

INTERLUDE

Ellen Sturgis Hooper, untitled poem ("I walk the busy street"), in *Poems* (published privately [Edward William Hooper, 1872]), in The Tappan Papers, bMS Am 1221, call no. AC8.H7663.872p, MH-H.

I walk the busy street—the sight and sound
Of stirring life outwearies every sense—
Dull cares, hot words, hard work are all around,
Hearts filled with strife, nerves strung to action tense.

High over all—a strange unwonted guest,
The pure young moon hangs in a day-lit sky,
Placid and tender as on evening's breast—
How like to thee, whose gentle pressure nigh
Speaks to a rude vexed world of harmony.

"*How It All Lies before Me To-day*"

Transcendentalist Women's Journeys into Attention

SARAH ANN WIDER

Evoking late-afternoon walks shared with Sarah Clarke on the shores of Lake Michigan, Margaret Fuller describes sunsets that embody time and place. Not only were they particular to 1843; they suggested landscapes far from the prairies and writings thousands of years old. Fuller writes, "Sunset, as seen from that place, presented most generally, low-lying, flaky clouds, of the softest serenity, 'like,' said S. [referring to Sarah Clarke], 'the Buddhist tracts'" (*SL*, 22). Only a month earlier, the first translation of one of those "Buddhist tracts" had appeared in *La Revue Indépendante*. Half a year later Elizabeth Palmer Peabody would translate a section for the *Dial*.[1] Their mutual friend Caroline Sturgis, who had accompanied Fuller and Clarke for the first part of their journey to the Great Lakes, placed an "Oriental Mythus" (her phrase) centrally within the philosophical understanding she was developing for herself and others.

Rereading *Summer on the Lakes* a few years ago, I found Clarke's remarkable comparison. I had never seen it before. Or rather, no matter how many times I had read the passage, I never attended to it. This time I stopped, wondering how Clarke's attention had been drawn to this aspect of Asia. What enabled her to see "the Buddhist tracts" in the sunset sky? Around the same time, I read Caroline Sturgis's undated poem "How It All Lies before Me To-day" in manuscript at the Houghton Library and wondered what had drawn her attention to the Hindu traditions from which she cast her "Oriental Mythus."[2] The presence of goods from the China and India trade? A teacher, Elizabeth Peabody, who used a text featuring the history of India? Waldo Emerson and his reading? All of the above? How does one follow another's attention? Especially when that attention may have left scant record?

The Latin roots of the word "attention" (*ad tendere*) tell us that when we attend to something we stretch toward it. I mull over the many ways these thinkers ask us to reach toward what is around us, whether in our minds, on the page, in a desert arroyo, or amid the chaos of injustices in which we daily live. Based less on argument and more on observation, drawing more from synthesis than analysis, attentiveness trades not in the definitive but in the evocative. And yet there is nothing as potentially ephemeral as attention. Where does it go? How is it shaped or structured into a form that does not destroy its very nature of momentary being?

For transcendental women educators and artists, few questions sparked greater attention. For the purposes of this chapter, I have selected a redoubtable trio: Margaret Fuller, Sarah Clarke, and Caroline Sturgis.[3] Each was deeply interested and involved in the others' work even before all came together for Fuller's Conversations at Elizabeth Peabody's bookstore. They had long attended to each other's thoughts. The interwoven nature of their lives and their shared philosophic, educative, and aesthetic projects is full, fascinating, and well beyond the scope of this essay. I draw attention to only a few signal moments. First, Fuller and Clarke meeting when Fuller was ten and Clarke twelve, and Fuller noting even then Clarke's excellence as a visual artist.[4] Then there were early 1830s conversations around the dinner table at the boardinghouse kept by Clarke's mother: taking part were Clarke and her brother James, as well as boarders Elizabeth and Mary Peabody, historian Jared Sparks, and educator Horace Mann, with Margaret Fuller and Waldo and Charles Emerson joining the company from time to time. Finally, there were reading parties and historical conferences developed and taught by Peabody that included Clarke and Sturgis as participants and attracted Fuller's collegial interest. For both Clarke and Sturgis, these events may well have been the source for their later aesthetic and philosophic approaches as well as an early fostering of their interest in Asian texts.[5]

Sharing a fascination with how attention could be given form, these three women developed a range of possibilities, some specifically focused on and for women (Fuller's Conversations as well as Peabody's reading parties and historical conferences). As Peabody vowed, as Fuller concurred, and as Phyllis Cole has pointed out elsewhere in this volume, there would be "no silent ladies" in their gatherings. Attendance meant response. Other genres of attention engaged audiences through different modes, language translation among them.[6] Then, there were other kinds of translation: experience into language and experience into drawing. Through the verbal and visual sketches in *Summer on the Lakes*, Clarke and Fuller instruct the reader-viewer on how to replace prejudice with open-mindedness by keeping the eye moving. Similarly, Sturgis envisions a philosophical tradition centered on the motion of thought through matter.

For all the transcendentalists, attentiveness was multidimensioned, often involving literal attendance at a lecture, conversation, or concert. It encompassed the patient rendering of minute detail and the equally patient rendering of expansive abstraction. It kept trust with a temporality that was both timely and salient, and asked of the individual a wide and wild flexibility of observation. Part and parcel of that flexibility was an insistence on expansive reading of the philosophical and aesthetic traditions from every time and place. Little wonder that Emerson featured a series of what he called "Ethnical Scriptures" in the *Dial*.[7] Seeking to "collate" the wisdom literature of "different ages and races," he was in keeping with the approach pioneered by historian Hannah Adams in the late eighteenth century in her *Alphabetical Compendium of the Various Sects* and developed more radically by Elizabeth Peabody through both her historical conferences and her collection of books and periodicals for the Foreign Circulating Library.[8] Adams, setting forth the guiding principles of her work in 1784, emphasized the importance of impartial presentation. When quoting sources, she would not include sections where authors passed judgment on their material.[9] Peabody, however, found that Adams did not live up to her own guidelines. Citing Adams's commonly used work on U.S. history, *A Summary History of New England* (1799), she noted that it "might have been entitled, 'The Providence of God in New England'" (*LEPP*, 17).[10] Peabody would champion an increasingly "no-strings-attached" breadth—a true eclecticism that probed a subject of inquiry without relying on prior judgment.

That was a keystone of transcendental attentiveness. For such attention to yield new thought, immediate judgment had to take a back seat. Provisionality was essential. In Caroline Sturgis's words, what the individual sought to say was "how it all lies before me to-day." To perceive what was in the moment—to attend to that, and not to one's prior convictions or others' interpretations—asked for a rigor as keen as the sharpest analysis. Could you describe what you saw and resist the temptation on the instant to represent it as something else you had already seen or to promptly coin an interpretation? Public and published forms pushed for such conclusiveness: the sermon with its moral teachings, the essay with its reasoned discourse. Although possibly spurred by attentiveness, such forms did not express attentiveness itself. That remained for the more provisional and dialogic forms: the conversation, the letter, the journal, the sketch, the privately circulated poem.[11]

Just at the time when I could direct a period of attentiveness toward these women of transcendentalism, another experience began to shape my understanding. Health taught me to understand attention differently. Anyone who experiences the occasional migraine knows what I'm saying. Those with intractable migraine comprehend the lay of the land even more closely. How often we must think about Fuller. When pain splits your brain, it is no surprise that attention takes on dimensions it never before assumed. And in the aftermath when the pain subsides and the nausea settles, and sound no longer jabs and light no longer jars, there are the hours of a mind rendered different. It muses. Unable to rush, unable to zero in and go for the analytic edge, it is luxuriantly inclusive. Not quite the transparent eyeball, but worth imagining in that way.

In the new rhythm of days accompanied by migraine, the old forms of attention are dismayed. The singular focus on which, as scholars, we often pride ourselves no longer works. Or it works in one clear direction: the shortest path between oneself and another migraine is uninterrupted concentration. And so one looks again. Sees differently. Values what is accessible in the moment. Looks to observation. Brings together small pieces separated by the absence of an argument. Calls attention to the sentence or paragraph or verse that has not yet developed our attention. What other forms might attention take beside the well-known undivided version that it is now impossible to sustain? The time within thought opens. Intermezzi arise from interruptions. Insight opens into different forms of relation, ones that rest on the closely observed detail and that embrace provisionality as part and parcel of all we can say. Before attention dims, if we are lucky, we can each say, with Caroline Sturgis, "how it all lies before me today." No more. No less.

Attention as a Moving Force

Returning to Fuller's Lake Michigan sunsets, I follow the movement of attention in her description. From sunset she moves with temporal familiarity into the night sky. She pictures the sudden burst of a shooting star that could not "astonish" the presiding serenity. She concludes the section with what many would have seen as an extravagant comparison: "Yes! it was a peculiar beauty of those sunsets and moonlights on the levels of Chicago which Chamouny or the Trosachs could not make me forget" (*SL*, 22).

I pause here, in part, for the palpable future in Fuller's sentence. In what time does she stand? Her imagined, impersonal reader might well see the comparison as based in life experience. "Could not make me forget": it sounds as though she has made that comparison in person, observed sunsets in both places, and found that the one in no way overshadowed the other. But that choice of "could" over "would" opens a double possibility, as her friends well knew. Here were both the lost trip to Europe and the longed-for one come true. The future implied by "could not" suggests a reality that will become indisputable.

What of the comparison itself? To this day, there are those among us (perhaps you, perhaps me) who can't help a private guffaw. The shores of Lake Michigan and the Alpine peaks? Who is she fooling? Never having been present at one of those sunsets in either of those places, I leave the question to others' (highly subjective) experience. It does make me itch, though, for a guidebook from Fuller's day (or ours) in order to hear the patent descriptions of sunsets in tourist spots. It also returns me to the whole of Fuller's passage that explores the dangers in initial response. As with her difficulty "seeing" Niagara Falls, perception itself has already been overinfluenced. At Niagara, she never quite gets the book images out of her line of sight. Prior experience holds her attention captive, even though the experience is two-dimensional. She has already read so many words on Niagara and seen so many sketches of the famous falls that the physical place remains in their shadows. In the prairies, a similar "a priori" frames her experience, but only her initial experience. At first she takes in only "the very desolation of dullness." In that frighteningly circular way we all know, she only knows how to see how she knows how to see. Her prior landscape determines what she sees—whether that view has been crafted from daily walking or daily reading. Had those internalized points of reference remained her standard, she would have continued to see an impoverished waste of "vast monotony" (*SL*, 22). Her published description, however, proceeds differently from her own experience. She does not let the reader see monotony first. Preceding any comments on "dullness" is a vivid description of flowers that leaves the reader in a dazzle of color and light. Only once she has given us so much detail does she turn 180 degrees to her first response.

The writer's and the reader's experiences are kept purposely separate. Most of Fuller's audience would have been reading through their own East Coast lenses that would have framed the view in monotony, but she does not privilege the familiar. Neither does she omit it. Monotony remains part of the experience, and a focus-changing experience at that. She presents both, modeling for her readers how we attend to the shifting rhythms between the familiar and the unknown. On the lakeshore she walks "with slow and unexpecting step," not walks but "traces." As if learning a new pattern, she follows the thin boundary again and again. This is a pattern with seemingly no end: "There was a grandeur in the feeling that I might continue that walk, if I had any seven-leagued mode of conveyance to save fatigue, for hundreds of miles without an obstacle and without a change" (*SL*, 22).

Clarke created no etching of this moment for *Summer on the Lakes*. The representation of sunset or flowers may well have seemed futile in a black-and-white form. She would instead render the prairies in a manner complementary to Fuller's descriptions. Considering one of Clarke's two prairie etchings (*Rolling Prairie of Illinois*), you find a similar emphasis on movement. To preclude the response of "dullness," Clarke shapes the etched lines so that the eye is offered motion wherever it looks. The grass hillocks are composed of fine curvilinear strokes. The nearby stalks of grass spread up and away. Birds are skimming in foreground and distance. Even the clouds participate, though this is difficult to perceive in our modern reproductions.[12] The contour lines of the sketch allow the viewer to wander through the prairie, up one ridge or down another, up to the rise and under the trees. Here is a visual equivalent of Fuller's physical manner of attentiveness: "to trace with slow and unexpecting step."

Both Clarke and Fuller replace monotony with possibility: the "unexpecting step" that might continue indefinitely. As Fuller remarks, "there was a grandeur in the feeling." No longer an "encircling vastness" like some Miltonic Chaos, the place is now the center for a "lovely, still reception . . . nothing but plain earth and water bathed in light."[13] Breaking free from preconception occurs only through the steady process of learning a place on its own terms. She comments: "It is always thus with the new form of life; we must learn to look at it by its own standard. At first, no doubt my accustomed eye kept saying, if the mind did not, What! no distant mountains? what, no valleys? But after a while I would ascend the roof of the house where we lived, and pass many hours, needing no sight but the moon reigning in the heavens, or starlight falling upon the lake" (*SL*, 22). Demonstrating for her reader how dangerous the eye can be, she illustrates the insidious way it convinces the mind that everything can be seen in only one way. Now of course, this is not any eye, but the accustomed version.

Taking the custom out of our own eye may be no easy task of extraction. How often, after all, do we "change our minds" in any real sense of that phrase? And yet, whether you're Fuller describing the prairies or Thoreau inviting us to know beans, it's a direct path, if a time-engrossing one. Their attention to the most particular detail is key. Only when the eye rests long enough on unfamiliar elements around it can it begin to see anew. And as with both Thoreau and Fuller, movement is integral. One cannot stand still. Their "rest" is filled with movement—walking, hoeing. It is a place for the "-ing," a world of continuous present but no hard conclusions. There is nothing mysterious in the process. It means opening attention in a new direction, stretching toward what one does not yet know.

Attending, Observing, and Representing

By the summer of 1843 Clarke knew a great deal about such attentiveness. Observer and participant, she attended in multiple capacities to the varieties of thought and expression in and around Boston. Her mother ran the boardinghouse in which Horace Mann and Elizabeth and Mary Peabody took rooms. The conversations around that boardinghouse table were lively and engaged. Sarah gave drawing lessons at Alcott's Temple School. She was one of the adult students in Peabody's historical conferences.[14] When her brother James took a ministerial position in Kentucky, she served as his best source of information, a witty and canny observer of the "Newness" back home. In addition to being a skillful copyist and engraver, she was encouraged to undertake a career in original painting by none other than the then-premier American painter

Washington Allston. Writing to James, she records the conversation from this vocation-making day. She had brought two paintings for Allston to see. Of the second, she reports, he said: "'Ah! Why, this I like better than the other. The same unity of tone, and this shows a feeling for nature. Miss Clarke,' (turning round), 'on such an occasion as this I should not hold myself justified in saying anything less or more than the truth exactly. I should do very wrong to say more than the truth, but I don't hesitate to advise you to make landscape painting your profession. You will be successful in it, and you will find it a profitable profession.'"[15]

It may well have been Clarke's success as a painter that prevented later generations from placing her firmly within the transcendentalist circle.[16] Barbara Novak's monumental study of nineteenth-century American landscape painting established the common cultural milieu in which visual and verbal artists worked, and yet, as Albert von Frank points out in his chapter on visual arts in the *Oxford Handbook of Transcendentalism*, it has been difficult to get beyond "assertions of affinity" (*OxH*, 441). Scholar Gayle Smith's work opened many doors into the role of painting within transcendentalism, but few of us have figured out how to walk through them. Nancy Stula's *At Home and Abroad: The Transcendental Landscapes of Christopher Pearse Cranch (1813–1892)*, based on an exhibit at the Lyman Allyn Art Museum in New London, Connecticut, and featuring essays by David Robinson and Novak, is the only sustained study to date of a visual artist within the transcendentalist circle.[17]

To this day in our criticism, we face difficulties interpreting the transcendentalists' relationships to various forms of art. In our focus on Emerson and Thoreau, with their interesting distrust of human creativity (fine in creating, worrisome as creation), we have seen through their eyes and by their standards. The art piece is always problematic. In addition, both men endorsed the primacy of nature over art. What Fuller or John Sullivan Dwight wrote about music as the highest form of expression, what Sturgis explored in terms of form itself, or what Clarke and Cranch embodied on canvas in the way of philosophy have been seen as less transcendental than romantic, more European-derivative than part of the "Newness" in which each thinker variously participated.

There is also the matter of *which* "transcendentalisms" have received critical attention. In her landmark discussion of Caroline Sturgis's and Margaret Fuller's shared commitment to art, Kathleen Lawrence reminds us that we have only begun to explore the "interdisciplinary and female driven aspects" of what she so aptly terms "aesthetic transcendentalism."[18] Continuing this work are Ivonne García's chapter on Sophia Peabody and Sterling Delano's consideration of Marianne Dwight in this volume.

In Clarke's case the matter is complicated by the absence of her work. A list of her paintings in her brother's papers at the Houghton Library tantalizingly names sixty-six canvases along with some of their owners, but of those I can account for only two: a landscape acquired by the Boston Athenaeum and the painting she gave to Emerson in 1843.[19] Of this painting, Emerson wrote to Fuller in May, just before she and Clarke left on their western journey: "I beg you to congratulate Sarah Clarke on my behalf on the rich summer that opens before her, & tell her that I am very often her debtor indoors & on rainy days for the sunlight & foliage which she has brought from the forest & fixed by good enchantments on the canvass of this valued picture. I have often intended to write & thank her; Meantime you must convey this message" (*LE*, 3:176).

Another element in Sarah Clarke's work—in this case her written observations—also suggests why she has been sidelined. The satiro-comedic element in transcendentalist expression deserves more attention than we have given it, whether that means revisiting caricatures of Cranch's or the dry wit of Sarah Clarke describing Emerson's lectures and Bronson Alcott's conversations as "intellectual coteries" that she would willingly forfeit in favor of Fuller's Conversations ("LS," 27 October 1839). There is much more to say about how those within the Newness sought to keep it honest, unpretentious—and "new."

While Clarke did not hesitate to deflate the aggrandizement surrounding habituated attendance at an Emerson or Alcott event, she had not always been so willing to forgo Emerson's lectures. In earlier seasons, not only did she unfailingly attend them but they superseded her own work. Writing to James on New Year's Eve / New Year's Day 1837–38, she notes how her intended painting has gone by the wayside. At the same time, she is not worried over the consequences. She trusts what has presently captured her attention: "I had intended by this time to have painted some of my Western views in oils."[20] "But these lectures," she continues, "take up half my time and all my thoughts; but I shall not lose by it. Is it not the characteristic of a true work of art that it takes you captive for the time, and carries you out of yourself, that it may restore you to yourself raised and improved?" ("LS," 31 December 1837–1 January 1838).

Characterizing Emerson's lectures as "a true work of art" (she would elsewhere liken them to a gallery of paintings), Clarke found herself engrossed with matters of the American Scholar. She writes, "I am at present pervaded and dissolved by one idea,—that is, Emerson of *man thinking*." If ever we as twentieth- and twenty-first-century readers have wondered how women of the nineteenth century responded to that phrase, here at least is one woman directly applying those words to herself. It was by no means easy. Her letters record the varied difficulties she faced on her way to becoming a self-reliant painter. At the center was what she called "the central difficulty of self-culture" ("LS," 11 February 1838). Listening to Emerson's lectures, she found no direct answer though she noted possible aids to reflection along the way. Reporting on the lecture that we know as "The Head" but that she designates "'The Power of Thought'—on the function of the soul and the discipline it requires," she comments on two essential "rules": "The first is to sit alone. Consider it a necessary of life to have an apartment where you can be alone every day, even if to do so you must sell your coat and wear a blanket. . . . The other rule is to keep a journal." She allows that this second recommendation is nothing new, "recommended by every teacher to every learner, and yet," she adds, "it comes with new force from him." Her own experience with journal keeping had never yielded much fruit: "I so detested a record of the feelings and that part of self which passes away." Apparently, the new force she heard in Emerson's words was his focus on what she called a "journal of the intellect." Here one could record the permanent—the working of intellect that outlasts the transient elements of self. She concludes her report on the lecture with a passage that seems designed to stand as one of those passages for such a journal: "The most interesting inquiry to us is, how we can come into possession of our inheritance, which is *truth*. I answer, by sincerity. If we express honestly and fully that which is within us, we shall then start from a new point. The universal law of God seems to be, Use all the truth you have, and you shall have more" ("LS," 31 December 1837–1 January 1838).

What Clarke repeats from the lecture is no mere transfer of words from one lecturer to another. This discussion of "inheritance" is timely. Not only does this lecture date from the 1830s period of burst economic bubbles and bank collapses, but it also reminds us of the shaky legal ground upon which a woman's monetary inheritance stood. What she remembered as Emerson's words on inheritance spoke directly to her situation. In a family with five sons and one daughter, there was little doubt where an inheritance would have landed, had there been one. Her only guaranteed inheritance was an abstraction. Unlike other kinds of abstractions, however, this one was accompanied by a "how-to" manual. Perhaps it would not seem practical to us. It certainly would not seem practical to most of my business-minded students, but for Clarke it succinctly expressed her situation. Expression was key. Not limited to language, it required individual directness. She needed to call forth outer form from inner substance.

For Clarke, not only was this calling forth artistically difficult for anyone, but it raised every question about what authorized a person, particularly a woman, even to attempt such work. What were the consequences? Could one accept and then act on them and also earn money through them? As she wrote in late August 1838, shortly after hearing Emerson's July address at the Divinity School: "As for trusting in my own genius, I do not think I am deficient in that point." She assures James that she feels no self-doubt along those lines. She then responds to his encouragement with words that both encourage and dead-end. She quotes him back to himself, reaffirming her "right" to "fairly try the experiment and see what [she] can do." However, she brings him up short against his assumptions. He assumed she could readily divide her time and manage well as a part-time artist, shrinking the expectations of women's duties just a little, but not too far. Relying on her own self-knowledge, she sees this as an impossibility: "The question with me is, Have I a right to give myself up, time and thoughts, body and soul, to this interest, to leave nothing of myself for any social purpose, to sever all the ties that bind me to my kindred and my race? You will say that so much is unnecessary: that I need not be so one-sided as that; that I can consecrate a part of myself to art, and leave the rest to satisfy the calls of duty. But, if I know myself, it is not so." While her brother claims she need not think of her work with such fixed focus, she assures him that it can be done in no other way. Hers is not a situation where attention can be divided, especially when she needs to contribute to the maintenance of the household. And yet she finds a way through the discord of societal and individual response by a consonance of thought that harmonizes the two. Such resonance strikes action from words. She writes: "But latterly, here is Mr. Allston advising me to make it my profession, and promising me success. Here is Mr. Emerson saying, 'It is your first and highest duty to obey your instincts: satisfy the wants of your own soul, and you will do right'" ("LS," 20 August 1838).[21]

From there Clarke began working closely with Allston. Not surprisingly, Emerson opposed the decision, urging her to work out each artistic difficulty on her own: "Mr. Emerson asked me a question such as I might have expected from him: he asked me, 'How can Mr. Allston help you?' 'But *how* can he help you?' Clearly he disbelieves in any help but self-help. For my part, I have arrived at that time of life, as mother's phrase is, when I do not disdain to receive help from an Allston. To be sure, it is far grander to get out of your difficulties alone and have all the glory of it; but meantime one might starve in the forest, before one could find the way out. 'Art is long, Life is short'; and now I have found the true application of that saying. It is because life is so short that one cannot do everything for one's self" ("LS," 20 August 1838).[22] Facing her own questions of vocation, woman thinking, self-knowledge, and practicality, she sets aside worries of overinfluence. Time is a factor, and she has none to spare.

Here is a practical self-reliance that does not blush at collaboration. That her decision in no way compromises her work appears in a letter to James a year later. As she points out, experimentation may be intriguing, but it can also be fruitless:

> I have never yet told you anything about my Allstonian experiences. I hope one day to show you some fruits of that season, for I feel now as if I could paint the universe, having got hold of a most philosophical and clear method of going to work. I have hitherto wasted so much time in trying experiments that I am fully prepared to appreciate the value of a worthy plan. I might have wasted years in study and not

> have discovered what Mr. Allston has shown me in a few days. He has painted an entire landscape before my eyes and answered every question I chose to ask him with the utmost frankness. I was glad to hear him say that he never painted a picture that did not cost him his whole mind, for it justified my original impression that there is a whole world of thought belonging to each picture. In particular he said that the Eliot landscape cost him a world of study, far more than he meant it should when he began it. ("LS," 18 September 1839)

Clarke's self-knowledge and experience are amplified by Allston's comments that every painting "cost him his whole mind." She recasts this in terms of her understanding: behind every painting is a "whole world of thought." She now feels ready to "paint the universe" with a method both clear *and* philosophical. Rather than leaning on Allston's experience, she has transformed it. It came into her life: it goes out from her truth.[23] For her, moments of attention—whether spent on the shores of Lake Michigan or in the woods of Kentucky—were expressed through a "philosophical and clear method" that yielded landscapes of the "whole mind."

That, of course, is a matter of opinion. A matter for speculation. Can we see it in her paintings? Who did? There is precious little known response to Clarke's work.[24] We have her theory. What about her practice? I sit here wondering: What would enable us to see her art on her own terms, even if we had ready access to works now known only by a list among her brother's papers? Her own terms set high stakes for visual art: what is drawn from the mind, what is realized in visible forms. Formal matters were elemental in her work as a painter. The landscape on canvas conveyed a "world of thought." Using a method that was at once technically grounded and philosophically based, she translated the universe.

Clarke's interest in form also appears in her written philosophical inquiries. In a letter to good friend Mary Peabody (not yet Mann), she responds to Mary's discomfort at the verbal picture Emerson had painted in one of his lectures. In a passage most familiar to us from "Experience," known to them from the lecture "The Heart" in the *Human Culture* series of 1837–38, Emerson described the individual's inviolable solitude in a way that apparently bothered Mary. She wrote to her friend Sarah, asking if she too experienced such dis-ease at the picture he painted of two people meeting only at points. Sarah's reply was a frank "no." Such descriptions did not bother her in the least because the feeling was absolutely familiar. She comments to Mary: "'Did I feel faint?' you ask—No, Mary—when he spoke of the loneliness of the soul I felt that what he said was so true—almost so trite that it scarcely made an impression on me, and I did not remember it till you reminded me of it—This I have always felt—A perfect intercourse is a thing so far from my experience that I scarcely believe in it—It is ever true that 'we meet only at points'—and when the points do touch an electric spark of communication is felt which is a novel & delightful sensation enough—and that I suppose we call friendship & love—Is it not so?—But what do they amount to after all in comparison with the years of lonely converse with ourselves."[25] Emerson's words seemed "almost so trite" that she made no note of them for herself. It was not until Mary reminded her that the passage came to mind. Allowing that there might be such moments of "perfect intercourse," she unflinchingly acknowledges the daily reality of the singular, solitary self. She pictures the self alone in conversation with itself alone.[26]

Clarke's words to Mary suggest no interest in rendering thought as biography. She explores human existence from her own perception, but without suggesting that her observations can be neatly explained away by particular events. After she describes the years of self-conversation, she introduces other metaphors for an absolute solitude that nonetheless incorporate an underlying shared essence. She gives Mary the image of the ocean: each person a drop of water, each person separated from the other drops. Contained. Formed. The essence remains the same yet separated by boundaries that cannot be crossed. She writes, "I have often felt a thrill of wonder at the thought that my soul is forever separated & boxed up—and made into an individual—and this feeling is so strong & constant that it comes near to a remembrance of the time when we were really a part of the whole—drops in the ocean of life—'now spilled, and which cannot be gathered.'" To be individual—indivisible—in Clarke's understanding means a distinct yet double experience of form. It is a thought that is also a feeling. The thought of the soul—what it is to be individuated—and the memory of the feeling when one was not.

Tending the "Primal Fire"

If for Sarah Clarke the matter of form was in the certainty of separation, for Caroline Sturgis constant flux guaranteed that nothing remained bounded for long. Those who have read Sturgis's poetry and prose know her philosopher's bent and her longstanding interest in the relation between genius and form. As Lawrence discusses, Sturgis was not only a visual artist herself but someone interested in assembling works of art that spoke to each other. Rather than just assuming the "society" life and "collecting" mania attributed to her, we must look instead at what she chose to do in her writing, her painting, and her collecting. While Lawrence looks to the visual arts, I turn to Sturgis's writing, and in this particular case a long, unpublished, philosophical poem she titled "How It All Lies before Me To-day."[27]

Her titling phrase speaks volumes. It suggests a landscape: how it lies before her. One can think about a possible Miltonic reference: "the world was all before them." Or a landscape as might have been painted by Sarah Clarke, "sunlight & foliage which she has brought from the forest & fixed by good enchantments on the canvass." It also suggests there will be no hasty conclusions, to borrow Thoreau's phrase. She writes comprehensively yet provisionally. The poem itself is evocatively structured. It is written in terza rima, Dante's form. This is no poetic muscle flexing, but a choice that aptly matches form with thought. Sturgis's stanzas again and again take up the constant metamorphosis of thought into expression, back into thought, and then into further expression. For example, from the beginning of the poem:

> The primal Thought within itself must move
> Divide itself, to know itself in Love
> Receive itself, that Truth may Truth approve,
>
> Of Segment life begin the endless chain,
> Matter, evolving laws to form, attain
> And thought is symbolized to think again.

The form is liquid yet contained. The tercets with their self-continued rhyme (aaa, bbb, and so on) and constant iambic create an undulating rhythm. Something is realized, then rethought, realized, then rethought, then realized. Without thought rendered into form, Sturgis implies, thought would end. Matter literally creates new thought rather than simply reiterating the old in new forms. Here she parts company with those philosophies that would view form and matter as secondary. She makes it essential to creation: "Matter, evolving laws to form, attain / And thought is symbolized to think again."

In the poem, Sturgis takes up questions of original creation as well as matters of unity. Just what is the relationship, or perhaps more aptly, what are the relationships among the one and the many? She challenges established assumptions about the derivative and secondary nature of manifestation. In her thinking, there is no such hierarchy. She celebrates a complexity that allows for multiple iterations occurring simultaneously. The process of thought realized is never ending and overlapping. She writes,

> A song within a song mars not the sense
> Note behind note makes music more intense;
> Let this for complex schemes be the defence.

As the last line suggests, she is well aware that some would fault her perspective for its complexity. There is no Occam's razor in her world. She, however, feels no need to apologize. The image she chooses and carries further into this later section of the poem focuses on music, evoking the music of the heavenly spheres as well as the art form that such transcendentalists as Margaret Fuller and John Sullivan Dwight deemed the highest form of expression. A few stanzas later she links the individual to "natural desire," which in turn predicts a Dickinsonian going out upon circumference:

> And all my life is natural desire
> A kindred stirring of the primal fire
> Which drives me under, deeper, farther, higher.
>
> And as the thoughts in me a centre crave,
> The centre a circumference would have,
> Each wish be planted in a fruitful grave.
>
> Even so those stars in spheral music bound
> A home within the universe have found,
> And satellites to perfect the endless round.

Worth noting is the underlying restlessness that drives this perpetual process. The speaker's desire is not so much fire stolen from the gods as it is an innate dynamism. While Sarah Clarke envisions the solitary drops of water separated from each other, Sturgis imagines fire as the elemental force. Its apt rhyme with "desire" suggests a kinship that yields both energy and light. Desire, in Sturgis's representation, need not be smothered. Distinguished by its activity, it speaks for her definition of the self: a force moving below surfaces as equally as it moves above them.[28]

Consider the final tercets in Caroline Sturgis's poem:

> And all that was not taught in the first home
> That thou art child of the creative power,
> Is in thy turn to *be* creative power
>
> The constant flux of constant energy
> Now refluent not only *through* but *from* thee
> Will make it perfect happiness to be.

The individual *is* creator, a lesson not learned in "the first home," a phrase that may well refer to the instabilities in Sturgis's own home.[29] It may also take us to Wordsworth, but it upends the Wordsworthian reference. The child who fathered the man had not understood his creative prospects. In these lines, lives move in a different manner—through transmigration, for example. Now were it not for other references in the poem, I would be cautious about bringing in such a possibility. But the following lines illustrate the multiple worlds upon which Sturgis drew:

*Upon itself the Only One did brood
The One Alone discerned its solitude
And cast a Lotus Flower upon the flood;

The flower bloomed, *a* good within *the Good*,
The One Alone forgot its solitude,
The life-beat made a circle on the flood.

And thought on thought began the endless dance,
And Love on Love, broke up the primal trance,
And day made night, and Certainty made chance.

Ancient of Days, and in the moment new,
The Eternal Spirit in an endless view,
Doth self-enfolded arms in self developed forms pursue.

*The First of all, says the Oriental Mythus,
Brooded on itself like a sea of milk. Presently the need
Of creating was felt and a Lotus flower was cast forth,
the first existence amid the Essence.[30]

I turn first to the footnoted explanation. Written as a quatrain, these lines name her source. Of course, it is a name comprising a great abstraction. Her "Oriental Mythus" cites no text, no verse. She combines her sources here and throughout this poem. It is a tour de force of "wisdom traditions," her own "Ethnical Scriptures" beginning with a Neoplatonic world, creating a blend of ideas, taken mostly from the Vedic tradition (what she calls "the Oriental Mythus"), evoking Christianity, though never by name and strikingly without a Christ, and making certain there is a prominent place for the Greek Muses. Hers is a way of inclusiveness. Remarkable within the poem (though not remarkable for Sturgis) is the absence of hierarchy. She does not prefer one tradition over another; she presents each as another manifestation of fundamental reality:

All cantos of the poem but repeat
The words which at the first our questions greet
To love and to be loved; to think and to be thought

In her poem, there is no system of "progress" or "advance." All the world's traditions stand, equally valued.[31]

Through Sturgis's poem, I reach a conclusion, and yet her poem foregrounds no such conclusion. Its title holds true to the end. Provisionality is its element. To borrow Clarke's words, the poem represents a "world of thought," but it never presumes to be definitive. The composition may well have cost the writer her "whole mind" of that moment. Each work of formed expression invariably did, but did not exhaust the mind itself. Whether Fuller tracing the shore of Lake Michigan to learn bodily what she had only experienced negatively, or Clarke coming to every landscape with a mind newly re-formed, or Sturgis celebrating "the constant flux of constant energy," each thinker cultivated an attentiveness that did not destroy what it expressed. With minds always in motion, they opened worlds of perception to which we are still learning to attend.

NOTES

In the spirit of Mary Moody Emerson: "Good conversation makes the soul." While our twenty-first-century days do not allow the weekly possibility of conversational gatherings or the art of thought-full letter writing practiced by Emerson and the many women she knew and influenced, the correspondence I have shared with Phyllis Cole, Jana Argersinger, and Elizabeth Addison keeps that vital thread of transcendental attentiveness thriving. I am grateful for their insight, their interest, and, in the case of this essay, their always thought-provoking, thought-extending suggestions. They truly put the "vision" back into "revision." Phyllis kindly let me read an earlier draft of her essay on Peabody published elsewhere in this volume, and the conversations that preceded and followed were my Sarah Clarke equivalent to heralding a new year. To Alan Hodder, I am also grateful for his comments, which clarified what this essay both could and could not do. Finally, though never final, I am incalculably indebted to the women scholars who have made my own work possible. There are too many "Exaltadas" to name, though I will single out Helen Deese, Phyllis Cole, Elizabeth Addison, Susan Belasco, Nancy Simmons, Leslie Wilson, and Megan Marshall.

1. Eugène Burnouf, "Fragments des Prédications de Buddha," *La Revue Indépendante*, 25 April 1843, 520–34; "The Preaching of Buddha," *Dial* 4, no. 3 (1844): 391–401.
2. Caroline Sturgis, "How It All Lies before Me To-day," poem, in Correspondence and Manuscripts, Caroline Sturgis Tappan papers, bMS Am 1221 (314), MH-H; not to be reproduced in whole or in part without permission.
3. In an earlier version of this paper, the trio was a quartet that included Elizabeth Palmer Peabody, whose careful work developing the holdings of the Foreign Circulating Library at her West Street Bookstore made possible much of the transcendentalists' attentiveness to varied philosophical traditions. Her own role as translator of the section of *The Lotus Sutra* that appeared in the *Dial* in 1844 (the first appearance in English of any of the Buddhist sutras) has yet to be fully explored. Also for future study is the topic of women reading the debates surrounding Buddhism in the nineteenth century.
4. Fuller writes: "I saw a head of her [Rebecca Clarke's] daughters painting which looked very natural Five or six pencils and brushes lay upon a window sill—and a portrait was upon a wooden frame. I saw also a beautiful landscape[.] This young ladys name is Sarah[.] She has a singular taste for painting" (*LMF*, 1:96).
5. One of the texts Peabody used with pupils in her history studies was A. H. L. Heeren's *Historical Researches in the Politics, Intercourse, and Trade of the Principal Nations of Antiquity* (Oxford: D. A. Talboys, 1832–33). Megan Marshall notes Peabody's reference to this work in Peabody's 1882 "My Experience as a Teacher" (*Peabody Sisters*, 532).
6. Peabody and Fuller were signal among transcendental translators, Peabody primarily for her translation of Joseph Marie de Gérando's *Self-Education; or, The Means and Art of Moral Progress* (Boston: Carter & Hendee, 1830), a book that would strongly influence

the transcendentalists. In this arena, Fuller is best known for her work on Goethe and his circle. Other women in the transcendental translation circle would include Eliza Cabot Follen with her work on Fenelon.

7. Robert Richardson calls the "Ethnical Scriptures" the "boldest new feature" introduced into the *Dial* under Emerson's editorship (*Emerson: The Mind on Fire* [Berkeley and Los Angeles: Univ. of California Press, 1995], 379). With selections from *The Laws of Menu*, Confucius, and *The Lotus Sutra* (translated by Peabody), the series ran from July 1842 to the final issue in 1844. The phrase itself lived on and was used, for example, by second-generation transcendentalist Moncure Conway in the title of his collection *The Sacred Anthology: A Book of Ethnical Scriptures* (New York: Henry Holt, 1874).
8. Ralph Waldo Emerson, *Dial* 3, no. 1 (1842): 82. Adams's book went through several editions. Published first in 1784 under the title *An Alphabetical Compendium of the Various Sects which Have Appeared from the Beginning of the Christian Era to the Present Day*, it was issued in an expanded second edition in 1791 under the title *A View of Religion, in Two Parts*. Two more American editions as well as three British editions appeared in the author's lifetime. For the complex history of these editions, see Gary D. Schmidt, *A Passionate Usefulness: The Life and Literary Labors of Hannah Adams* (Charlottesville: Univ. of Virginia Press, 2004).
9. Adams notes: "The reader will be pleased to observe, that the following rules have been carefully adhered to through the whole of this performance. 1. To avoid giving the least preference of one denomination above another: omitting those passages in the authors cited, where they pass their judgment on the sentiments, of which they give an account" (*A Dictionary of All Religions and Religious Denominations, Jewish, Heathen, Mahometan and Christian, Ancient and Modern* [New York: James Eastburn; Boston: Cummings and Hilliard, 1817, Advertisement], n.p.).
10. Marshall also notes the unsatisfactory personal meeting between the sixty-five-year-old Adams and the fifteen-year-old Peabody (97).
11. I am grateful to Phyllis Cole for conversations on these issues of attentiveness and provisional form.
12. I have consulted the etchings Fuller sent to Emerson when they were deciding which should be included (MH-H Ms Am 1280.235 [244], Ralph Waldo Emerson Memorial Association deposit), as well as Abba May Alcott's 1844 copy of *Summer* (MH-H AC85 Al 191 Zz8440). In both, the skies with their various clouds are beautifully present as are other details: rain, variations in light on prairie grass, detailing on canoes, and expression on faces.
13. Worth highlighting is Fuller's use of the word "reception." One of those quintessentially transcendentalist concepts, it appears at exclamatory and declarative moments in Emerson's essays. See, for example: "A thrill passes through all men at the reception of new truth" ("The Over-Soul," in *CW*, 2:166). Also worth much more consideration is how some of the transcendentalists (for example, Emerson) gendered this concept feminine, and how others (Fuller, both Ellen and Caroline Sturgis) used but also resisted such gendering.
14. Peabody spoke highly of Sarah Clarke as a friend. Writing to her sister Mary in the year 1833, Peabody noted that the friendship with Clarke was one of the few things of great value in an otherwise "most unsatisfactory year," and six weeks later she mentioned the "divine letters" Clarke had written to her (*LEPP*, 121, 124).
15. Sarah Clarke to James Freeman Clarke, 11 June 1838, "Letters of a Sister," MH-H bMS Am 1569.3 (12), not to be reproduced in whole or in part without permission; hereafter

cited parenthetically as "LS." Clarke's letters were prepared for publication under the title "Letters of a Sister (1831–1840)" by her niece Lillian F. Clarke and published in the Unitarian periodical *The Cheerful Letter* between 1903 and 1910. The periodical was the written arm of the Unitarian women's group "The Cheerful Letter Exchange." Formed in 1891, the group sought to extend education to women who had little access by sending books, as well as letters, along with its monthly newsletter. Clarke's letters thus appeared at the turn of the twentieth century for women struggling to expand their own education. The copy I have consulted is in the Houghton, and rather than the periodical itself, it is solely the printed letters pasted onto the pages of a large scrapbook-like volume. Robert Hudspeth identifies these as the corrected proof-sheets for the original printing (*LMF*, 1:203). The whereabouts of Clarke's original letters are unknown.

16. In his biographical entries for *Dial* contributors, George Willis Cooke observes that Clarke was "one of the first women to take up art as a profession" (*An Historical and Biographical Introduction to Accompany "The Dial"* [1902; New York: Russell and Russell, 1961], 2:68). Cooke mentions her as a colleague to artists Harriet Hosmer and Margaret Foley in Italy. Clarke also receives a very brief entry in J. L. Collins's *Women Artists in America: Eighteenth Century to the Present* (Chattanooga: Univ. of Tennessee Press, 1973), n.p., which reports that she was "known for her landscape paintings." As yet, few scholars have attended to Sarah Clarke. While she often comes up in biographical discussions of Fuller and Peabody and also figures in Emerson biographies, she has remained on the margins, though it seems her friends did not see her in that way. Beyond Joel Myerson's "'A True and High Minded Person': Transcendentalist Sarah Clarke" (*Southwest Review* 59 [Spring 1974]: 163–74), the only other work specifically focused on Clarke is Joan Alice Kopp's brief but helpful biography written for the centennial of the Clarke Library in Marietta, Georgia (founded by Sarah Clarke). See *Sarah Freeman Clarke: Woman of the Nineteenth Century* (Marietta: Cobb Landmarks and Historical Society, 1993). See also Myerson's "Sarah Clarke's Reminiscences of the Peabodys and Hawthorne," *Nathaniel Hawthorne Journal* (1973): 130–33.
17. Barbara Novak, *Nature and Culture: American Landscape Painting, 1825–1875* (New York: Oxford Univ. Press, 1980); Gayle L. Smith, "Emerson and the Luminist Painters: A Study of Their Styles," *American Quarterly* 37, no. 2 (1985): 193–215; Nancy Stula, *At Home and Abroad: The Transcendental Landscapes of Christopher Pearse Cranch (1813–1892)* (New London, Conn.: Lyman Allyn Art Museum, 2007).
18. Kathleen Ann Lawrence, "Soul Sisters and the Sister Arts: Margaret Fuller, Caroline Sturgis, and Their Private World of Love and Art," *ESQ: A Journal of the American Renaissance* 57 (2011): 79–104.
19. *Kentucky Beech Forest* (ca. 1839)—most likely one of the "Western views in oils" that Emerson's lectures had kept Clarke from working on—now hangs in David Dearinger's office at the Boston Athenaeum. I am grateful to Dr. Dearinger, Susan Morse Hilles Curator of Paintings and Sculpture and Director of Exhibitions; to Hina Hirayama, Associate Curator of Paintings and Sculpture; and to Catharina Slautterback, Curator of Prints and Photographs for their generous help with the Clarke materials.
20. Not to be confused with the sketches Clarke made during a later trip with Fuller, these would have dated from her visit to James in the winter of 1836–37 during his ministry in Kentucky.
21. Myerson reads this passage differently, markedly contrasting Emerson's and Allston's comments. In the context of Clarke's ongoing discussions with her brother, I see Clarke reconciling the dissonance. Together, Emerson's and Allston's words licensed the all-

consuming nature of her art: with painting as her profession she satisfied her soul, depended on no one, and in fact benefited others.

22. Allston's work created a debate among transcendentalists over how to value it, where to place it, and whether to claim it as part of their element. See C. P. Seabrook Wilkinson, "Emerson and the 'Eminent Painter,'" *New England Quarterly* 71, no. 1 (1998): 120–26; as well as von Frank's focus on the 1839 Allston exhibition ("The Visual Arts," in *OxH*, 441–52). As he points out, Allston's work seems "to have emboldened the feminist work of two generations of Transcendentalist women" (448).
23. See Ralph Waldo Emerson, "The American Scholar," in *CW*, 1:55.
24. In addition to the comment from Allston that Sarah Clarke reported to James in her 1838 letter, the most detailed remark comes from Emerson, expressing thanks for the painting Clarke gave him shortly before leaving with Fuller on the journey that would issue in *Summer on the Lakes*.
25. Sarah Clarke to Mary Peabody, MH-H bMS Am 1569.8 (147); not to be reproduced in whole or in part without permission.
26. At the end of "Illusions," Emerson writes, "And when, by and by, for an instant, the air clears, and the cloud lifts a little, there are the gods still sitting around him on their thrones,—they alone with him alone" (*CW*, 6:174).
27. The poem has never been published, nor do we know how frequently it may have circulated among friends.
28. Worth further study is the restlessness evoked by women in the transcendentalist group. While accounted for in part by their interest in motion and its essential importance to thought, there is also a tonal difference that I have found particularly striking in the poetry of both Caroline and Ellen Sturgis.
29. The Sturgis home was a complicated one. In 1826, the highly favored son William died in a freak boating accident, and Sturgis's mother never recovered, eventually moving out of the Boston home altogether. Sister Ellen was sharply criticized during this period for not showing appropriate grief. Father William was by all accounts an aloof parent whose real interest was exploration: not only playing a seminal role in the China trade, he was deeply interested in the American continent and the contest with Russia for the fur trade in the Northwest.
30. The lotus holds deep significance for both Hindu and Buddhist traditions. Here, Sturgis clearly draws on Hinduism.
31. In her day, Sturgis shared this position with very few. Of Emerson, Alcott, and Thoreau, Alan Hodder observes: "In contrast to the Transcendentalist minister Theodore Parker, who viewed Eastern religions in a more critical light, or even Elizabeth Palmer Peabody, whose assessment was somewhat guarded, the three Concordians welcomed the religious and literary contributions of India and the Far East with undiluted favor" (*OxH*, 34). Peabody's assessment is indeed interesting. While clearly maintaining the superiority of an ideal Christianity (*LEPP*, 303–5), she was nonetheless instrumental in guaranteeing that others would be able to come to their own conclusions by reading the texts for themselves.

INTERLUDE

Sarah Helen Whitman, from "Emerson's Essays, by a Disciple," *United States Magazine and Democratic Review* 16 (June 1845): 600.

Every new discovery in physics teaches that all difference is phenomenal. The integrity of being is detected under manifold disguises. The farther we push our inquiries into the different departments of science, the more obvious are the analogies subsisting between them. In nature all the lines blend and converge towards a common centre. The moment we attempt to distinguish and define, to draw lines and affix boundaries, we are perplexed and baffled by her fluidity and sameness. In the crystal we already detect a paradigm of vegetable forms, in the vegetable an approach to the sentient instinct, while sensation and volition present strange and subtle analogies with electricity.

The discovery of the dependence of the chemical affinities of bodies on their electric states—the detection of electric forces in magnetic phenomena—the close analogies subsisting between light, heat, and sound, all point to one primal energy in nature, the agent in all natural phenomena, as in the mind that perceives them—for mind itself, in so far as we are acquainted with its mode of being, is but a subtle force vibrating to the impulsion of other forces external to itself.

"*We have abolished* domestic servitude"

Women and Work at Brook Farm

STERLING F. DELANO

When George Ripley and Charles Anderson Dana arrived at Clinton Hall in New York City in early April 1844, its sheer size, and the hustle and bustle of the streets around it, likely gave them pause to reflect. Just a few days before, Ripley and Dana had been at "home" in the Brook Farm community in West Roxbury, Massachusetts, where the largest building was an aging farmhouse and the most common sounds were the lowing of cattle and the chatter of the woodpeckers and scarlet tanagers now returning to the two-hundred-acre farm, signaling the beginning of spring. Standing in front of the imposing four-story Greek Revival building located not far from the expanding commercial area around Wall Street, the two men would undoubtedly also have been reminded of the persistent financial difficulties that had plagued the Brook Farm community since its organization three years before, nearly to the day, by Ripley and his wife, Sophia. It was the community's mounting indebtedness, in fact, that had prompted Ripley and Dana to make this trip to New York to trumpet Brook Farm's various achievements to potential financial supporters. They would also attempt to position Brook Farm at the vanguard of the utopian fervor then sweeping across the country.[1]

The early years of Brook Farm's existence—the so-called transcendentalist period from April 1841 to December 1843—had been financially difficult ones for several reasons. As minister of the Unitarian Church on Boston's Purchase Street since his ordination by the Harvard Divinity School in 1826, George Ripley was one of the most widely respected theologians in New England when he resigned from his pulpit in order to begin his social experiment. But Ripley embarked on the venture in West Roxbury without any hands-on farming experience. That explains, in part, the unfortunate decision to locate the community on the Ellis property in West Roxbury. George and Sophia Ripley had only the happiest associations with the Ellis farm because they had vacationed there on several occasions and were smitten by its beauty and serenity, not to mention its convenient proximity to Ripley's good friend Theodore Parker, who was ministering the Second Church in West Roxbury. It was of course no secret to locals why, for generations, the Ellis property had been a dairy farm: its stony and infertile soil was not hospitable to crop farming. No amount of manure, as Ripley and the Brook Farmers had been discovering, would ever change that fact.

But the community faced other problems too. Not only was George Ripley not a farmer, he had no hands-on experience in worldly matters. His enthusiasm for the Brook Farm community, moreover, invariably trumped his better judgment. Nathaniel Hawthorne noted the problem right away in 1841, just a few months after moving to the community himself. Ripley's zeal, he observed, would "not permit him to doubt of eventual success."[2] Thus the doors to the community were wide open from the start. From the modest fifteen or sixteen of the faithful who had set up housekeeping with the Ripleys in April 1841 (Hawthorne among them), the number of boarders, resident students, and members quickly grew to sixty just one year later. By the end of 1843 there were nearly one hundred people living at Brook Farm, and more on their way. In order to accommodate the swelling population, new buildings had to be constructed. The new construction, however, meant additional indebtedness because the community's coffers had been virtually empty from the start.

Such a quick snapshot of the early years of Brook Farm's existence is not intended to suggest that life in the community was mostly a drudge and a grind. From all accounts it was anything but, especially for women, whether single or married. Surviving reminiscences do not speak about hunger and want. They invariably recall the "happy and wholesome" lives enjoyed at Brook Farm, and they particularly celebrate the opportunities available to women that were not available anywhere else in the United States. Carol Kolmerten puts it succinctly in her study of gender in American Owenite communities when she notes that "women at Brook Farm enjoyed the best advantages that American culture had to offer."[3]

And just what were some of those "advantages"? For one thing, Brook Farm women enjoyed freedom from the prevailing social and religious expectations that defined the "cult of true womanhood" in antebellum America. The mere fact that Brook Farm women were living in the West Roxbury community was already a violation of the "cardinal virtue" of domesticity. The editor of one of the popular women's magazines of the period did not hesitate to admonish his readers—clearly with a direct nod at communities like Brook Farm—that women should "not look away from [their] own little family circle for the means of producing moral and social reforms, but begin at home." It was not merely that a woman's place was in the home. Woman, according to Barbara Welter, was a "hostage in the home."[4] That was hardly the case for the fifty-eight women and girls (forty of them unmarried) who were living at Brook Farm in the mid-1840s.

From its very beginnings, Brook Farm has been celebrated for the quality of the social and educational opportunities it provided to women. The record of this aspect of community life is so extensive that it would be impossible to repeat it here. Nevertheless, it is worth indicating, if only very briefly, the kinds of activities women enjoyed at Brook Farm.

Students of Brook Farm are always hard-pressed to find even a single reminiscence of the community that does not recall, with great fondness, the rich variety of social activities that were the staple of life there. Interestingly, nearly all the reminiscences are by women who lived at Brook Farm—some for a month, some for a year, and some for several years.[5] Piano recitals, for instance, occurred nearly every week, thanks to John Sullivan Dwight, a gifted musician who in 1841 had renounced his Unitarian pulpit in Northampton, Massachusetts, to join the Ripleys in West Roxbury. Dwight regularly entertained his fellow Brook Farmers on one or the other of two pianofortes in the community. Dwight also conducted the Brook Farm choir, whose performances of his original arrangements of Mozart and Haydn often provided the morning "wake-up call" to community residents.

Evenings also featured charades, a popular entertainment at Brook Farm. These after-supper diversions might involve just a few of the communitarians or large groups who competed against one another. On weekends there might be full-scale dramatic tableaux, complete with period costumes and props, involving the efforts of many members of the community. For those who preferred more intimate gatherings, there were coffee and dessert parties, and even an oyster party on at least one occasion. For those who preferred a contemplative evening, books from George Ripley's extensive personal library—one of the largest in New England—were there for the taking.

Brook Farmers spent a great deal of time outdoors too, no matter the season. When they were not working they could be found picnicking, rowing on the nearby Charles River (or skating on it in winter), walking in the pinewoods that bordered the north side of the farm, or venturing over to West Roxbury on Sundays to hear Parker preach. Outdoor masquerade parties, such as the one Hawthorne immortalized in "The Masqueraders" chapter in *The Blithedale Romance*, often occurred in the spring and autumn. In October there were also husking parties in the barn (Margaret Fuller enjoyed one of these in 1842), and in April or May there were outdoor celebrations to mark the arrival of spring. Lindsay Swift was entirely right when he noted in his early study of the community that "enjoyment was almost from the first a serious pursuit of the community."[6]

As stimulating and enriching as these social activities were, however, it was the educational opportunities available to women at Brook Farm that really set the community apart from all others in antebellum America. A wide variety of courses were always available to women, including classes, for example, in philosophy (moral, natural, and intellectual), foreign languages (Greek, Latin, Italian, French, Spanish, and German), astronomy, history, drawing, and music. The teachers for some of these classes, in fact, were Brook Farm women themselves. Sophia Ripley taught history and Italian; Amelia Russell taught French and dancing; and Hannah Ripley, George's cousin, taught drawing, as did Marianne Dwight, John S. Dwight's sister, after she moved to Brook Farm in 1844. Dwight told a friend in September 1844, for instance, that "countless" classes were being organized in the community, "enough to make one's brain whirl."[7]

Such recollections suggest the unusual, even extraordinary, range of social and educational opportunities available to women at Brook Farm. It is not unreasonable to suggest either that frequent Brook Farm visitor Margaret Fuller had the West Roxbury community in mind when writing her essay "The Great Lawsuit. *MAN* versus *MEN. WOMAN* versus *WOMEN*," the basis of her foundational book *Woman in the Nineteenth Century* (1845). The essay was published in the *Dial* not long after Fuller's weeklong visit to the community in October 1842. Fuller wrote, "What a woman needs is not as woman to act or rule, but as a nature to grow, as an intellect to discern, as a soul to live freely, and unimpeded to unfold such powers as were given her when we left our common home."[8] Women at Brook Farm had uncommon opportunities to grow, to discern, and to unfold. This is certain. What has been less certain, however, is whether women there were also "free" to choose the work they performed. To what extent were women constrained by cultural expectations about gender? Did Brook Farm women, despite the freedom and opportunity available to them in the community, ironically devote themselves mainly to domestic work? Did they work harder than men? Did married women work harder than single women? For the answer to these and other related questions, we need first to return to Ripley and Dana and their visit to New York City in 1844.

By the end of 1843 it was no longer possible to muffle the sounds of the proverbial wolf clawing at Brook Farm's door. Desperate circumstances called for decisive action. It was therefore decided to convert Brook Farm into a Fourierist Phalanx, that is, a community pledged to the utopian socialist principles of French visionary and mathematician Charles Fourier. The decision to do so, however, had less to do with ideology than it did with financial exigency. Ripley hoped that the conversion would result in much-needed monetary support from such New York–based Associationists as Horace Greeley and Albert Brisbane, among others. (American proponents of Fourier's utopian socialist theories preferred being known as Associationists rather than Fourierists. They did not want to be tarred with, among other things, the Frenchman's controversial views regarding sexual relations between men and women.) Ripley further hoped that Brook Farm would be designated a "Model Phalanx" (Phalanx was Fourier's term for community), thereby prompting additional financial support from Associationists around the country. In early January 1844 Brook Farm's original Articles of Agreement and Articles of Association were revised and amended, and on 18 January 1844 a new *Constitution of the Brook Farm Association for Industry and Education* was published. The publication of the constitution marked the end of the so-called transcendentalist period of Brook Farm's existence and the beginning of its Fourierist period.[9]

When Ripley and Dana traveled to New York in early April 1844, financial circumstances at Brook Farm were even worse than they had been just a few months earlier because there were now more mouths to feed. The General Convention of the Friends of Association in the United States in New York provided a timely opportunity to lobby for Brook Farm's importance in the rapidly expanding Associationist movement that was spreading across the United States.

The three-day gathering of Associationists in New York attracted delegates from Maine, Massachusetts, western New York, Pennsylvania, and Virginia. Notable among the few dozen attendees devoted to the cause were William Henry Channing, the nephew of Unitarian divine William Ellery Channing; Horace Greeley, editor and co-owner of the influential and increasingly powerful *New York Daily Tribune* newspaper; and Albert Brisbane, the foremost expositor in America of Fourier's utopian socialist theories. George Ripley was appointed president of the proceedings, and Dana was elected one of the vice presidents. On the third day of the convention, before the delegates retired to the popular Apollo Saloon nearby to commemorate Fourier's birthday on the 7th of April, Dana was given the floor to speak.

Dana would not talk, he told those gathered, about the promise or the potential of the Brook Farm community. Instead he would "make some remarks on the practical results of Associationism."[10] He would do so as a member of the oldest Association in the United States. He was not there to make a speech; he was there to describe what the Brook Farm community had actually achieved since its inception three years earlier. He would not brag, and he would not boast: "I shall give you some simple, plain truths, without any exaggeration—simple facts." Dana cited three. The first in order of these "simple facts" had to do with labor in the community, specifically that the Brook Farmers had "abolished *domestic servitude*." Second, the Brook Farmers had "secured thorough education for all"; and third, they had "established justice to the laborer, and ennobled Industry."[11]

From the very beginning, one of the actuating goals of the Brook Farm community, Dana told the delegates, had been to abolish domestic servitude.

"We have now for three years lived at Brook Farm," Dana proudly announced, "and have carried on all the business of life without it."[12] There were no servants at Brook Farm, and there was no "mean and degrading labor." All members of the community were the servants of each other—"no man is master." All work at Brook Farm was honorable, no matter how debasing it might be considered in conventional society. The Brook Farmers had therefore "reversed the order of society": "He who digs a ditch or discharges any other repulsive duty, is not at the foot of the social scale [at Brook Farm]—he is at the head of it." All labor at the West Roxbury community was compensated equally, no matter how lofty or how menial. The members of the community who mucked the stables in the barn received the same wage as the teachers in the Brook Farm School. All members of the community received the same wage—women the same as men, the young as well as the old—because all work at Brook Farm was dignified. At Brook Farm, domestic servitude had been abolished.

Dana's claim, to be sure, was no mere boast. When in June 1845 Ripley and Dana launched the *Harbinger*, a weekly paper devoted to the cause of Associationism and Fourierism, they immediately reprinted a series of articles from the *New York Daily Tribune* that detailed the plight of women in the New York City workplace. Tens of thousands of women, the articles claimed, were working twelve- to fifteen-hour days for pitifully low wages. These women lived in squalid housing and had no opportunity for recreation or education. "Hundreds are annually driven to infamy and ruin by absolute destitution."[13] That was certainly not the case at Brook Farm, as the community's labor records make clear.

One of the legacies of the decision in January 1844 to pledge Brook Farm, to the extent possible, to Charles Fourier's utopian socialist principles is a surviving record of labor activities for the twelve-month period from May 1844 to April 1845 that sheds important, and largely unexamined, light on day-to-day work patterns at Brook Farm—and, perhaps more interestingly, on the kind of work performed by every man, woman, and child listed in the record.[14] Close examination of the labor record also provides particularly valuable information about women's work activities at Brook Farm for the twelve-month period.

Let's begin with some general observations about the labor record for May 1844 to April 1845. There are 122 names listed of people who worked the equivalent of one full day or more in the community during the twelve-month period.[15] In fact, 119 of the 122 people listed actually worked fifty hours or more during the twelve months. Virtually none of the more "recognizable" Brook Farm names—such as Nathaniel Hawthorne, George William Curtis and his brother Burrill, Georgiana Bruce (Kirby), Isaac Hecker, Abby Morton, and

George P. Bradford—appear in the record because these people had departed the community before Brook Farm's conversion to Fourierism in early 1844.

Of the 122 names listed, 58 are women or girls and 64 are men or boys. In no single month did everyone on the list perform work at Brook Farm. The "busiest" month of the twelve-month period was November 1844, when 92 people were credited for work performed. The smallest number of people working in the community in any single month was during August 1844, when just 66 people received credit for work performed. These numbers are not surprising. Autumn is a busy time on a farm, whereas August is a relatively quiet time. Moreover, many Brook Farmers would have been away from the community during the summer months. In any case, the average number of people who worked each month is nowhere near the 122 listed in the labor record; the average in fact is 79 people. The movement of people in and out of the community during this twelve-month period was obviously just as fluid as it seems to have been throughout the nearly seven years of Brook Farm's existence.[16]

The labor record makes perfectly clear that the West Roxbury community was not only hospitable to families but had family and kinship at its core, despite the considerable number of single or unmarried people who lived there.[17] Seventy-nine people have the same surname as at least one other person listed in the labor record. These include husbands and wives without children; husbands and wives with children; mothers and daughters; a father and daughter; brothers and sisters; and sisters. To be more precise, seven pairs of husbands and wives without children appear in the record (Mary Ann and William Cheswell, a carpenter; Alpha and James Clapp, a bricklayer; Hannah and Nathaniel Colson, a shoemaker; Cynthia and Buckley Hasting, a grocer; Mary and Castalio Hosmer, a shoemaker; Sophia and George Ripley; and Mary and John Sawyer, a broker—a woman's "occupation" is rarely listed). Six husbands and wives with at least one child are listed (Rebecca and John Codman, a machinist, and children Charles, John, and Sarah; Augustina and Peter Kleinstrup, a cabinetmaker and gardener, and daughter Louisa; Eliza and Jean Palisse, a manufacturer, and son Edgar; Caroline and Flavel Patterson, a carpenter, and daughter Ann; Maria and Minot Pratt, a farmer, and children Frederick, John, and Caroline; and Jane and Lewis Ryckman, a shoemaker, and daughter Jean).

Five mothers were also present at Brook Farm with children but without husbands between May 1844 and April 1845. It is not known whether these women were widowed or divorced. At least one was definitely still married, and that was Mary Dwight, who moved to the community with her daughters Marianne (she later changed her name to Mary Ann) and Frances (Fanny) in April 1844. Son John Sullivan Dwight had been living at Brook Farm since November 1841. John the elder, however, for whatever reasons (Mary and John were not estranged), never lived at Brook Farm for any extended period of time, although he did stay there occasionally. The other mothers with children but no husbands were Mary Macdaniel and daughters Frances (Fanny) and Eunice (who married Charles Dana in 1846); a Mrs. Patterson and daughter Helen; Catherine Sloan, a seamstress, and daughter Catherine; and Amelia Whitehouse and daughters Amanda, Julia, and Sarah.

Nathaniel Swasey, it should be added, arrived at Brook Farm alone with his daughter Jane in late October 1844, but they both departed just a few months later in February 1845. During their brief residence, Jane was credited with 121 hours for domestic work, and she accrued 31 hours in the Waiters Series, which was a popular work activity, especially for unmarried women and men. (Work at Brook Farm was divided into "Groups" and "Series." These are discussed in detail below.) Jane was also credited for 34 hours in the Second Mechanical Group, which likely involved sewing, dressmaking, and other "fancy" work. Her father Nathaniel devoted all 215 of his total hours to the Mechanical Series, although it is not certain in which industry (see below).

Of the 58 women listed in the labor record, 40 were single, although 3 of the 40, it appears, were widows. (No wonder Margaret Fuller's friend Marcus Spring once remarked, "If I were a single man I should certainly go to Ripley's [that is, Brook Farm])."[18] I have been able to determine the ages of 29 of the 40 women. Thirteen were younger than 21 years; 11 were between ages 21 and 40; and 5 were 41 years or older. The youngest worker at Brook Farm was Maria and Minot Pratt's 7-year-old daughter Caroline (about whom more below). The oldest single woman at Brook Farm during the twelve-month period was George Ripley's sister, Mary Ann, who celebrated her forty-seventh birthday the same month that the labor record was begun in May 1844.

Of the 64 men listed in the labor record, 51 were single. So 91 of the 122 people—or 75 percent—who worked at Brook Farm between May 1844 and April 1845 were not married (40 women and 51 men). I have been able to determine the ages of 40 of the 51 men. The average age of a single man at Brook Farm between May 1844 and April 1845 was 25.7 years. This is virtually identical to the average age of a single woman, which was 25.1 years of age. The majority of Brook Farm men—30 of them—were between the ages of 21 and 40. Eight were younger than 21 years. Just 2 single men were more than 41 years old. The oldest unmarried man in the community was Job Tirell, a carpenter, who was 49. The youngest were Maria and Minot Pratt's children: John, who at 11 years of age certainly did not know that he would one day marry Anna Alcott, the eldest of Bronson and Abba Alcott's four daughters; and Frederick, who was 13.

On that early April day in 1844 when George Ripley and Charles Dana were making their way to New York City to attend the convention of Associationists at

Clinton Hall, John Sullivan Dwight's sister Marianne was arriving at Brook Farm with her mother, Mary, and sister, Frances (or "Fanny" as most friends called her). Marianne Dwight would turn out to be the most prolific letter writer who ever lived at Brook Farm. Over the next three-and-a-half years, she would send off more than one hundred letters from Brook Farm (eighty were published in *Letters from Brook Farm, 1844–1847*) to her brother, Frank, and to her dear friend Anna Q. T. Parsons, whose parents would not permit her to reside at the West Roxbury community, perhaps because they were concerned about the propriety of their daughter living in such immediate proximity to so many unmarried men. In any event, Marianne Dwight's letters are variously informative, gossipy, humorous, insightful, and personal. Of all the letters that have survived, hers provide the most vivid account of day-to-day life at Brook Farm during the Fourierist period. The letters of the intelligent, committed, resourceful, and determined Dwight tell us a great deal about the life of a single woman in the West Roxbury community.[19]

Just two weeks after arriving, Marianne Dwight wrote to her brother Frank describing a typical day in her newfound life as a communitarian. Her brief account provides a lively description of a typical workday—at least for Dwight, and presumably for most other Brook Farmers—at the West Roxbury community:

> Now my business is as follows (but perhaps liable to frequent change): I wait on the breakfast table (½ hour), help M[ary] A[nn] Ripley clear away breakfast things, etc. (½ hour), go into the dormitory group till dinner time,—half past twelve. Then from half past one or two o'clock until ½ past five, I teach drawing in Pilgrim Hall and sew in the Eyrie. At ½ past five go down to the Hive, to help set the tea table. Afterwards I wash tea cups, etc, till about ½ past seven. Thus I make out a long day of it, but alternation of work and pleasant company chats make it pleasant. (7–8)

As if her day were not busy enough, Dwight goes on to tell Frank that she was about to join a "flower garden group," and that she would soon begin "assisting Miss [Amelia] Russell in doing up muslins" (8).

Dwight's description of her busy schedule prompts some obvious questions. Is her day typical or exceptional for a Brook Farm woman? Were all or most Brook Farm women just as busy as Dwight? And what about Brook Farm men? Were they equally busy? Answers to these questions can in fact be found in the labor record.[20]

By compiling the total number of hours worked by each person at Brook Farm for the twelve-month period from May 1844 to April 1845, we can determine who the hardest-working members of the community really were. Table 1 is a list of the ten hardest working, in terms of total number of hours worked,

TABLE 1

Ten Hardest-Working Brook Farmers, May 1844–April 1845

	Name (M=married; S=single)	*Gender*	*Hours Worked*
1	Ripley, Mary Ann (S)	Female	3,042
2	Cheswell, MaryAnn (M)	Female	2,877
3	Codman, Rebecca (M)	Female	2,858
4	Ryckman, Jane (M)	Female	2,832
5	Dwight, Frances (S)	Female	2,825
6	Dana, Anne (S)	Female	2,788
7	Baldwin, Peter (S)	Male	2,773
8	Dwight, Mary (M)	Female	2,770
9	Codman, Sarah R. (S)	Female	2,678
10	Pratt, Maria (M)	Female	2,675

during the twelve-month period. What is immediately striking about table 1 is, of course, that nine of the ten hardest-working Brook Farmers were women. To anyone familiar with the ethos of antebellum American society and its culture of domesticity, this will hardly be a surprise. But here for the first time is documented proof that women, and not men, did the heavy lifting, so to speak, at Brook Farm, at least for the twelve-month period for which we have extensive documentation. Does this mean, then, that Charles Dana's boast in New York in April 1844 that the Brook Farmers had abolished domestic servitude was nothing more than an exaggeration intended to impress his fellow delegates?

To return to the table for a moment before answering that question, it should be noted that five of the women are married, and four are not. The one man on the list, Peter Baldwin, was Brook Farm's baker, so most, if not all, of his 2,773 hours of work were credited as a domestic activity. The table, abbreviated as it is, suggests right away that, while unmarried people may have made up 75 percent of the population at Brook Farm between May 1844 and April 1845, family was nonetheless very much the heart of community life. Mary Ann Ripley, George's sister, was the hardest-working member of the community, when measured in hours. Not far behind her were Mary Dwight and her daughter Fanny, and Rebecca Codman and her daughter Sarah. Anne Dana was the eighteen-year-old sister of Charles, and Maria Pratt was the wife of Minot, both of whom were original shareholders and had been with the Ripleys from the beginning of Brook Farm's existence.

Before jumping to hasty conclusions, however, about women and work at the West Roxbury community, it is important to expand the context slightly and look at the next ten hardest-working members of the community in terms of total number of hours worked, as shown in table 2. The first observation to make is that seven of the next ten hardest-working Brook Farmers were men. The initial impression of community work from the first table is now different. Of the twenty hardest-working members of the community, twelve were women, and eight were men.

A second observation to make is that table 2 further reinforces the point above about the importance of family in Brook Farm's daily operations. Seven of the second ten hardest-working members of the community were directly related to the ten hardest-working members in the first table.

If we broaden the context a bit more and include the next ten hardest-working people, we discover that nine were men, as shown in table 3. So, in fact, of the thirty hardest-working Brook Farmers for the twelve-month period from May 1844 to April 1845, seventeen were men and thirteen were women. Once again, three family names from this table are already quite familiar from the previous two tables: Codman, Ripley, and Dwight.

The point of citing these data, however, is not to argue that women worked harder than men, or that men worked harder than women at Brook Farm. The real point to make is that Charles Dana's claim about abolishing domestic servitude in the West Roxbury community may not have been an exaggeration at all. We can determine more precisely whether it was or not if we examine the kind of work that women and men actually performed in the community. Was work at Brook Farm prescribed along traditional gender lines? Women to the kitchen,

TABLE 2

Second Ten Hardest-Working Brook Farmers, May 1844–April 1845

	Name (M=married; S=single)	*Gender*	*Hours Worked*
11	Dwight, Marianne (S)	Female	2,666
12	Ripley, George (M)	Male	2,538
13	Salisbury, Charles (S)	Male	2,506
14	Dana, Charles (S)	Male	2,460
15	Ryckman, Jean (S)	Female	2,436
16	Cheswell, William (M)	Male	2,435
17	Teel, William (S)	Male	2,404
18	Pratt, Minot (M)	Male	2,381
19	Whitehouse, Sarah (M)	Female	2,374
20	Westacott, Robert (S)	Male	2,372

TABLE 3

Third Ten Hardest-Working Brook Farmers, May 1844–April 1845

	Name (M=married; S=single)	*Gender*	*Hours Worked*
21	Colson, Nathaniel (M)	Male	2,339
22	Capen, Ephraim (S)	Male	2,331
23	Reynolds, Jeremiah (S)	Male	2,329
24	Codman, John (M)	Male	2,322
25	Ripley, Sophia (M)	Female	2,321
26	Codman, John T. (S)	Male	2,298
27	Dwight, John S. (S)	Male	2,271
28	Cheever, John (S)	Male	2,254
29	Tirell, Job (S)	Male	2,214
30	Butterfield, John (S)	Male	2,198

please, and men, grab those spades and hoes! Did women engage primarily in domestic work? Were men responsible for the agricultural and mechanical labors in the West Roxbury community?

When Marianne Dwight described her very busy schedule right after her arrival at Brook Farm in April 1844, she referred to a "dormitory group" and a "flower garden group," and she also remarked that "alternation of work" made it less tedious, even pleasant. She was alluding to the organization of labor in the community into "Series" and "Groups," a system instituted when it was decided to embrace Fourierism and, to the extent possible, incorporate some of Charles Fourier's utopian socialist principles into Brook Farm life.

Fourier believed that unrelieved and relentless work, performed daily and mechanically, is contrary to human nature and deadens the soul. Human nature, Fourier believed, is composed of twelve "passions" (what he characterized as five sensitive passions, four social passions, and three regulating passions). One of the twelve passions was what Fourier called the "butterfly passion." We do our best work and accomplish the most when we are able to flit like a butterfly from one activity to another, wherever our passions naturally attract us. It is contrary to human nature to work at the same activity day after day after day, à la Melville's Bartleby, the scrivener. Individual growth and development require variety and change. Alternation of work is therefore healthy and desirable.

Beginning in May 1844, work at Brook Farm was divided into Series and Groups. These are Fourier's terms. A Series was any kind of general activity, such as farming, that comprised a number of different Groups, such as a ploughing group, a planting group, a weeding group, a hoeing group, a harvesting group, and so on. Work at Brook Farm was divided into six Series: an Agricultural Series, a Mechanical Series, a Domestic Series, an Educational Series, a

Waiters Series, and a Second Mechanical Series.[21] This last Series, formally organized in September 1844, was composed almost exclusively of women, whose efforts at making dresses, decorating lampshades, tailoring, and such began to generate significant income for the financially beleaguered community.

So what kinds of Groups made up the different Series at Brook Farm? Beyond the Groups in the Agricultural and Second Mechanical Series, the Mechanical Series consisted mainly of a shoemaking group, a sash-and-blind group, and a Britannia-ware group. The Domestic Series certainly included a baking group, a washing and ironing group, a refectory group, and a dormitory group, among others. It was hoped that the "Mechanical Series," particularly, would generate a reliable stream of income for the community. Unfortunately it did not.

The Waiters Series was just that: a group of young women and men who waited tables at mealtimes, which typically were occasions for lively conversation and banter, as well as much fraternizing between men and women. The Waiters Series, not surprisingly, was particularly popular with Brook Farm's unmarried residents. Of the twenty-nine people who devoted ten or more hours to the Waiters Series, twenty-six were unmarried. Eleven of the twenty-nine were men. It might be expected that women would log the most hours in the Waiters Series because it was a domestic activity, but it was actually Charles Dana who accrued the greatest number of hours at 247, followed closely by Eunice Macdaniel, who devoted 238 hours to this Series. Evidently more than dirty plates passed between Dana and Macdaniel: they married each other in March 1846. So did four other "waiters" who worked together in this Series. Marianne Dwight married John Orvis in December 1845—the only marriage ever performed at Brook Farm—and Sarah R. Codman married Jonathan Butterfield, a printer, two years after they left the community.

The Educational Series was actually the celebrated and progressive Brook Farm School, which consisted of three different programs. The "infant program" was for children below the age of six. Preschool programs throughout the United States today owe much to this early model. It provided childcare for parents so they could work at the farm. The "primary program" was for children six to ten years of age. The "preparatory program" was for boys and girls who were "fitting" (preparing) for college. Of the eighteen Brook Farmers who provided more than 100 hours of instruction in the school, thirteen were women.

The Brook Farm School was widely recognized for the quality and extensiveness of its curriculum, as well as for the superior instruction available there. This is not so surprising when we remember that George Ripley, John S. Dwight, and George P. Bradford were all graduates of both Harvard College and the Harvard Divinity School. Charles Dana too had managed to complete two years at Harvard College. No other American community in the 1840s—eighty-four existed, at one moment or another, in that decade—could boast such highly educated teachers. The fact is, nonetheless, that it was Brook Farm's women who were the real backbone of the school, especially Sophia Ripley, Fanny and Marianne Dwight, Amelia Russell, and Anne Dana. And although they could not boast Harvard degrees themselves, these women were paid exactly the same wages as the men.[22]

It is instructive now to examine the Series to which Brook Farmers were attracted by their "passional" nature. The Brook Farm Labor Record for May 1844 to April 1845 not only lists every hour worked by every person in the community for the twelve-month period, it also lists each Series in which those hours were invested. An examination of this part of the labor record further refines what we know about women and work at Brook Farm.

Table 4 compiles the hours that the ten hardest-working Brook Farmers devoted to each of the six Series. What catches the eye right away in this table is the preponderance of hours that women devoted to the Domestic Series. It has already been noted that Peter Baldwin was Brook Farm's baker, so few or none of his hours in this Series were spent washing and ironing or cleaning rooms with the Dormitory Group. Unfortunately, the labor record only identifies in which Series hours were accrued. It does not tell us to which Groups within a Series an individual devoted his or her time.

Before any hasty conclusions are drawn about gender and domestic work at Brook Farm, it should be remarked first that it is not at all surprising that women chose to perform virtually all the community's domestic work. Who would realistically expect otherwise, given the ethos of the age? The real point is not that women handled nearly all the domestic activities at Brook Farm. Rather it is that women were not required to do any work they did not want to do—domestic or otherwise. That was Dana's point when he spoke to his colleagues in New York in April. There was no domestic servitude at Brook Farm because women were free to engage in whatever kind of labor appealed to them. This may seem a minor distinction, but it is a critical one.

While it is true that many Brook Farm women typically chose to do domestic work in the community (just as men often chose agricultural work), it is also important to observe that domestic work was certainly not the only kind of labor that women did. Individual labor records make this perfectly clear. For instance, Jane Ryckman was credited with a very substantial 943 hours in the Mechanical Series. Also in that Series, Mary Ann Cheswell logged 321 hours and Mary Dwight 192. Dwight's daughter Frances devoted 152 hours to the Mechanical Series. Mary Dwight also found time to devote 261 hours to the Agricultural Series, where Mary Ann Ripley also spent 76 hours of her time during the year. What this table indicates is not just that women completed the bulk

TABLE 4

Ten Hardest-Working Brook Farmers, May 1844–April 1845: Individual Labor Records

Name	*Waiters Series*	*Agricultural Series*	*Mechanical Series*	*Domestic Series*	*Education Series*	*Second Mechanical Series*	*Miscellaneous**
Ripley, Mary Ann	29 hrs	76 hrs	43 hrs	2,481 hrs	0 hrs	24 hrs	369 hrs
Cheswell, Mary Ann	0 hrs	0 hrs	321 hrs	2,108 hrs	3 hrs	174 hrs	271 hrs
Codman, Rebecca	0 hrs	8 hrs	91 hrs	2,287 hrs	81 hrs	204 hrs	187 hrs
Ryckman, Jane	16 hrs	0 hrs	943 hrs	1,181 hrs	40 hrs	121 hrs	531 hrs
Dwight, Frances E.	161 hrs	0 hrs	152 hrs	1,515 hrs	651 hrs	291 hrs	55 hrs
Dana, Anne	126 hrs	15 hrs	18 hrs	1,923 hrs	281 hrs	0 hrs	425 hrs
Baldwin, Peter	0 hrs	257 hrs	27 hrs	2,188 hrs	0 hrs	0 hrs	301 hrs
Dwight, Mary	0 hrs	261 hrs	192 hrs	1,387 hrs	0 hrs	863 hrs	67 hrs
Codman, Sarah R.	228 hrs	0 hrs	71 hrs	2,111 hrs	158 hrs	64 hrs	46 hrs
Pratt, Maria	0 hrs	0 hrs	51 hrs	2,032 hrs	0 hrs	7 hrs	585 hrs

* The Miscellaneous column records hours of labor not directly assigned to one of the six Series. For example, time devoted to serving on any of Brook Farm's many different committees—each Series had its own operational committees—would be credited in the Miscellaneous column. One other important point is that the hours listed for an individual in each Series occasionally do not add up to the total number of hours worked by that individual in the tables listed above. That is because the Functional Series is not included in the Series tables.

of the community's domestic chores but that work in the community was not prescribed along gender lines. Each woman or man chose freely, according to "passional" inclinations.

Table 5, listing the individual labor activities of the next ten hardest-working Brook Farmers, further illustrates this point. Two men, William Cheswell, a carpenter, and William Teel, a shoemaker, logged the most hours in the Mechanical Series, as might be expected, but it should also be noted that Cheswell devoted 126 hours to the Second Mechanical Series—a Series in which women, by far, accrued the most hours—and William Teel was credited with 171 hours in the Domestic Series. Similarly, Minot Pratt, who accumulated 1,445 hours in the Agricultural Series, also devoted 607 hours of his time to the Domestic Series. Three other men on the list also spent considerable time doing work in the Domestic Series. Cabinetmaker Robert Westacott accumulated 215 hours; Charles Dana was credited with 183 hours; and Charles Salisbury, a farmer who gave 2,088 hours to the Agricultural Series, also devoted 147 hours to the Domestic Series.

And what about the three women listed in the table—Marianne Dwight, Jean Ryckman, and Sarah Whitehouse? All three obviously spent considerable time working in the Brook Farm School. Dwight also devoted 131 hours of her time to labors in the Mechanical Series, a Series that attracted Jean Ryckman even more, as her 407 hours of work there indicate.

One name that does not appear in any of the tables above is Caroline Pratt, the daughter of head farmer Minot Pratt and his wife, Maria—not unexpectedly, given that she was just seven years old when the labor record began in May 1844. Caroline, or "Carry" as the Brook Farmers usually called her, was a student in the Brook Farm School, and she would have been the "poster child" for Associationism and Fourierism in America had there been such an honor. Her work record from May 1844 to April 1845 would certainly surprise many parents of younger children today. Carry worked 514 hours at Brook Farm during the twelve-month period, in addition to attending school. Carry was quite an example too of Fourier's "butterfly passion." While obviously not old enough to work in the Education Series, she did manage to log hours in every other Series. Most of her time went to the Domestic Series (301 hours), but she also spent 94 hours in the Agricultural Series, 32 in the Waiters Series, 34 in the Mechanical Series, and 19 in the Second Mechanical Series. She was also credited with 44 hours of Miscellaneous work. All this from a seven-year-old child. Her older brother John, by the way, who was just eleven years old, logged 889 hours of work at Brook Farm during the same twelve-month period, and her eldest brother Frederick, who was thirteen years old, contributed 761 hours of work at the farm during the year. No wonder the Ripleys were so disappointed when

TABLE 5

Second Ten Hardest-Working Brook Farmers, May 1844–April 1845: Individual Labor Records

Name	*Waiters Series*	*Agricultural Series*	*Mechanical Series*	*Domestic Series*	*Education Series*	*Second Mechanical Series*	*Miscellaneous**
Dwight, Mary Ann	21 hrs	0 hrs	131 hrs	1,415 hrs	521 hrs	503 hrs	75 hrs
Ripley, George	0 hrs	301 hrs	14 hrs	31 hrs	591 hrs	0 hrs	1,031 hrs
Salisbury, Charles	5 hrs	2,088 hrs	165 hrs	147 hrs	0 hrs	0 hrs	101 hrs
Dana, Charles	241 hrs	587 hrs	6 hrs	183 hrs	521 hrs	3 hrs	584 hrs
Ryckman, Jean	38 hrs	0 hrs	407 hrs	1,404 hrs	193 hrs	105 hrs	289 hrs
Cheswell, William	0 hrs	38 hrs	2,202 hrs	0 hrs	7 hrs	126 hrs	62 hrs
Teel, William	78 hrs	29 hrs	2,035 hrs	171 hrs	0 hrs	0 hrs	91 hrs
Pratt, Minot	0 hrs	1,445 hrs	203 hrs	607 hrs	9 hrs	0 hrs	117 hrs
Whitehouse, Sarah	35 hrs	0 hrs	31 hrs	1,749 hrs	253 hrs	191 hrs	101 hrs
Westacott, Robert	0 hrs	19 hrs	1,995 hrs	215 hrs	32 hrs	0 hrs	111 hrs

* The Miscellaneous column records hours of labor not directly assigned to one of the six Series. For example, time devoted to serving on any of Brook Farm's many different committees—each Series had its own operational committees—would be credited in the Miscellaneous column. One other important point is that the hours listed for an individual in each Series occasionally do not add up to the total number of hours worked by that individual in the tables listed above. That is because the Functional Series is not included in the Series tables.

Minot and Maria Pratt decided to leave Brook Farm in April 1845 and move the family to nearby Concord.

If Carry Pratt might have served as the poster child for Associationism and Fourierism in America, then Marianne Dwight would certainly have been the ideal choice for a poster highlighting what Brook Farm could mean for women. Dwight spent three-and-a-half years there, arriving at the beginning of the Fourierist period in April 1844 and staying until its ultimate collapse in October 1847. Dwight's extensive correspondence is the most detailed surviving record that we have of day-to-day life at Brook Farm, but it is also of course a record of her own life there, specifically the opportunities afforded by the community to nurture her talents, and to "LIVE IN ALL THE FACULTIES OF THE SOUL," as Elizabeth Palmer Peabody had so memorably phrased it in an early article promoting Brook Farm.[23]

Immediately upon her arrival at Brook Farm, Dwight complained to brother Frank about the amount of work that needed to be done. There were "so few women to do the work," she said, "that we have to be nearly all the time about it" (8). Two weeks later she complained again to her friend Anna Q. T. Parsons, although already her disgruntlement had been softened by the fact that it was "so pleasant" at Brook Farm, "even with all the work!" (13). Dwight was twenty-eight years old when she arrived, so her expectations likely had been tempered by experience. By July she could say to brother Frank that she liked her life in the West Roxbury community "better than any" she had "ever before realized," although, she recognized, "the ideal of true life is ever *before* me—we cannot yet attain unto it" (26). Two months later she reported to Frank again, this time to say: "I would not exchange this life [at Brook Farm] for any I have ever led. . . . Life is so full and rich here, that I feel as if my experience were valuable, and I were *growing* somewhat faster than when I lived in Boston" (41).

Dwight's sudden enthusiasm for Brook Farm life was probably due, in part, to the countless social and educational opportunities that were open to her and other women (and men). But her comment to Frank about personal growth must also have been inspired by the work she was doing in the community, specifically the opportunities that had already been made available to her for exercising her considerable natural gifts. Sophia Ripley, Amelia Russell, and other women recognized those gifts right away, and they immediately enlisted Dwight to be a member of a group "for making fancy articles for sale in Boston" (38).

At a time when Brook Farm was sorely in need of regular sources of income, Dwight and the "fancy group" began manufacturing such things as women's caps, collars, and under-sleeves, which they sent to one or two merchants in Boston for sale. Dwight assured Frank in early July 1844 that their manufacture was "quite workmanlike," and that they "realize[d] considerable money (!!)" from it. For Dwight, however, the real goal of doing "productive labor" and earning money was the higher goal to which it could lead, and that was "nothing less than the elevation of woman to independence, and an acknowledged equality with man" (32). When she wrote to Parsons in August, Dwight was quite emphatic about what women needed to do: "Women must become producers of marketable articles," she stated. "Women must make money and earn their support independently of man" (32).

Toward that end, Dwight and several other women borrowed "twenty-five or thirty dollars." With the loan, the "fancy group" purchased materials and "made up in one week about forty-five dollars worth of elegant and tasteful caps, capes, collars, under-sleeves, etc., etc.," which they sent to a Boston merchant who agreed to "take all" they could produce (32).

Dwight immediately began imagining the possibilities for marketing the fancy goods. If they succeeded, she told Parsons, other women would want to come to Brook Farm to "take part in [their] fancy work." More women would mean a better distribution of work for the women already at Brook Farm, which, in turn, would mean more time to create new goods. Eventually, Dwight thought, profits would accumulate so much that other branches of business could be started, and "all [their] proceeds" could "be applied to the elevation of woman forever" (32). If woman could become the equal of man, Dwight wondered, "what intellectual developments may we not expect?" This, Dwight told Parsons, was really the great work of Association.

Dwight's greatest natural gift was her ability to paint, particularly with watercolors. Her favorite subjects were the flora and fauna that she found at and around Brook Farm. In spring she painted the brown star cluster of the wood anemone against its thin green leaves. In May there were blue violets, and in June the delicate pinkish lantern bulbs of mountain laurel before they burst into flower. July at the farm showcased the purple and yellow pointed bulbs of woody nightshade. And in August and September there were touch-me-nots, fringed gentians, and blue asters. Individual leaves also caught Dwight's eye. At Brook Farm, dogwood, witch hazel, maple, oak, and whortleberry leaves were plentiful, depending on the time of year. Birds were everywhere too, and Dwight painted the American goldfinches, hummingbirds, blue jays, and scarlet tanagers that visited the farm in different seasons.[24]

These paintings of flora and fauna on lampshades, fans, card-boxes, and the like quickly became very popular. More importantly, they generated relatively substantial, much-needed income for the Brook Farm community. In January 1845, Dwight informed brother Frank that she was "engaged to paint some lamp shades to send into Boston" (71). The lampshades were such a hit that Dwight found herself devoting most of her time to producing them. In mid-February, she wrote to Frank, "I have given my chief attention this week to the lamp shades, have painted nine" (77). Less than two weeks later, she wrote to Parsons that she was painting six to seven hours a day. "I have more demands for lamp shades and other painted fancy things than I can at present supply," she told her friend. "I seem to have got myself into business at present" (80).

It quickly proved to be a financially rewarding business. Dwight and the Brook Farmers priced each painted lampshade at one dollar, and evidently prospective buyers were not deterred: "My lamp shades continue in great demand," Dwight told Frank in March 1845. Dwight and the Brook Farmers charged even more for painted fans—"a dollar and a half apiece"—probably because they were more detailed and required more work. (Dwight charged "fifty cents a sheet" for painted wildflowers.)

We can only wonder today just how extensive Dwight and the Brook Farmers' success might have become had circumstances in the community not turned out as they did. In early November 1845, Brook Farmer John Allen returned to the community from a visit to Boston, where his son Fred had became infected with smallpox. By the time it was realized that Fred's nagging cough was not simply a cold but smallpox, the boy had already infected many people in the community. "Our carelessness," Dwight sadly acknowledged to Anna Parsons in late November, "has been very blamable" (135).

The outbreak was devastating to Brook Farm. The school had to be shut down, and other operations all but came to a halt. Many had to be quarantined. By the time the crisis finally passed several weeks later, hard winter was settling in. Former students did not return to school; new ones were difficult to find. Snow-covered roads and ice made it difficult to move "fancy goods" and other marketable items, such as Dwight's lampshades and fans, to Boston merchants.

Students of Brook Farm already know the tragic story of the troubled and protracted year-and-a-half following the outbreak of smallpox, so it need not be repeated here. It is enough to say that the devastating fire that destroyed the nearly completed 175' x 40' "unitary dwelling" in March 1846—following so quickly after the smallpox—was too much for the heavily indebted Brook Farmers. Seven thousand dollars had been invested in the "Phalanstery," and the building had never been insured. Multiple schemes for righting the community were tried. But recovery was not to be.

For Marianne Dwight, Sophia Ripley, Georgiana Bruce (Kirby), Amelia Russell, and many other women who had lived at Brook Farm, there was at least the satisfaction of having discovered a quality of life that women elsewhere could hardly begin to imagine—a life that was free from domestic servitude, and a life that provided social, educational, and vocational opportunities for personal growth for women the same as for men. This uniquely nurturing and affirming community enabled Brook Farm women to know the "solemn joy" that comes, as Marianne Dwight herself realized in 1845, from "the consciousness that there is something worth living for" (97). It is not too much to say that, for women, this consciousness was more likely to be discovered at Brook Farm than anywhere else in the antebellum United States.

NOTES

I want to express my sincere thanks to Joel Myerson and Leslie Perrin Wilson for their careful reading of an earlier version of this chapter.

1. Eighty-four utopian communities were in existence, at one moment or another, in the 1840s. As Ralph Waldo Emerson so keenly observed to Thomas Carlyle at the beginning of the decade, "Not a reading man but has a draft of a new Community in his waistcoat pocket." See Robert Fogarty, *Dictionary of American Communal and Utopian History* (Westport, Conn.: Greenwood Press, 1980), 173–95; and *The Correspondence of Emerson and Carlyle*, ed. Joseph Slater (New York: Columbia Univ. Press, 1964), 283.
2. Nathaniel Hawthorne, *The Letters, 1813–1843*, ed. William Charvat et al., in *The Centenary Edition of the Writings of Nathaniel Hawthorne*, ed. Thomas Woodson et al., 23 vols. (Columbus: Ohio State Univ. Press, 1963–97), 15:553.
3. Carol Kolmerten, *Women in Utopia: The Ideology of Gender in the American Owenite Communities* (Bloomington: Indiana Univ. Press, 1990), 175. Kolmerten's remark refers to single women, but it certainly applies with equal force to all women at Brook Farm.
4. T. S. Arthur, *The Lady at Home* (Philadelphia: J. & J. L. Gihon, 1847), 178; Barbara Welter, "The Cult of True Womanhood: 1820–1860," *American Quarterly* 18 (Summer 1966): 151. Welter identifies four "cardinal virtues" by which a woman judged herself and was judged by others: piety, purity, submissiveness, and domesticity. Brook Farm women were certainly pious, pure, and domestically inclined, but not at all in the contemporary sense of these terms in middle-class antebellum New England. And Brook Farm women were certainly not submissive. Since Welter's article in 1966, of course, antebellum women's history (and beyond) has been virtually rewritten. For studies showing the greater complexity of women's lives, see for instance Monika M. Elbert, ed., *Separate Spheres No More* (Tuscaloosa: Univ. of Alabama Press, 2000); and Sandra Harbert Petrulionis, *"To Set This World Right": The Antislavery Movement in Thoreau's Concord* (Ithaca, N.Y.: Cornell Univ. Press, 2006); Marshall; and Wayne.
5. See, for example, Georgiana Bruce Kirby, *Years of Experience* (New York: Putnam's Sons, 1887), 89–189; Amelia Russell, *Home Life of the Brook Farm Association* (Boston: Little, Brown, 1900); Marianne Dwight, *Letters from Brook Farm, 1844–1847*, ed. Amy L. Reed (Poughkeepsie, N.Y.: Vassar College, 1928); Ora Gannett Sedgwick, "A Girl of Sixteen at Brook Farm," in *The Brook Farm Book*, ed. Joel Myerson (New York: Garland, 1987), 263–83; and "Rebecca Codman Butterfield's Reminiscences of Brook Farm," ed. Joel Myerson, *New England Quarterly* 65 (December 1992): 603–30.
6. Lindsay Swift, *Brook Farm: Its Members, Scholars, and Visitors* (New York: Macmillan, 1900), 53.
7. Dwight, *Letters from Brook Farm*, 40; this collection of Dwight's letters is hereafter cited parenthetically.
8. Fuller spent a week at Brook Farm in October 1842, "where [she] gave *conversations* on alternate evenings with the husking parties" (*LMF*, 3:97). Fuller's essay appeared in the *Dial* 4 (July 1843): 14.

9. Brook Farm did not officially change its name to Brook Farm Phalanx, however, until May 1845.
10. Dana's "Address" was printed in full in Albert Brisbane's *The Phalanx*, along with all the convention proceedings, in the number for 20 April 1844, 113–15.
11. Dana distinguished the third point from the first, about domestic servitude, by noting that Brook Farmers performed labor for the benefit of all, not "for the benefit of the capitalist, as it is in civilized society" ("Address," 114).
12. Ibid.
13. See, for example, "The Anarchy of Labor," 2 August 1845, 115; "Labor in New York: Its Circumstances, Conditions and Rewards," 6 September 1845, 202; 13 September 1845, 218; 20 September 1845, 232; 27 September 1845, 246; 4 October 1845, 259; and 11 October 1845, 280. Conditions for women at the Lowell Mills in New England were not much better. See Thomas Dublin, "Women, Work, and Protest in the Early Lowell Mills: 'The Oppressing Hand of Avarice Would Enslave Us,'" *Labor History* 16 (1975): 99–116.
14. The labor records are among the Brook Farm Papers of the Massachusetts Historical Society. I am particularly grateful to Peter Drummey for the valuable assistance he has unfailingly provided over many years. The Brook Farmers kept a detailed log of labor activities because, as Dana noted in his remarks in New York in April, all labor was dignified and deserved equal compensation. The log tracked the actual labor performed by each person living in the community from May 1844 to April 1845, literally to the minute. No other extended labor records have survived from the Brook Farm community—if, in fact, they ever existed.
15. This number does not include four people—three men and one woman—who are listed in the labor record but who did not work the equivalent of one full day during the twelve-month period. The names of a few of Brook Farm's paying boarders, such as Charles King Newcomb and several of its resident students, such as Theodore Parker's ward, George Colburn, do not appear anywhere in the labor record.
16. For example, when Marianne Dwight wrote to her friend Anna Q. T. Parsons in late August 1844 to invite her to visit Brook Farm, she remarked: "[I do not] know when you would most enjoy coming, our population is so changing. . . . Amelia Russell is now absent. . . . Fanny Macdaniel has gone to New York, and will probably stay a fortnight or longer" (30). The common cold, it might be noted, plagued the Brook Farmers as often as it does us today and accounts for much missed work time. When someone caught a cold it seems to have spread immediately from one end of the community to the other.
17. Brook Farm was not unique in this regard. Christopher Clark has noted, for example, that Dolly Stetson and her husband James, members of the Northampton (Massachusetts) Community, were related to "no fewer than twenty-seven individuals" in the community over the course of its existence (1842–46). See "A Mother and Her Daughters at the Northampton Community: New Evidence on Women in Utopia," *New England Quarterly* 75 (December 2002): 556.
18. Spring's remark is quoted in Lillie Buffum Chace Wyman and Arthur Crawford Wyman, *Elizabeth Buffum Chace, 1806–1899*, 2 vols. (Boston: W. B. Clarke, 1914), 1:92–93.
19. Dwight's unpublished letters from Brook Farm are at the Massachusetts Historical Society. See also Sterling F. Delano and Joel Myerson, "Letters from Brook Farm: A Comprehensive Checklist of Surviving Correspondence," *Resources for American Literary Study* 31 (2006): 95–123.

20. I am grateful to former graduate student Carol F. Capitani, who initially "crunched" the numbers recorded in the Brook Farm Labor Record. I have since substantially revised those tabulations based on information not available when they were first calculated.
21. There was also a Functional Series but it is not included here because relatively few Brook Farmers ever accrued work hours in it. The Functional Series seems to have been administrative in nature because the people who accrued the most hours were Mary Ann Ripley, George Ripley, and Charles Dana.
22. It is true that other notable antebellum "utopian" communities promised gender equality, but they rarely practiced it. See, for example, Jean Pfaelzer, "The Sentimental Promise and the Utopian Myth: Rebecca Harding Davis's 'The Harmonists' and Louisa May Alcott's 'Transcendental Wild Oats,'" *ATQ*, n.s., 3 (1989): 85–100; and Kolmerten, *Women in Utopia*.
23. Elizabeth Palmer Peabody, "Plan of the West Roxbury Community," *Dial* 2 (January 1842): 361–72.
24. Amy L. Reed included one of Dwight's paintings when she published eighty of Dwight's letters in *Letters from Brook Farm, 1844–1847*. The black-and-white image of a columbine, however, hardly does justice to the original, which was painted in bright watercolors.

INTERLUDE

Margaret Fuller, from "The Liberty Bell," in *The Liberty Bell, by Friends of Freedom*, ed. Maria Weston Chapman (Boston: Anti-Slavery Fair, 1846), 80–88.

It was a legend of Germany, that, in the time when the faith of Christendom was lively, and her heart aspiring to be devout, if she had not sufficient clearness of mental view to avoid great mistakes as to the way, a certain society of knights had vowed, with the straitest vow, their service to the oppressed in every part of their country. And so faithful was their adherence to this vow, that Heaven took them under its especial care and allowed them supernatural assistance, that they might multiply good deeds more and more. In their chapel hung a bell, whose silver blazonry chronicled the acts of many who had imitated their Master not only in purity and self-denial, but, also, in active benevolence towards their fellow-men. Its silver sound was, in itself, almost a prayer. It was a beautiful and solemn sight when this sound called many votaries to kneel before the altar. . . .

And those hearts, once thus awakened, retained a sensibility so delicate that when any act of oppression was about to be perpetrated on the earth, the votary of this most holy order, who was nearest, heard in the air the warning sound of that consecrated bell. Then did he immediately long, with all his force, to embrace the occasion,—not counting the cost, not to be deterred by weariness, sickness, or scenes of happiness to be forsaken. The means of reaching the scene where his devoir was to be done, were instantly afforded him. On the land a white steed bore him, on the waters white swans impelled his bark. . . .

This legend made a deep impression on me, and though, even in the fairest visionary time of youth, I never met in the greenwood or descried upon the stream one of those chosen servants, with his attendant snowy steed, or swan, and the seal of the shining ones upon his brow, yet I believed such an association could not have died out. . . .

One day I read, in the album of a distinguished contemporary, this signature,—"Dan. O'Connell, of the Order of Liberators." Of this Daniel, I, at that time, knew little; not enough to judge whether he, like the great Israelite, was one able to brave the fiery furnace, and the lion's den, and the silken lures of a court, and speak truth always with a poet's power. But it flashed upon me at once, that the Order to which he vowed himself must be that of the Consecrated Bell, under a new form.

Yes! it is surely so. We know too much now to be content with merely freeing individual victims from their chains. We know enough to war with the errors which forge them. We must liberate men, but we must also establish the principles of liberty for man. We need not the white steed to show us the way; it is now too well marked to be missed by any who choose to see it.

But now, more than ever, do we need the consecration of the spirit which should precede, the pure tone of conscience which shall direct, our action! . . .

We stand, it has been said, in a time of revolution; so do men ever. Yet that this is a moment of great and peculiar importance, we do believe. Principles cannot die; but the earthly embodiment of one of the greatest that give man his claims to spiritual hope, lies gasping with a wound that threatens a long trance, or convulsion. Never did the earth more need the salt to show its savor. Bring the sacred bell; and at its sound must move, before the sincere worshipper, millions of spirits yet unborn to the woes of this world; the scenes of centuries to come demanding his agency to avert evils that shame imagination. Bring, then, the silver bell; but ye who obey its summons, believe, also, that the time demands, and God commands, a deeper, larger wisdom, a severer devotion than those that enabled Milton and Washington to leave us their legacy. We have it to pay over, principal and interest, to our heirs; the mint is ready; let not the pieces which bear the name of Texas be stamped on the reverse with slavery, and the lone star be given for a throne to him who has forfeited the title of Lucifer, except as bitter mockery. Let it not be so, if well-considered purpose, if flame-like ardor and purity of life, can prevent it. Or, if you feel yourselves unfit to aid in this cause, consider well whether you forever forego admission to the Order of Liberators, since, if you forbear this test of service, you incur a vast debt to humanity, which fate may not, in your own age, afford you opportunity to cancel. Consider well, but not slowly, for the time is short.

Sentimental Transcendentalism and Political Affect

Child and Fuller in New York

JEFFREY STEELE

In the 1840s, after Lydia Maria Child and (later) Margaret Fuller moved from Massachusetts to New York City, their writing changed dramatically. Deeply invested in questions of social reform, they found that urban conditions exposed them to a new, challenging set of problems: not just slavery and the struggle for woman's rights but also widespread poverty, accelerating immigration, capital punishment, the need for prison and asylum reform, and sectarian conflict. Child's 1843 volume *Letters from New-York* and Fuller's 1844–46 *New-York Tribune* essays reveal the ways in which they adapted their writing to the complex demands of the city and to new opportunities provided by liberal urban publications. As an editor and writer for the *National Anti-Slavery Standard* (where her New York letters first appeared), Child was deeply committed to analyzing and changing the political values of her contemporaries. But she also attempted to broaden the reach of the *Standard* by turning it into a "family newspaper" that combined antislavery essays with a broad range of "literary and miscellaneous matter." Child's column "Letters from New-York" (later repackaged as a book) furthered her aim of reaching a wide audience.[1] Similarly, Fuller's work as literary editor and front page columnist for Horace Greeley's *Tribune* "afford[ed] . . . her a far more various view of life than any [she] ever before was in" (*LMF*, 3:256). Like Child, she was profoundly affected by the challenge of reaching an expansive audience and shaping their opinions.

In their urban journalism, both Child and Fuller moved far beyond their transcendentalist roots into rhetorical modes anchored in their struggle for social justice. Emerson had taught them a powerful discourse of personal transformation and human dignity, but what his writing lacked was a coherent analysis of the structures shaping public behavior and values. Pioneering a hybrid mode of writing that I have termed "sentimental transcendentalism," Child and Fuller combined the transcendentalist commitment to the self-reliant self with a more general awareness of how public feelings shape political action. What became clear to them in the city was that social change has an *affective*, as well as an intellectual, component. People's hearts, as well as their minds, needed to be changed; for, otherwise, they would remain frozen in habituated patterns of perception and behavior. This made it necessary to generate patterns of self-awareness that would enable the public to see and *feel* themselves in a different light. As Child and Fuller discovered, existing discourses of sentimentalist reform, focused on political sympathy, provided a powerful tool for measuring collective emotional responses. But often, such discourses tended to mystify the precise dynamics of social change. The challenge facing Child and Fuller was to mesh their transcendentalist commitment to personal growth with an understanding of the public feelings motivating civic life.

Readers of Lydia Maria Child have long noted that her writing contains both sentimentalist and transcendentalist strands. Her earliest writing, books such as *Hobomok* (1827), relied on sentimentalist patterns of response by promoting "sympathetic relationship," "the role of the heart," and the power of maternal love.[2] But as she developed, Child was also deeply influenced by the ideas of such transcendentalists as Ralph Waldo Emerson and Margaret Fuller. In the 1820s, Child was introduced to Emerson by her brother Convers Francis; and, by the 1830s, she was attending Emerson's lectures in Concord.[3] Child's *Letters from New-York* is so filled with transcendentalist echoes that her editor, Bruce Mills, characterizes the book as a "revealing expression of Transcendentalist thought," expressing Child's belief (along with Emerson) in "the divinity of the individual."[4] But Child's dual investment in sentimentalism and transcendentalism has long posed a problem for her readers. On the one hand, Mills stresses the transcendentalist dimension of her writing, arguing that she moved from sentimentalist models of reform to a "Transcendentalist . . . literary method" that "further enhanced the ability to move readers."[5] Adopting the opposite view, Heather Roberts acknowledges Child's spiritual commitments but finds in her writing an overriding deployment of political sympathy.[6] Most recently, Travis Foster has begun to merge these two critical perspectives by arguing that Child developed a mode of what he terms "transcendental sympathy" modeled on "universal love." But rather than exploring the implications of this insight, Foster ultimately narrows his critical focus to moments when this transcendentalist legacy is supplanted by a conventional, middle-class perception.[7] But if Child's goal in New York (as Laura Mielke phrases the problem) was "to unite the transcendental pursuit of truth and the reformist goal of social perfection," we have yet to determine how these two supposedly antithetical agendas functioned together.[8] While it is easy to demonstrate that Child, along with Fuller, based her rhetoric of reform upon a model of either shared sentiment or transcendentalist idealism, readers have found it difficult to explain how these two modes combined, giving focused sentiment a universalizing power equivalent to that found in Emerson's writing.

I offer the term "sentimental transcendentalism" to this critical conversation in order to remind us that Child (and Margaret Fuller) created a distinctive discourse that *blended* Emerson's commitment to transcendentalist vision with a political sympathy binding readers together. What resulted from this dual literary investment was a hybrid mode of writing that supplemented Emerson's commitment to the expansion of individual being by adding to it a consideration of public feeling. Child reveals, in the process, a strain of transcendentalist insight that was latent but not fully developed in Emerson's writing. Imagining like Emerson a universal ground of being, she insists (in a move that revises Emerson) that this ground is registered in moments of collective *feeling*. In order to pursue this aspect of Child's writing, I shall contrast the concept of "affect" to personalized conceptions of "sympathy" or "sentiment." This critical move is necessary because many readers continue to characterize sentiment and sympathy as individualized responses, a projection of feeling *onto* a suffering other, without attending to the linkage *between* such personal response and more general climates of thought and feeling.

The generalization of sentiment beyond individual response is an important strategy for writers who focus on feeling as a political instrument. Utilizing the primary tool of moral suasion, both William Lloyd Garrison and Frederick Douglass stress that their readers need to address social injustice with a feeling heart and not a heart of stone. Child shares this commitment to public feeling, as she moves beyond private sentiment into the examination of the condition of *public* feeling as a key indicator of social justice. One of the primary goals of her *Letters from New-York* is to measure the changing condition of what she calls *"the public heart"*[9]—the transcendent, collective foundation of feelings and values that circulate throughout society. The concept of "affect" is the key to understanding the way that both Child and Fuller link transcendentalist insight to such sentimentalist response. "Affect" is a useful category, because it generalizes and desubjectifies the personalized concept of "sentiment." In the words of Gregory J. Seigworth and Melissa Gregg, critical discourses that mobilize affect as a structure of shared feeling and human potential "have progressively left behind the interiorized self or subjectivity." Instead, they turn to "atmospheres of sociality, crowd behaviors, contagions of feeling, [and] matters of belonging."[10] We find a similar agenda in the writing of Child and Fuller, as they consider the collective feelings that shape the political will, reinforcing apathy or motivating political action.

One of the places where Child found an idea of collective being was in Ralph Waldo Emerson's concept of the Over-soul. Imagining a universal field of transcendent, spiritual energy, Emerson consistently asserted that the key to self-reliance lies in the ability to tap into the potentially expressive energies in this fount of divine energy, what he characterized in *Nature* as "the unfathomed sea of thought and virtue" (*CW*, 1:28) and in "Self-Reliance" as the lap of "immense intelligence" (*CW*, 2:37). Frequently, Emerson associated linkage to the Over-soul with the influx of an illumination and with the acquisition of "divine wisdom" (*CW*, 2:38). He even went so far as to assert that in "the hour of vision . . . [t]he soul raised over passion . . . perceives the self-existence of Truth and Right" (*CW*, 2:39–40). At such moments, Emerson suggested that the perception of Truth involves the suspension of feeling in favor of a pure process of unimpassioned illumination. The goal, he argued, is to aspire to apprehend the "divine idea which each of us represents"—a realm of truth found in the "highest mind" (*CW*, 2:28). Absorbing the concept of the Over-soul, Child learned from Emerson that connection to a universalized ground of being could link the self to generalized standards of spiritual truth and social justice. But, from other moments in his writing, she learned something more. Despite Emerson's emphasis upon the importance of the "soul" being "raised *over* passion," he also argued in places that collective feeling might play an important role in social reform. In "Man the Reformer," for example, he asserted that the reform impulse opens "a secret door into the heart" and can shine "new light . . . in upon a thousand hearts" (*CW*, 1:146). Commercialism and commodification, he insisted later in the essay, lead to "a sequestration from the sentiments of generosity and love" (*CW*, 1:148). Elsewhere, in "The Over-Soul," Emerson evocatively characterized the Over-soul both as "the influx of the Divine mind into our mind" *and* as the "common heart" (*CW*, 2:166, 160).

Emerson's dual characterization of the Over-soul as divine foundation and "common heart" suggests that Child's merger of transcendentalism with sentimentalism amplifies affective tendencies already found in his writing. But, in Emerson's case, the turn toward affect remained latent and unactualized. Emerson referred to affect, the "common heart," as an ideal without deploying feeling and affect as tools of political perception. Vision and affect remained separate, as parallel but unconnected streams, as Emerson talked about feeling without actually performing it. The problem with such a position is highlighted by Elspeth Probyn: "An abstract way of approaching affect and emotion," she observes, "places the writing itself in an uninterested relation to affect. This is a contradiction in terms—affects are inherently interested."[11] What Child found in Emerson was an abstract model of social affect, but what she supplied in *Letters from New-York* was an engaged awareness of the affective forces that energize abstraction, putting it into motion. While Emerson's concept of the Over-soul contained a latent idea of affect, Child developed it by using concepts of affect and shared feeling to amplify individual moments of sentiment, making them more audible. In the process, she established a collective emotional field that was analogous to the collective spiritual field (the Over-soul) that Emerson used to gather together individual moments of illumination. This rhetorical move created the ideal literary medium for measuring the distance between images of perfected being and the unjust social and political conditions that limited the self's development. The move toward social justice, whether the abolition of slavery or the amelioration of urban poverty, depended on the dual capacity to imagine more equitable conditions and to mobilize a collective will (energized through affect) that might change the world.

At key moments in *Letters from New-York*, Child replicates many of Emerson's central insights. She observes that one must be true to one's "own genuine, inward experience" and not be seduced by the hollow forms pursued by most individuals (*LNY*, 58). "The outward," she asserts elsewhere, "is but a seeming and a show; the inward alone is permanent and real" (*LNY*, 56). "True culture" for most individuals, she summarizes, "consists in the full and free development of individual character, regulated by their *own* perceptions of what is true, and their *own* love of what is good" (*LNY*, 154; emphasis in original). One should follow "the oracle *within*" (*LNY*, 101; emphasis in original) and not be influenced by "public" opinion, "trading interest," and "local prejudice" (*LNY*, 102). In general, Child follows Emerson in contrasting "public opinion" against "inward *perceptions*" (*LNY*, 101; emphasis in original). Her general tendency (like that of Emerson and Fuller) is to map the changing condition of the inner self by contrasting an inner illumination against what she depicts as an outer realm of "simulation and false shows" (*LNY*, 57). Exposed to the "despotic sway of custom and public opinion" (*LNY*, 177), Child observes, we are surrounded by what seems to be "the false environment of civilized life" (*LNY*, 164). While such passages seem to reify concepts like "custom" and "public opinion" as external forces, Child reminds her readers that they already exist *within* an individual's mind as collective social energies that—like the Over-soul—intersect with the self.

In order to address the impact of collective values, Child shows her readers that both spiritual illumination and the awareness of social pressure reside in the same place—in human sensibility. Contrasting the soul's "pure aspirations" against habituated patterns of "selfishness" (*LNY*, 168), she centers attention upon the overall "spirit" of both the self and society (*LNY*, 34). Identifying her own transforming sensibility as a tool that might register the impact of social injustice and human suffering, Child stresses the importance of "see[ing] with the heart" (*LNY*, 173). Defining it as one of her literary goals "to speak to hardened and suffering hearts" (*LNY*, 74), Child frequently focuses upon her desire to maintain a sympathy for the "beseeching looks" and "hungry eyes" she encounters (*LNY*, 59). But it is important to note that Child generalizes sentiment into a concept of *public* feeling. Using her heart as an organ of moral perception, she insists that she is registering not only the permutations of her own emotional response to the city but also the larger structures of affect that orient its population. She contends, for example, that "[her] heart" is linked to "the universal heart of man" (*LNY*, 115). Registering the various phases of what she terms "the public heart" (*LNY*, 63), she measures the interweaving of private feeling with public affect.

In Letter 16, for example, Child records the emotional impact of a fire that destroyed an acquaintance's garden. Demonstrating one of the key aspects of sentimental writing, she ponders the way in which one's sense of loss is affected by personal relationships. "Our real losses," she reflects, "are those in which the heart is concerned" (*LNY*, 71)—a passage that confirms Joanne Dobson's argument that the sentimental focuses on the "ties that bind." According to Dobson, "The principal theme of the sentimental text is the desire for bonding, and it is affiliation on the plane of emotion, sympathy, nurturance . . . for which sentimental writers and readers yearn."[12] Often, the straining and fracturing of relational ties (whether through oppression or death) become the primary focus of sentimentalist writing. In such cases, the loss or suffering of a child, friend, or significant other provides the primary topic upon which the heart dwells. But what is important to notice is that Child does not stop with her *personal* emotional response. Instead, she generalizes her sorrow into a principle of collective feeling, a definition of affect that helps her readers map the invisible climate of "moral sentiment" that shapes their response to the world (*LNY*, 152). "*Our* hearts are aching," she observes, "for all round *us* comes a voice of wailing from the homeless and the impoverished" (*LNY*, 73; emphasis added). At such moments, expressions of private sentiment turn into reflections on public affect.

This process of generalization becomes highly visible when Child considers the corruption of public feeling into debased forms. Journeying to Blackwell's Island, she notices that the criminality of many young men is shaped by the affective "contagion" of "the fierce, speculating spirit of the age" (*LNY*, 128). Such public feeling corrodes the heart, which becomes "petrified" (*LNY*, 125). Arguing that the prisoners she encounters have the same "passions" as her readers (*LNY*, 129), Child focuses on the way in which the human heart is shaped by the affective ground in which it is located. Elsewhere, her understanding of the disastrous consequences of corrupted public feeling is even more evident in her discussion of the bloodlust intensified by executions. In Letter 31, for example, she analyzes the violent waves of sentiment that coursed throughout the crowd on the day of John C. Colt's planned execution for murder. The "spirit of murder," she observes, "was rife among the dense crowd eager for blood" (*LNY*, 137). After Colt avoided execution by committing suicide, the prison caught on fire—an event that Child uses to symbolize the public feeling corrupting the crowd. The flames, she reflects, were like "angry spirits" that "had escaped on fiery wings." This release of affective energy, she notes, influenced her as well: "Society had kindled all around me a bad excitement, and one of the infernal sparks fell into my own heart" (*LNY*, 138). Touching the "hearts of men," these "diabolical passions" released an uncontrollable excitement (*LNY*, 139). In the next letter, Child generalizes her understanding of the affective energies swirling through the crowd. A "contagion of murder" had mobilized them (*LNY*, 143), she reflects, and led to the "fierce exaggerations of an excited populace" (*LNY*, 144). Reflecting further on the problem of affective contagion, Child endeavors to map an alternative model of affect that might reshape "public opinion" (*LNY*, 145). Instead of being ignited by "the germ of murder," the populace needs a different model of emotional intensity—a "divine spark" that is "kindled" instead "by an atmosphere of love" that "flows out upon others" (*LNY*, 144, 146).

Although critical discussions of *Letters from New-York* have tended to stress Child's personal responses to the city, recently scholars have begun to comment evocatively upon her engagement with public feeling. Heather Roberts, for example, focuses on the way in which the traumatizing effects of urban suffering threaten to overload Child's sympathies, precipitating a struggle "to keep her heart open to suffering." But despite this emphasis upon the personal, Roberts also gestures toward structures of affect, noticing Child's evocation of the "public heart" as "a communal affective space" and her attempt to create an "angelic economy" (Child's term) of shared sympathy.[13] But what is missing in Roberts's insightful analysis is an explanation of how generalizing concepts such as "angelic economy" link private emotional responses to larger structures of public feeling. Foster goes much further than Roberts in examining how Child's *Letters* evoke a collective ground of being. In his words, she develops "a nuanced form of Emersonian transcendentalism" that "invites her readers not only to place themselves into the position of a suffering other but also to imagine themselves simultaneously occupying infinite space." In the process, Foster argues, Child generates a model of "transcendental sympathy" modeled on a "universal love" that collapses "the walls of class and sect." But as Foster's essay continues, he finds it increasingly difficult to reconcile Child's personal responses with her investment in a universalized model of sympathy. Eventually, he asserts (in a classic formulation of "urban shock"), Child found "urban space . . . a horrific medium that dissolves bodily autonomy" and "threatens self-reliance." In response, he argues, she retreated to "the separate and autonomous individual that characterizes bourgeois, liberal subjectivity." The linchpin of Foster's argument is his analysis of Child's visit to the display of American Indians at P. T. Barnum's American Museum. Overwhelmed by this display, Foster asserts, Child fell back on a concept of "racialized bodies" that distanced her isolated subjectivity from the individuals on display.[14]

For both Roberts and Foster the general and the specific, as well as the spiritual and the material, become antagonists at key points in Child's letters. But by emphasizing individual moments of response, they downplay the dynamic interconnection of transcendentalist illumination and affect that circulate throughout Child's book. Rather than defining moments of transcendentalist illumination or political sympathy as ultimate goals, Child uses them as a means to further a larger political end—to transform the consciousness of her readers by developing a critical awareness that detaches them from any single perspective. It is not enough to experience moments of divine ecstasy or to feel the pain of urban sufferers, Child suggests, unless one sees that each moment provides an alternative perspective, opening up a different existential horizon. For example, Child shows her readers that the understanding of sentiment changes when it is brought into contact with universalizing models of affective being. This move from the specific to the general enables her readers to distinguish private sentiments from larger regions of value. From this perspective, the cultural work of Child's text depends upon her ability to dramatize the collective structures of feeling that can either intensify positive social cohesion or lead to disturbing moments of social conflict and selfishness. Measuring specific moments of feeling against general models of affect, she brings into visibility public feelings that orient the individual and shape her being in the world.

Such doubling of awareness is part of Child's overall strategy in *Letters from New-York*. Rather than remaining in any single moment of individualized awareness, she multiplies viewpoints in order to detach her readers from habituated patterns of perception. In the process, Child exemplifies what Sarah Ann Wider (in this volume) characterizes as the "multidimensioned" quality of transcendentalist "attentiveness" (158). She teaches her readers to view the world critically, not only with their eyes but through multiple organs of perception including the spirit, the heart, and memory. Child insists that critical insight depends upon the capacity for double vision, developing a dialogic and binocular sense of the competing frameworks of value that shape the lived world. The process of seeing "*within* a landscape" (*LNY*, 16; emphasis in original), Child reminds her readers, involves the capacity to register qualities that are not immediately perceptible to the eyes. At times in her text, such perception involves the intuition of the transcendentalist "God *within* us" (*LNY*, 16; emphasis in original). At other moments, the process of seeing beyond immediate phenomena leads her to examine the lingering historical traces that many people fail to perceive. In Letter 28, for example, she uses historical memory to measure present contemporary urban disorder against the traces of earlier times. "Maiden-lane," where "the sky" is "shut out with bricks and mortar," was once the place where "young Dutch girls" did their laundry; the "Bowery," now overwhelmed by the din of "a thousand wheels," used to be a place of orchards and open fields (*LNY*, 79). Doubling her readers' vision, Child detaches them from the overwhelming impact of contemporary social conditions at the same time as she destabilizes the perception of contemporary urban scenes by pairing them with earlier but nearly forgotten landscapes.

At times, this doubling of vision creates important ideological effects in Child's text. Visiting the Jewish synagogue on Crosby Street, she found herself surprised by the mixture of ancient ceremony with contemporary dress. For Child, this "heterogeneous jumbling of the Present with the Past" was liberating, because "it broke the illusion completely." Rupturing habituated modes of perception, it unshackled her mind, allowing it to become "unfettered by narrow prejudice" (*LNY*, 25). This cognitive shift is analogous to what the twentieth-century Marxist playwright Bertolt Brecht aimed for in the theater. Creating forms of staging and acting that seemed unnatural to his audience, Brecht designed plays that evoked what he termed an "alienation effect." By "alienating the familiar," he argues, such theatrical forms were "designed to free socially-conditioned phenomena from that stamp of familiarity which protects them from our grasp today." The actor, he continues, "appears on the stage in a double role."[15] Such doubleness, Child also demonstrates, alters one's relationship to the visible world. For example, she highlights the importance of double vision in her account of a visit to a famous historical site in upstate New York. Measuring contemporary scenes against the vivid "impress of former days," Child begins to see doubly. A "dim remembrance," she reflects, "throws back, through the transparent present, the images of the world in marked outline; and thus you enjoy a two-fold world" (*LNY*, 109). Just as the modern railroad cuts through "hereditary acres," this doubled perception cuts through "old seed-fields of opinion, theological and political" (*LNY*, 110). Opening a cut or rift in the present, it destabilizes the "dream-state" of the contemporary world.

My reference to society's dream-state is meant to evoke Walter Benjamin's ground-breaking analysis in *The Arcades Project*. The collective awareness of society, he argues, is intoxicated by the phantasmagoria of cultural forms inducing consumption and conformity. Resisting this deadening of awareness, Benjamin asserts by way of Marx that "the reform of consciousness consists *solely* in . . . the awakening of the world from its dream about itself."[16] Such moments of awakening bring into focus an understanding of the cultural forms that have seduced perception. It is striking that Benjamin characterizes the process of awakening as a sudden "flash" that alters awareness: "What has been," he writes, "comes together in a flash with the now to form a constellation."[17] This conjunction of the past and the present parallels the "two-fold world" that Child found at times in her urban and rural excursions. Like Benjamin, she is not able to prolong these brief flashes of recognition, but what lingers is a mediated view of the world as a site perceptible through multiple organs of perception. No longer invested solely in visible experience or moments of intense sentiment, Child is then able to evaluate the limitations of the perceived world through the "lenses" of competing viewpoints, whether spiritual, affective, imaginative, or historical. Each moment of conjunction compares daily experience with differently constructed life-worlds, alternate universes of being and value. In Edward Soja's terms, this process shatters the "illusion of opaqueness" that "reifies space" by constructing—in its place—a "demystification of spatiality" that reveals the hidden structures of ideology, investment, and affect that are ordinarily invisible to the eye.[18]

We find similar patterns of demystification throughout Child's text. On the first page, she reminds readers that the "splendour of Broadway" tends to obscure the perception of "the blind negro beggar" sitting close by, while awe at the "stately mansion" can overwhelm awareness that it is the home of a "slave trader" (*LNY*, 9). Only by doubling vision can we see through visible appearances by attending to the uninterrogated affects embedded in our sense of "splendour" and awe. Each flash of critical awareness is akin to what Emerson termed "gleams of a better light" (*CW*, 1:43). But instead of punctuating the flow of everyday experience (which for Emerson was often pastoral), Child's flashes stop the overwhelming rush of *urban*—not rural—experience. Pulling figures from the ever-flowing crowd, "those who have flitted across [her] path," Child resists the urban shock that threatens to imprison the self within a sense of solitary and "vanishing" identity (*LNY*, 44). The danger, she recognizes, is that such isolation within the walls of *individual* identity blocks both self-reliance and an understanding of the self's relational ties to the productive matrix of public feelings.

In order to disrupt the overwhelming flow of experience, Child fractures the tempo of everyday perception. Placing "picture[s]" in "the halls of memory," she creates different "forms of composition . . . and event" that evoke the stark contrast between the city's "rapid fluctuation, and never-ceasing change" and images of frozen time (*LNY*, 46, 42, 43). Constructing breaks in the temporal flow, she detaches the reader from the deadening pressure of immediate reality. By weighing daily sights against other vistas and remembered scenes, Child generates political insight by seeing beyond "the surface" into what she terms the "deep foundations" of everyday life (*LNY*, 10). Pointing toward realities beyond what can be "proved to the senses" (*LNY*, 83), beyond the world in which "we live . . . entirely in the body," she opens up vistas of what she terms "the soul" (*LNY*, 86). But, as we have seen, these reflective regions depend not only on transcendentalist insight but also on the deployment of memory and affect. At such moments, Child shows her readers, the reflective self moves beyond the visible to other planes of awareness that reveal the invisible heart of the self and society.

The danger, Child suggests through *Letters from New-York*, is that this capacity to see doubly, through appearances, might collapse into a single plane of monocular and monologic vision. Anxious reactions—such as those to the ever-flowing crowd or to the American Indians on display in P. T. Barnum's American Museum—trap the self in a detached mode of perception that reinforces a sense of personal isolation. As Foster has noted, such moments of solitude often replicate individual, self-interested values that contradict the overall political agenda of Child's book. But rather than faulting Child for limited moments of isolated perception (the overall critical stance of both Roberts and Foster), it is important to recognize that she reminds her readers that such personal isolation is a politically dangerous stance, leading to selfishness, solipsism, and political apathy. Registering lessons learned in part from Emerson, Child critiques such isolated viewpoints throughout *Letters*, asserting over and over again that the key to motivating social change lies in the ability to maintain a sense of *shared* perceptions and motives. Part of this sharing involves Child's deployment of both transcendentalist paradigms of the Over-soul and Christianized models of universal love—a mixture that facilitates her "sentimental transcendentalism." But both models, in Child's usage, depend upon her understanding of the dynamics of affect, the emotional and moral climates that mobilize people and direct their lives.

The emotional rhythm of everyday life, Child shows her readers, is crucial, for the public mood touches every part of our being. It can shape structures of care or lead us into moments of carelessness and apathy that grow out of the belief that one's private feelings do not relate to the larger world. A striking analogue to Child's concerns is found in the study of "morale" that has emerged out of military science. Public feelings make a difference, strategists have discovered. Acts of "psychological warfare" can destroy a community's morale and ability to focus on concerted action.[19] As a result, the control of morale (both one's own and the enemy's) is now perceived as a strategic necessity by military and political leaders. Child, like other antislavery advocates, was engaged in a different but analogous battle. Her "front-line" was the city—the place where public moods shape people's willingness to resist social injustice or reinforce their sense that feelings are a private resource that can be hoarded just like money. From this perspective, the target of *Letters from New-York* is the possessive individualism that believes it can own the self or slaves—pieces of disposable property enclosed within impermeable boundaries. But when we view Child's text through the lens of affect, we understand that such enclosure mystifies the relational and emotional ties that make a person part of a community. They generate a fixation on visible surfaces and a blindness to the invisible relays of affect and ideology that shape human culture and everyday experience.

Like Child, Margaret Fuller dedicated much of her New York writing to the analysis of the structures of feeling shaping everyday life in New York. The temptation, when considering her *New-York Tribune* columns, is to detach her social essays from the rest of her literary production, much of which was devoted to analyzing artistic, musical, and literary works. But the study of artistic expression and aesthetics, Ben Highmore reminds us, has always contained an important political potential. Dealing with "the affects, the body, and the senses," aesthetics includes within its purview a focus on the "forms of perception, sensation, and attention." Aesthetic awareness, Highmore suggests, has the potential to examine "the orchestration of perception, sensorial culture, [and] affective intensities." Such critical awareness, he contends, can bring into visibility the "affect horizons" and perceptual structures mediating everyday life.[20] In both her reform essays and her reviews of artistic works, Fuller shares this concern with the structuring of experience. What her New York essays reveal is a sustained attempt to reconfigure social perception by addressing the shared structures of imagination and public feeling that configure the public's motives, goals, and values. Like Child, she asserts that communal affects have become corrupted. The ensuing corrosion of spirit has cut individuals off from both self-reliant action and shared political commitment.

From the beginning of her residence in New York, Fuller showed her readers that social change involved the linkage of transcendentalist illumination to what John Protevi terms "political affect." Arguing that emotion is the "necessary partner" of cognition, Protevi asserts that affects help us to "navigate" and "constitute" the world; "affective cognition," he continues, "is the sense-making of bodies politic."[21] This concern with the role of public feeling is evident in Fuller's review of Emerson's *Essays: First Series*, where she argues for the combination of transcendentalist insight *with* feeling. "Here is, undoubtedly, the man of ideas," Fuller observes, "but we want the ideal man also; want the *heart* and genius of human life to interpret it" (*MFC*, 5; emphasis added). While admiring Emerson's profound discourse of self-culture, Fuller considers the political danger of allowing one's life to be "sometimes obstructed or chilled by the critical intellect" (*MFC*, 6). Committed to the solitary pursuit of Truth, she cautions, one might focus exclusively on "the life of [one's own] soul" and not be able to "arouse" the community to "nobler energy" (*MFC*, 6, 2). One can find this concern with the limits of solitary transcendentalist illumination as early as the dialogue between "Self-Poise" (Emerson) and "Free Hope" (Fuller) in *Summer on the Lakes*. "Thou art greatly wise," Free Hope tells her Emersonian auditor, "yet I find not in your theory or your scope, room enough for the lyric inspirations, or the mysterious whispers of life. To me it seems that it is madder never to abandon oneself, than often to be infatuated; better to be wounded, a captive, and a slave, than always to walk in armor" (*EMF*, 148). Breaking the armor of possessive individualism, Fuller asserts, one needs to "beat with the living heart of the world" (*EMF*, 149). This concern with the world's "heart" is evident in many of Fuller's New York essays. In "Thanksgiving," for example, she notices that "the impulse of social or political reform" is "now sensible in the *heart* of the civilized world" (*MFC*, 11; emphasis added), which registers the movement of shared concern that she characterizes as "religious sympathy" (*MFC*, 12). Only those who approach society's outcasts with "the whole heart" (*MFC*, 13), she asserts, can alleviate social suffering.

Elsewhere, Fuller expands her presentation of political affect by linking public feeling, intelligence, and will. After visiting the inmates at the Bloomingdale Asylum for the Insane, for example, she connects "the emancipation of our wills"—a transcendentalist imperative—to "the miraculous power of Love, when guided by pure faith . . . and intelligence."[22] It is striking that, in the same essay, Fuller characterizes the antithesis of such focused awareness as the dysfunction of "a mind which does not see far enough to connect partial impressions." Overwhelmed by "mania" or "prejudice," those inflicted with such cultural myopia lack the capacity to coordinate their mental functions. As a result, their "attention is . . . distorted in some morbid direction" (*MFJ*, 80). In opposition to such scattered or distorted attention, Fuller continues her analysis of affective insight in her reviews of artistic and literary works. In "Critics and Essayists," she asserts that the examination of "public taste" demands the combination of "imagination, refined perceptions, and . . . judgment" (*MFC*, 439). Characterizing the critic's sensibility as a tool that can register public ideas and feelings, Fuller articulates a concept of enlightened feeling that melds together reason and emotion. In Elizabeth Barrett Browning's poetry, she reflects, "Personal feeling is . . . enlightened by Reason" and "ennobled by Imagination" (*MFC*, 20). Linking the awareness of her readers to what she terms "the field of general human interest" (*MFC*, 33), she encourages them to use their awareness of affect as a tool to register the moral tone, as well as the material condition, of their world.

Recognizing the disabling charge that feeling may be reduced to a private, apolitical response, Fuller observes in her essay "Prison Discipline" that some may consider such affects as the "spirit of mercy" a form of "'sickly sentimentality.'" But "the spark has been struck," she continues, "and . . . the fire glows, grows, rises, and begins to cast a light around" (*MFJ*, 105). At such moments, Fuller shows her readers that social change depends on shared feeling, not just abstract analysis. The glowing "spark" of reform illuminates many hearts. It is not just a private feeling, but a collective awareness of political affect registered through shared sensibility. "Sensibility," Protevi tells us, "is the openness to the world, our ability to sense aspects of situations." An important part of such awareness, he continues, is our recognition of "the virtual" through "our feeling for the genesis and future of situations."[23] Nearly all students of affect agree that it opens up this sense of the virtual. Registering "actual lines of potential," Kathleen Stewart observes, affects map "the trajectories that forces might take."[24] We find this concern with virtuality in Fuller's use of affect both to measure the moral tone of society and to articulate the direction of future social change. "One thing is certain," she reflects: "we live in a large place, no less morally than physically; wo [*sic*] to him who lives meanly there and knows the exhibitions of selfishness and vanity as the only American facts" (*MFC*, 127). The need, she argues elsewhere, is to comprehend the "genius of the time," which is "working through myriad organs, speaking through myriad mouths." One of the most important such "organs," she reminds her readers, is the heart, for a new tone has been struck, that of "brotherhood," which "must be well pronounced and learnt *by heart*" (*MFC*, 175).

Fuller's concern with public feeling is even more evident in her reform essays. Recounting a visit to the institutions on Blackwell's Island, in her essay "Our City Charities," she focuses on the affective dimension of "public attention" (*MFC*, 102). The first step toward social change, she argues, is to bring these inmates and prisoners into the field of attention, for "they should be looked at by all" (*MFC*, 98). But vision alone, she reminds her readers, is not enough, since many visitors—she notices—visit the hospitals and asylums only to subject their inhabitants to "careless scrutiny" and "the gaze of a stranger." Such unimpassioned vision, Fuller cautions, only reproduces social ills. What is needed is the application of a "deeper religion at the heart of Society," a deployment of affect as "intelligent sympathy" and "love" (*MFC*, 99). Fuller's concept of "intelligent sympathy," like that of enlightened feeling, combines reason with passion, understanding with affect; it becomes a form of what Protevi characterizes as "affective cognition."[25] Turning to the precarious position of women released from prison, Fuller's essay "Asylum for Discharged Female Convicts" presents one of her most impassioned arguments for such focused public feeling. Appealing "to all" (*MFC*, 135), she imagines the city as a region of cloistered individuals who have lost the capacity to connect their own sorrow to the general suffering of others. "Their pleading eyes," Fuller reflects, "we meet or seem to meet as we pass through the thoroughfares of this great city." But enclosed within their own *private* subjectivity, each passing individual is cut off from the experience of others. Fuller breaks the walls of solitude by articulating her desire to "awaken the *heart* to a deep and active interest" (*MFC*, 136; emphasis added). Focusing her readers' awareness on the inmates at Blackwell's Island, she defines a potential locus of shared sympathy that merges collective attention with public feeling.

"One of the most compelling problems now facing those studying the city," Nigel Thrift argues, "is how to take affect into our urban accounts. . . . [Cities] are shot through with and continually generate affect. Yet, only recently have we begun to think of cities in this way or to consider how affect is mobilized."[26] Focusing on what Thrift terms "the affective fabric" of society,[27] Fuller attends to the daily interactions that shape the moral tone of a community. In contrast to Child, she is less interested in the deployment of individual sentiment than in critical reflection on the public feelings that shape daily interactions. One of the most striking places where Fuller brings into focus the affective disposition of her readers is in her 1845 sketch "Prevalent Idea that Politeness is too great a Luxury to be given to the Poor." Writing about some rude behavior that she witnessed on one of New York's ferry boats, she weighs the impact of living in a city where a wealthy woman feels free to berate a poor boy for apparently neglecting a child. The woman's "insolent rudeness" (*MFC*, 128), Fuller reflects, is a key index of society's moral tone (that is, its prevailing affective register). Taking this incident as an opportunity to bring into focus the state of urban public feeling, she considers what it might mean to live instead in a society characterized by "graceful courtesy" (*MFC*, 129). The inhabitants of such a place, she concludes, would pass through the city "with an open eye and open heart," "a heart alive to affection" (*MFC*, 130). As Fuller knew all too well, such emotional responsiveness is difficult to maintain in a place where "callousness" is often "produced by the sight of more misery than it is possible to relieve." The danger, which Child also recognized, is that "the heart, at first so sensitive, tak[es] refuge in a stolid indifference against the pangs of sympathetic pain, it had not force to bear" (*MFC*, 377). But despite the real threat of apathy and indifference, Fuller struggled in many of her New York essays to articulate a critical sensibility able to use its awareness of affect as a tool registering the moral and political condition of society. As a means of bypassing what Roberts has characterized as "compassion fatigue,"[28] she connects personal sympathy to the deployment of a *collective* public feeling where a multitude—not just the solitary self—shares the burden of care.

Fuller's investment in the mapping of affect is particularly evident in her discussions of the different moral tones pervading nineteenth-century countries. At such moments, her writing anticipates Protevi's evocative argument that "affective cognition is the sense-making of bodies politic."[29] For example, Fuller's essay "1st January, 1846" surveys the affective condition of European nations in the 1840s. "France," she observes, "is in an uneasy dream," while Russia is "animated by despotic will." Ireland, she reflects, is experiencing a "general panic" caused by the potato famine (*MFC*, 327). But Fuller reserves her most pointed commentary for the United States, a nation contaminated by slavery and imperialistic aggression toward Mexico. "Our nation," she laments, "has indeed shown that the lust of gain is at present her ruling passion. . . . A large portion of our citizens, or their parents, came here for worldly advantage, and have never raised their minds to any idea of destiny or duty. More money—more land! is the only watchword they know" (*MFC*, 328). Condemning the ruling passion of "national aggrandizement" (*MFC*, 424) in her cynical 1846 essay "Victory," Fuller condemns the war fever fueling the Mexican War. "The wolves of war rage abroad," she observes, "without the slightest excuse from hunger"

(*MFC*, 425). What deeply concerned Fuller was the generalized corruption she perceived in the moral tone of America. In one of her reviews, she reflects on the "gross materialist tendency in our time and place" (*MFC*, 53). The country's "heart," she complains elsewhere, "is made shallow and cold, her eye dim, by the pomp of circumstance" and "the love of gross outward gain" (*MFC*, 474). "The nation," she observes, "wrap[s] itself in callousness and stop[s] its ear to any cry but profit or loss" (*MFC*, 464).

The danger, Fuller concludes, is that the body politic might be overwhelmed by moral "disease," an "infection" that might contaminate public feeling and permanently damage the country. "A mighty sea of life swells within our nation," she asserts, "and, if there be salt enough, foreign bodies shall not have power to breed infection there" (*MFC*, 150, 55). While at first glance this observation seems to reflect a nativist response to the overwhelming tide of immigration, what it casts into relief is a concern less over the influx of foreign bodies than with the inpouring of unwholesome affects and ideas.[30] The United States is passing through an important transition state, Fuller recognizes, a moment when imported corruptions might reinforce tendencies already present in the country, such as the "plague-spots" caused by slavery and "the conduct of this nation toward the Indians" (*MFC*, 465). While Fuller imagines "salt" as a substance that might cure national corruption, elsewhere she characterizes this antidote in affective terms, as "soul." "It takes a great deal of soul," she considers "to keep a huge body from disease and dissolution" (*MFC*, 474). "Our only hope," she affirms elsewhere, "lies in rousing, in our own community, a soul of goodness, a wise aspiration, that shall give us strength" (*MFC*, 54). Reflecting on the "diseased substance" of the country's affective "body," she asserts that what is needed is "a heart of force and purity to assimilate" (*MFC*, 253) the different, discordant elements making up the nation. What is wanted, Fuller declares, is "a dissemination of all that is best, intellectually and morally, through the whole people" (*MFC*, 334). Only through such affective reformation can the country's "transition state" lead to "a nobler era" (*MFC*, 235).

If I have lingered over Fuller's amplification of sentiment into a concern for public affect, it is to remind her readers that her best-known work, *Woman in the Nineteenth Century*, shares the double emphasis I have characterized as "sentimental transcendentalism." Fuller's indebtedness to Emerson in this book is unmistakable, especially at the moment when her alter ego, Miranda, asserts that her father taught her "self-reliance" (*EMF*, 262). Feminizing Emerson's plea for spiritual independence, Fuller asserts that woman as well must develop "a standard within herself" (*EMF*, 258). In this way, "incarcerated souls" might learn "self-dependence" and "the power of self-poise" (*EMF*, 311). But at the same time that Fuller develops an eloquent plea for female self-reliance, she also attends to the affective structures that have inhibited the concentration of attention on women's rights. The "gleams" of transcendentalist insight, she observes, are too often "obscured by the mists of sensuality" and "the dust of routine" (*EMF*, 268). The "tone of feeling" toward women, she laments, is similar to the attitude "towards slaves" (*EMF*, 258). Women have been encouraged to develop "vanity" and a "love of dress, love of flattery," and "love of excitement" (*EMF*, 329). At their weakest, they have been subjected to the "brute passions of man" and have experienced the sexual degradation of becoming their "sold and polluted slaves" (*EMF*, 330, 319). All of these terms—"sensuality," "tone of feeling," "love of excitement"—use the awareness of such affective conditions as a "daguerreotype plate" registering the impact of society's moral tone. Measuring the state of public feeling, they reveal the collective sensibility that has shaped the condition of women's lives.

At the same time that Fuller gauges the corrosion of public values, she uses affect to imagine alternative structures of being. Women, she argues, need a "free genial atmosphere" (*EMF*, 267). In order to change their lives, they need to realize that they possess "moral power" (*EMF*, 341). Too often this idea of "moral power" has been reduced to the timeworn category of female "influence," but Fuller is aiming much higher. Like the writers and reformers who follow her, she sees herself engaged in a struggle for the soul of the nation. One of her contributions to this national conversation (later amplified by such writers as Harriet Beecher Stowe) is found in her assertion that the nation needs to change its affective structure, becoming oriented by a maternal care that would replace selfishness and materialism.[31] Directing attention toward women suffering in prison, she exhorts her female readers: "Seek out these degraded women, give them tender sympathy, counsel, employment. Take the place of mothers, such as might have saved them originally" (*EMF*, 329). But perhaps an even more striking image of transformed being is found in Fuller's conception of "Las Exaltadas," the exalted ones (*EMF*, 334). Exaltation, we should remember, is a condition of both spiritual and emotional intensity. It is the combination of insight with affect that gives power to this image of transfigured being. For it reminds us that social change depends both on the transformation of insight and the reshaping of public feeling.

In their deployment and examination of political affect, Child and Fuller traveled a long way from their transcendentalist roots. Maintaining a commitment to the spiritual and intellectual growth of individual souls, they supplemented their concern with self-reliance with a growing awareness that the affective medium in which the soul takes root and flourishes is more complex than Emerson's concept of the Over-soul. The cultural climate of attitudes and opinions, they both realized, has a direct effect on individual change. In order to bring that climate into focus, both writers examined the public affects shaping "habituated" attitudes (*MFJ*, 106) and the imagined contours of human potential. This shift in emphasis had a number of important effects. One of the most striking of all is the way it alters the awareness of time, bringing into focus an awareness of history. "Man postpones or remembers," Emerson reflects in "Self-Reliance"; "he does not live in the present, but with reverted eye laments the past, or heedless of the riches that surround him, stands on tiptoe to foresee the future. He cannot be happy and strong until he too lives with nature in the present, above time" (*CW*, 2:39). Acknowledging Emerson's call for direct intuition and immediate creative action, Child and Fuller saw something else as well: that Emerson's plea for the immediacy of self-reliance necessitated the rejection of historical factors that he characterized as "society," "customs" (*CW*, 2:29), "dead institutions" (*CW*, 2:30), and social "usages" (*CW*, 2:32). It is probably no accident that Emerson linked his plea for direct action with a rejection of what he termed "feminine rage" (*CW*, 2:33), for his list of inhibiting factors includes the very factors that women's rights activists and female reformers took as the center of their collective attention. Child and Fuller realized that it was not enough to live solely in the present, basking in the influx of divinely inspired truth. For the lives they saw around them manifested both the residual effects of social injustice and the virtual outlines of hope. While transcendentalist illumination registered the ecstasy of personal empowerment, it needed to be combined with affect in order to communicate the exaltation of renewed *social* being. Transcendentalism was the perfect tool for depicting transformation, but what it required in order to measure the limits of social justice was also a heart.

NOTES

1. Carolyn Karcher, *The First Woman in the Republic: A Cultural Biography of Lydia Maria Child* (Durham, N.C.: Duke Univ. Press, 1994), 273, 274.
2. Laura L. Mielke, "Sentiment and Space in Lydia Maria Child's Native American Writings, 1824–1870," *Legacy* 21, no. 2 (2004): 174, 175.
3. Karcher, *First Woman in the Republic,* 15, 258.
4. Bruce Mills, Introduction to *Letters from New-York* by Lydia Maria Child, ed. Mills (Athens: Univ. of Georgia Press, 1998), xix, xxvii.
5. Mills, Introduction, xix, xxvii.
6. Heather Roberts, "'The Public Heart': Urban Life and the Politics of Sympathy in Lydia Maria Child's *Letters from New York,*" *American Literature* 76 (December 2004): 749–75.
7. Travis Foster, "Grotesque Sympathy: Lydia Maria Child, White Reform, and the Embodiment of Urban Space," *ESQ: A Journal of the American Renaissance* 56, no. 1 (2010): 1–32.
8. Mielke, "Sentiment and Space," 179.
9. Lydia Maria Child, *Letters from New-York*, ed. Bruce Mills (Athens and London: Univ. of Georgia Press, 1998), 63, emphasis added; hereafter cited parenthetically as *LNY*.
10. Gregory Seigworth and Melissa Gregg, "An Inventory of Shivers," in *The Affect Theory Reader*, ed. Melissa Gregg and Gregory Seigworth (Durham, N.C.: Duke Univ. Press, 2010), 8.

11. Elspeth Probyn, "Writing Shame," in *Affect Theory Reader*, 74.
12. Joanne Dobson, "Reclaiming Sentimental Literature," *American Literature* 69 (June 1997): 267.
13. Roberts, "'Public Heart,'" 766, 759, 751.
14. Foster, "Grotesque Sympathy," 7, 8, 13, 19.
15. Bertolt Brecht, "A Short Organum for the Theatre," in *Marxist Literary Theory*, ed. Terry Eagleton and Drew Milne (Oxford, U.K.: Blackwell, 1996), 121–23.
16. Karl Marx, quoted in Walter Benjamin, *The Arcades Project*, trans. Howard Eiland and Kevin McLaughlin (Cambridge, Mass.: Harvard Univ. Press, 1999), 438, 456.
17. Benjamin, *Arcades Project*, 462.
18. Edward W. Soja, *Postmodern Geographies: The Reassertion of Space in Critical Social Theory* (London: Verso, 1989), 7, 61.
19. See Ben Anderson, "Modulating the Excess of Affect: Morale in a State of 'Total War,'" in *Affect Theory Reader*, 161–85.
20. Ben Highmore, "Bitter after Taste: Affect, Food, and Social Aesthetics," in *Affect Theory Reader*, 122, 121, 128, 136.
21. John Protevi, *Political Affect: Connecting the Social to the Somatic* (Minneapolis: Univ. of Minnesota Press, 2009), 26, 33.
22. *Margaret Fuller's New York Journalism*, ed. Catherine C. Mitchell (Knoxville: Univ. of Tennessee Press, 1995), 82, 81; hereafter cited parenthetically as *MFJ*.
23. Protevi, *Political Affect*, 51.
24. Kathleen Stewart, *Ordinary Affects* (Durham, N.C.: Duke Univ. Press, 2007), 2.
25. Protevi, *Political Affect*, 51.
26. Nigel Thrift, "Transurbanism," *Urban Geography* 25, no. 8 (2004): 730.
27. Nigel Thrift, "But Malice Aforethought: Cities and the Natural History of Hatred," *Transactions of the Institute of British Geographers*, n.s., 30 (June 2005): 140.
28. Roberts, "'Public Heart,'" 766.
29. Protevi, *Political Affect*, 51.
30. For an extensive analysis of Fuller's conception of the body politic, as contrasted with the views of contemporaneous nativists, see chap. 9 of Jeffrey Steele, *Transfiguring America: Myth, Ideology, and Mourning in Margaret Fuller's Writing* (Columbia: Univ. of Missouri Press, 2001).
31. The classic discussion of such female moral power is found in chap. 5 of Jane Tompkins, *Sensational Designs: The Cultural Work of American Fiction, 1790–1860* (New York: Oxford Univ. Press, 1985), where she develops the concept of "sentimental power."

INTERLUDE

Elizabeth Oakes Smith, from *Bertha and Lily; or, the Parsonage of Beech Glen* (New York: Phillips, Sampson, 1854), 282–83.

"You look rich, and fresh, and seductive, even to me [said Bertha to Julia]. Were I a man, I could not fail to love you." (Here Bertha turned her clear eyes to my face, and the blood mounted to my temples.) "For myself, poets and artists call me beautiful; but the common observer sees nothing in any way attractive in my looks."

"But these are the highest authority. They would paint you for a Sibyl, me for a Venus," whispered Julia to herself.

"I am glad to suggest beauty always. I believe it a great and desirable gift. It is a part of the harmonies. . . .

"I love to think lilies belong to me . . . the beautiful water-lily, I mean. This flower is so lovely to me, that I find no words to express what it suggests. A soul-life, an inner consciousness, a sphere of unstained purities—of translucent, transparent harmonies—away from the external senses, which I cannot describe. . . . If I place my hands upon each side of my head, over the region of hope, and love, and ideality (according to Dr. Buchanan's theory), I fall into a soft, dreamy state. This is so delicious, that one of less integrity of life might be tempted to repeat it. I seem to float in air—my senses are cottoned upon me—faint music and exquisite odors float about me. The Lily at once throws me into the same state."

(S)exchanges

Julia Ward Howe's *The Hermaphrodite* and the Gender Dialectics of Transcendentalism

MONIKA ELBERT

The finest people marry the two sexes in their own person. Hermaphrodite is then the symbol of the finished soul.

—Ralph Waldo Emerson, *Journals* (April 1843)

Male and female represent the two sides of the great radical dualism. But, in fact, they are perpetually passing into one another. Fluid hardens to solid, solid rushes to fluid. There is no wholly masculine man, no purely feminine woman.

—Margaret Fuller, *Woman in the Nineteenth Century* (1845)

Men and women are made of the same clay, and in the same image.

Julia Ward Howe, "Why Are Women the Natural Guardians of Social Morals?" (ca. 1896)

Perhaps surprisingly, the purpose of Julia Ward Howe's fragmentary "Laurence manuscript" (recently published as *The Hermaphrodite*) comes into new perspective when read alongside Henry David Thoreau's classic *Walden*. Howe composed her manuscript in 1846–47, as Thoreau was reaching the end of his two-year residence at Walden Pond, and in it she registered some of the same troubling aspects of transcendentalism—the tension between a public and a personal self, exacerbated by preordained or prescribed gender roles—that plagued Thoreau in his hermitage.[1] Both felt spiritually isolated as they embarked on their excursions inward—for Thoreau, during his solitary moments at Walden, and for Howe, in transgressive moments of writing.

Howe's writing at this moment was of two kinds, both the subversive "Laurence manuscript" and the safe haven of personal letters and journals. She was living metaphorically in her own hermitage, in order to tackle questions about social obligations and personal needs and to imagine a life inspired by the divine within. Far from solitary, she was overwhelmed by mothering duties and household chores, but she wrote to sisters Louisa and Annie to express her sense of confinement and her desire to escape the burdens of "woman's work" so that she could reconnect with her deeper self. "My heart will be much taken up with my babies," she wrote; "as for my soul, that part of me which thinks and believes and imagines, I shall leave it alone till the next world, for I see it has little to do in this." And again: "Is not my life full enough of business, of flannel petticoats, aprons, and the wiping of dirty little noses? Must I sew and trot babies and sing songs, and tell Mother Goose stories, and still be expected to know how to write?"[2] In the same way that Thoreau attempted to retreat from the masculine world of commerce and industry, Howe wanted to escape the housewife's drudgery, and she would have liked the kind of writer's retreat Thoreau found at Walden.[3] Ironically, it is during this time, the winter of 1846, that Howe found refuge from domestic duty in secret writing of *The Hermaphrodite*. Yet in one of those confessional letters to her sister, she expressed a fear that the pedestrian nature of life had robbed her of creativity: "My fingers are becoming less and less familiar with the pen, my thoughts grow daily more insignificant and commonplace" (*JWH*, 122).

In this essay I would like to argue for *The Hermaphrodite* as a transcendentalist text and a beginning point for Howe's longer career as a feminist writer. Howe's fragmentary novel explores the gender questions that haunted her until she found her public voice later in life. Her early forays into transcendentalist thinking would save her in the maddening years of her first creative phase, which included the private writing of the Laurence fragment in 1846–47 and the more public collection of poems circulated in *Passion-flowers* (1854). These years saw Thoreau's arc of creativity on *Walden* as well, from his two-year retreat to publication of his book. Thoreau (1817–62) and Howe (1819–1910) were in similar positions as apprentices to transcendentalism, disciples following the master teachers Emerson and Fuller to discover their own truths. Looking first at their intertextual dialogue will open larger questions about Howe's career and its relation to transcendentalism as a whole.

Howe's transgressive writing, like Thoreau's "dropout" phase at Walden, shows the journey she must take, as her protagonist Laurence does, to abandon the false veneer of society and to reclaim her soul. As Gary Williams notes in his introduction to the recently discovered novel, Howe feels that she has "waked up" (as she puts it in a letter of late January 1847), having come to terms with the deadening chores of a housewife and the lack of sympathy from her husband. Though Williams suggests that the protagonist Laurence, who drives his would-be lover Emma mad, reflects Samuel Howe's coldness, I argue that Laurence also reflects the questing Julia, who feels desexed, unappreciated, and imprisoned in prescribed social roles.[4] The theme of awakening is shared by Thoreau and Howe in their works of personal questing. Thoreau, shunning the world of man's commerce, proclaims the necessity of learning "to reawaken and keep ourselves awake" as we await the dawn.[5] In *The Hermaphrodite*, Howe's protagonist expresses a similar goal as he tolerates the "slumbers of the soul" in waiting "for the divine voice to awake [him] to higher and nobler musings" (64). As pilgrims on the journey to awakening, Thoreau and Howe (through Laurence) strip away masks of civilization and endure several deaths and rebirths along the way.

Both Howe, in her questioning of the domestic realm, and Thoreau, in his temporary abandonment of the commercial realm, could be perceived as rebellious, if not monstrous, in their desire to transgress gender spheres. While Thoreau enjoys keeping house, preparing meals, and being domestic at Walden, Howe enjoys shirking her domestic responsibilities by writing.[6] Valarie H. Ziegler notes that the rejected Emma labels Laurence a "monster" when he does not react to Emma's charms and when she realizes he is a hermaphrodite. I agree with Ziegler that Howe most likely felt monstrous too: "The fear of being a monster herself was an anxiety with which Julia had long struggled; her own desires to enter the male world of writing and lecturing were suspect in an age that assumed women's natural place was in the home."[7] Howe must have felt hopeless about asserting herself when her husband Samuel bantered with his friend Charles Sumner about "pitying unmarried women." Julia, mother several times over, writes to her then-pregnant sister Laura a less-than-hopeful letter describing the men's insensitivity: "Oh my dear friends, thought I, if you could only have one baby, you would change your tune" (*JWH*, 116). Not just mothering but housekeeping seemed onerous to Howe; though resorting to "Catharine Beecher's cookbook," she is still vexed by the art of cooking and proclaims, "This was not what her hand was made for" (*JWH*, 110). In *The Hermaphrodite* such gendered discontents are magnified into an alter ego who must struggle with the constraints upon both genders.

Howe's protagonist Laurence is in the chrysalis stage between child and adult, between boy and girl—a stage of development that transcendentalists find symbolically resonant with promise.[8] The text starts with his being considered sexless by his parents; shortly thereafter, at college, he is discovered to be "one of those unsexed souls" (15) and then likened to Apollo (whom Fuller had conceptualized as a feminine male) and "the lovely hermaphrodite in the villa Borghese" (16).[9] These comparisons nearly drive him mad. He acknowledges to his rival Wilhelm that he is "no man, no woman, nothing" and then has a further rude awakening when his father gives his patrimony to a younger brother, whose sex as a male is certain. Laurence hears the story about how he was born "imperfect" and given the "name and rights of a man" only for expedience (22, 29). His father's patrimony, not financial but psychological, impresses on him the need to be a male and to shun the feminine qualities that connect him to the poetic realm, which had brought some recognition when he was at school. His father recommends the profession of the ministry, a noteworthy choice given that the church has often been viewed as feminized.[10] Hating the woman within himself, he initially grapples with his maligned manhood; and with his father's "odious slur upon [his] manhood," Laurence sets out "to distinguish [himself] in the eye of the world as [his father] had never done" (35). Secluding himself in a hermitage in the woods, Laurence feels the liminality of his situation, but sequestered from society and liberated from social and gender expectations, he returns to a simple, childlike state and reflects, "How was it that when I had understood and reasoned as a child, I had felt as a man?" (59).

Like Thoreau taking over Emerson's Walden property in an attempt to live deliberately, Howe's Laurence escapes civilization and lives on the estate of a deceased Count who had clearly led a transcendentalist lifestyle. Indeed, the Count had balanced his time between solitude, study, and frugality on the one hand and social interaction and beneficence on the other, while his remaining library contains Swedenborg and other authors on "the mysterious questions of the soul's relations with God" (39). The Intendant from the village makes Laurence swear to what sounds in part like a transcendentalist oath. Apparently, the Count had made provisions for the questing individual to take up the abode (and it sounds much like Emerson's leasing his land to Thoreau): "The hermitage cannot be hired . . . but it is free to any one who will comply with the Count's terms as recorded on the wall" (40). This spiritual platform directs the pilgrim to dine simply ("he must eat no flesh, he must drink no wine"), avoid luxurious clothing and shun worldly goods ("no goodly garment his state shall show" and "to gold . . . he must bid farewell"), become self-reliant and work independently ("no menial here his hest shall wait"), avoid sexual contact ("in his bed no mate"), and focus on spiritual growth ("in holy study his days must pass") (40–41). Following these precepts, the individual should find "good" in "body and soul" as the "angel of peace" stands guard. Laurence is conscious of his wounded masculinity and anticipates the time "when [his] unripe manhood shall have put on maturity" (41). The remainder of the novel finds Laurence battling the gender demons within.

Howe's Laurence appears to undergo a mental breakdown as he tries to eradicate fleshly desire and in the process becomes obsessed with it. Much of his thinking, like Thoreau's thinking about body and soul in "Higher Laws," is informed by dualistic Christian concepts of good and evil as expressed through the privileging of spirit and a repugnance for the flesh.[11] What confounds Thoreau about the bifurcation of spirit / flesh in "Higher Laws" drives Laurence into an introspective state that nearly kills him. Denying himself bodily pleasure is a way in which Laurence tries to forget his hermaphroditic state: "The curse of my existence, the cruel injustice of nature had for the time quite faded from my remembrance—my body was become a matter of such small consequence to me, that I cared little after what manner it was made" (46). One might well think about the physically numbing (and ongoing) birthing state that weighs upon Howe's body as she is writing this manuscript.

Julie Ward Howe among the Transcendentalists

Howe, unlike Thoreau, did not carry her questing into card-carrying transcendentalism, but her early exposure to transcendentalist ideas allowed her to explore notions of duality and sometimes helped reconcile the paradoxes she found in her own life. Though Howe wrote her fragmentary novel before Thoreau published *Walden* in 1854, there are uncanny resemblances between Howe's questing Laurence, the authorial persona of Thoreau, and Howe herself. It is a resemblance based upon parallel if also distinct cultural encounters.

Howe's move to Boston from New York City in the late 1830s, after the death of her father, had afforded her the opportunity to commune with the best transcendentalist minds (including Emerson, Fuller, Bronson Alcott) and with the Unitarian minister Theodore Parker, and she knew the writings of such influential mystics as Swedenborg. Through Parker's definition of divinity as androgynous she learned about the creative possibilities of transcendentalism. As she records in her 1899 *Reminiscences*, "I am almost certain that Parker was the first minister who in public prayer to God addressed him as 'Father and Mother of us all.'"[12] In *Reminiscences*, an introspective Howe discusses the liberating effect of Parker's sermons (in 1845), as she broke away from her Calvinist upbringing and shocked her "society friends." Reading his sermon "The Transient and the Permanent in Christianity," Howe was "surprised" to find it "reverent and appreciative in spirit, although somewhat startling in its conclusions" (*Rem*, 81). It was a time heady with transcendentalist thought: "The remembrance of Mr. Emerson's Phi Beta address ["The American Scholar"] was fresh in my mind. This discourse of Parker's was a second glimpse of a system of thought very different from that in which I had been reared" (*ibid.*).

Margaret Fuller's thinking also resonated with Howe, even if she did not quite comprehend the Conversation she attended in Boston until later in life, when she tackled the same questions. Howe would summarize the import of the Conversations, especially for women, in her biography of Fuller (1883). In *Reminiscences*, Howe recalls a church service by the Unitarian minister Frederick Henry Hedge that she attended with Fuller in 1842. She was surprised by Fuller's assertion that Hedge's transcendentalist thinking was not radical enough: "it was high ground for middle ground" (*Rem*, 146). Fuller herself staunchly advocated for Julia Ward Howe's literary gifts; upon reading one of Howe's early poems (now lost), she responded: "It is the record of days of genuine inspiration,—of days when the soul lay in the light, when the spiritual harmonies were greatly apprehended. . . . I can hardly realize that the Julia Ward I have seen has lived this life. It has not yet pervaded her whole being, though I can recall something of it in the steady light of her eye" (*JWH*, 69). Fuller urged Ward to publish the poem, which she believed would interest "many persons" in Fuller's circle.

Though Howe did not immediately publish, she found a new personal faith on the Boston movement's periphery. Later, by 1868, Howe had more fully found her "daemon" (or genius). When she delivered a lecture with a distinctly transcendentalist bent on "polarities" ("Doubt and Belief") to the Boston Radical Club, she perceived with delight that Bronson Alcott and Emerson, among the audience, understood her meaning completely. During the turbulent years for Howe, the 1840s, which found her constrained by the material circumstances of marriage, motherhood, and household affairs, she expressed her desire for something deeper in spiritual terms: "I am glad . . . to feel myself still a pilgrim of something that is neither house nor lands, nor children nor health. What that something is I scarce know. Sometimes it seems to be one thing and sometimes another" (17 May 1847, *JWH*, 126). In 1848, as her son turned seven weeks old, Howe lamented: "I will rather give up the world and cut out Beacon Street, but an hour or two for the cultivation of my poor little soul I must and will have" (*JWH*, 131). Howe was aware of the liberating but also conflicting messages of transcendentalism. Her novel *The Hermaphrodite* is an attempt to reconcile the differences and tensions that transcendentalism embodied—with its inadvertent insistence on dualities—between flesh and spirit, between public and private, between intellect and intuition, between civilization and nature, and between male and female.

Howe was among the women seekers of the movement. Thoreau recollects that, during his time at Walden, he found himself more "himself," and more at home in the woods, when the young women and children came to visit him: "Girls and boys and young women generally seemed glad to be in the woods. They looked in the pond and at the flowers, and improved their time. Men of business, even farmers thought only of employment, and of the great distance at which I had dwelt from something or other; and though they said that they loved a ramble in the woods occasionally, it was obvious that they did not." Thoreau goes on to chide the "restless committed men, whose time was all taken up in getting a living or keeping it" (*Walden*, 153). If he seems to identify his woods as especially congenial to women, for the women their rambles were a break from gendered expectation. We know that Thoreau could only live in the woods for so long before the business of life and publishing called him back to the marketplace realm of men. Just so, Howe, Thoreau, and Laurence, all of them pilgrims on a quest to be awakened to a more creative life by rethinking gender roles, found themselves torn between the polarities construed as active and passive. As an apprentice, Thoreau finally had to break with Emerson, who never did reconcile the dualities of gender. On the other hand Howe did not as an apprentice have to break completely with Fuller: she found that Fuller's "sibylline" transcendentalism afforded her flexibility to define herself in a more wholesome / holistic manner.

The quintessential split between the prototypical male and female transcendentalists, which emerges in the Laurence fragment, can also be seen in the strained relationship between Emerson and Fuller. Fuller's assertive yet intimate personality forces Emerson to wonder about his own gender predilections. Though he says in an April 1843 journal entry that "the finest people marry the two sexes in their own person," and that "hermaphrodite is then the symbol of the finished soul," his life does not embody this idea. He pays lip service to the idea of gender balance, and he is still intent upon differentiating harshly between "masculine women" and feminine men. Most condescendingly, he describes Harriet Martineau as a woman whose male side is overdeveloped: "Man can never tell woman what her duties are: he will certainly end in describing a man in female attire, as Harriet Martineau a masculine woman solved her problem of woman." He unwittingly describes himself in a journal entry: "A highly endowed man with good intellect & good conscience is a Man-woman & does not so much need the complement of Woman to his being as another. Hence his relations to the sex are somewhat dislocated & unsatisfactory. He asks in Woman, sometimes the Woman, sometimes the Man."[13] This self-portrait ultimately explains his strained, "somewhat dislocated and unsatisfactory," relations to the opposite sex; these problems arise because, in asking the woman to be "sometimes the woman, sometimes the man," he cuts himself off from his own experience of being sometimes the woman, sometimes the man. Intellectually, he posits: "In the spiritual world we change sexes every moment. You love the worth in me; then I am your husband. . . . Meantime I adore the greater worth in another, and so become his wife." But he never allows himself to experience such sexchanges on an emotional level. He sees the mind as an androgynous organ: "the eye,—the mind, is always accompanied by these forms, male and female."[14]

If Emerson expresses the mystical idea that "hermaphrodite is . . . the symbol of the finished soul," it is Fuller's sense of androgyny (in flux and action) that will prove most liberating for Julia Ward Howe. Ironically, in comparing Emerson with Fuller, Howe does finally assign more masculine power to Fuller. In a memorial lecture on Emerson presented at the Concord School of Philosophy, Howe describes their skills of elocution in gendered terms, and Fuller comes out the victor: "I should say that Mr. Emerson's patient and cautious nature made his position a less aggressive one than that of his brilliant contemporary. Margaret's eloquence, which gave expression to the quick and vehement action of her mind, was less favorable to the formation of reserved judgment than was Mr. Emerson's more deliberate speech. Eloquent on foot Mr. Emerson was rarely or never."[15] Howe is more temperamentally aligned with Fuller, to whom she pays homage in various writings, most notably in her biography, *Margaret Fuller (Marchesa Ossoli)* (1883), which, though it does cite various passages from the Emerson / Channing memoirs, also includes her summation of Fuller's work and her own interjections about the enduring value of Fuller's thinking, especially to women. Howe again distinguishes between Emerson and Fuller, maintaining that Fuller was "a priestess of life-glories" with her passionate discourse, whereas Emerson "had also a priesthood, but of a different order."[16] She discusses Fuller's sibylline qualities as an orator, and later, in her introduction to *Love-Letters of Margaret Fuller, 1845–1846* (1903), she proclaims, "Among the titles bestowed on women of unusual gifts, that of Sibyl appears to me to suit best what we know of her."[17]

Though it is obvious in Howe's biography that by then she was very much acquainted with Fuller's writings on women's rights, both "The Great Lawsuit" of 1843 and the expanded version, *Woman in the Nineteenth Century*, of 1845, it is not clear whether Howe had such a grasp on Fuller's work when she was writing her Laurence manuscript (1846–47). However, she was knowledgeable about Fuller's empowering ideas from her Conversations, which informed the writing of both texts. In the poem "Sibyl," published in 1854 in *Passion-flowers*, Howe seems to have Fuller in mind: "Since the maternal saint I worshipped / Did look and love her last, / No woman o'er my wayward spirit / Such gentle spell has cast." Howe concludes by having the speaker ask the Sibyl to take her hand, to vitalize her: "For, though human by my nature / You've made it half divine."[18]

While Fuller would show throughout *Woman in the Nineteenth Century* that intuition seems to be more or less the province of woman, and intellect that of man, she thought that both sexes could partake of each type of wisdom (since "all soul is the same") (*WNC*, 68). Aware that "the intellect, cold, is ever more masculine than feminine," Fuller finds promise in the intermingling of gender traits: "warmed by emotion, it [intellect] rushes towards mother earth, and puts on the forms of beauty" (*WNC*, 61). Howe summarizes Fuller's ideas about the sexes almost verbatim: "The growth of man is twofold,—masculine and feminine. These terms, for Margaret, represent other qualities, to wit. Energy and Harmony, Power and Beauty, Intellect and Love" (*Marchesa*, 155).[19] Like Fuller, Howe is hopeful and predicts a more utopian time in the future, when the sexes will be deemed equal: "Where there is duty, there must be right, and men and women alike are entitled to fulfil their highest duty, and to claim, in fulfilling it, the noblest right to which humanity is heir."[20] Throughout Howe's later works, optimism resonates, but in the Laurence fragment, her early work, hope for the future is not strong, possibly as a result of her repressive marriage as well her observation of other women and men around her in the Boston world of the mid-1840s.

The Monster Within: Confronting the Sexless Self

Two discordant voices struggle within Laurence—one sounding like the idealist and the other the materialist of Emerson's and Thoreau's transcendentalist philosophy. On the one hand, Laurence tries to convince himself that he is above Nature: "God hath appointed that trees should grow and flourish, that animals should wax fat, and increase—their existence and its ends are alike material and finite, but it were shame that the soul of man should be satisfied with pleasures and destinies like theirs" (46). He himself strives to become "the embodiment of a spiritual essence" and not "a simply sentient and material creature" (ibid.). In extreme rejection of the physical world, he feels "choked with the solid, asphyxiating gases of . . . materiality" and longs to "breathe the air of sublimated spirituality" (47). However, this vehement attack on the physical world leads to a crazed crescendo. Looking for a kind of Over-soul, "the soul of the Universe," leads him to renounce flatly the workings of feminine Nature, who, in his frenzied state, appears to lead him away from God: Laurence finds fault with the "hysterical nurse of ours, called Nature," though she is "good in her way," and seeks release "from her jurisdiction" (ibid.). But the practical side of his psyche responds to his aversion toward Nature, and that practical voice resounds with a cautionary tale: "Clearly, it is God's will that you carry this poor mortality with you as far as you are able. Your mother Nature is not to be turned off with a pension. Dutifully and with filial piety must you provide for her wants and pleasures . . . or she may rise up against you with horrible energy" (47–48).

The discourse of the mortification of the flesh puts Laurence into a trance-like stupor, his spirit overcoming his body: "while my body was unconscious and incapable of motion, my mind seemed to penetrate with rapid progress into regions unknown before me" (48). It takes a visitor, in the shape of the young, gentle, and feminized Ronald, to lead him away from his "deserted hermitage" and remove him from self-imprisonment. Laurence has just had a vision about a "beautiful child" (a "diaphanous" sexless youth, the type Alcott celebrates), and he sees Ronald as a heavenly guide, spirit incarnate, who will bring him home, back to earth. In retrospect, Laurence will see his life as an ascetic hermit as an "unnatural mode of life" (46). What finally drives him out of his state of torpor is his acquaintance with the forester Rudolf (Ronald's servant), who restores Laurence to physical health. Significantly, Laurence is appalled when the boy Ronald first mistakes him as a woman and asks him to keep his hair long (51).

He then argues with Ronald that he does not want a "woman," not even the motherly Lischen, to tend him—"I cannot suffer the presence of a woman" (52)—recalling, no doubt, the deceased sentimental Emma (whose death he has caused by his androgynous display).[21] Laurence chooses instead the hunter Rudolf to heal him: described as "a man of sense" (54), he is much like Thoreau's manly French Canadian woodsman, "in whom the animal man chiefly [is] developed" (*Walden*, 146). Laurence recovers and gains strength from the magnetic, beastly power of the huntsman and his dogs, who display an excess of animal vitality. Soon Laurence's appetite returns, and he declines gruel in favor of meat and wine. He feels reborn as he bathes in icy waters and then climbs a hill to witness sunrise: his early-morning vision awakens him to a momentary reconciliation of spirit and matter: "Heavenly comfort streamed in upon my soul with the morning rays—my heart turned to God . . . and He spake to me through the double medium of soul and of sense" (56). Here, Laurence finds peace, reconciling "soul and sense," but this constant shifting between body and spirit, sometimes manifest as female or male polarities, haunts him until the end of his journey.

On leaving his solitary life at "the deserted hermitage," Laurence must, like Thoreau at the end of his "Solitude" chapter, recognize that he is intrinsically connected to Nature. Thoreau acknowledges that it is the feminine realm, not the aggressive male allopathic world, that will sustain him: "What is the pill which will keep us well, serene, contented? Not my or thy great-grandfather's, but our great-grandmother Nature's universal, vegetable, botanic medicines, by which she has keep herself young always" (*Walden*, 138). To approach the rejuvenating spirit at the heart of transcendentalist thought, one must finally accept Nature and one's nature. Transcendentalism feeds off a continuous cycle of excess and repression, often expressed in terms of gender conventions (logic pitted against feeling, individuality countered by community). In "Higher Laws," Thoreau delineates the enemy as female—"Nature is hard to be overcome, but she must be overcome" (*Walden*, 221). This misogynistic vision in some phases of transcendentalism, that Mother Nature "must be overcome," and the quandary of privileging male reason over female intuition also lie at the heart of Howe's novel. Though Laurence attempts to achieve the transcendence that Thoreau would later envision in "Higher Laws," the difficulty of such transcendence is apparent in his encounters with the two male companions and guides he meets on his journey, the sensitive Ronald and the hardened Berto.

The feminine youth, Ronald, leads Laurence away from the primitive but natural (and healing) Rudolf. Laurence continues to be obsessed with defining his masculinity against Ronald's feminized boyishness, bragging that he could hurl a stone in a more manly fashion, announcing, proudly, picking up the heaviest stone, that his "is no woman's throw" (61). Arriving at the castle of Ronald's father, Raimond, Ronald proudly asserts that his "nature" is "masculine," his "habits, anti-gregarious" (63). Laurence applauds the Lord of the Manor for being "no woman fancier" and he avoids all connections with the servant women (68). He does feel "a return to the common life of humanity" with the other scholars and thinkers at court (65). But in becoming Ronald's main tutor, he teaches him through transcendentalist ventures into the woods to find truths not available to Ronald's other preceptors. Laurence takes pride in forming the young Ronald's intellect—"I had taught him to reason"—but Ronald's emotional side teaches Laurence "to hope and to enjoy." Ronald's overemotional approach to Laurence makes Laurence feel unmanned, when, for example, he tries to kiss Laurence (68). Ronald is also wont to cling to Laurence "like a child to his mother" (72). This all horrifies Laurence, but this drama comes to a crescendo as Laurence, visiting Ronald at university, is indeed rendered womanly when asked to play the part of Juliet in the school play. Laurence finds a strange delight, "a nameless pleasure" in portraying the woman, and gives a "fervent expression to the glowing words of the Italian woman-child" (81). His true identity, as not-male, is detected, and the young Ronald fights a duel on his behalf but implores him, in private, to be a "sweet, warm, living woman" to him (86). Drugging the love-struck Ronald with wine, Laurence escapes.

Before Laurence's narrative ends, he acts the part of a woman, in the company of Berto's three sisters, and acquiesces to feminine Nature. He also relinquishes any last vestige of patrimony when he ultimately renounces his father, who, finally feminized and softened through grief, tries to reclaim Laurence, his only surviving son, after Laurence's brother Phillip dies. Berto, as cynical spokesperson, with pragmatic and essentialist views, represents the folly of reductive transcendental thinking about women: "Who ever by reason convinced a woman, much less a girl? Born to feel, and not taught to think, they are ever the slaves of their own impulses, and they become the slaves of men, nor do they give up on caprice, until it is trampled under foot by its successor" (101). Berto, though, is instrumental in Laurence's development, as he introduces him to his sisters, who will disprove Berto's theory about gender.

Fuller, playing devil's advocate, uses similar rhetoric (to Berto's) when she proclaims, "Women of genius, even more than men, are likely to be enslaved by an impassioned sensibility" (*WNC*, 61). Fuller is more hopeful than Howe in reconciling the two halves of "the great radical dualism" in the androgynous image of the feminized poet (her portrait of Shelley, for example, which is comparable to Howe's Laurence as the sensitive class poet or the dramatic actor playing Juliet) or in the archetype of the Virgin Mary (wise but nurturing). Fuller also provides examples of gender transference: "Nature provides exceptions to every rule. She sends women to battle, and sets Hercules spinning"

(*WNC*, 69). However, Fuller also shows the difficulty of such gender reconciliation: male and female "are perpetually passing into one another," but in pronouncing that "fluid hardens to solid, solid rushes to fluid" (*WNC*, 68–69), she shows that one quality is dominant, and that one experiences the other part of the gender duality only in dialectical moments—when fluid turns to solid and vice versa. One quality does not partake of the other.

This type of gender dualism is finally accepted in Howe's novel, in Book 3, when the doctor "Medicus," attending to the dying Laurence, pronounces "Laurent [*sic*]" (erstwhile disguised as "Cecilia") neither man nor woman: "I shall say that he is rather both than neither" (195). The obsession with defining his gender finally leaves Laurence at an impasse. Berto argues for Laurence's masculinity to the end, but the more enlightened sister Briseida, referring to Swedenborg, finally resolves the issue by simply calling Laurence "one undivided, integral soul," needing not to seek his other earthly half but "only to adore the God above . . . and to labour for its brethren around it" (195–96).

In language that recalls Thoreau's discourse about boyhood and hunting in "Higher Laws," Berto, the mouthpiece for phallocentric thinking in Book 2, describes the need to retain some barbarian aspects of nature in order to defend one's manhood—to thwart the feminizing influence of the mothers: "Every man should be a savage once in his life, because every individual, to be a genuine man, should go through all the phases through which necessity has led the race" (97). In this context, "savage" nature is seen as positive, whereas the feminizing influence of maternal nature is deemed negative (as controlling): "Man is born naked to the intent that he should begin life as a naked barbarian. To be sure, mothers will thwart the benevolent purpose of nature, but they cannot change it" (ibid.). Berto, in this passage, maintains that "civilized" man will give up the toys of childhood—as Thoreau also maintains boys will give up hunting and fishing when they reach manhood; Nature will be overcome. But the equivocal meanings of Nature torment the transcendentalists. Thoreau mocks the man who needs stimulants and instead advocates for the Vedic scriptures on purity; and Laurence, in the early part of Howe's novel, asserts, "It is the cold and dull of temperament who need the genial flow of wine" (64), though pages before, Laurence has been awakened from his slumbers by Rudolf's offering of wine. Thoreau is drawn to the physical, manly strength of the French Canadian woodsman, but he finally finds his brute instinct repulsive: "I never . . . could get him to take the spiritual view of things; the highest that he appeared to conceive of was a simple expediency, such as you might expect an animal to appreciate" (*Walden*, 150). Similarly, when the reclusive Laurence comes out of his hermitage (in Book 1), he finds the forester Rudolf's brute strength appealing: "He and his rude master were more congenial to me for the time than even the gentle Ronald—there was in them such a vigour and fulness of animal life" (55).

In the dialectical process of transcendentalist living, Laurence must renounce this brute force and accept a gentleness belonging to Ronald (another sort of hermaphroditic soul), behavior antithetical to male modes of being. There is no union of the spirit and the flesh, female and male, only moments of living each, separately, dialectically.

The puritanical emphasis on cleanliness and purity in transcendentalist writings bears on the matter of Nature. The Roman Berto tries to teach the fastidious Laurence the acceptance of dirt as a part of Nature; Thoreau is unable to reconcile the "spiritual" with the "primitive" instincts, even though he evinces a desire to do so ("I reverence them both" [*Walden*, 210]). Berto actually has accepted all-encompassing Nature, as he has lived in Nature: "Cleanliness is, philosophically speaking, nothing but the absence of dirt. . . . Dirt is the law of nature, cleanliness is that of civilization. I have now made acquaintance with dirt, and esteem it highly conducive to health" (187). Significantly, when Berto returns, sullied, from the countryside, Laurence refuses to embrace him, "the unclean beast" (186), and in not accepting the similarly sensual and reptilian side of himself, he quickly moves toward death. For Laurence, dirt stays dirt; cleanliness remains cleanliness, and never the twain shall meet—an attitude that parallels the thinking of Thoreau, in "Higher Laws," where he reverences both the "spiritual" and the "savage," though he ultimately privileges "the civilized" over the "wild" (*Walden*, 210–11).

Berto's message, unheeded, offers the more wholesome attitude toward "savage," unclean nature. Berto indulges in drunkenness once a year (during Carnival) to access this savage state and then to repudiate it. Thus, he embodies the dialectic of transcendentalist principles more successfully than Laurence, as he critiques consistency and calls for an open mind: "I abhor onesidedness, fixed idea, and all the insanities of the learned. For them, the earth should stand still, for me, it turns round, and shews me a new face every day" (95). With confidence, Berto celebrates himself: "I desire to do entire justice to every fibre of my brain, every nerve and muscle of my body, and I therefore give to each its appointed time of training and exercise" (95). But it is precisely the carnivalesque mode, liberating in Berto, that also allows Laurence to disguise himself as a woman, as "Cecilia," and become "sister" to Berto's three sisters—experiencing for the first time familial love.[22]

Laurence, throughout the narrative, has been the outcast transcendentalist male, solitary and unsure of his manhood, fearful of the feminizing aspect of Nature and, at the same time, like the transcendentalist woman, Fuller or Howe, an outsider who wants to enter the misogynist transcendentalist clubhouse and who thus must renounce (in part) a female persona, at least temporarily. Before he dies, though, Laurence learns the lesson of "Higher Laws," as suggested by *Woman in the Nineteenth Century*: "There is no wholly masculine man, no purely feminine woman" (116). Berto and Briseida (Berto's wisest sister) grapple with the definition of Laurence, as male or female, even as he lies on his deathbed; Berto argues for his logic / masculinity (190) and Briseida for his "tenderness of heart" / femininity (191). She implies that Laurence, for the first time referred to as "she," is more like one of the girls: "It is true that she can reason better than most women, yet is she most herself when she feels, when she follows that instinctive, undoubting sense of inner truths that is only given to women and to angels." Just as Laurence does not successfully reconcile the two sides in life, his friends cannot affix one definition on him, though the doctor in attendance argues for androgyny: "I cannot pronounce Laurence either man or woman . . . but I shall speak most justly if I say that he is rather both than neither" (195). The doctor speaks for the reconciliation of polarities, which is, after all, the theoretical goal of transcendentalism.

Laurence's (impending) death, however, shows the grotesque confrontation of opposites and illustrates the impracticability of transcendentalist teachings. Suffering a strange transcendentalist crucifixion, Laurence is more aware of polarities than of rapprochement: "a cross is not formed otherwise than of two loves or two desires which cross each other or conflict" (197). The two halves of the "great radical dualism" (to borrow from Fuller) seem to cancel each other out in Laurence's case, and Howe's final verdict about transcendentalism in *The Hermaphrodite* is that the contradictions cannot be resolved if one insists on binary oppositions. One might also recall Emerson's final indictment of Thoreau's conflicted and at times rigid personality and wonder whether Emerson is reflecting on his own shortcomings, or obsessions with defining manhood: "There was something military in his nature, not to be subdued, always manly and able, but rarely tender, as if he did not feel himself except in opposition."[23] The cloistered life of a transcendentalist pilgrim—as seen in Laurence's reclusive lifestyle, in the early hermitage of the Count, in the transcendentalist clubhouse of Ronald's (father's) estate, and later in the cloistered circumstances of Berto's sisters—is also questioned, as it leads to a variety of self-centeredness, not compatible with political activism or social change. Laurence has sought a communal setting, early on, at dramatic events at school; an intellectual community at Ronald's father's castle; then brotherhood with Ronald and Berto; and, finally, sorority with Berto's sisters. But as Laurence laments toward the end of the narrative, "For me there was no companion, and no companionship" (163). In attempting to bring his disparate gender sides into accord, he denies the possibility of finding a soul mate with similar disparate traits. As Howe will later proclaim in her essay "The Halfness of Nature," "The halfness of the individual is literally shown in the division of sex."[24] And though she suggests that "the two halves were never historically" one, they were "ideally" one. She finds marriage to be "one of the most difficult and delicate achievements of society," as each person needs to come to terms with the other half of self: "Either party, striving to dwarf the other, dwarfs itself." A successful marriage, "the supreme of Nature and the sublime of institutions," allows for gender reconciliation: "The ideal human being is man and woman united on the ideal plane."[25]

Laurence does not reconcile the social / solitary polarities that characterize Emerson's advice in "Self-Reliance"—"the great man is he who in the midst of the crowd keeps with perfect sweetness the independence of solitude."[26] There was something, too, about Thoreau's self-centeredness or aloofness, spawned sometimes by the transcendentalist ethos, that the socially dynamic Howe found offensive. Recollecting Emerson's memorial lecture on Thoreau, Howe voices her discontent: "I remember hearing Mr. Emerson, in his discourse on Henry Thoreau, relate that the latter had once determined to manufacture the best lead pencil that could possibly be made." When asked why he would not make the pencil available to interested parties, Thoreau, according to Emerson, responded: "Why should I do this? I have shown that I am able to produce the best pencil that can be made. This was all that I cared to do."[27] Howe finds this a striking example of "selfishness and egotism" and is surprised that such censure "did not appear to have entered into Mr. Emerson's thoughts" (*Rem*, 290, 291).[28] Just so, Laurence's death represents his life—"a deadness and numbness" take "possession of [his whole body], and his eyes are "rigidly fixed upon a single point of vision" (197). Moreover, in diary jottings of 1843 (not coincidentally the year of her marriage) that anticipate her writing of the Laurence manuscript, Howe reveals the key to Laurence's solitary soul in terms of gender balance and social interaction: "Having learned the extent of that which can be accomplished by a solitary mind, it remains for him to learn how much more can be effected by the conjunction of two that form one" (199).[29]

This idea would haunt Julia Ward Howe in such later lectures and essays as "The Halfness of Nature": "Where, oh where," she asks, "shall I find that infinite companionship, which my life should have earned for me?" This lament sounds very much like Laurence's, when he pleads his own case of loneliness. Howe realizes later in life: "The man remains incomplete his whole life long. Most incomplete is he, however, in the isolations of selfishness and of solitude."[30] The answer to Laurence's question might lie in Briseida's final pronouncement that the "undivided" and "integrated" soul in Laurence should not "seek on earth its other moiety" but live to serve God and the community (195–96). Just so, Howe finds ultimate communion with society by joining the greater feminist cause as her marriage gradually dissolves, and certainly after her husband dies. Not finding in marriage the opportunity to unite her male / female polarities, she finds unity within and becomes the perfect hermaphrodite later in life, not the freakish and hopeless hermaphrodite she had envisioned as a young wife and mother, while secretly writing *The Hermaphrodite*.

Reconciling Self with Society

Howe, in her later work as a public voice of feminism, remained ever hopeful in moving toward transcendentalist change and progress: "Life is a perpetual marriage of real and ideal, of endeavor and result," she declares in "The Halfness of Nature," and "The ideal human being is man and woman united on the ideal plane."[31] Though she could imagine and articulate these reconciliations abstractly in her later work, in the unsure phase during which she was writing *The Hermaphrodite*, Howe could not imagine Laurence (and perhaps herself, given her many misgivings about being a woman) as anything but monstrous. The young Howe had to contend with the ire of her husband Samuel after her anonymous publication of *Passion-flowers* (1854); she wrote her sister Louisa, "I really thought . . . that he would have driven me to insanity, so horribly did he behave."[32] After the death of her husband in 1876, she began to reconcile feminine sensitivity with masculine confidence—finding a public voice (which her husband had forbidden) to defend womanhood through her work in the woman's suffrage movement (which the later, more politicized Fuller would have applauded).[33] At first she, like the recently emancipated Frederick Douglass, could not access her public voice easily in public meetings attended by both men and women: "When they requested me to speak, which they did presently, I could only say, 'I am with you'" (*Rem*, 183). Nonetheless, for the first time she did not feel freakish but rather experienced "relief" from a "sense of isolation and eccentricity." "For years past," she maintained, she had wanted "to lend [her] voice to the convictions of [her] heart." In becoming a spokesperson for women, she found a resolution to her earlier conflicts: "I now found a sphere of action in which this mode of expression no longer appeared singular or eccentric, but simple, natural, and, under the circumstances, inevitable" (*ibid.*). Even in her role as presiding chair of the New England Women's Club, she worked steadily to reconcile differences, commenting that even though men and women came together from different parts of the nation, "the comparisons elicited by our meetings ha[d] more and more tended to resolve imagined discords into prevailing harmony" (*Rem*, 189).

Fuller, the woman Howe so admired, might have found it fitting to see the social activist Howe as the liberating "Virginia" of the coming age: "The woman who shall vindicate their birthright for all women; who shall teach them what to claim, and how to use what they obtain?" (*WNC*, 104). Like Fuller, Howe redefined "true womanhood" as she looked for empowerment within. Howe recalled that, during the first "two thirds" of her life, she had "looked to the masculine idea of character as the only true one": "I sought its inspiration, and referred my merits and demerits to its judicial verdict." But in the last part of her life, she saw a new "domain" of "true womanhood": "woman no longer in her ancillary relation to her opposite, man, but in her direct relation to the divine plan and purpose, as a free agent, fully sharing with man every human right and every human responsibility" (*Rem*, 372). This epiphany evokes Briseida's conclusion in *The Hermaphrodite* that the sexless soul must connect to the divine plan and serve humanity.

Fortunately for Howe, during the last part of the nineteenth century, gender roles were less prescribed, and she actually lived to celebrate the progress that had been made. In the treatise *Modern Society*, based on lectures she had delivered at the Concord School of Philosophy, Howe reiterates key transcendentalist tenets and pays homage to her transcendentalist teachers. She concludes by expounding on women's freedom: "Of all the changes which I can chronicle as of my own time, the change in the position of women is perhaps the most marked and the least anticipated by the world at large." Though suffrage was not yet granted to women, Howe acknowledges increased opportunities resulting from the efforts of earlier reformers, and she credits the change, in no small part, to the endeavors of the transcendentalists: "Horace Mann was its apostle, Theodore Parker was its prophet, Margaret Fuller, Lucy Stone, and a host of wise and true-hearted women . . . have been its female saints."[34]

Howe bequeaths the future generation of women "a noble standard of womanhood" and then insists that "the standard of manhood really derives from that of womanhood."[35] In a speech titled "The Future of American Women," included in the *Woman Suffrage Movement* volume, Howe uses the apocalyptic rhetoric of hopeful transcendentalism—as Fuller had ended with the "Virginia" prophetess to come, and Thoreau with the seventeen-year locust, the burrowing bug, and the morning-star imagery. Howe alludes to the passing of time in Nature in order to inspire optimism for cultural change: "The metamorphoses of the seasons, the course of stars and planets, and in minute life, the hatching of the bird from the egg, the resurrection of the worm in the butterfly—all of these should prepare us to expect and understand metamorphoses in the moral world." Hopeful in the women of the new generation who are "equipped with courage and with culture," she provides them with maternal and self reliant archetypes that Fuller had offered previously. Howe refers to the Virgin Mary as representing the woman who has "hidden in her heart the secret of hopes which seemed too great for life to realize." And then she evokes the virgin goddess Diana, as she envisions women as the vanguard of the future: "Women, now is your time. Remember, the crescent which crowns Diana, images also the golden sickle of the reaper." She exhorts the crowd of women to act in the public arena, to effect change: "In the institutions which are coming, your wheat will be bound with the precious sheaves that nourish the multitudes, and the chaff of the traditions which have enslaved you will be burned with unquenchable fire."[36] But Howe is also aware of man's responsibility and includes him as an equal partner in change: "man and woman alike are entitled to fulfil their highest duty, and to claim, in fulfilling it, the noblest right to which humanity is heir." If Thoreau proclaims, at the end of *Walden*, that the "the sun is but a morning star" and awaits the brighter day (333), Howe, at the end of her life, feels that she has witnessed the beginning of that day and looks forward to the changes that will appear at "high noon": "Friends, behold the dawn! The brighter day is already here. Prepare to set your thoughts and deeds in order fit for the splendor of its high noon."[37]

NOTES

1. Gary Williams notes that Howe probably began writing the *Hermaphrodite* manuscript "in the winter of 1846–1847, about three years after Julia Ward's marriage to Samuel Gridley Howe and after the births of her first two (of six) children" (Introduction to *The Hermaphrodite*, by Julia Ward Howe, ed. Gary Williams [Lincoln: Univ. of Nebraska Press, 2004], x). Williams traces the first jottings of this unpublished novel to 1843, the year Howe married. All further references to *The Hermaphrodite* cite this edition and are noted parenthetically in the text.
2. *Julia Ward Howe, 1819–1910*, ed. Laura Elizabeth Howe Richards, Maud Howe Elliott, and Florence Howe Hall, 2 vols. (Boston: Houghton Mifflin, 1916), 1:122 (17 August 1846, 1 December 1846); this volume is hereafter cited parenthetically by page number as *JWH*.
3. See Dana Nelson's essay about the middle-class white man's attempt to redefine manliness during this time period; Thoreau manifests the anxieties that competitive marketplace masculinity could provoke ("Thoreau, Manhood, and Race: Quiet Desperation versus Representative Isolation," in *A Historical Guide to Henry David Thoreau*, ed. William E. Cain [New York: Oxford Univ. Press, 2000], 61–94). Male transcendentalists in particular liked to comment on and defend Thoreau's manhood. Bronson Alcott, for example, claimed, "Thoreau is persistency manly and independent as of old" (11 September 1856 entry from "Bronson Alcott's Journals: Selected Thoreau Entries from 1848 to 1862," comp. Bradley P. Dean, in *The Thoreau Reader*, http:thoreau.eserver.org, accessed November 20, 2013.
4. Williams, Introduction to *The Hermaphrodite*, xxv. I would suggest that Laurence's battle with his father reflects Howe's own struggle with Samuel, who sought to silence her. In a diary entry, Howe reveals how "paralyzed" she felt in this relationship: "I never knew my husband to approve any act of mine which I myself valued. Books—poems—essays—everything has been contemptible . . . because it was not *his way* of doing things" (quoted in Gary Williams, *Hungry Heart: The Literary Emergence of Julia Ward Howe* [Amherst: Univ. of Massachusetts Press, 1999], 232).
5. Henry David Thoreau, "Where I Lived, and What I Lived For," in *Walden* (1854), in *WHT*, 90.
6. For an excellent essay on Thoreau's "domesticity," see Cecilia Tichi, "Domesticity on Walden Pond," in *Historical Guide to Henry David Thoreau*, 95–122.
7. Valarie H. Ziegler, *Diva Julia: The Public Romance and Private Agony of Julia Ward Howe* (New York: Trinity Press International, 2003), 112.
8. Transcendentalist Bronson Alcott, in his observations about children, remarks on this liberating stage of adolescence: the liminal state between the unsexed child and the gendered adult. In a strange, mystical passage, Alcott describes this chrysalis stage, which

is common to the prepubescent child and also necessary for the awakening of the transcendentalist, who transcends gender boundaries. This moment appears to hold the key, in his view, for reaching a balance between the "instinct" relegated to females and the "intellect" assigned to males (*Concord Days* [Boston: Roberts Bros., 1872], 87).

9. "Man partakes of the feminine in Apollo, woman of the masculine in Minerva" (*WNC*, 69).
10. See, for example, historian Ann Douglas's argument for an alignment between ministers and sentimental women in *The Feminization of American Culture* (New York: Macmillan, 1977).
11. Richard J. Schneider also takes up the question of duality in Thoreau and discusses his contradictory views of nature and chastity; see "*Walden*," in *The Cambridge Companion to Henry David Thoreau*, ed. Joel Myerson (New York: Cambridge Univ. Press, 1995), 92–106. For a discussion of divine / earthly duality in Howe, and on Howe's participation at the Concord School of Philosophy, where she, along with Ednah Cheney, was seen as a "Transcendentalist 'professor,'" see Therese B. Dykeman, "The Philosophy of Halfness and the Philosophy of Duality: Julia Ward Howe and Ednah Dow Cheney," *Hypatia: A Journal of Feminist Philosophy* 19, no. 2 (2004): 18.
12. Julia Ward Howe, *Reminiscences, 1819–1899* (Boston: Houghton Mifflin, 1899; reprint, Fairford, U.K.: Echo Library, 2010), 84; hereafter cited parenthetically as *Rem*. Howe attended transcendentalist lectures by Emerson and Conversations with Fuller. In January 1842, in a letter to her sister, a youthful and giddy twenty-two-year-old Julia exclaims, "I have had hardly the least dash of Transcendentalism, and that of the very best description, a lecture and a visit from Emerson, in both of which he said beautiful things, and tomorrow (don't be shocked!) a conversation at Miss Fuller's, which I shall treasure up for your amusement and instruction" (*JWH*, 71–72).
13. Ralph Waldo Emerson, *JMN*, 8:380 (April 1843), 381; (March–April 1843), (14 June 1842), 175.
14. Ralph Waldo Emerson, "Swedenborg; Or, the Mystic," in *CW*, 4:72–73; "Nature," in *CW*, 1:28.
15. Julia Ward Howe, "Emerson's Relation to Society," in *The Genius and Character of Emerson: Lectures at the Concord School of Philosophy*, ed. F. B. Sanborn (Boston: Osgood, 1884), 289.
16. Julia Ward Howe, *Margaret Fuller* (*Marchesa Ossoli*) (Boston: Roberts Brothers, 1883), 85; hereafter designated parenthetically as *Marchesa*.
17. Julia Ward Howe, introduction to *Love Letters of Margaret Fuller, 1845–1846* (New York: D. Appleton, 1903), v.
18. Julia Ward Howe, "Sibyl," in *Passion-flowers* (Boston: Ticknor, Reed, & Fields, 1854), 99, 100.
19. Also see *WNC*, 99.
20. Julia Ward Howe, "'Let There Be Light': Speech on Woman Suffrage" (1905), in *Julia Ward Howe and the Woman Suffrage Movement: A Selection from her Speeches and Essays*, ed. Florence Howe Hall (Boston: Dana Estes, 1913), 220–21.
21. The sensitive Emma of Laurence's school days, who is ultimately destroyed by the discovery of the "sexless" Laurence, has some powers of elocution that were characteristic of Fuller, as Howe will even describe them later in her biography of Fuller. In the novel, Laurence comments on Emma's dramatic presence: "Unlike most women, she possessed the twofold gift of being graceful alike in speech and in silence—her voice was full of music, her words full of power, but when she listened, her features all spoke; and you read the eloquent answer in her eye long before you heard it from her lips" (9).

22. Though I perceive the bonding here as sororal between Laurence and Berto's sisters and between Howe and Fuller, Dorri Beam, in this volume, shows the possibility of a more erotic bonding between transcendentalist women as well.
23. Emerson, "Thoreau," in Joel Myerson, "Emerson's 'Thoreau': A New Edition from Manuscript," in *Studies in the American Renaissance, 1979,* ed. Myerson (Boston: Twayne, 1979), 90.
24. Julia Ward Howe, "The Halfness of Nature," in *Is Polite Society Polite? and Other Essays* (Boston: Lamson, Wolffe, 1895), 172.
25. Ibid., 173. This concept is quite similar to Fuller's vision of the ideal marriage, "the fourth and highest grade of marriage union," a spiritual union that allows both partners to thrive on their individual journeys (*WNC*, 48). And Fuller also celebrated difference: "Harmony exists in difference, no less than in likeness" (47).
26. Emerson, "Self-Reliance," in *CW*, 2:31.
27. Actually, Howe does not recall here the precise wording of the line from the memorial sermon on Thoreau. Emerson quotes Thoreau saying: "Why should I? I would not do again what I have done once" ("Thoreau," 394). This sounds more like Thoreau justifying himself according to the transcendentalist credo that one does not traverse the same path twice.
28. To give the male transcendentalists Emerson and Thoreau credit, they did become more political after their solitary incubation periods, advocating quite vocally on the lecture circuit for the eradication of slavery.
29. These jottings are cited from appendix 1 of Williams's edition.
30. Howe, "Halfness of Nature," 170.
31. Ibid., 170, 173.
32. Julia Ward Howe, quoted in Williams, *Hungry Heart*, 173.
33. Howe helped found the New England Women's Club in 1868 and also the New England Woman Suffrage Movement, over which she presided from 1868 to 1877 and from 1893 to 1910. She inaugurated the *Woman's Journal* in 1870 and served as editor from 1870 to 1890.
34. Julia Ward Howe, *Modern Society* (Boston: Roberts Brothers, 1881), 84, 85.
35. Ibid., 87.
36. Julia Ward Howe, "The Future of American Women," in *Julia Ward Howe and the Woman Suffrage Movement*, 187, 188.
37. Howe, "Let There Be Light," 220–21. This, a woman's suffrage speech, full of promise for the future, solidifies the idea of sisterhood Howe endorsed. And, tellingly, daughter Florence takes on the mission as she collects Howe's writings.

SECTION 3
Wider Circles of Vision and Action

INTERLUDE

Eliza W. Farnham, from the preface to *Life in Prairie Land* (New York: Harper Brothers, 1846), iii–vii.

To those who read the volume first, and afterward, in some idle moment, turn back to the preface, I need not say that I have been impelled in every step by love of my theme. That will have been apparent enough to them, without any such declaration. I have loved the West, and it still claims my preference over all other portions of the earth. Its magnitude, its fertility, the kindliness of its climate, the variety and excellence of its productions are unrivaled in our own country, if not on the globe.

In these characteristics, it presents itself to my mind in the light of a strong and generous parent, whose arms are spread to extend protection, happiness, and life to throngs who seek them from other and less friendly climes. Setting a high value upon these resources, I rejoice to hear of emigration to the country possessing them—not alone because those who go will find there abundance for the supply of their natural wants, but because the influences with which it will address their spiritual natures are purifying, ennobling, and elevating. If nature ever taught a lesson which the endwarfed, debased mind of man could study with profit, it is in these regions of her benignest dispensations. The burden of her teaching here, is too palpable to be wholly rejected by any. Even vulgar minds do not altogether escape its influence. Their perceptions become more vivid, their desires more exalted, their feelings purer, and all their intellectual action more expanded. . . .

It must not be forgotten, however, that a large class of minds have no adaptation to the conditions of life in the West. This is more especially true of my own sex. Very many ladies are so unfortunate as to have had their minds thoroughly distorted from all true and natural modes of action by an artificial and pernicious course of education, or the influence of a false social position. They cannot endure the sudden and complete transition which is forced upon them by emigration to the West. Hence a class may always be found who dislike the country; who see and feel only its disadvantages; who endure the self-denial it imposes without enjoying any of the freedom it confers; who suffer the loss of artificial luxuries, but never appreciate what is offered in exchange for them. Persons so constituted ought never to entertain for a moment the project of emigration. . . .

I had no such experience, for I loved the country, and when compelled to return to the crowded and dusty marts of the East, I did so with many and deep regrets; and these still linger and mingle largely with the emotions of my life. The writing of these sketches has, therefore, been a labor of love. While engaged upon them, I have lived again in the land of my heart. I have seen the grasses wave, and felt the winds, and listened to the birds, and watched the springing flowers, and exulted in something of the old sense of freedom which these conferred upon me. Visions, prophetic of the glory and greatness which are to be developed here, have dwelt in my mind and exalted it above the narrow personal cares of life.

It is the enjoyment afforded by this kind of emancipation which so endears the Western country to those who have resided in it. It steals upon the heart like what it is, the very witchery of nature; so that those who are susceptible to it, feel the charm but not the inconvenience through which it is invoked. Such persons delight in the perfection and beauty of the natural, and these suffice them.

Green Exaltadas

Margaret Fuller, Transcendentalist Conservationism, and Antebellum Women's Nature Writing

DANIEL S. MALACHUK

In the last two decades, scholars have established transcendentalism as a motive force for two major nineteenth-century political movements, abolitionism and women's rights.[1] This scholarship rightly returns us to the first mature understanding of transcendentalism, the understanding that thrived between Henry David Thoreau's 1860 declaration, as he sided with John Brown's radical abolitionism, that the North "was suddenly all transcendental" and Caroline Dall's 1897 observation that feminism, like transcendentalism, asserted "the inalienable worth of man, and of the immanence of the Divine in the Human."[2] While twentieth-century critics largely lost sight of transcendentalism's political commitments, today these commitments are at the center of scholarly appraisals of the movement, with a special focus on three canonical authors: Ralph Waldo Emerson, Henry David Thoreau, and Margaret Fuller.

Many postbellum critics also understood transcendentalism as a motive force for a third major movement, environmentalism, but we have yet to regain this insight. That conviction about "the Divine in the Human" has instead been identified by ecocritics as exactly what one of the transcendentalists had to renounce before he achieved ecological awareness: that is, once Thoreau "de-transcendentalized," environmentalism began. In a 1991 founding text of ecocriticism, Max Oelschlaeger spotted in *Nature* (1836) damning proof that for the "conventionally anthropocentric" Emerson "nature is mere putty in human hands," while for the admirably "ecocentric" Thoreau the "idea of wilderness goes beyond transcendentalism." According to this version of environmental history, Thoreau, late in his career, glimpsed what for Oelschlaeger and other ecocritics is a central tenet: that the dominant reality for environmentalism must be natural systems, not humanity. As Lawrence Buell concurred in his influential 1995 *The Environmental Imagination*, Thoreau, finally and rightly, "became increasingly interested in defining nature's structure . . . for its own sake, as against how nature might subserve humanity, which was Emerson's primary consideration."[3] And, so, where in the recovered political history of transcendentalism the three canonical authors now properly share equal billing, in the ecocritical version of American environmentalist thought, Emerson plays the anthropocentric foil to the properly de-transcendentalized and ecocentric late Thoreau—and Fuller rarely appears.[4]

Heading in the opposite direction, this essay argues that the transcendentalists' conviction about the Divine in the Human is the core not only of their recovered politics but also of their neglected environmentalism. A more complete account of this transcendentalist environmentalism would attend at length to Thoreau, who needs to be remembered not as a late-blooming ecocentrist but as an unrepentant transcendentalist naturalist—regretting as late as 1853, for example, that he did not tell the American Association for the Advancement of Science that, for him, the most interesting "branch of science" was that "which deals with the higher law" (that is, the Divine in the Human).[5] Thoreau's major environmentalist declaration, the late-career "Walking," which begins with a pledge "to speak a word for . . . wildness," explicitly contends that to preserve the world we must make better use of wildness—that "in Wildness is the preservation of the world" (*Excursions*, in *WHT*, 202). "The importance of wilderness" for Thoreau, as biologist Daniel B. Botkin explains this often-misinterpreted passage, "is in the way it enriches people and civilization."[6] Indeed, Thoreau makes his humanist priorities immediately apparent in the sentences that follow, emphasizing the wild's multifarious uses—from "the tonics and barks that brace mankind" to the founders of every eminent state that "have drawn their nourishment and vigor from a . . . wild source." The passage, in short, is about as clear a vindication of "anthropocentrism" as you are likely to find, but it is, importantly, a *transcendentalist* anthropocentrism: like Emerson and Fuller, Thoreau urged what he called in *The Maine Woods* the "highest use" of nature so as to enable us to realize the Divine within, or (to use Fuller's favored phrase from Johann Wolfgang von Goethe) *Bildung*, the central project of transcendentalism.[7]

Of course, what Thoreau means by a "higher use" of nature is the very opposite of what contemporary free-market capitalists mean by the cynical phrase "wise use." Nonetheless, Thoreau does advocate that we use nature, though more often in higher ways and less often in lower ways. This framing of the human–nature relationship may be out of step with today's ecocriticism, but Thoreau's (and Emerson's and Fuller's) emphasis on "higher uses" of nature puts them historically at the very vanguard of a much bigger movement, indeed, at the core of the modern environmentalist movement: conservationism. First formally articulated (in the United States) in George Perkins Marsh's 1864 *Man and Nature*, conservationism had a lengthy prehistory, as a variety of historians are now demonstrating: from early conservationist thought among antebellum natural historians, farmers, and gardeners to the classical pastoral and georgic traditions, particularly as articulated by the romantics as the "middle landscape"—that "somewhere 'between' . . . the opposing forces of civilization and nature," as Leo Marx put it in his classic 1964 *The Machine in the Garden*. One can locate the transformation of these classical modes (specifically the georgic and the pastoral) into conservationism as far back as the seventeenth-century landscape painters, as Simon Schama has done, but most scholars agree that conservationism started in earnest with those European and American romantics who were so repulsed, on the one side, by the industrializing city that they dramatically shifted the middle landscape back toward the other side, the wild, which becomes, as Thoreau puts it, a kind of "tonic," without which "our village life would stagnate" (*Walden*, in *WHT*, 317).[8]

The main concern of the first section of this essay, however, is Margaret Fuller's contribution, and so it elaborates only briefly on the most distinctive aspect of the conservationist philosophy of transcendentalism as a whole. Many earlier writers had of course praised the middle landscape, even contending with Jefferson that "those who labor in the earth are the chosen people of God," but it was the three canonical transcendentalists who most powerfully explicated the middle landscape's central purpose to be the cultivation of the Divine in the Human, or *Bildung*.[9]

This essay's longer second section expands the circle of writers participating in transcendentalist conservationism by demonstrating how Margaret Fuller's distinctive emphases were shared not only by Emerson and Thoreau but even more by a small set of other women who, like Fuller, wrote about nature in the American West between the mid-1830s and the early 1850s. Sharing the transcendentalists' conservationist belief that the middle landscape is the best place for *Bildung*, these writers were cannier than Emerson and Thoreau about gender. And, at a time when most everyone was writing about nature-as-feminine and humanity-as-masculine, that canniness enabled these female writers to propose more nuanced human–nature relationships than one finds in Thoreau and Emerson. As Annette Kolodny observed in what remains the most important study of these writers, they of course eschewed "the psychosexual dynamic of a virginal paradise" that characterized so much antebellum male writing about nature, but so did Emerson and Thoreau.[10] What Emerson and Thoreau did not always avoid, however, was the other extreme, the "cult of true mothernaturehood" (to adapt a phrase). Writing against that grain, these female writers were able to refine three additional qualities of transcendentalist conservationism beyond the emphasis on the middle-landscape *Bildung*, qualities that are present but muted in the writings of Emerson and Thoreau: a realism about the degree to which nature encourages *Bildung* and corresponding sensitivities about the challenges of both communal (especially democratic) agency and individual agency in creating middle landscapes.

This achievement gives the present essay its title. Of the three most prominent transcendentalists, it was only Fuller who began to imagine in any detail how people might realize conservationism's middle landscape. In her 1845 *Woman in the Nineteenth Century*, she called for a movement of "Exaltadas," young women who would absorb the "teachings of the woods and fields" before saving "the world" (*WNC*, 79, 80): conservationist women whose "service" would be "action and conservatism" (*WNC*, 91). Like Thoreau, Fuller aimed to use nature to preserve "the world," but she was able to imagine more precisely how this might be done. And she accomplished this by doing what Emerson and Thoreau never did: going west and writing a book—the book before *Woman in the Nineteenth Century*—about how nature was and was not being used to preserve the world. This essay is about that book, *Summer on the Lakes, in 1843*, and several more like it written by Fuller's allied "green Exaltadas."

In 1964, Leo Marx famously portrayed Thoreau's *Walden* as a strictly literary pursuit of a middle landscape, but others have since read it as a serious pursuit of real landscapes, including (to take just one example) Thoreau's earnest experiment in "The Bean Fields" as one in "sustainable agriculture."[11] In that chapter, Thoreau describes his field as "the connecting link between wild and cultivated fields": "as some states are civilized, and others half-civilized, and others savage or barbarous, so my field was, though not in a bad sense, a half-cultivated field" (*Walden*, 158). Emerson, too, was more interested than is usually recognized in the middle landscape, including farms, as when he writes in "The Young American" (1844) about the East "imbib[ing] . . . European culture," the "rocky West . . . intruding a new and continental element into the national genius," and between the two a "looked-for American genius": "How much better when the whole land is a garden, and the people have grown up in the bowers of a paradise" (*CW*, 1:229). So too in *Summer* does Fuller find all over western Illinois that "half-cultivated field." In Geneva, Illinois, she is struck by the environs of a country home: "There is that mixture of culture and rudeness in the aspect of things as gives a feeling of freedom. . . . This habitation of man seemed like a nest in the grass, so thoroughly were the buildings and all the objects of human care harmonized with what was natural. The tall trees bent and whispered all around, as if to hail with sheltering love the men who had come to dwell among them" (*EMF*, 92). In Oregon, Illinois, she notes, nature's abundance means the farmer "can afford to leave some of it wild, and to carry out his own plans without obliterating those of nature" (*EMF*, 105).

Such paeans to the middle landscape, however, are ubiquitous in antebellum American literature. What the transcendentalists specifically contributed to early conservationism was the suggestion that these kinds of places, used properly, were the ideal sites for *Bildung*, a *Bildung* that aspired to spiritual as well as intellectual insight (unlike Goethe's version, as Fuller made clear in the preface to her translation of *Eckermann's Conversations with Goethe* [1839]).[12] In his 1836 *Nature*, Emerson offers the first and most systematic consideration by a transcendentalist of these ascending uses of nature, from (as the chapter titles make clear) the lowest use of "commodity"; to "beauty," "language," "discipline," and "idealism"; and finally to the highest use, "spirit." We "know the uses of . . . a few plants," Emerson writes in that last chapter, but "is not the landscape . . . a face of him [God]?" (*CW*, 1:39). "I think we must regard the *land*," Emerson writes in "The Young American," "as a commanding and increasing power on the citizen, the sanative and Americanizing influence, which promises to disclose new virtues for ages to come" (*CW*, 1:229; emphasis in original). Thoreau, too, argues in several other texts besides *Walden* and "Walking" that the wild should ultimately be tapped for spiritual self-realization. In *The Maine Woods* he proposes preserving New England forests "not to hold the king's game merely" as in Old England "but to hold and preserve the king himself also, the lord of creation,—not for idle sport or food, but for inspiration and our own true re-creation" (*Maine Woods*, in *WHT*, 156). "Recreation" is a favorite synonym of Thoreau's for "higher use"; in the unfinished "Wild Fruits" he contends that "each town should have a park, or rather a primitive forest [to] stand and decay for higher uses—a common possession forever, for instruction and recreation."[13]

Fuller also proposes the middle landscape as the best place for *Bildung*, so long as we use nature in higher ways. Early in *Summer*, Fuller, awaiting inspiration at Niagara Falls, observes a regrettable scene: "A man . . . walked close up to the fall, and, . . . with an air as if thinking how he could best appropriate it to his own use, he spat into it." Such "love of *utility* . . . will not," she hopes, "be seen on the historic page to be . . . truly the America" (*EMF*, 73; emphasis in original). She develops this hope later in the book through a dialogue between her favored character, "Free Hope," and several others, including "Good Sense." "Good Sense" urges us to recognize that "all around us lies what we neither understand nor use" and to "confine ourselves" to that and "be completely natural." "Free Hope" responds: "Who sees the meaning of the flower uprooted in the ploughed field? The ploughman who does not look beyond its boundaries and does not raise his eyes from the ground? No—but the poet who sees that field in its relations with the universe" (*EMF*, 146).[14]

In the transcendentalist oeuvre, though, one of the most important but neglected portraits of the middle landscape as the site of *Bildung* may be "Ganymede to His Eagle," a poem by Fuller in *Summer*. Ganymede is arguably a prototype of the Exaltadas introduced the next year in *Woman in the Nineteenth Century*. In the opening pages of *Woman*, long before she introduces those Exaltadas, Fuller refers to the person who has "ascertain[ed] and fulfill[ed] the law of his being" serving as "an angel or messenger" to the rest of us (*WNC*, 5). Later in the book, however, Fuller despairs that, in the United States, "where humanity was, at last, to have a fair chance to know itself, and all men be born free and equal for the eagle's flight," the annexation of Texas for the expansion of slavery has jeopardized what such angelic go-betweens can in fact accomplish (*WNC*, 97). It is in the very next paragraph that Fuller issues her call for "Exaltadas": the new angelic / aquiline figures who will "save the country from this disgrace" (*WNC*, 98).

In *Summer*, written the year before the annexation of Texas, Fuller expresses more robust hopes for two such go-betweens, Ganymede and his eagle, though Fuller already worries that the United States is a problematic launching pad for *Bildung*. Before the poem, Fuller describes a Fourth of July visit to a bluff near Oregon, Illinois, known as the "Eagle's Nest," where she had "never felt so happy" to have been "born in America"; at the same time she decries the recent removal of Black Hawk and his people from this same place (*EMF*, 100–101). Similarly, in the four paragraphs that follow the poem, Fuller at once recalls the holiday's "laughter," "sweet thoughts," and "pleasing fancies" but also how the patriotic celebrations involved the "the usual puffs of Ameriky" (*EMF*, 104).[15]

However, if the nation as a whole is an ambiguous site for *Bildung*, the region of western Illinois is not. Fuller's admiration extends to both its natural and its cultural qualities: the "fine, park-like woods . . . carpeted with thick grasses and flowers" but also the families returning from Sunday services (*EMF*, 99); the view of bluffs whose rocks "touch it with a wildness and liberality" but also the homesteads like "a double log cabin" that to Fuller's "eye" is "the model of a Western villa" (*EMF*, 100). Fuller stresses that this home is the work of both humans and nature: "Nature had laid out before it grounds which could not be improved [and w]ithin, female taste had veiled every rudeness—availed itself of every sylvan grace" (*EMF*, 104).[16]

But it is in the actual poem that Fuller most fully dramatizes her vision of go-betweens, enabled by the middle landscape, spreading the message of *Bildung*. Consider first the specific work of Fuller's proto-Exaltadas in the poem's story, especially in contrast to two rival Ganymedes Fuller must have known. Goethe's 1789 "Ganymede" is narrated entirely by the shepherd boy himself, who begins as in a classical pastoral lying facedown upon the spring grass but then finds himself whisked aloft, still backward, by a force unidentified until the final lines: "Clouds, in your lap, / Upward, / Embraced embracing! / Upward to your breast, / All-loving father!"[17] While Goethe's poem can be interpreted as balancing Xenophon's spiritual version of the myth (the rapturous knowledge of God) and Plato's homoerotic version, it leans toward the latter. Fuller's Ganymede pursues a more spiritually rapturous *Bildung*, though she may have hoped the androgynous Ganymede would appeal as a model to both female and male readers. Her Ganymede does not directly engage Jove but rather his "destined brother friend" (*EMF*, 101), an eagle; Jove has declared both "the chosen servants of his ministry"—the messenger eagle "to express the verdict of Olympian laws," Ganymede to provide water so that the eagle may sing those laws, and the two together thus "weav[ing] the needed chain to bind [earth] to heaven"(*EMF*, 103). Far from experiencing rapture (sensual or spiritual), however, Ganymede in Fuller's account is still troubled, portrayed by a speaker in the opening stanza with "a strange pain . . . written on his brow" (*EMF*, 101), a notable departure from the bland façade of the title figure in the 1817 *Ganymede* by Danish sculptor Bertel Thorvaldsen (mentioned in the subtitle [ibid.]). Following the opening stanza, the rest of the poem is spoken by Ganymede, who pleads for the eagle to return, until the final stanza, in which the opening speaker comes back to add her plea that the eagle return with the song to reward the boy's laborious work of *Bildung*, "bear[ing] him often to the serene heights, / Where hands that were so prompt in serving thee / Shall be allowed the highest ministry / And Rapture live with bright Fidelity" (*EMF*, 103).

Fuller imagines this rapture (notably active and moral compared to Goethe's) beginning "on the height called the Eagle's Nest, Oregon, Rock River, July 4th 1843," as the subtitle reads (*EMF*, 101). But she reminds us in various ways throughout the poem that Ganymede, like the bluffs themselves, has his roots in the middle landscape below. Ganymede has filled the eagle's vase a "hundred times . . . / Since the full noon o'er hill and valley glowed" (ibid.), reminding us of the world below. He likens life before seeing the eagle to "May, / Longing for summer that must mar its bloom," a metaphor nudged into the promise of unknown growth: "For, what the rosebud seeks tells not the rose" (*EMF*, 101–2). Before seeing the eagle, Ganymede dwelt in a land of "Eternal youth, where flowers are the fruit" (*EMF*, 102), but now he will bloom more completely. Lightning occasionally tells "the secrets of its fiery frame," notably striking both "the sacred spire" and "the sacred grove" below (ibid.), which ties bluff and land together and teaches Ganymede that "the creation" as a whole has "but just begun, / New leaves still leaving from the primal one" (ibid.).

Fuller thus finds a number of ways to signal that this boy's—and humanity's—heavenward growth is rooted in a middle landscape of May, flowers, fruits, groves, and leaves. As she wrote a year later in her journal, "Last year this day was the Ganymede . . . day": "the full music of soul amid that resplendent beauty of nature" (*WNC*, 198). Far, then, from exemplifying "a mode of optimism that overcomes the limits of the transcendental idealism she has brought from home,"[18] *Summer*, and particularly the Ganymede poem, reveals Fuller to be the quintessential transcendentalist conservationist: she insists that

Ganymede's realization of the Divine in the Human—"the full music of soul"—springs specifically from the "resplendent" middle landscape.

As it had been for millennia, in the antebellum period the quintessential middle landscape of the garden was gendered feminine, whether figured as a cultivated settlement shy of the wilder masculine frontier or the delicate picturesque opposite the strenuous sublime.[19] All three of the major transcendentalists readily co-opted the garden's gender ideology to convey the middle landscape's allure in provocative but culturally resonant ways. For example, in the famous passage from "Walking" cited earlier, Thoreau first feminizes "wildness" (as the wolf nursing Rome's founders) into a middle landscape but then implies that it became both too feminine (in falling to the Goths) *and* not feminine enough (by recalling that the Goths themselves were breastfed in the forest) (*Excursions*, 202).[20]

That said, Thoreau and Emerson were often complacent about gender ideology, and so as conservationists working at a time when nature was routinely gendered female and humanity male, their complacency led to less-nuanced depictions of the human–nature relationship. Postbellum readers of the transcendentalists sensed this. For example, Thomas Wentworth Higginson, a biographer of Fuller and champion of Thoreau's environmentalism, ultimately favored Fuller's conservationist phrasing, or so his 1886 *Out-Door Papers* suggests. Higginson was attuned to Thoreau's allegiance to the middle landscape—he defended Thoreau in 1879 against the charge of "hat[ing] civilization" by pointing to his final decision in *The Maine Woods* to return from wild "barrenness" to the "partially cultivated country."[21] And he was undoubtedly familiar with Thoreau's delicate observation in *Walden* that "fishermen, hunters, woodchoppers, and others, spending their lives in the fields and woods, in a peculiar sense a part of Nature themselves, are often in a more favorable mood for observing her . . . than philosophers or poets even, who approach her with expectation" (*Walden*, 210). But he still chose Fuller's *Summer*, not Thoreau's *Walden*, to make the following point:

> The sentimentalist . . . say[s,] "if the object is . . . the enjoyment of Nature, why not go and enjoy her, without any collateral aim?" Because . . . if we have a collateral aim, we enjoy her far more. . . . Margaret Fuller's fine saying touches [this] point,—"Nature will not be stared at." Go out merely to enjoy her . . . and you begin to suspect yourself of affectation. . . . Go out under pretence of shooting on the marshes or botanizing in the forests; . . . swim with her, ride with her, run with her, and she gladly takes you back once more within the horizon of her magic.[22]

Thoreau and Fuller were articulating a similar idea, but Thoreau's humans with collateral aims become "a part of" Mother Nature. Fuller's nature is more complexly feminine, "not [to] be stared at" because she is severe, modest, coquettish, or perhaps all of these things. Fuller's easy play with nature's gender arouses Higginson's own conservationist imagining that we remain in complex relation with nature rather than apart from or one with "her." This nuanced sense of gender enabled Fuller, and the other green Exaltadas, to convey vividly how best to build, sustain, and use the feminized middle landscape.

Fuller would formally introduce the "Exaltadas" in the 1845 *Woman*, but their more patently green prototypes appear in *Summer*. With the exception of the androgynous Ganymede, Fuller proposes for this role young women in the West. Regretting the Northeastern orientation of the first-generation settler—"accustomed to the pavement of Broadway, [she] dare not tread the wildwood paths for fear of rattlesnakes!" (*EMF*, 106)—Fuller looks instead to the second, the daughter who will "diffuse around her" a "new" kind of "elegance . . . , original, enchanting." This new agent of the middle landscape will be "really skilled to make home beautiful and comfortable," but also possess the "bodily strength to enjoy plenty of exercise, the woods, the streams, a few studies, music, and the sincere and familiar intercourse" (*EMF*, 107). If in *Woman* Fuller takes Queen Isabella's material sponsorship of Columbus as a sign that the United States "must pay back its debt to Woman, without whose aid it would not have been brought into alliance with the civilized world" (*WNC*, 38), in *Summer* she examines just how these young women—"women as creators of a nation," as Susan Rosowski has argued[23]—are bringing the land and the civilized world "into alliance."

Though both Thoreau and Emerson wrote texts interrogating the classical tradition of *translatio studii et imperii*, the Western transfer of empire and learning, and published travel writing about places to the north (Maine, Quebec) and east (Cape Cod, England), neither actually wrote at any length about the West.[24] Fuller herself went west and published a full nonfiction account of the women she saw there, something few other women did between the mid-1830s and the early 1850s.[25] The next part of this essay considers some of these other accounts: Mary Austin Holley's *Texas: Observations, Historical, Geographical and Descriptive* (1833); Harriet Martineau's *Society in America* (1837) and *Retrospect of Western Travel* (1838); Caroline Kirkland's *A New Home, Who'll Follow?* (1839), *Forest Life* (1842), and *Western Clearings* (1845), all on Michigan; Eliza Farnham's *Life in Prairie Land* (1846), on Illinois; Susan Fenimore Cooper's *Rural Hours* (1850), on rural New York; and Alice Cary's *Clovernook; or, Recollections of Our Neighborhood in the West* (1851), on Ohio. These texts, like those by Emerson and Thoreau, celebrate the higher uses of nature in the middle landscape as conducive to *Bildung*; showing this will be the first aim of this part of the essay. However, the authors of these texts also share Fuller's three distinctive gifts as a transcendentalist conservationist, to which the essay finally turns: that is, they offer a greater realism about nature's participation in *Bildung*, and they attend carefully to the consequent challenges to both communal and individual agency in the middle landscape. The remainder of this essay draws on *Summer* and these other texts written by and about the green Exaltadas to demonstrate each of these four points in turn.

First, then, the green Exaltadas believed like Emerson and Thoreau that the middle landscape was the place for *Bildung*. Erika Kreger has noted this in the texts of Cary, Cooper, and Kirkland. Where Marx focuses on the "pastoral[s] of failure" written by Eastern men, Kreger shows that these women wrote "pastorals of possibility that, even when depicting the flaws of a given settlement, argue for the attainability of the ideal middle ground." Kreger observes how Kirkland situates "Montacute" (her fictionalized Pinckney, Michigan) in the middle landscape between the "city comforts 'apt to make us proud, selfish, and ungrateful' and the 'unwatched and unbridled license which we read of in regions nearer to the setting sun.'" The same is true of the others, as Kreger shows: Cary describes Clovernook (outside Cincinnati) as equidistant from "those old empires" to the east (characterized by "tyrannous laws" and "hereditary acquaintance") and "the far west where pioneers are still busy with felling the opposing trees [and] it is not yet time for the [pastoral] reed's music"; Cooper also praises her upstate New York village in *Rural Hours* as a middle landscape, having "a cheerful, flourishing aspect, yet rural and unambitious."[26]

Most modern critics have looked past these women's interest in middle landscapes as sites for *Bildung*, however, and instead treated their tributes to settlement as uncomplicated expressions of manifest destiny ideology. In *The Land before Her*, Kolodny notes that such prairie promotionalists as Fuller and Farnham (in Illinois) and Holley (in Texas) point to that seemingly ready-made middle landscape as proof that God has customized it for white habitation. Fuller cannot resist describing the Rock River country of Illinois, for example, as "the very Eden which earth might still afford," Kolodny remarks.[27] Kreger, too, argues that Cary, Cooper, and Kirkland "all idealize this 'middle landscape' in their community narratives and, as women of their time, occasionally fail to recognize any inconsistencies in pairing progressive and pastoral goals."[28] That much of this literature is too comfortable with American imperialism is true; Fuller's own ambivalence in *Summer* about indigenous populations is typical in this regard, as Jessie Bray shows.[29] It is also true that these authors sometimes represent the middle landscape as a providential gift, as when Kirkland writes of "the harmony which the Creator has instituted between the animate and inanimate works of His hand."[30]

Nonetheless, read within the conservationist tradition, these texts reflect an impressive awareness of the middle landscape as something not *found* (as a gift from God) but rather *made* by men and women in collaboration with nature, and thus easily marred. For example, the green Exaltadas writing specifically about wooded areas worry exceedingly about deforesting that landscape. Kirkland, whom Fuller read before writing *Summer* (as Kolodny notes), and later praised for her "valuable suggestions for the future" (*MFC*, 267), not only objects in *Forest Life* to the settler who sees in trees "only obstacles which must be removed" but finds in this mentality a flawed understanding of the purpose of the middle landscape.[31] For these lower-use advocates, Kirkland protests, "not one tree [can] be suffered to cumber the ground," their "very notion of advancement . . . inseparably connected with the total extirpation of the forest."[32] Similarly, Cooper, an author Fuller did not live to read, asserts in "A Dissolving View" (1852) that "the hand of man generally improves a landscape," but "when he endeavors to rise above his true part of laborer and husbandman [and] assumes the character of creator . . . he is apt to fail."[33] In *Rural Hours* (1850), Cooper defends the carefully made and then conserved middle landscape as beneficial to both humans and nature; to continue to remove trees in a more settled community, particularly "when the hills are becoming more bare every day [and] timber and fuel are rising in prices, and new uses are found for even indifferent woods," is to defy "common sense."[34]

And so, pace Kolodny and others who interpret such tributes to middle landscapes as entirely imperialist, these prairie pastoralists perceive the middle landscape as a fragile creation by humans. Yes, Holley and Farnham write about the prairie as a paradise regained, but they also are troubled by the male preference to (in Holley's words) "cut away every tree of a clearing" and thus remove "the noble giants of the forest [that] serve as true parasols to the dwelling they ornament." Observing the "files of earnest men, with hard hands and severe, calculating faces, pass[ing] toward [Illinois] from the east," Farnham worries that nature's "former aspect" will "fade away beneath the despoiling hand that labor would lay upon her charms."[35] Fuller, too, despairs in *Summer* that the settlers' "mode of cultivation will, in the course of twenty, perhaps ten, years, obliterate the natural expression of the country" (*EMF*, 96). At the same time, she still believes that any *successful* middle landscapes on the prairie require the collaboration of humans and nature. Her poem in *Summer* about Dixon, Illinois, "The Western Eden," does not marvel at nature's readymade middle landscape (as the misleading title implies) but instead emphasizes that "'improvement' yet has made no blot, / But Nature all-astonished stands, to find / Her plan protected by the [conservationist] human mind" (*EMF*, 97).

The distinctive quality of transcendentalist conservationism, though, is the more specific contention that the middle landscape nurtures not just Jeffersonian virtues but *Bildung*. The green Exaltadas believe this, too, though in contrast to the transcendentalists, they generally rely upon either orthodox Christianity or Goethean naturalism to describe self-culture. Cooper would be an example of the former. In *Rural Hours* she offers her book as "a sort of rustic primer" to lead readers "to something higher," by which she means not just a general ethic of "simplicity" ("a quality as yet too little valued or understood in this country") but also Christianity. "A careless indifference to any good gift of our gracious Maker," Cooper warns, "shows a want of thankfulness, as any abuse or waste, betrays a reckless spirit of evil."[36] Her sectarianism is even more precise in *The Rhyme and Reason of Country Life* (1854): "No system connects man by more close and endearing ties, with the earth and all it holds, than Christianity," certainly not "all the gods with which Homer peopled his narrow world."[37]

Leaning toward Goethean naturalism is Eliza Farnham. Like Cooper in *Rural Hours*, Farnham recommends the middle landscape as a moral site; she notes that settlers in Illinois "have fewer artificial luxuries than the inhabitants of the older regions," which promotes "a simple [rather] than a complicated style of living." Like Cooper, Farnham shifts to a higher use of nature, but her discourse is Goethean: "My cathedral [is] the overhanging cliff, my temple the eloquent shades. . . . Living much with nature, makes me wiser, better, purer, and therefore, happier."[38] In *Society in America*, Harriet Martineau similarly complains that the settler's use of nature rarely rises above exploitation; for example, she bemoans the absence of "higher objects in life" in the settlement of Texas. Her hopes for higher uses of nature are most evident in "Economy," which opens part 2 of volume 1 of *Society*. "It is an absorbing thing to watch the process of world-making," Martineau writes, meaning "both the formation of the natural and the conventional world." Describing the formation of caves and waterfalls and even "a sort of scum on the waters" of the Mississippi that "betoken the birth-place of new land," Martineau concludes these phenomena have much to teach us about conventional (that is, human) world-making. Unfortunately, though, these wildernesses have been "dispensed to savages" who lack a critical perspective on them, or to "busy [white] colonists" who find themselves "pressed by bodily wants" or who "drive out the red man, and drive in the black man . . . think[ing] only of cotton and of gold." "The philosopher should come [west]," Martineau decrees, before the "primitive glories of nature" are "effaced," and "find combinations and proportions of life and truth which are not to be found elsewhere." So, too: "The painter should come and find combinations and proportions of visible beauty. . . . The architect should come, and find suggestions and irradiations of his art. . . . The poet should come. . . . [These regions] should not be left to the vanishing savage, the busy and the sordid."[39] Like Goethe, both Farnham and Martineau urge a search for truth and beauty; unlike the transcendentalists, they do not also urge a search for the Divine.

Second, while the green Exaltadas may differ in their philosophical accounts of the "higher uses," they are all more realistic than Emerson and Thoreau about the limits of nature's collaboration in "our own true re-creation," as Thoreau optimistically puts it. The male transcendentalists certainly have moments of doubt about nature's transformational power—for instance, Thoreau's "Higher Laws" chapter in *Walden*—but the green Exaltadas, most of all Fuller, significantly enrich our appreciation of this otherwise muted aspect of transcendentalist conservationism. Fuller's review of Schoolcraft Jones's *Ellen: Or, Forgive and Forget* (1846) is a prime example of this realism of the green Exaltadas. Fuller explicitly challenges the "current superstition that country people are more pure and healthy, in mind and body than those who live in cities" (*MFC*, 333). "Our groves and fields have no good fairies or genii who teach . . . the truths . . . that can alone preserve the village, as the city, from the possession of the fiend," Fuller contends. Instead, those truths require "the schoolmaster," who "knows not only 'reading, writin', and 'rithmetic,' but the service of God and the destiny of man" (*MFC*, 334).[40]

Turning to the third and fourth points, this chastened sense of just what nature can and cannot contribute to the middle landscape is especially striking in the green Exaltadas' writings about the future of democracy and about the role of individual women. Kirkland, for example, with her epigraph to the 1839 *A New Home*—"A show, as it were, of an accompanable solitariness, and of a civil wildness," from one of the first modern English pastorals, Sir Philip Sidney's *Arcadia* (1593)—immediately signals her awareness of the historical challenge of building a rural yet sociable democracy.[41] And in her 1844 *Forest Life*, Kirkland again demonstrates her keen sense of the challenge of "civil wildness." She praises the nascent democracy in Montacute as "increas[ing] the spirit of self-dependence" but also recognizes that "evils [still] grow out of . . . the blind pursuit" by the majority "of one form of good to the neglect of all others." Kirkland likely alludes here to an earlier chapter in *Forest Life* that describes the majority's desecration of the town's common, exactly the kind of local wilderness that Thoreau urges every village to save as a "tonic." After opening this chapter with a dark poem by Thomas Cole, the Hudson River School painter, decrying how "Each hill and every valley is become / An altar unto Mammon," Kirkland declares, "I wish our people cared more for the beautiful!" She explains the impasse the town has reached about its "public square": "We cannot approach unanimity in deciding what kinds [of shade-trees to plant] so that blackened stumps are likely to continue the sole ornaments of our Prado." While Kirkland hopes "the fine remnants of the original forest [are] allowed foothold on this roomy earth," she is frankly pessimistic about the choices of democratic communities, predicting that the original forest, too, "must fall ere long before the 'irresistible influence of public opinion.'" For "the Western settler," Kirkland erupts, "'[c]learing' is his daily thought and nightly dream." At times, Kirkland's critique of majoritarian cultures is as sociologically acute as those found in "Self-Reliance" and "Civil Disobedience," as when she details (like these more famous texts) all the strategies—especially the psychological—employed by a tyrannous majority. There is force, of course, but Kirkland is more disturbed by the "pretended blunders" "resorted to in order to get rid of those [trees] marked for preservation," as well as the way in which the few trees remaining "become the frequent subject of wondering remark": "'Well! I *should* think there was oak-trees enough without keeping them in a body's door-yard! Jus' like the woods!'"[42] In contrast, as sharp as they are on the threat of social and political conformity in urban and suburban environments, when Emerson and Thoreau turn to more rural ones, they rely less on sociology than on fantasy. Much more could be mentioned here, but consider two typical instances. In *A Week on the Concord and Merrimack Rivers*, Thoreau rejects "Conscience . . . bred in the house" for one "Turn[ed] out doors, / Into the moors."[43] But how exactly do people with outdoor consciences collaborate? Thoreau is silent. So too is Emerson in his 1844 "Politics," where he hopes that "wild liberty develops iron conscience" (*CW*, 3:124).

Like Kirkland, Fuller is less naive, remarking that the abundance of resources in Illinois has hardly eliminated the threat of attack by "some chance Vandal" (*EMF*, 105). Fuller may have had Emerson's "wild liberty" fantasies specifically in mind when she pointedly wrote him during her travels about a mother and her three daughters in "what they call a 'claim fight'": "Some desperadoes laid claim to her property which is large[;] they were supposed to belong to the band who lately have been broken up by an exertion of Lynch law. She built shanties in the different parts, she and her three daughters each took one to defend it. They showed such bravery that the foe retreated" (*LMF*, 3:130). Wild liberty and the outdoors do not so easily breed conscience in Kirkland's and Fuller's accounts.

In *Summer*, Fuller pays tribute to the collective effort needed to build middle landscapes via her portrait of Morris Birkbeck, an Englishman whose 1816 "English settlement" in southeastern Illinois prospered due to the liberal loan policies he offered those who joined the community, and whose abolitionist editorials and then efforts as secretary of state (under the second Illinois governor) kept proslavery forces at bay. As she draws to a close her two most important chapters on the middle landscape in *Summer*, chapters 3 and 4, Fuller apologizes: "I have fixed my attention almost exclusively on the picturesque beauty of this region . . . [b]ut I ought to have been more interested in the housekeeping of this magnificent state, in the education she is giving her children, in their prospects" (*EMF*, 132). Alluding to Illinois's early brush with slavery, Fuller urges the state's citizens to remember Birkbeck, whose books—*Notes on a Journey in America* (1818), *Letters from Illinois* (1818), a second *Letters from Illinois* (1822), and the antislavery pamphlet *An Appeal* (1823)—she read in preparing this tribute (*EMF*, 133–35). "He thought all the creatures of a divine love ought to be happy and ought to be good," she begins. More specifically, Birkbeck's aspirations for

Illinois were those of a transcendentalist and an abolitionist, which she suggests by reference to his belief in "liberty of law" (Fuller's own formulation, thrice-repeated in *Woman*, for pursuing individual growth while respecting society [*WNC*, 5, 46, 70]) as well as to his "two thoughts": "Freedom, the liberty of law, not license; not indolence, work for himself and children, and all men, but under genial and poetic influences;—these were his aims. How different from those of the new settlers in general! And into his mind so long ago shone steadily the two thoughts, now so prevalent in thinking and aspiring minds, of 'Resist not evil,' and 'Every man his own priest, and the heart the only true church'" (*EMF*, 133). In addition to his transcendentalist (that is, abolitionist and radical Protestant) credentials, Birkbeck was a farmer; that combination leads Fuller to close her tribute with the hope that "Illinois will yet . . . regard this man, who knew so well what *ought* to be, as one of her true patriarchs, the Abraham of a promised land" (*EMF*, 134).

Fourth and finally are the portraits of individual agents in the middle landscape offered by the green Exaltadas. Little need be said here about Emerson's notorious unwillingness to particularize his self-reliant individual in any detail. Thoreau, too, is reluctant to offer specific alternatives to "lives of quiet desperation" (*Walden*, 8). "I would not have any one adopt *my* mode of living on any account," he writes (*Walden*, 71). But the conclusion to "Slavery in Massachusetts" may best serve to exemplify Thoreau's hesitation to flesh out his self-reliant individual, preferring to cede agency to nature. Repulsed by the American state's concessions to slave power, Thoreau offers a white water lily as an "emblem of purity . . . to show us what purity and sweetness reside in, and can be extracted from, the slime and muck of the earth." Alluding to the plant's Linnaean name (*Nymphaea odorata*), Thoreau proposes that the conventional world has given rise to a rival species, "*Nymphoea Douglassii*," named after the Kansas-Nebraska Act supporter, Stephen Douglas. Darkly amusing, Thoreau's dueling lilies also reveal a flustered political imagination, according to which humanity has little or nothing to contribute to the middle landscape. There is the corrupt flower of masculine civilization, and then there is the pure flower of feminine nature; there is the Fugitive Slave Law written by men, and then there are the higher laws that have "prevailed longest and widest" in nature. Because these higher laws "still prevail," Thoreau does finally hope "that the time may come when man's deeds will smell as sweet." However, Thoreau illustrates an active nature's deeds, not a passive if perceptive humanity's. "If Nature can compound this fragrance still annually, I shall believe her still young and full of vigor, her integrity and genius unimpaired, and that there is virtue even in man, too, who is fitted to perceive and love it" (*Reform Papers*, in *WHT*, 108).

Thoreau's imagination may be limited here by his apparent reliance on such sources as Sarah Josepha Hale's 1833 *Flora's Interpreter*, which codifies the white water lily as "purity of heart."[44] Smugly sure that Fuller's early death was the just desert for those "who wander from the Rock of Salvation, Christ the Saviour," Hale dedicated her life to upholding the gender identities that the green Exaltadas challenged as obstacles to building better middle landscapes.[45] At their best, Emerson and Thoreau challenged these obstacles too, but more often their gender conformism kept them loyal to the cult of true mother-naturehood, a sphere separate from the masculine world, and one that Emerson and Thoreau trusted would simply "breed" conscientious citizens.

Compare Kirkland's emphasis on the individuals who build middle landscapes in *A New Home*. While the majority may seek to denude the commons, the women of Montacute are inspired by the local wildflowers to build a garden, which (Kirkland notes) is achieved "all by female effort." To the individual woman only, Kirkland concludes, must be credited the resolve "to throw over the real homeliness of her lot something of the magic of [the] IDEAL."[46] Or, compare another of Fuller's own green Exaltadas. In the 1846 review of *Ellen* discussed above, Fuller turns from that novel to another, *Metallek*, for evidence of how nature can, indeed, ennoble us through one more angel figure.[47] Through much of this novel, Fuller admits, "you follow the hunter in his path, walking through the noblest and fairest scenes only to shoot the poor animals that were happy there." "But," she declares, "when we come to the girl who is the presiding deity, or rather the tutelary angel of the scene, how are all discords harmonized; how all its latent music poured forth!" In contrast to the nasty hunter, this girl teaches us the higher uses of nature: "Pure and brilliantly blooming as the flower of the wilderness, she . . . shares, while she sublimes, its nature. She plays round the most vulgar and rude beings, gentle and caressing, yet unsullied; in her wildness there is nothing cold or savage; her elevation is soft and warm. Never have we seen natural religion more beautifully expressed; never so well discerned the influence of the natural nun, who needs no veil or cloister to guard from profanation the beauty she has dedicated to God and which only attracts human love to hallow it into the divine" (*MFC*, 335). Fuller's "natural nun" not only shares the flower's nature but actively "sublimes" it.

At the end of his bean-farming experiment, Thoreau objects, like the green Exaltadas, to that avaricious farming by which "the landscape is deformed." But he ultimately identifies the cure in what the farmer should *not* do. Thoreau's middle landscape—that "half-cultivated field"—will effectively build itself: "this broad field which I have looked at so long looks not to me as the principal cultivator, but away from me to influences more genial to it, which water and make it green." "We should receive the benefit of [the sun's] light and heat," he declares, "with a corresponding trust and magnanimity" (*Walden*, 166).

The green Exaltadas also occasionally forget the farmer. Fuller has her own classic "into the wild" moment—her 1840 recollection (written for Emerson, notably) of storming out of church and into the woods until a sun beam "passed into [her] thought a beam from its true sun, from its native sphere": "I saw there was no self [and] I was for that hour taken up into God" (*EMF*, 11). But mostly, the green Exaltadas remember the farmer, as well as a range of other agents, often young women, who will build the middle landscape. In a poem prefacing *Forest Life*, Kirkland pays tribute to "sympathy," "bestowed by bounteous Heaven, / [which] Links in one chain the hearts of human kind." Looking around for proof of world-preserving power, Kirkland finds it in "the dance beneath the trees / With forest-girls their simple carols singing."[48] Fuller, too, often pays tribute to nature and people creating the middle landscape together. Writing an unknown correspondent in 1840 to explain the aims of transcendentalists, she explains, "Their hope for man is grounded on his destiny as an immortal soul [and i]t was not meant that the soul should cultivate the earth, but that the earth should educate and maintain the soul."[49] But Fuller the conservationist elsewhere makes clear that humans have their part to play too, and no small one; theirs (as she writes in *Woman*) will be "the holy work that is to make the earth a part of heaven" (*WNC*, 5). Fuller's green Exaltadas thus seek both to ascend like Ganymede and to descend like Fuller herself, down from the Abruzzo Mountains into the foothills of Rieti and finally into Rome, to join in building a new republic.

NOTES

The author is indebted to the editors, Bob Burkholder, and Jessie Bray for their feedback on this essay.

1. For recent work in this area, see Phyllis Cole's "The Nineteenth-Century Women's Rights Movement and the Canonization of Margaret Fuller," *ESQ: A Journal of the American Renaissance* 44 (1998): 1–33; Cole's "Woman's Rights and Feminism," in *OxH*, 222–40; and Len Gougeon's "Emerson and the Reinvention of Democracy: A Lesson for the Twenty-First Century," in *New Morning: Emerson in the Twenty-First Century*, ed. Arthur S. Lothstein and Michael Brodrick (Albany: State Univ. of New York Press, 2008), 162–78.
2. Henry David Thoreau, *Reform Papers*, ed. Wendell Glick, in *WHT*, 147; Caroline Wells Healey Dall, *Transcendentalism in New England: A Lecture Delivered before the Society of Philosophical Enquiry, Washington, D.C., May 7, 1895* (Boston: Roberts Brothers, 1897), 25.
3. Max Oelschlaeger, *The Idea of Wilderness: From Prehistory to the Age of Ecology* (New Haven: Yale Univ. Press, 1991), 135, 136, 293; Lawrence Buell, *The Environmental Imagination: Thoreau, Nature Writing, and the Formation of American Culture* (Cambridge, Mass.: Harvard Univ. Press, Belknap Press, 1995), 117. This critique of ecocriticism's handling of the transcendentalists echoes two essays from *Conservation Reconsidered: Nature, Virtue, and American Liberal Democracy*, ed. Charles T. Rubin (Lanham, Md.: Rowman & Littlefield, 2000): Rubin's preface, ix–xix; and Bob Pepperman Taylor's "Henry David Thoreau's Use of Nature," 183–205.

4. When she does appear—as in Lance Newman's "Margaret Fuller's *Summer on the Lakes, in 1843* and the Condition of America," *Romanticism on the Net* (May 2005): 38–39, http://www.erudit.org/, accessed 1 December 2013—Fuller, too, must renounce transcendentalism before being judged worthy of serious consideration. For example, Fuller's greatest importance was her "experimentation with ontological alternatives to the idealism [that is, transcendentalism] that hobbled Emerson" (para. 21). Much more promising is Robert E. Burkholder's recent suggestion that Fuller's "calls for harmonious human interaction with the land . . . anticipate Aldo Leopold's 'land ethic'"; see "Nature Writing and Environmental Activism," in *OxH*, 644.
5. Henry David Thoreau, *Journals*, ed. John C. Broderick et al., 8 vols. to date, in *WHT*, 5:469.
6. Daniel B. Botkin, *No Man's Garden: Thoreau and a New Vision for Civilization and Nature* (Washington, D.C.: Island Press, 2001), 218.
7. Henry David Thoreau, *The Maine Woods*, in *WHT*, 121. On Thoreau's higher-use environmentalism, see Daniel S. Malachuk, "Thoreau and the Higher Uses of Nature," in *Literature, Writing, and the Natural World*, ed. James Guignard and T. P. Murphy (Newcastle-upon-Tyne, U.K.: Cambridge Scholars, 2009), 14–32. On the importance of *Bildung* to Fuller and Emerson, see David M. Robinson, "Margaret Fuller and the Transcendental Ethos: *Woman in the Nineteenth Century*," *PMLA* 97 (January 1982): 83–98.
8. On early American conservationism, see Richard W. Judd, *The Untilled Garden: Natural History and the Spirit of Conservation in America, 1740–1840* (Cambridge, U.K.: Cambridge Univ. Press, 2009). Leo Marx defines the middle landscape in *The Machine in the Garden: Technology and the Pastoral Ideal in America* (New York: Oxford Univ. Press, 2000), 23; see also Simon Schama, *Landscape and Memory* (New York: Knopf, 1995). On Thoreau's interest in the middle landscape, see Daniel S. Malachuk, "'A Still More Perfect and Glorious State': Thoreau's Maine," in *Maine's Place in the Environmental Imagination*, ed. Michael Burke (Newcastle-upon-Tyne, U.K.: Cambridge Scholars, 2008), 43–67.
9. See *The Political Writings of Thomas Jefferson*, ed. Merrill D. Peterson (Charlotte: Univ. of North Carolina Press, 1993), 61.
10. Annette Kolodny, *The Land before Her: Fantasy and Experience of the American Frontiers, 1630–1860* (Chapel Hill: Univ. of North Carolina Press, 1984), 3.
11. Marx, *Machine in the Garden*, 265; Buell, *Environmental Imagination*, 129.
12. See Bell Gale Chevigny, *The Woman and the Myth: Margaret Fuller's Life and Writings*, rev. and exp. ed. (Boston: Northeastern Univ. Press, 1994), 176–77.
13. Henry David Thoreau, *Wild Fruits: Thoreau's Rediscovered Last Manuscript*, ed. Bradley P. Dean (New York: Norton, 2000), 238.
14. Thoreau similarly asks: "Is it the lumberman, then, who is the friend and lover of the pine, stands nearest to it, and understands its nature best. . . . No! no! it is the poet . . . who makes the truest use of the pine" (*Maine Woods*, 121).
15. Fuller takes the holiday's symbolism seriously; see also her 1845 "Fourth of July," in *MFC*, 149–51. "Ganymede and His Eagle" is the neglected first of a series of otherwise famous Fourth of July protest texts in antebellum literature: Thoreau's *Walden* (the experiment begun 4 July 1845); Frederick Douglass's "What to the Slave Is the Fourth of July?" (delivered 5 July 1852); and Whitman's *Leaves of Grass* (published 4 July 1855).
16. In a letter to her brother, Fuller writes that Oregon, Illinois—with bluffs that "touch the heavens" and a river that is "nowhere broken or injured by the hand of man"—might be ideal, "if we two," she notes, "could live and you have a farm which would not be a twentieth part the labor of a N England farm, [and with] our books and our pens, and a

little boat on the river." See *LMF*, 3:133. Fuller's attention to the middle landscape did not blind her to the natural beauty of Illinois; see Sarah Wider's chapter in this volume.

17. *Goethe: The Collected Works, Volume 1: Selected Poems*, ed. Christopher Middleton (Princeton: Princeton Univ. Press, 1983), 33.
18. Newman, "Margaret Fuller's *Summer*," para. 15.
19. On the former, see Kolodny, *Land before Her*; and on the latter, Angela Miller, *The Empire of the Eye: Landscape Representation and American Cultural Politics, 1825–1875* (Ithaca, N.Y.: Cornell Univ. Press, 1993), 248.
20. On breastfed Goths as classically intriguing, see Schama, *Landscape and Memory*, 85.
21. The language is Thoreau's as quoted by Thomas Wentworth Higginson in *Short Studies of American Authors* (Boston: Lee & Shephard, 1880), 24.
22. Thomas Wentworth Higginson, *Margaret Fuller Ossoli* (Boston: Houghton Mifflin, 1884), 30.
23. Susan Rosowski, "Margaret Fuller, an Engendered West, and *Summer on the Lakes*," *Western American Literature* 25, no. 2 (1990): 141.
24. In *The Poetics of Imperialism: Translation and Colonization from "The Tempest" to "Tarzan"* (Philadelphia: Univ. of Pennsylvania Press, 1997), Eric Cheyfitz explains the central place of *translatio studii et imperii* in American imperialist ideology. In "The Radical Emerson: Politics in 'The American Scholar,'" *ESQ* 34 (1988): 37–57, Burkholder shows Emerson to be critical of it.
25. According to Susan Clair Imbarrato, no women published nonfiction about the West through 1830; see *Traveling Women: Narrative Visions of Early America* (Athens: Ohio Univ. Press, 2006), 2.
26. Erika M. Kreger, "Rustic Matters: Placing the Rural Community Narratives of Alice Cary, Susan Fenimore Cooper, and Caroline Kirkland in the Context of the Nineteenth-Century Women's Sketchwriting Tradition," in *Susan Fenimore Cooper: New Essays on "Rural Hours" and Other Works*, ed. Rochelle Johnson and Daniel Patterson (Athens: Univ. of Georgia Press, 2001), 193–214, esp. 196, 199, 204 (quoting Alice Cary), 207 (quoting Susan Fenimore Cooper).
27. Kolodny, *Land before Her*, esp. 8 (quoting Fuller).
28. Kreger, "Rustic Matters," 195–96. On the middle landscape as ideological, see Miller, *Empire of the Eye*.
29. Jessie Nichol Bray, *"A More Perfect Indian Wisdom": Transcultural Exchange in the Writings of Henry D. Thoreau* (PhD diss., Univ. of South Carolina, 2010, 97–103). See also Ivonne García's reading of Sophia Peabody's transcendentalism in this volume.
30. Caroline Kirkland, *A New Home—Who'll Follow?* (New York: C. S. Francis, 1839), 233.
31. Kolodny, *Land before Her*, 131.
32. Caroline Kirkland, *Forest Life*, 2 vols. (New York: C. S. Francis, 1844), 1:43.
33. Susan Fenimore Cooper, "A Dissolving View," in *The Home Book of the Picturesque; or, American Scenery, Art, and Literature* (New York: Putnam, 1852), 82.
34. Susan Fenimoore Cooper, *Rural Hours* (New York: Putnam, 1850), 213.
35. Kolodny, *Land before Her*, 104; Mary Austin Holley, *Texas: Observations, Historical, Geographical and Descriptive* (New York: Arno Press, 1973), 48–49; Eliza Farnham, *Life in Prairie Land* (New York: Arno Press, 1972), 405, 404.
36. Cooper, *Rural Hours*, 406n, 216, 217.
37. Susan Fenimore Cooper, *The Rhyme and Reason of Country Life* (New York: Putnam, 1854), 28–29.
38. Farnham, *Life*, 68–69, 209.

39. Harriet Martineau, *Society in America, in Two Volumes* (New York: Saunders and Otley, 1837), 1:332, 156, 157, 158–59.
40. Five years earlier, Fuller had admired her brother's description of nature but could not resist adding: "You go to an extreme in your denunciations of cities and the social institutions. . . . One may be gossiping and vulgar and idle in the country,—earnest, wise and noble in the city. . . . I see very distinctly that the city also is a bed in God's garden" (*LMF*, 2:263).
41. Kirkland, *New Home*, n.p.
42. Kirkland, *Forest Life*, 227, 41, 42–43, 43, 44.
43. Henry David Thoreau, *A Week on the Concord and Merrimack Rivers*, in *WHT*, 74.
44. Sarah Josepha Hale, *Flora's Interpreter, or The American Book of Flowers and Sentiments*, 4th ed. (Boston: Marsh, Capen, and Lyon, 1835), 223.
45. See Barbara Welter, "The Cult of True Womanhood: 1820–1860," *American Quarterly* 18 (Summer 1966): 154 (quoting Sarah Josepha Hale). Contrast Fuller's exploration of "the potential of floridity as the site of feminine alterity," in Dorri Beam, *Style, Gender, and Fantasy in Nineteenth-Century American Women's Writing* (Cambridge: Cambridge Univ. Press, 2010), 34.
46. Kirkland, *New Home*, 231–32.
47. Fuller likely means Osgood Bradbury's *Metallak: The Lone Indian of the Magalloway* (Portland, Me.: C. W. Child, 1844).
48. Kirkland, *Forest Life*, 1:6.
49. Fuller, quoted in Chevigny, *Woman and Myth*, 182–83.

INTERLUDE

From *The Journals of Charlotte Forten Grimké*, ed. Brenda Stevenson, in The Schomburg Library of Nineteenth-Century Black Women Writers (New York: Oxford Univ. Press, 1988), 113, 154, 174–75, 181–82, 229–30.

Friday, November 24, [1854]. Lizzie [Church] and I finished reading "Memorable Women," by Mrs. Crosland. . . . The character of Margaret Fuller interested me greatly; there is a charm even in reading of a nature so earnest and impassioned, combined with the richest mental endowments and possessing with all its defects so many qualities that were truly lovable, and worthy of the highest praise.

Sunday, November 26, [1854]. Finished reading "Ida May." It is extremely interesting but I do not think it compared with "Uncle Tom's Cabin." Still it shows plainly the evils of slavery, and may do much good. I read it with pleasure, as I do everything which is written in opposition to this iniquitous system. This evening listened to one of the most eloquent and radical anti-slavery lectures that I have ever heard. It was given by Rev. Mr. [Charles] Hodges of Watertown, one of the few ministers who dare speak and act as freemen, obeying the Higher Law, and scorning all lower laws which are opposed to Justice and Humanity.

Sunday, April 6, [1856]. I have been reading Margaret Fuller's "Woman in the 19th Century," and liked it much. I am a warm admirer of the noble-hearted writer. She says so much about Goethe's writings that I felt more than ever anxious to read them, and have must [*sic*] commenced his "Wilhelm Meister," translated by Carlyle; but I am rather disappointed in it. Wilhelm seems to me to be so deficient in strength of character. The little Mignon I think is a beautiful though very singular character. I have a presentiment that I shall like the second volume better. I know, however, that these works lose very much of their beauty by translation. Oh, when shall I be able to read them in the original. I do most earnestly desire to; and I *will* if I live a few years longer. I am determined!

Christmas Day, December, 1856. Spent the day very delightfully at the [Anti-Slavery] Fair.—Saw many beautiful things and many interesting people. Had the good fortune to be made known to three of the noblest and best of women;—Mesdames [Maria W.] Chapman, [Eliza Cabot] Follen, and [Lydia M.] Child; who were very kind and pleasant to me. . . . Mrs. Follen has a real *motherly* kindness of manner. She is a lovely looking silver haired old lady; Mrs. Chapman's irresistible sweetness and grace of manner, I have no words to describe. Mrs. Child smilingly told me that she visited our house once,—when *I* must have been a "wee toddling." She is not quite so spiritual looking as one would expect to see the author of "Philothea," but is a very charming person nevertheless.

Sunday, January 1, [1857]. Wrote to—Miss [Harriet] Martineau! Am astonished and shocked at my own presumption.—But felt impelled to write by one of those Spirit movings' which will not be resisted. Have always greatly admired and loved Miss Martineau, and have thought of her much since seeing her exquisite work at the Fair. . . . It may give her some pleasure to hear in this way from a young colored girl in a distant land.

Wednesday, June 17, [1857]. Went to Byberry [near Philadelphia]. On the boat met Miss [Elizabeth] Peabody, and Mattie Griffiths, the author of "Autobiography of a Female Slave." Miss P.[eabody] read to us an account of her last visit to Washington Allston. It was beautifully written and deeply interesting. Miss P.[eabody] is certainly a highly cultivated and intellectual woman. She converses finely . . . Miss G.[riffiths] is a plain and unpretending young lady; but she is pleasant and I like her much. Miss P.[eabody] was the principal talker. She gave us her spiritual experiences, which were really quite wonderful. . . . On reaching the city, Mrs. P.[utnam] and I were *refused* at two ice cream saloons, successively. Oh, how terribly I felt! Could say but few words. Mrs. P.[utnam] told one of the people some wholesome truths, which cannot be soon forgotten. It is dreadful! dreadful! I cannot stay in such a place. I long for N.[ew] E.[ngland].

"Each Atomic Part"

Edmonia Goodelle Highgate's African American Transcendentalism

ERIC GARDNER

This essay begins to rediscover Edmonia Goodelle Highgate's engagement with American transcendentalism. As a recovery of a transcendentalist woman's work, the essay recognizes that the study of Highgate's writing—especially her publications between 1865 and 1867 in the African Methodist Episcopal Church's weekly *Christian Recorder*—needs to be placed firmly within the larger reconsideration of women and transcendentalism. And so it shares this volume's sense that "unfolding the divinely human faculties of the self" was a different experience for women than for men in nineteenth-century America (10).

That said, in part because Highgate was a Black woman and the texts studied here were written for a Black-run and Black-oriented newspaper, this essay queries the race of those women "unfolding the divinely human faculties of the self" and grapples with the possibilities and limits that nineteenth-century African Americans—and African American women specifically—might have found in exploring transcendentalism.[1] I open by briefly reflecting on the absence of African Americans in the scholarship of transcendentalism and then articulating broader concerns tied to Lara Cohen and Jordan Stein's recognition that "recovery requires more than the excavation of forgotten texts; it also requires the knowledge to read them."[2] Thus I pair the biographical treatment of Highgate with discussion of her publication venue to examine how she initially entertained and then moved to adopt and revise transcendentalism as a mode for understanding, explaining, and trying to change her world. The discussion here attends especially to Highgate's exploration of concepts of truth, individuality, and collective action—with emphasis on race and gender—in four key *Recorder* pieces: "Waiting for the Cars," "A Spring Day Up the James," "Truth," and "On Horse Back—Saddle Dash, No. 1." Such recovery work is often incremental, and so this essay, like the volume in which it appears, is a beginning rather than an ending—a statement of how much more work there is to do.

References to African Americans—particularly African American women—are few and far between in the landmark *Oxford Handbook of Transcendentalism* (2010). Famous fugitives with Boston connections—Thomas Sims, Shadrach Minkins, William and Ellen Craft, and Anthony Burns—receive the most attention, though such discussion is very brief. Frederick Douglass, William Cooper Nell, and a few others are also mentioned. Many of these references occur in Sandra Harbert Petrulionis's excellent chapter, "Antislavery Reform." The *Handbook*'s limited treatment of Blackness is not extraordinary in the scholarship of American transcendentalism; indeed, as a monumental work that richly diversifies our scholarship, the *Handbook* is arguably *more* attuned to the interplay between white, mostly male New Englanders and "other" voices.[3] Much of this same critique could be applied to a host of recent attempts to widen our understanding of transcendentalism. The master narrative here is clear, though assumed rather than stated: African Americans, and especially African American women, had little to do with transcendentalism. When they did, they often represented conceptual problems for (white) transcendentalists to address—such as the problems of slavery and the Fugitive Slave Law—rather than standing as individuals engaged with questions of philosophy, social theory, and aesthetics. Even the best of the much-welcomed scholarship revisiting the nexus of transcendentalism and antislavery activism—for example, Petrulionis's *To Set This World Right* (2006)[4]—does not place Black people as potential or actual transcendentalists, even though it sees them as historical actors.

I begin with a recognition, building from generations of African Americanist scholars, that this unspoken narrative of absence needs to be spoken—and that, when spoken, it may well turn out to be a narrative of occluded presences. Think of the myriad portraits of George Washington—for instance, Edward Savage's *The Washington Family*—with a Black person somewhere in the background: African Americans "hidden," as it were, in plain sight. I admit at the outset that I do not know the shape and extent of Black engagement with transcendentalism: you don't know what's at the edges of a canvas—much less what's slightly off the canvas but still in the original, larger scene—until you look. Such acts are, by necessity, as fragmentary as the extant archive, and of course we are just starting to look.

It *is* essential that we look. Consider, for example, how scholars of Herman Melville have benefited from the questions of African Americanists—and vice versa—with results ranging from Sterling Stuckey's *African Culture and Melville's*

Art (2008) to Robert S. Levine and Samuel Otter's exciting collection *Frederick Douglass and Herman Melville: Essays in Relation* (2008).[5] While much of the previous generation of African Americanist recovery centered on finding African American texts, authors, and contexts—and while continuing such work remains essential—part of the project of recovery for this generation may be recognizing that Black folks were often present in diverse nineteenth-century debates in even the seemingly "whitest" of spaces.

Earlier recovery efforts have laid the groundwork for our search for Black transcendentalists. Carla Peterson's *"Doers of the Word"* (1995) pushed us to rethink Black engagement with the nineteenth-century American lecture circuit. James Horton and Lois Horton's pioneering *Black Bostonians* (1979) and Elise Lemire's *Black Walden* (2009) established Black presences in the geographic heart of transcendentalism.[6] A generation of scholarship on Frederick Douglass—especially following Robert S. Levine's germinal *Martin Delany, Frederick Douglass, and the Politics of Representative Identity* (1997)—has caused most to acknowledge, if not fully study, Douglass's long engagement with romanticism, European revolutions, post-Enlightenment and post-Calvinist faith-based social action, and even the edges of transcendentalism.[7]

Beyond the now-canonical Douglass, we could also consider—though we haven't yet—transcendentalist traces in the texts of such Black activists as William Cooper Nell and Charlotte Forten.[8] Nell interacted regularly with Theodore Parker throughout the 1850s and, for example, wrote movingly in the 22 June 1855 *Liberator* of a wedding where Parker told a young couple that "a true marriage was the union of hearts" and that "they should study each other's character, and make cheerful recognition of what each found superior in the other, and thus develop true life."[9] Forten's lively journals record the experience not simply of reading Emerson's essays but of hearing several transcendentalists lecture. Forten even speaks of reading Fuller's *Woman in the Nineteenth Century* and declares that she is "a warm admirer of the noble-hearted writer."[10] In short, Edmonia Goodelle Highgate's transcendentalism shouldn't be surprising or unknown; to recover that work, we need both "excavation" and contextualization.

Highgate has not fallen totally out of American history. Several studies of Black education mention her, and select historians have sketched a basic biography, from which this essay builds.[11] The first child of Charles and Hannah Francis Highgate, she was born in 1844 in New York. Pennsylvanian Charles Highgate was a barber, though the family also rented out rooms. Hannah Highgate was born in Virginia—though whether slave or free remains unclear.[12] Barbering potentially placed Charles Highgate among those African Americans edging toward the middling classes and gave him some mobility.[13] While the Highgates advertised a "genteel boarding house" in Albany in the late 1840s, by 1850 they were planning to move to Syracuse.

The Highgates engaged with local Black and antislavery communities and the region's nascent Black print culture. Their boarding advertisements, for example, appeared in Frederick Douglass's *North Star*. Hannah Highgate joined Caroline Loguen (wife of Jermain Loguen, activist and future bishop of the African Methodist Episcopal Zion Church) and Julia Garnet (wife of firebrand Henry Highland Garnet) on a committee of women who planned an 1849 fundraising fair to aid Black activist Samuel Ringgold Ward's reform newspaper *Impartial Citizen*.[14] In March 1853, Charles was named to a committee to draft resolutions for an anticolonization meeting in Syracuse.[15] Evidence also suggests that the Highgates' sense of reform—like that of many Black abolitionists—touched a number of issues beyond African American rights.

Little is known about Edmonia Highgate's youth in this activist family, though education was clearly emphasized. Highgate graduated from Syracuse High School—apparently the only African American in her class—in 1861.[16] Though she earned teaching credentials, she could not find a position in Syracuse because of her race and instead began teaching in Montrose, Pennsylvania, and then in Binghamton, New York. Her siblings shared her commitment to education; four would become teachers. The family also seems to have been close, especially after the untimely death of Charles Highgate Sr. in May 1861.[17]

The family's position among Syracuse's faith communities is less clear. One might assume that they attended services at Loguen's church, and they may well have done so.[18] The Highgates also seem to have interacted regularly with Samuel Joseph May, white antislavery stalwart and Syracuse's Unitarian pastor. However, in April 1857, Hannah Highgate joined Syracuse's Plymouth Congregational Church; Edmonia followed her in February 1858.[19] The mostly white church had been founded in 1853 and was headed by Oberlin graduate Michael Strieby, a committed white abolitionist.[20] Strieby thought well enough of Edmonia Highgate to write a recommendation to the American Missionary Association (AMA) on her behalf in January 1864. Highgate's later letters to the AMA and the *Recorder* show a strong commitment to her faith but also what seems to be a flexibility of association—an ecumenical willingness to work wherever she found a liberationist theology in action—and she could have been active in any or all of these venues.

She was clearly already exploring questions of faith and social action. In seeking recommendations for her AMA application, she wrote to a friend, "You may have heard some rumor of my wavering in some points, in a true orthodox belief, but I wrote out a full statement of my views to Bro. Strieby, and his dear wife will tell you that it was satisfactory to him."[21] Before and as she composed this "full statement," there would have been a host of conduits to transcendentalism. As Philip Gura argues, "We cannot overestimate the excitement the Transcendentalists' ideas generated and the commitment they engendered," even as "to many people . . . the Transcendentalists were unsettling, and as often ridiculed or reviled as respected."[22] The issues of Douglass's *North Star* that advertised the Highgates' rooms contain no less than a dozen references to Emerson alone—including several quotations. It is especially tempting to think of one of Highgate's parents reading aloud from the three paragraphs of *Nature*'s section "Beauty" that appeared in the 25 February 1848 *North Star*—perhaps even running Highgate's four-year-old finger over some of the words.

In a broader sense, Syracuse's print culture included several reform undertakings (from the first incarnation of Ward's *Impartial Citizen* to temperance papers), and the city boasted both bookstores and a school library. Syracuse was also a regular stop on lecture tours—one made attractive to transcendentalists and reformers by Samuel J. May's presence.[23] May himself could have introduced the young Highgate to transcendentalist ideas, texts, and even figures: Strieby's recommendation noted that, were further testimonials needed, "Rev. Samuel J. May of Syracuse [was] well acquainted with her," and Highgate herself listed May as a reference.[24] While much of her youth was framed by more conventional Protestant influences, even these—within African American traditions—would have pushed her to think about intersections between self-improvement and community activism. Highgate's struggle was likely never one of choosing between Emerson's (and Fuller's, albeit different) individualism and Brownson's (and Peabody's) collectivism—the binary Gura and others have suggested—but one of bringing the two into balance.

Highgate's teaching may have offered some of that balance: a way to develop intellectually while giving back to the community (and sidestepping expectations of marriage). Teaching also provided a bridge from being a listener and reader to being a (public) speaker and writer. By the end of March 1864, Highgate had arrived in Norfolk, Virginia, a crucible not only for her own sense of public work but for the education of the newly freed. Highgate was assigned to be part of an experiment: an AMA school fully staffed by African Americans, which included Sallie Daffin (a graduate of Philadelphia's Institute for Colored Youth), Clara Duncan (an Oberlin graduate), and principal Blanche Harris (another Oberlin graduate). While this configuration did not last long, the four women grew close under the stress of long hours, low pay, poor classroom conditions, students who had been traumatized by slavery and the Civil War, and the ongoing war itself. Presaging her later exploration of trauma and community responsibility, Highgate wrote an AMA supervisor that June to report: "The most earnest months of my existence were the two last. . . . I have been able to get so near to so many of my people who have spent most of manhood's and womanhood's freshness in slavery. There are peculiar crushing emotions which, at first, check even my utterance but go away and leave me with such deep compelling motive power to 'do with my might whatsoever my hands find to do.'"[25] Though the letter ended with "Oh how inspiring the thought that these dear souls are 'forever free,'" those "peculiar crushing emotions" and the simple physical exhaustion took their toll. As the hot Norfolk summer wore on, Highgate was struck with what fellow teacher Daffin—in an 8 October 1864 *Christian Recorder* letter—called "a terrible malady, 'aberration of mind,'" and had to be taken back to Syracuse. Daffin praised Highgate deeply—"there is no teacher who will be more universally missed than Miss H"—but also mourned the more general fact that "laborers [were] falling rapidly in the field."[26]

Under this strain, Highgate could have chosen to return to a more localized private life. Instead, within days of returning to Syracuse, she spoke to the National Convention of Colored Men, which spent four days considering the upcoming 1864 presidential election and African Americans' future generally. The list of delegates—all men—reads like a Who's Who of Black reform: Frederick Douglass was elected president of the convention; among the delegates for Massachusetts were John S. Rock and William Wells Brown; for New York, publisher Robert Hamilton as well as Henry Highland Garnet and Jermain Loguen; for Pennsylvania, editor of the *Christian Recorder* Elisha Weaver and educator/activist George Vashon. The only other woman invited to speak was Frances Ellen Watkins Harper.[27] The main thrust of Highgate's speech seems to have been unremarkable: the published proceedings refer to her as "an accomplished young lady of Syracuse" and note only that she "urged the Convention to trust in God and press on, and not abate one jot or tittle until the glorious day of jubilee shall come."[28]

More interesting is Highgate's self-positioning as a speaker. According to an account of her speech in the 26 October 1864 *New Orleans Tribune*, she opened by telling "her audience that her age was twenty" and that "she would not be quite in her place, perhaps, if a girl as she [was], she should tell the Convention what they ought to do." Nonetheless, "she had, with others, *thought* about what had been proposed and those thoughts she would tell them," albeit with demure phrasing ("jot or tittle"). The *Tribune*'s sense of her health—"Miss Highgate was unwell, and labored under a little difficulty in speaking"—underscores that, rather than being defeated by her "terrible malady," she was consciously entering a broader public sphere, even as she recognized that her gender and age (as well as her race) might call on her to do a bit of rhetorical dancing. By March 1865, she was setting up a school for the newly freed in Darlington, Maryland, and she had already published her first two pieces in the AME *Christian Recorder*.

Highgate's choice of venue is worth discussion, in part because the nineteenth-century Black press remains beyond the ken of many critics and historians. Highgate did have publishing choices, albeit choices limited by racism. Beyond Black papers such as the New York City *Weekly Anglo-African*, white reform venues like the *Liberator* might have offered space. In light of these possibilities, a nineteenth-century denominational organ may seem a curious location for an African American woman exploring transcendentalism—especially given that this specific denomination was in some ways much more doctrinally conservative than, say, Unitarianism. (The first and subsequent versions of the AME *Discipline* affirm the trinity, the depth of original sin, and the importance of the Lord's Supper.)[29]

Still, by the 1860s, the African Methodist Episcopal Church had spent decades crafting a liberationist theology out of a stunning combination of folk practices, responses to exclusionary tactics of white denominations, ideas at the nexus of the Enlightenment and post–American Revolution revivals, and deep engagement with diverse revisions of Calvinism, various Episcopalian sensibilities, and especially the participatory nature of Wesleyan Methodism. AME leaders *were* extremely radical in their racially egalitarian reading of scripture and their application of such through liberationist practice. Further, while the church sometimes severely limited women's participation and did not offer women formal roles in the church hierarchy until later in the nineteenth century, the AME press sometimes allowed real debate on such questions, and the church's diffuse structure and emphasis on itinerancy allowed different church entities to work within a broad tent.[30] The early 1860s thus saw oral, written, and print debates about basic issues of both the theory and the practice of faith—from whether "African" should be part of the denomination's name to how church doctrine should address the Civil War. When Highgate was writing for the *Recorder*, the AME tent was becoming even larger, in part because the church was often only a few steps behind the Union advance and the *Recorder* often traveled in the packs of African American soldiers and the carpetbags of teachers and activists. In this frame, the *Recorder* published across an amazing generic spectrum—sermons, essays, letters, poetry, short fiction, and even longer serialized fiction—including texts as doctrinally diverse as future bishop Benjamin Tucker Tanner's serialized biography of St. Cyprian, letters memorializing Unitarian stalwart Thomas Starr King, and even a reprinted article from the *Independent* that, with some humor, describes how Lyman Beecher "labored for the conversion of Theodore Parker!"[31]

Moreover, like Douglass's periodicals, the *Recorder* published a range of material about transcendentalism, including a large excerpt from *Walden*—"A Battle between Ants"—in March 1863, an extended extract from Thoreau's 1842 *Dial* piece "Natural History of Massachusetts" in May 1864, and brief quotes from several transcendentalists (though not Fuller) at various times. The *Recorder*'s treatment of Emerson is especially interesting. A 23 March 1861 item titled "Modern Literature" copied from the *Methodist Quarterly*, for example, devotes this single sentence to him: "Emerson is a brilliant but Christless heathen." A piece in the 29 June 1861 *Recorder*—reprinted from the *Westminster Review*—notices *The Conduct of Life* and concludes: "Mr. Emerson has much in common with the mocking-bird of his own woods; . . . in the present volume he is evidently dominated by that disreputable . . . Walt Whitman; many a page might be transferred to the notorious 'Leaves of Grass,' . . . which he christened the first fruit of American poetry."[32] Not all of the *Recorder* comments are this critical. The paper's own 1 June 1867 review of Emerson's *May Day, and Other Poems* assumes some reader familiarity with Emerson and transcendentalism. It opens: "Few writers . . . evoke more decided opinions of their writings than Ralph Waldo Emerson. The transcendental philosopher-poet has been ardently admired or thoroughly disliked by all who have carefully read his essays or his poems."[33] Perhaps the most positive treatment in the *Recorder*, this review concludes that portions of the title poem "ha[d] seldom been surpassed in power of description and delicacy of delineation of the sensations (if we may use the paradox) of inanimate nature."

Given the range of texts touching on transcendentalist concepts and practitioners, some of Highgate's *Recorder* readers would have been prepared to consider the ideas she would explore and the references she would make.

Highgate's first *Recorder* letters—the 4 February 1865 "Salvation Only in Work" and the 25 February 1865 "Waiting for the Cars"—show the seeds of her engagement with transcendentalism in print: a broadly romantic sensibility applied to the wider American polity that meshes with the paper's uplift framework but does not move fully into transcendentalist territory. "Salvation" reads like a piece on personal recovery—from "anguish, that cuts down to the soul's quick, and baptizes it in the life-blood of sorrow, and almost dethrones reason"—though it makes little explicit personal reference. Opening with a quote from Elizabeth Barrett Browning's *Aurora Leigh*,[34] it argues that "work is the grand regenerator" and declares that "Nature has a balm for laborers." While Highgate's later writing would articulate more fully the kinds of work she hoped would prove (re)generative, she was already recognizing trauma in the midst of slavery and the Civil War as having both individual and collective impact.

"Waiting for the Cars" offers more extended first-person commentary and political application. Written during a three-day wait in a railroad depot caused by deep snow as she journeyed to her new teaching job in Maryland, the piece begins by refining her rhetorical entry as a speaking / writing woman: the essay will focus on her "meditations and thoughts" but contain "nothing . . . a la Gail Hamilton or Fanny Fern."[35] Highgate tells readers that "the dignity of existing in the present has been uppermost in [her] mind for a long time," and she recognizes that such "dignity"—"the moral grandeur of having a heartache as one's companion through life, because of the sacrifices we are daily making for freedom's cause"—is exhausting. It also affords, simultaneously, the "sublime privilege" of "sounding one's soul depths" and of "forgetting self, losing personal identity, and becoming atomic parts of personified principle." This intertwining of pain, deep self-reflection (romantic rather than Calvinistic), and both celebration and "forgetting" of self leads to Highgate's first and only direct use of the word "transcendental" in her *Recorder* texts, one that might make Emersonian individualists uncomfortable: "O, the unseen forces that press upon us from every side, and urge us to make what is termed 'transcendental'—the simple rule for controlling each atomic part of the nation!"

Highgate's sense of "atomic" here links individualism and community activism, and she never suggests that the nation fully swallows the "atoms." While briefly leaning toward "forgetting self," the essay actually works to a sense of self guided by principle, giving principle body and individual voice: "Being loyal to one's self is loyalty to the cause of liberty, to the country, and to the Union, whose . . . keystone is *Justice*." It is especially notable that the collective repeatedly figures as national: while at later points in her writing, she doubles that sense to reflect both the nation and, in the common African Americanist rubric, the "nation within a nation," here she speaks of *being* American, of what seems a mutually constitutive conception of how Americans should behave and how America should treat its members. Of "first" importance in this, she asserts, is "trueness to one's own God ideal." This truthfulness makes "justice . . . the rule." The turn here is striking: "forgetting self, losing personal identity, and becoming atomic parts of personified principle" can only happen when one is true to the individual self and to "one's own God ideal." Highgate seems to be working out a sense of an Over-soul with implications for community and for duty to others, a layering of entities including principle, nation, collective / community, and individual.

Taking these concepts to their logical conclusion, she asserts that women and people of all races must be included as "atomic parts"—each finding *and* exercising truth within individualized circumstances—and argues that "we can't be true to ourselves and false to our brother." Highgate thus claims that African Americans must both recognize truth and demand such from "the occupants of the highest place in the body politic": "Are the men in New York state true," she asks rhetorically, "if they do not compel . . . the legislature to grant them unconditional franchise? Do not those noble and brave men who face the cannon . . . demand . . . for their children that for which they fight and die . . . ? Are Black laws, though milder in expression, any more ornamental on the statute book of New York State?" African Americans, she writes, cannot be "true" to themselves if they are "so easily satisfied, when [they] have but a cracker thrust at [them]—a whole loaf being what [they] demand." White people cannot be true to themselves or to the nation's other "atomic parts" if they do not share that loaf. Being an "atom" may require something like the submission to principle that Christopher Newfield explores in *The Emerson Effect*, but that "submission" is, for Highgate, inherently active: giving one's self fully to truth means working for the actuation of truth in arenas personal *and* political and in collectives not always committed to principle and not always welcoming to all of their "atoms." This is not Newfield's "restrictive liberalism."[36]

Highgate's next set of contributions—which call for future research and discussion—step away from direct philosophy and suggest that Highgate was experimenting with various voices and genres. Her 1 April 1865 "A Stray Waif from the Port of Grace" plays with the kind of newsy letter mixing humor and political commentary on which the *Recorder* thrived, and her "Congojoco" is a rare example of early Black women's serialized fiction. While the first of this story's three chapters seems to have appeared in the now-missing 13 May 1865 issue, the second and third are extant in the 20 and 27 May issues, and they tell a wartime tale of shipwreck, disguise, and spurned love within a sentimental framework.

Even as "Congojoco" was being serialized, truths that challenged understanding and expression in any mode—romantic, sentimental, or transcendental—pushed into Highgate's life. In 1864, her brother Charles—whom the *Recorder* calls "one of the best boys in Syracuse"—had been allowed to join a majority-white regiment, the locally raised New York 185th. In fighting associated with the Appomattox Campaign on 29 March 1865, he was shot five times, and he died on 2 April. The 20 May 1865 *Recorder* reports that he "fought bravely" and quotes the *Syracuse Standard*'s story of "the brave colored boy" who had given "his whole bounty" for enlisting "to his mother, for use of the family."

In the wake of these events, Highgate sent another piece to the *Recorder* that appeared in the same 27 May 1865 issue as the final installment of "Congojoco." While it does not name her brother Charles, it is very much about him. It opens by contrasting "bright, joyous April" with "national sorrow" and "recent trophies and grand victories" with "many, many hearts . . . mourning." "How many mothers, wives, and sisters," she asks, "read telegrams or letters saying: 'He fell on the field making a desperate charge' or"—and here is the telling detail—"'terribly wounded in five places!'" Highgate ends this first paragraph imagining national wholeness at the sacrifice of some "atoms"—"Our pangs in this freedom birth of America are agonizing, yet we rejoice, for the cost endears the end"—but the paragraphs that follow cast doubt over such resolution.

Though the piece's title—"A Spring Day up the James"—suggests calming, meditative travel- and nature-writing, the trip Highgate describes is horrific: "Reader," she asks, "did you ever go to the front to search for your beloved wounded?" Notified that Charles had been *wounded*, Highgate seems to have gone to find him before learning of his death. She "started up the James" with members of the U.S. Christian Commission, as "a young lady, unattended, going to the front" was "something unusual." The account of this journey is both very much in the present and deeply tied to the past, especially when she passes Jamestown—"so famous in this history of American Slavery . . . a most miserable, unimportant dilapidated little town, but ever notable as being the birth-place of the monster which has swallowed our brothers . . . spoiled our maidens, and beaten our mothers, robbed and killed their babies." In a direct invocation of the kind of liberation historiography John Ernest writes about, Highgate declares, "Thank God for the privilege of telling it!"

Traveling through "the darkness of that night, the rain pouring down in torrents," she finally reaches the Fifth Corps hospital. "Fear and hope in conflict" face her "at every step," and then she finds clerks who "kn[o]w the whole story": "Oh, how they hated to say that 'your brother died of his wounds two weeks ago.' But we felt it to be the truth, and their pale lips confirmed it. We then knew how sublime . . . it is to suffer and be strong." Still, even this sublime grief, this sense of being an atom within a personified principle, is interrupted: the "rough tent" in which Highgate waits for return transport is dominated by two Southern white women, "livid because their husbands' property had been taken"; as the wait is prolonged, the words of "kind friends who had wept with us" are replaced by "the groans of the dying" and the passing of "a large concourse of southern female friends . . . who sneered at the Yankee flag."

"A Spring Day" thus becomes a fearsome rewriting of "Waiting for the Cars," both in Highgate's painfully slow progress to the Fifth Corps hospital—which, remember, includes a journey through the birthplace of U.S. slavery—and then her war-torn wait to follow her brother's body home. Both multiply mark the limits of the travel narrative as genre—that is, they are as much about waiting to travel as about traveling, a fascinating commentary on African Americans' frustrated mobility in multiple senses of that word. "A Spring Day" illustrates the war's destruction of travel as pastime and highlights the violence of regional (and racial) boundaries. While "Waiting for the Cars" unevenly begins to see a collectivist joining of transcendental atoms through the discovery and practice of self-culture and "truth," here the pain of truth and falseness threatens to explode any possibility of wholeness. Even those women with whom Highgate shares the tent and who might understand the heavily gendered image of a "freedom birth" are divided, battling. What seems an abstract problem of the individual and the collective in "Waiting for the Cars" is made all too real by the physicality of the Fifth Corps hospital and the dead "brave colored boy" Charlie Highgate, to say nothing of the fact that Edmonia Highgate may have resembled some of the "property" at the core of the Southern women's complaints.

This piece's exploration of how truth might be conceptualized marks another of Highgate's central challenges to transcendentalism. As Katherine Adams says of Margaret Fuller, much transcendentalist thought argues that difference (in terms of race, gender, class, nation) must be "transcended," left behind, set aside as a "worldly thing." Here and later, Highgate recognizes that barriers based on difference have the power to block transcendence; breaking those worldly barriers—through not only self-actuation but community activism—is thus crucial for any practice of and toward truth.[37]

In her own last words of the text, Highgate seems almost to throw up her hands in defeat: "God, thou are past finding [unintelligible words] the afflictions with which thou visitest on thy children." And then she turns again to the poetry of Elizabeth Barrett Browning—this time a slightly altered version of the second-to-last stanza of "De Profundis," Browning's poem mourning her drowned brother Edward. Highgate introduces the passage with "Waiting, weeping, hoping, yet," and then concludes her "Spring Day" with these lines:

> I praise Thee while my days go on,
> I love Thee while my days go on,
> Through dark and death, through fire and frost,
> With emptied arms and treasures lost,
> I thank Thee while my days go on.[38]

Given the physical and metaphysical strain of these events, it isn't surprising that more than two months passed before Highgate again published in the *Recorder*. In what was becoming a kind of cycle, the majority of her next group of contributions returned to reporting local news, first from the upper South and then from her new home in New Orleans, where she took charge of what her 17 March 1866 *Recorder* piece describes as "a flourishing school . . . called after our eloquent champion, Frederick Douglass," and housed in a former "slave pen." That 17 March "Letter from New Orleans" and her 7 July and 18 August "New Orleans Correspondence" of the same year emphasize the complexities of "reconstruction," trace increasing racial tensions, and mark the difficulties—even dangers—of Highgate's physical world. She wrote her 18 August 1866 letter, a frightening account of the 30 July 1866 riot in New Orleans, "during a lull in the grand saturnalia of blood." Louisiana's Radical Republicans (including several African Americans) had reconvened the state constitutional convention of 1864—nominally an illegal maneuver—to fight the state's newly enacted Black codes and refusal of Black suffrage. Those gathered in support were, in Highgate's words, "assailed by armed policemen, who shot into the crowd . . . killing and wounding white and colored." "Your correspondent," she added in the third person, "did what she could of wound-dressing until near midnight. Some ten died, to say nothing of those who . . . were locked up."[39] With New Orleans under martial law and African American activists under threat, Highgate left the Crescent City for Lafayette Parish, more than a hundred miles away in what she describes as the state's "western interior."

Her two essays from Lafayette Parish show her most direct engagement with transcendentalism. They simultaneously pray that transcendentalist approaches might address the national and individual trauma engulfing her, mark her recognition of the raced and gendered boundaries of such approaches, and attempt to revise transcendentalism so that it can cross those boundaries to reach the ideals of (collective) truth and justice. Her 27 October 1866 piece takes its title from the concept that dominates Highgate's earlier philosophical work in the *Recorder*; it is simply labeled "Truth." The text carries an epigraph from the second volume of *Memoirs of Margaret Fuller*: "There is a species of cactus, from whose outer bark, if torn by an ignorant person, there exudes a poisonous liquid; but the nations who know the plant, strike to core, and there find a sweet and refreshing juice that renews life."[40] Highgate credits the quotation thus: "So wrote one of the most highly gifted beings that ever existed, namely Margaret Fuller Ossoli." What follows is a dense and rich consideration of the title concept that cites the Bible, Hugo, and Carlyle and that weighs gender, individuality, community, nature, and nationhood.

A cornerstone is that "deep in the inner heart of hearts nature holds her secrets of the true." Highgate's concept of nature is Emersonian—perhaps even Thoreauvian—and suggests a reading of, among other texts, Emerson's "Circles":

> Nature, all nature, proclaims truth. Her beautiful symbolic forms teach it. Notice with me the doctrine in her consecutive whirls of stars, that are loop-holes in the floor of the Eternal; in those same circles in the layers of the tree trunks; in the corolla; in the arrangement of leaves on the stem and in the leaf-bud; in the wavelets in the stream; in the strata of the various incrustations of the earth; in every stone; in the drops that descend to fertilize the earth; in the formation of the human eye; in magnetism and electricity, and none the less so in the most delicate circlets in the abdominal bud just at a time when the human verges nearest the Divine Creator.
>
> What, we ask, do these whirls and circles teach? These are but symbols of the affectionately clasped arms that speak of love. Nature is too true to do otherwise than repeatedly proclaim the grandest of her laws.

Highgate's gendering of the natural here is not random: one of her final calls in the piece is "Woman, be true to your most delicate conception of your mission even if you become a Heloise!" And this move, like the broad developing sense of an Over-soul in her earlier work, is part of her push to articulate a functional place in the broader national collective and a conception of fully realized, natural selfhood available to women—*all* women. Note again her "Notice with me." Inviting collective vision, she asserts that "every one who is forming their characters, and aiding others in the formation of theirs, should worship truth."

Such a statement's presence in an evangelical newspaper layers the phrase "aiding others": this is not only an idealistic hope; it is a concrete call to engage in education and both individual and community action. Arguably, the study of nature, the practice of self-culture, and the engagement in worldly struggles for truth go hand in hand, and so for Highgate, the definition of an American scholar / citizen must cross boundaries of gender and race. This wider conception of just who might find the truth makes Highgate redouble her imperatives: "Sacrifice everything to truth. Seldom, if ever, accept expedience in its place, or in our own souls. All outside is reflected or shadowed. . . . All else will be swallowed up in . . . eternity; but truth has an individuality, which is changeless."

Thus, crystallizing the collectivist and activist sensibility of truth hinted at in "Waiting for the Cars" and "A Spring Day," she writes that "the pith of every motive should be truth," not just for individuals but for nations. Playing at the edges of truth or trying to cover the truth could be as dangerous as tearing Fuller's cactus bark: "ignorant person[s]" could cause the plant "to exude a poisonous liquid"; indeed, "whole nations have endeavored to keep back and disguise" the truth and have thus suffered. This is why Highgate's battle is so important: "No description in the Apocalypse," she asserts, "can adequately picture the inner bill" for the "crime" of denying truth. Truth must be "the core, the heart, the summit, and the foundation" of every action, and "those who seek for it must throw the plummet with a steady, strong hand, into the middle of the stream." "It has no creation," Highgate continues, "for it is of God. It may lie latent in the soul of a people or individual, but it cannot die." If nations "are to stand the inevitable test," truth must be "in the lowest and strongest stratum of their foundation"; individuals committed to truth must link their atomic selves to (re)create that foundation—submitting to principle, but also (or, more properly for Highgate, simply and inherently *and*) practicing activist integration of principle in all locations. And because nature's "grandest law" is love—self-love and the love of community—Highgate ends with this stunning sentence: "Personal truth would save this nation, and the world." As much ideal as concrete, this call suggests that transcendentalist praxis must be politically active, must break the barriers erected in the name of race and gender to reform and re-form the nation and the world.

The piece Highgate sent to the *Recorder* after "Truth" seems at first glance lighter in tone; its play, though, actually explores the limits of humor in ways similar to the rewriting of the travel narrative as genre in "A Spring Day" and extends and challenges the ideas of "Truth" by placing them directly in Highgate's immediate (and dangerous) personal and political moment. Appearing in the 3 November 1866 *Recorder* and titled "On Horse Back—Saddle Dash, No. 1,"[41] the piece initially narrates a "quick gallop" to "these grand old October woods," brought about by Highgate's feeling of a "teacher's *ennui*" from "trying with all [her] might to instruct these very French, little and large Creoles." Showing her own Northern and middle-class biases but also attempting humorously to recognize again the difficulties facing transplanted teachers, she admits, "But for my roan, I would break down as a harp unstrung." Even her horse, she writes, "was Creole, and I am afraid rather *confederate* in his tendencies," for "when I was feeling lost, almost[,] to my surroundings in some meditations of an intensely union cast, he had the bad taste to get into a fence leaping mood." But she "conquers" the horse and then offers "meditations": "I plunged into the thickest of the oak tree forest with its exquisite drapery of gray hanging moss. The old dame must have anticipated some children visitors, for she had swings ready made, formed of the thick inter-lapping vine-like branches . . . , reaching from treetop to treetop all through these woods. What delightful order! Oh, if dear Henry D. Thoreau were here, wouldn't he go into a rhapsody! But he is here in spirit."

Albeit again under the veil of humor, Highgate feels obliged to defend this sense of "ministering spirits": "Yes, they are 'ministering spirits' [but] don't imagine me a modern spiritualist after the 'affinity-seeking,' 'wife and husband leaving' stripe. . . . I detest 'table rappings and crockery breaking,' especially the last, for I have broken so much." She also reminds readers, however, how quickly the transcendental "coalescing" of like spirits can be stopped by race and gender bias. Initially, her mind is taken by "a cluster of scarlet blossoms"—"How I wish my Philadelphia friends had these!" But she cloaks these potentially transcendentalist desires to enfold and share nature's beauty with what seems a flip internal racism: "All negroes like red; so pash on, pony, I must have those flowers." A later passage suggests this line is both self-aware and designed to force readers to think about Blackness and these potentially transcendent woods, woods nonetheless dangerous for African Americans: "Some rebel equestrians just passed, and fired four times almost in my face." Highgate's report of being shot at—by whites attempting to frighten her away from teaching in Lafayette Parish—also found its way into much more direct reports to the AMA, as did terrifying accounts of her students being shot at and sometimes actually shot.[42] Surely this account brings forward memories of Charlie Highgate—the young Black man shot five times by rebels, a synecdoche for the pain of war and "freedom's birth"—and of

"A Spring Day" for both Highgate and some of her readers. As in "A Spring Day," the trauma Highgate invokes is simultaneously individual, collective, and even national—and, in all, tied to both the battles for truth and the battles against racism. It is the trauma of an (African) American and so also an American trauma.[43]

Again humor conveys unspeakable horror and bravery: "But who is going to let grape[shot] keep them off horse back or off duty?" Highgate demonstrates that she can engage in Emersonian or Thoreauvian wit and suggests that such wit comes from a place of power—a power to actualize the self that "rebels" (even after the war's conclusion) want to deny African Americans through any means necessary. Like Thoreau's, her humor is detached and matter-of-fact, but it simultaneously emphasizes that she cannot detach herself from the matter-of-fact nature of racial violence.

Highgate deals with her world's gender discrimination in similar fashion. After recognizing "how independent one feels in the saddle," she asserts the stupidity of "such long riding skirts . . . so inconvenient when you have to ford streams." She calls out, "Oh, fashion, will no Emancipation Proclamation free us from thee!" Even the piece's expected sentimental resolution is set amid frightening humor: "Hasn't He promised to keep His workers? 'Then to doubt would be disloyal; to falter would be sin!' Oh! I forgot to say my roan did not understand English any better than my scholars do. When I said, 'Whoa, pony,' he would gallop." Such levity is not simply a coping mechanism; it becomes a mode for addressing the past and potential traumas outlined in such texts as "A Spring Day," for marking a community ("His workers") even as it reveals the fractures in that community (her "very French" scholars cannot "understand"), and for telling and actuating individual and communal truths in the pursuit of truth.

Highgate's "Saddle Dash" is in God's hands, nature's hands—though perhaps neither of these entities understands her "English" enough to protect her, either. If Henry David Thoreau's spirit is here, it is as fleeting as it is potentially wondrous. It also cannot keep Highgate in a woodsy reverie. As if the grapeshot were not enough, the world of work and the needs of the newly freed (and so the collective need for truth) command her presence: "Oh! It is time for my night school." And the call of that world, in which she tries to enact transcendental ideas, requires that she pass sharecroppers at work in cotton fields—"so anxious are they to get places of their own"—on her way to teach her threatened scholars in a location she worries "northern radical spoken friends" may have forgotten.

Only four of Highgate's contributions to the *Recorder* after "On Horse Back" have surfaced,[44] and they return largely to the local news–centered form described above. Further trouble in Louisiana and the consolidation of her family in Mississippi led her to move there to teach, but by late 1869, she had returned North to lecture. She addressed the Massachusetts Female Anti-Slavery Society in February 1870, wrote to white abolitionist and supporter Gerrit Smith about the possibility of giving temperance lectures, and contemplated returning to Mississippi for a position at the AMA's new college, Tougaloo, though death prevented this last. Fuller consideration of her final years and the search for texts connected to those years are tasks for our future.[45]

The story of Edmonia Highgate has no neat ending, and I thus conclude by highlighting several strains of transcendentalist potential flowing from her. Most biographers offer an account of Highgate's tragic death that veers toward a cautionary tale of the power of racism and gender bias. Dorothy Sterling's summary is both succinct and foundational: "Highgate had fallen in love with a white man, John Henry Vosburg," who "was married, with two children and a wife in a mental institution"; by 16 October 1870, "Edmonia Highgate, the young woman of shining promise, had died penniless and alone, in an abortionist's shabby boarding house . . . [and] in her trunk the coroner found *Virginia and Other Poems* by John Henry Vosburg."[46] This account, relying on Highgate family letters to Gerrit Smith and the *Syracuse Daily Courier*, concludes that both racism and gender bias allowed Vosburg to "betray" Highgate, "abandoning her to the abortionist's blade."[47] In many ways, Highgate was, in Sterling's words—quoting Highgate's brother-in-law Albert T. Morgan—"murdered 'with the world as an accessory.'"[48] Still, the ease with which we have accepted the *Courier*'s lurid account suggests that this "ending" calls for more scrutiny.

The end of Highgate's story has an intimate parallel in her sister Caroline's brief notoriety. Teaching in Mississippi, Caroline Highgate fell in love with Albert Morgan, a white Union veteran, Reconstruction-era sheriff of Yazoo County, and Mississippi state senator. The couple married 3 August 1870, and the union was reported widely—usually in negative and insulting terms.[49] The Morgans' story is cited fairly widely in histories of Reconstruction.[50] What goes missing from such work, though, is a close consideration of Caroline Highgate's philosophy and voice. She may have explored some of the same questions as Edmonia; later, she became a "mental healer, Christian Science practitioner, and dramatic reader."[51] Perhaps Edmonia Highgate's transcendentalism was a familial affair.

This legacy may contextualize the work of one of Caroline's daughters, poet Angela Morgan—a figure mentioned briefly by Sterling but not explored by Highgate scholars.[52] Morgan—born Nina Lillian Morgan (ca. 1874–1957)—lived her adult life as white and was both a writer and a peace activist. Her papers suggest that her mother Caroline "was not only her constant companion but [illegible] her spiritual guide and inspirer."[53] New York Public Library archivist John Stinson summarizes her work: "She was strongly influenced by the American transcendentalist movement and, through her mother, by Swedenborg. . . . She came to regard poetry as a vehicle for the expression of cosmic truths and ultimately for the spiritual transformation of mankind. . . . She was a social visionary who opposed war, capital punishment, the economic exploitation of the poor, and the oppression of women, and who pleaded, in her most serious poems, for a world of peace, social justice and human brotherhood."[54] Critical treatment of Morgan's work, however, has been thin, and no one has fully explored her ties to the Highgates—much less to her aunt's engagement with transcendentalism.

The question of female genealogies that informs this volume foregrounds the need to reconsider African American engagement with transcendentalism over time. We do not fully know whom Edmonia Highgate influenced or how. One fascinating possibility is Frances Ellen Watkins Harper, whom Highgate met at the 1864 Syracuse convention and who involved herself closely with the *Recorder* during the 1860s. African Americanists have long noted that, while Harper worked with the AME Church throughout her life, she attended services (and had her funeral conducted) at Philadelphia's First Unitarian. They have not, however, discussed its pastor. Without remarking any connection to Harper, historians of transcendentalism, on the other hand, have long recognized minister William Henry Furness's position at the nexus of Unitarianism and transcendentalism and his close friendship with Emerson. Harper's work reveals transcendentalist traces, but, as with so many Black figures, critics have left such traces unexamined, in part because of the assumption that those interested in concrete reform could not also engage with transcendentalism's idealism.[55]

Asking about Harper should lead us to ask as well about later figures—as Katherine Adams does with Pauline Hopkins in this volume. But it should also lead us to wonder why transcendentalism and African American women's writing became so distanced in our literary criticism and history—and, in a more immediate sense, why Hopkins and Highgate were, in some ways, so far apart. While this, too, is work for another day, I want to suggest that Highgate embraced the possibility that she could be an Exaltada—that transcendentalism might be adapted to make room for her race, her gender, and her own unique self—at a moment of great hope for Black America, a moment before the nation was fully "reconstructed" into a Jim Crow state. Highgate wrote at a time—however brief—when she could pray with some degree of optimism that "personal truth would save this nation, and the world."

NOTES

The author thanks the volume editors, Katherine Adams, Michael Borgstrom, Jodie Gardner, and Paul Teed. Some of the research for the essay is tied to a larger project partially supported by a fellowship from the National Endowment for the Humanities; any views, findings, conclusions, or recommendations expressed here do not necessarily reflect those of the National Endowment for the Humanities.

1. On the *Recorder*, see Eric Gardner, "Remembered (Black) Readers," *American Literary History* 23 (Summer 2011): 229–59. In light of the complexities of the *Recorder*'s pagination, for clarity's sake, I refer to *Recorder* texts by title and date but not page. Quotations come from microfilm of original issues, as online transcriptions are not always accurate.

   My capitalization of "Black" is a conscious challenge to most style manuals, which place both "Black" and "white" in lowercase. Echoing Gabrielle Foreman's "A Note on Language" in *Activist Sentiments: Reading Black Women in the Nineteenth Century* (Urbana: Univ. of Illinois Press, 2009), I make this decision "as a matter of practice and principle" and to recognize difference rather than essentialize it (xv). To help explain her rationale, Foreman quotes a sentence from T. Thomas Fortune's 1906 speech "Who Are We?" that I've long found persuasive: "I AM A PROPER NOUN, NOT A COMMON NOUN." Fortune's claim calls attention to the long misnaming of Black people; it is simultaneously an assertion of humanity and an implicit argument about the evils of a society that would make such an assertion necessary from *any* person. But while Fortune's linking of capitalization and personhood might seem to suggest that "white" should be capitalized, too—in the spirit of equity and consistency—his implicit argument reminds us that "Black" and "white" folks were not (and are not now) treated equitably or consistently in American society. Consider the resonances of the capitalized phrases "Black Power" and "White Power," for example. I similarly submit that placing both "Black" and "white" in lowercase suggests a state of consistent equity that we simply haven't reached. This essay repeatedly recognizes how white denials of Black humanity shaped Highgate's life and world, and so its approach to capitalization acknowledges both how much she had to tell *all* people about human struggles and how deeply such attempts to be a "proper noun" challenged white power structures.
2. Lara Langer Cohen and Jordan Stein, introduction to *Early African American Print Culture*, ed. Cohen and Stein (Philadelphia: Univ. of Pennsylvania Press, 2012), 16.
3. According to the introduction, "contributors were encouraged not to review standard coverage of topics but to provide new perspectives on old themes, explore new directions, open new topics, and point to work demanded by a new century" (*OxH*, xxv).
4. I single out Sandra Harbert Petrulionis's *To Set This World Right: The Antislavery Movement in Thoreau's Concord* (Ithaca, N.Y.: Cornell Univ. Press, 2006) because of its smart emphasis on "civic context" (3), though Len Gougeon's strong work on Emerson and antislavery and Albert J. von Frank's pioneering *The Trials of Anthony Burns* (Cambridge, Mass.: Harvard Univ. Press, 1998) also deserve note.
5. See Sterling Stuckey, *African Culture and Melville's Art: The Creative Process in "Benito Cereno" and "Moby-Dick"* (New York: Oxford Univ. Press, 2009); and Robert S. Levine and Samuel Otter, eds., *Frederick Douglass and Herman Melville: Essays in Relation* (Chapel Hill: Univ. of North Carolina Press, 2008). Just as students of transcendentalism can benefit from considering Black presences, so can African Americanists from considering transcendentalism. A brief example: One of Highgate's most important works ("A Spring Day up the James") appeared on the same page of the 27 May 1865 *Recorder* as a chapter from Julia Collins's *The Curse of Caste*. That placement should prompt us to rethink the contexts and paratexts of Collins's recently recovered serialized novel. See *The Curse of Caste*, ed. William Andrews and Mitch Kachun (New York: Oxford Univ. Press, 2006).
6. See Carla L. Peterson, *"Doers of the Word": African American Women Speakers and Writers in the Antebellum North (1830–1880)* (New York: Oxford Univ. Press, 1995); James O. Horton

and Lois E. Horton, *Black Bostonians: Family Life and Community Struggle in the Antebellum North* (New York: Holmes & Meier, 1979); and Elise Lemire, *Black Walden: Slavery and Its Aftermath in Concord, Massachusetts* (Philadelphia: Univ. of Pennsylvania Press, 2009).

7. See Robert S. Levine, *Martin Delany, Frederick Douglass, and the Politics of Representative Identity* (Chapel Hill: Univ. of North Carolina Press, 1997).
8. Bases for such work would be *William Cooper Nell: Selected Writings, 1832–1874*, ed. Dorothy Porter Wesley and Constance Porter Uzelac (Baltimore: Black Classic Press, 2002); and Charlotte Forten's *Journals*, ed. Brenda Stevenson (New York: Oxford Univ. Press, 1988).
9. *William Cooper Nell*, 412. On Theodore Parker, see Dean Grodzins's *American Heretic* (Chapel Hill: Univ. of North Carolina Press, 2002); and Paul Teed's *A Revolutionary Conscience* (Lanham, Md.: Univ. Press of America, 2012).
10. Forten, *Journals*, 154, 113.
11. The root of most work on Highgate is Dorothy Sterling's treatment in *We Are Your Sisters* (New York: Norton, 1984). Ronald Butchart's "Edmonia G. and Caroline V. Highgate: Black Teachers, Freed Slaves, and the Betrayal of Black Hearts," in *Portraits of African American Life since 1865*, ed. Nina Mjagkij (Wilmington, Del.: Scholarly Resources, 2003), adds to Sterling's work and also appears revised in Butchart's *Schooling the Freed People* (Chapel Hill: Univ. of North Carolina Press, 2010). Milton Sernett's consideration of Highgate at the end of *North Star Country* (Syracuse: Syracuse Univ. Press, 2002) is valuable but brief. See also Clara Merritt DeBoer's *His Truth Is Marching On* (New York: Garland, 1995); and Linda Cabral's PhD dissertation "Letters from Four Antebellum Black Women Educators," Univ. of Massachusetts at Boston, 2006. One of Highgate's letters—published as "Louisiana" in the *American Missionary* 9 (March 1867): 56–57—appears in the resources for teachers for *Reconstruction: The Second Civil War*, part of the PBS series *American Experience*.
12. Edmonia Highgate's tombstone indicates her birthdate; some sources list her birthplace as Syracuse, others as Albany. Select later sources assert that Hannah Highgate was white, even though she herself referred to the newly freed as "my people" in a letter to the American Missionary Association; see H. F. Highgate to George Whipple, 23 April 1865, American Missionary Association Archive, Amistad Research Center, Tulane University (hereafter cited as AMAA). See also the 1850 Federal Census of Albany (Ward 6), New York, 357B; the 1860 Federal Census of Syracuse (Ward 7), New York, 934; and issues of the *North Star* for 1848 and 1849 containing the Highgates' boarding advertisements.
13. I read the Highgates' economic circumstances differently than Butchart, who takes the absence of property amounts in an 1860 census listing—a common lapse by census takers—to mean that the Highgates had little money ("Edmonia," 3–4).
14. "Fair in Aid of the Impartial Citizen," *Impartial Citizen*, 5 September 1849, 2.
15. Jermain Loguen was deeply radicalized by this point because of his work with the Underground Railroad and his participation in the 1 October 1851 "Jerry Rescue," in which an interracial group liberated William Henry—called "Jerry"—who had been arrested as a fugitive. See Sernett, *North Star*, 137–45.
16. Edward Smith, *A History of the Schools of Syracuse* (Syracuse: C. W. Bardeen, 1893), 325.
17. The family remained connected even as its members dispersed widely. See Sterling, *We Are Your Sisters*, 300; Butchart, "Edmonia," 4–5, 7; Butchart, *Schooling the Freed People*, 45, 47–48; death notice for Charles Highgate, *Syracuse Standard*, 7 May 1861; "Obituary" for Charles Highgate Jr., *Christian Recorder*, 20 May 1865; "State Normal School," [Jackson, Miss.] *Clarion*, 7 April 1886, 1.

18. Highgate's initial connection to the AME Church might have been through Loguen, who sometimes straddled the AME / AMEZ divide.
19. See *Trustee Minute Book, 1853–1875*, Corporate Records of Plymouth Congregational Church, 20, 135, 149, and 150.
20. See "Rev. Michael E. Strieby, D.D.," *American Missionary* 53 (April 1899): 1–6.
21. Edmonia Highgate to Ira Cobb, 22 January 1864, AMAA.
22. Gura, xii.
23. A graduate of Harvard Divinity School and Bronson Alcott's brother-in-law, Samuel J. May is mentioned in most histories of transcendentalism. A committed Unitarian and abolitionist, he shared the platform, for example, with Douglass and Emerson at the famous 1844 meeting of the Concord Female Anti-Slavery Society. See Petrulionis, *To Set This World Right*, 41–47.
24. Michael E. Strieby to Simeon S. Joycelyn, 24 January 1864, AMAA; and Edmonia Highgate to George Whipple, 18 January 1864, AMAA.
25. Edmonia Highgate to George Whipple, 1 June 1864, AMAA. Highgate alludes here to Ecclesiastes 9:10. On this period, also see Sterling, *We Are Your Sisters*, 295–96; and DeBoer, *His Truth*, 51–53.
26. DeBoer reports: "Clara Duncan accompanied [Highgate] home to Syracuse. Highgate was deranged much of the time and allowed no one but Duncan to care for her" (*His Truth*, 55).
27. See *Proceedings of the National Convention of Colored Men* (Boston: George C. Rand and Avery for the Convention, 1864); and "National Convention of Colored Men," *New Orleans Tribune*, 26 October 1864, 1.
28. *Proceedings*, 15.
29. *The Doctrines and Discipline of the African Methodist Episcopal Church* (Philadelphia: Richard Allen and Jacob Tapisco for the African Methodist Connection in the U.S., 1817).
30. Because the *Recorder* was charged with linking together the massively diffuse Church, contributions arrived from a broad geographic range that guaranteed even further diversity. See Eric Gardner, *Unexpected Places* (Jackson: Univ. Press of Mississippi, 2009), 76–83, 88–90; as well as the work of Frances Smith Foster.
31. "Dr. Beecher's Views on Universalism," *Christian Recorder*, 25 April 1863.
32. "The Westminster Review on Ralph Waldo Emerson," *Christian Recorder*, 29 June 1861.
33. "Emerson's New Poems," *Christian Recorder*, 1 June 1867.
34. Highgate quotes lines 161–68 of Book 3 of *Aurora Leigh* ("Get leave to work / In this world—'tis best for you all"); she likely saw one of the many American editions of Elizabeth Barrett Browning's poem, such as *Aurora Leigh, and Other Poems* (New York: C. S. Francis, 1857).
35. Highgate's invocation of these writers is telling. Mary Abigail Dodge ("Gail Hamilton") and Sara Willis Parton ("Fanny Fern") were widely known for ardent women's rights arguments, often delivered with dazzling wit and thoughtful negotiation of popular sentimentality.
36. Christopher Newfield, *The Emerson Effect: Individualism and Submission in America* (Chicago: Univ. of Chicago Press, 1996), 4.
37. Compare this to Fuller's assertion in *Woman in the Nineteenth Century*: "If the negro be a soul, if the woman be a soul, appareled in flesh, to one Master only are they accountable. There is but one law for souls, and if there is to be an interpreter of it, he must come not as man, or son of man, but as son of God." Or her thinking that "we must have units

before we can have union" (*WNC*, 20, 60). On Fuller's sense that difference must be set aside for unity's sake, see Katherine Adams's essay in this collection and her *Owning Up: Privacy, Property, and Belonging in U.S. Women's Life Writing* (New York: Oxford Univ. Press, 2009).

38. This poem first appeared in Browning's posthumous *Last Poems*. Highgate likely saw one of the American editions published by James Miller (successor to C. S. Francis), such as *Last Poems by Elizabeth Barrett Browning with a Memorial by Theodore Tilton* (New York: James Miller, 1862). In Browning's original, "death" is actually "dearth." I have not yet found evidence as to whether this was an error by Highgate or the *Recorder* or a deliberate revision of the poem. I have located a handful of other versions with "death," including one contemporary with Highgate: a quotation of four stanzas from Browning's poem in the "Editor's Table" of the February 1861 *Ladies' Repository* (392).
39. While I take issue with its conclusions, James G. Hollandsworth Jr.'s *An Absolute Massacre* (Baton Rouge: Louisiana State Univ. Press, 2001) is the fullest treatment of the riot.
40. The epigraph is part quotation and part paraphrase. In addition to appearing in *Memoirs*—see, for example, the 1852 Phillips, Sampson edition (2:108)—it appears in Eliza Farnham, *Woman and Her Era* (New York: A. J. Davis, 1864), 1:237.
41. It is unclear whether Highgate planned more "saddle dashes"; some issues following the 3 November 1866 *Recorder* are missing or incomplete.
42. Edmonia Highgate to Michael Strieby, 17 December 1866, AMAA; reproduced in Sterling, *We Are Your Sisters*, 298–99.
43. Highgate's sense of the ways trauma can shape insight should be compared especially with Fuller's. See, for example, the treatment of the Seer of Prevorst in *Summer on the Lakes*: notably, though the Seer gains "sight" during and after great pain, she is "immersed in the inward state" (*SL*, 90); Highgate sees her individual trauma as part and parcel of racial and national collective trauma and thus as a spur to reach outward.
44. More may exist, and Highgate may have contributed to periodicals beyond the *Recorder*, the *American Missionary*, and the *National Anti-Slavery Standard*. This volume's awareness of the importance of both published and unpublished writing should also remind us of the need to continue recovering Highgate's work.
45. See Sterling, *We Are Your Sisters*, 299–300; Butchart, *Schooling the Freed People*, 47; and Butchart, "Edmonia," 7. Highgate's speech to the Massachusetts Anti-Slavery Society is reported in *National Anti-Slavery Standard*, 5 February 1870, 1–2.
46. Sterling, *We Are Your Sisters*, 302, 304.
47. Butchart, "Edmonia," 10. See also the 17 October 1870 *Syracuse Daily Courier*.
48. Sterling, *We Are Your Sisters*, 304. Sterling quotes a 21 October 1870 letter from Albert T. Morgan to Gerrit Smith.
49. See, for example, the 30 July 1870 *Weekly Arizona Miner* (which copied a piece from the 21 June 1870 *Georgia Weekly Telegraph*); the 6 August 1870 *Cleveland Daily Herald*; and even the 30 July 1870 *Frank Leslie's Illustrated Newspaper*.
50. Part of the story's wide dissemination is tied to Morgan's own account of his time in Mississippi, *Yazoo; or, on the Picket Line of Freedom* (1884)—which was republished in 1968 and again in 2000.
51. Butchart, "Edmonia," 10; Richard Current, *Those Terrible Carpetbaggers* (New York: Oxford Univ. Press, 1988), 411–12. Some critics have begun to trace components of Christian Science to transcendentalism; see, for example, Albert von Frank, "Religion," *OxH*, 131.
52. Sterling, *We Are Your Sisters*, 305.

53. Walter McNitt and Christopher Leonard, "Finding Aid for the Angela Morgan Papers, 1893–1957," Bentley Historical Library, University of Michigan, n.p. See also John D. Stinson, "Finding Aid for Angela Morgan Papers, 1901–1957," New York Public Library.
54. Stinson, "Finding Aid," n.p.
55. See, for example, Frances Smith Foster, ed., *A Brighter Coming Day: A Frances Ellen Watkins Harper Reader* (New York: Feminist Press, 1990), 22. Furness is noted in Gura, 99–104, and mentioned in several other studies. Harper's poem "Youth in Heaven" carries an epigraph from Swedenborg, her poem "Let the Light Enter" moves from the last words of Goethe, and select speeches address key questions of transcendentalism.

INTERLUDE

Elizabeth Bancroft, from *Letters from England, 1846–49* (London: Smith, Elder, 1904), 26–28, 85–88, 169–70.

To [her sons] W[illiam] D. B[liss] and A[rthur] B[liss]

London, November 29, 1846

After a long interval I find again a quiet Sunday evening to resume my journal to you. . . . Nothing could be more delightful than London. . . . We have some of the best specimens of English society, too, here just now, as the Whig ministry brings a good deal of the ability of the aristocracy to its aid. The subjects of conversation among women are more general than with us, and [they] are much more cultivated than our women as a body, not our blues. They never sew, or attend, as we do, to domestic affairs, and so live social life and understand it better.

To Mrs. W. W. Story

London, March 23, 1847

My dear Mrs. Story: I should have thanked you by the last steamer for your note and the charming volume which accompanied it. . . . The poems, which would at all times have given me great pleasure, gave me still more here than they would if I were with you on the other side of the Atlantic. I am not cosmopolitan enough to love any nature so well as our American nature, and in addition to the charm of its poetry, every piece brought up to me the scenes amidst which it had been written. How dear these associations are your husband will soon know when he too is separated from his native shores and from those he loves. . . . I shall look forward with great pleasure to seeing him here, and only wish you were to accompany him, for your own sake, for his, and for ours. His various culture will enable him to enjoy most fully all that Europe can yield him in every department. My own regret ever since I have been here has been that the seed has not "fallen upon better ground," for though I thought myself not ignorant wholly, I certainly lose much that I might enjoy more keenly if I were better prepared for it. . . . There are certain sympathies of country which one cannot overcome. On the other hand I certainly enjoy pleasures of the highest kind, and am every day floated like one in a dream into the midst of persons and scenes that make my life seem more like a drama than a reality. Nothing is more unreal than the actual presence of persons of whom one has heard much, and long wished to see. One day I find myself at dinner by the side of Sir Robert Peel, another by Lord John Russell, or at Lord Lansdowne's table, with Mrs. Norton, or at a charming breakfast with Mr. Rogers, surrounded by pictures and marbles, or with tall feathers and a long train, making curtsies to a queen.

[To her uncle I. P. D.]
Friday, March 17th, [1848]
Things look rather darker in France, but we ought not to expect a republic to be established without some difficulties. . . . You cannot judge of the state of France, however, through the medium of the English newspapers, for, of course, English sympathies are all entirely against it. They never like France, and a republic of any kind still less. A peaceful and prosperous republic in the heart of Europe would be more deprecated than a state of anarchy. The discussion of French matters reveals to me every moment the deep repugnance of the English to republican institutions. It lets in a world of light upon opinions and feelings, which, otherwise, would not have been discovered by me.

Caroline Healey Dall and the American Social Science Movement

HELEN R. DEESE

When in 1860 the second-generation transcendentalist Moncure Conway began in Cincinnati a new publication, resonantly titled the *Dial*, its first issue included his laudatory review of Caroline Healey Dall's *"Woman's Right to Labor"; or, Low Wages and Hard Work*. What touched Dall most about the notice was Conway's remark that reading the book made him feel "Margaret Fuller's mantle did not pass into heaven with her."[1] Dall commented in her journal, "How unfit I am to be named with Margaret, I know very well, but it was pleasant to find one person, inclined to throw *her* mantle over me." Then she added the significant clause: "and it brought ~~one~~ ^a^ tear of strong resolve to my cheek."[2]

Caroline Healey Dall (1822–1912) was perhaps the most self-conscious and the most direct early inheritor of Margaret Fuller's feminism. As her response to Conway's nomination indicates, she was more than open to her role as Fuller's successor, despite the modest disclaimer. Her association with Fuller stretched back to the time when, as an impressionable young woman of eighteen in the spring of 1841, she sat enthralled, though not intimidated, in Fuller's Conversation group. These few weeks represented almost all of her direct interaction with Fuller, and she never felt personally close to her mentor—indeed, she believed that Fuller disliked her. But the young Caroline Healey recognized immediately the significance of this experience, and the mature Caroline Healey Dall forever after regarded it as a pivotal point in her development. Her private judgment of Fuller, expressed in her journals only months after Fuller's death, was that "there is no American woman that stands near her" (*Selected Journals*, 1:131). Publicly, reviewing a new edition of *Woman in the Nineteenth Century* in 1855, Dall called the work "the deepest thought and clearest utterance of our noblest woman."[3]

Subsequently, in a series of lectures, articles, and books in the 1850s and 1860s, Dall proceeded to become a major apologist for Fuller.[4] Writing for the new *Dial*, she linked Fuller's influence directly to the American women's rights movement, observing that Fuller's 1844 *Dial* article "The Great Lawsuit" "stated with transcendent force the argument which formed the basis of the first 'Woman's Rights Convention' in 1848." She elaborated: "Nothing has since been added to her statement; nothing can ever be taken away from it: and every new step in the movement crowns her brow with a new laurel; for to her it was left to make a complete, scholarly exposition of [the woman] question."[5] Similarly, in the *North American Review* Dall called *Woman in the Nineteenth Century* "the most brilliant, complete, and scholarly statement ever made upon this subject."[6] In the 1890s, when Dall was in her seventies, she again brought Fuller to public attention, publishing first her own notes from the Conversation series (*Margaret and Her Friends*, 1895) and then a lecture she had recently delivered to the Society for Philosophical Enquiry in Washington, D.C. (*Transcendentalism in New England: A Lecture*, 1897). In the latter work Dall undertook to construct a revisionist *feminist* history of the transcendentalist movement, one that presented Fuller's role as central.

Choosing to foreground what she called the "aggressive and reformatory" in Fuller,[7] Dall used that legacy to help validate her own career path. First, she read in Fuller's thought an impetus to unlimited choices and action by women. Of Fuller's broad appeal for woman's recognition of her own possibilities and for society's removing the barriers to their fulfillment, Dall wrote (quoting Fuller), "Let principles be once firmly established, and particulars will adjust themselves."[8] The seed Fuller planted, Dall observed, had already borne fruit in the appearance of professional women in many nontraditional fields, in new opportunities for education, and in the beginnings of the women's rights movement. Fuller had not specifically spelled out the new vocations that would open to women nor all the educational opportunities due to them, and she had not forecast the conventions, petitions, lobbying, and extended campaigns that would be necessary to achieve these ends. But the principles she enunciated, including her statement of "the first clear, uncompromising, scholarly demand for the civil rights of her sex," certainly implied them. Dall saw the practical reform activities of herself and others as the working out of "the fearlessness of [Fuller's] suggestions."[9]

Second, Dall used her own published history of transcendentalism to highlight the emphasis of the movement and of Fuller herself on reformative action. Daring to recast Emerson's definition of transcendentalism ("Idealism as it appears in 1842") into her own version, "Idealism *made practical* as it appeared in 1842," Dall went on to stress the socially conscious, reforming side of Fuller herself.[10] Subtly taking issue with Octavius B. Frothingham's earlier and much fuller history of the movement, *Transcendentalism in New England: A History* (1876), which presented Fuller as "The Critic," Dall rejected its depiction of her as intellectualized and detached. She fumed at this limited and limiting category and countered it by emphasizing Fuller's practical transcendentalism, often seen in her attempts to improve the lives of other women. At Brook Farm, Dall pointed out, Fuller had "interested herself in the single women longing for something better than they knew, and without resources." Fuller followed the lives of such women and "in several instances known to [Dall], helped them to independence." Likewise, in New York she offered aid to women at Sing Sing prison through both public addresses and private counseling. And in Italy she not only became involved in the Italian Revolution and wrote its history but also superintended a hospital. Dall's point was to rectify an error made by Frothingham and other interpreters of Fuller: the "common feeling that she valued intellect above character, and felt neither sympathy nor affection for commonplace persons." According to Dall, "The very reverse of this was true."[11] Besides Frothingham, Dall must have had in mind her own experience with Charles Robinson, a Unitarian minister personally acquainted with Fuller, who in 1858 "baffle[d] any memory" of Dall's about Fuller by saying that "she had no republicanism about her, that she despised common people" (*Selected Journals*, 2:198). Dall's defense stressed that (like Anne Hutchinson, whom Dall saw as a precursor of transcendentalism) Fuller was distinguished not only by her intellectual achievement but by her practical service, especially to other women. Thus Dall framed Fuller's reputation to fit the legacy that she herself had claimed from her, as the inspirer of what Dall aptly called "practical 'Exaltadas.'"[12]

Building on Fuller's principles and personal example, Dall forged for herself an identity as an avant-garde reformer. She pressed a feminist agenda through expanded avenues, venturing into forums and employing tactics that Fuller never attempted. In the process, she constantly pushed the boundaries of what her contemporaries considered acceptable behavior by a woman. Lecturing from a public platform in Boston, Worcester, and elsewhere in New England, she argued the justice of woman's claim to equal educational, occupational, and legal opportunities. Immersing herself in the organized American women's movement beginning in the mid-1850s, she embraced an early leading role, organizing, presiding at, and participating in public meetings. Further, she took part in political action, addressing a legislative committee, writing and circulating petitions, and lobbying legislators. And, like Fuller, she argued her position from the printed page. Then, in the mid-1860s, Dall turned her energies to the establishment of a social science movement in America. This initiative was an instance of the general transition from the older style of romantic, idealistic reform movements of the early nineteenth century to a fact-based, scientific approach to societal problems. This relatively unexplored phase of Dall's career will form the focus of this paper.[13]

Caroline Dall was a founding mother in 1865 of the American Social Science Association (ASSA), a society devoted to the study of a broad range of social issues that was soon holding national conventions attracting the foremost thinkers on social questions. The purpose of the organization was not to carry out reforms but to bring to light the facts relating to societal problems so that they might be addressed by public action. In other words, the ASSA saw itself as providing the raw material—the results of inspections, surveys, studies, and observations conducted by experts—that would enable society to understand and thus to deal effectively with these issues. Dall participated in the planning of the organization before its inception, took part in its earliest meetings, served on multiple committees, wrote the statement of purpose, and had a major role in writing its bylaws. The other founders and early leaders who worked alongside Dall were almost entirely male, including Massachusetts Institute of Technology president William B. Rogers, eminent statistician Edward Jarvis, *Boston Commonwealth* editor and secretary of the Massachusetts State Board of Charities Frank Sanborn, educator George B. Emerson, Governor John A. Andrew, former governor Emory Washburn, political economist and former state legislator and congressman Amasa Walker, educator of the blind Samuel Gridley Howe, and recent past president of Trinity College Samuel Eliot. In her association with these men of eminence and power, Dall refused to be simply the organization's token woman. Instead, she aggressively prosecuted her agenda—a crucial part of which turned out to be ensuring meaningful roles for women in the organization's leadership. In the process, Dall honed political skills that often allowed her to gain her ends. While her assertiveness did not always endear her to coworkers, it does appear that she was effective. Indeed, in general Dall's personality seems to have been better suited to working with men—who did not so often take her abrasiveness personally—than with women.[14]

Dall's preparation for this work began as early as her teenage years in Boston's West Church (Unitarian). There she taught in a Sunday School and acted as a sort of rudimentary social worker, making investigative and charitable visits to the families of her students, most of whom were from economically disadvantaged circumstances. This model was the legacy of Joseph Tuckerman, a Unitarian minister renowned for his work with the poor. Still in her teens, Dall became an admiring disciple of the transcendentalist preacher Theodore Parker, whose jeremiads concerning Christian duty to "the perishing classes"[15] must have intensified her commitment. This orientation toward serving the underclass was likely responsible at least in part for Dall's original attraction to her future husband, Charles Henry Appleton Dall, in whose ministries to the poor in Baltimore and Portsmouth, New Hampshire, Caroline would figure largely. Dall was also the inheritor of the principles of self-culture and self-reliance that had come to her through association with such Unitarians / transcendentalists as her West Church ministers Charles Lowell and Cyrus A. Bartol, Ralph Waldo

Emerson, Elizabeth Palmer Peabody, and Margaret Fuller. Thus it was with an eye not only to improving conditions for society's needy class but also to working out her own destiny and enabling other women to do so as well that Dall took up this work. Her guiding principle of self-trust was often put to the test within the organization, as she found it necessary to fight for the position and standing from which to address effectively such questions as public health and sanitation, conditions and treatment of the institutionalized, and the plight of urban women workers. The field of social science allowed her to integrate the basic principles of transcendentalism with her commitment to addressing the problems of the poor.

In the late 1850s Dall became aware of the beginnings of a social science movement in Great Britain. In an 1860 lecture she observed that the women's cause in England was in some respects in advance of that in America, noting the prominent and public role women played in the National Association for the Promotion of Social Science (NAPSS), an organization founded in October 1857. Seizing on what seemed like an opportunity for women in a new field in which no entrenched male establishment yet existed, she challenged her fellow Americans, "If England can organize associations like these, so can we."[16]

Dall had several connections to the British movement. She probably learned about the NAPSS through her contact with British feminists and their publication *The English Woman's Journal*, for which she served for a time as the American agent.[17] Two of the founders of the association, Barbara Bodichon and Bessie Rayner Parkes (later Belloc), and their lesser-known associates Isa Craig and Sarah Lewin corresponded with Dall for several years beginning in 1858.[18] In addition, at least as early as the spring of 1859 Dall was acquainted with the work and publications of well-known and highly regarded English reformer Mary Carpenter. The daughter of the Unitarian minister in Bristol, Lant Carpenter, she founded a reform school for girls and later one for boys. Carpenter, whose primary patron was Lady Byron, exchanged publications with Dall and participated prominently in the earliest NAPSS meetings. Another of Dall's English correspondents, the journalist and reviewer Edward Peacock, published a glowing review of her *Woman's Rights under the Law* in an 1862 issue of the *Social Science Review*.[19] And still an additional source of Dall's knowledge of the organization was her husband Charles, who, stopping over in England between India and America in the summer of 1861, attended a Social Science "soiree" and passed along to his wife an invitation from Mary Carpenter to attend the upcoming NAPSS meeting in Dublin, offering what Dall called "half a year's salary."[20] Dall was unable to attend.

Dall's interest in such an organization was no doubt piqued in part by her own difficulties in obtaining published materials with facts and figures that could form the basis for effective reform. She had been appalled when in February 1859 she investigated the holdings of the Boston Athenaeum relating to the status of women: "I could not help laughing when I got there—" she wrote. "There were about a dozen wretched pamphlets & thin books—fewer than on my own poverty stricken shelves!" (*Selected Journals*, 2:207). As an organizer (from her teens) of several Sunday School libraries and as an inveterate user of collections, Dall had a real interest in library arrangement and acquisitions. And so a few weeks later she began a campaign to fill this vacuum, concentrating her efforts on the Boston Public Library, only five years old at the time. She began by consulting with Boston Unitarian ministers Ezra Stiles Gannett, Robert C. Waterston, and Samuel H. Winkley (the latter two of whom conducted ministries to the poor) in an effort to get "*one* alcove of the Library devoted to reports upon all matters relating to Societary Reform, Government—Reports &c—and organising it in such a manner—as should be available for all persons interested in Pauperism—Vice or Employment as a Social Question" (*Selected Journals*, 2:224). Not receiving much encouragement, two days later she wrote a letter of inquiry to the librarian, Edward Capen, regarding the library's holdings in the area of social science; and on 25 March she composed a letter with accompanying "Memorial" to the Trustees of the Public Library proposing that a Department for Social Science be established, with a special alcove set aside for books and pamphlets relating to it.[21] She urged that the library acquire additional relevant materials, particularly censuses and "Reports, whether of governments, Parliamentary or Philanthropic Committees, or Societies for the Prevention of Pauperism, Idleness or Crime, especially the Reports published in England, Scotland, Ireland, France and Germany," that would provide statistics and other facts useful to researchers. She suggested that one person be assigned the oversight of this department and noted that the time for action was ripe, while social science was in its infancy and the organization of the library still "plastic."[22]

Soon after Dall approached Waterston, he reported having spoken about her plan to both Capen and George Ticknor, one of the library's founders, and assured her that "both replied as if they intended to carry it out" (*Selected Journals*, 2:227–28). But a month later she received an apparently discouraging letter from the board of trustees that prompted her to go directly to the library's superintendent, Charles Coffin Jewett. Here she had no better success. She was, she wrote, "a good deal amused by the interview and the look of consternation on [Jewett's] face, when I told him, the Board would hear fm me again" (*Selected Journals*, 2:229). She did, in fact, continue "push[in]g" her "Memorial" but also "bearing some disappointments" (*Selected Journals*, 2:230). She enlisted other prominent Bostonians (the lecturer E. P. Whipple and the minister Thomas Starr King) in her campaign, but despite all her efforts Dall did not ultimately succeed in establishing a special department for social science. Two decades later she recalled that "Mr. Ticknor only relinquished the idea because space could not be found."[23] Still, she had raised awareness of the need for acquisitions in the area and had associated herself publicly with the cause of social science.

And thus it was that (by Dall's account) in the spring of 1865, as the war was drawing to a close, three Boston men, Charles F. Barnard, Thomas C. Amory, and William A. Babcock, perhaps among others, approached her with the idea of forming some sort of organization to consider the kinds of societal problems that the British NAPSS was addressing and that they believed were becoming more acute. Both Barnard and Babcock ministered to the poor at the Warren Street Chapel; Amory was a former Boston alderman and state legislator and civic activist. Dall, a reluctant recruit to what she called "a Social Science committee," saw little chance of success for the plan in the hands of its proponents, who in her judgment "had not the influence nor the character necessary to form such an association." Accordingly, having asked the originators if they "were enough in earnest to allow it to be formed by other persons" and having received their cheerful assent, she approached Franklin B. Sanborn, secretary of the Board of State Charities, a bureau established in 1863. She asked if he would be willing to serve on the committee if she could secure the permission of Governor John A. Andrew to use "the machinery" of the board in this endeavor. Andrew agreed, Sanborn agreed, and in September 1865 Dall began attending various organizational meetings. She helped to hammer out the constitution and was assigned the task of writing an address for the first public meeting. She noted wryly that she was appointed part of a "*Committee*" to draft this report, which she knew actually meant that she would have to write it: "when every man on the Committee was too indolent to prepare the statement of purposes,—I consented to do the work, rather than have all go to shipwreck," she recorded.[24]

But even in this organizational phase Dall ran into trouble. She realized early on that two of the other founders, Thomas Amory and pioneering dermatologist James C. White, thought her reputation as a woman's rights woman to be "not . . . favorable to the work," and they objected to her taking part in the public meeting. When Dall, acknowledging that "the less [she] had to do the better," nevertheless was unwilling that *no* woman participate and proposed that she simply read her own ten-minute report, the reaction was starkly sexist: "Such a blank silence & vapid speech as fell on the Committee! 'It would prejudice the public if an official act, were performed by one of the 'woman party[']] &c &c &c—." Dall eventually acceded to the "*official* point" of their objection, withdrawing her proposal, but her retreat "did not disarm the enemy—for he evidently preferred that no woman shd read anything." Dall, now in the uncomfortable position of seeming to promote herself, refused to back down, knowing that there was too much at stake: "I was obliged to insist—& to decline serving otherwise, at the risk of seeming anxious to put myself forward," she recorded in her diary, continuing, "There is only a choice between Dr Zakrzewska &

myself—&, of course they wd prefer me to Dr Z. It was impossible to make them feel as I did, that if I did not secure this privilege for women now—it would be forever lost. A reactionary conservative movement has already begun since the war. What is not seized & held *now* of such advantage—will be conceded. They objected to inviting Dr Zakrzewska & Dr Sewall to the meeting—but I carried that point."[25] Further, when Dall proposed that the topics for discussion in the Department of Education should include institutions of higher education that admitted women, such as Antioch, Oberlin, and Vassar, her fellow committee members "struck out these three names on the ground that they represented *sectarian institutions*." But Dall knew that this was but a smokescreen and that "the prejudice against the woman movement lay at the base of all." Not since the earliest days of the women's movement had she "encountered so disagreable a state of things," she noted, and she left the meeting "with a raging headache" (*Selected Journals*, 2:603). This incident marked only the first of many such internecine battles that Dall was to fight within the leadership of the social science movement. Her journal entries detailing her role in the ASSA, in fact, are peppered with the rhetoric of struggle, if not of warfare: "hard battle," "disagreable work," "hard work," "hard struggle," "hard time," "hard fight," "fought hard," "very hard fight," "internecine war"—these are typical descriptors of her experience.[26]

Undeterred by the apparent determination of the male leadership of the organization to minimize the role of women, Dall audaciously turned her energies to ensure that women held positions of leadership in the ASSA. She had persuaded Abigail W. May to serve on the organizing committee. May, already involved in charitable work in Boston, would become a distinguished reformer, working for the establishment of obstetrical clinics and holding key positions in the U.S. Sanitary Commission and the Freedmen's Aid Society. Now in the wake of the 22 September committee meeting in which the antifeminist bias of other members became apparent, Dall took deliberate and decisive action to ensure a significant female presence on the board of directors. Fully realizing the peril to women's cause of their exclusion from leadership, and knowing she would be out of town when the committee next met, she wrote a passionate letter to Sanborn, who had missed two previous meetings. She exhorted him that if he "ever had a duty in [his] life" it was to be at the next meeting: "For if this association starts on false principles it will be far worse than having none inasmuch as it will deprive us for years of anything better." She explained the conflict over women's participation at the earlier meeting and noted the "ungracious position" she was in, "obliged either to push [her]self or lose the principle." Neither Amory nor White "in spite of protestations wanted *one* woman on the Board," she explained to Sanborn: "Work by *degrees* said Mr A. Find one woman who is fit, said Dr. W.—which I thought cool in Abby May's presence to say nothing of mine." Dr. White said he would have no objection to a woman director "if we had a Florence Nightingale here—and the only reason we have not *one* F.N.," Dall fulminated, "is because we have so many—! Think of such an objection—in a country which has had Miss Dix—Miss Wormley—Miss Woolsey & Mrs Winthrop—Miss Carey & Miss Gilson!!" Eventually, she told Sanborn, the men consented to have two women (out of twelve members) on the board, but she and May pressed for three and were finally (if, as it turned out, temporarily) successful, though Dall noted ruefully, "of course we ought to have had five."[27]

Dall's letter demonstrated considerable political shrewdness. She believed that neither Amory nor White should be officers, but she knew that leaving out White would "make an enemy," so she thought he could be marginalized by making him secretary to the Department of Public Health. When the question arose as to which department each of the women would be associated with, Dall proposed Mary Eliot Dwight Parkman, widow of Dr. Samuel Parkman, for the Department of Public Health, noting that she was not sure she could have succeeded "with a less able candidate," but she was confident that "Mrs. P." could "fill any post." Then she attempted to put the committee members on the spot by being "rude enough to propose [Abby May] in her presence" for the Department of Education, but this strategy failed as the men "demurred." Her letter advised Sanborn to come to the meeting with an ally and to "look sharp as to the *men*" they selected for the board. "Make up your mind to sacrifice other things if needful for this is *very* important," she pressed him, "but don't yield this woman question." She concluded, "The only salvation for the whole thing is that you should go and speak *as a man*—what it is disgusting for me to say as a woman."[28]

Sanborn, heeding Dall's exhortation, attended the meeting. He notified Dall that not all the officers had been chosen but that he proposed Dall for the office of general director, that is, one without any attachment to any specific department, and the committee had unanimously approved. He thought that the "spirit of the committee [was] now what it should be with reference, to the share that women are to take in the matter." He could not predict what would happen at the upcoming public meeting, "but if women will attend it they can control this point."[29]

The initial public meeting took place on 4 October 1865, at the House of Representatives chamber of the State House in Boston, Governor Andrew presiding. By Dall's recollection almost half a century later, a thousand invitations were issued and six hundred persons were actually present to form the organization named the "American Social Science Association."[30] Several states were represented, and among the attendants were "many ladies, several of whom took part in the proceedings, while many enrolled themselves as members of the association" (among the enrollees was "Mrs. R. W. Emerson").[31] Dr. James C. White read the report of the Committee of Arrangements written by Dall (which the committee would not allow her to read); Dall remarked, "[White] murdered my Address but I had the pleasure of hearing it praised on all sides, by people who didn't know who wrote it." And although she claimed to have come to the meeting "without intending to open [her] mouth," she was constitutionally incapable of such a thing and "took a fair share in the debate" (*Selected Journals*, 2:607). In reporting the meeting, an anonymous writer for the new periodical the *Radical* noted "a very happy mixture of Radicals and Conservatives, and a fair proportion of women," adding that "in the British Association some of the most eminent members are women—Florence Nightingale and Mary Carpenter being two of them."[32]

In the course of the meeting Governor Andrew named Dall one of thirteen members of the nominating committee. Allying with one other member, Boston police court justice Edwin Wright, she boasted, "between us, we engineered every nomination." She managed, she declared, to secure the office of president for William B. Rogers, founder and first president of the Massachusetts Institute of Technology, when others pressed for a New Yorker. Importantly, she was able to retain on the board one woman other than herself—Mary Dwight Parkman—"by a joke—for when they questioned—her powers—& proposed a man—I said she had one power that he had not—namely—the power to work with Dr [Samuel Gridley] Howe!" (*Selected Journals*, 2:607). (Howe was to head the Public Health Department in which Parkman would serve.) The *Radical*, clearly attempting to play up the role of women, pointed out, "of the five directors, two are women."[33] Though the statement was technically true, it did not tell the whole story: the roster of officers was heavily loaded with men, since it included not only the five directors but the president, four vice presidents, and four secretaries (one each for the departments of Education; Public Health; Economy, Trade, and Finance; and Jurisprudence and the Amendment of Laws), a recording secretary, a corresponding secretary, and a treasurer, all of them male. On the whole, Dall was pleased with the initial meeting, but she could not have been sanguine as to the difficulties ahead.

And difficulties there were. Appointed to a committee with Sanborn and President William B. Rogers to prepare an address for the next general meeting, Dall found a few days later that Sanborn and Rogers, whom she thought of as allies, had prepared the report without consulting her or notifying her of their meeting. She learned this fact shortly before the report was submitted to the Executive Board, not even having time to read it beforehand. "In a committee of women," Dall seethed in her journal, "this would not have passed unnoticed—but I let it pass—because it would be put down to the sensitiveness of women—if I said one word, about it" (*Selected Journals*, 2:614). The slights to women continued: when, a few weeks later, George B. Emerson reported that the directors wished to elect a woman counselor to each of the departments, "*except that of law*," he probably expected Dall to be pleased. But Dall, who had after all written a book titled *Woman's Rights under the Law*, "rose & objected & carried [her] point" (*Selected Journals*, 2:615).

At the second public meeting of the ASSA at the Lowell Institute in Boston on 27–28 December 1865, Dall became the first woman to deliver a paper before the organization. This event was a major victory, following on the loss of her hard-fought battle to have a woman on the program at the first meeting. Among papers by Harvard president Thomas Hill (on problems in education), Philadelphia economist and sociologist Henry C. Carey (on national resources and trade policy), University of Michigan professor of medicine Alonzo B. Palmer (on sanitary education), statistician Edward Jarvis (on life expectancy), Frank Sanborn (on prison discipline), psychiatrist Isaac Ray (on the treatment of the insane), and others, Dall, as the designated librarian of the association, presented a paper on the need for a social science library. She stressed the difficulty in America of obtaining relevant printed materials, noting that the Boston Public Library held only a small, insufficient collection, and she spoke, reportedly "with earnestness," on the need for funds to purchase such a library. Dall did not relinquish the platform without seizing the opportunity to assert "the desire of the Association to welcome women as members, and to receive suggestions and papers from them."[34]

For the next few years, the ASSA seemed to prosper, at least in terms of the eminent persons, including academics, physicians, economists, lawyers, administrators of hospitals, correctional institutions, and institutions for the insane, who associated themselves with it. The organization held meetings in New Haven, Boston, New York, and Albany. Dall realized her goal of getting another woman on the board, as Abby May, previously rejected for a directorship, became a special secretary. And Dall's own role in the organization was clearly a central one. In fact, she served as one of its workhorses. She was appointed, for example, one of a committee of three to prepare bylaws (the other members being Emory Washburn and Samuel Eliot). Also, she was commissioned by George B. Emerson to produce a paper on lodging houses for women workers (*Selected Journals*, 2:612, 615). And she herself observed that she, Sanborn, Eliot, Washburn, and James J. Higginson "appear[ed] to do all the business" (*Selected Journals*, 2:614). At a Boston meeting in March 1867 she delivered an address on the work of Mary Carpenter in India and, perhaps more substantially, at the November 1867 New York meeting a paper on lodging houses for working women. The latter presentation she thought "enthusiastically received" by "a very fine audience" (Ms. Journals, 13 March 1867, 19 November 1867). Judging from newspaper accounts of the meetings of the late 1860s, Dall was one of the most frequent contributors to discussions and debates, a precedent she had set from the very first meeting; most of the time, but not always,[35] she was the only woman mentioned as participating in this way.

One of Dall's greatest triumphs during this period occurred in October 1867 at the third annual meeting of the association, when the corresponding secretary, Samuel Eliot, delivered an address that Dall declared to be "forever memorable." And no wonder: a major portion of the speech addressed the woman question, with Eliot prophesying, "Gone is the once overruling conviction that the place of the woman was in the family alone, and that except for feats of fashion or offices of charity, she had no social position." His argument echoed Dall's own plea for equality in three areas: "Let the expansion of woman's life go on, fearlessly on. Let every opportunity of improving herself be given to her. Let her be educated as she seeks to be; let her be employed as she seeks to be; let her be endowed with the civil privileges which she seeks to obtain."[36] Eliot's rhetoric also echoed Margaret Fuller's famous "let them be sea-captains, if you will" dictum. Dall was exultant: Invoking the memory of Charles G. Loring, a Boston attorney and reformer who had recently died, she remarked, "It seems as if the mantle of C. G. L. had fallen upon him." (Loring was a friend of Dall and a supporter of women's rights.) She doubted "whether either of these distinguished men, would ever have read a Woman's rights' book—if [she] had not asked them, and [her] 'Right to Labor' was the first that either of them ever saw." Remembering that she had been in the audience when Eliot graduated from Harvard in 1839, she continued:

> How little I thought, when my admiring eyes, gazed up at Samuel Eliot, as he gave his graduating oration at Cambridge—that I should ever speak in public or that he would uphold me when I did so. How little Alden Bradford thought when he sent me little complimentary notes in my girlhood, that his grandson & I would ever fight shoulder to shoulder in such a cause—![37] and ah! when I felt a year ago, as if every member of the Ex[ecutive] Com[mittee] was against me—as if they barely *bore with* me & my views, how little I thought—that my much faith and patience—nay if they will my obstinacy & egotism—were to be so blessed by God! (Ms. Journals, 9 October 1867)

Upon hearing Eliot's second delivery of the talk in New York, Dall thought it was "even more touchingly beautiful, and more decided in every respect than before." She could not help taking some credit: "Certainly, our Association has done a great deal for him. Two years ago, he would not have advocated the Franchise for Women—" (Ms. Journals, 19 November 1867).

In November 1868 Dall traveled to Chicago to take part in the inaugural meeting of the Western Association for the Promotion of Social Science. Her chief role seems to have been that of a senior expert or consultant. At the opening session she improvised an address to the group of about two hundred, offering advice on organizational matters—on the advertising of meetings, for example, the need to raise money to print the papers presented (which the ASSA had not yet managed), and the necessity of choosing for discussion "subjects which are practical and interesting to working people." And she warned emphatically, "You will also fail if you do not call in women to your help." "Mrs. Dall had no hesitation in asserting," a local newspaper reported, "that women knew more . . . than men" about such topics as lighting and cooking in public institutions, and that "states would save money by putting women on these committees." Her remarks were described as "lengthy, and judging from the manner in which they [were] received, exceedingly practical"; the newspaper reporter suggested, however, that the "rather *ex-cathedra* manner in which they were delivered" was a novelty for a Western audience.[38] As for Dall: "It was very strange to me," she marveled, "to find myself constantly referred to, and to see how important such counsel as I gave was considered."[39]

On the next evening she delivered her talk on lodging houses for women to the largest audience of the meeting, including "many ladies," a fact "evidently owing," according to a newspaper account, "to the interest excited by Mrs. Dall's well-known reputation as a philanthropist." In her paper Dall highlighted the dangers to young women who came to the city to work for low wages. As long as women's labor was undervalued, she argued, it would be necessary for philanthropy to come to their aid if they were not to be forced into prostitution in order to survive. To address this problem in the long term, she urged that women be taught collective action, encouraged to become small-scale capitalists, and when necessary assisted by capitalists. Not only should affordable housing be available to working women, but it was desirable to provide attached restaurants and stores offering meals and ready-made clothing. Dall was concerned not only that prostitution be prevented but also that protection and counsel be offered to those already "driven to take the first steps in a life of shame." In this effort she thought female preachers would be useful, as well as associations on the model of what she had proposed in Boston, "A Committee of Counsel and Comfort." Such an entity would offer to these women "a warm sisterly sympathy," encouragement, and confidentiality. The newspaper noted that "the paper of Mrs. Dall was listened to with the greatest attention and was received with hearty applause."[40]

Dall took seriously her position in Chicago as role model, adviser, even troubleshooter. Listening to papers by two men on prostitution and reformatories for women, she felt that both had "weak spots," but she uncharacteristically refrained from saying so: "I would not have criticised them for the world—It took a great deal of courage on the part of both these men, to treat these subjects in public."[41] When an impasse developed over who would serve as president of the organization, the secretary turned to Dall. The dispute, he told her, "threatens to crush the whole thing," for "both parties are stiff": "It is for you and I, to find a way out of it." The nominating committee had proposed Dr. Edward Beecher, oldest sibling of the famous Beecher family, but he proved unacceptable to a group that objected on principle to a clergyman's holding the position. Dall "determined without consulting any body to appeal to Dr Beecher himself": "I made my appeal—Most nobly and sweetly he responded."[42] Beecher withdrew, and penologist Zebulon R. Brockway was elected president.[43] Dall congratulated herself: "If ever I had a right to be grateful for the work of one day, I may for this!"[44] She remained somewhat dazed by the attention she was receiving in Chicago, observing, "The tone of the press in regard to me is most remarkable, and that of the Association still more so." So valuable were her services to the fledgling organization that one member commented on her "great executive ability" and another offered to pay her expenses if she would stay in Chicago a month.[45]

Dall's social science work during this period was not wholly focused on organizational and parliamentary matters. Along with other members, she visited various institutions of correction, hospitals, and asylums in order to observe facilities, living conditions, and treatments. Especially aware of such issues as ventilation, lighting, cleanliness, and food, she often voiced her views on these matters to the authorities. During a group visit to the New York House of Refuge at Randall's Island in New York, a juvenile facility considered a model institution, she found "two things to complain of—The wretched rusty tins, out of which they ate—and the accommodations for bathing, which were simply vile—better suited to pigs than human beings, especially women." She "spoke [her] indignation loudly" and the next evening was surprised to receive from Bradford K. Pierce, chaplain to the House of Refuge, the message, "Your visit to Randall's Island will result—in securing private baths for the girls, and proper table furniture for all the inmates!" Here was an achievement that would make a real difference in people's lives. Dall was justifiably jubilant: "Thank God! That was worth coming to New York for. . . . It will be a great thing to introduce these changes into the institution which was the first of its' kind in the world & is still the largest" (Ms. Journals, 20 and 21 November 1867).

Dall's determination to place women in leadership positions in the ASSA was again threatened in 1870. The current president of the association, Samuel Eliot, whose landmark speech on women's issues Dall had so joyfully welcomed in 1867, attempted, she believed, to engineer a coup that would have excluded women, and herself in particular, from the board. When the other two members of the nominating committee supported the slate proposed by Eliot that included no women, Dall objected. Attempting a compromise, she proposed a slate that would include Mary Dwight Parkman and Abby May but not herself, but the two male members refused. Not to be silenced, Dall then delivered a minority report at the meeting. The *Boston Daily Advertiser* reported that she

> protested against the [proposed slate] as containing the name of no woman. This was contrary to precedent from the beginning, the coöperation of the ladies always heretofore having been welcomed. She feared that if the precedent now proposed were assented to by the society, it would result in establishing a custom of having gentlemen only upon the board of government. Such a result would defeat and render valueless her own labors in the cause continued through many years. Her constant hope and aim had been through social science to open a way and afford an opportunity for the exercise of woman's talents and industry. The action of the majority of the committee she considered not only unwise, but a discourtesy also to the ladies who had faithfully served the association in the offices they had held. In the protest she thus made, she had no desire to secure her own name a place on the board, but could not consent to a reëlection after what had transpired. She wished her sisters on the board might be retained.[46]

Several men answered by protesting that the proposed changes to the board were simply in the interests of "efficiency," but T. W. Higginson took up the women's cause. He supported Dall's proposal to add Parkman and May to the list of directors, noting that he would also have added Dall's name had she not declined reelection. This motion passed without opposition, and thus by Dall's own proposal she had excluded herself from the board but at the same time preserved the principle of women's participation for which she had fought so strenuously.[47] The whole matter, not surprisingly, frayed personal relationships among the directors. Dall believed she was the target of the attempted changes, for she had been opposing alterations to the constitution that Eliot wished to push through. After winning the vote, she endeavored to smooth things over with Eliot, but in vain: "I went up to Dr Eliot, & put out my hand. He would not take it—I began much surprised to say—'Dr Eliot if at any time *you* had wished me to resign—['] when he interrupted me hastily, saying—'You have a right to make your point—but you are wholly wrong—to give the matter a personal turn.'" When she approached Higginson in order to warn him against certain constitutional changes that Eliot was proposing, "He started back, and as if he tho't I were coming to complain of not being elected—said—'I can't help it, Mrs Dall, there are only these two [women] & yourself, and you're such an *intensely* unpopular person!'" This unkind cut clearly staggered Dall, but she gathered herself and responded in her journal: "I do not believe I am an *unpopular* person. I believe I have had one or two bitter enemies say Towne &

Eliz. Peabody—& Mrs Severance, who have done their best to prejudice people against me. I deserved Towne's enmity for my folly & indiscretion. I did *not* deserve that of Peabody or Severance." But she did wish that "only one kind person had cared enough for me to tell me what was wanted [that is, her resignation] & avoid the scandal!" (Ms. Journals, 12 October 1870). A few days later, still coming to terms with the trauma, she wrote in her journal, "I had better forget it all." But she could not help adding, "The sense of injury is very deep" (Ms. Journals, 16 October 1870).

Two years later the ASSA was in deep trouble, though for reasons not entirely clear. Certainly financial problems plagued the organization from the beginning, but apparently there was also some sort of discontent with the leadership. Dall wrote: "The Executive Committee of the Social Science Association are preparing a great wrong. They are going to suppress the Association instead of resigning their offices" (Ms. Journals, 14 October 1872). A month later "the troubled affairs" of the association were put in the hands of a committee of six: the famous zoologist Louis Agassiz and early founders James M. Barnard, Thomas C. Amory, Frank Sanborn, Abby May, and Caroline Dall (Ms. Journals, 9 November 1872). A month after that, Dall was reinstated in her old position and the constitution substantially restored to its original state (Ms. Journals, 9 December 1872). Unfortunately, however, this was but the beginning of even more internecine warfare. Women's role in the organization was an issue that seemingly would not die. Though Dall must have taken some pride in the fact that by 1873 seven of the seventeen directors of the ASSA were women,[48] when the association met in Philadelphia in 1876 she was "disgusted" to find that neither of the arranged evening social gatherings, one at the Penn Club and the other at the home of publisher and historian Henry C. Lea, was open to women. And as late as 1899 in Washington, D.C., where she then lived, Dall received a letter from T. W. Higginson alerting her to the fact that the ASSA was organizing a new National Institute of Arts and Letters, which would exclude women. He published a protest in the *Nation*, and Dall wrote a letter of resignation to the secretary of the ASSA, "a painful duty after thirty-five years' service" (Ms. Journals, 26 and 31 August 1899). But some weeks later, learning that the Institute (the forerunner of the American Academy of Arts and Letters) had separated itself from the ASSA, she withdrew her resignation, writing, "So ends the farce!" (Ms. Journals, 4 October 1899).

The fortunes of the ASSA continued perilous; by 1877 Dall feared that it would be disbanded for lack of funds, and she found the prospect "distressing & depressing to the last degree" (Ms. Journals, 24 February 1877 and 31 March 1877). Hearing a committee recommendation that Sanborn, unless willing to serve without salary, be peremptorily dismissed from his position as secretary, she was indignant. She moved for a special meeting of directors and for a new committee to report on the association's finances and the cost to retain Sanborn for the remainder of his term. Achieving these goals, at the next meeting she "carried all [her] points one by one," partly with the help of William B. Rogers, whom, as she noted, "Sanborn had had the sense to exhume for the occasion." Dall was glad to have helped prevent "the nightmare of a dishonorable end" (Ms. Journals, 27 May 1877 and 2 June 1877). The association went on to conduct apparently viable meetings that Dall attended in 1877 at Saratoga, in 1878 at Cincinnati, and in 1880 at San Francisco.

Dall's move from Boston to Washington in 1878 meant that her most active period in the organization was over. In 1882 she learned that she had been dropped as a director and member "on the pretext," as she called it, that she had not paid her dues in two years. She blamed Sanborn for the affront and clearly felt a sense of entitlement to special consideration. But at the next meeting she paid her dues and was restored to office (Ms. Journals, 28 June 1882 and 4, 6, 7 September 1882). Though hardly active in the official business of the organization thereafter, she continued to be listed as one of the directors and to attend meetings when possible. At the meeting in Washington in April 1902, when almost eighty, she appeared as "the only relic of the old management" and participated in the discussion ("burning with indignation"), apparently for the last time. It was "badly managed," she observed (Ms. Journals, 22, 24, 25 April 1902).

An analysis of the causes of the demise of the ASSA (it languished until 1909) is beyond the scope of this paper. Briefly, it may be observed that, as Goldman has pointed out, the association never attracted significant support from the political establishment,[49] but most essentially what happened is that professionalization and specialization overtook it. The ASSA was the mother of numerous organizations, spun off in the late decades of the nineteenth century, that populate today's American professional landscape, including among others the American Economic Association, the American Prison Association, the American Historical Association, the American Sociological Society, the American Political Science Association, the National Conference of Social Work, and the American Academy of Arts and Sciences. It would, in fact, be difficult to conceive of an American organization that has had a comparable impact.

In the decades of her active service in this area, Dall largely succeeded in making the ASSA a forum and social science a field of endeavor open to women. In addition, she used the organization as a vehicle to push for such women's issues as affordable housing, equal wages, and opportunities for higher education. In the larger context of transcendentalism and transcendentalists, Dall's social science work occupies a territory toward the far end of the spectrum beginning in individualism and ending in social action. Her transcendentalism was transcendentalism on the ground, in the trenches, as it were, of insane asylums, prisons, and city slums. It concerned itself with women's wages, living conditions, and education, with prostitution and sanitation, with juvenile offenders and tramps. It vividly illustrates, in fact, Dall's own definition of transcendentalism as "idealism made practical."

Thanks to Dall's unusually detailed journal accounts, we are allowed to view the inner workings of the American social science movement—but from her own point of view, of course. This is at once a limitation, for the account is certainly not strictly objective, and an advantage: through it we share in the experience, emotional as well as intellectual, of Dall's often lonely crusade. We see her basking in the compliments of her contemporaries, as when one enthusiastic admirer, she notes, "undertook to promise me, any position I would like to fill, on the part of the world in general & Boston in particular" (*Selected Journals*, 2:644); or when the reformer Lady Amberley (future mother of Bertrand Russell) met Dall during an American visit and, in Dall's words, said "she had been told everywhere that I was the fountain head, in matters of the soc sci." (Ms. Journals, 30 October 1867). But there was clearly a human toll to be paid. Dall's assertiveness, so necessary to pushing her agenda, at the same time made her "unpopular," as Higginson had ungraciously informed her. Each triumph she enjoyed was, it often seemed, balanced by many disappointments. In part because of her domestic circumstances (Dall was essentially an abandoned wife and a single mother) and in part because of her controlling and difficult personality, Dall traveled a largely solitary road: she generally faced the forces of sexist discrimination alone, and there were few if any to share the joy of her victories. Yet she clearly felt the sacrifice worth it. Hearing a paper delivered at an 1881 ASSA meeting by Josephine Shaw Lowell (sister of Robert Gould Shaw and widow of Charles Russell Lowell Jr.), the first woman commissioner of the New York State Board of Charities, Dall rejoiced in the fact that her own work had helped make such positions possible for women (Ms. Journals, 26 July 1881). She was aware of a rising generation poised to consolidate the gains for which she had fought. In the field of social science Dall had, in fact, found a new way to promote the cause of women, in large part by simply demonstrating her own competence, dedication, and ferocious persistence.

NOTES

1. Moncure Conway, review of *"Woman's Right to Labor"; or, Low Wages and Hard Work*, by Caroline Healey Dall, *Dial* 1 (January 1860): 70.
2. *Selected Journals of Caroline Healey Dall, Volume 2: 1855–1866*, ed. Helen R. Deese (Boston: Massachusetts Historical Society, 2013), 283; hereafter cited as *Selected Journals*. References to yet unpublished passages from Dall's journals are from the Caroline Healey Dall Journals, Dall Papers, MHi (hereafter cited as Ms. Journals). I am grateful to the Massachusetts Historical Society for permission to quote from these papers.
3. Caroline Healey Dall, "Woman in the Nineteenth Century," *Una* 3 (1855): 105.

4. Other scholars who have considered Dall's role as apologist for Fuller include Judith Mattson Bean, "'A *Presence* among Us': Fuller's Place in Nineteenth-Century Oral Culture," *ESQ: A Journal of the American Renaissance* 44 (1998): 79–123; Phyllis Cole, "The Nineteenth-Century Women's Rights Movement and the Canonization of Margaret Fuller," *ESQ* 44 (1998): 1–33; Wayne; and Mary De Jong, "Required to 'Speak': Caroline Healey Dall and the Defense of Margaret Fuller," in this volume.
5. Caroline Healey Dall, "The Late Lawsuit: Men and Women vs. Custom and Tradition," *Dial* 1 (May 1860): 286. A version of this article appeared as "'The Great Lawsuit': Men and Women vs. Custom and Tradition," in Dall, *Historical Pictures Retouched* (Boston: Walker, Wise, 1860), 249–64.
6. Caroline Healey Dall, "Margaret Fuller Ossoli," *North American Review* 91 (July 1860): 127. An expanded version of this article appeared as "Margaret Fuller," in Dall, *Historical Pictures Retouched*, 226–48.
7. Dall, "Margaret Fuller Ossoli," 127; repr., "Margaret Fuller," in *Historical Pictures Retouched*, 243.
8. Dall, "Late Lawsuit," 293; repr., "'The Great Lawsuit,'" in *Historical Pictures Retouched*, 264.
9. Dall, "Late Lawsuit," 291, 292; repr., "'The Great Lawsuit,'" in *Historical Pictures Retouched*, 261.
10. Caroline Healey Dall, *Transcendentalism in New England: A Lecture Delivered before the Society for Philosophical Enquiry, Washington, D.C., May 7, 1895* (Boston: Roberts Brothers, 1897), 23; emphasis added. For a fuller discussion of Dall's positioning of Fuller in the history of transcendentalism, see Helen R. Deese, "Transcendentalism from the Margins: The Experience of Caroline Healey Dall," Capper and Wright, 527–47.
11. Dall, *Transcendentalism in New England*, 37–38. Elsewhere, Dall stated that after Fuller had supported the education of her brothers, she had made "large gifts or loans of money" to women in distress ("The Hawthorne Book Censured," *Springfield Daily Republican*, 15 December 1884), though it is difficult to imagine when Fuller would have had access to such funds.
12. Dall, *Transcendentalism in New England*, 38; Caroline Healey Dall, *The College, the Market, and the Court; or, Woman's Relation to Education, Labor, and Law* (Boston: Lee & Shepard, 1867), 116.
13. Dall's place in the social science movement has often been undervalued; she receives short shrift, for example, in the primary published history of the American Social Science Association (Thomas L. Haskell, *The Emergence of Professional Social Science: The American Social Science Association and the Nineteenth-Century Crisis of Authority* [Urbana: Univ. of Illinois Press, 1977]). This oversight has to some degree been rectified in articles by William Leach, Nancy Bowman, and Lawrence Goldman that draw heavily on the Dall Papers. Leach and Bowman trace Dall's career from the women's movement to social science, and Goldman gives full credit to the central role she played in the formation and early history of the ASSA (Leach, "From Personal Disunion to Social Community: The Feminist Career of Caroline Dall," in *True Love and Perfect Union: The Feminist Reform of Sex and Society* [New York, 1980], 263–91; Bowman, "Caroline Healey Dall: Her Creation and Reform Career," in *Women of the Commonwealth*, ed. Susan Lynne Porter [Amherst: Univ. of Massachusetts Press, 1996], 121–46; Goldman, "Exceptionalism and Internationalism: The Origins of American Social Science Reconsidered," *Journal of Historical Sociology* 11 [1998]: 1–36).
14. An account of Dall's eventually troubled relations with dozens of her acquaintances is beyond the scope of this paper, but among those with whom she had major fallings-out

were Elizabeth Palmer Peabody, Caroline Severance, Marie Zakrzewska, and Julia Ward Howe.

15. See, for example, Theodore Parker, *A Sermon of the Perishing Classes in Boston: Preached at the Melodeon, on Sunday, August 30, 1846* (Boston: Butts, 1846).
16. "Mrs. Dall's 'Fraternity' Lecture," *Liberator*, 26 October 1860, 170.
17. The founding of the NAPSS is described in the *English Woman's Journal* 1 (August 1858): 390–91.
18. Letters from these women appear sporadically in the Dall Papers, MHi, from September 1858 through October 1865.
19. Edward Peacock, review of *Woman's Rights under the Law*, by Caroline Healey Dall, *Social Science Review*, 27 December 1862, 462–63.
20. See Bessie Rayner Parkes to Dall, 16 July 1861, Dall Papers, MHi; and *Selected Journals*, 2:343.
21. Dall's desire for a separate social science division must be understood in the context of the library's organization: even several years later, social science was subsumed under the division heading "Religion and Ethics" (*Fourteenth Annual Report of the Trustees of the Public Library* [Boston: n.p., 1866], 14).
22. Copies of Dall letter, 25 March 1859, and of "Memorial A," Dall Papers, MHi.
23. "The Proceedings," *Library Journal* 6 (1881): 117. Dall attended and participated in the discussion of the Conference of Librarians in Washington, D.C., in February 1881, where she made this comment. She would no doubt take some satisfaction in the fact that one end (an alcove, in fact) of the grand Bates Hall of today's Boston Public Library is devoted to the Social Sciences Department.
24. See Dall's journal entries for 3 April 1910 and for 6, 9, 20, 22, and 25 September 1865 (*Selected Journals*, 2:600, 602–4).
25. Marie Zakrzewska, a pioneering German-born American physician, was founder of the New England Hospital for Women and Children. Dall seems to suggest that there was bad blood between Zakrzewska and the male medical establishment. Lucy Ellen Sewall, a protégée of Zakrzewska, worked as an attending physician at the New England Hospital for Women and Children.
26. *Selected Journals*, 2:602; Ms. Journals, 26 March 1867, 14 October 1868, 31 October 1868, 30 January 1869, 25 December 1872, 12 September 1874, 14 October 1874, 31 October 1874.
27. Dall to Sanborn, 24 September 1865, Dall Papers, MHi. Dorothea Dix, famous advocate for humane treatment of the mentally ill, served during the Civil War as superintendent of army nurses. Katherine P. Wormley, Jane Stuart Woolsey, Mary Cary, and Helen Louise Gilson were all distinguished Civil War nurses. I have not identified "Mrs Winthrop."
28. Dall to Sanborn, 24 September 1865, Dall Papers, MHi.
29. Undated fragment of a letter from Sanborn to Dall, Dall Papers, MHi (filed with items dated 11 October 1865).
30. Ms. Journals, 3 April 1910. Apparently the planning group had originally envisioned only a local association; in her account of this meeting Dall speaks of "the new idea of a *National* Association" (*Selected Journals*, 2:607). In fact, for a time at least, there existed both a Boston and an American Social Science Association, and it is sometimes difficult or impossible to separate the two in Dall's journal accounts.
31. "The American Social Science Association," *Radical* 1 (1865): 105; American Social Science Association, *Document Published by the Association, with an Abridgment of the Transactions, Part 1, 1865–6* (Boston: Wright & Potter, 1866), 8.
32. "The American Social Science Association," *Radical* 1 (1865): 108.

33. Ibid.
34. "American Social Science Association. Second General Meeting," *Radical* 1 (1865): 227–29.
35. The *Lowell (Mass.) Daily Citizen and News*, for example, mentions a "Mrs. Dr. [Sarah H.] Young of Lowell," who vigorously took issue with a paper at the third annual meeting in Boston that dealt in part with "the Physical Organization of Women in relation to the Laws of Human Increase." Mrs. Young stated her belief that "infidelity and excesses of men had as much to do with the deterioration of the physical organization of woman as the style of dress, or want of exercise" (11 October 1866, 2).
36. Eliot repeated his speech at the Fifth General Meeting of the ASSA in New York on 19 November 1867, and it was printed as "Address at the Fifth General Meeting," in American Social Science Association, *Documents Published by the Association*, pt. 2, 1866–67 (Boston: Wright & Potter, 1867); quotations on 77 and 79.
37. Alden Bradford, clergyman, author, and Massachusetts Secretary of State, was Dall's neighbor as she was growing up; Samuel Eliot was his grandson.
38. Unidentified newspaper clipping, Scrapbook 6, Dall Papers, MHi.
39. "Journey to the West" Journal, 11 November 1868, Caroline Wells Healey Dall Papers, 1829–1956 (MC351), Box 5, Folder 76v, Schlesinger Library, Radcliffe Institute, Harvard University. I am grateful to the Schlesinger Library for permission to quote from these papers.
40. Unidentified newspaper clipping, Scrapbook 6, Dall Papers, MHi.
41. "Journey to the West" Journal, 12 November 1868.
42. Ibid., 11 November 1868.
43. *Congregationalist and Boston Recorder*, 26 November 1868, 1.
44. "Journey to the West" Journal, 11 November 1868.
45. Ibid., 12 and 13 November 1868.
46. "Annual Meeting of the American Social Science Association," *Boston Daily Advertiser*, 13 October 1870, 4.
47. Ibid.
48. The president, nine vice presidents, secretary, and treasurer were, however, all men.
49. Goldman, "Exceptionalism and Internationalism," 19–20.

INTERLUDE

Elizabeth Stoddard to Margaret Sweat, 14 April [n.d.], Rare Books and Manuscripts, Allison-Shelley Collection, Special Collections Library, Pennsylvania State University Libraries.

Mattapoisett

14 April—

My dear Mrs Sweat

It seemed to me a beautiful finish to a letter, that ending of yours—"yours as you left me"—

How few lovers, friends, acquaintances dare or can say this.

I have thought of you—since I heard from you, have held a letter in futurity for you.

I arrived home Sunday morning, hoping my long tarrying into the spring in New York might save me cold stormy weather. Yesterday a furious snow storm fell upon us—and to day winter [rules?] and [shines?] I miss my New York occupations and enjoyments so much! It is with pain I fit myself into my place here—I can only send forth regular trains of thought—nothing returns to the Dépot—

Sky and sea, books and work, riding and walking, eating and sleeping are the texts of my life here—

The interior effect of life is however progressive—This you well know, since you say you are contemplative. You seem for companionship to be situated as I am at home. Is it not most difficult to find an intellectual woman sympathizer?

I am nigh disgusted with the search—

Why will you not visit me this summer? I should like to see you—I shall be home much of the hot season—I have been thinking of taking a voyage but it is a great thing to decide upon to cross the seas—and I hardly think I shall go. I intend to go to Portland some time this year—I hope Mrs. Ruggles may go to P. with me.

What books are you reading—I have latterly been sitting at the feet of Emerson—though after all his philosophy is narrow—beginning and ending in self. I like him, he is a wonderful [spurrer?] on to self-culture—

I have now to read Schlegels history of literature, Schillers aesthetic [Prose?], Philip Van Artevelde & Goethes Essays on Art. I am afraid they will break my head—Twice I have read Browning's Paracelsus—without making anything more of it than breaking stones—

I hope we are to converse together—many things are there for us both to say. I want to enter into your *humanity* now—to have more blood in our friendship, it will come of association—Do write me.

In thinking of you in the cold winter I am reminded of [Olianna?]—the northern winds, the snow [ribbed?] round &c—yours truly
EDB

Transcendental Erotics, Same-Sex Desire, and Ethel's Love-Life

DORRI BEAM

Margaret Jane Mussey Sweat's 1859 novel, *Ethel's Love-Life*, has been variously identified as a legible "treat[ment] of Lesbianism," as a rendering of the physical intensity of women's friendship in a world of female love and ritual, and as a fiction that evinces the increasing pathologization of erotic friendships between women.[1] It is little surprise that this strange and compelling novel should prompt such a range of responses. *Ethel's Love-Life* energetically embodies the fluidity of its own mid-nineteenth-century moment, upholding Sharon Marcus's astute insistence on the Victorians' "particular indifference" to "a homo / hetero divide for women" by situating the title character in a "love-life" that figures women and men without clear discrimination.[2] And yet it is also a harbinger of the cultural change to come, as it pointedly attends to passionate love between women. Sweat's novel makes apparent that our ways of thinking about sexuality in the early to mid-nineteenth century have proven inadequate, particularly our impulse to categorize relationships according to a homo / hetero binary and our related desire to taxonomize relationships as sexual or nonsexual.

Attempting to dispense with anachronistic questions of sexual identity in "romantic friendship," recent scholarship has observed that nineteenth-century Americans held in sight a different binary—the spiritual versus the carnal—as far more determining of a relationship's cultural acceptance than its hetero- or homoeroticism.[3] But such novels as Sweat's remind us that this historical binary is not to be subsumed under our own nonsexual / sexual binary. Rather than drawing our attention to the emotional, intellectual, and "spiritual" at the expense of the erotic and sexual (as studies of romantic friendship often do), or casting the spiritual as a sublimation of sexual desire as our modern sensibilities demand,[4] *Ethel's Love-Life* opens new, postsecular critical arenas in which, as Elizabeth Povinelli has suggested, to "multiply the ways we can coordinate spirituality and sexuality."[5] For many Americans of the nineteenth century the carnal was a surprisingly narrow category, while the spiritual was a supple and capacious realm permeated with pleasure and sensation and bearing its own relationship to embodiment. In featuring the reach and power of spirit and casting even the social and sexual realms in its terms, Sweat's novel actively builds on, and elaborates in unprecedented detail, a transcendentalist model of sexual relations that allows her to articulate and portray erotic love between women.

Sweat's novel is of interest, then, not as a historical illustration of the intensity and physical intimacy of women's friendships but as an articulation of the sexual results of the transcendentalist urge toward a world attuned to the spiritual needs of the self. In fact, a utopian social architecture emerges from Sweat's desire to think through and portray more flexible sexual arrangements. If George Ripley's Brook Farm erected a social system based on Fourier's privileging of personal passion but excised the sexual consequences from its official doctrine, *Ethel's Love-Life* reunites radical American experimentalism with passional freedom, entertaining both structural and philosophical challenges to monogamy. An expert Francophile, Sweat wed her interest in social theory to her study of George Sand's novels (a critical essay of hers was appended to a translation of *Antonia*). Through Sand, Sweat recognized the potential of the novel form as a testing ground for social theory. She used the form, merging it with a transcendentalist-inflected interest in the social dynamics of epistolarity, to work out the larger social consequences of her own system of spiritual attraction. In *Ethel's Love-Life*, a spirituo-sexual vision comes alive at the intersection of transcendental idealism and social thought, a meeting place that has prompted lively debate in recent years. Rather than charting a turn from religious radicalism toward social activism, the progressive trajectory from spiritual to secular matters favored by many critical treatments of transcendental politics, the novel demonstrates how crucially spiritual matters could underpin and shape a social vision—and in so doing, it illuminates such a dynamic in figures like Margaret Fuller.

Transcendental Erotics

Margaret Sweat was not a card-carrying transcendentalist, but her life and work register the reach and resonance of transcendentalist thought in its second generation. Sweat was a married intellectual who maintained a network of friends in the literary world, most notably with author Elizabeth Stoddard. She boasted fluency in four languages and was one of the few women who reviewed books for the venerable *North American Review*. Her only novel, *Ethel's Love-Life*, is intensely introspective in nature. Composed as a series of letters from the title character to her fiancé Ernest, it closely examines "the presence of love in its various manifestations" across her relationships with several men and women, including a tempestuous affair with a woman named Leonora that provokes the most comment today.[6] The lavish, unscrolling study of the inner workings of the self—a type of "cardiagraphy," as Sylvester Judd called his own rare instance of a transcendentalist novel—might alone mark the novel's transcendentalist debt.[7] But Sweat's novel also displays a deeper and more philosophic relation, for it is the phenomena that undergird transcendental philosophy—the peak experience of visionary ecstasy, the experience of feeling, power, and pleasure in a realm not compassed by the body—that drive the book's articulation of social and sexual experience.

Sweat offers a nontheistic account of how one's spirit moves, is felt and experienced, and the insight it brings, thus yielding a view of the self and relationality with fascinating consequences for same-sex relations, as this often-quoted passage demonstrates:

> Women love each other with as much fervor and excitement as they do men. When this is the case, there is generally rare beauty both in the feeling and in its manifestations, great generosity in its intuitions and the mutual intercourse is marked by charming undulations of feeling and expression. The emotions awakened heave and swell through the whole being as the tides swell the ocean. Freed from all the grosser elements of passion, as it exists between the sexes, it retains its energy, its abandonment, its flush, its eagerness, its palpitation, and its rapture—but all so refined, so glorified, and made delicious and continuous by an ever-recurring giving and receiving from each to each. (*EL*, 82)

This passage wishes to delineate a form of sexual activity that exists beyond "the grosser elements of passion" between the sexes, and such gestures have classically led scholars such as Lillian Faderman to posit a unique form of spiritual passion between women.[8] For Faderman, that passion is sexless and noncarnal. And yet, we can't assume we know what Sweat would exclude or include among those "grosser elements." In the meantime, *something* in this passage is swelling and heaving, flushing and palpitating.

Modernist legacies affecting the way we look at language (suspiciously, if it is sinuous rather than sinewy), as well as the way we look at sexuality, tempt us to see Sweat's language either as a canny dance of revelation and withholding or as an unconscious compensation for something that cannot be said directly. But Sweat's novel asks us to take the language at face value, for the book is in fact entirely concerned with the meaning, movement, and sensation of this force—alternately called "the magnetic current," "the subtle element," and the "sensational powers" (*EL*, 58, 58, 62). For in Sweat's novel, the "flows" and "currents" of sexual desire are forces of the soul rather than of the sex organs, and they thus make possible a fascinating spectrum of sexual economies: as we will see, receptivity and activity belong not to women and men, respectively, but to kinds of souls, and furthermore, they can be combined in one person.

What is so striking about the novel is not only its almost blithe dismissal of events or external details ("external changes and external sounds and sights have often passed before me as a panorama, tame and spiritless compared to the turmoil and excitement which filled my inner world" [*EL*, 42]) but its relentless commitment to describing the surges of attraction and repulsion that Ethel and her lovers experience. This descriptive repertoire is never carnal, yet it is utterly sensual and sensational. The agents in the story *are* fluids, vibrations, and fields of energies emanating from the people who have passed into or out of Ethel's life. Given the eroticized nature of her relations, one might wish for a little more real "sweat" and a little less "spiritual fluid," but throughout, Ethel's love-life is cast in the language of force fields, fluids, and other attributes of spirit, according to mid-nineteenth-century vocabularies. Her self-writing labors not to re-create her self as an actor in a social world but to make her self palpable to herself. She makes this concept explicit by characterizing her dreams as "a sort of double consciousness" in herself, through which she is "able to pause and examine, as it were, each subtle change in emotion" (*EL*, 73). By this, she does not mean she reflects on her emotional state at various points in time. She examines her emotion as a tangible thing, a subtle substance that moves, expands and contracts, and varies in consistencies. She watches as its bulk impinges on others, requiring in turn various reactions in the physical composition of their own emotions. Feeling and desire become tangible forces to measure, to trace, to chart, to touch with and be touched by.

Sweat partakes of a view of the capaciousness of spirit that was widespread in this period, drawing in particular on the transcendentalist philosophy that the spirit is an entity that moves beyond the body, that is larger than the individual self and linked to a vast network or ecology of spirit through streams of relation. In the second letter of the book, Ethel describes the way she is constitutionally caught up in atmospheric changes: "magnetic influences sway me; I become, as it were, a portion of the storm, feeling its wild unrest, responding to its unearthly voices, obeying its weird suggestions" (*EL*, 41). These romantic "storm within" clichés are denaturalized by the literalism they accrue as the letters build a portrait of Ethel via near-exclusive recourse to such internal meteorological reports. Passages of this kind posit a theory that the self is unbounded and best known when shorn of attributes of the person. It is connected to the world through an unquantifiable interior energy, an energy that is in fact part of the world, akin to and even indistinguishable from the forces that drive atmospheric changes. Sweat shows us how romantic intellectuals brought such ideas to bear on the social world of personal relations.

I take Sweat's depiction of Ethel's tangible, motile interiority to stem from a popular language of spirit as a substantive, sensual fluidity. Many Americans of this period believed that spirit could be sensed and that through spirit one could experience an expanded menu of feeling and sensation. As I have argued elsewhere, these ideas were confirmed and developed by accounts of the trance state offered in popular manuals on mesmerism and by those individuals (often women) who experienced it as a healing technique.[9] These accounts frequently relate a peeling off and abandonment of the physical body to achieve a more pleasing, sensuous state, often explicitly described as a "spirit body," unlike the limited physical body in its capacity for experience and pleasure. Emerson himself evokes such mesmerist conceptions of spirit and body when he writes in "Friendship" that a friend's "essence is not less beautiful than their appearance, though it needs finer organs for its apprehension" (*CW*, 116). Even as he distinguishes between physical and spiritual attraction, Emerson restricts the distance between them: attraction to another's essence works much like attraction to his or her body—it is equally sensual but relies on finer sensory capacities attuned to another register of sensation. The "jets of affection" and "irradiations" between friends that Emerson's essay recounts are limited when we take them as merely metaphors; taken more literally, they chart the pleasures, reducible to neither pure spirit nor utter sensuality, available under Emerson's theory of relation (*CW*, 114, 113). When Ethel similarly speaks of her spiritual makeup and its palpitations, attractions, and pleasures, her language derives from by-then-established ideas, rooted in mesmerist discourses, of spirit as subtle but palpable and as a zone through which to touch and relate to others.

In *Woman in the Nineteenth Century*, Margaret Fuller deploys this model of energy, or spirit, to work out a feminist understanding of gender, body, and self. When Fuller claims that "male and female represent the two sides of the great radical dualism," she imagines masculinity and femininity as essences or energies that constitute the self but do not originate in the body. "But in fact," or in the person, Fuller goes on, male and female are transitive forces rather than fixed characteristics of the person: "They are perpetually passing into one another. Fluid hardens to solid, solid rushes to fluid. There is no wholly masculine man, no purely feminine woman." Just as Emerson insists that we not nail a word or meaning to a form, so Fuller insists that gender can never be fixed to anatomy because "history jeers at the attempts of physiologists to bind great original laws by the forms which flow from them." While physiologists may make a "rule" that binds gendered characteristics to a male or female body, nature, Fuller declares, delights in exceptions ranging from women warriors to lactating fathers. And Fuller enjoys nature's "still gayer pranks," which "deprive . . . organs" of "a necessary end," permitting people to "read with the top of the head, and see with the pit of the stomach," special visionary dispensations allowed particularly via mesmeric trance. This central passage on Fuller's gender theory moves from "organizations" (the way social roles are divided) to "organs" to reveal the notable dissonance between the social organization of a sex / gender system based on the perceived bimorphism of the anatomical body and the much broader horizon of possibility demanded by the soul's unrestricted capacities: "Let us be wise and not impede the soul. . . . Let it take what form it will, and let us not bind it by the past to man or woman, black or white." Spiritual embodiments and genderings, in other words, will be infinitely more varied than the two-option human body (as demonstrated by the Seeress when she "behold[s]" the "feminine form behind the man, sometimes the reverse," or by Linnaeus's daughter, who can see "the soul of the flower exhaling from the flower"). Fuller thereby lifts gender from biology and makes it newly available for examination and reframing (*EMF*, 310–11).

Fuller's voice becomes a conduit for universal energies as, throughout *Woman in the Nineteenth Century*, she reads "the signs of the times" with the authority of a divinator, examining "tokens" and poring over newspaper leaves to unlock the future (*EMF*, 260, 277). Like clairvoyants, Fuller strains to discern and channel the spirit behind the person, especially as it pertains to the significance of Woman. The "Woman" of Fuller's title is an essentialized form of the feminine, but it could never be represented in a single woman. She understands this essence to operate as a transcendental energy akin to Emerson's Over-soul, one that persons access and experience but never contain as an individual embodiment; nor could social forms crudely capture it in any particular role or position.

If Woman, or the feminine half of Fuller's "great radical dualism," were allowed equal conceptual play, Fuller prophesies, "the divine energy would pervade nature to a degree unknown in the history of former ages, and that no discordant collision, but a ravishing harmony of the spheres would ensue" (*EMF*, 260). Fuller's "harmony of the spheres" points to the cosmic location of the balance she seeks to right while wittily signaling its distinction from contemporary discussions of the gendered spheres of social roles. Unlike that social model, her "ravishing harmony" balances without fixing either side of the dualism, placing both energies in perpetual reciprocating movement, a process that continually renegotiates their relation. Fuller's cosmic balance was to provide the law that would fuel the dynamism of the relation between Man and Woman as conceptual ideals of gender within cultural discourses, while also productively accommodating internal gender diversity. Fuller summons this ravishing harmony to her incanted, prayer-like lines—"Let it take what form it will, and let us not bind it by the past to man or woman, black or white. Jove sprang from Rhea, Pallas from Jove. So let it be" (*EMF*, 311). Using chiasmus as she did in the lines "fluid hardens to solid, solid rushes to fluid," Fuller performs the rhythmic arrangement of parts that meet in perpetually repeating oscillation, fueling a dynamic movement that surpasses the sum of its parts (*EMF*, 310). Fuller thus signals the sensational presence of cosmic energies that, properly summoned, course through her lines as they will course through each person, transforming both lines and persons into calibrations of divine principles. Fuller's transcendentalism allows her to reframe sensational experience itself. In these moments of ecstatic vision that provide the backbone of *Woman in the Nineteenth Century*, Fuller constructs an ecology of self that pleasurably extends and expands when social obstacles are removed in dream or vision and the self pours out of its bounds, especially the body. Like many Americans of this period, Fuller was drawn to the idea that spirit has its own phenomenologies: it is, in this view, a richer amalgam of the material and immaterial, the self and the not-self, than we have been inclined to understand, and Fuller taps this vein for her feminist politics.

Sweat's novel shows us how this notion of sensual spirit put in place a sexual economy fundamentally different from the paradigm, based on the heterosexual opposition of male and female, that still largely structures our own time and place. What is so striking about Sweat's economy, especially given the novel's content, is that—something like Fuller's "ravishing harmony"—it does not bind receptivity and activity to one's genital morphology, or sex, and does not correlate them to gender, precisely because one's relational essence is not bound by or to the body. Equally striking is how systematically Sweat has worked out this economy of erotic exchange. First, Ethel explains, one's capacities for the superfine element are the primary determinant of intimate relations:

> It is quite extraordinary how great a difference there is, not only in the proportion of active, outgoing, magnetic power in different individuals, but also in the simply receptive element. Some who can give seem absolutely incapable of receiving—the most delicate and subtle returning fluid fails to win entrance at the door which opens but for egress to those within. . . . Others seem to have so large a capacity of reception and are so open to all floating magnetic forces, that it is a matter of continual wonder that the accumulation does not pour forth of its abundance. . . . But the two powers in persons of each class remain always distinct; the first cannot receive, the second cannot give. (*EL*, 62–63)

Again, the book is not generalizing about male and female anatomy, or about masculinity and femininity. Receptivity and activity are essences of character or temperament or, in the book's terms, qualities of one's spiritual makeup. What could be trite protopsychology about active and passive types is made more interesting by the unexpected love-matches that result. When receptivity and activity are unassigned to bodies or to genders, one can look for the panoply of relations Ethel experiences. She resists seduction by the greater "force" of her own powers; she declines being the object of love in a relation where she cannot also return the passion; and she can speak of "mingling . . . some of [her] superfluous inner energies with [the] prostrate and enervated susceptibilities" of an unnamed woman (*EL,* 62). Ethel takes us through her love-life to show the variety of matches available to her, a variety characterized by a range of spirituo-sexual combinations. Hetero- and homoerotic variation is a subset of these combinations, but it is not the primary taxonomic axis of Ethel's relations.

Ethel also posits a third possibility that does not depend on the difference between the parties or a fixed characteristic in the individual. She continues, "There are, however, exceptional natures capable of both giving largely and receiving fully, in which the flux and reflux of the magnetic element is as the mighty tide of ocean, not like the tributary flowing of the river, bound on its unreturning errand to the sea." "These natures," she claims, are like systems within themselves: they "move grandly on through their own orbits, rejoicing in their own fulness and planetary serenity of steady force, and render a large obedience to the great laws which regulate the universe" (*EL,* 63). Ethel, Leonora, and Ernest are such "spherical natures," able to enjoy the fullest range of intimacies and, as Ethel's love-life demonstrates, the greatest variety of combination. If her theory of receptivity and activity seems in some way conventional, depending on a sexual economy of opposites that is built into spiritual anatomy, this third possibility disrupts such a dependency, allowing for other configurations—significantly including love between similar constitutions. Like Fuller, Sweat understands "gendered" characteristics and desires to originate from the soul rather than the body. Such desires are continually negotiated in interaction with others, rather than being static features of a fixed identity.

Marylynne Diggs maintains that Leonora, like Ernest, takes a "male" role toward Ethel and desires an exclusive relationship, characteristics that convince Diggs that Sweat has identified Leonora as a gender invert, according to a medicalized definition.[10] But Sweat outlines a very different understanding of same-sex relations that is not dependent on gender inversion. Ethel writes, "The electricity of the one flashes and gleams through the other, to be returned not only in *degree* as between man and woman, but in *kind* as between precisely similar organizations" (*EL,* 82–83; emphasis in original). Between women there is not only reciprocity in the degree to which each partner gives or takes but also identicality in what is exchanged. To be sure, it appears the spiritual element can somehow indicate its "kind" as from a woman or a man. That kind, on the other hand, still does not seem to limit the nature or the range of its expressions of intimacy. Here Sweat effectively avoids setting up the opposition between hetero- and homosexuality that informs our own cultural norms. In Sweat's formulation, hetero- and homosexual relations are not antithetical; they are interchangeable, but homoerotic relations can add a degree of intensity. Nor does Sweat's formulation rely on the idea that sexual attraction requires a relation of opposites. Instead, the attraction of like to like has the greatest charge in her system. It requires the presence neither of a man nor of masculinity.

Sweat's novel is not focused on the eroticization of gender or gender difference because differentials are not linked to bodies (in the case of receptivity and activity) and because differentials are not stable across one's relations (in the people capable of both receptivity and activity). And finally, in love between women, difference itself is at least theoretically unnecessary—there sameness carries the added eroticized charge. Thus, Sweat's model dispatches with a dimorphic model of gendered sexuality by uncoupling desire from anatomy; it acknowledges the possibility of internal gender diversity in her third, mixed category of person; and it explicitly allows for, and even exalts, the exchange of passion between constitutions that are alike, evincing no regard for the erotics of gender difference, the very basis of heteronormativity.

Like Fuller, Sweat begs the questions: What if desire is not attached to anatomy or social roles? What if gender has no basis in bodily morphology? What ways of living would such a framing allow? How can we imagine life—pleasures, bodies, feelings, power—differently and perhaps more justly? Sweat's exuberant defense of passion and her detailed delineation of its pathways gives us a view of the kind of social experience that a sexual investment in spirit could promote.

Contextualizing Same-Sex Desire: Beyond "Romantic" or Sapphic

Sweat's novel in fact seems to capture this history at a striking moment. On the one hand, Ethel's breezy tone suggests the relative acceptance with which her spirituo-sexual theory and its various applications would meet, at least among the cosmopolitan intellectuals Sweat probably counted as her audience. On the other hand, Sweat takes noticeable care to detail and demonstrate the workings of the spiritual element behind each instance in the love-life, and there seems an almost scientific urge to test her theory on the widest array of relations possible. Sweat makes a studied effort to work out and test the belief she presents, and she pays special attention to love between women.

The issues the novel explores percolated in the epistolary relationship between Sweat and Elizabeth Stoddard in the 1850s, prior to the novel's publication.[11] Sweat's letters have unfortunately not come to light, but Stoddard's letters to Sweat reveal the friends' mutual interest in transatlantic romantic philosophy, including the thought of Emerson, Carlyle, Goethe, Schiller, and Cousin; their attempts to work out identities as intellectual women vis-à-vis gendered roles in social circles and domestic life; and their intensely introspective concern with their own temperaments and moods. These interests are the framework within which they probe and explore their relation to each other. Like Sweat's novel, the correspondence reveals the ease with which women could move between hetero- and homoerotic relations and their compatibility within the space of the same letter and life. Sweat had in fact married before the correspondence began, and Stoddard married midway through. But the correspondence also reveals a self-conscious interest in love between women—whether it would offer an alternative to the gender constrictions of heterosexual marriage and whether it might be a more pleasurable and satisfying arrangement.

Stoddard enthuses in one letter over meeting Charlotte Cushman, the renowned actress, and her partner at the time, Matilda Hays, a translator of George Sand's novels (Sweat was also involved in promoting Sand's work in English), expressing her admiration of both women, particularly Cushman: "She is a wonderful creature, most splendidly superior, odd, brilliant energetic and independent. I never saw a woman I was so much attracted by." Stoddard is particularly intrigued by Cushman's comment on her partnership: "One thing she said I remember, that only a woman knows how a woman should be loved." Stoddard turns to other literary matters momentarily but seems to return to this train of thought when she suggests to Sweat: "I wish I could see you. I sit by my sea-window, all is calm and pleasant. I would you had no husband almost so that we could be partners in divers concerns." Stoddard interjects the thought of "my Wilson," a favorite brother, and how Sweat will love him too when he brings Stoddard to Portland on a visit. Stoddard then dwells on her "deep and luxuriant feeling," much as Ethel lays claim to exceptional capacities in her letters: "I have stronger passionate powers than most women, therefore I run riot in these matters."[12] And like Ethel's, Stoddard's feeling is here suggestively fluid in its objects. "These matters" remain unspecified: it is not clear whether her brother or her female friend / would-be partner has opened this well of feeling, but she celebrates its intensity and extravagance, its disregard for expected paths and thresholds. My point is not to suggest that a portrayal of Stoddard or of the Stoddard-Sweat relationship underwrites *Ethel's Love-Life* but to highlight the conspicuous interest displayed here in identifying love between women. The correspondence suggests that Sweat's novel is driven by an attempt to articulate, describe, and theorize the workings of passion and how it might accommodate various relations at a historical juncture when those relations—whether romantic friendship, erotic love, or marriage—are in flux.

I suspect Sweat's effort to delineate her system of magnetic attractions in such detail evolves in part from a desire to strike a self-conscious distance from two opposing contemporary models: first, the French "Sapphic novel" tradition (in which Sweat was well-versed, judging from her library and book reviews); and second, what Sharon Marcus has identified as the pervasive naturalization of female homoeroticism as a feature of femininity, rather than gender aberrance, within a British context.[13] Appearing keen to pose her own transcendental erotics against both views, Sweat at the same time seems to have felt some tension in moving a step beyond naturalized romantic friendship to suggest that homo- and heteroerotic relations are interchangeable aspects of a love-life—a tension the novel registers in a perplexing combination of longing for and condemnation of Leonora. Ethel censures Leonora for an unspecified "betrayal" while simultaneously avowing Leonora's enduring and immutable claim to her love. When Ethel calls Leonora "monstrous" and "treacherous," Diggs avers, Sweat is ambivalently drawing on an emerging medical identification of lesbianism as pathological and counternormative.[14] I would reorient this claim to propose instead that Sweat thus signals her awareness of the novels of Gautier and Balzac, and that if we impose a choice between resisting or accepting a pathologized sexual identity, we obscure the novel's resistance to any such codification.

Building a representation of Leonora as an "earthly" type, as a sensual woman full of social and intellectual ambition, the novel implies that she pursues a particularly carnal kind of love—a representation that aligns her with the explicit sexuality of French Sapphism and contrasts sharply with British depictions of women's relations, which are rarely explicitly sexual. Exactly what the novel might be condemning in Leonora's character is thrown into question, however, by Ethel's own experience with women: "I have had my passionate attachments among women. . . . I have loved so intensely that the daily and nightly communion I have held with my beloved ones has not sufficed to slake my thirst for them, nor the lavishness of their love for me been able to satisfy the demands of my exacting nature" (*EL*, 84). Ethel also awards a special and permanent place to Leonora in her heart, claiming: "Our subtle essences mingled and assimilated too thoroughly ever to be entirely disunited. . . . I know . . . that I visit her in the night hours [in dreams] as she visits me . . . that there is an invisible bond which still unites each to the other" (*EL*, 91–92). These are hardly the words of someone who disavows the intensity, sensuality, or significance of love between women. But while Ethel casts love for women as often unique, it is not the opposite of love for men as is implied in the Sapphic novel and later instituted in medical models. And while Ethel describes love between women as often hotly passionate, her passion is never premised on an exclusive and physical attraction to women's bodies—the novel abjures the reduction of any kind of passion to the narrow hypersexualization of the Sapphic model. The Sapphism that accretes to Leonora's character, then, does not appear to introduce homophobic constructions of erotic relations but rather threatens to reify forms of eroticism that Sweat prefers to experience as fluid, nonexclusive, uncategorizable, and nonidentitarian. At the same time, the British model of romantic friendship fails to acknowledge, at least explicitly, the sexual basis for affinity that Sweat develops. Sweat is driven to articulate a love-life that includes women and to anatomize a sexual culture that can support less reified forms of passion.

That Sweat is actively constructing a responsive social vision becomes apparent when we place her novel next to other reform writing of the period. Sweat's discursive use of the language of hydraulics, electricity, and magnetism to map the fluid circuits of interpersonal, and sexual, relations places her directly in conversation with a cadre of other social reform engineers. Figures from John Humphrey Noyes, the founder of Oneida, to Sylvester Graham, the health reform advocate, sought to understand sexuality in terms of social economies that became the basis for larger social blueprints. These social engineers, though positing very different systems, attempted to structure sexual relations by redistributing their "flows." Noyes defended his system of reserving male climax in hydraulic terms: "It economizes the love principle. There need be no waste of it. . . . The entire power is confined for use—utilized as water is by a perfect dam—and made to turn machinery."[15] Graham, eager to guard the floodgates of desire, unleashed in its stead a cataclysmic vocabulary of paroxysms, tornadoes, and cataracts to counter the dangers of sexual release, especially the undirected release of masturbation.[16] Sweat is clearly conversant in the economics of sexuality they engage, but her design eschews their theories of conservation. Indeed, Ethel informs Ernest (who has had less love-life than she) that though he is "rigidly locked up within," she is "the master-key to open the gateway to the pent-up flood." She encourages him to "pour forth the swelling floods without measure and without stint," and she will "ride upon the mounting waves" (*EL*, 125). Ethel espouses a potentially radical notion of love and desire as positive forces rather than as pathologies in need of control, bringing her own blueprint in line with Fourier, the social philosopher most influential to the articulated social visions of transcendentalism—including not only George Ripley's Brook Farm but Margaret Fuller's feminism as well.[17] Like Fourier, Sweat is concerned with how attraction works, the social relations it forges, and the basis such relations create for social life. Such attraction, in her view, forges the "true" course of spiritual energies rather than disrupting social harmony.

Novel Social Architectures

As Emerson noted, Fourier's theory externalized spiritual order onto a model of social relations, carrying it "outward into its correspondence in facts," imagining the elaborate social architecture that observance of spiritual dictates and passional agency would build (*CW*, 10, xxx). In fact, Fourier's major contribution to radical thought was quite simply his challenge to the structure of Western society. Fuller herself remarked that Fourier's importance was as "a seer of divine order, in its musical expression." As she perceived it, the cosmic order Fourier projected hinged on the "arrangement of groups and series" through which, he asserted, passion could move freely, knitting persons together in social and industrial pursuits like the notes on a musical scale (*EMF*, 314). (Like Sweat, and indeed Fuller, Fourier drew on music, as well as magnetism and planetary movement, to derive the cosmic laws by which passion was bound.) While the practical details were baroque and often bizarre, Fourier's organization of social life into "series" to accommodate the posited need for variety in passional pursuit, whether sexual or occupational, leveled a simple yet profound challenge to the binary and static form of the monogamous heterosexual couple at the base of Western society—a challenge aimed at unfolding the true geometry of social life. With the serial form operating as his primary mechanism, Fourier opened the stasis of monogamous love to allow for variety over time and refused the fixed roles based on binary opposition of man and woman by allowing for a spectrum of personalities that affected attraction to either roles or mates.

In their own challenges to the sex and gender complementarity of marriage, both Fuller's and Sweat's efforts align with Fourier's formal restructuring of social relations as they posit a spectrum of sex and gender positionalities and, crucially, allow persons room to move along the spectrum. Sweat's dissection and categorization of spiritual types and the varieties of love relations that result is reminiscent of Fourier's even more elaborate multiplication of personality types into sets that correlate to levels of attraction and varieties of relational bonds. Similarly, what Charles Capper calls Fuller's theory of "proportional androgyny," in which gender is never pure or exclusive but instead a "preponderance" of masculinity or femininity, rests on a serialized span of possible combinations indebted to Fourier's model (Capper 2, 35). The form is evident in the "zodiac" Fuller claims in *Woman in the Nineteenth Century* to "see before [her]," "a zodiac of the busts of gods and goddesses, arranged in pairs": "The circle breathes the music of a heavenly order. Male and female heads are distinct in expression, but equal in beauty, strength, and calmness. . . . Could the thought, thus expressed, be lived out, there would be nothing more to be desired. There would be unison in variety, congeniality in difference" (*EMF*, 272). Fuller stretches the dualism of masculine and feminine over a series of positions, each with a male and a female version that are not, she states, oppositional "complement[s]" but reciprocating "companion[s]" (*EMF*, 269)—another instance of the "ravishing harmony" she seeks, now proliferated. The consequence of Fuller's division of gender types according to the proportion of a quality, rather than its definitive absence or presence, is that she understands gender to be a matter of degree rather than of positive category.

In another example, Fuller attempts to define the poles of masculinity and femininity, breaking out of the prose style of *Woman* to order them visually in verse-like arrangement:

> The growth of man is two-fold, masculine and feminine.
> As far as these two methods can be distinguished they are so as
> Energy and Harmony.
> Power and Beauty.
> Intellect and Love. (*EMF*, 343)

Even as Fuller repeats a dualistic gender structure within each line, the lines as a set work to proliferate the terms of the dualism. That is, she begins to serialize, if we think of this list form as neither a linear progression nor a random catalog but instead a series of varied repetitions of a form. When she goes on to suggest that "if these two developments were in perfect harmony, they would correspond to and fulfill one another, like hemispheres, or the tenor and bass in music," she positions gender duality on a scale that ascends and descends through a variety of notes, a musical scale that we are perhaps to hear in her verse-like list as well (*EMF*, 343). *Woman in the Nineteenth Century* itself is arguably the trail of Fuller's repeated visionary instantiation of similar series of women, from contemporary instances, to historical, to mythological, to fictional, in each of which she seeks to divine the full "scale" of woman's potentiality. The goal is not to present role models but—in a manner more like Fourier's than she might wish to acknowledge—to project those forms that would allow spiritual energies to flourish. Fourier's passions are not far from the gendered forces, male and female, that move through Fuller's version of the soul, yielding the human variety—a variety visible in the series of women she repeatedly lays out—that society has yet to accommodate fully.

A similar adjustment has the fairly profound consequences we have seen in Sweat's novel, where a variety of personality types, seemingly divorced from their biological sex, provide the grounds for conceiving sexual attraction as based on something other than dyadic anatomical difference. Sweat does not carry her schematization of coupling and attraction far enough to propose an explicit plan for a new communal organization on the order of Fourier's Phalanxes or Noyes's experiment at Oneida, nor does she project a visionary order on the same scale as Fourier or Fuller; indeed, she works within a novelistic focus on a single individual's interior life. And yet, Sweat surely understood her novel to defend the freedom and priority of the passions, and her blueprint for sexual relations carries the charge of the utopian and reform impulses—the vision of social change—belonging to the philosophers and discourses she engages.

In fact, when Sweat chose a novel as the vehicle for her ideas, it was not a decision she thought would lessen their significance as social vision. In the 1870 critical essay published with a translation of George Sand's *Antonia*, Sweat argues that novels occupy "a high position among the social forces of the time" and "have become a favorite medium for the dissemination of new theories, the discussion of difficult social questions, and the promulgation of new remedies for human ills." She points to "romances which elucidate the mysteries of Mesmerism and Fourierism; of Communism and Agrarianism; or set forth in Protean forms the conclusions of aristocratic Atheism or fashionable Pantheism." Sweat endorses a theory that locates the novel's social force not in a realist commentary on life-as-it-is but in an idealized rendition of life as it might be or should be: "We find in [Sand's novels] no servile copy of narrow imitation, but the great facts of nature as seen through the idealism of art."[18] What Sweat has in mind, however, is neither the morally perfectionist mode we might associate with "idealization" nor the divorce from material life of which we often accuse philosophical idealism. What Sweat practices in her own novel and condones in Sand's is utterly in keeping with the transcendental politics I have been describing: an artistic mode that conveys social relations in their abstracted, imagined essence, not to escape material conditions but to examine the roots of social ills or project how "new theories" might play out in their "Protean forms."

Ethel's Love-Life itself is assessed in much the same terms eleven years earlier in the *North American Review* (where Sweat was a frequent reviewer): "The style is natural, that is to say, not such a style as any young lady ever employed in writing to a young man, but such as would of necessity be adopted by the somewhat intensified and idealized heroines of fiction, if they lived and wrote love-letters. It requires a finer and higher art by far to produce a work like this, than to jot down the gossip and incidents that form the staple of an ordinary novel."[19] The reviewer does not claim that Ethel is an impossible paragon of moral virtue but rather that heroines of fiction can be intensified versions of their real-world counterparts and that Sweat has successfully styled the feelings and expression of her heroine in a likewise elemental form. The reviewer claims that, despite its status as fiction, Sweat's novel is an "autobiography" in a "profounder sense," not because it is based on actual events but because it is based in some kind of felt truth ultimately "beyond the reach of fiction."[20]

Though Ethel is an exceptional heroine in her capacity to feel, it is not character or plot that sets in motion the formal embodiment of the novel's idea, as it might in a Sand novel; in Sweat's novel, such features of story are far too thinly rendered. It is the circuits of feeling themselves that *Ethel's Love-Life* abstracts to demonstrate the law it wishes to examine. Sweat renders feeling in an idealized form—that is, as a literal essence, a palpable energy that circulates without clear origin in the physical body or particular events. And by rendering feeling in an essential, elemental form and as itself a physical agent, Sweat intends to chart interpersonal economies as they should be, relatively free from external circumstance and social convention.

According to Sweat's theory, we can expect the novel's idealism to instantiate its idea formally and place its theory in motion. Sweat meets this criterion through her use of the epistolary form, which plays a special role in the embodiment of both circulatory love and the social economy it creates—"set[ting] forth in Protean forms" the "conclusions" of the spirituo-sexual dynamic the novel is at pains to illuminate. Letters, in theory at least, could circulate like the fluid magnetism of the interpersonal economy Sweat describes. In her letters to Sweat, Stoddard writes appreciatively on the "neutral ground" of the letter: "To you I appear differently, I do so, because you are ignorant of the leavings and tendencies of my life. We meet on neutral ground and it is a relief."[21] Stoddard suggests the bond she shares with Sweat has a special intimacy precisely because they commune primarily through letter writing, rather than in person with material "leavings" and social contexts distracting from or even determining their interaction. Sweat's novel likewise portrays the letter as a distinctive medium through which Ethel can channel her interiority and feeling and "paint" it for others, as she often says.

The notion of the letter as a different and more accurate kind of "portrait" is one to which Sweat often returns, and it is also one that recurs in other correspondence of the period. Letter writing was in fact integral to one network of bonds that looms large in histories of transcendental friendships and is described by its participants in both utopian and eroticized terms: the circle of friends including Fuller, Emerson, Anna Barker, Samuel Ward, and Caroline Sturgis. According to Fuller's biography, Fuller's own social magnetism forged the circle, but her circulation of others' letters sustained it. She managed Emerson's inclusion by passing on to him bundles of letters each friend had written to her—"such pictures as you have sent me," as he called the letters, moved and attracted him (*LE*, 2:168). Letters, in Fuller's circle, Sweat's novel, and Stoddard's correspondence, become "pictures" of selves, but what is visible are not the trappings of the person—of flesh, features, clothes, or even actions. Instead, in letters, the beauty—and sensuality—of the soul might easily shine through the "mere features" (*CW*, 6, 160). Ethel's letters discuss no actual events but unfurl, letter after letter, the workings of her brain and heart, as if in imitation of the waves and undulations of feelings she endlessly describes, sent forth bodilessly across time and space. Sweat's epistolary form is in perfect consonance with her theory of interpersonal relation, for letters held out the possibility of transcending the person, and especially the conventional social and gendered identities—of male or female, husband or wife, bachelor or maid—that might otherwise limit one's social and erotic circulation.

That letters commonly traveled beyond the named addressee enhances this depiction of their circulatory qualities and pushes against our own tendency to treat them as "private."[22] They could knit together an array of relations. As Elizabeth Hewitt argues, nineteenth-century writers for whom "issues of social mediation are paramount repeatedly turn to letter writing as both practice and theoretical model for conceiving of social reciprocity."[23] In Fuller's circle, letters helped link Emerson to a circuit of affection that reconceived the dynamics of social reciprocity at the foundation of society. As David Robinson, Larry Reynolds, and Caleb Crain have, in different ways, persuasively argued, Fuller was, in Robinson's words, "defining intimacy as something shared and not restricted to a couple"—in an experiment aimed beyond private desires for an open relationship.[24] It offered a utopian model for how transcendentalists might imagine social and sexual relations in a way that challenged the existing system of monogamy and, for Fuller, the gender roles it entailed.

Ethel's Love-Life certainly extends this transcendentalist conception of friendship, but the degree to which it challenges monogamy or shapes a larger social vision beyond the individual encounter requires some examination—for the novel's defense of passion, the variety of the love-life, and the transitivity of eroticized gender roles are in tension with Ethel's accession to marriage. While Sweat delineates a theory of affection that can obviate sex or gender as a basis for coupling, in her vision, unlike in Fuller's epistolary experiment, the couple remains the basic relational unit, and Ethel's marriage seems to enshrine a lasting, singularly affinitized couple. Yet the epistolary form might be seen to set forth "conclusions" shaped by the sexual dynamic Sweat examines, for this serialized rendering of the love-life structures an affectional economy that does not consistently view intimate love as a singular lifetime event, and it implicitly supports the more radical tendencies of theories of "spiritual affinity" to allow for love in a variety of forms and situations. Such a view can have serious consequences for the institution of marriage that Sweat would almost certainly not endorse. Her novel nonetheless registers the incongruity of passional agency with the institution of marriage, especially the traditional loss of the female self, a fear of which also surfaces frequently in Stoddard's letters to Sweat.

The novel's embodiment of passional agency, devoid of sex or gender markers, in its epistolary form brings this tension between the love-life and the marriage to the fore. On one hand, all of Ethel's letters are directed to her fiancé, Ernest. As a whole, they seem to collect and collate Ethel's love-life in order to subsume it in the ultimate relation with the ultimate addressee, in which she claims to "crown but one king" (*EL*, 81). The love-life is retrospect and the marriage prospect. Ethel purports to be "exorcis[ing]" her past in a narrative of conversion into the marital fold (*EL*, 75). Though Sweat's concept of sexual relations that are not determined by gender and sex allows Ethel to claim a basic equality, an economy of equal give and take with Ernest, other signs suggest that the emerging "companionate" marriage will reestablish gender complementarity and with it the fixed, unequal role Ethel had evaded in her love-life. The occasion of the letter writing—offering her "love-life" to her future husband—seems to separate her from her past with its heterogeneity, the dynamism of its great relational struggles and triumphs, and its even greater self-indulgence. On the other hand, if letters were regularly "forwarded" to other friends (who, like the reader in this fictional economy, receive them and look on), we cannot assume that the one-way correspondence of a woman to her future husband formally channels the writer's affection into a single outlet. And we cannot help but feel the sheer exhibitionism in Ethel's voluminous discourse and the ringing silence of Ernest, effects that actively compete with the notion of Ethel's absorption in marriage and beg the question of Sweat's tone.

On a larger scale as well, epistolarity mounts a significant challenge to the monogamy, and the expected subordination of homoerotic relations, with which the novel proposes to conclude. Instead of exorcising the past, the letters seem to relive it, formally working to "open" Ethel's love-life to her marital partner and connect her past loves with the present one—to associate it, in the strong sense of that word. In this way, the letters mitigate the exclusivity of the marital bond. Additionally, Sweat's decision to serialize Ethel's love-life, to structure the novel on the premise that Ethel is delivering an account in regular installments, places the marriage as another installment in a series, as one in a nonhierarchical gathering of equivalent representations. The serial form reinforces Ethel's insistence, as she recounts her various relationships, on their discrete significance to her life (as when she affirms that marriage will not supersede Leonora's claim to a specific place in her heart). Thus, while the novel defines intimacy as restricted to a couple, intimacy is rendered in the novel as a distinctly serial form, one in which Fourier's theory of variety in association is tangible: intimacy occurs not as an isolated and singular event but in a series of encounters between an array of couples. In this arrangement, marriage depends for significance on its mutual relationship with other couplings rather than on its place as the culmination of events, to which all other events were leading. The matches proliferated by the sequence of letters unfold from the bi-(tri?-)sexual love-life that the novel relates and from the multiple possibilities that inhere in Sweat's theory of interpersonal relation. Though Sweat would not have endorsed free love, divorce, or communal love, these are some of the likely results of the sexual economy she puts forth in her novel. It is testimony to her committed view of the work a novel can perform that she gives play to her social and sexual theory, to its range of potential consequences, in the structure of *Ethel's Love-Life*.

One wonders whether, like the originator of the serial form, Scheherazade of *The Arabian Nights*, Ethel indefinitely effects a teleological delay, with another letter and yet another, of the moment marriage will end the series (she is not yet married at novel's end). Ethel's writing stylistically and generically, as intensively wrought first-person expression in serial format, continues to manifest both her agency and her sensitivity as eroticized presence. Again and again, Ethel speaks of the pleasure of looking at herself, likening its delights to those "a spectator may feel in watching the movements of a champion on whom he feels an immutable reliance" (*EL,* 50). She "fill[s] up all but the corners of the sheets" she posts with "continually repeated pictures" of herself, and wonders if her correspondent "grow[s] weary of contemplating this face that so pertinaciously places itself" before him; yet she goes blithely on "from one reminiscence to another, pleasing [her]self," she says (*EL,* 198, 148–49). Ethel's "accumulations" of both spiritual energy and prose continue to inundate, spilling into her one-way stream of communication with Ernest, and indeed threatening to tax the reader with an overwhelming volume of Ethel-ness (*EL,* 125).

One could argue that in forever churning out magnetic missives closely examining her own inner workings, the narrator of *Ethel's Love-Life* finally evinces the solipsism and self-isolation of late-stage transcendentalist reverie. Instead, I have argued that Sweat's novel is a distinctively vivid example of the social vision that transcendental idealism might serve, and indeed is a rare example of how the novel form might be deployed to fashion a world founded on its tenets and examine the social effects of its beliefs. Sweat's text helps reconstruct the very genealogies of transcendentalist thought, bringing into view the ways in which Fuller, perhaps more than any other leading transcendentalist, yoked ideas about spirit, ecstasy, and passion to the social field and to social meanings, particularly concerning gender, relationality, and subjectivity. It asks us to consider how transcendental commitments could put under erasure the boundaries between the "ideal" and the social worlds, and between the spirit and the body, for socially transformative purposes. Sweat takes such ideas and applies them to the specific issue of newly articulating, in the face of other competing discourses, a theory of same-sex desire.

Indeed, *Ethel's Love-Life* reminds us that sex and gender are at their very basis "genealogical" concepts—that is, they must be understood as embedded, circumstantial, and themselves dependent on a nexus of historical and social relations. Challenging our homo / hetero framework, the novel accesses a broader, nonbinary sexual morphology by locating sexual attraction in the realm of the psyche or spirit, a move that can work to constitute sexuality rather than, as much scholarship would argue, evade it. In Sweat's formulation, persons can meet on a terrain in which affect and pleasure, the erotics of receptivity and activity, are never simply determined by gender or sex and can thus open onto the alternative sexual—and social—relations of *Ethel's Love-Life.*

NOTES

1. See Lyle Wright, *American Fiction, 1851–1875: A Contribution toward a Bibliography* (San Marino: Huntington Library Press, 1978), 322 (entry 2413); John D'Emilio and Estelle B. Freedman, eds., *Intimate Matters: A History of Sexuality in America* (Chicago: Univ. of Chicago Press, 1998), 126; Carroll Smith-Rosenberg, *Disorderly Conduct: Visions of Gender in Victorian America* (Oxford: Oxford Univ. Press, 1986); Marylynne Diggs, "Romantic Friends or a 'Different Race of Creatures'? The Representation of Lesbian Pathology in Nineteenth-Century America," *Feminist Studies* 21, no. 2 (1995): 317–40.
2. Sharon Marcus, *Between Women: Friendship, Desire, and Marriage in Victorian England* (Princeton: Princeton Univ. Press, 2007), 13. Instead of seeing women's relationships as potentially subversive of sexual or gender norms and therefore protolesbian, Marcus finds homoeroticism to be a pervasive aspect of Victorian society—and in fact one of the codes of femininity.
3. See, for example, Jonathan Ned Katz, in *Love Stories: Sex between Men before Homosexuality* (Chicago: Univ. of Chicago Press, 2003).
4. Axel Nissen, for example, describes "romantic friendship" as a "period term" that indicates a shift of focus away from sexual and erotic, and toward emotional, intellectual, and spiritual, aspects of relations (*Manly Love: Romantic Friendship in American Fiction* [Chicago: Univ. of Chicago Press, 2009], 7–8). Caleb Crain argues that Emerson subsumes his homoerotic feelings in Platonic spiritual rhetoric. Crain describes "a holy divorce" between sexual feeling and its transubstantiation in literary writing, in his view the last resort of homoerotic feeling in the nineteenth century (*American Sympathy: Men, Friendship, and Literature in the New Nation* [New Haven: Yale Univ. Press, 2001], 227).
5. Elizabeth Povinelli, "Sex in a Secular Age: Can Sex Be a Minor Form of Spitting?" in *The Immanent Frame: Secularism, Religion, and the Public Sphere* (blog), Social Science Research Council, 13 December 2007, http://blogs.ssrc.org/tif/2007/12/13/can-sex-be-a-minor-form, accessed 2 November 2013.
6. Margaret Sweat, *Ethel's Love-Life: A Novel* (New York: Rudd & Carleton, 1859), 151; hereafter cited parenthetically as *EL*.
7. Sylvester Judd, quoted in Gura, 194.
8. Lillian Faderman, *Surpassing the Love of Men: Romantic Friendship and Love between Women from the Renaissance to the Present* (1981; New York: Harper Collins, 1998). Martha Vicinus, in *Intimate Friends: Women Who Loved Women, 1778–1928* (Chicago: Univ. of Chicago Press, 2004), treats many of the same relationships, describing them as sexual and positing a tension between religious, spiritualized love and carnal desire.
9. See Dorri Beam, *Style, Gender, and Fantasy in Nineteenth-Century American Women's Writing* (Cambridge: Cambridge Univ. Press, 2010), chap. 2.
10. See Diggs, "Romantic Friends," 329.
11. The correspondence lasted from 1851 until 1854, when the friendship ended abruptly. See Jennifer Putzi, "'Two *Single* Married Women': The Correspondence of Elizabeth Stoddard and Margaret Sweat, 1851–1854," in *Letters and Cultural Transformations in the United States, 1760–1860*, ed. Theresa Strouth Gaul and Sharon M. Harris (Surrey, U.K.: Ashgate, 2009), 117–36.
12. Elizabeth Stoddard to Margaret Sweat, 4 June [1852], in *The Selected Letters of Elizabeth Stoddard*, ed. Jennifer Putzi and Elizabeth Stockton (Iowa City: Univ. of Iowa Press, 2012), 3–6.

13. Marcus, *Between Women*. My discussion of the Sapphic novel is indebted to Marcus's "Comparative Sapphism," in *The Literary Channel: The Inter-National Invention of the Novel*, ed. Margaret Cohen and Carolyn Dever (Princeton: Princeton Univ. Press, 2002), 251–85.
14. Diggs, "Romantic Friends," 326.
15. John Humphrey Noyes, quoted in Louis J. Kern, *An Ordered Love: Sex Roles and Sexuality in Victorian Utopias; The Shakers, the Mormons, and the Oneida Community* (Chapel Hill: Univ. of North Carolina Press, 1981), 278.
16. See Sylvester Graham, *A Lecture to Young Men on Chastity: Intended also for the Serious Consideration of Parents and Guardians* (Boston: G. W. Light, 1838).
17. See Zwarg, 125–60; and Phyllis Cole, "Woman Questions: Emerson, Fuller, and New England Reform," in *Transient and Permanent: The Transcendental Movement and Its Contexts*, ed. Charles Capper and Conrad Edict Wright (Boston: Massachusetts Historical Society, 1999), 408–46.
18. Margaret Sweat, "The Novels of George Sand," in *Antonia: A Novel*, by George Sand, trans. Virginia Vaughan (Boston: Roberts Brothers, 1870), 1–23 (after the novel), esp. 2–3 and 22. Sweat's assessment anticipates Naomi Schor's in *George Sand and Idealism* (New York: Columbia Univ. Press, 1993).
19. Unsigned review of *Ethel's Love-Life*, by Margaret Sweat, *North American Review* 89 (July 1859): 276.
20. Ibid.
21. Elizabeth Stoddard to Margaret Sweat, [June?] Thursday 24th [1852], in the Allison-Shelley Collection, Rare Books and Manuscripts, The Pennsylvania State Univ. Libraries, State College, Pa.
22. See Eve Bannett, *Empire of Letters: Letter Manuals and Transatlantic Correspondence, 1680–1820* (Cambridge: Cambridge Univ. Press, 2005).
23. Elizabeth Hewitt, *Correspondence and American Literature, 1770–1865* (Cambridge: Cambridge Univ. Press, 2004), 3.
24. David M. Robinson, "'In the Golden Hour of Friendship': Transcendentalism and Utopian Desire," in *Emerson and Thoreau: Figures of Friendship*, ed. John T. Lysaker and William Rossi (Bloomington: Indiana Univ. Press, 2010); Larry Reynolds, "Hawthorne's Labors in Concord," in *The Cambridge Companion to Nathaniel Hawthorne*, ed. Richard H. Millington (Cambridge: Cambridge Univ. Press, 2004), 10–24; Crain, *American Sympathy*. See also Kathleen Lawrence on Emerson's continuing "relational experiment," one of "passionate soul-mates," with Caroline Sturgis ("'The Dry-Lighted Soul' Ignites: Emerson and His Soul-Mate Caroline Sturgis as Seen in Her Houghton Manuscripts," *Harvard Library Bulletin* 16 [Fall 2005]: 37–68, esp. 55).

SECTION 4
Late Voices and Legacies

INTERLUDE

Elizabeth Cady Stanton, from "Reminiscences," no. 27, *Woman's Tribune*, 21 June 1890, 170.

When I see so many of our American women struggling to be artists, who cannot make a good loaf of bread, nor a palatable cup of coffee, I think of what Theodore Parker once said when art was a craze in Boston. "The fine arts do not interest me," said Theodore Parker, "so much as the coarse arts, which feed, clothe, house and comfort a people. I should rather be a great man as Franklin, than a Michael Angelo—nay, if I had a son I should rather see him a mechanic, who organized use like the late George Stephenson, in England, than a great painter like Rubens, who only copied beauty. In short, I take more interest in a cattle show, and feel more sympathy with the Pope's bull than his *bul-lum*. Men talk to me about the absence of art in America. You remember the stuff that Margaret Fuller used to twaddle forth upon that theme, and what transcendental nonsense got delivered from gawky girls and long-haired young men. I tell them we have cattle-shows and mechanics' fairs, and plows and harrows, and sawmills, sewing-machines and reaping-machines, threshing-machines, and planning machines. There is not a saw-mill in Rome. I doubt if there is one in the Pontifical States."

Required to "Speak"

Caroline Healey Dall and the Defense of Margaret Fuller

MARY DE JONG

Cd. there be a greater tribute to the universality of Margaret's life than the testimony of the many strong *women who find as you, a wonderful kindredness of experience with her. I have been struck with it very much. I have felt it profoundly myself.*

—Anna Q. T. Parsons to Caroline Dall (1852)

While writing the biography *Nathaniel Hawthorne and His Wife* (1884), Julian Hawthorne chose to publish a version of his father's 1858 notebook entry that records and expands upon American sculptor Joseph Mozier's denigrating remarks about Sarah Margaret Fuller and Giovanni Angelo Ossoli, with whom Fuller had formed an intimate relationship in Rome by late 1847.[1] In a self-justifying letter in the *Boston Evening Transcript*, Julian stated that he had expected to arouse "a fluttering in the dove cotes of Margaret's surviving friends, and of the later disciples."[2] There was more than a "fluttering." Fuller's friends and admirers generated an energetic published controversy that lasted into June 1885, longer than most scholars realize. In that controversy Caroline Healey Dall was a key but generally unrecognized participant. Although Dall's personal interactions with Fuller were confined to Fuller's early 1841 Conversations about Greek mythology, and Dall realized that Fuller disliked her, she nevertheless "loved" Fuller.[3] Eventually she assumed responsibility for defending Fuller's character and her legacy as a feminist and transcendentalist.

According to Julian's biography, Mozier described Ossoli to Nathaniel Hawthorne as a handsome, barely literate simpleton who falsely claimed to be a marchese. Fuller was drawn to him despite her "cruel and bitter scorn of intellectual deficiency." Mozier further alleged that she lost her literary "power" and could not write the history of the Roman Revolution she had led her friends to expect. As if solving the mysteries of Fuller's attraction to such a man and her "total collapse," Nathaniel Hawthorne articulated his view that she had merely overlaid her "coarse," "in many respects defective and evil nature" with extraordinary learning and talents, arrogating to herself the act of self-creation. She must have yielded to sexual passion for Ossoli and fallen "as the weakest of her sisters might." Thus *Nathaniel Hawthorne and His Wife* insinuated that she had not properly married Ossoli and declared that such a moral and intellectual breakdown revealed she was "a great humbug."[4] The biography became available for review in late October 1884.

The Hawthorne-Fuller controversy broke as reviewers quoted Julian's excerpts from his father's notebooks. Hawthorne had disparaged acquaintances on two continents, but the two-and-a-half-page Fuller-Ossoli passage became the most notorious in the United States.[5] Gary F. Scharnhorst, author of a forthcoming biography of Julian Hawthorne, characterizes the affair as a "tempest in a Boston teapot."[6] It was that, but also more. The storm gathered in various locations and spread beyond Boston. Fed by unpublished letters enclosing clippings from periodicals, the controversy revived questions about Fuller's character that prompted personal calls and cross-country letters as well as printed arguments. In this essay, I focus on the campaign waged by Dall, Fuller's most persistent public advocate.

Thomas R. Mitchell's *Hawthorne's Fuller Mystery* credits Dall with an early protest but understandably does not explore the extent and vigor of her efforts to challenge Julian Hawthorne.[7] Julian's hostility and the heat of indignation that Dall felt and propagated show that Fuller's reputation mattered. Tracing Dall's agitation on Fuller's behalf, this essay demonstrates that epistolary exchanges and face-to-face interactions shaped the public discourse. Letters served as arguments, tools for research, and drafts of published documents. Supporters of both Fuller and Nathaniel Hawthorne used periodicals to shape public opinion. Such insights are accessible largely because Dall preserved a trove of manuscripts and a scrapbook of clippings that document responses to Julian's book.[8]

Dall's correspondence, journal, and scrapbook of periodical clippings with the cover title "Hawthorne versus S. M. Ossoli C. H. Dall et. [*sic*] al." reveal that intermittently, from 1841 onward, Dall thought, spoke, and wrote about Margaret Fuller. Scholars of women transcendentalists have recognized that she regarded Fuller as a model.[9] I wish to add that Dall identified with her and came to think of herself as "Margaret's" proper biographer. Scrapbook 9—"made," she inscribed on an introductory sheet dated November 1899, "at a time when I expected to write Margaret's memoir"—collects twenty-three clippings of commentaries on *Nathaniel Hawthorne and His Wife*.[10] Among these are Dall's three letter-reviews, published in the widely circulated *Springfield Republican* on 15 December 1884; the *Unity*, a Chicago Unitarian paper, also 15 December; and the *Louisville Commercial*, documented by an undated clipping with the dateline 18 December 1884. Her notices insist on the question of who should defend Fuller.

Calling Julian's biography "the great literary sensation of the season," Dall, then living in Washington, D.C., summoned three first-generation transcendentalists to charge to Fuller's defense: it was "not proper," she declared, "for any of Margaret's younger friends to come to the rescue of her honor, while Dr. Hedge, William Henry Channing, and James Freeman Clarke are still alive."[11] Frederic Henry Hedge met Fuller in 1823 and became a lifelong friend.[12] Channing and Clarke, intimates and frequent correspondents of Fuller during different periods, were coeditors with Ralph Waldo Emerson of the first book-length biography, *Memoirs of Margaret Fuller Ossoli* (1852). Emerson had died in 1882, and when Dall summoned the two survivors, Channing was terminally ill in London.[13] Fuller's older friends were dying out.

Dall had already decided it was "proper" for a *particular* younger friend to recruit additional defenders by more personal means. On 29 November 1884 she wrote letters "about S. M. F." to Clarke and Hedge (Register). Three days later she fired off her review to the *Springfield Republican* and "wrote burning hot with indignation to Sarah Clarke in Marietta [Georgia] concerning Hawthorne's vile aspersions upon Margaret Fuller" (Journal, 2 December 1884). Next she called, bearing coals, on fellow Washingtonian Augustus A. Hayes, a *Harper's* author whose wife Emily Roelker Fuller was the daughter of Fuller's brother William Henry.[14] Hayes "drew [her] into a corner," she narrated with dramatic flair, to say that he had assisted Julian with research for the biography. "'Imagine how disgusted I was,'" Hayes complained, to learn of his "'vile thrust'" at Emily's aunt! Emily Hayes declared that she would not read Julian's book (Journal, 4 December 1884). The Hayeses apparently abstained from public protest, but Dall's protest had barely begun.

Dall's astute letters to the press anticipated from the beginning all the major points of dispute of the larger 1884–85 controversy: Nathaniel Hawthorne's authority to judge Fuller, Mozier's credibility, Julian Hawthorne's exposure of private writings, Fuller's personal qualities, and Fuller's marriage. I will indicate how each of these issues appeared to the larger circle of interested readers and to Dall herself, at some points incorporating recent scholarship.

Hawthorne was renowned for his careful observation and analytical acumen. Fuller was better known as a remarkable woman intellectual and speaker than as an author, though the reading public was aware of *Woman in the Nineteenth Century* (1845), in part because many late-century women lecturers cited it orally and in print.[15] This landmark feminist text, collections of Fuller's other writings, and *Memoirs* had been repeatedly reprinted by late 1884.[16] Even among friends, though, a question lingered: Who *was* that multifaceted woman? An unsigned paragraph in the *Boston Evening Transcript* illustrates the difference in the two authors' reputations as well as the writer's frustration at Fuller's resistance to definition:

> Of all Margaret Fuller's contemporaries none has shown so much insight into character in general as Hawthorne, and his judgment of her, severe as it is, wonderfully reconciles all the others which, conflicting in many ways, have puzzled those who never saw her, and who, when declaring that they found little in her works, have been silenced with "You should have heard her! You could only know Margaret through her conversation." He said, "She was a great humbug."

After quoting a few more lines, this paragraphist expressed relief at Hawthorne's penetration: "This explains everything," the full range of traits that made Fuller famous. "It is not a pleasant solution of the riddle, but it is better to know precisely what sort of an Isis is behind the veil."[17] For such readers it was sufficient to label Fuller a pagan maternal goddess. Deference to Hawthorne's acuity was so great that the *Boston Herald* could call his statements about Fuller in his Roman journal "facts" that the public needed to counterbalance against two recent adulatory biographies, Julia Ward Howe's *Margaret Fuller (Marchesa Ossoli)* (1883) and Thomas Wentworth Higginson's *Margaret Fuller Ossoli* (1884).[18] Readers less certain of Hawthorne's authority were left to ponder his ruthless assessment, apparently based on Mozier's allegations.

Deliberately inciting debate, Dall attacked the defamers' weakest claim, that Fuller's friends could say little in her favor. "We may at least ask," she wrote, "what Hawthorne meant" by asserting that Fuller "had not left in the hearts and minds of those who knew her any deep witness of her integrity and purity." During her own cross-country trip in 1880, Dall countered, numerous people "poured into [her] listening ear many a noble story of Margaret Fuller"; she was "made welcome in many obscure places because [she] had known and honored her" ("Hawthorne Book"). In early 1885, friends and relatives, including nephew Frederick T. Fuller, marshaled personal knowledge and private writings to affirm Fuller's virtues and establish that she was esteemed by many—including, in 1842–44, Sophia Peabody and Nathaniel Hawthorne.[19]

Dall could only inquire why Hawthorne took Mozier's word. Subsequent defenders who knew Mozier or knew of him pronounced him a habitual gossip. Until the definitive scholarly edition of Hawthorne's *French and Italian Note-Books* appeared in 1980, most readers could not know that Julian had obscured his father's depreciation of Mozier.[20] Nor could they know that Mozier spread falsehoods about other Americans in Italy while feigning cordiality; for instance, in 1847 and 1861 he "publish[ed] slurs against" Hiram Powers in the American press.[21]

Nathaniel Hawthorne and His Wife prompted general discomfort by exposing private writings, especially Nathaniel's cutting statements about individuals still living in 1884. According to Dall, Julian seemed to violate others' privacy "with a sort of elation" ("Hawthorne Book"). Stinging remarks in his self-justifying letters published in the *Boston Evening Transcript* suggest that the antifeminist Julian did relish attacking Fuller. He stated that he would have been "disappointed" if his book had not disturbed her admirers, for she represented a "class" of persons who considered themselves superior and whose worshippers denied their faults.[22]

Fuller's advocates could not deny that she challenged prevalent middle-class gender norms—selflessness, conventional domesticity, and sexual purity—epitomized in Julian's biography by Sophia Hawthorne. Emerson's remarks in the 1852 *Memoirs* on Fuller's eccentricities and "mountainous ME" supported common views of her as mystical and arrogant, at least prior to her sojourn in Italy during the political upheavals that swept Europe in 1848–49.[23] In Italy, old and new friends agreed, she was gentle, generous to suffering strangers, and affectionate with Ossoli and their son born in 1848. Today's scholars, less likely to equate mildness or premarital chastity with estimable character, valorize as evidence of her expanded analytical powers the new patterns of thinking articulated in her 1846–50 articles for the *New-York Tribune*.[24] But friends who memorialized her in print at midcentury did not applaud her radical ideas and behaviors, such as critiquing nonegalitarian marriage and suggesting that violent revolutions are necessary for the birth of democracies. Nor did her mid-1880s defenders uphold a radicalized Fuller. Like the editors of *Memoirs*, biographers Howe and Higginson and other late-century admirers stressed her dedication to her family after her father's death. Although Higginson portrayed Fuller as an intellectual who acted on her convictions, he devoted two chapters to her marriage and motherhood.

Dall had directly observed the marriage issue dividing the women's movement.[25] As a follower of the press, she knew that many contemporaries deplored radicals' attacks on the institution of marriage.[26] Nevertheless, to confront the rumor that Fuller had postponed or dispensed with matrimony, she asked why the Hawthornes apparently accepted Mozier's insinuation of unsanctioned sex over the word of respected author-artist William Wetmore Story and disregarded "Margaret's own distinct utterances" that she had married Ossoli ("Hawthorne Book"). Likewise conscious of public opinion, Julian protected his father's reputation for purity of mind by obscuring his explicit depiction of Fuller as a sexual being.[27] In 1885 he claimed that his father did not think or "[mean] to insinuate that the unfortunate woman was never legally married to Ossoli."[28] Caroline Dall and James Clarke did not believe him.

Dall learned of friends' versions of Fuller's marital history from Sarah Clarke. In 1849 Fuller confided her secret marriage and motherhood to a friend in Italy, Emelyn Eldredge Story, wife of William Wetmore Story. Emelyn undertook to quell rumors in the United States with a letter to Maria White Lowell relating what Fuller had told her. Story saw documents purported to prove the marriage but later could not recall the date of the ceremony or of Fuller's revelations. Story further testified that she and William respected Ossoli as a dutiful, courageous soldier and a devoted husband. Lowell circulated this information among interested parties,[29] making a copy for Fuller's friend Sarah Clarke, who in turn copied excerpts for Dall (Clarke to Dall, 14 December 1884, Letters). Story's affirmation of the legitimacy of the Ossoli marriage was quoted in *Memoirs* and again in Higginson's pointedly titled *Margaret Fuller Ossoli*.[30]

Only readers of Fuller's extant correspondence about her union with Ossoli and their desire for secrecy could know that her "distinct utterances" about her marriage, as Dall phrased it, were few and inexplicit. Bell Gale Chevigny observes that even after disclosing her relationship with Ossoli and the existence of their child to relatives and close friends, Fuller usually avoided or delayed stating that Ossoli was her "husband."[31] Although her union with a man of limited education who did not speak English clouded prospects for successful integration into American society, she announced she would return to publish her manuscript on the Risorgimento and support her family by writing. Some well-wishers aware of the gossip advised her to prolong her stay in Italy, among them Emerson, who offered to arrange for her book's publication.[32] Emerson and the other editors of the 1852 *Memoirs* fretted over the questions of whether and when she legally married Angelo's father. Believing that she rejected wedlock on principle, Channing altered manuscripts at his disposal to protect her reputation.[33] When Julian revived the specter of sexual impropriety, Dall's outrage sparked a campaign of letters that would soon extend far beyond Washington.

Dall's ongoing tactic was to mobilize others. Even before her initial challenge to Julian was in print, she launched private missives to discredit him. In early December 1884, she was "writing letters—full of indignation yet about Hawthorne's assault on Margaret" (Journal, 5 December 1884). Over the next twelve weeks, until 2 February, she contacted Fuller's friends, acquaintances of her own, and other persons who might become public defenders of "Margaret" or opponents of Julian. On 16 December she "spent [her] eve[nin]g in writing and mailing to parties interested in that—and the Fuller-Ossoli scandal" (Journal, 16 December 1884). ("That" refers to errors in Julian's genealogies of the Hawthornes and Peabodys.) Her register for 16 December specifies that she sent "Letters enclosing Protest against Hawthorne's 'Roman Journal'" to A. A. Hayes, Sarah Clarke, and Hedge.

She also wrote "Letters enclosing Protest" to three publishing firms that might stand by Fuller or address potential damage to Nathaniel Hawthorne's reputation: Houghton, Mifflin & Company of Boston (successor to James R. Osgood & Company, the original publisher of *Nathaniel Hawthorne and His Wife*), which had also published Higginson's memoir of Fuller and was bringing out the Riverside Edition of Hawthorne's collected works; Roberts Brothers, Boston publisher of Howe's biography of Fuller, three collections of Fuller's essays, and reprints of *Memoirs* and *Woman in the Nineteenth Century*; and Mary Louise Booth at Harper & Brothers in New York City.[34] Booth edited *Harper's Bazar* for Harper's, publisher of popular books and magazines. Less overtly than Dall, Booth supported women's rights,[35] and the two women had previously corresponded (for instance, Letters, 5 June 1860, 8 November 1861, 14 February 1867). The "Protest" that Dall distributed to publishers was probably a clipping of her review in the *Republican*.

Next she wrote to Sarah Clarke and the *Louisville Commercial*, and sent a "Hawthorne letter" to the *Boston Evening Transcript* (Register, 17 December 1884). The *Transcript* of this period did not print a Hawthorne item attributed to Dall, but the *Commercial* did: a clipping titled "The Bookmakers" appears in scrapbook 9. In it Dall reiterated that "the older men" who loved Fuller should defend her honor. She could not expect Channing, Clarke, and Hedge to see her reproof in a Kentucky paper, but as a professional writer she knew that her review of Julian might be copied by other periodicals, extending the territory for protest.

Booth acknowledged her letter (Letters, 18 December 1884), saying nothing about the controversy. Dall may have received other responses to her "Protest" messages, for within the next week she sent "3 letters" to Roberts Brothers, "3 letters for Harpers" to Booth, and "3 letters" to "A. Smith" of Houghton Mifflin (Register, 19–25 December 1884). (Azariah Smith was then in charge of advertising and trade releases favorable to the company's reputation.)[36] Or, without encouragement from these firms, she may have forwarded letters of complaint that others had sent her. Dall's letters to these publishers have not been found; nor have any direct replies. Whether her protests had printed consequences is unknown. *Harper's Bazar* maintained silence, but *Harper's Weekly* regretted the "great injustice" done to Fuller.[37] Whatever the editors' and publishers' reasons for ignoring or noticing Julian's treatment of Fuller, it is significant that Dall exerted herself to enlist the national media.

The correspondence among Fuller's defenders in 1884–85, here examined for the first time, demonstrates how much Dall and other transcendentalists valued Fuller's character and intellect. Sarah Clarke of Marietta, Georgia, and her brother James F. Clarke, Jamaica Plain, Massachusetts, consulted one another and other friends before going to print. Opposing Julian may have been painful, for both had maintained long friendships with the Peabody sisters, Elizabeth, Mary, and Sophia.[38] James wrote Sarah on 9 December 1884 that he would "probably" answer Julian's "outrageous attack" on Fuller and that he expected Hedge and Higginson to publish protests. Later he added, "I received your answer to Hawthorne, which I like much, & will have printed immediately."[39] A frequent contributor to periodicals, James had contacts. On 11 December he reported that the *Transcript* was pleased to have Sarah's statement of the pro-Fuller "side" and that he would send her a printed copy. James and his wife had deleted Sarah's reference to "'the spiteful fling' of Mr. Hawthorne." "We thought it true," he wrote, "but that it would wound poor *Rose*" (Julian's sister).[40] The Clarkes did not call Julian "Mr. Hawthorne."

Sarah's sole published contribution to the controversy cited personal knowledge and quoted from Story's testimony about Fuller's marriage. Contradicting Mozier's allegations about the Ossolis' lowly rank, she declared that Giovanni was "a gentleman"; she claimed acquaintance with "many" people who respected him. Although Hawthorne "allowed himself to be . . . deceived" by "an inveterate gossip," he "was too wise to publish anything so crude." Sophia Hawthorne, too, while editing her husband's notebooks for publication in 1868–71, had "wisely omitted things not characteristic of his genius or his normal temper." Unfortunately, their son lacked Nathaniel's wisdom and Sophia's "delicate discrimination."[41] In short, Clarke blamed Julian for digging up a locust of slander that had slept for twenty-six years. Copied in other periodicals, including the *Springfield Republican* of 29 December and the *Woman's Journal* of 10 January, her article reached a varied readership.

Clarke credited Dall, saying, "Your letter decided me" to seek publication. Probably in response to questions from Dall, she stated that "three American families" could invalidate Mozier's slander of the Ossolis. Revealing more to Dall than to her print audience, Clarke stated that when she knew the Moziers in Rome, they did not calumniate Fuller and Ossoli, "except that Mr Mozier spoke with contempt of his abilities as well as of his poor education." She suggested that Mozier "touched his pictures no doubt more and more coarsely to flatter the prejudices of Hawthorne." Brother James, Hedge, and Higginson would answer Julian, she related. Sarah intended to make no further public statements, but she continued to correspond with Dall about the controversy. After sealing this letter, she opened it to copy four pages from Story's account. Asking Dall not to publish this "private letter," she stated that she had given Higginson permission to publish (Letters, 14 December 1884). Evidently she favored Higginson as a Fuller apologist. Dall nevertheless held her post.

Clarke asked Dall why she had not written her projected life of Fuller. Years later, Dall wrote an explanation on Sarah's letter: Fuller's family had asked her to write a memoir and turned over all "Margaret's" papers for a year. She recalled: "I told Mrs. Fuller that I did not think I ought to do it—as Margaret had never loved *me*. 'She would have loved you dearly had she lived to return'—was her reply." But Richard Fuller's death made the project financially "impossible" (Letters, 23 December 1884).[42] On a sheet at the head of scrapbook 9, she recorded different reasons: Julian's biography contradicted "many facts" that "have come to my knowledge. . . . Elisabeth [*sic*] Peabody was engaged to Hawthorne before he saw Sophia." Dall continued, "I gave up my intention of writing about the Hawthornes because no two members of either family could agree as to dates." It was "impossible to give any guarantees for my narrative" (scrapbook 9, 24 November [18]99). At this time Dall may have been finding excuses for a persistent reluctance or inability to immerse herself in a difficult project with the potential to drain her personal resources. As her note reveals, by 1899 the histories of Nathaniel Hawthorne and Elizabeth Peabody were intertwined in her mind with writing Fuller's life.

In 1884–85, while Dall was corresponding with Fuller loyalists in Massachusetts and Georgia, nudging Hayes in Washington, and stoking the press to enlarge her campaign, the friends were communicating among themselves and forwarding items to her. In March 1885, Sarah Clarke wrote Dall: "The Hawthorne-Fuller controversy has, I believe, expanded into a volume—and I dare say it has helped the sale of the Memoir. I saw a brief word from Story, which said all that was needed about Ossoli."[43] Clarke was signing off as a public vindicator. Three weeks later, she stated that Higginson had explained to her, evidently persuasively, that further protest might provoke "a reaction in Julian's favor" (Letters, 9 March and 31 March 1885).

Earlier moves against Julian were detailed in James Clarke's 20 December 1884 letter to Sarah. Higginson had placed a "capital article on the Hawthornes" in the *Woman's Journal*,[44] and Elizabeth Palmer Peabody, Julian's aunt and an admirer of Fuller, had contacted Hedge. Peabody forwarded to James a "severe letter" she had received from Hedge, which James quoted at length:

> "You seem to suppose that his [Julian Hawthorne's] publishing that extract . . . was an error of judgment—nothing more. Alas! I am compelled to believe that that [*sic*] it was done with malicious intent. He does not inherit his mother's sweet spirit, but the evil nature of his father, as shown in his writings & impressed on me by personal observation. That Hawthorne senior should have inscribed in his journal a monstrously [perverse?] judgment of Margaret, though not intended for publication, betrays either utter want of [insight?], or natural malig-

> nity, or both. . . . That Julian should publish it, is an [illegible] iniquity. But Margaret's writings & her biography speak for themselves.[45]

In other words, Hedge refused to collar a man tainted by hereditary evil.

James's own reply to the most notorious passage of *Nathaniel Hawthorne and His Wife* appeared in the New York *Independent*, a widely circulated interdenominational paper; the *Boston Evening Transcript* copied it the next day. Clarke, a seasoned controversialist, did not abuse the Hawthornes or Mozier but adopted Sarah's view that the sculptor was "full of the gossip of the studios." He stated that Julian had damaged his father's name by quoting caustic remarks from the notebooks.[46] A few other commentators agreed that the controversy injured Nathaniel.[47] Julian's reviews were primarily positive, however, suggesting that his father's standing was not seriously jeopardized. As America's literary canon was "institutionalized" during the late nineteenth century, enterprising publishers promoted Hawthorne as a "classic" American author.[48] However, as we shall see, some reviewers shored up his reputation.

James Clarke's 11 January 1885 letter to Sarah reveals how much he had disciplined his anger to write temperately for the *Independent*. He called Julian's recent self-defense "supercilious & insolent." Analyzing the elder Hawthorne's language, Clarke concluded that he "must either have meant that Margaret was not married, or that she married him to gratify a mere passion." Upon Mozier's "falsehood" about Ossoli he constructed "an elaborate hypothesis" that Fuller merely bedecked herself with virtues. "This stuff is received as gospel," Clarke fumed, "because it came from Hawthorne!"[49]

Dall also tried to enlist the anger of Frederic Henry Hedge of Cambridge. In December 1884 Hedge replied to three letters from her, one enclosing her review in the *Springfield Republican*. He related that Christopher Pearse Cranch—a poet-artist who socialized with Fuller in Italy—showed him Hawthorne's "outrageous libel," quoted in the *New York Times* as if every word were true. Hedge would not answer Julian because he was "too busy," but he had "given liberty to use [his] name as witness to the falsity of Hawthorne's statement" (Letters, 2 December [1884]). Soon he was explaining to Dall that he lacked personal knowledge of contested matters of "fact" such as the Ossoli family's social status, and that the assessment of "Margaret's character" was a "matter of opinion." The public could perceive his esteem for her as "biassed [*sic*]" by friendship; his words would be ineffectual. (Dall privately called his rationalizations "very sophistical" and expressed pain at his coldness [Journal, 16 December 1884, 4 January 1885].) He reported that Elizabeth Peabody had asked him to "advise" Julian to omit the Fuller passage from later editions—"as if [the fault] were mere lack of judgement [*sic*]," rather than "infernal malice." Advising Julian would be futile. (To Dall he did not confide his sense of the elder Hawthorne's "evil nature.") But he had already chided the editor of *Every Other Saturday* for publishing a paragraph that portrays Ossoli as a faux marquis. (It begins, "And so Margaret Fuller was no countess at all.")[50] He also asked that editor, an acquaintance, to copy Sarah Clarke's protest in the next issue (Letters, 15 December 1884).

Dall did not let Hedge off. His next reply acknowledged her rejection of his reasoning but testily resisted one of her arguments: "Whether Margaret's 'pen would have flown' to defend me had I been assailed I cannot say. . . . It did not fly to vindicate Emerson when [he was] assailed by the critics." (Hedge was recalling the controversy over Emerson's 1838 "Divinity School Address.") He counted himself out of the debate, professing to be "satisfied with [his] reticence" because Sarah's article (he enclosed a copy) surpassed anything he could write—given, he reiterated, his lack of "personal knowledge" and "facts" (Letters, 19 December 1884). Annoying him and perhaps troubling his conscience, Dall may have provoked a step—contacting an editor—that he would not otherwise have taken.

Every Other Saturday (1884–85), edited by Horace Parker Chandler, was a family-oriented Boston periodical with varied literary and religious content.[51] Hedge could reasonably suppose Chandler would oblige him by copying Sarah Clarke's letter, for his endorsement of the magazine as worthwhile was quoted in several mid-1884 issues. But Chandler did not comply with Hedge's request. Avowedly nonpolitical and usually noncontroversial, the magazine undertook to educate and entertain the middle classes. The 8 November 1884 issue printed an illustration of Hawthorne against the background of his home, the Wayside, as part of a series on nineteenth-century authors. In late 1884 and early 1885 the magazine implicitly endorsed *Nathaniel Hawthorne and His Wife* by freely using it as a source of anecdotes and quotations for its "About Books" and "Owl's Nest" columns and explicitly did so by defending Julian's biography against Higginson's critique of the insular Hawthorne marriage in the *Atlantic Monthly*.[52] Taken all together, the Hawthorne-related texts in Chandler's magazine reflect the older Hawthorne's canonization and the younger's gender conservatism.[53]

Chandler's periodical reinforced messages propagated by prominent media like the *New-York Tribune*, the paper that in the 1840s had employed Fuller as literary editor and foreign correspondent. The *Tribune*'s review of Julian's biography characterized Nathaniel Hawthorne as "the pure-minded and honest gentleman" who was "the greatest original writer our country has produced." This genius had "a positive aversion" to the transcendentalist Fuller, a dislike "somewhat justified" by her effort to persuade Hawthorne to take Ellery and Ellen Fuller Channing as boarders at the Manse in Concord during the newlywed Hawthornes' idyllic residence there. Hawthorne's "rather harsh analysis of her character and career," which the reviewer quoted for more than an inch of column space and paraphrased for another inch, "is, perhaps, quite as trustworthy, as the unduly worshipping estimates of her followers." This review even praised Julian's "good taste."[54] His worshipful tributes to his father's genius and parents' mutual devotion evidently compensated for his cruel and petty uses of private writings because, as a great American author, Nathaniel Hawthorne was indispensable. His prestige is further evidenced by the choice of Hedge and the Clarkes to suppress their views on his imperfections. The multiple reissues of *Nathaniel Hawthorne and His Wife* and its favorable critical reception indicate that to people invested in Hawthorne as an exemplar of American belles-lettres, Fuller was dispensable.[55] Among transcendentalists and supporters of women's rights, she was esteemed to the end of her century as an advocate and model of human and particularly female potentials.[56]

Unlike Hedge, Cranch, a resident of Cambridge in 1884, was a conspicuous combatant. As we have seen, he descended upon Hedge, waving a copy of the *New York Times* review of Julian. He wrote Higginson, "I have called twice at your house" to discuss "the abominable libel" against the Ossolis. His sister-in-law in New York had sent him a clipping of the *Times* review with "a very indignant letter about it." Cranch and "others" (he named only Hedge) believed that the offending passage should be refuted in the *Times*, ideally by Higginson, who as Fuller's biographer held "all the facts of her life in Rome fresh in [his] memory." Julian's "motive," Cranch "presume[d]," was "to make his book sell,"[57] a charge he would twice repeat in print. This letter both establishes that strategies were discussed in Cambridge and confirms Higginson's authority among Fuller's defenders.

Cranch wrote Dall three times between 11 December 1884 and 27 January 1885, at least twice in response to letters from her. He regretted that Nathaniel Hawthorne's "malevolence" had been "dragged into the public light" and reported on his consultations with Higginson and Hedge. At first Cranch believed that Fuller's biographer, not her friends, should defend her (Letters, 11 December 1884). Dall must have proposed that a rebuttal be placed in the *Times*, for Cranch argued that doing so would merely "call attention to" Julian's book (Letters, 16 December 1884). Using the *Times* had already been rejected in Cambridge, where Fuller's admirers strategized face to face. Dall could only read from afar about the campaign she had worked to mount and sustain.

Seeing the Hawthornes' remarks "going the rounds in several newspapers," Cranch erupted in the *Boston Evening Transcript* of 9 January 1885. Mozier's false statements, he suggested, may have turned Nathaniel against Fuller, a former friend, leading to his "gross and merciless libel." Julian had apparently selected "this unsavory extract from his father's private journal" to increase sales.[58] A month later, Cranch's second published response reinforced James Clarke's argument that the scandal would damage "only the author and the abettor of the libel."[59] Writing to his brother, Cranch expressed satisfaction with friends' efforts: "I think by this time young Hawthorne has his quietus, for he sees that public opinion is against him. Last night I was at a meeting of a Cambridge Club where Colonel T. W. Higginson gave an admirable lecture on her life, and Rev. Dr. Hedge added some reminiscences of his own."[60] While Cranch watched the controversy playing out locally, Dall took a larger view, trying to turn up the heat on both coasts by sending a "Hawthorne article to Pasadena, Cal.," and a letter "about Margaret" to Emily Fuller Hayes (Register, 2 February 1885 and 13 February 1885).[61]

Dall heard from Higginson because Cranch forwarded him one of her letters. Higginson and Dall had worked together as reformers, but their personal interactions were occasionally strained. In 1860 Higginson publicly lost his temper with her at a Boston women's rights meeting. He censured her, the co-organizer, for inviting too few female speakers; pointed out two factual errors in her address; and charged that carelessness with facts was her "habit." Though badly shaken, she handled the scene with aplomb. Privately analyzing his "insane" outburst, she thought "perhaps" he resented her success.[62] Or perhaps she projected her own competitiveness onto him.

Soon after Higginson's *Margaret Fuller Ossoli* appeared in spring 1884, Dall wrote him a letter articulating a sense of her claim on Fuller's biography. It had been "very hard for [her]" when Howe was chosen to write on Fuller for Roberts Brothers' "Famous Women" series, for Dall felt she better understood and sympathized with the subject. Higginson's book was "by far" superior—but left "a great gap" that only she "could fill." If he called on her, she would explain how she acquired "all the Fuller Mss." for a year "yet did *not* write the life [she] promised Margaret's mother." (An implicit message: I read those papers before you did.) For now she must add "two things," one a compliment and the other her opinion that "the *date*" of Fuller's marriage might be "ascertained" in Rome. Then, taking the self-assured tone that alienated many acquaintances, she added a third point and a fourth and a fifth, each a challenge to or correction of Higginson's work.[63] When Higginson addressed Dall in March 1885, he had already published two sharp criticisms of *Nathaniel Hawthorne and His Wife*.[64] He tried to dissuade her from joining battle in print, for "the general feeling hereabouts [Cambridge] is that so much has been written against J. H. as to put him a little in the light of a hero—or at least of the 'underdog.'" With this argument, we recall, he persuaded Sarah Clarke to publish no more. In his next letter Higginson "hope[d]" that Dall would not address "the *fact* of [Fuller's] marriage." "The old ill-natured suspicions" lingered among older readers, but "the younger generation" need not know that the matter was disputed. His biography "carefully avoided" the issue, with the Fuller family's approval. Repeating himself, he "earnestly" advised Dall not to "reopen the question of the *fact* of her marriage" (Letters, 17 March and 21 March 1885).

Higginson asserted his priority as biographer—or Dall's carelessness as reader—by pointing out that his book cited the Maria Lowell letter that she spoke of. (As shown, Dall received portions from Sarah Clarke.) He continued, "Any discussion of Ossoli's character, any indication of the good *judgment* of her marriage, would be in point—although even this is somewhat belated" (Letters, 21 March 1885). Like other conscientious late-century biographers, Higginson could be scrupulous with facts yet protective of his subject. He knew that Fuller's marital status before and after Angelo's birth still mattered socially and that subtlety and tact were not Dall's customary weapons.

She soon acquired new information about the sources and repercussions of *Nathaniel Hawthorne and His Wife*. A Washington acquaintance informed her that Elizabeth Peabody had given family papers to Julian as he worked on the biography. After examining the first printed copy, sent to her by the publisher, Peabody begged her nephew to minimize the harm to his parents by "expung[ing] the passage concerning Margaret from future editions, with an acknowledgment of the indiscretion of printing it"—"and there," Dall wrote, "she [rests?] her hand, she will do no more" (Journal, 5 April 1885). Actually, the aggrieved Peabody did more. Getting no satisfaction from Julian, she appealed to Hedge, again to be disappointed, as Hedge declined to correct Julian. She also sent Anna Q. T. Parsons of Roxbury a letter "full of her own feeling on the Hawthorne Fuller matter—which Anna wishe[d]to print" (Dall, Journal, 5 April 1885). An old friend of Peabody and an admirer of Fuller, Parsons was also Dall's friend.[65] Dall's language suggests impatience with Peabody, but she must have recognized that Julian's aunt dreaded further squalls.

There were additional complications, some of them known to or inferred by Dall. As Nathaniel Hawthorne's patron and friend in the late 1830s, Elizabeth Peabody believed that she was also his fiancée. But Hawthorne turned his attention to her sister Sophia and insisted that the failure of understanding or breach of agreement with Elizabeth be concealed from Sophia. According to Dall, Elizabeth told her of being jilted and intimidated, a story that Dall wrote out more than once—for instance, in her journal for 21 March 1872, which states that Nathaniel censored Elizabeth's letters before letting Sophia see them.[66] On the cover sheet of scrapbook 9 Dall wrote, "I have seen a letter from [Hawthorne] to [Peabody] acknowledging the fact [of their engagement] & warning her not to let Sophia know it—[this letter] she brought to me . . . in great distress of mind" (24 November 1899). Some of Hawthorne's collected letters reflect disagreements between the Hawthorne household and Elizabeth Peabody.[67] Although Julian did not disclose the matters outlined here, Elizabeth deplored his handling of his father's notebooks.[68]

Peabody's friends gave her a public forum for challenging the male Hawthornes' depiction of Fuller. In June 1885, Ednah Dow Cheney of Jamaica Plain placed in the *Boston Evening Transcript* part of a letter Peabody had written in 1870 to "an invalid friend," probably Anna Parsons.[69] Cheney had known Parsons, Peabody, and Dall for many years.[70] "E. D. C." (Cheney) introduced Peabody's "reminiscences" of "Margaret" by referring to the recent "discussion" in the *Transcript* of Fuller's "character." (Defenders had stopped naming Julian and his book.) She explained that after Peabody spoke at the New England Women's Club's 1870 celebration of Fuller's life, she wrote out her remarks for the absent friend. Although Peabody "ha[d], naturally enough, been entirely silent in the late controversy," Cheney suggested that she "[would] not object to the publication of some extracts." This document, unnoticed in previous studies, should be read as part of the written record of the Hawthorne-Fuller controversy. Dall so understood it, for she placed a clipping in scrapbook 9. Peabody recalled Fuller as a dutiful, self-sacrificing daughter and sister, a happy wife, and a "great soul." Without naming Nathaniel or Julian Hawthorne, she contested their portrayals of Fuller as a self-obsessed "fraud."[71]

Peabody's assertions saw print as a result of collaboration among Fuller's admirers—Cheney, Parsons, and possibly Dall—though in 1885 Dall lived in Washington and was alienated from Peabody and Cheney.[72] I entertain the possibility that Dall participated because she shared with Parsons a history of strategizing about how they might influence interpersonal conflicts and public issues (for instance, Journal, 18 November 1850 and 15 August 1857). Visiting Boston in late 1885, Dall called on Parsons, a reformist friend since the 1850s (Journal, 12 November 1885).

The previously unexamined portions of the Dall-Fuller story related here enrich our understanding of relatively familiar incidents and materials. Dall's interventions in the scandal were consistent with her characteristic determination and her attitude toward Fuller from the early 1850s. After eagerly awaiting Fuller's *Memoirs*, Dall confided to Parsons her disappointment in the chapters by Channing and Emerson. In the "Autobiographical Romance," however, she found that her experiences and Fuller's ran "parallel"; she identified with Fuller, who, like herself, was pressured into early intellectual attainments, suffered disturbing dreams and "subsequent nervous depression," and wanted to "grow" (Register, 6 March 1852).[73] Four days later, in an extraordinarily detailed journal entry expanding on the Fuller portions of her letter to Parsons, she stated, "In Margaret Fuller's Autobiography I see my own life renewed"—from her rigorous education to marriage with a loving but intellectually limited man.[74] Thereafter, defending a second self in "Margaret," Dall validated herself. This sympathetic identification goes far to account for Dall's advocacy of Fuller as well as her lectures and publications defending other women who suffered, struggled, and were "misunderstood," a recurring word in her discourse about extraordinary individuals.[75] Parsons's reply to Dall in 1852, which provides the epigraph for this essay, suggests that others felt "kindredness of experience" with Fuller as well.[76]

Dall's defense of Fuller was not, then, merely an episode of the 1880s, but a significant vocation of her adult life, eventually extending through almost sixty years. After the publication of Fuller's *Life and Complete Works* (1860) in six volumes, Dall defended Fuller against friends—the editors and other witnesses represented in *Memoirs* (the "Life" of the set)—who exposed her personal flaws and, Dall believed, spread misconceptions. She argued that although Fuller was imperfect like every human being, she overcame many of her weaknesses and therefore became a model of self-development.[77] By then it must have seemed clear to Dall that another life of Fuller and more lives like Fuller's were needed. She had recurring thoughts, as we have seen, of writing a memoir informed by her experiential and sympathetic knowledge.

Still monitoring Fuller's reputation in the 1890s and beyond, Dall deployed her skills as an agitator to secure publication for *Margaret and Her Friends* (1895), her record of Fuller's 1841 Conversations on Greek mythology, an experimental series that admitted men. That series failed, Dall suggested, because some participants apparently failed to listen or to understand one another, taxing her patience as well as Fuller's. Furthermore, some of the men, Emerson especially, wandered off the topics Fuller announced.[78] In *Transcendentalism in New England*, a lecture delivered in 1895 and published in 1897, Dall challenged Octavius Brooks Frothingham's historical book of the same title, arguing that Frothingham underestimated Fuller, Hedge, and Thoreau and asserting that New England transcendentalism began with Anne Hutchinson and ended with the death of Margaret Fuller. Yet she called herself "a Transcendentalist of the old New England sort" and concluded, "The glory of Margaret's life did not perish."[79]

Fuller's self-reliance came into question with the publication of *Love-Letters of Margaret Fuller, 1845–46* (1903), a collection of letters she wrote to New York businessman and aspiring writer James Nathan, with whom she claimed a spiritual affinity and whose confidence and affection she desired.[80] Although Dall had hoped to "remain mute," the silence of Fuller's other friends and the imminent auction of the manuscript letters to Nathan required Dall to "speak": "The responsibility was laid on me, many years ago, by Margaret's mother" and brother Richard, she asserted. Again Dall's story behind her unwritten biography of Fuller changed in detail, but its essence for her remained the same. Disturbed by "aspersions" against Fuller's character, Margaret Crane Fuller and Richard repeatedly urged Dall to write a "simple, straightforward narrative" of her life. When she demurred, saying, "'I fear I should not do her justice,'" Mrs. Fuller took her hands, kissed her forehead, and uttered words she had "silently worn like a crown" ever since: "'Mrs Dall, if Margaret were alive to-day she would choose you above all others. She would entreat you to do her this justice to quiet the malignant tongues.'" "I could not resist this," Dall recalled. Just after she began writing, however, Richard died. She never finished the book—not, in this telling, because of the Hawthornes or Peabodys but because "no publisher would take it," and she could not pay for its publication. That was "a sore disappointment." Since she "was at that time thought worthy to defend Margaret," she must "do it now."[81] Fully explicit here is her self-identification as the appropriate—indeed, designated—custodian of Fuller's reputation.

Discrediting the *Love-Letters*, which represented only part of one side of the correspondence and incorporated texts that may have been "tamper[ed] with," she argued that Fuller overestimated Nathan's worth and tried to "lift" him above mercenary concerns. The letters, if correctly understood—that is, as Dall interpreted them—were not "love letters" in the usual sense. "What personal affection she felt [for Nathan]," Dall concluded, was "maternal," comparable to her later feelings for Ossoli.[82] Years would have to pass before Fuller's readers could acknowledge her complex sexuality. In 1903 Dall was protecting her against the easy and still disreputable inference that she hungered for sexual experience. Wasn't that the Hawthornes' most inflammatory charge against Fuller's honor, more disturbing than Mozier's implication that she deceived friends into thinking she was writing a history of the Roman Revolution?

Calling on an ailing Dall in 1910, Higginson encountered the disappointed Fuller biographer. She deprecated Howe's biography, then announced that papers to be published after her own death would "place Margaret in a far higher light than had ever been shown before." She had also obtained Rebecca Spring's promise not to publish a potentially damaging document, one that could be "misunderstood," about Fuller's relationship with Nathan. Commenting in his notes that Dall (1822–1912), like most "old people," was repeating herself and had little new to offer, Higginson (1823–1911) worried, "I fear posthumous revelations, after Hawthorne's inexplicable note about M. F."[83] For Higginson, as for Dall, doing justice to Margaret Fuller required research, contacts, and vigilance.

NOTES

1. On Joseph Mozier, see Thomas Woodson, "Explanatory Notes," in Nathaniel Hawthorne, *The French and Italian Notebooks*, Centenary Edition (Columbus: Ohio State Univ. Press, 1980), 14:753n153. This edition is hereafter cited parenthetically as *CE*. Hawthorne's infamous 3 April 1858 entry appears in *CE*, 14:153–57; see Woodson, "Explanatory Notes," 153–57 and 770–72.

2. Julian Hawthorne, "Hawthorne and Margaret Fuller," *Boston Evening Transcript*, 2 January 1885, 4.
3. Caroline Healey Dall, MS, "Conversations upon the *Mythology of the Greeks*," quoted in Joel Myerson, "Caroline Dall's Reminiscences of Margaret Fuller," *Harvard Library Bulletin* 22 (October 1974): 416.
4. Nathaniel Hawthorne, quoted in Julian Hawthorne, *Nathaniel Hawthorne and His Wife* (Boston: Houghton, Mifflin, 1884), 1:259–63.
5. Gary Scharnhorst's "'We Remember No Biography Having So Many Poorly Concealed Antagonisms': Character Assassination in Julian Hawthorne's *Nathaniel Hawthorne and His Wife*," *Nathaniel Hawthorne Review* 36, no. 2 (2010): 35–40, identifies other objects of scorn. Most print reviews did not mention Fuller. My discussion of readers' responses draws upon Scharnhorst, *Nathaniel Hawthorne: An Annotated Bibliography of Comment and Criticism before 1900* (Metuchen, N.J.: Scarecrow Press, 1988); Joel Myerson, *Margaret Fuller: An Annotated Secondary Bibliography* (New York: Burt Franklin, 1977); Myerson, *Margaret Fuller: An Annotated Bibliography of Criticism, 1983–1995* (Westport, Conn.: Greenwood, 1998); and dozens of reviews.
6. Scharnhorst, "'We Remember,'" 33.
7. Thomas R. Mitchell, *Hawthorne's Fuller Mystery* (Amherst: Univ. of Massachusetts Press, 1998), 29–30.
8. Key documents among the Caroline Wells Healey Dall Papers, 1811–1917 (MHi) are identified parenthetically in the text: the letters Dall received as Letters; the record of letters she sent as Register; her journal as Journal. Scrapbook 9 is identified within the text.
9. Myerson, "Caroline Dall's Reminiscences," 415.
10. Julian's three retorts are counted. I did not count a few brief, unidentified clippings.
11. Caroline Healey Dall, "The Hawthorne Book Censured," *Springfield Republican*, 15 December 1884, 2; hereafter cited in the text as "Hawthorne Book." The entire review appears on p. 2 of the *Republican*.
12. Joan von Mehren, *Minerva and the Muse: A Life of Margaret Fuller* (Amherst: Univ. of Massachusetts Press, 1995), 25–26, 121, 134, 278.
13. Octavius Brooks Frothingham, *Memoir of William Henry Channing* (Boston: Houghton, Mifflin, 1886), 3:413–19. Dall noted Channing's passing in her journal entry of 24 December 1884.
14. Thomas Fuller Genealogy, http://www.surnameguide.com/fuller/thomas_fuller_genealogy.htm, accessed 3 June 2011.
15. Judith Mattson Bean, "'A *Presence* among Us': Fuller's Place in Nineteenth-Century Oral Culture," *ESQ: A Journal of the American Renaissance* 44 (1998): 79–123.
16. Mitchell, *Hawthorne's Fuller Mystery*, 13–14.
17. "High Tea," *Boston Evening Transcript*, 15 November 1884, 6.
18. "Margaret Fuller in a New Light," *Boston Herald*, 23 November 1884, 12.
19. Frederick T. Fuller, "Hawthorne and Margaret Fuller Ossoli," *Literary World*, 10 January 1885, 11–15. To my knowledge, this is the only rebuttal of Mozier's claim that Fuller's manuscript on the Roman Revolution never existed (ibid., 14).
20. Woodson, *CE*, 14:153–57, 770–72. Julian suppressed Nathaniel's reservations about Mozier's "veracity" (*CE*, 14:492–93) and made "several significant omissions and revisions" while lifting the notorious passage from the notebook (*CE*, 14:766). See also Mitchell, *Hawthorne's Fuller Mystery*, 21–23.
21. Richard P. Wunder, "The Irascible Hiram Powers," *American Art Journal* 4, no. 2 (1972): 10–15.

22. Julian Hawthorne, "Mr. Hawthorne and His Critics," *Boston Evening Transcript*, 5 February 1885, 4.
23. Ralph Waldo Emerson, *MMFO*, 1:236.
24. Larry J. Reynolds and Susan Belasco Smith, eds., introduction to *"These Sad but Glorious Days": Dispatches from Europe, 1846–50* (New Haven: Yale Univ. Press, 1991), 1–35; Bell Gale Chevigny, "To the Edges of Ideology: Margaret Fuller's Centrifugal Evolution," *American Quarterly* 38, no. 2 (1986): 173–201.
25. Helen R. Deese, "Caroline Healey Dall and the American Women's Movement, 1848–75," *American Nineteenth Century History* 3, no. 2 (2002): 9–10, 15, 25n7.
26. Larry R. Reynolds, in "Hawthorne and Emerson in 'The Old Manse,'" *Studies in the Novel* 12 (1991): 60–81, examines challenges to marriage.
27. Woodson, *CE*, 14:766.
28. Julian Hawthorne, "Hawthorne and Margaret Fuller," 4.
29. von Mehren, *Minerva*, 324, 382n22.
30. *MMFO*, 2:281–93; and Thomas Wentworth Higginson, *Margaret Fuller Ossoli*, 2nd ed. (reprint, New York: Chelsea House, 1981), 243–46. Higginson quotes two letters by Story.
31. Bell Gale Chevigny, "The Long Arm of Censorship: Myth-Making in Margaret Fuller's Time and Our Own," *Signs* 2, no. 2 (1976): 455.
32. von Mehren, *Minerva*, 328–29.
33. Chevigny, "Long Arm of Censorship," 452–56. Fuller and Ossoli were probably secretly married after Angelo's conception. See Capper 2, 365–67 and 601n4. Von Mehren examines the "marriage narratives" in Fuller biography, *Minerva*, 340–95, and she provides new documentary evidence of an eventual marriage in "Margaret Fuller, the Marchese Giovanni Ossoli, and the Marriage Question," *Resources for American Literary Study* 30 (2005): 104–43.
34. Mitchell lists reprints in *Hawthorne's Fuller Mystery*, 13–14.
35. Maurine H. Beasley, "Booth, Mary Louise," in *American National Biography Online*, www.anb.org, February 2000, accessed 25 June 2011.
36. Ellen B. Ballou, *The Building of the House: Houghton Mifflin's Formative Years* (Boston: Houghton Mifflin, 1970), 256.
37. [George W. Curtis], "Margaret Fuller and Hawthorne," *Harper's Weekly*, 24 January 1885, 15. Curtis was a friend of Fuller. A review of Julian's biography in *Harper's Magazine* 70 (February 1885): 489–90, does not mention Fuller but remarks that Nathaniel Hawthorne sometimes lacked "amiability."
38. Joel Myerson, "Sarah Clarke's Reminiscences of the Peabodys and Hawthorne," *Nathaniel Hawthorne Journal* (1973): 130–33.
39. J. F. Clarke to Sarah Clarke, 9 and 10 December 1884, in James Freeman Clarke Correspondence, MS Am 1569, (1267), MH-H; hereafter cited as Clarke Correspondence.
40. Clarke Correspondence, 1269.
41. Sarah Clarke, "Margaret Fuller Ossoli and Hawthorne," *Boston Evening Transcript*, 12 December 1884, 4.
42. When Dall agreed to write is unknown. See Caroline Healey Dall, *Margaret and Her Friends: Or Ten Conversations* (1895; reprint, New York: Arno Press, 1962), 13–14; Joel Myerson, "Mrs. Dall Edits Miss Fuller: The Story of *Margaret and Her Friends*," *PBSA* 27, no. 2 (1978): 194 and 194n28; and von Mehren, *Minerva*, 344. Mrs. Fuller died in 1859, Richard in 1869.
43. Clarke referred to William W. Story, whom George Alfred Townsend quotes in "Story on Margaret Fuller's Husband," *Cincinnati Enquirer*; copied in *Boston Daily Advertiser*, 26 February 1885, 2.

44. Clarke wrote Higginson: "Your notice of Hawthorne & Wife was admirable. I have bought several copies to send to [illegible] friends" (25 December 1844, in Clarke Correspondence, 508).
45. James F. Clarke to Sarah Clarke, 20 December 1884, in Clarke Correspondence, 1270, quoting Frederic Henry Hedge.
46. James F. Clarke, "Hawthorne and Margaret Fuller," *Independent*, 1 January 1885, 1–2.
47. For example: "The Hawthorne-Fuller Case," *Literary World*, 10 January 1885, 10; and John W. Chadwick, "Mr. Julian Hawthorne," *Christian Register*, 26 March 1885, 195.
48. Mitchell, *Hawthorne's Fuller Mystery*, 15–16.
49. James F. Clarke to Sarah Clarke, 11 January 1885, in Clarke Correspondence, 1271.
50. *Every Other Saturday*, 6 December 1884, 429.
51. On Chandler, see Ednah C. Silver, in *Sketches of the New Church in America on a Background of Civic and Social Life* (Boston: Massachusetts New Church Union, 1920), 267–68.
52. "The Outlook," *Every Other Saturday*, 14 February 1885, 49, attacks [Higginson], "Nathaniel Hawthorne and His Wife," *Atlantic Monthly* 55 (February 1885): 259–65.
53. In *Hawthorne's Fuller Mystery*, 19–20, Mitchell notes Julian's disapproval of expanding roles for women.
54. "The Real Hawthorne," *New-York Tribune*, 16 November 1884, 4.
55. Mitchell, *Hawthorne's Fuller Mystery*, 27–28. Mitchell states, "after 1884," most of Fuller's books went out of print (39). That does not prove Julian destroyed her reputation, as Mitchell contends. Fuller's audience differed from Hawthorne's. Phyllis Cole writes, "A vital memory of Fuller's life and thought . . . persisted among advocates of women's rights for more than half a century" after 1850 ("The Nineteenth-Century Women's Rights Movement and the Canonization of Margaret Fuller," *ESQ: A Journal of the American Renaissance* 44 [1998]: 2).
56. Cole, "Nineteenth-Century Women's Rights," 1–33; and Bean, "'A *Presence*,'" 79–123.
57. Christopher Pearse Cranch to Thomas Wentworth Higginson, 2 December 1884, Margaret Fuller Ossoli Papers, MS Am 1452 (7), Boston Public Library.
58. Christopher Pearse Cranch, "Hawthorne and Margaret Fuller," *Boston Evening Transcript*, 9 January 1885, 6.
59. Christopher Pearse Cranch, "Hawthorne and Pharisaism," *Boston Evening Transcript*, 10 February 1885, 6.
60. Christopher Pearse Cranch, quoted in *The Life and Letters of Christopher Pearse Cranch*, ed. Leonora Cranch Scott (1917; reprint, New York: AMS Press, 1969), 352.
61. These documents are unlocated.
62. Helen Deese, ed., *Daughter of Boston: The Extraordinary Diary of a Nineteenth-Century Woman: Caroline Healey Dall* (Boston: Beacon Press, 2005), 295–96.
63. Caroline Healey Dall to Thomas Wentworth Higginson, 12 May 1884, Rare Books and Manuscripts, Ms Am 1450 (211), Boston Public Library.
64. Thomas Wentworth Higginson, "Wedded Isolation," *Woman's Journal*, 20 December 1884, 407; see also n. 52 above.
65. Peabody's letter to Parsons has not been found. Parsons had been Peabody's pupil (Ronda, 53).
66. Marshall, 357–62, 412–14, 552n358.
67. For example: *The Letters, 1857–1864* (1987), ed. Thomas Woodson et al., *CE*, 14:115–16, 589–93.
68. Publicly and privately, Peabody argued that Hawthorne's notebooks reflected "impressions" and "mere facts," not settled opinions. See *LEPP*, 424–30; and Minna Caroline

Smith, "Elizabeth Peabody: Reminiscences and Interests of Her Active Life," *Boston Daily Advertiser*, 25 August 1887, 4.

69. Parsons's invalidism is mentioned in Dall's papers—for example, Parsons to Dall, Letters, [2?] September 1851, 18 November 1853, and 11 April 1858; and Journal, 24 November 1854.

70. Parsons and Cheney became friends in 1851 through the School of Design for Women. See Ednah Cheney, *Reminiscences* (Boston: Lee & Shepard, 1902), 72. On Cheney and Dall see Helen R. Deese, ed., *Selected Journals of Caroline Healey Dall* (Boston: Massachusetts Historical Society, 2006), 6n10. Cheney and Peabody both participated in Boston's Radical Club.

71. "Miss Peabody's Reminiscences of Margaret's Married Life," *Boston Evening Transcript*, 10 June 1885, Scrapbook 9. Dall also clipped Rebecca B. Spring, "Margaret Fuller," *Harper's Monthly* 71 (June 1884), 146–47, a previously unnoticed document in the controversy.

72. Deese, introduction to *Selected Journals*, 1:xxvii, xxxix, 538, xix.

73. Dall copied this letter into her log, not her usual practice.

74. Dall, *Selected Journals*, 1:359.

75. Deese surveys Dall's lectures and publications in the introduction to *Selected Journals*, 1:xxxiii–xxxviii. Deese graciously directed me to important passages in Dall's journals when most were unpublished.

76. Anna Q. T. Parsons to Caroline Healey Dall, 8 April 1852, Caroline Wells Healey Dall Papers, 1811–1917, MHi.

77. Caroline Healey Dall, "Margaret Fuller Ossoli," *North American Review* 91 (July 1860): 119–29.

78. Tiffany K. Wayne discusses Dall's shifting of "blame" for the series' failure to the male participants (Wayne, 23–26).

79. Caroline Healey Dall, *Transcendentalism in New England: A Lecture*, reprint of an article from the *Journal of Speculative Philosophy* 23, no. 1 (Boston: Roberts Bros., 1897), 32, 38. On this lecture, see Helen R. Deese, "Transcendentalism from the Margins: The Experience of Caroline Healey Dall," in Capper and Wright, 527–47.

80. von Mehren, *Minerva*, 206, 208–14.

81. Caroline Healey Dall, "Margaret Fuller's Letters," *Springfield Republican*, 10 December 1903, 7.

82. Dall, "Margaret Fuller's Letters," 7. To a less protective reviewer, the letters bespoke a "sentimental friendship," some flirtation on Nathan's part, and "sisterly," "motherly," and lover-like feelings on Fuller's side ("Margaret Fuller and Milton: The Love Letters of Margaret Fuller," *Springfield Republican*, 16 December 1903, 11).

83. Thomas Wentworth Higginson, "Interview," Fuller Papers, box "Miscellaneous A," bMSAm 1086 (1), MH-H. Individual items within this box are unnumbered. Thanks to Phyllis Cole for calling this document to my attention. Fuller was traveling with Rebecca and Marcus Spring when her relationship with Nathan ended. Published "revelations" originating with Dall have not been identified. I am testing a hypothesis about Dall's intentions.

INTERLUDE

"Address of Mrs. [Julia Ward] Howe," from *Ednah Dow Cheney: Memorial Meeting, New England Women's Club, February 20, 1905* (Boston: George H. Ellis, 1905), 3–6.

Of Mrs. Cheney's girlhood I know only what she has told me. She was early attracted by Margaret Fuller. At the age of sixteen, having a sum of money at command, she invested it by becoming a pupil of that remarkable woman. Early in their intercourse, Margaret asked, "Is life rich to you?" "It is since I have known you," was Ednah's reply. In years that followed she was fed with the fine spirit of Transcendentalism, which left its impress upon her life. I had no acquaintance with her before her marriage, but met her soon after this at some meetings of women which Theodore Parker held in his famous study. . . .

She became, as you all know, one of the founders of this club. I also enjoyed this honor, but was not, as she was, one of those who pledged the financial backing which was necessary for the starting of the enterprise. It was on this new ground that I first gained some acquaintance with her noble qualities. . . . She fully appreciated the varieties of human taste and inclination; and, while she could philosophize soundly and deeply, she could also appreciate the need of relaxation and amusement. We were all younger thirty years ago than we are now. I remember some club charades, in one of which Mrs. Cheney personated Father Hyacinthe, who was in Boston at that time. In another I played the part of Punch to her Judy, and Susan Hale, inimitable in her comic vein, personated the devil, who carries Punch away in requital for his evil deeds. . . .

In my club life and in my suffrage work, Mrs. Cheney was a prominent figure, always wise, always helpful. But it was in the Association for the Advancement of Women that I became most intimately associated with her. . . . For the space of twenty-five years we held an annual congress, in which the officers and speakers were women. We went north as far as Canada, west to Colorado, south to New Orleans. In this last-named city Mrs. Cheney read a paper on her beloved Margaret Fuller, of whom she always spoke with a deep feeling of reverence and gratitude. On these occasions Mrs. Cheney would wear beautiful Cheney silks and rich laces. She had no fondness for dress, but understood its importance sufficiently to care to make always a suitable appearance. The beauty of her head needed no adornment. Her presence in public assemblies was impressive, her countenance and demeanor expressing the calm dignity of her character,—a dignity tempered, if I may say so, by the deepest and tenderest humanity.

Let me imagine, for a moment, that we are starting on one of our long-distant trips. I come from my Boston home. Ednah Cheney meets me at the station, with a little group of cheerful, determined sisters, who have set their faces toward Canada, Denver, or New Orleans. . . . As we journey, our band is re-enforced by members who join us at various stopping-places. . . . Ednah Cheney, Maria Mitchell, Abby May,—with such women to show, it made little difference to the company assembled if our trunks, with best dresses, had been delayed in transportation. Talk of the man with the hoe! We were the women of the plough. To us it was given to draw the furrow and drop the seed from which have sprung up clubs and federations scarcely to be numbered.

"A Woman's Place"

The Transcendental Realism of Mary Wilkins Freeman

SUSAN M. STONE

In an 1895 oration on Margaret Fuller, Ednah Dow Cheney praised the leader of Conversations for the "force of her intellect," a force achieved "not by borrowing the peculiar weapons of man, but by using her own with courage and skill." Such a leader of women, Cheney told her national feminist audience, had "planted . . . the seeds of thought, principle, and purpose" in her own life as a teenager at the Conversations, "and I owe it to her to speak in her name, to try to make her life again fruitful in others."[1]

Cheney gave a particularly direct and eloquent account of Fuller's influence, even as she tried to extend it. But others, among them feminist writer Mary Wilkins Freeman, followed Fuller more implicitly in the 1890s, even joining Cheney in the instruction of younger women. In Freeman's 1899 essay "Good Wits, Pen and Paper," she sounded notes of transcendental self-reliance in offering the following advice to would-be female writers: "break free from dullness and complacency," "sharpen your eyes and ears to see and hear everything," "write in [your] own way," "look upon the scene with American eyes," "learn to be your own mentor."[2] Though Freeman was born two years after Fuller's death, and though she penned mostly fiction and lived much of her life in small villages rather than Boston, she and her work resonate with Cheney's contemporary account of Fuller. In Freeman's written work and role as mentor to others, Fuller's transcendental feminist "seeds" also bloomed and grew.

This study is situated between the tracing of influence and the discovery of a broader cultural intertextuality between the two writers: it repositions Freeman as a New England–focused, feminist transcendental realist more than a generation removed from, yet writing in proximity and response to, Margaret Fuller and the networks of Boston women that sustained Fuller's memory and work.[3] Transcendental realism, a vein of the broader realist movement, provides a new angle of vision for the consideration of literary work after the

Civil War as a response to a continuing transcendental call or ethos. Without genre-based, geographic, or chronological restrictions, yet cognizant of the ways in which later authors' perspectives are multiply influenced, the concept of transcendental realism offers opportunities for fresh interpretations of both familiar and lesser-known writing, and it acknowledges the legacy of transcendentalism via common thematic connections and literary aims shared by the core figures and later writers and activists. Among the continuities especially relevant to Fuller and the women writing after her are insistence upon truth and accuracy of vision, promotion of self-culture, celebration of the real and commonplace, discovery and interpretation of intuited divinity, and—through these common concerns—use of literary work to reform society.[4] In her stories, Freeman models what Charles Capper argues is the "central defining characteristic" of literary transcendentalism: "its collective commitment to change people's lives by changing their minds."[5]

Historically intense debates and shifts in scholarly evaluation of Freeman's works underlie my claim of her kinship with Fuller's feminist transcendentalism. Freeman's initial champions, realists Hamlin Garland and William Dean Howells, as well as twentieth-century critics F. O. Matthiessen, Fred Lewis Pattee, and Van Wyck Brooks, applauded her verisimilitude and attention to detail, focusing on her description of familiar rural settings and New England character types. So admired was Freeman for these accomplishments that, in 1925, she was awarded the inaugural William Dean Howells Medal by the American Academy of Arts and Letters; today an inscription on the Academy's bronze door is still "Dedicated to the Memory of Mary E. Wilkins Freeman and the Women Writers of America."[6] Two years later her longtime publisher, Harper & Brothers, crowned her career by producing *The Best Stories of Mary E. Wilkins*. However, though Freeman maintained a high level of popularity and critical approval for another decade after these accolades, much of her corpus then drifted out of publication and was reclassified as "local color," minor realism, or regionalism, most likely because she dealt predominantly with women's lives in rural settings. Fortunately, late twentieth-century scholars Marjorie Pryse, Josephine Donovan, and Susan Allen Toth rejected these judgments, revived interest in Freeman's work, and reaffirmed her place among the major realists of her era. Additionally, these newer Freeman scholars repositioned her alongside Sarah Orne Jewett and Charlotte Perkins Gilman as an early feminist and psychological realist.[7] With their valuable essays and new anthologies of Freeman's works, as well as a pair of revealing literary biographies and a collection of previously unpublished letters, Freeman's rich life and struggles as a writer emerged alongside new feminist views of her fiction.[8]

The discovery of transcendental impulses in the work of a fictional realist arose from these various phases of reassessment, with Freeman's biographers

Edward Foster and Perry Westbrook first to establish ties between her writing and that of Ralph Waldo Emerson and Henry David Thoreau. In turn, the transcendental ideologies of intuition and self-reliance have been discovered as important resources in Freeman's inward-turning feminist character studies.[9] In the words of her 1906 novel title, many of her characters live *By the Light of the Soul*. Building on these breakthroughs of literary, social, and biographical criticism, I turn to Freeman in relation not only to Emerson but also to the precursor who united feminist and transcendental thematics, Margaret Fuller.[10]

Although the link was not explored critically for a half-century after her death, Mary Ella Wilkins Freeman encountered and embraced literary transcendentalism in formative years.[11] Born in 1852, Freeman spent her childhood and early adolescence in Randolph, Massachusetts, a farming town just fifteen miles south of the transcendentalists' Boston hub, and then during her young womanhood lived in Brattleboro, Vermont. Raised by strict Congregationalist parents, by the age of nineteen she was avidly reading and discussing Emerson and Thoreau in active resistance to the village ethos, along with her equally inquisitive friend Evelyn "Evie" Sawyer (Severance). She had just returned to Brattleboro from a disappointing year at Mount Holyoke College, which pleased her no more than it had Emily Dickinson a quarter-century before. As she recalled afterward, she "did not behave at all well" at the religiously orthodox school, due to "monotony of diet and too strenuous goadings of conscience." Thereafter her real education came through reading, as she and Evie ranged widely not only in the transcendentalists but also (across gender and genre) in Poe, Goethe, Dickens, Thackeray, Harriet Beecher Stowe, and many poets.[12] Of all these writers, however, it was Emerson that Freeman explicitly acknowledged in her 1913 essay "The Girl Who Wants to Write," describing herself as from early years "committed to the teaching of 'Nature,' 'The American Scholar,' and 'Self-Reliance.'"[13]

Freeman certainly enacted a girl's version of "Self-Reliance" in becoming a writer. She first tried out the literary marketplace in her early twenties because of her family's economic need. Then her instincts guided her to move from poetry and children's fiction to short stories for adults. In 1883 came the miracle of acceptance and a check for $25 from editor Mary Louise Booth at New York's prestigious *Harper's Bazar*. A series of other stories followed in the same magazine for women, followed by inclusion in the even more illustrious *Harper's New Monthly*, and in 1877 *Harper's* published her first book-length collection of stories. In the meantime, however, she relocated her life and base for writing from the family's pragmatically chosen location in Vermont back to their ancestral home in Massachusetts. An early romance had failed, and both parents and all her siblings had died. After a period of bitter doubt and loneliness, Freeman took her father's modest inheritance and moved in 1884 into the Randolph home of her closest childhood friend, Mary John Wales.[14] Randolph and her friendship with Wales would ground her life for years afterward.[15]

Along with Freeman's rising stature as a writer, these cherished ties would also provide the base from which a village writer could take on Boston's literary establishment. As she wrote to Booth in 1888, the year after her book appeared, she was relying on the connections of an avid supporter from the city to "meet some Boston people." "She knows all the people I want to meet, Miss Jewett, and Mrs. Fields etc. and they are to take me out to Concord to take tea with the Emersons. Won't it be lovely?" Ralph Waldo Emerson had died six years before, so it was to the shrine of his house and the conversation of his wife and daughter that Freeman was making her pilgrimage. But she later paid homage to both the father of American transcendentalism and his family through her characters Mr. and Mrs. Emerson in "The Lost Ghost," a story about a Boston family relocating to the country.[16]

Nothing comparable to the acknowledgment of Emerson specifies Freeman's reading of Fuller, though the young woman's wide survey of books is likely to have included her. More to the point, Freeman pursued her writing career in settings where old transcendentalism, new realism, and Fuller's feminist works were actively embraced at once. Even the New York world of *Harper's* knew and defended Fuller. Mary De Jong, in the essay preceding my own in this collection, shows editor Mary Louise Booth receiving vehement defenses of Fuller from Caroline Healey Dall amid the 1884–85 scandal of Julian Hawthorne's attack. At exactly the same season, Freeman traveled to New York for the first time and met Booth, after months of exchanging letters.[17] Even more personally, in the Boston region that she had newly chosen for her writing life, recent biographies of Fuller, as well as the newspaper blitz arising from Hawthorne's attack, would have made her story and ideas vivid to an up-and-coming woman writer. The best clue, however, is Freeman's listing to Booth of the people she "wanted to meet" beyond the Emersons: Sarah Orne Jewett and Annie Fields. Freeman succeeded in becoming a visitor to the powerful literary salon centered at Fields's home on Charles Street. In turn, Fields introduced her to older writers like Jewett, and she directly advocated for Freeman's literary productions with her husband, influential *Atlantic Monthly* editor and book publisher James T. Fields.[18]

Annie Fields, as Rita Gollin shows, was "in many senses a facilitator—between authors as a hostess, and, as a writer, between generations who could become acquainted with one another." Fields herself compared the conversations in her salon with Fuller's, celebrating the transcendentalists while also drawing in Elizabeth Stuart Phelps, Sarah Orne Jewett, and Mary Wilkins Freeman. "And so the ball rolls on," she exulted.[19] If her aims were not openly political, they certainly were woman centered and feminist. This long-running, multigenerational group—fueled by friendship, rooted in love of literature and transcendentalism, and united around issues of gender and reform—included many who were friends, students, or avid readers of Fuller, such as Cheney, Louisa May Alcott, Lydia Maria Child, Elizabeth Peabody, Julia Ward Howe, Eliza Farnham Pratt, and Jewett.[20] In such a company of New England writers in the late 1880s, Fuller would have been a name to conjure with. One especially influential mediator of Fuller in the Fields circle may have been Harriet Beecher Stowe, whom Freeman had first read almost two decades before, shortly after the publication of *Oldtown Folks* (1869). As Monika Mueller points out, in that novel Stowe had diverted the thematics of female self-reliance to the New England village in presenting such "Fullerian virgins" as Miss Minerva Randall, who could both navigate a ship and read Greek and Latin.[21] In later years, at Annie Fields's salon, the two authors could talk directly about their respective New England heroines.

A larger cultural world of Boston women also strengthened the bonds among authors fostered by Annie Fields. The politically oriented American Woman Suffrage Association was located in Boston, and the New England Women's Club (NEWC) also brought together writers and reformers with society ladies and seekers. This group was so devoted to Margaret Fuller that they celebrated her birthday. Again personal friendships supported cultural connections. Through Booth, Freeman enjoyed acquaintance with Antoinette Brown Blackwell, the first female Congregational minister in the United States, who became a leader of Boston's feminist organizations, extending her reach from the NEWC to suffrage advocacy and publication. Freeman's Brattleboro friend Evie Sawyer Severance, still close by letters, was related by marriage to Caroline Seymour Severance, a New England Women's Club's founder. Fields, Alcott, and other writers also belonged.[22]

The culture of women's clubs was integral to both literature and reform. Freeman repeatedly acknowledged its importance, both to herself and to others. She was apparently not an official member of the New England Women's Club despite connections to the group. However, once she married in 1902 and moved to New Jersey, Freeman and her sisters-in-law participated actively in Metuchen's "Quiet Hour Club"; once more they read Emerson's "Self-Reliance," while also discussing the pros and cons of coeducation and considering the moral value of opening museums, libraries, and art galleries on Sundays. Their lively conversations on literature and philosophy attempted, as Margaret Klawunn claims, to "bring together the women in Metuchen for mental culture, social intercourse, and a sympathetic understanding of whatever women [were] doing along the lines of progress." As an active member of this all-female association, which followed the patterns of Boston's NEWC and New York City's Sorosis, Freeman herself promoted "female culture," debated philosophy, encouraged public speaking, and created literature alongside other notable women, including the group's founder, Hester M. Poole. More than a simple book circle, the club called upon each woman to lead a discussion, to research and speak publicly about literature, to write, and to prepare women for activity outside the home.[23]

Freeman, then, experienced an immersion in Fuller-influenced cultural groups, reinforcing the personal reading of Fuller's work that may have come even earlier in her life. The result is that in both her fiction and her criticism, self-reliance is seen and tested explicitly through the lens of gender. Her work promotes *women's* autonomy in opposition to prescriptive environments, pondering as well such concerns of the overlapping feminist and transcendental communities as individual inspiration, personal protest, and democratic principles. Until recently these intersections would have seemed surprising, given the fifty-year gap between the transcendentalists' pre–Civil War peak of influence and Freeman's life and work. The plausibility of reading her texts in such a light, however, grows alongside other studies in this collection on the later nineteenth-century literary work and reform of Elizabeth Peabody, Caroline Dall, Julia Ward Howe, Louisa May Alcott, and Pauline Hopkins, all significantly linked to antebellum transcendental, abolitionist, and feminist legacies. As Cheney recalled, "seeds of thought" had come to life across decades in the ongoing careers of both elders and new protégées. Fuller's ideas were available for Freeman's new and original imagining of "a woman's place."

Most significantly, Freeman shared with Fuller a scrutiny of the feminist implication of self-reliance for the dual conditions of a woman's life, marriage and singlehood. *Woman in the Nineteenth Century* had laid down the challenge that "union" was possibly only for "those who are units," that a woman's first obligation was "as a nature to grow, . . . as a soul to live free and unimpeded." Her Miranda, a fictional type of herself, embodied such possibilities in independence from men. Although Fuller's essay also idealizes four ascending types of marriage, from household partnership to union of spirit, her argument often dwells on the thwarted circumstances of wives. The wife of the "irritable trader" has no opportunity to speak for herself, and an old woman who has lived with her husband for forty years in a hut on a mountain cannot say why she has accepted "so barren a spot." "[I do] not know," the old woman replies. *"It was the man's notion."* Fuller comments to her reader, "I would not have it so."[24]

Neither would Freeman "have it so." Herself a single woman for most of her years, she created female characters isolated in rural New England, trying to navigate a village-based, postwar world short on men, money, and tolerable marriage possibilities. The result is visible both in her most widely anthologized stories and in her lesser known, newly available work. Among the best-known fiction, for example, "A New England Nun" represents the case of a happily single woman declining long-promised marriage, while "The Revolt of 'Mother'" presents a woman finding voice and power against her husband's "notion." The present study focuses on two of Freeman's fictional pieces among the many that might be viewed through this lens: the relatively familiar story "A Conflict Ended" (1886) and the newly recovered "Juliza" (1892), which Mary R. Reichardt notes was never included by Freeman in one of her original collections.[25] The first ends in a pair of marriages, the latter in a remarkable charting of unmarried vocation. In these negotiations of spinsterhood and marriage, Freeman explores what Leah Blatt Glasser has characterized as a battleground of "conflicts between defiance and submission, self-fulfillment and self-sacrifice."[26] Such characterization of women's battles is positioned as well amid the concern for creativity, identity, mentoring, and voice that would inform Freeman's advice to would-be writers in "Good Wits, Pen, and Paper" (1899).

The impulse to allegorize that led Freeman to name a fictional family "Emerson" finds even wider expression in "A Conflict Ended," where the names of characters and settings seem to allude playfully to her feminist and transcendental precursors. One suitor is George Elliot (male nom de plume of the female British realist); his fiancée is Margy (diminutive of Margaret); and the customer for whom she is creating a hat "Mis' Fuller." The drama unfolds in the village of Acton: can it be a coincidence that a real Acton lies alongside Concord in eastern Massachusetts?[27] But the town name has a wider possible implication as well, as the two heroines "act on" their convictions in negotiating marriage. Such a reading is supported by the older heroine's name, Esther, alluding clearly to the Old Testament exemplum of female voice and confrontational bravery. And her would-be male partner is Marcus Woodman, who combines Roman rigidity and New England woodenness under the shared "mark" of a defective historical Christianity.[28]

At once pathetic and humorous, "A Conflict Ended" opens with conflict-causer Marcus, who has refused to enter the Acton Congregational Church for a decade, stubbornly sitting on its steps during services, sacrificing his engagement to Esther Barney, his social status, and his productive place in the community because he does not like the "new" minister. Despite initial praise for his nonviolent action, Esther is careful to distinguish between this potentially Thoreauvian behavior, born of principle, and his later presence on the steps, which she attributes to a gendered, foolish resistance to change. Marcus, she declares to Margy, has "got so much mulishness in him it makes him seem almost miraculous." His peculiar behavior is no less than an addiction, which he has taken to "the way other men take to smoking and drinking" (*SSS*, 78, 88). Through Esther's vernacular voice, Freeman is offering a critique of both male intransigency and Protestant divisiveness, two New England traditions she had personally and culturally witnessed.

In fact the story's real miracles and creative acts of resistance are the work of women, as Marcus's stubborn passivity liberates and inspires Esther. She has long since dismissed earlier thoughts of marriage to him and claimed her own place in the community as owner of a millinery shop, thereby serving and socializing within an active, multigenerational circle of single and married women, including Marcus's mother. But she continues to care for him, and one Sunday, amid his step-sitting vigil, Esther tries to get Marcus to accept her parasol as protection from both the sun and the condescension of the parishioners' glares. Narrative language depersonalizes her act of will as the exercise of an "intense, nervous nature" against his even greater force. She is initially unsuccessful because the two middle-aged lovers "were on such different planes that [her will] slid by his with its own movement; there could be no contact even of antagonism between them." The word "movement" is central here, resonating with the larger women's movement toward new ideas and opportunities. Movement opposes fixity, and Esther is its agent. For a second time she holds out the parasol, now pointing it at him "like a weapon" (*SSS*, 75).

Caught off balance and forced to pay attention, Marcus awkwardly accepts the parasol and looks to her for approval. In a delightful reversal of Victorian-era gender roles, Esther becomes his rational, powerful, forward looking protector and Marcus a literal *homme covert* protected in the shade of her feminine accessory.[29] Later offering to join Marcus's protest on the steps, Esther might seem to concede, but actually she continues the challenge that allows him to move forward literally, figuratively, and philosophically: he confesses to long weariness with his vigil, marries Esther in a spirit of open communication, and enters the church at last (*SSS*, 88–89). Esther's action prompts Marcus to realize what she has always known but only recently been able to communicate; she has managed to change not only herself but also her partner. In Fuller's terms, Esther and Marcus each have become genuine and equal "units," forming a "union" of value to both of them.

Alongside the negotiations of this couple, Esther's new millinery shop assistant, Margy Wilson, also responds to an offer of marriage from George Elliot. Margy rejects self-sacrifice and takes her fledgling feminism a step farther than her mentor-employer. George has assumed that his unpleasant mother (also a defector from the Congregational minister's fold) will live in the same house with them, but Margy tells Esther that she is "going to have it an understood thing that [she is] going with George, and [she] ain't going with his mother." George will have to choose between the two women in his life. "I don't care," Margy assures Esther, "I'll show him I can get along without him" (*SSS*, 77, 78). From start to finish, however, Margy cannot get along without Esther; she needs her guidance and friendship. Each makes the other better. As Reichardt comments, for Freeman "women's relationships . . . are at once more fundamental, substantial, and tenacious than women's relationships with men."[30]

The story's wider transcendentalist and feminist implications emerge as the two women talk. Telling Esther that she is out of sorts and looking for an outlet, Margy "go[es] right to work on Mis' Fuller's bonnet." Rather than staying with the grain—of the velvet and of the town—Margy realizes that she is agitated and unable to follow established patterns. She repeatedly "cuts everything bias," but Esther tells her to "never mind" because patterns "ain't much anyway" (*SSS*, 78). In the end, what Margy creates is both liberating for her and most likely satisfying for Mis' Fuller, who will be the first in Acton to try something new. Although at one point Margy says that she has "about made up [her] mind it's a woman's place to give in mostly" to George and his mother (*SSS*, 79), she uses the conditional words "about" and "mostly" in a way that tells of her less accommodating side: the conversations with Esther have sparked inner dissatisfaction, and she is still seeking out an egalitarian union. In what Susan Allen Toth calls her "positive drive toward fulfillment," Margy becomes a better version of herself and her mentor.[31] She prompts Esther to think about her relationship with Marcus again in a new light, thus initiating a two-way process of thought. Ultimately, Margy's mother-in-law-to-be ends up living with another son, and marriage plans with George proceed.

This happy ending is given a new, unconventional meaning—for Margy and for the story as a whole—because it is so much the product of women's wills. "A Conflict Ended" represents a much wider body of Freeman's work precisely in the extent of its conflict, of women vocally rebelling against the status quo and claiming agency. Biographer Edward Foster quotes an unpublished manuscript—unusual within Freeman's corpus for its first-person voice—that appears especially to express the author's own kindred thoughts. This fragmentary text is also noteworthy in phrasing resistance as response to metaphysical circumstance, in a manner worthy of Fuller or Dickinson. "I am a rebel and what is worse a rebel against the Overgovernment of all creation," declares the narrative voice of "Jane Lennox." "I even dare to think that, infinitesimal as I am, . . . I, through my rebellion, have power. All negation has power."[32]

"Juliza," written in 1892 but unpublished in Freeman's lifetime, expresses that rebellion in a much more fully realized fictional world. It also extends the exploration of love, work, self-culture, and socially prescribed gender limitations begun in "A Conflict Ended." In this story the nonconformist title character ultimately chooses to devote herself to public speaking rather than to a man and marriage, although the path to this decision is not at all straightforward. Through her gifts of oratory and intellect, Juliza Peck recalls both Fuller and the women abolitionists' claiming of public voice; she might even be traced back through Fuller to such romantic prototypes as Germaine de Staël's Corinne, whose verbal artistry fills the public spaces of Rome.[33] Unlike her giggling, fashion-focused, man-chasing peers, Juliza Peck, a "heavily built" young woman "with a certain importance about her," has been home-schooled by her "majestic" mother in relative isolation from the oppressive, patriarchal mores of Stony Brook (another name with connotations of rigidity).[34] In her education and resulting self-dependence, she is the most like Fuller's Miranda of all Freeman's heroines, though the formation of these traits comes from a mother rather than a father. Juliza's relation to the town is primarily through her public renditions of poetry, performed with an elocutionary skill that itself has been taught by her mother. As a result of inwardness and independence, however, she is ignorant of the power hierarchy and "breaks the rules" of the separate spheres.[35] Soon conventional expectations are reversed in humorous but critically significant ways.

In a courtship scene reminiscent of, yet even more confrontational than, those in "A Conflict Ended," Juliza frets over her childhood friend Frank Williams, whom she mistakenly supposes to be her intended husband. She is concerned at his inability to take care of himself rather than her own prospects for married life. "What makes you act so?" she asks Frank, as they walk home together from one of her brilliant, well-attended oratorical performances. He has become hungry, irritable, and befuddled by "tryin' to do the cookin'" while his mother lies ill. As his despair builds, Juliza, the epitome of common sense, decides that "there ain't but one thing to do"—marry Frank to rescue him from his own ineptitude (*US*, 24–25). Assuming that he will also be persuaded by this logic, she voices her willingness. An awkward moment ensues, and Frank must, in keeping with his name, be "frank." Hesitatingly, he suggests to Juliza that "there's something to be considered besides common sense, sometimes," thus alerting her to the possibility that he might love someone else. Confused about his answer and a bit nervous about what this breach of propriety might do to her public reputation, Juliza still does not regret being turned down. On the contrary, in a response closely akin to that of Freeman's more famous "New England Nun," she sighs with relief that Frank has dismissed her proposal, and she goes home to have her mother explain exactly why Frank "don't want to marry" a strong woman like her (*US*, 26). Even though the mother has produced this independent and intellectual daughter, she is shocked at Juliza's breach of traditional courtship protocols:

> "Juliza Peck, you didn't ask Frank Williams to marry you?"
> "No, I didn't ask him; I told him I would."
> "Do you know what you've done?"
> "What?"

> "What? You've made yourself a laughin' stock all over Stony Brook."
>
> "I don't see why I have, I'm sure."
>
> "Don't you know girls don't tell young men they'll marry 'em unless they're asked."
>
> "I don't see why they don't."
>
> "You needn't tell me you didn't know better than that." Juliza turned about, and fronted her mother calmly.
>
> "No I didn't, an' I don't," said she. "I don't see why it's any worse for a girl to speak than 'tis for a man." (*US*, 27)

Juliza is exploring what Martha J. Cutter, in her analysis of "The Revolt of 'Mother,'" calls the "frontiers of language."[36] Sure of herself and her words, Juliza rejects conventional ideas about courtship, takes the initiative, and proposes marriage. Assuming that Frank, like Marcus in "A Conflict Ended," needs her protection and guidance, she becomes centered and purpose driven. Through speech much like that of Sarah Penn, the rebellious "Mother" in Freeman's best-known work, Juliza becomes a profound "speaking subject," one described by the narrator in masculine, even phallic, terms as a "massive pillar" of "certain dignity" (*US*, 29). Unsatisfied with the cultural norms, she seeks to "redefine a linguistic frontier" and cut through the mentality of separate spheres.[37] Yet, unlike "Mother," Juliza begins her act of rebellion with this sort of speech, rather than arriving at it late in life and marriage. Moreover, it is significant that, out of respect for her mother's abilities and "energetic fire," Juliza makes her marriage proposal knowing that she is less needed at home than with Frank, whom the narrator depicts in traditionally feminine (and debilitating) language as "shrinking," "hesitating," "feeble," "blushing," and "constrained" (*US*, 28–30). Fuller's sense of the sexes as a "great radical dualism . . . perpetually passing into one another" is here explored in directly subversive terms.[38]

Granted a reprieve from a potentially unfulfilling partnership, Juliza looks inward and experiences a sense of liberty and clarity; her soul expands, her mind soars, and she becomes not just an actor but active. Like Miranda and the "Fullerian virgins" in Stowe's fiction, she arrives at acute personal insight once the distraction of courtship is removed.[39] Like Esther and Margy in "A Conflict Ended," she stops asking questions and starts giving orders. Indeed Freeman's protagonist, in Alicia Suskin Ostriker's famous feminist description, is "stealing the language" of men,[40] appropriating and altering it to celebrate herself, to communicate better with men, and to transcend prescribed gender roles. She understands—and helps her mother, Frank, and the reader to understand—that she does not need or want a man to support her economically or emotionally, although she is more than capable of doing so for him, if she should so choose.

But the story does not end with this feminist victory alone. Juliza is of a new generation and creates her own rules. Frank is of the old order and needs both a wife to tend to him and a lesson about the potential for different types of mutually satisfying male-female relationships. Hence, despite her mother's initial objections, Juliza does what needs to be done: she claims control not only of her own fate but also of Frank's. In a feminist version of *Cyrano de Bergerac*, Juliza enthusiastically takes on Frank—and his courtship of the woman he actually loves, Lily Emmons—as a project. Frank is comically clueless about how to communicate with the opposite sex and relies upon Juliza's writing and speaking skills to win Lily's consent. Juliza's mother, old-fashioned around the edges despite her dominant position in marriage and her training of Juliza, is not so easily convinced that this act—and Juliza's resolution to remain unmarried—are good things. She sees Juliza as defying not just one but three established social conventions: first, that adult women should be married and dependent upon men; second, that women should never tell males what to do or presume to speak for them; and third, that performing for self-gratification "ain't a woman's place" (*US*, 33). Undoubtedly, Freeman makes these issues prominent because she knew of—and worried about—many women like Juliza's mother who denied their own daughters, sisters, or neighbors the opportunity to live for themselves. Her own mother had experienced a loss of identity and security through culturally decreed marriage, a fate that Freeman regretted and hoped to avoid.[41]

The conclusion of "Juliza," therefore, is triumphant, transcendent, and significantly radical, including negotiation of marital status and more. Juliza's coaching of Frank Williams succeeds, and the "new" Frank is able to communicate clearly and effectively not only with Juliza but also with Lily. As a result, the couple marries in the very church that serves as Juliza's venue for public recitations, and they ask her to honor them not with a wedding *present* but with a wedding *presentation* (*US*, 35). Her mesmerizing speech at her would-be fiancé's marriage to another is a personal and public success, showing that there are alternatives for the young women in her generation that were unavailable to their mothers. Indeed, the dazzling Juliza is such a commanding presence at the altar that, when the last word falls from her mouth, "everybody listen[s]," and the bride and groom are "forgotten" (*US*, 36). The quirky, headstrong, working "spinster" has found a voice that all must hear and respect. With her creativity, integrity, unconventionality, and strength of determination, Juliza has done the nearly unthinkable in small-town Stony Brook—and in American literature and society of the day—she has upstaged a marriage. She leaves the church committed to her *self*, her art, and her audience. The townsfolk are moved deeply by Juliza, and her mother also becomes proud of her daughter's achievements.

Like a successful minister or spiritual leader, she has, from the pulpit, delivered an important message, unveiled the spark of divinity within, and inspired all to change and grow. As Beth Wynne Fisken comments of another heroine, she "shine[s] with an inner light reflecting a higher spiritual plane."[42] Tellingly, Juliza's transformative victory and that of Freeman's protagonist Esther are won in—or on the steps of—traditionally patriarchal churches. Such institutions saw significant intellectual activity and reform between 1870 and 1900. As Phyllis Cole notes, during this time "transcendentalism enjoyed prolonged vitality in the religious, literary, and benevolent work of Boston's feminist community," and many of the debates begun by Fuller continued within the domain of churches.[43]

Through her hybrid characters and the balancing points they attain—between old and new, masculine and feminine, individual and community, private and public—Freeman offers literary and life options for her readers and severely critiques the gendered limitations that hemmed in American women of the nineteenth century. Single, Juliza thrives. Because of the foresight of the two widow-aunts for whom she was named, Julia and Eliza, Juliza does not need economic help from a man to be secure in life. She has a well-equipped home and money to live on; she may freely pursue her artistic calling, develop her voice, and nurture her soul because women from an earlier generation, themselves married at some point yet seeing beyond their own limits, have provided a way for her. Like Sarah Penn on a much grander scale and outside of marriage and motherhood, Juliza is "goin' to think [her] own thoughts an' go [her] own ways, an' nobody but the Lord is goin' to dictate to [her] unless [she has] a mind to have him."[44]

Indeed Juliza resembles Freeman herself, who in 1889 remarked to a friend that, "as far as the signs of the time go, I do not see any reason to apprehend that I ever shall be married." In a sad irony, Freeman did agree in 1902, at the age of fifty, to try marriage with her longtime suitor, Dr. Charles Freeman, but with disastrous consequences. Any promise of marital "union" vanished within a few years, as her former friend, advocate, and intellectual equal became a controlling force in her career and an aggressive alcoholic. As a result, both Freeman's writing and her emotional health suffered, and—afraid, outraged, humiliated—she eventually had Charles committed to the New Jersey Hospital for the Insane, seeking legal separation in 1922.[45] Although this happened long after the writing of "Juliza," Freeman already seems sensitive in it to the possible pitfalls of marriage, or at least to those of the wrong marriage. It is particularly poignant, then, that through Juliza, Freeman urges women to be emotionally supportive of their unmarried peers, should they choose—or be forced—to live independently. Without this sort of understanding, Freeman argues, women run the risk of being their own enemies. In an effort to prevent such outcomes—as did Fuller in her Conversations, Fields in her salon, and Freeman and Poole in their "Quiet Hour Club"—Freeman paid the generosity of her writing forward, educating women and men, single or married, about the potential benefits associated with improving themselves as individuals in relation to the larger world.

Both Freeman and Fuller, whose texts and voices cross from the private to the public realm, have much in common with Juliza and with Freeman's protagonists in "A Conflict Ended." These heroines see independence and education as spiritual goals, ends for which women should fight—even against other women, if they are in the way. Each views pursuit of these aims as God given, embracing the belief that woman needs "as a nature to grow, as an intellect to discern, as a soul to live freely and unimpeded, to unfold such powers as were given her."[46] Like Freeman and Fuller, they do not disallow the possibility of actualizing these goals in marriage, but they repeatedly question the institution and celebrate female autonomy. They obey their inner voices, rejecting compulsory marriage and tradition for tradition's sake and abhorring silence and forced subservience. Reaching across the literary and literal generations, these characters challenge cultural norms and create new ways of being.

Both, furthermore, wrote in their respective times as literary voices in close proximity to the political and cultural networks of nineteenth-century feminism. As Cheney noted in her 1895 address on Fuller—contemporary with the high point of Freeman's career—a collective understanding among women was building. Freeman contributed to it by creating characters who, in Toth's words, fought for "a measure of individual freedom" amid tension "between need for independence and social insistence on conformity, between private fulfillment and social duties." Glasser further suggests that Freeman explored these needs from within, articulating "the psychology of women's conflicts as she knew them," "giving voice" to them and "open[ing] a door to what the 'spinster' of her time generally kept 'in a closet hidden, like a skeleton.'"[47] Freeman's protagonists may have come from small towns, but they pioneered modern ways for readers of nationally circulated magazines.

Still committed to these values in her sixties and even more invested in the process of mentoring future generations of women authors, Freeman expanded on the themes of her earlier "Good Wits" essay in "The Girl Who Wants to Write: Things to Do and Avoid" (1913). As well as recalling her early love of Emerson's essays, she instructed the aspiring woman author to record "above all things, the truth as far as she can see it, as clearly as she can see it," and to seek out "American viewpoints." Such precision and genuineness, she noted, may help to shape a "distinctly national literature." Here Freeman sounded a chord not only with Emerson but also with Fuller in her "Short Essay on Critics," published in the *Dial*'s opening issue more than seven decades before. Freeman warned her female audience to be wary of the power of literary critics, like Fuller applauding their proper function, but counseling that it would be a "great mistake to listen too much to individual criticisms of literary efforts and be swayed by them." On the contrary, she cautioned that reviewers often had preset agendas for judging the unsuspecting author's creations, and these were antithetical to originality. If the hopeful woman writer could hold fast to her own vision and write originally, "as if she were running a race in the sight of the world," she stood the best chance of success. Freeman adhered to the transcendentalist's belief in "inward law" over "outward rule." If the girl-author truly wanted to achieve greatness and satisfaction, Freeman advised, she must listen to her own voice and discover courage, or she would "defeat her own ends." It is always better, Freeman reasoned, "to go your own gait, although you may toddle and limp, than to go the gait of another." That pace would lead to the ultimate prize, "liberty."[48]

Within Freeman's feminist works, one finds both the ideal truth of transcendentalism and the descriptive truth of realism. Her conscious aim, she declared in 1887, was "making [her female] characters true and having them say and do just the things they *would* say and do" in real life. Howells applauded this goal and praised Freeman's interpretation of everyday scenes, her "unity of spirit," and her "community of characters," but he declared at the same time that every "sketch is like the sentences of Emerson . . . an infinitely repellent particle." Indeed her transcendental impulse extends from style to content. In Freeman's fictional women and girls, Howells finds, "at last are real interests, passions, ambitions," and "figures . . . drawn with exquisitely satisfying veracity."[49] Freeman's truths were inner expressions of self-trust and outward accounts, whether humorous or indignant, of repression and injustice. These truths united in promotion of the advancement of women and other individuals who had been denied active choice. Like Fuller, Freeman "would have every barrier thrown down . . . every path laid open."[50] She advanced personal and social change, yearned for philosophical insight, applauded individuality, and offered alternatives. Freeman is both a transcendental realist and, in the spirit of Fuller's definition, an "Exaltada." She succeeds at representing women who, like their real fin-de-siècle counterparts, act and react. They move from inner self-discovery to public voices and action. Each at her chosen speed, they move toward personal and communal victories, each running her own "race in the sight of the world."

NOTES

1. Ednah Dow Cheney, "Lecture Given at the Congress of the American Advancement of Women," in *Reminiscences of Ednah Dow Cheney* (Boston: Lee & Shepard, 1902), 193–94.
2. Mary Wilkins Freeman, "Good Wits, Pen and Paper," in *What Women Can Earn: Occupations of Women and Their Compensation*, ed. Grace H. Dodge et al. (New York: Frederick A. Stokes, 1899), 23–29.

3. See the introduction to Monika Mueller, *George Eliot U.S.: Transatlantic Literary and Cultural Perspectives* (Madison, N.J.: Fairleigh Dickinson Univ. Press, 2005) on this productive approach to comparative literary study. Mueller argues that Eliot not only writes in direct response to the texts and philosophies of Hawthorne, Stowe, and Fuller but also encompasses "unconscious, socially prompted types of text formation, archetypes, popular culture," even "ideas in the air" (20). Freeman, with Howells, Stowe, and Eliot herself as likely mediators of Fuller, does the same.
4. Transcendental realism is an idea I developed in "Transcendental Realism: The Thoreauvian Presence in Howells's *A Modern Instance*," *Studies in American Fiction* 27, no. 2 (1999): 149–57; the concept was explored more fully in my dissertation, "Transcendental Realism: Natural Environment and Social Reform from Ralph Waldo Emerson to Mary Wilkins Freeman," PhD diss., Univ. of South Carolina, 2001.
5. Charles Capper, "Margaret Fuller as Cultural Reformer: The Conversations in Boston," *American Quarterly* 39, no. 4 (1987): 509.
6. Edward Foster, *Mary E. Wilkins Freeman* (New York: Hendricks House, 1956), 189. On the William Dean Howells Medal, see Brent Kendrick, *The Infant Sphinx: Collected Letters of Mary E. Wilkins Freeman* (Metuchen, N.J.: Scarecrow Press, 1985), 370–71 and illustration after 268.
7. See Susan Allen Toth, "Defiant Light: A Positive View of Mary Wilkins Freeman," *New England Quarterly* 46 (1973): 82–93; Marjorie Pryse, ed., *Selected Stories of Mary E. Wilkins Freeman* (New York: W. W. Norton, 1983) ; and Josephine Donovan, *New England Local Color Literature: A Women's Tradition* (New York: Frederick Ungar, 1983). Freeman admired the work of Gilman, and she both admired and socialized with Jewett, who wrote on multiple occasions to Freeman praising the younger writer's short stories.
8. Biographies include Foster, *Mary E. Wilkins Freeman*; and Perry Westbrook, *Mary Wilkins Freeman* (Boston: Twayne, 1988). For letters, see Kendrick, *Infant Sphinx*. Selected recent feminist studies include Mary R. Reichardt, *A Web of Relationship: Women in the Short Fiction of Mary Wilkins Freeman* (Jackson: Univ. of Mississippi Press, 1992); Reichardt, *Mary Wilkins Freeman: A Study of the Short Fiction* (New York: Twayne, 1997); Martha J. Cutter, "Beyond Stereotypes: Mary Wilkins Freeman's Radical Critique of Nineteenth-Century Cults of Femininity," *Women's Studies* 21, vol. 9 (1992): 383–95; and Leah Blatt Glasser, *In a Closet Hidden: The Life and Works of Mary E. Wilkins Freeman* (Boston: Univ. of Massachusetts Press, 1996).
9. Foster, *Mary E. Wilkins Freeman*, 33–34, 52; Westbrook, *Mary Wilkins Freeman*, 8, 13, 60–62, 126–28. Westbrook further asserts Emerson's influence on the representation of nature in Freeman's *Six Trees* and *Understudies* (112–17). On the theme of "self-reliance" in Freeman's fiction, see also Rosamond Smith, "The Celebration of Self-Reliance in the Fiction of Mary Wilkins Freeman," PhD diss., Univ. of Alberta, 1975; and Beth Wynne Fisken, "'Unusual' People in a 'Usual Place': 'The Balking of Christopher' by Mary Wilkins Freeman," *Colby Library Quarterly* (1985): 99–103. For more on Freeman's transcendentally inspired nature writing, see Robert M. Luscher, "Seeing the Forest for the Trees: The 'Intimate Connection' of Mary Wilkins Freeman's *Six Trees*," *American Transcendental Quarterly* 3 (1989): 363–81; and Terrell F. Dixon, "Nature, Gender, and Community: Mary Wilkins Freeman's Ecofiction," in *Beyond Nature Writing: Expanding the Boundaries of Ecocriticism*, ed. Karla Ambruster and Kathleen R. Wallace (Charlottesville: Univ. of Virginia Press, 2001).

10. The only sustained study I have found that explores links between Fuller and Freeman is Mary Bortnyk Rigsby's dissertation, "Margaret Fuller's Feminist Aesthetic: A Critique of Emersonian Idealism in the Works of Fuller, Alcott, Stowe, and Freeman," PhD diss., Temple Univ., 1991, one section of which focuses on Freeman's *Pembroke* (1894).
11. As a young woman, she changed her second name to "Eleanor," her mother's name. Although Freeman produced many of her works prior to marriage, I use her married name rather than "Wilkins" throughout because she preferred it.
12. Foster, *Mary E. Wilkins Freeman*, 7–8, 24–33; Freeman to Helen L. Todd, 6 March 1907, quoted 31.
13. Mary Wilkins Freeman, "The Girl Who Wants to Write: Things to Do and Avoid," *Harper's Bazar* 47 (June 1913): 272.
14. Foster, *Mary E. Wilkins Freeman*, 39–40, 50–56, 59–63; cf. Westbrook, "A Young Writer in New England," chap. 1 of *Mary Wilkins Freeman*.
15. Freeman's complex relationship with Wales, with whom she lived for almost two decades prior to her marriage to Dr. Charles Freeman and also during its troubled periods, parallels the "Boston marriage" of her colleagues Sarah Orne Jewett and Annie Fields, as well as Fuller's romantic friendships with Anna Barker and Caroline Sturgis. See especially Kendrick, introduction to *Infant Sphinx*, on the relationship with Wales and the absence of extant letters between them; and Glasser, "The Tenderness of One Woman for Another," chap. 6 of *In a Closet Hidden*.
16. Mary Wilkins Freeman to Mary Louise Booth, 15 May 1888, in Kendrick, ed., *Infant Sphinx*, 88. On Booth's career, see Paula Bernat Bennett, "Mary Louise Booth and *Harper's Bazar*," in *Blue Pencils and Hidden Hands: Women Editing Periodicals, 1840–1910*, ed. Sharon M. Harris with Ellen Gruber Garvey (Boston: Northeastern Univ. Press, 2004), 225–40. Freeman's "The Lost Ghost" appeared in the collection *"The Wind in the Rose-Bush," and Other Stories of the Supernatural* (New York: Doubleday, Page, 1903).
17. Foster, *Mary E. Wilkins Freeman*, 62.
18. For discussions of this group, see Josephine Donovan, *New England Local Color Literature*, 38–49; Deborah Evans, "Annie Adams Fields," in *American Women Prose Writers, 1870–1920*, ed. Sharon M. Harris, Heidi L. M. Jacobs, and Jennifer Putzi, vol. 221 of *Dictionary of Literary Biography* (Detroit: Gale Group, 2000), 120–27; and Rita K. Gollin, *Annie Adams Fields, Woman of Letters* (Boston: Univ. of Massachusetts Press, 2002).
19. Gollin, *Annie Adams Fields*, 123; Fields quoted on 155.
20. Evans, "Annie Adams Fields," 122–24. Fields was also a hostess and biographer of male writers, including Emerson, but her detailed diary shows that her salons were exclusively for women (quoted in Julia Sprague, *History of the New England Women's Club, from 1868 to 1893* [Boston: Lee & Shepard, 1894], 123–24).
21. Mueller, *George Eliot U.S.*, 83.
22. See Phyllis Cole, "Woman's Rights and Feminism," in *OxH*, 222–40, on Fuller's web of influence into the early twentieth century through Howe, Cheney, Higginson, Alcott, Paulina Wright Davis, and others in a "generation of dissenters" (230, 237).
23. Kendrick, *Infant Sphinx*, 268; Margaret Klawunn, "The 'New Women' of Suburbia: A Study of the Quiet Hour Club of Metuchen, New Jersey," *Journal of Rutgers University Library* 46 (1984): 91–100. A well-known advocate of suffrage, Poole was not only a writer but also the founder of the International Council of Women in 1888 and a member of Sorosis (91–92). Freeman actively joined the Quiet Hour Club in 1902 but may have had earlier involvement during visits to her longtime friend Charles Freeman's town.

24. *EMF*, 321, 261–64, 282–89, 346; emphasis in original.
25. Reichardt, *Mary Wilkins Freeman*, 30.
26. Glasser, *In a Closet*, xvi. See also chap. 6, "Sometimes I Think I Am a Monster," for Freeman's experience of unmarried life and depiction of it in her fiction.
27. In this reading of the 1886 story, Freeman clearly knew of Fuller by text or at least reputation even before her 1888 pursuit of the "Boston people" who upheld Fuller's legacy.
28. Mary Wilkins Freeman, "A Conflict Ended," in *Selected Short Stories*, ed. Pryse. Page references will hereafter be cited parenthetically as *SSS*.
29. On the laws of "coverture," see for instance http://www.library.hbs.edu/hc/wes/collections/women_law/, accessed 15 November 2013.
30. Mary R. Reichardt, "'Friend of My Heart': Women as Friends and Rivals in the Short Stories of Mary Wilkins Freeman," *American Literary Realism* 22, no. 2 (1990): 54.
31. Toth, "Defiant Light," 90.
32. Untitled ms., n.d., quoted in Foster, *Mary E. Wilkins Freeman*, 142–43. Among Freeman's stories of rebellion, see for instance "The Church Mouse," "Old Woman Magoun," "Mistaken Charity," "A Poetess," "The Secret," "A Modern Dragon," "On the Walpole Road," "An Honest Soul," *The Portion of Labor*, *Pembroke*, and *By the Light of the Soul*. For a related study, see Carol Holly, "Reading Resistance in Mary Wilkins Freeman's 'A Poetess,'" *American Literary Realism* 39, no. 2 (2007): 95–108.
33. See *EMF*, 297, for Fuller's praise of de Staël's influence on "little rugged girls" in "the obscurest schoolhouse in New England": "They may never through life hear her name, but she is not the less their benefactress."
34. Mary Wilkins Freeman, "Juliza," in *The Uncollected Stories of Mary Wilkins Freeman*, ed. Mary Reichardt (Jackson: Univ. Press of Mississippi, 1992), 21; hereafter cited parenthetically as *US*.
35. See Lucia Cherciu, "'A Veritable Guest to Her Own Self': Mary Wilkins Freeman's Humorous Short Stories," *Journal of the Short Story in English* 35 (2000): 25.
36. Martha J. Cutter, "Frontiers of Language: Engendering Discourse in 'The Revolt of "Mother,"'" *American Literature* 63 (June 1991): 279–91.
37. Cutter, "Frontiers of Language," 280.
38. *EMF*, 310.
39. Mueller, *George Eliot U.S.*, 83.
40. See Alicia Suskin Ostriker, *Stealing the Language: The Emergence of Women's Poetry in America* (Boston: Beacon Press, 1986).
41. Young Eleanor Wilkins agreed to marry her husband Warren a year after her father's death, but instead of financial security, Warren brought his subsequent family a shared embarrassment over their "increasingly shabby homes and parsimonious existence" (Glasser, *In a Closet Hidden*, 6; Reichardt, *Web of Relationship*, 8).
42. Fisken, "'Unusual' People," 150.
43. Cole, "Woman's Rights and Feminism," 235.
44. Freeman, "The Revolt of 'Mother,'" in *SSS*, 134.
45. Freeman, quoted in Glasser, *In a Closet Hidden*, 56; for an account of her marriage and separation, see 174–77, 200–204.
46. *EMF*, 261.
47. Toth, "Defiant Light," 128, 133; Leah Blatt Glasser, "'She Is the One You Call Sister': Discovering Mary E. Wilkins Freeman," in *Between Women: Biographers, Novelists, Critics, Teachers and Artists Write about Their Work on Women*, ed. Carol Ascher, Louise DeSalvo, and Sara Ruddick (New York: Routledge Press, 1994), 187–88.

48. Freeman, "Girl Who Wants to Write," 272; see also Fuller, "A Short Essay on Critics," in *Transcendentalism: A Reader*, ed. Joel Myerson (New York: Oxford Univ. Press, 2000), 294–300.
49. Freeman, quoted in Reichardt, *Mary Wilkins Freeman*, 143; William Dean Howells, "Editor's Study," *Harper's Monthly Magazine* 75 (September 1887): 639, 640, and 83 (June 1891): 155.
50. *EMF*, 260.

INTERLUDE

Letter from *Woman's Era*, Conference Souvenir Number, vol. 2, no. 5.

August 1895

SALEM, 2 July 1895.

The Woman's Progressive Club of Salem was formed June 12, '95. The purpose of this club is to broaden and strengthen the moral, social, intellectual and religious life of its members, and through them to make itself a power for good, not only in their home, but abroad in other fields; also to help those who have not had the advantages of home influence and education, thereby assigning them to a higher plan of living.

As our club is of very recent formation, the report is necessarily brief, but as the days and months pass by we shall be enabled to accomplish some good. Our club consists of 17 members, who are wide awake, enthusiastic, and interested in helping to solve the various problems of our day and time.

ANNIE L. BLANCHARD, *Pres.*

ANNA M. BARBADOES, *Sec.*

Black Exaltadas

Race, Reform, and Spectacular Womanhood after Fuller

KATHERINE ADAMS

Much has been achieved in this country since the first Declaration of Independence. . . . But the noble sentiment which she expressed in her early youth is tarnished; she has shown that righteousness is not her chief desire, and her name is no longer a watchword for the highest hopes to the rest of the world. . . . We want shining examples.

—Margaret Fuller, "Fourth of July," *New-York Tribune* (1845)

The silence in the house was painful. These were representatives of the people for whom God had sent the terrible scourge of blood upon the land to free from bondage. The old abolitionists in the vast audience felt the blood leave their faces. . . . "Go down, Moses, way down in Egypt's land, Tell ol' Pharaoh, let my people go," sang the woman. . . . Spell-bound they sat beneath the outpoured anguish of a suffering soul. All the horror, the degradation from which a race had been delivered were in the pleading strains of the singer's voice. It strained the senses almost beyond endurance. It pictured to that self-possessed, highly-cultured New England assemblage as nothing else ever had, the awfulness of the hell from which a people had been happily plucked.

—Pauline Hopkins, *Of One Blood* (1905)

To articulate the past historically does not mean to recognize it "the way it really was" (Ranke). It means to seize hold of a memory as it flashes up at a moment of danger.

—Walter Benjamin, "Theses on the Philosophy of History" (1940)

Spectacular womanhood was for Margaret Fuller an instrument of reform. She wielded it by staging her own famously "magnetic" person before friends and students and by embedding examples of iconic femininity throughout her writings, where myriad figures from history, literature, and an envisioned future stand side by side. For Fuller, such displays could communicate a transcendent ideal and, through its irresistible force, effect change: "Never have I known minds so truly virgin," she writes of the "Exaltadas," an imagined future class of "maiden[s]" from whom, she prophesied, "would issue a virtue by which [the world] would, at last, be exalted too" (*WNC*, 91).[1] Central to Fuller's idealist project is the conception of femininity as a long-suppressed resource that must now serve where masculinity has failed. In her masterwork, *Woman in the Nineteenth Century*, she declares that "the time is come when Eurydice is to call for an Orpheus, rather than Orpheus for Eurydice," and promises that Adam will be redeemed by "the Virgin Mother of the new race" (*WNC*, 12, 60). However, Fuller also warns that Woman is not yet ready to lead, to reveal Truth. Something—Eurydice's captivity, Eve's shame—always delays the promised transformation. My first epigraph, taken from an 1845 *New-York Tribune* column in which Fuller denounces the annexation of Texas as a slave state, begins to indicate how the reformer theorizes Woman's obstructedness (*MFC*, 149–50). It presents another example of Woman impeded in her mission. As an allegorical figure for the U.S. nation-state, she is charged with the exceptionalist task of conveying freedom's ideal to her global audience. But Liberty's image is obscured by unrighteous "desires" that coincide with the "tarnish" of slavery. In her, as in the original Eve—who necessitates a new Eve to serve as "Virgin Mother of the New Race"—corrupt female sexuality and racial unfreedom converge in an overdetermined condition of corporeal excess. Fuller calls for "shining examples" capable of engendering "salvation." But this vision is set in an unknown future, a receding horizon of transcendence, a telos beyond history and the tarnished bodies that inhabit it.

Sixty years later, Dianthe Lusk, the heroine of Pauline Hopkins's 1905 novel *Of One Blood*, performs in Boston's Tremont Temple.[2] In the extraordinary scene from my second epigraph, Hopkins stages her own version of a spectacular womanhood that draws nationalist identification and encodes a national truth. Like Fuller's tarnished Liberty, Dianthe performs a revelation of meaning that acts powerfully upon its listeners. Like Liberty again, her image is racially inflected. Hopkins chooses the Tremont Temple for its long association with antislavery and racial justice activism; and Dianthe appears with the Fisk Jubilee Singers to celebrate the anniversary of emancipation. But while Fuller poses racial meaning against (and as a way of making legible) an untarnished and implicitly disembodied future, Hopkins links Dianthe's racialized performance to an intensely embodied experience of a collective present and an intensely affective identification with a national past. Liberty struggles to lead us forward into incorporeal whiteness, while Dianthe plunges us backward into the blackness of hell.

This essay focuses on representations of spectacular femininity in writing by Hopkins and other black women activists from the turn of the twentieth century, putting these into conversation with Fuller to consider how gender and race shape conceptions of U.S. history, progress, and reform. Specifically, I find in Fuller an early version of a narrative of progress that aligns blackness with subjection to history, and whiteness with transcendence. Fuller imagines reform as a millennialist shift from horizontal into vertical temporality, an escape from historicity. However, by casting this shift in racialized and reproductive terms, Fuller also relies upon what philosopher Walter Benjamin refers to as "historicism": a view of history as a linear and unified progression through "empty" or "homogeneous time" and toward a receding, idealized future.[3] Half a century after Fuller, Hopkins disrupts the racialist historicism that shaped her own reform culture and rejects its promise of corporeal transcendence. Like Benjamin, who characterizes historical narrative as a "triumphal procession in which the present rulers step over those who are lying prostrate," she exposes the way historicism naturalizes hegemonic power, erases its violent constitution, and silences its victims ("TPH," 256). In the traumatic impact of Dianthe's song, Hopkins portrays the "flash[ing] up" of memory that disables a linear and progressive national narrative. The song flashes from the past, but also—as Benjamin would have it—from the emergency of the now ("TPH," 255). The "hell" to which the white ex-abolitionists are subjected sharply corrects the plantation nostalgia that such concerts promoted but also reconfigures the audience's relation to the present "moment of danger," defined by rampant lynching and legislative reversals. In its excruciatingly corporeal effect, the song's merging of past and present also establishes what Daphne Brooks identifies as a "contact zone" between singer and audience.[4] The racialized "strains" of Dianthe's voice re-embody themselves in the white listeners' "strained senses"; blood spills in the 1860s and drains from 1890s faces (*OOB*, 453–54). Time folds. But nonlinearity is not transcendence. While Fuller rejects historicity (subjection to history) but not historicism (a linear and progressive model of history), Hopkins rejects historicism but not historicity.

In the most famous of his theses on history, Benjamin describes an angel whose "face is turned toward the past":

> Where we perceive a chain of events, he sees one single catastrophe which keeps piling wreckage and hurls it in front of his feet. The angel would like to stay, awaken the dead, and make whole what has been smashed. But a storm is blowing in from Paradise; it has got caught in

> his wings with such a violence that the angel can no longer close them. The storm irresistibly propels him into the future to which his back is turned, while the pile of debris before him grows skyward. This storm is what we call progress. ("TPH," 257–58)

Taking my cue from Benjamin's angel, I consider Hopkins's use of spectacular womanhood as not only a counterhistory that corrects hegemonic accounts of the past or a counterpublicity that confronts hegemonic accounts of the present—though it performs both functions. I approach it also as an intervention into racialist historicism (a conception of history that both relies on and produces racial meaning) that resists the storm of progress. Hopkins demands that we recognize history *and* historiography as repeating catastrophes produced upon and through racialized-feminized bodies, and locates reform in the radical temporality of the now.

Although Hopkins never mentions Fuller, their biographies reveal a tantalizing array of near connections. Both writers worked within a nineteenth-century tradition of women's reform historiography that, while far from univocal—especially concerning race—was extremely self-referential. Although Fuller died more than a decade before Hopkins's birth, both grew up in or near Boston, immersed in that city's intellectual and reform cultures. Also significant here is that both women were spectacular in their own right. Fuller's friends and critics often remarked on her powerful oratory and forceful personality; and, as the Dianthe scene demonstrates, Hopkins's early theatrical career deeply influenced her journalism and novels.[5] Both were punished for their public visibility. Fuller was criticized as harridan and egoist, and Hopkins was famously ousted from an editorship at the *Colored American Magazine* by Booker T. Washington, a coup that critics attribute to gender and Hopkins's refusal to placate white readers.[6] A further link via spectacular (and punished) femininity exists in Zenobia, the character from Nathaniel Hawthorne's *Blithedale Romance* whom many nineteenth-century readers took for a portrait of Fuller. Hopkins overtly draws from *Blithedale* in *Of One Blood*—both novels feature mesmerism and men who use it to manipulate women—and one is tempted to ask if Fuller's commanding public persona lurks anywhere in Dianthe's DNA.[7] All speculation aside, I propose that juxtaposing Hopkins and Fuller within these common contexts will shed light on race-gender intersectionality in reformist conceptions of history, progress, and futurity.

In what follows I begin by expanding on Fuller's treatment of spectacular womanhood and inscription of racialist historicism. I then consider how ideas and problems that underwrite Fuller's logic also play out within the white and black women's club movements during the second half of the century—a context shaped by Fuller's posthumous influence *and* Hopkins's political activism. I conclude with Hopkins's first novel *Contending Forces* (1900), where, in the character of Sappho Clark, she deploys the spectacle of the mixed-race female body against historicist delusion, showing how historiography and racial meaning organize and produce each other, and offering the disruptive alternative that Benjamin calls *jetztzeit*, or now-time.

Neither Fuller nor Hopkins was unusual in linking public displays of womanhood to reform. Among U.S. women, this tradition goes back at least to Judith Sargent Murray's 1790s essays for *The Gleaner*, which catalogue exemplary women from history to illustrate a capacity for more rigorous education and more challenging civic obligations; and, as Linda Kerber notes, Murray's precedents begin as early as Christine de Pizan's 1405 *Book of the City of Ladies*.[8] In Fuller's time, many writers employed what Nina Baym terms a "strategy of compilation," citing historical women in service to a wide array of causes, including both support of and opposition to women's rights.[9] Fuller's lists are similar in content to those produced by her contemporaries. But she distinguishes herself in posing her exemplars as catalysts for millennial progress—as both female role models *and* vehicles of national salvation. Like the Virgin Mary or Lady Liberty, Fuller's spectacular women solicit universal—not just female—identification and stand for ideals and goals that far exceed women's welfare. More, as conduits of sublime meaning they promise to displace their audience from the historical setting in which such welfare might signify. Iconic in the sense of religious statuary, Fuller's spectacular woman is a point of translation between the secular and divine, a relay beyond history and into millennialist nationalist ideality:

> Without attaching importance, in themselves, to the changes demanded by champions of women . . . [w]e would have every path laid open to woman as freely as to man. Were this done and a slight temporary fermentation allowed to subside, we should see crystallizations more pure and of more various beauty. We believe the divine energy would pervade nature to a degree unknown in the history of former ages, and that no discordant collision, but a ravishing harmony of the spheres would ensue. (*WNC*, 20)

In this, Fuller's spectacular women reflect both a convention of women's reform historiography and a nationalist iconographic tradition that positions female allegorical figures at the receding horizon of national ideality. Figures like Columbia, Justice, and Liberty represent principles that the nation's actually existing democracy can never make manifest—principles with which we identify in a mode of always-already deficit, in which ideality obtains in incommensurability with the present. They instantiate the dual temporality found in John O'Sullivan's essay "The Great Nation of Futurity," or in Ralph Waldo Emerson's salute to "This new yet unapproachable America": "what a future it opens" (*CW*, 3:41). In these images and narratives, the future is both chronologically ahead and synchronically latent. Extending Baym's argument that catalogues of famous women demonstrated "women have a place in history," we could say Fuller's catalogues claimed for women a place simultaneously in *and* beyond history, a place at the intersection of vertical and horizontal temporalities.[10]

This logic of two-timing idealist futurity often worked in a manner suggestive of Benjaminian historicism and its "triumphal procession[s]" of dominant power ("TPH," 256). As Thomas Allen has argued, temporal narratives like O'Sullivan's allowed nineteenth-century Americans to reconcile democratic, anti-imperialist rhetoric with the political realities of continental expansion. Slavery and Indian genocide could be glossed over by a vision that displaced national progress from a spatial/geographical frame to a temporal frame in which futurity became a "utopian horizon . . . where the nation's contradictions would resolve themselves into a coherent republic."[11] Here, Fuller adds an extra, and brutal, twist. Rather than merely eliding injustice, her formulation of postponed-and-latent national ideality *requires* it. The racial subjugation that tarnishes her examples of iconic womanhood, Liberty most overtly, stands as the necessary condition—the obstacle *and* opportunity—for transcendence. In *Woman in the Nineteenth Century* and *Summer on the Lakes* (1840), respectively, Fuller appropriates the historical unfreedoms of enslaved blacks and displaced American Indians to symbolize both the unfreedoms of (tacitly white) women and the way these impede the transformative effect of the (tacitly white) principal of "Woman." Important here is that Fuller theorizes women's oppression not just in terms of alienated civil and political rights but also, more fundamentally, with reference to the embodied, embedded condition that necessitates such rights and prevents women from manifesting Woman.

Thus, in the passage from *Woman* quoted above, Fuller characterizes historical "changes demanded by the champions of women" as important not "in themselves" but as steps toward the activation of "divine energy" and "ravishing harmony." It is from this more metaphysical account of women's oppression that Fuller develops a racialist historicist narrative. She envisions a progressive, linear movement through and beyond history, in which nonwhiteness tropes not just historical unfreedom but historicity *as* unfreedom. Hence the state of unreadiness that so often characterizes Fuller's iconic Woman: Eurydice's captivity in the underworld, Liberty's tarnish, Eve's state of fallen grace—these figure transcendence as a project rather than a condition, and whiteness as historicist progression.[12]

To be sure, this logic of racialist historicism does not account for the full breadth of Fuller's thinking about racial injustice or racial difference. She read widely, and critically, in the literature on Native Americans, and if she sometimes appropriates their hardships in *Summer* to represent white women's unfreedom, she also succeeds at subjecting gender and racial oppression to what Christina Zwarg terms a "double exposure" in which neither is subordinated to the other (Zwarg, 170). Although Fuller never embraced the antislavery movement, she acknowledged that it "command[ed her] respect."[13] She even contributed a piece (reprinted in this volume) to the 1846 edition of *The Liberty Bell*, the abolitionist gift book edited by Maria Weston Chapman. Here again slavery matters chiefly as a catalyst for spiritual becoming, and reform's purpose is to "establish the principles of liberty for man" rather than "merely freeing individual victims from their chains" (204).[14] And yet, alongside the places where Fuller subordinates her condemnation of slavery—figuratively or explicitly—to women's reform or the nation's exceptionalist destiny, there are others like the passage from *Woman* (also discussed in this volume's introduction) where she exhorts future Exaltadas to fight the annexation of Texas and consequent expansion of slavery, specifying that this be done not only as an opportunity for women's self-development "but on the ground of right" (*WNC*, 98).[15]

Nor is Fuller the lone or originary racialist historicist. Below I discuss the similar logic of social Darwinism with its vision of white national progress driven by violent opposition to black bodies.[16] But a more closely related case is *Uncle Tom's Cabin*, published six years after *Woman*. Jane Tompkins famously defends the novel on the grounds that Harriet Beecher Stowe's "eschatological vision" of history accurately reflects the antebellum imagination, specifically in pointing beyond social and political circumstances to "a single timeless reality" governed by the struggle between good and evil.[17] James Baldwin likewise finds that Stowe's novel is governed by Manichean logic, but in his reading that logic's purpose is to displace the "terrifying" ambiguity of human subjectivity onto black caricature so as to affirm white national futurity. As the victim of Stowe's "virtuous rage" and "merciless morality," Uncle Tom has much in common with Fuller's spectacular Woman.[18]

According to her student Caroline Healey Dall, Fuller's "very existence was a stimulus to endeavor; and hundreds of women became practical 'Exaltadas.'"[19] Posthumously, Fuller continued to stimulate through her writings and her memorialized example. As Phyllis Cole has shown, Fuller was "canonized" after her death by a variety of white women's organizations. Suffragists, temperance workers, marriage reformers, and clubwomen took her up as a rallying point for female reform and emulation. Through this widespread "symbolic appropriation," Fuller herself acquired the status of spectacular womanhood, engendering progress and new forms of belonging.[20]

The American Woman Suffrage Association (AWSA) is especially interesting here, both because it pursued a particularly intense style of memorialization, which Cole characterizes as "the cult of Fuller," and because it was based in Hopkins's hometown, Boston, and led by white reformers who worked closely with that city's black clubwomen.[21] Support for the black franchise was a key factor in the schism that brought Lucy Stone, Julia Ward Howe, and others to break with the National Woman Suffrage Association (NWSA) and organize independently. Stone and Howe were important advocates of racial justice, recognized as allies in the antilynching campaign. Both spoke frequently at black women's club meetings, and a biography of Stone appears in the first issue of the movement's journal, *Woman's Era* (named for the Boston club). Another AWSA member, Ednah Cheney, who had been Fuller's student and toured the country giving lectures about her former teacher into the 1890s, was even more involved in the black clubs. Cheney attended meetings, wrote frequently for *Woman's Era*, and delivered an invited lecture at the Boston club's inaugural gathering. A black school in South Carolina and a black club in Tuskegee bore her name.[22]

And yet, even with so much apparent potential for transmission, there is no explicit sign that Fuller mattered to black clubwomen. In his essay for this volume, Eric Gardner demonstrates that educator Edmonia Highgate found inspiration in Fuller's writing for her own transcendentalist publications in the *Christian Recorder* immediately following the war. Three decades later, nary a mention of Fuller appears in *Woman's Era* (beyond one reference to the Ossoli Circle, a white club in Knoxville, Tennessee)[23] or in surviving speeches and essays by movement leaders Victoria Earle Matthews, Anna Julia Cooper, or Fannie Williams. This despite the fact that transcendentalism makes quite a prominent showing—Bronson Alcott earns several accolades, Brook Farm is selected as the special focus of a girl's study group, and Emerson is quoted widely.[24] Hopkins, who often memorialized Boston's activist history, published a biography of Fuller's close friend Lydia Maria Child in 1903. And her close engagement with *The Blithedale Romance* in *Of One Blood* strongly suggests she knew of Fuller's reputation. So Fuller may be most significant to a study of black women's postbellum reform writing—Hopkins's in particular—in her marked absence from it. Even omitting the racial inflection of her millennialist historiography, Fuller's lack of involvement in racial justice was likely sufficient to exclude her from black activists' "usable past." Indeed, Cole suggests Fuller was adopted by the NWSA and AWSA in part *because* she was among the few antebellum reformers not closely affiliated with the antislavery movement.[25]

Like Fuller, however, black clubwomen made the display of women's "shining examples" a central strategy of reform; and their ideas about how this practice would shape futurity often resonate strongly with hers, indicating that gendered iconicity and its relation to temporality were recurring concerns across differing periods and areas of nineteenth-century women's reform. Scholars have thoroughly established the importance of public visibility in black women's activism at the end of the nineteenth century. In such works as *A New Negro for a New Century*, biographies and photographs of exemplary black women were deployed against the racist, sexualized imagery that pervaded the white-dominated mass culture. Exhibitions of photographic portraits traveled the nation, a mode of resistant black publicity designed, as Gabrielle Foreman shows, to "shape collective memory"; and club lectures constantly urged the necessity of exemplary self-display.[26] This emphasis on public image concerned more than providing black role models. In 1897 Victoria Earle Matthews announced to the Society of Christian Endeavor the "tremendous awakening of the Afro-American womanhood . . . from the double night of ages of slavery in which it was locked in intellectual and moral eclipse" and declared this emergence "one of the most promising facts in our national life."[27] Like Fuller, Matthews and other black clubwomen viewed femininity as a transformative force finally coming into its full and publicly recognizable powers, poised to advance not just female and black but also national progress. For leaders like Josephine Ruffin and Margaret Murray Washington, women were suited to this work by their propensity to serve: "it is especially fitting that the women of the race take the lead . . . for the benefit of all humanity."[28] Others saw themselves rectifying the failed efforts of black men, impatient, like Fuller's Eurydice, of waiting for their Orpheus to lead. "All too long has the way been blocked by bold incompetents," asserted one clubwoman in *Woman's Era*.[29]

Yet black clubwomen differed from Fuller and her AWSA acolytes by not linking spectacular femininity to an exit from historicity. I have argued that Fuller's female spectacles stand at the intersection of horizontal and vertical temporalities, intervening against historical existence rather than modeling progress within it. Cole finds a similar conceit in Fuller's AWSA "canonization." While the New York–based NWSA valued Fuller for her social and political critique, the Bostonians remembered her as a mystic. Howe and Cheney especially invoked Fuller as a "priestess" who would instigate "spiritual transformation." Cole compares the two styles of memorialization as history (New York) versus biography (Boston), which seems especially apt in light of Emerson's claim, as he prepared *Representative Men* for publication, that he wanted "to draw characters, not write lives."[30] Fuller, too, wanted to offer portraits not structured by time, to delineate essence rather than manifestation; and when celebrated as "a central symbol of . . . higher female holiness" she became such a portrait herself. In contrast, black clubwomen typically theorized female spectacle as wielding extrahistorical force upon historical context. Thus, if Matthews's "Awakening of Afro-American Women" seems initially to describe mystical emergence rather than social change, the benefits she promises will follow are decidedly secular and material. The spiritualizing tone drops away as Matthews methodically lists the social and political institutions black women will transform.

There are obvious explanations for this differing understanding of public femininity. For one, white womanhood offered ideological content that black womanhood did not. The former was already deeply associated in the national imagination with ideality and transcendence, both cultural symbol and reproductive vehicle for white futurity. This is the normative cultural function of True Womanhood that Fuller attempted to appropriate and retask toward a radical critical agenda. The meanings assigned to black femininity, conversely, were something reformers fought to overcome. They enshrined images of middle-class black femininity to counteract racist caricatures of savagery and sexual promiscuity. Most pressing, Matthews and her fellow activists operated in the context of unprecedented social, political, economic, and physical violence against blacks. With a far more urgent stake in historical change, these reformers were unlikely to view the proper recognition of black women as merely a step, "without . . . importance, in [it]self," toward the millennium (*WNC*, 20).

In places—and especially where it dovetails with social Darwinism—black clubwomen's emphasis on change *within* history risks reinscription of what I am referring to as "racialist historicism." Social Darwinists argued that blacks were not only less evolved than whites but actually incapable of evolving. If extinction were delayed by a welfare state or social reform, civilization itself would be held back.[31] Here is a racist narrative of progress that literalizes the racialist logic found in Fuller; by its logic a primitive and recalcitrant blackness signifies against white futurity but also serves as the impurity that drives eugenic / eschatological transcendence. Black clubwomen contended variously with social evolutionary narratives. At meetings and in periodicals they discussed the merits of particular theories and developed their own studies of racial development. The second issue of *Woman's Era* announces, for example, that Victoria Matthews was surveying race leaders across the nation to gather the "true statistics of our people morally."[32] Such projects were risky, given the racial bias that pervaded the supposedly objective discourse of science: another article quotes W. E. B. Du Bois on the corruption of sociology "by that strange American disorder, colorphobia." In this light, we might interpret the widespread determination among black clubwomen to hold a national convention as a form of evidentiary strategy. In her speech opening the first national gathering, Ruffin acknowledged the inadequacy of countering racist statistics with "individual effort." The convention was therefore vital, she argued, for presenting "an army of organized women standing for purity and mental worth." Through this "dignified showing," women's public bodies would stand proof against the equation of blackness with degeneration and whiteness with evolutionary progress.[33]

But gestures of exemplary display could also affirm historicist evolutionary logic by advocating the transcendence of racialized embodiment in bids for inclusion—a strategy by which, as Patricia Williams puts it, "castration from blackness becomes the initiatory tunnel . . . to participation in the pseudo-celestial white community."[34] Clubwomen and uplift reformers frequently enumerated the changes wrought in black women by the three decades since their emergence from what Matthews calls "intellectual and moral eclipse." This deprived blacks of historiographic resources by defining current racial value against its putative former absence. It also located progress, and its necessity, in black womanhood rather than structural oppression—a formulation that is most troubling where it maps onto black female bodies and the "tarnish" of sexuality. Lecturing Tuskegee clubwomen on the accomplishments of the American Missionary Association, Margaret Washington tracks racial advancement as an effect of black female purity, contrasting the "true honored womanhood" of her fellow clubwomen with its postbellum counterpart: "Thirty years ago, over two millions of our women were set free from bondage of soul and body. With few exceptions . . . none had been taught lessons that tended to improve womanhood. . . . [W]ith no deep realization of their deplorable condition, [m]any drifted here and there, often falling by the wayside, too helpless amidst their environment to have a desire to lead purer, nobler lives." Although Washington attributes freedwomen's degradation to slavery's "insidious influences," she also aligns enslavement with savagery. More significant, she charts a linear temporality, locating the past in shameful, burdensome black female embodiment—a state of ignorant and "helpless" contingency, incapable of forward movement and enthralled, like Fuller's Liberty, by wayward "desire"—while staking the future in "true" womanhood.[35]

As we have seen, this is not the only way clubwomen cast the relationship between progress, blackness, and female bodies. Yet it represents a thread that Hopkins found prominent enough to merit critique. In her 1900 novel *Contending Forces*, she associates such rhetoric with Mrs. Willis—a critical portrait of the Woman's Era Club president, Josephine Ruffin—who calls on clubsisters to "eliminat[e] immorality from our midst."[36] "Thirty-five years of liberty have made us a new people," Willis admonishes. "The marks of servitude and oppression are dropping slowly from us; let us hasten the transformation of the body by the nobility of the soul" (*CF*, 153). For Hopkins, I argue, this model of reform, predicated upon the production and erasure of women's "marked" bodies, represents the racialist historicist narrative she aims to disrupt.

Hopkins, who was a member of the Woman's Era Club and contributed to the periodical bearing its name, shared many of the views on public womanhood that it shared with Fuller. She, too, portrays women's developing powers as a precipitating condition for social progress and corrective to men's inadequate leadership. "If our race ever amounts to anything," says the heroine of *Contending Forces*, Sappho Clark, to her friend Dora Smith, "it will be because such women as you are raised up to save us" (*CF*, 100). Also, as Sappho's phrase "raised up" suggests, Hopkins often imagines women's power as a fusion of spirituality and public visibility: in "Famous Women of the Negro Race," for example, she describes female vocalists as "half-deserted shrines . . . leading the upward flight."[37] The quasi-religious iconicity of these images seems again to resonate with Fuller's spectacular women and their power to translate between horizontal and vertical temporalities. But like the clubwomen discussed above, Hopkins resists the transcendent potential of iconic femininity. Rather than escaping historicity, her spectacular women intensify it.[38] Dianthe and Sappho, especially, project a presence so dense with what Brooks calls "historically thick black identity" that it warps temporality and confounds hegemonic constructions of meaning.[39]

Benjamin's conception of now-time, or *jetztzeit*, helps us understand Hopkins's experiments with a temporality that is both nonlinear and nontranscendent. For although *jetztzeit* has often been misread as an irruption of sacred or transcendent meaning—partly because Benjamin associates it with "messianic time"—its source is crucially not extrahistorical. As Sami Khatib argues, now-time differs from eschatological or millennial time, both of which occur at the conclusion of history, in that it constitutes a "loop" or "contraction" within historical time; now-time is made up of historical and materialist memory, enabled by historically contingent consciousness, and provoked by historical-political necessity.[40] Also important, now-time militates against a "providential" vision of history as teleological, progressive, and divinely intentioned.[41] Benjamin's angel of history looks backward, but *not* because if only the storm of progressive historicism were less overwhelming he could stop the recurring damage once and for all, freeing everyone to look forward together. Benjamin places the debris of the past "before" the angel—choosing a preposition that works in English and the original German, *vor*, to designate both a temporal past and a spatial future.[42] This violent history will not be resolved in service to transcendent futurity. "For Benjamin," Khatib points out, "the past is never ontologically fully constituted, it can be rewritten, re-opened at a certain critical moment, at the moment of the 'now of recognisability.'"[43] The explosions of *jetztzeit* that occur in Hopkins's novels disrupt providential—or otherwise historicist—narratives by revealing both their racist subtext and their production of racial meaning. This latter effect holds special significance for scholarship on early black historiography, which has focused primarily on alternative historical or temporal narratives devised to express the silenced experiences and desires of a putative preexistent black racial identity.[44] Hopkins compels us to take the question a step further. In her scenes of temporal disruption, historiography and blackness emerge as mutually constitutive structures of meaning.

This interpretation of Hopkins as nonprogressivist and nonracialist may seem surprising, given her predilection for light-skinned heroines. Dianthe passes for white in *Of One Blood*, and Sappho's description in *Contending Forces*, "tall and fair, with hair of a golden cast, aquiline nose, rosebud mouth," implies she could do the same (*CF*, 107). Early commentators found a racist evolutionary subtext in such portraits: progress measured as distance from black corporeality.[45] But, as Hazel Carby first argued, Hopkins's focus on mixed-race women is also legible as an insistence on the legacy of white male sexual violence against black women.[46] Both Sappho and Dianthe embody a counterhistory of trauma that, as Sappho's lover Will Smith points out, is both individual and national (*CF*, 299). This history contradicts hegemonic racial knowledge by resignifying whiteness from mark of advancement to mark of injury. Indeed, it fundamentally disrupts racial knowledge by disabling the polarizing temporal logic of racialist historicism—black past / white futurity. Hopkins's spectacularly mixed-race heroines reveal, in Lisa Marcus's words, "the whiteness of black origins, how blackness in the United States has been, literally and forcefully, fathered by whiteness."[47]

As sites of historical repetition and simultaneity, both Sappho and Dianthe signal the radical temporality of now-time: in their persons the past and present converge. In *Of One Blood*, Dianthe marks a pattern of violation: the rape of her grandmother by a white owner echoes in her mother's incest-rape by the same man, and in Dianthe's mental and physical incest-rape by her brothers. *Contending Forces* traces a similar pattern through Sappho. The novel opens in the early 1800s with the brutal rape of Grace Montfort and the destruction of her family, motivated by white greed. That origin story repeats with the biography of Luke Sawyer, whose family members are raped and murdered by more resentful whites, and again with Mabelle Beaubean's story told by Luke at an antilynching rally. As a girl, Mabelle is abducted, raped, and impregnated by her white uncle—here again incest figures the inward fold, temporal and generational, of white racial violence. When her father threatens to prosecute, his family is slaughtered and only Mabelle and Luke escape. The story nearly repeats a fourth time when Mabelle—now living as Sappho Clark—is threatened sexually by John Langley. In the repetition of violated women and devastated families we see not a "chain of events" across time but "one single catastrophe which keeps piling wreckage," embodied by black women ("TPH," 257).

This typology of violence presents an extraordinarily dark account of history and futurity. Yet it is precisely in her embodiment of this history that Sappho has power to intervene in historicist consciousness. As Dianthe's song provokes an agonizing revelation of past and present, so does Sappho's image force hidden truths and histories to awareness. A crucial example involves "one learned doctor" who guesses at the origins of her light complexion. The doctor is Arthur Lewis, Hopkins's fictionalization of Booker T. Washington, whose accommodationist politics oppose Will Smith's Du Boisian convictions (their rivalry suggests one interpretation of the novel's title). Watching Sappho, Lewis suddenly intuits her past, and "in that moment," the narrator declares, "a cloud passed from before his mental vision, and he beheld in all its hideousness the cankering sore . . . stamping the lie upon the Constitution." "Expediency and right must go hand in hand," he realizes. "There is no room for compromise" (*CF*, 202). Here, Sappho's image disperses Lewis's racialist historicist delusion—his Washingtonian theory of black underdevelopment and "politics of [white] emulation."[48] She enables a "flash[ing] up" of racial / national memory to reveal the error of his views, and the true path of "no compromise" that Hopkins herself fiercely advocated in defiance of the real Booker T. Washington.

Sappho's power to disrupt hegemonic historicist consciousness manifests dramatically at the novel's climax—an antilynching meeting arranged by the American Colored League. Hopkins devotes three chapters to this episode, restaging an actual event from May 1899 that Lois Brown identifies as the novel's genesis. The original meeting was truly "a moment of danger" where the victors threatened to commandeer the historical record. Proceedings began with William Northen, a Georgia politician, who took two hours—twice his allotted time—to deliver a white supremacist history of Reconstruction. He addressed "negro lawlessness, white victimization . . . and the impossibility of achieving interracial harmony in the South" unless blacks submitted as dependents to the superior white race.[49] But Northen's central argument concerned white womanhood: "Is there no tender word for the defenseless women of the south who carry with them a living shame in a living death?"[50] Compared to the depravity of black rapists, Northen argued, lynching was an understandable and lesser evil. After Northen came Bishop Benjamin Arnett, a black politician from Ohio. But with only twenty minutes remaining, Arnett gave a fumbling, impotent performance. Northen's racialist historicism carried the day, imposing a narrative of black history even more defeating than Washington's gradualism, Brown observes, because it offered no hope of ever achieving equality with whites.[51] Incapable of evolving, blacks could not expect progress toward citizenship—would, in fact, *obstruct* progress if not restrained, particularly in the threat they posed to white women, the symbol and reproductive basis of white futurity.

In her fictionalization of Northen as "The Hon. Herbert Clapp," Hopkins preserves his emphasis on white femininity, quoting him at length. Clapp likewise invokes the "hellish diabolism" of the black "fiend" and demands "sympathy for the pure and virtuous woman who carries with her a living shame."

But Clapp also improvises on Northen by reminding the audience of "all the benefits conferred upon the Negro at the South" and asking, "Where find excuses for such ingratitude?"—a query suggesting that Northen's true concern is not white women but the white supremacy they represent (*CF*, 248). Hopkins then adds her own speakers, including Luke Sawyer, who takes the platform to deliver an impromptu recitation of Mabelle / Sappho's tragic history and galvanizes the crowd. After Luke comes Will Smith with a call to action—"We must *agitate*" (*CF*, 272).

Hopkins's revision of the antilynching rally enacts both a counterhistory and a counterhistoriography. In the first mode, she restages the event to redeem Arnett's failure and challenge Northen's version of what "all history shows" (*CF*, 246). Through Will, she disputes Northen's claims about the benefits and benevolence of slavery, the savagery of one race, and the purity of the other (*CF*, 263–73). Will's closing reference to "the anti-slavery apostles [who] went everywhere, preaching the word fifty years before emancipation," provides the crowning touch to Hopkins's counterhistory (*CF*, 272). But she invokes those same figures at the outset of the rally in a very different aspect when she describes the stage "heavily draped in American flags" with "pictures of the anti-slavery apostles peer[ing] out at the audience from the folds of the national colors" (*CF*, 243–44). Here the apostles approach their audience timidly, nearly obscured by the symbol of national union—much like Arnett (represented in the scene by Lewis) overcome by Northen's triumphal historicism. Another history by and of male heroes will not suffice. The crisis of racialist historicism calls for a counterhistoriography—an alternate theory of historical narrative. As John Ernest puts this, "African American historians . . . could not hope to simply correct the record; they needed to enter into the theater of history . . . to shift or disrupt the social rituals of historical propagation."[52]

Hopkins enters the "theater of history" quite literally by posing Mabelle against Northen / Clapp's deployment of spectacular white womanhood. These iconic images represent another pair of "contending forces" as competing sites of historiography. On one side, imperiled white womanhood symbolizes a white national futurity threatened by political and social amalgamation. On the other, the female embodiment of a traumatic black past calls forth a collective memory and awakens the audience from the spell of historicist delusion. Mabelle's history provides more than a corrected version of the past. If Northen's bespoiled white woman, like Fuller's tarnished Liberty, embodies a nation locked in historicity and held back from historicist / millennial progress ("The Negro in American civilization is a problem of a vast deal more import than we are inclined to believe," he warns—"The problem is national" [*CF*, 247]), Mabelle's story trumps this effect by reconfiguring time and space. It transports the audience out of the linear temporality of history-as-progress and into immediacy with the past as it informs the present. The "murmurs of discontent" during Northen's speech give way to acutely embodied participation during Luke's: "The house was filled with the cries and groans of the audience. Sobs shook the women, while the men drank in the words of the speaker with darkening brows and hands which involuntarily clinched themselves in sympathy with his words" (*CF*, 254, 258). Like Dianthe's audience, Luke's inhabits the past physically and affectively. They "drink" and "digest" it, "grief-convulsed" and "groaning" (*CF*, 258, 261). Luke concludes by folding moments of racial, national, and personal "suffering" from the past and the future into an unbearable present tense of pain that permits no fantasy of future escape, only the resolve to act:

> I ask you what you think the American Colonies would have done if they had suffered as we have suffered and are still suffering?
>
> Gentlemen call for peace. . . . When the grave has closed over me and my memories, I shall have peace. . . . Contentment . . . is impossible; justice alone remains to us. (CF, 262)

Although Mabelle transforms the antilynching rally, she—like the iconic white womanhood she counteracts—is present only by male proxy. In fact, Luke reports that Mabelle has died in childbirth, true to the formulae of the tragic mulatta, the seduction plot, and—as Jennifer Putzi demonstrates—the abolitionist novel, in which erasure of racially and sexually tainted bodies signifies movement toward community freedom. Luke is mistaken. Unlike Uncle Tom, Mabelle / Sappho lives in defiance of the racialist and misogynist structure of progressive historiography.[53] Hopkins, that is, refuses to reinscribe Fuller's and Stowe's "merciless doctrine" upon Sappho's body.[54] And by keeping Sappho on stage in her novel—and emphasizing Mabelle's absence from the rally stage—she asks us to recognize how such bodies serve in productions of both historical and racial meaning.

All of the key relationships in *Contending Forces* are shaped by the specular economy that develops around Sappho as a visible record, a historiographic sign, of miscegenation and rape. Everyone stares at Sappho with varying mixtures of pleasure and desire and appropriates her image into a past or future they wish to inhabit. "She has the sweetest and saddest face I ever saw," muses Dora. "I have read of the woman with a story written on her face, but I never believed it anything but a fairy tale" (*CF*, 89). Dora's is the most benign reading of this ilk, but even she finds discomfiting aesthetic gratification in the tragic story Sappho embodies. More disturbing is the burst of grotesquely misplaced nostalgia with which another character identifies the origin of our heroine's image: "'I knowed it,' cried Mrs. White, as she triumphantly glanced around the room. 'Ol' New

Orleans blood will tell on itself anywhere'" (*CF*, 108). Most significant here is the rapist uncle who appropriates Sappho physically and epistemically into the legal past of slavery: "'It is my belief that [Negresses] were a direct creation by God to be the pleasant companions of men of my race,'" he explains when confronted. "'Now, I am willing to give you a thousand dollars and call it square'" (*CF*, 261). While the first two examples remind us, dissonantly, that Sappho's mixed-race blood signifies a past of subjection, the third reveals that it is the past that subjects and racializes her. By reading meaning onto her body, the uncle reconstitutes a pre-emancipation temporal frame that gives him ownership of her and cancels the racial ambiguity of their blood relation. The blackness that the uncle imposes both produces and is produced by the racial order of an antebellum past: blackness as the past, the past via blackness.

However, Hopkins refuses to stage a sacrifice of sexualized, racialized, historically contingent embodiment toward the fulfillment of Woman as the "Virgin Mother of the new race." In fact, the novel associates that mandate with another kind of injurious gaze. When Mrs. Willis counsels other clubwomen to "hasten the transformation of the body" and eliminate the "marks" of immoral sexuality in order to lead the race forward, she focuses particularly upon Sappho: "'It is a blessing to look at you. Beauty like yours is inspiring'" (*CF*, 153, 155). She reads in Sappho the very transformation she calls for—a beauty with transcendent meaning ("a blessing") and power to lead ("inspiring"). But providing such a display requires that Sappho conceal her traumatic history at great personal cost—when Mrs. Willis deflects the girl's confidence this erasure of Sappho's "marks" is not freeing but isolating and burdensome. Will Smith also asks Sappho to represent transcendent femininity. Declaring his love, he "glance[s] at the fair face beside him with something like awe" and feels "he [stands] in the presence of a saint" (*CF*, 309–10). Like Mrs. Willis, Will imagines Sappho as his future—in marriage and in reform work, "yoked in all exercise of noble end"—and refuses to share her burden of history: when Sappho tries to confide in him, Will interrupts, "I do not care for the past" (*CF*, 402, 312). Mrs. Willis and Will reverse the injury done by her uncle by reading Sappho into ahistorical spiritualized femininity. Yet, by noting how Will's gaze "feasts" on Sappho's beauty, Hopkins implies a comparable act of appropriation. His misreading remains complicit with racialist historicism, valuing progress away from taint, historicity, or the taint of historicity and toward the unmarked and saintly "fairness" it constitutes upon her.

Rather than shed her traumatically racialized body, Sappho incorporates it into exemplary womanhood: "in the years which followed," sermonizes the narrator, "she learned to value the strong, chastening influence of her present sorrow, and the force of character it developed, fitting her perfectly for the place she was to occupy in carrying comfort and hope to the women of her race"

(*CF*, 347). But this faith that Sappho's survival will bring "comfort and hope" to others disregards the community's resistance to its terms. When Sappho flees to a New Orleans convent, a nun counsels a return to concealment of her shameful history and to providential historical consciousness: "You are not called upon to make too many sacrifices. God sees your heart and will reward you in his own good time" (*CF*, 352). Will, especially, struggles to incorporate Mabelle's past into his conception of the future: "How could he bear to think that his beautiful Sappho—his pure girl-love, had been subjected to such brutality. . . . He could not suffer more and live" (*CF*, 330). *Contending Forces* does not simply valorize marked female embodiment as that which embraces history and leads the way forward within it. In his fourteenth thesis on history, Benjamin writes:

> History is the subject of a structure whose site is not homogenous, empty time, but time filled by the presence of the now. Thus, to Robespierre ancient Rome was a past charged with the time of the now which he blasted out of the continuum of history. The French Revolution viewed itself as Rome reincarnate. It evoked ancient Rome the way fashion evokes costumes of the past. Fashion has a flair for the topical, no matter where it stirs in the thickets of long ago; it is a tiger's leap into the past. This jump, however, takes place in an arena where the ruling class gives the commands. ("TPH," 261)

Like Robespierre, Hopkins finds revolutionary resources in nonlinear temporality and specifically in a past "charged with the time of the now." But she also recognizes temporality as a contested territory where every "leap" courts danger. Sappho's spectacular image warps the continuum of historicism, opening space in which to challenge the racial and gendered meanings that historiography organizes and is organized by. But it also positions her as sacrificial object in the arena of hegemonic culture. Benjamin's ambiguous reference to "a tiger's leap" is instructive. It figures counterhistorians as both aggressors out to slaughter the historicist faithful and potential gladiators themselves, next in line for martyrdom before the "ruling class." In *Of One Blood* and *Contending Forces*, where Dianthe, Mabelle, and their audiences literally convulse in agony, where Sappho faints at the moment Luke recalls her death, it seems clear that the leap is not merely conceptual or critical; it is ontological and excruciatingly corporeal (*CF*, 261–62). For Hopkins, racialist historicism is more than a false construct that obscures a true past and can be rejected or corrected. It is an evolutionary/eschatological fantasy written on and through embodiment, a corporealization of race-gender codes. It *is* the violence that it conceals.

Sappho's failure to die or otherwise transcend her tainted body conveys Hopkins's refusal to endorse a vision of reform in which femininity and blackness move in opposite directions, one toward transcendence, the other toward the past. It reveals, as well, the historicity of historiography by portraying what such a vision has cost black women whose bodies have borne both the trauma of the past and the violent un / re / writing of its record. Although two reform projects are underway at the conclusion of *Contending Forces*—one headed by Arthur Lewis, one by Will Smith, both focused on the realization of black potential—the novel's most radical conceptualization of reform differs from these. It focuses not on hopeful futurity but on the harrowing temporality of the now, where history—the corporealization of historiography and its race-gender inscription—lies.

NOTES

1. For other discussions of spectacular femininity in Fuller's writing and self-presentation, see Katherine Adams, *Owning Up: Privacy, Property, and Belonging in U.S. Women's Life Writing* (New York: Oxford Univ. Press, 2009), 31–70; and Julie Ellison, *Delicate Subjects: Romanticism, Gender, and the Ethics of Understanding* (Ithaca, N.Y.: Cornell Univ. Press, 1990).
2. Pauline Hopkins Brown, *Of One Blood*, in *The Magazine Novels of Pauline Hopkins* (New York: Oxford Univ. Press, 1988), 452–54; hereafter cited parenthetically as *OOB*.
3. Walter Benjamin, "Theses on the Philosophy of History," in *Illuminations: Essays and Reflections*, trans. Harry Zohn (1968; New York: Schocken Books, 2007), 261; hereafter cited parenthetically as "TPH."
4. Daphne Brooks, *Bodies in Dissent: Spectacular Performances of Race and Freedom, 1850–1910* (Durham, N.C.: Duke Univ. Press, 2006), 300–302.
5. For more on this connection, see Lois Brown, *Pauline Elizabeth Hopkins: Black Daughter of the Revolution* (Chapel Hill: Univ. of North Carolina Press, 2008); and Brooks, *Bodies in Dissent*.
6. See Jill Bergman, "'Everything we hoped she'd be': Contending Forces in Hopkins Scholarship," *African American Review* 38, no. 2 (2004): 181–99.
7. Such a lineage would necessarily pass through both Zenobia and Priscilla—Zenobia's inverted image—since Dianthe becomes the object of manipulation and mesmerism soon after her triumphant performance at the Tremont Temple. My gratitude to Jennie Kassanoff for pointing out this connection.
8. Linda Kerber, *Toward an Intellectual History of Women* (Chapel Hill: Univ. of North Carolina Press, 1997), 117.
9. Nina Baym, *American Women Writers and the Work of History, 1790–1860* (New Brunswick, N.J.: Rutgers Univ. Press, 1995), 217.
10. Baym, *American Women Writers*, 217.
11. Thomas Allen, *A Republic in Time: Temporality and Social Imagination in Nineteenth-Century America* (Chapel Hill: Univ. of North Carolina Press, 2008), 23.
12. For a more detailed version of this argument, see Adams, *Owning Up*, esp. chap. 2.
13. Margaret Fuller, quoted in Phyllis Cole, "Woman Questions: Emerson, Fuller, and New England Reform," in Capper and Wright, 426.
14. Margaret Fuller, from "The Liberty Bell," in *The Liberty Bell, by Friends of Freedom*, ed. Maria Weston Chapman (Boston: Anti-Slavery Fair, 1846), 85.

15. An early passage, for example, characterizes the "monstrous display of slave-dealing and slave-keeping" as failures that "only seemingly impede" the nation's destiny to "elucidate a great moral law" (*WNC*, 13).
16. According to Kelley Wagers, the 1884 founding of the American Historical Society began with Andrew Dickson White's aim to "uncover the 'great lines of historical evolution' through a 'rewriting of history from the American point of view'" ("Race, Nation, and Historical (Re)Form in *The Souls of Black Folks*," *Arizona Quarterly* 64, no. 1 [2008]: 78).
17. Jane Tompkins, *Sensational Designs: The Cultural Work of American Fiction, 1790–1860* (New York: Oxford Univ. Press, 1985), 134.
18. James Baldwin, "Everybody's Protest Novel," in *The Norton Anthology of African American Literature, Second Edition*, ed. Henry Louis Gates Jr. and Nellie Y. McKay (New York: Norton, 2004), 1702.
19. Caroline H. Dall, *The College, the Market, and the Court* (Boston: Lee & Shepard, 1867), 116.
20. Phyllis Cole, "The Nineteenth-Century Women's Rights Movement and the Canonization of Margaret Fuller," *ESQ: A Journal of the American Renaissance* 44 (1998): 2.
21. Cole, "Canonization," 17.
22. A tribute to Stone and Cheney appears in the first issue of *Woman's Era* (1, no. 1 [1894]), and an article praising Howe's antilynching stance appears a year later (2, no. 4). All *Woman's Era* citations can be located at Emory University's electronic Women Writers Resource Project: http://womenwriters.library.emory.edu/browse.php?field=publisher&value=%22Woman's%20Era%20Club%22, accessed November 10, 2013.
23. Sylvia Mann Maples, "Club Notes: Tennessee," *Woman's Era* 2, no. 2 (1895): 13.
24. See "Chat with Girls" on the Brook Farm study group (*Woman's Era* 1, no. 2 [1894]); Emerson's "three rules for reading" in "Chat with Girls" (1, no. 1 [1894]); and Fannie Barrier Williams's Emersonian epigraphs in "Notes from Illinois" (1, no. 9 [1894]; 2, no. 2 [1895]; 2, no. 10 [1896]). Hopkins cites Emerson throughout *Contending Forces* and "Famous Women of the Negro Race."
25. Cole, "Canonization," 2, 14.
26. P. Gabrielle Foreman, *Activist Sentiments: Reading Black Women in the Nineteenth Century* (Chicago: Univ. of Illinois Press, 2009), 129. See also Brooks, *Bodies in Dissent*.
27. Victoria Earle Matthews, "The Awakening of the Afro-American Woman," in *With Pen and Voice: A Critical Anthology of Nineteenth-Century African American Women*, ed. Shirley Logan (Carbondale: Southern Illinois Univ. Press, 1995), 149, 154.
28. Josephine Ruffin, quoted in Francesca Sawaya, "Emplotting National History: Regionalism and Pauline Hopkins's *Contending Forces*," in *Breaking Boundaries: New Perspectives on Women's Regional Writing*, ed. Sherrie A. Inness and Diana Royer (Iowa City: Univ. of Iowa Press, 1997), 75–76.
29. "Mr. Fortune's Question," *Woman's Era* 1, no. 6 (1894): 9.
30. Cole, "Canonization," 19; Ralph Waldo Emerson, quoted in F. O. Matthiessen, *American Renaissance: Art and Expression in the Age of Emerson and Whitman* (London: Oxford Univ. Press, 1941), 71.
31. See Robert Knox's 1850 treatise, *The Races of Man: A Fragment* (Philadelphia: Lea & Blanchard, 1850).
32. S. Elizabeth Frazier, "Mrs. Wm. E. Matthews (Victoria Earle)," *Woman's Era* 1, no. 2 (1894): 1. See also the advertisement for a talk titled "Science of Human Beings" (*Woman's Era* 2, no. 1 [1895]: 1); and Mary V. Bass's "Nature or Environment" (2, no. 7 [1897]): 7.

33. W. E. B. Du Bois, quoted in Rebecca J. Cole, "First Meeting of the Women's Missionary Society of Philadelphia," *Woman's Era* 3, no. 4 (1896): 4; "Address of Josephine St. Pierre Ruffin, President of Conference," *Woman's Era* 2, no. 5 (1895): 14.
34. Patricia Williams, *The Alchemy of Race and Rights: Diary of a Law Professor* (Cambridge, Mass.: Harvard Univ. Press, 1991), 198.
35. Margaret Washington, "Call to the National Federation of A Fro-American [*sic*] Women," *Woman's Era* 2, no. 7 (1895): 2.
36. Pauline Hopkins, *Contending Forces: A Romance Illustrative of Negro Life North and South* (New York: Oxford Univ. Press, 1988), 153; hereafter cited parenthetically as *CF*.
37. Pauline Hopkins, "Famous Women of the Negro Race," in *Daughter of the Revolution: The Major Nonfiction Works of Pauline E. Hopkins*, ed. Ira Dworkin (New Brunswick, N.J.: Rutgers Univ. Press, 2007), 114–15.
38. In this Hopkins differs significantly from other nineteenth-century black historiographers. Early black historical narratives are often grounded in alternate, nonlinear temporalities. But these typically refer to sacred or biblical time, a temporal dimension that enables an imaginative escape from social history and a vantage point for reinterpreting experience within it. For recent overviews of nineteenth-century black historiography, see John Ernest, *Liberation Historiography: African American Writers and the Challenge of History, 1794–1861* (Chapel Hill: Univ. of North Carolina Press, 2004); Laurie F. Maffly-Kipp, *Setting Down the Sacred Past: African American Race Histories* (Cambridge, Mass.: Harvard Univ. Press, 2010); and Stephen G. Hall, *A Faithful Account of the Race: African American Historical Writing in Nineteenth-Century America* (Chapel Hill: Univ. of North Carolina Press, 2009).
39. Brooks, *Bodies in Dissent*, 290.
40. Sami Khatib, "Karl Marx, Walter Benjamin and the Spectre of the Messianic: Is There a Materialist Theory of Time?" in *Anthropological Materialism*, 22 November 2010. Available online at http://anthropologicalmaterialism.hypotheses.org/844, accessed November 30, 2013.
41. Ernest, *Liberation Historiography*, 10.
42. My thanks to University of South Carolina colleague Agnes Mueller for helping me track down Benjamin's essay in the original German and confirming the double action of *vor*.
43. Khatib, "Karl Marx, Walter Benjamin."
44. For two analyses that do explore the mutual constitution of historical and racial meaning, see Lloyd Pratt, who argues that black historiographers destabilized whiteness by challenging master narratives on time, history, and progress (*Archives of the American: Literature and Modernity in the Nineteenth Century* [Philadelphia: Univ. of Pennsylvania Press, 2010], 159); and John Ernest, who finds that the historical constitution of race becomes a "dynamic narrative principle" in black historical works (*Liberation Historiography*, 60).
45. See Gwendolyn Brooks, afterword to *Contending Forces: A Romance Illustrative of Negro Life North and South*, by Pauline Hopkins (Carbondale: Southern Illinois Univ. Press, 1978); and Houston Baker Jr., *Workings of the Spirit: The Poetics of Afro-American Women's Writing* (Chicago: Univ. of Chicago Press, 1991), 28.
46. Hazel Carby, *Reconstructing Womanhood: The Emergence of the Afro-American Woman Novelist* (New York: Oxford Univ. Press, 1987), 140.
47. Lisa Marcus, "'Of One Blood': Reimagining American Genealogy in Pauline Hopkins's *Contending Forces*," in *Speaking the Other Self: American Women Writers*, ed. Jeanne Campbell Reesman (Athens: Univ. of Georgia Press, 1997), 117–43, 120.

48. Kate McCullough, "Slavery, Sexuality, and Genre: Pauline Hopkins and the Representation of Female Desire," in *The Unruly Voice: Rediscovering Pauline Elizabeth Hopkins*, ed. John Cullen Gruesser (Urbana: Univ. of Illinois Press, 1996), 21–49, 25.
49. Brown, *Black Daughter*, 189, 185.
50. William Northen, quoted in Brown, *Black Daughter*, 184.
51. Brown, *Black Daughter*, 185.
52. Ernest, *Liberation Historiography*, 53.
53. Jennifer Putzi, "'Raising the Stigma': Black Womanhood and the Marked Body in Pauline Hopkins's *Contending Forces*," *College Literature* 31 (Spring 2004): 16–17.
54. Baldwin, "Everybody's Protest Novel," 1702.

Ednah D. Cheney, from the introduction to *Louisa May Alcott: Her Life, Letters, and Journals* (Boston: Roberts Brothers, 1889), iii–iv.

Louisa May Alcott is universally recognized as the greatest and most popular story-teller for children in her generation. She has known the way to the hearts of young people, not only in her own class, or even country, but in every condition of life, and in many foreign lands. Plato says, "Beware of those who teach fables to children;" and it is impossible to estimate the influence which the popular writer of fiction has over the audience he wins to listen to his tales. . . .

Of no author can it be more truly said than of Louisa Alcott that her works are a revelation of herself. She rarely sought for the material of her stories in old chronicles, or foreign adventures. Her capital was her own life and experiences and those of others directly about her; and her own well-remembered girlish frolics and fancies were sure to find responsive enjoyment in the minds of other girls.

It is therefore impossible to understand Miss Alcott's works fully without a knowledge of her own life and experiences. By inheritance and education she had rich and peculiar gifts; and her life was one of rare advantages, as well as of trying difficulties. Herself of the most true and frank nature, she has given us the opportunity of knowing her without disguise; and it is thus that I shall try to portray her, showing what influences acted upon her through life.

The Cosmopolitan Project of Louisa May Alcott

LAURA DASSOW WALLS

Evaluating stories together is one of the central human ways of learning to align our responses to the world.

—Kwame Anthony Appiah, *Cosmopolitanism* (2006)

The transnational turn in American literary studies has recently foregrounded the Atlantic Ocean's dual role as both barrier and highway. Louisa May Alcott and her contemporaries lived on an Atlantic highway bustling with new traffic: the cessation of war, technical developments that brought railroads and steamships, and emerging middle-class affluence all helped generate a new kind of global consumer culture. The aspiring New England housewife could select for her domestic environment the latest British novels, newest Paris fashions, finest China dishes, best West Indian sugar, and juiciest Cuban oranges. She could even dream of travel to Europe, a dream Louisa May Alcott gave to Amy of the impoverished March family in *Little Women*: "[I wish to] go to Rome, and do fine pictures, and be the best artist in the whole world."[1] Indeed, the success of this very book gave Alcott a foundation for her castle in the air: she herself took the grand tour of Europe, together with her real-life sister May, the model for Amy, who stayed on in Rome to study art and "do fine pictures."

But as Amy's yearning suggests, this emerging cosmopolitanism reached beyond consumers' tastes and transoceanic tourism. The political upheavals sparked by the United States' Declaration of Independence had precipitated a cascade of wars and revolutions across both hemispheres, which Alcott herself experienced most immediately during the American Civil War and through the influx of immigrants produced by the Irish and German diasporas. As the political boundaries of the United States expanded—Alcott lived to witness the annexation of Texas, the conquest of Mexico, the acquisition of Oregon Territory, and the purchase of Alaska—the question of who was "American" and who was "foreign" stayed both unsettled and profoundly unsettling. One response was an intensifying racist nationalism, the now-notorious hallmark of "manifest destiny" and anti-immigration legislation; but another was a nascent cosmopolitan ethos that imagined new forms of social solidarity across differences of race, class, and nation. Louisa's father Bronson Alcott spoke for this second response when he remarked that electricity, the telegraph and railroad, the press, and the freedom of world travel had brought a new breadth to modern life: "No life is insular now. Every thought resounds throughout the globe."[2] This new mobility of people and ideas had tremendous political consequences: "Our time is revolutionary," Bronson declared, for the "fellowship of all souls" was intent on laying the foundations for new institutions. "The firm of Globe Brothers & Co., prospers in both hemispheres, every citizen being a partner in the concern"—"the nations are leagued together on the basis of mutual assistance," basing alliances not on "force and fear" but on becoming "friends and copartners in conducting the world's affairs."[3]

Bronson's meditation on a league of nations places him in a long tradition of cosmopolitan thinking such as that voiced during the Enlightenment by Immanuel Kant. While watching the United States' battle for independence from Britain and the French Revolution devolve into yet another bloody world war, Kant proposed that only the lawful unfolding of human reason and free will could contain history's senseless march of war and conquest. Education and self-culture would balance and limit the predatory, expansionist impulse of modern trade and technology through a turn that would "league" all nations into a global civil society, what Kant called "a cosmo-political state," dedicated to protecting the freedom of all its members.[4] Rather than militarize national citizens for expansion and conquest, Kant's proposed new ethic of "universal hospitality" would forbid any nation to conquer or assault any other (Kant had in mind the French and British Empires), for ultimately "a violation of law and right in one place is felt in *all* others." This was not, in Kant's view, a hazy utopian dream but entirely practical, "a necessary completion of the . . . public law of mankind."[5]

Following Kant, generations of idealists have sought to realize his cosmopolitan ethic. In the United States, William Ellery Channing, Ralph Waldo Emerson, and Abigail Alcott's brother Samuel Joseph May all lectured before the American Peace Society, founded in 1828, whose efforts eventually contributed after World War I to the founding of the (painfully short-lived) League of Nations.[6] Cosmopolitanism advanced on the cultural front as well: once the 1815 Treaty of Ghent reopened transatlantic travel, ambitious young New England men—George Ticknor, Edward Everett, George Bancroft, Henry W. Longfellow—set sail for Europe, and the books, theories, and philosophies they brought back transformed the American intellectual landscape. Harvard rushed to add the exciting new European literatures to its curriculum, and beyond Harvard's gates sprouted informal reading groups dedicated to discussing the "new philosophy." Critics dubbed the most famous of them "the transcendentalists," using Kant's term to sneer at their strange and foreign ideas. But these very ideas inspired America's first great movement in literature, philosophy, and reform, which in turn carried cosmopolitan thinking around the globe, as books by Emerson, Thoreau, Fuller, Elizabeth Peabody, Louisa May Alcott, and others traveled the Atlantic back to Europe and beyond. Cosmopolitanism offered an ethical response to the global challenges faced by this generation of Americans, a response that tried, not to privilege the near and familiar by excluding or demonizing the "Other," but rather to value the Other and work toward connection and dialogue, even global political solidarity, across national boundaries and differences of race, class, and gender.[7]

Robert Weisbuch, in a book that anticipated the recent transatlantic approach to American literature, remarks on the "cultural thinness" that seemed to characterize America in contrast with the "thickness" of Europe.[8] But as Bronson Alcott suggests, America was hardly thin and (to use his word) "insular" but thick with planetary alliances and partnerships that put into play not only transatlantic geography but also the lengthening scale of history. Alcott's words reach from the eighteenth-century Enlightenment to the twenty-first-century thinking of Wai Chee Dimock, who locates national chronologies in geological "deep time" and national geographies on the face of the planet itself. In this planetary mode, the once-sovereign nation becomes "a crisscrossing set of pathways, open-ended and ever multiplying, weaving in and out of other geographies, other languages and cultures."[9] The once-sovereign author, too, becomes a complex weave, a thickening knot of converging and diverging pathways through deep time and planetary space.

Such pathways entwine Louisa May Alcott intellectually with her father, for Bronson Alcott incarnated his travels, both actual and intellectual, in the education and career of his famous daughter. Thanks to his compulsion to turn their home into a laboratory and his fatherly teachings into a scientific experiment, Louisa herself became the living, writing embodiment of a transatlantic metaphysical conversation. From this perspective, her fictions hardly divide neatly into "domestic" fictions versus "foreign" thrillers, a polarity that divides the globe itself between the national homeland and its threatening foreign agents, forcing women writers into the insidious role of civilizing imperialists.[10] Instead, nationalist anxieties and cosmopolitan hopes thread through all of Alcott's works, tying them together as moments in a long debate over how to domesticate the dangerous energies of cosmopolitan skepticism without surrendering its hopes for social solidarity.

Not just Louisa, however, is at stake here. Her choice to draw on the deep reservoir of cosmopolitical self-culture connects her with a complex network of transatlantic women, from Mary Wollstonecraft and Mary Shelley to Harriet Martineau, Elizabeth Peabody, Margaret Fuller, and beyond. Each of these writers found in cosmopolitical thought and action the resources to reconceive herself as an independent, self-unfolding intellectual as well as to conceive all women not only as full-fledged citizens of a planetary, cosmopolitical "league"—though that surely is breathtaking enough—but as agents whose work it could be to take Kant's ethical revolution from theory to fact. Men alone, as Fuller observed, could not solve the riddle of the times, for after all it was largely men who had created this riddle by their systematic silencing of women, the poor, the dark-skinned, the enslaved. It was up to women, for so long the marked and silenced Other of male power, to show the way, to bring that league into being at last.

Transcendentalist women engaged the cosmopolitical project in many ways. Elizabeth Peabody, for instance, leveraged her wide reading in European educational theory into reforms (such as the *Kindergarten*) that still mark the American classroom, and she stocked her Boston bookstore and forum with titles in English, French, German, Italian, Greek, and Latin, turning it into America's hub for transatlantic conversations.[11] Margaret Fuller, in her foundational work *Woman in the Nineteenth Century* (1845), leveraged world history, philosophy, and literature into what Phyllis Cole calls "a Romantic millennial vision of humanity fulfilled through woman's agency," an agency enacted by a roll call of revolutionary women that Fuller herself joined when she enlisted in the Italian Revolution of 1848.[12] Louisa May Alcott did not choose to reorganize the classroom, open a bookstore, or join a world revolution; instead, she filled homes and classrooms and bookstores with her novels and short stories, which collectively figure this transatlantic conversation as a high-stakes dialogue of ideas, with all futurity bound in the outcome. She worked, like Fuller and Peabody and other women of her day, to make the education of children central to a worldwide republicanism whose intergenerational goal was to transform conquest and power into a peaceful global domesticity.

Cosmopolitanism's most pressing dilemma is not how to imagine connections to the Other but how to *feel* them: how to go from loving one's family, friends, and neighbors to experiencing bonds of affection with distant foreigners and seemingly repellent aliens. The emotional bonds seem to stretch too thin, and finally to break, as if charity, like gravity, weakens with distance. The virtue of fiction lies in its ability to address this problem, to leap over distances and make the reader feel compassion for the Other—an ability that Harriet Beecher Stowe, for one, exploited to extraordinary advantage. Could a single writer change the world through literature?[13] John Matteson suggests that both Bronson and Louisa Alcott believed they could, an ambition they shared with an ancestor who in 1630 had crossed the Atlantic on the *Arbella* with John Winthrop and, presumably, stood on the deck to hear Winthrop declare that their new community must be bound into one body through love and Christian charity in order to stand as an ideal before the world, a "city upon a hill."[14] To this mythic Puritan ideal, Bronson added the teachings of the great Swiss educator Johann Pestalozzi, who famously counseled that "the role of an educator is to teach children, not subjects."[15] Pestalozzi's notions of the innate moral and spiritual intelligence of children inspired an educational reform movement that spread from Switzerland and Germany to Great Britain, and Bronson Alcott joined forces with Elizabeth Peabody to bring Pestalozzi's theories to the American classroom.

At their famous Temple School in Boston, they experimented with an innovative method of "teaching children, not subjects," by educing, or drawing out, a child's innate knowledge through the patient and searching (and, in Bronson's practice, sometimes coercive) form of the Socratic dialogue. As Cole details, Peabody had independently laid her own "groundwork for progressive, gender-equalizing pedagogy and reform," beginning with her reading in Herder, and it was she who made Bronson famous by featuring him in her *Record of a School* (1835). In this careful account of the school's pedagogical ideals and practices (which Megan Marshall calls "the first book of transcendentalist ideas to be published in America"), Peabody traces the unfolding of their students' minds and spirits under her own instruction in world geography and Alcott's in world literature: his close readings of the Bible, Spenser's *Faerie Queen*, Bunyan's *Pilgrim's Progress*, Milton, Coleridge, and Wordsworth all used imagination as, in Alcott's words, "the guiding energy of light and life to humanity." As one little boy exclaimed, "I never knew I had a mind till I came to this school!"[16]

Extending heart and head to all humanity was hard intellectual and cultural work. Pestalozzi insisted that education be practiced as an exact science, building on carefully cultivated sense impressions to develop, through reflection, complex ideas.[17] Yet Bronson worried that his pupils came to his classroom already compromised by conventional family practices of child-rearing; thus, starting with the Alcotts' first child, Anna, he carefully tried to control his own children's environment and meticulously recorded the results. His family laboratory continued to evolve as his reading in European philosophy expanded, and Louisa, his second child, was born under the star of Coleridge. Bronson filled nearly 300 pages with observations on her first twelve months of life. As she grew, he continued to educe her higher spiritual and creative powers through his ever-widening circle of reading, which included Coleridge, Wordsworth, Carlyle, Cousin, Goethe, Kant (at secondhand), Schiller, Herder, and Humboldt (a favorite at the Temple School), feeding all he read back into his educational theories.[18] Thus young Louisa was brought up as the incarnation of the very latest European romantic teachings, and she and her three sisters were proudly displayed as the products of the New Philosophy. In later years she told a droll tale of the day Emerson and Margaret Fuller dropped by to witness the results of Bronson's model educational methods: "As the guests stood on the door steps, a wild uproar approached and round the corner of the house came a wheelbarrow holding baby May arrayed as a queen; I was the horse, bitted and bridled and driven by my elder sister Anna, while Lizzie played dog and barked as loud as her gentle voice permitted." As the children "espied the stately group" before them, Louisa tripped, spilling the whole into a laughing heap, while mother Abigail climaxed the joke with a dramatic wave of her hand: "'Here are the model children, Miss Fuller.'"[19]

In *Little Women* (1868–69), Louisa herself would put her family on display as a model of the New Philosophy, but meanwhile, Bronson's experiments drove home the conflict between cosmopolitan ideals and American conventions. The Temple School, founded in 1834, was thriving until scandal erupted in December 1836, when Bronson (against Peabody's advice) published some overly frank allusions to human sexuality in *Conversations with Children on the Gospels*. Public outrage followed and enrollments plunged. Alcott finally closed the Temple School in June 1838 and in October opened a new school for the poor; but this, too, wilted when he admitted a black girl and his patrons withdrew their support. The Alcotts relocated to the more encouraging environment of Concord, where Bronson worked as a day laborer while Anna and Louisa enrolled in the Thoreau brothers' own innovative school. Emerson helped by opening his library to Louisa and funding her father's trip to England, where Bronson joined a group of Pestalozzi's English disciples, who had been so impressed by the records of the Temple School that they had named their own school "Alcott House" in his honor. It was one member of this group, Charles Lane, who helped Bronson found his very own city on a hill: Lane accompanied Bronson back to Massachusetts, where the two established Fruitlands, the utopian experiment in consociate family life that profoundly shaped Louisa May Alcott's own notions of family and education.

"Transcendental Wild Oats," Louisa's eventual account of the Fruitlands experiment—which began with great promise on 1 June 1843 and ended in defeat and despair the following January—is staged as a witty morality tale pitting the foolish improvidence of male idealism against the wise management of female pragmatism, making mother Abigail's resourcefulness and stalwart love for her husband the salvation of the family from destruction. Yet Louisa's actual journal entries from these months, when she was ten years old and just starting to write, show not failure but exhilaration in a cheerful, even idyllic, experiment in living and learning, where she was alternately embraced by philosophy and released to run joyously wild in nature. This more positive legacy of Fruitlands may be seen not in her bittersweet memoir but in her portrait of the fictional Plumfield, the utopian educational community that Louisa imagined for Jo March and Fritz Bhaer in *Little Men* (1871) and *Jo's Boys* (1886). What starts at the end of *Little Women* as a boy's boarding school matures (thanks to old Mr. Laurence's generous endowment) into a thriving coeducational college, with alumni indeed prospering in all hemispheres: Europe, South America, Australia, and California. At Plumfield, work and play, learning and living, go on around the clock, in a community of young people from diverse backgrounds bonded into a nurturing version of Lane's consociate family. As Matteson writes, "Where Fruitlands was experienced only by a handful of impractical dreamers, Plumfield has left its mark on the imaginations of generations of children, sowing seeds of idealism to sprout where they may."[20]

What Louisa barely registers in her childhood journal, and resolves in Plumfield, is the deep conflict between Lane's vision of the biological family as a transitory step to some larger, more inclusive association and Abigail Alcott's fierce defense of her own nuclear family. The conflict created a triangle with Bronson "oscillating uneasily in the middle," and while Abigail finally won, saving her family meant sacrificing Utopia.[21] Louisa, the child recording and remembering it all, thus experienced both the transformative force of European romantic philosophy and its fearsome power to tear apart traditional institutional and family structures. Remarkably, her writing centered on rehabilitating the same radical European ideals that had both shaped and threatened her childhood, as she literally domesticated those ideals into the close-knit, nurturing, mother-centered family of *Little Women*, which she then turned outward to reshape the world. That is, she was fully aware, in all her writing, of the double-edged quality of the ideals that had ruled her family during her childhood: in the resulting empowerment and destruction, she found a double edge and translated it into her various fictions.

In those fictions, Louisa frequently pairs two alternate social and literary attitudes, invoking a doppelgänger contrast between what Weisbuch calls "actualism" and "ontological insecurity." The first makes absences into virtues by making "actual" the mind's design: the very absence of historical institutions opens, in America, a space for implementing a utopian vision of what might be. Thus, in *Little Women*, the father's very absence (famously, Louisa writes him out of the first book by dispatching him to the Civil War) creates the conditions for a redesigned matriarchal family that implements the educational theories her own father had attempted and failed to complete. In effect, Louisa domesticates those theories into a form that, embodied and enacted not by designing and cold-hearted men but by practical and compassionate women, saves her father's ideals while correcting his absurdities and imbalances. In Louisa's retelling, the mind's design, that remote "city upon a hill," becomes a blueprint for a "pilgrim's progress" toward the new, reformed global family, a blueprint so attractive, and so definitive, that generations of readers have imagined their own lives in its terms.

Weisbuch's second stance, "ontological insecurity," could be manifested as both nervous and daring, fragmented and exploratory. As the nation's actual historical narrative became more and more disappointing, a bold and searching skepticism could offer "solace" to that narrative's dissatisfied devotees and make smug Victorian assurances seem "stupid and secretly frightened." His model here is, remarkably, Ralph Waldo Emerson, who in "The American Scholar" (addressed in 1837 to Harvard's all-male graduating class) presents "Man Thinking" against the British "Man Having Thought" or "Man Letting the Past Think for Him."[22] What better gloss on *Little Women*?—where Louisa transposes Emerson's prescription of "*Man* Thinking" into her dramatization of "*Woman* Thinking," enacting her own searching skepticism regarding her father's "Having Thought"? Margaret Fuller, who out-radicalized Emerson himself, would seem a still better model, certainly one more useful to Louisa—who, against Bronson's waywardness and insecurity, does not capitulate to convention but moves beyond it, and beyond her father too, defiantly practicing romanticism by other means. Louisa wields her revitalized romanticism as a weapon against the stifling Victorian conventions that everywhere attacked the salvific ideals she had grown up by and still held dear; and she does it by insisting that a revitalized romanticism is, essentially, gendered female.

Yet in Victorian America, a functioning family needs, to be sure, a strong male presence; Louisa does not mean to anticipate Charlotte Perkins Gilman's all-female Utopia, *Herland*. For her model she must therefore redesign the father as well as the mother, and for this purpose the shadowy Mr. March, that ghost of her own father, will not do. She interposes instead the benign and protective Professor Bhaer—bypassing her English Puritan inheritance entirely to supply instead a German romantic philosopher and teacher. From an Anglo-American perspective such a choice has seemed bizarre, but from a transnational perspective, it seems inevitable: Germany was the fountainhead for the "New Philosophy," and of all the transnational literatures available to Louisa, the German was by far the most important to her. As Christine Doyle has detailed, the influence of German literature on the March trilogy was deep indeed, making, as she says, "much more explicable the match between Jo March and Friedrich Bhaer."[23]

But when Louisa invented this key character, could she have had more than literary models in mind? I suspect she did: Charles Follen, Harvard's first instructor of German language and literature, bears some striking resemblances to Professor Bhaer.[24] Without Follen, those high-flown abstract German ideals would have remained philosophical imponderables, but in his presence they materialized into living human form, carrying conviction and passion into the hearts of those who knew him. That circle included not only Bronson Alcott and Margaret Fuller, who both studied German with Follen, but also Orestes Brownson (who openly acknowledged his deep debt to Follen), Frederick Henry Hedge, the Ripleys, Theodore Parker, the Peabody sisters, William Ellery Channing, and, most importantly, Abigail Alcott's brother Samuel May—indeed, Channing and May were Follen's closest friends. It is the warmth and excitement of an intimate old friend, a *felt* presence rather than abstract ideas, that Louisa conveys; through Follen / Bhaer, German ideals of cosmopolitan self-culture found their way not only into formal American educational systems but into the imaginative lives of generations of readers.

Bhaer's life story is only hinted at in *Little Women*. Jo discovers "that in his native city he had been a man much honored and esteemed for learning and integrity" (373), but the reader never learns why he left the dear home for which he still sighs. But everyone in the Alcott circle knew Karl Theodore Christian Follen's remarkable story, which Theodore Parker, in the *Dial*, called "a moral-heroic drama, in one act."[25] As a young man in Germany, Follen was a firebrand leader of the "Giessen Blacks," a radical student group whose platform is captured in his famous poem "The Great Song," a hymn to the people's overthrow of tyranny:

> Rush in, mighty angry ocean billows,
> Over slaves and tyrants who oppress thee;
> Be a nation, be a free state, be on fire![26]

Follen's deep learning and unbending integrity made him feared as the "handle" to the "axe" of revolution,[27] and he was hounded first out of Germany and then out of neutral Switzerland, where he had established himself as an honored professor of law and philosophy. He fled for his life to Paris. Then in 1824, at the urging of the Marquis de Lafayette, he shipped to the United States, where he anglicized his name to "Charles." Though drawn to the ministry, Follen was recruited to Harvard by Edward Everett and George Ticknor, who arranged his appointment as Harvard's first instructor of German. His supporters soon funded a five-year professorship, and Follen busied himself writing America's first textbooks of German grammar and literature. His religious and educational ideals drew him into William Ellery Channing's circle, and the two became intimate friends, putting Follen at the heart of the lively conversation that was birthing transcendentalism.[28] Conversation led to romance, as Eliza Cabot and Charles Follen fell in love, and though she was forty-one when they married, Eliza did bear one child, the beloved Charles Junior.

With his Harvard position, sparkling friends, and marriage into one of Boston's first families, Follen should have prospered, but once again his principles cost him his career. Late in 1833, a chance encounter with a black man shocked him into realizing the scope of slavery in his adopted country, and he went straight to see William Lloyd Garrison. Follen came away a convert, and within weeks he was invited to give the anniversary address of the New England Antislavery Society; copies of his searing speech were sent to every member of Congress. He feared his social activism would doom his Harvard appointment, and he was right. Though his classes were popular, Harvard's overseers did not renew his contract, and the Follens found the ranks of their Boston friends closed against them.[29] Forced into poverty, they pushed on hopefully, trying to found first a boys' school then a coeducational liberal college, moving from one ministry to another until Charles was called, in 1838, to East Lexington's transcendentalist-leaning Unitarian Church.[30] Here, at last, the Follens flourished. In 1840, the new church building Charles had lovingly designed and built was about to be dedicated when he was called away to lecture in New York. As he rushed back to Boston for the ceremony, the steamboat he was riding exploded into flames and sank, bearing him, with nearly all the passengers and crew, to a gruesome death.

It was Louisa's uncle Samuel May who arranged a memorial service at Channing's church, but Channing's own church board defied their wishes, locking the church's doors against any memorial to their controversial friend. May and Channing unlocked the doors and delivered their memorial nonetheless, May with a defiant eulogy and Channing a discourse raw in its grief and pain. So wounded was he by his own church's insult to his friend, and to their shared principles, that he never preached again but once. Eliza Cabot Follen, herself a teacher, author, and outspoken abolitionist,[31] assuaged her own grief by publishing her husband's papers and writing his biography, a massive and passionate monument to their love and respect for each other and to Charles's heroic faith in free speech and human rights. It also presented their marriage as a model of what Margaret Fuller would, two years later, call the "highest grade of marriage . . . the religious," a "pilgrimage toward a common shrine" that embraces both "intellectual communion" and "home sympathies and household wisdom," as the two pilgrims help "each other along the dusty way." Eliza's book hit its mark. Reviewing it for the *Dial*, in his own memorial to his old friend, Theodore Parker wished he could tear out "the pages of shame to the free State we live in"; but, he lamented, "what is done cannot be undone by silence."[32] Parker would come to embrace a socially activist, abolitionist religion very much like Follen's own.

The double martyrdom of Follen—once in reactionary Europe, again in the "free State" of Massachusetts—and the destruction of his loving family and model companionate marriage must indeed have shamed the conscience of many in Boston. Follen did not assimilate well to transcendentalism, and even now, for all his significance, he is little known. His fearless political radicalism and uncompromising defense of free speech at any cost made him obnoxious, even as his ardent gentleness, sweetness of presence, and self-deprecating humor made him impossible to dismiss. That he alone among the transcendentalists carried the full weight of German learning in philosophy, religion, and literature was undeniable: his was their one authentic native German voice, as his heavy accent made evident every time he opened his mouth. Yet he disliked their darling Goethe's apolitical aestheticism and argued vigorously against free religion, insisting that true radicalism was grounded not in atheistic materialism but in a life modeled on Jesus Christ. Both Emerson and Fuller dismissed him with contempt, but Parker wrote that Follen had "the mind of a giant, and an angel's heart." He was "less of a German than a Christian cosmopolite," concluded Peabody, and Bronson Alcott declared he was "[one of] the free men and the brave, by whom great principles are to be honoured amongst us."[33]

It is just this paradoxical combination—a Germanic John Brown who romps with children—that was captured by Louisa May Alcott. Her Professor Bhaer effectively brings Follen back to life, with his domestic side foremost: that is, her Bhaer is shaped less by her own memories (she was only eight when Follen died) than by Eliza Follen's.[34] Portraits of Follen, including Eliza's, repeatedly stressed his buoyant spirits even in disappointment, his lovable nature, and his playfulness with children, closely resembling Louisa's fictional character.[35] Her initial description of Bhaer is a virtual paraphrase of Eliza Follen: He was "in no respect what is called fascinating, imposing, or brilliant; and yet he was as attractive as a genial fire, and people seemed to gather about him as naturally as about a warm hearth. He was poor, yet always appeared to be giving something away,—a stranger, yet everyone was his friend, no longer young,—but as happy-hearted as a boy; plain and odd,—yet his face looked beautiful to many, and his oddities were freely forgiven for his sake" (372).

Two other moments from *Little Women* are particularly suggestive. First, at a "select symposium" one evening in Boston, Jo is allured by young atheists who spout the "Speculative Philosophy," quoting Kant and Hegel to reason religion away to "nothingness." Jo is herself tempted until the normally bashful Professor Bhaer "blaze[s] up with honest indignation, and defend[s] religion with all the eloquence of truth—an eloquence which ma[kes] his broken English musical, and his plain face beautiful." Though the "wise men" argued well, writes Alcott, Bhaer "stood to his colors like a man." And "somehow, as he talked, the world got right again to Jo; . . . God was not a blind force, and immortality was not a pretty fable, but a blessed fact" (374–75). This little episode neatly reprises both Follen's speaking presence, as reported by contemporaries, and the characteristic intellectual position evidenced in his published letters and sermons.

Second, Alcott conveys the same wistfulness that permeates Eliza Follen's biography: gentle self-deprecation, cheerful longing, *Heimweh* or the ache of loss. When the reader first meets Bhaer, he is humming his signature song, "'Kennst du das land,' like a big bumble-bee" (355). The song, a "poignant" expression of "longing for home," famously sung by the child Mignon in Goethe's *Wilhelm Meister*, won such popularity that it was set to music over a hundred times and was used in Gounod's opera *Faust*.[36] Alcott returns to it when she has Bhaer conclude a family evening—and begin his romance with Jo—by singing it once again:

> Mr. Bhaer sang like a true German, heartily and well; and Jo soon subsided into a subdued hum, that she might listen to the mellow voice that seemed to sing for her alone.
>
> "Know'st thou the land where the citron blooms," used to be the Professor's favorite line; for "das land" meant Germany to him; but now he seemed to dwell, with peculiar warmth and melody, upon the words,—
>
> "There, oh there, might I with thee,
> Oh my beloved, go";
>
> and one listener was so thrilled by the tender invitation, that she longed to say she did know the land, and would joyfully depart thither, whenever he liked. (480)

This is actually Eliza Follen's story of the moment her romance with Charles began. As Eliza tells it, the two were first introduced by their mutual friend Catharine Sedgwick, who was then visiting Boston: "The childlike earnestness, the sublime simplicity, of his character made an indelible impression upon me, as I saw him then for the first time. He did not seem a stranger to me. I believe he never seemed like a stranger to a human soul." Soon a "small number of ladies" invited Charles to join them at their weekly self-improvement sessions, to practice reading aloud. Asked at their first meeting to read, Charles demurred because of his poor English. Eliza invited him instead to recite a poem:

> No one present will ever forget his recitation of Göthe's "Kennst du das Land," especially the tender accents of his voice when repeating the words,
>
> "Dahin! dahin!
> Möcht' ich mit dir, O mein Geliebter, ziehn."
>
> It was indeed the cry of the homesick spirit after its father-land.[37]

This occurred late in 1826; Charles and Eliza were married on 15 September 1828. Louisa has in effect transposed herself, using Jo as proxy, into the role of Eliza

Cabot Follen, the *Geliebter* at Follen / Bhaer's side, granting her fictional Follen the very thing the real Follen longed for but could never have: a home that was a boys' school, a houseful of children whose latent energies he could awake and nurture—or as Follen himself said, in a letter relating his plans for a boys' school, "I should feel bound to educate them not only for college, but for life; I should study their natures, awake every dormant energy, cherish every generous sentiment, and lead them to form such habits and tastes as would qualify them to act an honorable part" in life (362). Furthermore, in the characters of Jo and Marmee, Alcott fictionalized not only herself and her mother Abigail but added many of the qualities evinced by Charles's wife Eliza. Alcott thus constructed the March / Bhaer families on the model of the ideal marriage portrayed so movingly by Eliza Follen: a domestic circle oriented to public service; the family as a hive of self-culture that educes the private self into public action; an unswerving commitment to an ethical life lived as a Christian, a "Pilgrim's Progress" (to recall the central narrative of *Little Women*) in which the tight-knit and insular domestic circle is broken by history to be recast, on a cosmopolitan scale, as a sacred rather than a secular plot, modeled on Christ as the perfected universal human being, messiah to a new world.

If Louisa's family ideal was intended to create a kind of American millennial transnationalism, then it makes particular sense that she would construct a German figure to embody the paternal partner of that family. The concept of literary nationalism itself had been a German import (via Herder, to begin with, and in person, via Follen himself). Through the Pestalozzians, German and Swiss ideas of childhood development were revolutionizing the American classroom, and it was the Follens' own close friend Elizabeth Peabody who took up the German innovation of the *Kindergarten* and promoted it into a standard feature of the American school system. During Alcott's lifetime, American graduate education also was reformed and reinvented by borrowing not from the British or the French but from the new German model, in which dedicated scholars pushed forward the frontiers of higher knowledge.[38] After all, as Weisbuch observed, relative to the British, America could only ever be a latecomer, a child forever thin in culture and history; but relative to the Germans, America could be a kind of adult Republican Mother to the German Fatherland, equal copartners in cultural, moral, religious, intellectual, and political reform, the one supplying practical power and the other genius: a companionate marriage on the national scale.[39]

If Louisa May Alcott had written nothing else, the story could conclude rather neatly right here, with her modulation of transatlantic romanticism into a distinctive and progressive American form—gender tensions resolved, a tragic history (if my suspicions are correct) posthumously redeemed. But her other writings, both sentimental and gothic, play out other sorts of cosmopolitan tensions, only some of them under control. To turn first to her more sentimental works: Both *Moods* and *Work* are domestic novels, women's fictions that chronicle, in Nina Baym's classic description, "the 'trials and triumph' . . . of a heroine who, beset with hardships, finds within herself the qualities of intelligence, will, resourcefulness, and courage sufficient to overcome them."[40] Both were begun during the Civil War, and while neither is in any sense a "war novel," they both center on the containment of warring inner energies that culminate in the play of violence on the world stage. For as Larry Reynolds has aptly observed, "one can regard the Civil War . . . as the final disturbance of the earthquake that convulsed Europe in 1848–49," making it not a parochial or exceptional American event but a national moment in a global revolution.[41] From this perspective, both novels offer a gendered realization of Kantian cosmopolitanism with a centrifugal spin: while the characters are American, their unruly and transgressive energies are associated with Europe, projecting them from domestic to world conflicts.

If the resolution of *Little Women* offends every generation of little readers by marrying Jo to that stodgy German professor rather than to her childhood sweetheart Laurie (modeled largely on "Laddie," a Polish expatriate freedom fighter whom Louisa had romanced in Europe),[42] the resolution of *Moods* is even more offensive. At least Laurie gets to marry the beautiful and worldly Amy, but the dashing and dangerous lover of *Moods* goes down to a violent death. Alcott here positions her protagonist, Sylvia Yule, between two very different men, each a study in virtue, forcing her to choose between them. One, the poet Geoffrey Moor, is a loose representation of Emerson (and her father Bronson) cast as a solid actualist nation-builder; the other, Adam Warwick, transforms Thoreau into a brilliant, noble, and militant Byronic lover, "the manliest man Sylvia had ever seen," the very image of attractive but unstable skepticism with more than a hint of John Brown.[43] Sylvia's affection for the fatherly Moor is overwhelmed when the heroic Warwick strides into her life, and as their romance kindles into fire, the pull between the two nearly destroys her—indeed, the original version of 1865 ended with her death as well as Warwick's, as if such a marriage could be sanctified only in heaven. But in the revised version of 1882, Alcott tames Sylvia's ungovernable "moods" until she can accept marriage with the gentle Moor, though it is still the fiery Warwick who teaches her how to fight and how to dare. Thus while the one literally domesticates her, the other calls out and embodies her deepest gender fantasy: "I long to be a man," Alcott confided to her journal as troops mustered in Concord to fight the Civil War (she herself would join the war as a nurse). Even as the war raged, and as she wrote her Sylvia-self (like her Jo-self) into proper feminine submission, she sent her violent masculine Warwick-self straight to Europe to fight gloriously alongside Garibaldi in the Italian Revolution of 1848: "a stalwart figure, bareheaded, stern-faced, sinewy-armed, fitfully seen through clouds of smoke and flashes of fire, working with a silent energy that seemed almost superhuman."[44] Warwick dies not in battle but on the journey home to America, in a shipwreck within sight of shore—dies, that is, like Margaret Fuller, America's *true* romantic revolutionary hero, who really *did* fight for the Italian Republic.[45] As Fuller fumed back in 1841, "I wish I were a man, and then there would be one" (*EMF*, 19).

For Warwick must surely die. As Larry Reynolds has shown, Alcott tamed him considerably in her postwar revision of *Moods*, yet even her toned-down Warwick threatens domestic peace with wild, demonic Sturm-und-Drang energies that, like the raging sea or the rampaging wildfire from which he, every time, saves Sylvia, run out of control, damage, scorch, drown, overwhelm, kill.[46] But in killing Warwick, Louisa in effect kills off part of herself—the revolutionary, heroic, cross-gendered Fuller part. This clearly will not do—so in *Work* (1873), she replays the character: now it is not Emerson but Theodore Parker, fictionalized as Thomas Power, who plays the foil to Thoreau, fictionalized this time as David Sterling. *Work* is an altogether different novel, not a Sturm-und-Drang fury but a true Bildungsroman, a female telling of Goethe's *Wilhelm Meister* (the protagonist, Christie Devon, even becomes an actress). Alcott's narrative voice is older, resolute, both more hopeful and more bitter, as she launches Christie into the world to endure its increasingly hard knocks, which educate her, and the reader, into the social limitations enforced against strong and independent women. At the crucial, suicidal moment, Parker / Power saves Christie by sending her to the home of the Sterlings, where she finds in David a curiously opaque soul, kind, quiet, loving, cultivating his flowers (he is a florist by trade), but also strangely contained and volcanic. Indeed, we learn his demonic energies once destroyed his family, forcing him to cultivate the iron will needed to subdue them. Thus, unlike Adam Warwick, David Sterling has controlled his violent tendencies enough to become a good son to his Quaker mother, a good brother, and, in time, a husband to Christie—for this time, Alcott does allow her male and female halves to meet and marry.

But is it a *good* marriage? We cannot know: once again, global forces take Alcott's domestic world into their teeth and shake it apart. After the Civil War has gone on long enough to exhaust the energies of eager and callow boys, the *men*—sober, saddened, disciplined men like David Sterling—must leave their wives and children and take up arms, not in a blazing, glorious, romantic fight but in a grim, brutal battle that slogs on for years. While Davy leads his troops, Christie serves as a nurse, and they romance each other on the fly during brief leaves. Then the inevitable happens. Davy is killed defending a black woman with her children, leaving Christie to raise their daughter Ruth in the bosom of yet another fatherless family. It is "'David's voice,'" the sound of the wind in his untouched flute, that gives Christie the courage to go on. In its "melodious sigh" she hears, as Alcott says in her elegy "Thoreau's Flute,"

> A potent presence, though unseen,—
> Steadfast, sagacious, and serene:
> Seek not for him,—he is with thee.[47]

How remarkable it is that, in all her domestic novels, Alcott invested her central male characters with futures and projects cut off by the untimely deaths of their biographical sources, as if she took it upon herself to complete in imagination what in the real lives of her models—Charles Follen, Margaret Fuller, Henry David Thoreau—had been so violently terminated.

Alcott's war of internal energies plays out rather differently in her "thrillers," where she again masks as the Byronic radical skeptic; but here, instead of devising wise compensations for disappointed world-building, over and over she subverts the whole complex, undoing the world altogether. In these gothic texts the double edge of romantic radicalism, again associated with Europe, is turned back on domestic society to create destruction in a mode evocative of Mary Shelley. The more lurid her metaphysical cross-dressing becomes, the more we can see how hard Alcott must work, in her "actualist" novels, to contain energies that she cannot wholly disavow. In its feminine form this erotic power is played out as Jean Muir in "Behind a Mask," her mischievous rewriting of Charlotte Brontë's *Jane Eyre*, which allures the reader into complicity as the Scottish governess seizes control of the smug, conventional upper-class American family.[48] In its masculine form this erotic power is unleashed in *A Long Fatal Love Chase* (1866) and its revision, *A Modern Mephistopheles* (1877), whose plots remind us that Alcott, who claimed Goethe as her favorite author, was capable of exploring a range of Goethean genres from Sturm und Drang to the Bildungsroman to Faustian tragedy. Remarkably, in reinventing *Faust* for her American audience, Alcott casts herself both as male Satanic villain—whose arsenal includes rape, stalking, suicide, murder, drugs, and sexual abuse—and as female victim. Furthermore, in this extension of self-splitting, her most violently transgressive energies are coded as European and worked out, not in domestic American sites, but across England, Germany, France, and Italy.

In comparing Alcott's domestic and gothic works, I'm struck that both her heroes and her seducers tend to be steeped in European Enlightenment and romantic texts, which is to say, she successfully imports the European metaphysical conversation even while bracketing it *as foreign*. In this, her approach functioned rather like George Ripley's anthology, *Specimens of Foreign Standard Literature* (1838–40), or Elizabeth Peabody's West Street bookstore, which was filled with titles in English, French, German, Italian, Greek, and Latin: both sites made cosmopolitanism available to literate Americans, while bracketing it as something set apart from the American mainstream. What distinguishes Alcott's benign subversives from her dangerous ones is how they *use* their transgressive knowledge. In *A Modern Mephistopheles*, for example, Helwyze deploys his library of foreign literature—Montaigne, Voltaire, Carlyle, Heine, De Quincy, George Sand, Goethe, Shakespeare, Dante, Byron, Browning, and Poe—as an instrument of metaphysical rape. By contrast, in *Work*, when Christie discovers in David's library, next to Milton and Montaigne, "several books in unknown tongues . . . half-hidden by volumes of Browning, Keats, and Coleridge," she is protected by her ignorance; she literally cannot read the queer foreign titles, and they stay (half-) hidden.[49] In *Little Women*, the danger is revealed when Jo's world is threatened by the specters of Kant and Hegel; here, it is Professor Bhaer who uses his own great European learning to slay the dragons of "Speculative Philosophy" and make Jo's world right again. In short, whereas in Alcott's thrillers the foreigner *infects* (rather as Charles Lane infected Fruitlands), in her domestic novels the foreigner *inoculates*, providing a homeopathic dose just strong enough to protect.

Alcott is walking a tightrope here. As Doyle observes, even today some readers object to the marriage of Jo and Fritz not because he is old and stodgy but because he is—gasp!—*foreign*.[50] Cosmopolitan projects have always had a double edge in the United States. On the one hand, the very concept of an independent United States was incited by a foreigner, Thomas Paine, who brought a global agenda for world revolution to bear on a local conflict; sure enough, the republicanism sparked by the American Revolution burned through France to Haiti, through North and South America, and on through Europe until it was arrested by the collapse of the Revolution of 1848. Similarly, for Follen, the Declaration of Independence was the gospel for *world* revolution. Thus he argued that slavery in the United States was intolerable not merely because it violated American, or even Christian, principles but because it gave the lie to the creed of his youth, the creed to which he had given his life: global revolutionary republicanism, the declaration that "all men are created equal," on which Kant himself had founded his absolute moral imperative. If even America couldn't uphold these principles—if *America* made them the laughingstock of the ruling classes of Europe—what hope was there? As Samuel May observed, for Follen it was more important to stand up to the Massachusetts legislature than to the Holy Alliance of Europe, for "the infringement of the liberties of speech by a democratic government would be more disastrous to the cause of freedom, than any encroachment on human rights by absolute monarchs."[51] It was America, not Europe, where the cosmopolitan stakes were highest.

Margaret Fuller understood this, which is why she agonized when Americans refused to help the Italian revolutionaries. To keep hope alive she imagined, in the last of her *New-York Tribune* dispatches, a New Era of "uncompromising revolution" so strong that no one nation, not even all of them together, could stop it: cosmopolitanism transformed from history to myth. Or as Follen had said in his last published essay: "A Congress and High Court of Nations" could be considered truly cosmopolitan only if it were founded on republican principles, securing liberty and equality to every human being, and recognizing power only "inasmuch as it is derived from and responsible to the people." "The true way," he declared, "to realize this sublime idea of a central board of international legislation and judicature, is to *republicanize the world*."[52] This means that intellectuals, teachers, and writers such as Paine, Fuller, and Follen were *all*, potentially, the handle to the axe. But even as "America" became the watchword for global Kantian cosmopolitanism, actual Americans, in a tradition dating back to President John Adams's Alien and Sedition Acts, knew that cosmopolitanism threatened the American Way. Louisa had witnessed the sacrifice of the Temple School on this altar, and as Channing and Parker admitted, the way Boston and Harvard had closed ranks on Charles Follen—attacked as one of those "foreigners throwing firebrands"[53]—shamed even the transcendentalists. One must beware of romanticizing these transatlantic waters. They are full of riptides; they drowned both Fuller and Follen. As Louisa wrote on, the national press was branding European immigrants as a threat to national security and the cosmopolitanism she was exploring as alien, seditious, subversive—and spreading like an infection. Even her intellectual fountainhead became a military superpower, as Wilhelm Meister transformed into Kaiser Wilhelm. The transatlantic polarization onto which she mapped her inner conflicts was intensifying to world war.

In short, Louisa May Alcott is grappling with a turbulent transatlantic world, playing out its fierce and hopeful energies on the level of imagination rather than philosophy. In the beginning, her families appear, conventionally enough, as female-centered, world-preserving domestic units insulated from masculine, world-disrupting, foreign energies, but as her heroines demonstrate again and again, those disruptive energies are already built in, intrinsic to self, family, and nation. As Alcott's characters struggle to negotiate them, her domestic spaces mature, at their best, into civil sanctuaries where wise women and good men repair to cultivate a world revolution. Conventional gender roles must also yield as Alcott's radical dualism, like Fuller's, invents new ones: gentle women may soldier; militant men dandle children, play the flute, and tend flowers. For the goal of her American nation-building is not to suppress revolutionary European romanticism but to *reclaim* it in a tempered, adult, and transgendered form, wielded as a quietly heroic weapon against Gilded Age smugness and xenophobia. Thus the Marches' insular feminized family evolves into the

Bhaers' global coeducational college; similarly, Alcott's novel *Work* concludes around the dinner table, where sits "a loving league of sisters, old and young, black and white, rich and poor, each ready to do her part to hasten the coming of the happy end," God's "great work" in the world.[54]

Alcott's closing image of a "league of sisters" bespeaks Eliza Follen's description of their own Wednesday evenings, when, though so poor they could serve their guests only water, the Follens opened their home to the brotherhood of all: "The artisan and the artist, the flattered favorites of the world, and its poor forgotten pilgrims, the homebound conservative, the republican stranger, whose home was the world, and the exiled philanthropist, the child and his proud grandparent, the learned and the unlearned, the grave and the gay, all met at our house, and passed a few free and happy hours in an unrestrained and friendly intercourse, recognising the bond of brotherhood which exists between the members of God's human family."[55] A beautiful and hopeful picture, if still not the whole picture, for as Alcott shows, this model Christian household, with all its lurking imperialism, was ever disrupted from within and embattled from without. Yet again and again, Louisa May Alcott's heroes lay down their lives in defense of what Bronson Alcott called the "fellowship of all souls," a fellowship that, as with poverty, gender, and race, marked a potential affiliation of strangers beyond the boundaries of family and nation.

Is this why we today still read Alcott as a living author? She hooks her characters into the same frightening historical uncertainties that continue to haunt us, not as inexplicable events from elsewhere, but as the playing out on the world stage of the intimate battles that still tear apart the street, the parlor, the bedroom, the dinner table. Her personal indeed becomes political, as inner conflicts, tyrannies, and brutalizations both petty and tragic are tested and sometimes—resolved: first in personal terms, as steps on the inner path to becoming an ethical person; but also in public terms, as steps on the elevating path that leads to the ethical defense of the human rights of all people. Like Fuller and the Follens, Alcott did not separate these two paths but integrated them as one single journey, an aspirational ideal that one must uphold by patient and redemptive labor: not a vault into a celestial paradise but a long, tough, earthly slog, made in concert one by one. It is this feature of her fiction, her repeated inward turn to education and self-culture, that marks Alcott as a cosmopolitan visionary, for as Kant had said, only this inward turn could lead outward to the flowering of a global civil society. But more: as Alcott's very earthliness, her progressive labor to bring forth the modern world, is illuminated by cross-Atlantic philosophies, so they in turn are grounded by her American pragmatisms. Practical power, and genius, united in the cosmopolitan project of our time: it seems Alcott's transatlantic project still has much work to do.

NOTES

1. Louisa May Alcott, *Little Women*, in *Little Women, Little Men, Jo's Boys* (New York: Library of America, 2005), 154 (hereafter cited parenthetically). Also see Daniel Shealy, introduction to *Little Women Abroad: The Alcott Sisters' Letters from Europe, 1870–71*, ed. Daniel Shealy (Athens: Univ. of Georgia Press, 2008), xvii–iii.
2. Amos Bronson Alcott, *Concord Days* (Boston: n.p., 1872), 22.
3. Amos Bronson Alcott, *Tablets* (Boston: n.p., 1868), 159.
4. Immanuel Kant, "Idea for a Universal History with Cosmopolitan Intent," in *The Philosophy of Kant*, ed. Carl J. Friedrich (New York: Modern Library, 1949), 116–18, 126.
5. Immanuel Kant, "Eternal Peace," in *Philosophy of Kant*, 446, 448.
6. My thanks to Larry Reynolds for pointing this out. See Edson L. Whitney, *The American Peace Society: A Centennial History* (Washington, D.C.: American Peace Society, 1928); and Valarie H. Ziegler, *The Advocates of Peace in Antebellum America* (Bloomington: Indiana Univ. Press, 1992).
7. Kant's ideal of cosmopolitanism can be cast negatively as the master narrative of Western economic and political domination, or envisioned as a way to wrestle with ethical obligations in a world that insists both on universality and on difference. The literature on cosmopolitanism is huge and growing rapidly. For a succinct discussion directed toward transcendentalism in particular, see Laura Dassow Walls, "Global Transcendentalism" (*OxH*, 513–23). For a useful entry into the broader literature, see Gavin Kendall, Ian Woodward, and Zlatko Skrbis, *The Sociology of Cosmopolitanism: Globalization, Identity, Culture and Government* (New York: Palgrave Macmillan, 2009); for an eloquent introduction, see Kwame Anthony Appiah, *Cosmopolitanism: Ethics in a World of Strangers* (New York: Norton, 2006).
8. The phrase is Henry James's; see Robert Weisbuch, *Atlantic Double-Cross: American Literature and British Influence in the Age of Emerson* (Chicago: Univ. of Chicago Press, 1986), xi, xx.
9. Wai Chee Dimock, *Through Other Continents: American Literature across Deep Time* (Princeton: Princeton Univ. Press, 2006), 3.
10. Alcott thus complicates Amy Kaplan's notion of "imperial domesticity" as detailed in her essay "Manifest Domesticity," *American Literature* 70 (1998): 586, 582.
11. For more on Peabody's extraordinary bookstore, lending library, and meeting house, see Marshall, 391–98.
12. Phyllis Cole, "Woman's Rights and Feminism," in *OxH*, 228.
13. The classic arguments for the revolutionary power of fiction are made by Cathy Davidson, *Revolution and the Word: The Rise of the Novel in America* (1986; New York: Oxford Univ. Press, 2004); and by Jane Tompkins, *Sensational Designs: The Cultural Work of American Fiction, 1790–1860* (New York: Oxford Univ. Press, 1985). More recently, Martha Nussbaum has offered a similar argument in defense of the humanities in *Not for Profit: Why Democracy Needs the Humanities* (Princeton: Princeton Univ. Press, 2010).
14. John Matteson, *Eden's Outcasts: The Story of Louisa May Alcott and Her Father* (New York: Norton, 2007), 11, 14.
15. Johann Pestalozzi, quoted in Richard Francis, *Fruitlands: The Alcott Family and Their Search for Utopia* (New Haven: Yale Univ. Press, 2010), 33.
16. Cole, "Woman's Rights," in *OxH*, 225; Elizabeth Peabody, *Record of a School*, ed. Megan Marshall (1835; Bedford, Mass.: Applewood Books, 2005), ix, 17, 70.

17. Frederick C. Dahlstrand, *Amos Bronson Alcott: An Intellectual Biography* (East Brunswick, N.J.: Associated Univ. Presses, 1982), 41.
18. Peabody, *Record*, 123, 98.
19. Louisa May Alcott, "Recollections of My Childhood," in *Little Women* (New York: Norton, 2004), 428–33, 431.
20. Matteson, *Eden's Outcasts*, 371.
21. See Francis, *Fruitlands*, esp. 278.
22. Weisbuch, *Atlantic Double-Cross*, xiv.
23. Christine Doyle, "Singing Mignon's Song: German Literature and Culture in the March Trilogy," *Children's Literature* 31 (2003): 50. For a revealing discussion of Fuller's own investment in German romanticism, particularly the way Goethe's fictional women allowed her to reimagine intellectual community, see Carol Strauss Sotiropoulos's essay in this volume.
24. Christine Doyle notes some possible, but not particularly persuasive, sources for Friedrich Bhaer in *Louisa May Alcott and Charlotte Brontë: Transatlantic Translations* (Knoxville: Univ. of Tennessee Press, 2000), 70.
25. Theodore Parker, "The Life and Character of Dr. Follen," *Dial* 3 (January 1843): 346. My biographical summary is based on Eliza Cabot Follen, *The Life of Charles Follen* (Boston: Hilliard, Gray, 1842); and Thomas S. Hansen, "Charles Follen," in *The American Renaissance in New England*, 3rd series, ed. Wesley T. Mott, vol. 235 of *Dictionary of Literary Biography* (Detroit: Gale Group, 2001), 132–39.
26. Charles Follen, "The Great Song," in Eliza Cabot Follen, *Life*, 595.
27. Eliza Cabot Follen, *Life*, 100.
28. Follen became a regular at Channing's "Friends of Progress" meetings with George Ripley, Orestes Brownson, Bronson Alcott, and Frederick Henry Hedge. And at Channing's Sunday School meetings at Boston's Federal Street Church, they were joined by Samuel May, Margaret Fuller, Elizabeth Peabody, and her friend Eliza Lee Cabot.
29. Why were the Follens ostracized? Sources suggest that Follen may have taken equality altogether too far: shortly before giving his address, he openly declared he would be happy if his son Charley were to "marry a negro." Elizabeth Peabody, in reporting the conversation to her sister Mary, registered her horror with exclamatory excess: "!!—!!—!!—Dr. Follen!!-!!" The multiple exclamation points might be variously interpreted, but Ronda asserts that "Peabody found this just as horrifying a thought as did most other members of the Unitarian elite, who closed ranks in forcing Charles and Eliza Follen out of Harvard College and Boston society" (263, 370n64). Marshall suggests that Mary Peabody feared Southern slave owners would dismiss abolitionists because they merely lusted after "'a black skin'" (528). In a clear attempt at damage control, Charles Follen worked, in the address itself, to distance himself from the "misrepresentation" that abolitionists encouraged intermarriage; see "Address to the People of the United States on the Subject of Slavery," in *The Works of Charles Follen*, ed. Eliza Cabot Follen, 5 vols. (Boston: Hilliard, Gray, 1841), 5:224. See also Anne C. Rose: "When new arrivals in Boston were no longer Unitarians from Salem but Germans infected with the idealism of their homeland, the elite used its money, college, and churches to protect itself from contamination" (*Transcendentalism as a Social Movement, 1830–1850* [New Haven: Yale Univ. Press, 1981], 20).
30. East Lexington was Theodore Parker's childhood home, and Follen replaced Emerson, who had been a supply preacher there (Dean Grodzins, *American Heretic: Theodore Parker and Transcendentalism* [Chapel Hill: Univ. of North Carolina Press, 2002], 17). In 1847

Caroline Healey Dall visited Follen's church, describing it as "one of the simplest and prettiest" she had ever seen (*Journals of Caroline Healey Dall*, ed. Helen Deese [Boston: Massachusetts Historical Society, 2006], 249).

31. Eliza went on to write more children's books, women's fiction, and antislavery tracts, as well as to edit both a children's magazine (*Child's Friend*) and an abolitionist journal (*Liberty Bell*).
32. *WNC*, 80–81; Parker, "Life and Character," 351.
33. Parker, "Life and Character," 345; Elizabeth Palmer Peabody, quoted in Gura, 31; *The Journals of Bronson Alcott*, ed. Odell Shepard (1938; Port Washington, N.Y.: Kennikat, 1966), 105.
34. There is no mention of Charles or Eliza Cabot Follen in Alcott's sketchy childhood journals, nor would such a mention be likely; by the time Louisa had matured, Follen was a distant family memory. Attempts to document whether she owned, or borrowed, a copy of Eliza Cabot Follen's biography of her husband have thus far been unsuccessful.
35. See *Works of William Ellery Channing* [Boston: American Unitarian Association, 1875], 616; Eliza Cabot Follen, *Life*, 274–75, 387.
36. Doyle, "Singing Mignon's Song," 58.
37. Eliza Cabot Follen, *Life*, 163–64.
38. Frederick Rudolph, *The American College and University: A History* (Athens: Univ. of Georgia Press, 1990), 333–34.
39. Weisbuch, *Atlantic Double-Cross*, xiii. Follen was one of many educated German expatriates who had grown up determined to fight for republican ideals in Europe, then were forced by a repressive state to seek shelter in the nation that seemed to embody their dream. See David E. Barclay and Elisabeth Glaser-Schmidt, eds., *Transatlantic Images and Perceptions: Germany and America since 1776* (Cambridge: Cambridge Univ. Press, 1997).
40. Nina Baym, *Woman's Fiction: A Guide to Novels by and about Women in America, 1820–1870* (Ithaca, N.Y.: Cornell Univ. Press, 1978), 22. Baym claims that the genre began in America with Catharine Sedgwick's *New-England Tale* (1822); Sedgwick, interestingly, was one of Charles Follen's first American friends, and it was she who introduced him to Eliza Cabot. Follen taught himself English by reading Sedgwick's novels, starting with *Redwood*, which he praised for its grace of style (Eliza Cabot Follen, *Life*, 149).
41. Larry J. Reynolds, *European Revolutions and the American Literary Renaissance* (New Haven: Yale Univ. Press, 1988), 53.
42. Matteson, *Eden's Outcasts*, 316–22.
43. Louisa May Alcott, *Moods*, in *The Portable Louisa May Alcott*, ed. Elizabeth Lennox Keyser (New York: Penguin 2000), 153–358, esp. 187.
44. Alcott, *Moods*, 345.
45. Reynolds, *European Revolutions*, 75; and *Righteous Violence: Revolution, Slavery, and the American Renaissance* (Athens: Univ. of Georgia Press, 2011), 146–47.
46. Reynolds, *Righteous Violence*, 134, 153–55. Reynolds points out that, in the revision of *Moods*, Alcott characterizes both Warwick and Sylvia as vulnerable to "storm and stress period[s]," the "moods" both must work to overcome (*Righteous Violence*, 154–55).
47. Louisa May Alcott, *Work: A Story of Experience* (1873; New York: Schocken, 1977), 442–43; and "Thoreau's Flute," *Atlantic Monthly* 12 (September 1863): 280–81. Thoreau's middle name was, of course, David. What shall we make of Louisa May Alcott's repeated reincarnations of Thoreau as both her deepest love and the embodiment of her own highest self?
48. See Doyle, *Alcott and Brontë*.

49. Louisa May Alcott, *A Modern Mephistopheles* (New York: Bantam, 1995), 85; *Work*, 224.
50. Doyle, "Singing Mignon's Song," 50.
51. Samuel May, quoted in Eliza Cabot Follen, *Life*, 402.
52. Charles Follen, "Peace and War," in *Works*, 5:369–70; emphasis in original.
53. Eliza Cabot Follen, *Life*, 342.
54. Alcott, *Work*, 442–43.
55. Eliza Cabot Follen, *Life*, 460. This passage is also quoted in Parker, "Life and Character," 353. Charles Follen was then a minister in New York City.

Selected Bibliography

PRIMARY SOURCES

Alcott, Abigail May. *My Heart Is Boundless: Writings of Abigail May Alcott, Louisa's Mother*. Ed. Eve LaPlante. New York: Free Press, 2012.

Alcott, Louisa May. *Alternative Alcott: Louisa May Alcott*. Ed. Elaine Showalter. New Brunswick, N.J.: Rutgers Univ. Press, 1988.

———. *Behind a Mask: The Unknown Thrillers of Louisa May Alcott*. Ed. Madeleine B. Stern. New York: William Morrow, 1975.

———. *The Journals of Louisa May Alcott*. Ed. Joel Myerson and Daniel Shealy. Boston: Little, Brown, 1989.

———. *Little Women, Little Men, Jo's Boys*. New York: Library of America, 2005.

———. *Louisa May Alcott on Race, Sex, and Slavery*. Ed. Sarah Elbert. Boston: Northeastern Univ. Press, 1997.

———. *Moods*. Ed. Sarah Elbert. 1865; New Brunswick, N.J.: Rutgers Univ. Press, 1991.

———. *Plots and Counterplots: More Unknown Thrillers of Louisa May Alcott*. Ed. Madeleine B. Stern. New York: Morrow, 1976.

———. *The Poems of Louisa May Alcott*. Introduction by Robert S. Nelson. Forest Hills, N.Y.: Ironweed Press, 2000.

———. *The Portable Louisa May Alcott*. Ed. Elizabeth Lennox Keyser. New York: Penguin, 2000.

———. *The Selected Letters of Louisa May Alcott*. Ed. Joel Myerson and Daniel Shealy. Athens: Univ. of Georgia Press, 1995.

———. *Work: A Story of Experience*. 1873; New York: Schocken, 1977.

Alcott, Louisa May, and May Alcott. *Little Women Abroad: The Alcott Sisters' Letters from Europe, 1870–1871*. Ed. Daniel Shealy. Athens: Univ. of Georgia Press, 2008.

Bancroft, Elizabeth Davis. *Letters from England, 1846–49*. New York: Scribner's & Sons, 1904.

Brook Farm Papers, MHi.

Brown, Pauline Hopkins. *The Magazine Novels of Pauline Hopkins*. New York: Oxford Univ. Press, 1988.

Buell, Lawrence, ed. *The American Transcendentalists: Essential Writings*. New York: Modern Library, 2006.

Butterfield, Rebecca Codman. "Rebecca Codman Butterfield's Reminiscences of Brook Farm." Ed. Joel Myerson. *New England Quarterly* 65 (1992): 603–30.

Cheney, Ednah Dow. *Louisa May Alcott*. Ed. Ann Douglas. 1889; New York: Chelsea House, 1980.

———. "Sarah Margaret Fuller." In *Reminiscences of Ednah Dow Cheney*, 192–210. Boston: Lee & Shepard, 1902.

———. "The Women of Boston." In *The Memorial History of Boston*, ed. Justin Winsor, 4:331–56. 4 vols. Boston: Ticknor, 1881.

Child, Lydia Maria. *An Appeal in Favor of That Class of Americans Called Africans*. 1833; Amherst: Univ. of Massachusetts Press, 1996.

———. *The Collected Correspondence of Lydia Maria Child, 1817–1880*. Ed. Patricia G. Holland, Milton Meltzer, and Francine Krasno. Millwood, N.Y.: KTO Microform, 1979.

———. *The History of the Condition of Women, in Various Ages and Nations*. 2 vols. Boston: J. Allen, 1835.

———. *Letters from New-York*. Ed. Bruce Mills. 1843; Athens: Univ. of Georgia Press, 1998.

———. *Letters from New York, Second Series*. New York: C. S. Francis, 1845.

———. *A Lydia Maria Child Reader*. Ed. Carolyn L. Karcher. Durham, N.C.: Duke Univ. Press, 1997.

———. *Lydia Maria Child: Selected Letters, 1817–1880*. Ed. Milton Meltzer, Patricia G. Holland, and Francine Krasno. Amherst: Univ. of Massachusetts Press, 1982.

———. *Philothea: A Romance*. 1836; Freeport, Me.: Books for Libraries Press, 1969.

———. "What Is Beauty?" *Dial* 3, no. 4 (April 1843): 490–92.

Church, Mary Van Wyck. "Memoir of Elizabeth Palmer Peabody." Ms. MHi.

Clapp, Eliza Thayer. *Studies in Religion*. New York: C. Shepard, 1845.

Clarke, Sarah. Letters. Ms. bMS Am 1569.8 (133). MH-H.

———. "Letters of a Sister." Ed. Lillian F. Clarke. In *The Cheerful Letter* (periodical 1903–10). Scrapbook of Clarke pages. MH-H.

———. "Margaret Fuller Ossoli and Hawthorne." *Boston Evening Transcript*, 12 December 1884.

Dall, Caroline Healey. Caroline Wells Healey Dall Papers, 1811–1917. MHi.

———. Caroline Wells Healey Dall Papers. Schlesinger Library, Harvard University.

———. *The College, the Market, and the Court; or, Woman's Relation to Education, Labor, and Law*. Boston: Lee & Shepard, 1867.

———. *Daughter of Boston: The Extraordinary Diary of a Nineteenth-Century Woman*. Ed. Helen R. Deese. Boston: Beacon Press, 2005.

———. "The Hawthorne Book Censured." *Springfield Republican*, 15 December 1884.

———. *Historical Pictures Retouched: A Volume of Miscellanies*. Boston: Walker, Wise, 1860.

———. *Margaret and Her Friends: Or Ten Conversations upon the Mythology of the Greeks*. 1895; New York: Arno, 1972.

———. "Margaret Fuller Ossoli." *North American Review* 91 (July 1860): 119–29.

———. *Selected Journals of Caroline Healey Dall*. Vols. 1 and 2. Ed. Helen R. Deese. Boston: Massachusetts Historical Society, 2006, 2013.

———, trans. *Spiridion*, by George Sand. *The Una*, July–Oct. 1855 (3:97–101, 113–15, 129–33, 155–60). Continued in *Saturday Evening Express*, 1858–59 (clippings in Scrapbook, Dall Papers, MHi).

———. *Transcendentalism in New England: A Lecture Delivered before the Society for Philosophical Enquiry*. Boston: Roberts Brothers, 1897.

Davis, Paulina Wright. *A History of the National Woman's Rights Movement, for Twenty Years*. New York: Journeymen Printers' Cooperative Association, 1871.

———. Paulina Wright Davis Papers, 1843–1890. Archives and Special Collections Library, Vassar College Libraries.

Dwight, Marianne. *Letters from Brook Farm, 1844–1847*. Ed. Amy L. Reed. Poughkeepsie, N.Y.: Vassar College, 1928.

Emerson, Ellen Tucker. *The Letters of Ellen Tucker Emerson*. Ed. Edith E. W. Gregg. 2 vols. Kent, Ohio: Kent State Univ. Press, 1982.

———. *The Life of Lidian Jackson Emerson*. Ed. Delores Bird Carpenter. 1980; East Lansing: Michigan State Univ. Press, 1992.

Emerson, Lidian Jackson. "Lidian Emerson's 'Transcendental Bible.'" Ed. Delores Bird Carpenter. In *Studies in the American Renaissance 1980*, ed. Joel Myerson, 91–95. Boston: Twayne, 1980.

———. *The Selected Letters of Lidian Jackson Emerson*. Ed. Delores Bird Carpenter. Columbia: Univ. of Missouri Press, 1987.

Emerson, Mary Moody. *The Almanacks of Mary Moody Emerson: A Scholarly Digital Edition*. Ed. Noelle A. Baker and Sandra Harbert Petrulionis. Prototype of ongoing project at http://marymoodyemerson.net/. Accessed 17 August 2013.

———. *Selected Letters of Mary Moody Emerson*. Ed. Nancy Craig Simmons. Athens: Univ. of Georgia Press, 1993.

Farnham, Eliza W. *Life in Prairie Land*. New York: Harper and Brothers, 1847.

———. *My Early Days*. New York: Thatcher & Hutchinson, 1859.

———. *Woman and Her Era*. New York: A. J. Davis, 1864.

Follen, Eliza Cabot. *Anti-Slavery Hymns and Songs*. New York: American Anti-Slavery Society, 1855.

———, ed. *The Child's Friend* (periodical). Boston: L. C. Bowles, 1843–58.

———. *The Life of Charles Follen*. 5 vols. Boston: Hilliard, Gray, 1842.

———. *Poems*. Boston: W. Crosby, 1839.

———, trans. *Selections from the Writings of Fenelon, with a Memoir of His Life*. Boston: Hilliard, Gray, Little, and Wilkins, 1829.

Forten, Charlotte. "Life on the Sea Islands." *Atlantic Monthly*, May and June 1864. Reprinted in *Two Black Teachers of the Civil War*, 65–89. New York: Arno, 1969.

Freeman, Mary Wilkins. "The Girl Who Wants to Write: Things to Do and Avoid." *Harper's Bazar* 47 (June 1913): 272.

———. "Good Wits, Pen and Paper." In *What Women Can Earn: Occupations of Women and Their Compensation*, ed. Grace H. Dodge et al., 23–29. New York: Frederick A. Stokes, 1899.

———. *Selected Short Stories of Mary E. Wilkins Freeman*. Ed. Marjorie Pryse. New York: Norton, 1983.

———. *The Uncollected Stories of Mary Wilkins Freeman*. Ed. Mary R. Reichardt. Jackson: Univ. Press of Mississippi, 1992.

Fuller, Margaret, trans. *Conversations with Goethe in the Last Years of His Life*, by Johann Peter Eckermann. Boston: Hilliard, Gray, 1839.

———. *The Essential Margaret Fuller*. Ed. Jeffrey Steele. New Brunswick, N.J.: Rutgers Univ. Press, 1992.

———. "The Great Lawsuit. Man *versus* Men. Woman *versus* Women." *Dial* 4 (1843–44): 1–47.

———, trans. *Günderode*, by Bettina von Arnim. Boston: E. P. Peabody, 1842.

———. "'The Impulses of Human Nature': Margaret Fuller's Journal from June through October 1844." Ed. Martha L. Berg and Alice de V. Perry. *Proceedings of the Massachusetts Historical Society*, 3rd Series, 102 (1990): 38–126.

———. Journal Fragment. S. Margaret Fuller Ossoli Papers (typescript), 1836–1850. Fruitlands Museum mss., Harvard, Mass.

——— *The Letters of Margaret Fuller*. Ed. Robert N. Hudspeth. 6 vols. Ithaca, N.Y.: Cornell Univ. Press, 1983–94.

———. "The Liberty Bell." In *The Liberty Bell 1846*, 80–88. Boston: Massachusetts Anti-Slavery Fair, 1846.

———. *Love-Letters of Margaret Fuller, 1845–46*. Ed. Julia Ward Howe. New York: D. Appleton, 1903.

———. *Margaret Fuller, Critic: Writings from the New-York Tribune, 1844–46*. Ed. Judith Mattson Bean and Joel Myerson. New York: Columbia Univ. Press, 2000.

———. Margaret Fuller Ossoli Papers. Boston Public Library.

———. Margaret Fuller Papers. MH-H.

———. "Margaret Fuller's 1839 Journal: Trip to Bristol." Ed. Robert N. Hudspeth. *Harvard Library Bulletin* 27 (1979): 445–70.

———. "Margaret Fuller's 1842 Journal: At Concord with the Emersons." Ed. Joel Myerson. *Harvard Library Bulletin* 21 (1973): 320–40.

———. "Margaret Fuller's Boston Conversations: The 1839–40 Series." Ed. Nancy Craig Simmons. In *Studies in the American Renaissance 1994*, ed. Joel Myerson, 195–226. Charlottesville: Univ. Press of Virginia, 1994.

———. "Margaret Fuller's Journal for October, 1842." Ed. Robert Habich. *Harvard Library Bulletin* 33 (1985): 280–91.

———. *Margaret Fuller's New York Journalism*. Ed. Catherine C. Mitchell. Knoxville: Univ. of Tennessee Press, 1995.

———. "Margaret Fuller's Translations from Goethe." Appendix. In Urbanski, *Margaret Fuller: Visionary*, 245–372.

———. *Memoirs of Margaret Fuller Ossoli*. Ed. R. W. Emerson, J. F. Clarke, and W. H. Channing. 2 vols. Boston: Phillips, Sampson, 1852.

———. *The Portable Margaret Fuller*. Ed. Mary Kelley. New York: Penguin, 1994.

———. Review of Washington Allston. *Dial* 1 (1840): 75.

———. *Summer on the Lakes, in 1843*. Ed. Susan Belasco Smith. 1844; Urbana: Univ. of Illinois Press, 1991.

———. *"These Sad but Glorious Days": Dispatches from Europe, 1846–50*. Ed. Larry J. Reynolds and Susan Belasco Smith. New Haven: Yale Univ. Press, 1991.

———. *The Woman and the Myth: Margaret Fuller's Life and Writing*. Ed. Bell Gale Chevigny. New York: Feminist Press, 1976. Rev. and exp. ed. Boston: Northeastern Univ. Press, 1994.

———. *Woman in the Nineteenth Century*. 1845. Norton Critical Edition. Ed. Larry J. Reynolds. New York: W. W. Norton, 1998.

Grimké, Charlotte Forten. *The Journals of Charlotte Forten Grimké*. Ed. Brenda Stevenson. In *The Schomburg Library of Nineteenth-Century Black Women Writers*. New York: Oxford Univ. Press, 1988.

———. Manuscripts of Poems and Diaries in the Francis James Grimké Papers. Moorland-Spingarn Research Center, Howard University.

Harper, Frances Ellen Watkins. *A Brighter Coming Day: A Frances Ellen Watkins Harper Reader*. Ed. Frances Smith Foster. New York: Feminist Press, 1990.

Hawthorne, Sophia Peabody. "'The Cuba Journal' of Sophia Peabody Hawthorne, Volume I, Edited from the Manuscript with an Introduction." Ed. Claire M. Badaracco. PhD diss, Rutgers Univ., 1978.

———. "Letters from Cuba"(*Cuba Journal*), journal MS in 3 volumes. Sophia Peabody Hawthorne papers. Berg Collection of English and American Literature, New York Public Library, Astor, Lenox, and Tilden Foundations.

———. Peabody Family Papers. Berg Collection of English and American Literature, New York Public Library, Astor, Lenox, and Tilden Foundations.

———. Peabody Family Papers (typescripts). Robert Straker Collection, Antiochiana, Antioch College.

———. "Sophia Hawthorne's Cuba Journal: Volume Three, 31 October 1834–15 March 1835." Ed. Claire M. Badaracco. *Essex Institute Historical Collections* 118 (1982): 280.

Higginson, Thomas Wentworth. *Margaret Fuller Ossoli*. Boston: Houghton Mifflin, 1884.

Highgate, Edmonia Goodelle. "On Horse Back—Saddle Dash, No. 1." *Christian Recorder*, 3 November 1866.

———. "Salvation Only in Work." *Christian Recorder*, 4 February 1865.

———. "A Spring Day Up the James." *Christian Recorder*, 27 May 1865.

———. "Truth." *Christian Recorder*, 27 October 1866).

———. "Waiting for the Cars." *Christian Recorder*, 25 February 1865.

Hoar, Elizabeth. "Elizabeth of Concord: Selected Letters of Elizabeth Sherman Hoar to the Emersons, Family, and the Emerson Circle." Ed. Elizabeth Maxfield-Miller. Part One: *Studies in the American Renaissance 1984*, ed. Joel Myerson. 229–98. Part Two: *Studies 1985*, 95–156. Part Three: *Studies 1986*, 113–98. Charlottesville: Univ. Press of Virginia, 1984–86.

Hooper, Ellen Sturgis. "Ellen H. Sturgis Hooper Poems" (mss.). Schlesinger Library, Harvard University.

———. *Poems*. Published privately by Edward William Hooper, 1872.

Hopkins, Pauline. *Contending Forces: A Romance Illustrative of Negro Life North and South*. 1900; New York: Oxford Univ. Press, 1988.

———. *Daughter of the Revolution: The Major Nonfiction Works of Pauline E. Hopkins*. Ed. Ira Dworkin. New Brunswick, N.J.: Rutgers Univ. Press, 2007.

Howe, Julia Ward. "Address of Mrs. Howe." In *Ednah Dow Cheney: Memorial Meeting*, New England Women's Club, 3–6. Boston: George H. Ellis, 1905.

———. "Emerson's Relation to Society." In *The Genius and Character of Emerson: Lectures at the Concord School of Philosophy*, ed. F. B. Sanborn, 286–309. Boston: Osgood, 1884.

———. *The Hermaphrodite*. Ed. Gary Williams. Lincoln: Univ. of Nebraska Press, 2004.

———. *Is Polite Society Polite? And Other Essays*. Boston and New York: Lamson, Wolffe, 1895.

———. *Julia Ward Howe, 1819–1910*. 2 vols. Ed. Lauren Elizabeth Richards, Maud Howe Elliott, and Florence Howe Hall. Boston: Houghton Mifflin, 1916.

———. *Julia Ward Howe and the Woman Suffrage Movement: A Selection from Her Speeches and Essays*. Ed. Florence Howe Hall. Boston: Dana Estes, 1913.

———. *Margaret Fuller (Marchesa Ossoli)*. Boston: Roberts Brothers, 1883.

———. *Modern Society*. Boston: Roberts Brothers, 1881.

——— *Passion-flowers*. Boston: Ticknor, Reed, and Fields, 1854.

———. *Reminiscences, 1819–1899*. Boston: Houghton Mifflin, 1899.

Kane, Paul, ed. *Poetry of the American Renaissance: A Diverse Anthology from the Romantic Period*. New York: George Braziller, 1995.

Kirby, Georgiana Bruce. *Years of Experience: An Autobiographical Narrative*. New York: Putnam's Sons, 1887.

McClymer, John F., ed. *This High and Holy Moment: The First National Woman's Rights Convention, Worcester, 1850*. Fort Worth, Tex.: Harcourt Brace, 1999.

Myerson, Joel, ed. *Fuller in Her Own Time: A Biographical Chronicle of Her Life, Drawn from Recollections, Interviews, and Memoirs by Family, Friends, and Associates*. Iowa City: Univ. of Iowa Press, 2008.

———. *Transcendentalism: A Reader*. New York: Oxford Univ. Press, 2000.

New England Women's Club Papers. Schlesinger Library, Harvard University.

Orvis, Marianne Dwight. *Letters from Brook Farm, 1844–47*. Ed. Amy L. Reed. 1928; Philadelphia: Porcupine Press, 1972.

Parsons, Anna Q. T. "Sketch of M. F.'s Character by a Seeress." March 1844. Fuller Papers, Boston Public Library.

Peabody, Elizabeth Palmer. *Aesthetic Papers*. New York: Putnam, 1849.

———. "Elizabeth Palmer Peabody to William Wordsworth: Eight Letters, 1825–1845." Ed.

Margaret Neussendorfer. In *Studies in the American Renaissance 1984*, ed. Joel Myerson, 181–211. Charlottesville: Univ. Press of Virginia, 1984.

———. "Emerson as Preacher." In *The Genius and Character of Emerson: Lectures at the Concord School of Philosophy*. Boston: J. R. Osgood, 1885.

———. "A Glimpse of Christ's Idea of Society." *Dial* 2 (October 1841): 214–28.

———. *Last Evening with Allston*. Boston: D. Lathrop, 1886.

———. *Lecture in the Training Schools for Kindergartners*. Boston: D. C. Heath, 1886.

———. *Letters of Elizabeth Palmer Peabody: American Renaissance Woman*. Ed. Bruce A. Ronda. Middletown, Conn.: Wesleyan Univ. Press, 1984.

———. "Miss Peabody's Reminiscences of Margaret's Married Life." *Boston Evening Transcript*, 10 June 1885.

———. "My Experience as a Teacher: Principles and Methods of Education." *American Journal of Education* 32 (1882): 721–42.

———. Peabody Family Papers. Berg Collection of English and American Literature, New York Public Library, Astor, Lenox, and Tilden Foundations.

———. Peabody Family Papers (typescripts). Robert Straker Collection, Antiochiana, Antioch College.

———. "Plan of the West Roxbury Community." *Dial* 2 (1842): 361–72.

———. *Record of a School*. Ed. Megan Marshall. 1835; Bedford, Mass.: Applewood Books, 2005.

———. *Reminiscences of Rev. William Ellery Channing, D.D.* Boston: Roberts Brothers, 1880.

———, trans. *Self Education: or, The Means and Art of Moral Progress*, by Joseph Marie DeGerando. Boston: Carter & Hendee, 1830.

———. "The Spirit of the Hebrew Scriptures." *Christian Examiner* 16 (1834): 174–202, 305–20; 17 (1834): 78–92.

. "A Tribute to Mary Moody Emerson." *Boston Evening Transcript*, 14 May 1863. Reprinted in *Notes on the History of Waterford, Maine*, ed. Thomas Hovey Gage, 54–57. Worcester, Mass.: privately printed, 1913.

———. "A Vision." *Pioneer* 1 (March 1843): 97–100. Reprinted in *Last Evening with Allston*, 62–72.

Ripley, Sarah Alden Bradford. Sarah Alden Bradford Ripley Papers. Schlesinger Library, Harvard University.

Ripley, Sophia. "Woman." *Dial* 1 (Jan. 1841): 362–66.

Russell, Amelia. *Home Life of the Brook Farm Association*. Boston: Little, Brown, 1900.

Sedgwick, Catharine Maria. Catharine Maria Sedgwick Papers, 1798–1908. MHi.

———. *Hope Leslie, or, Early Times in the Massachusetts*. 1827; New Brunswick, N.J.: Rutgers Univ. Press, 1987.

———. *Married or Single?* New York: Harper 1857.

———. *Means and Ends, or, Self-Training*. Boston: Marsh, Capen, Lyon, and Webb, 1839.

———. *A New-England Tale; or, Sketches of New England Character and Manners*. 1822; New York: Oxford Univ. Press, 1995.

———. *The Power of Her Sympathy: The Autobiography and Journal of Catharine Maria Sedgwick*. Ed. Mary Kelley. Boston: Northeastern Univ. Press, 1993.

Sedgwick, Ora Gannett. "A Girl of Sixteen at Brook Farm." In *The Brook Farm Book*, ed. Joel Myerson. New York: Garland, 1987.

Smith, Elizabeth Oakes. *Bertha and Lily; or, the Parsonage of Beech Glen*. New York: Phillips, Sampson, 1854.

———. Elizabeth Oakes Smith Papers. New York Public Library.

———. "Excerpts from the Diary of Elizabeth Oakes Smith." Ed. Joy Wiltenburg. *Signs* 9, no. 3 (1984): 534–48.

———. *Selections from the Autobiography of Elizabeth Oakes Smith*. Ed. Mary Alice Wyman. Lewiston, Me.: Lewiston Journal, 1924.

Sprague, Julia. *History of the New England Women's Club, from 1868 to 1893*. Boston: Lee & Shepard, 1894.

Stanton, Elizabeth Cady. "Reminiscences." No. 27. *Woman's Tribune*, 21 June 1890.

Stanton, Elizabeth Cady, and Susan B. Anthony. *The Selected Papers of Elizabeth Cady Stanton and Susan B. Anthony*. Ed. Ann D. Gordon. 6 vols. New Brunswick, N.J.: Rutgers Univ. Press, 1997–2013.

Stanton, Elizabeth Cady, Susan B. Anthony, and Matilda Joslyn Gage, eds. *History of Woman Suffrage*. 6 vols. 1881–1922; New York: Arno, 1969.

Stoddard, Elizabeth. Manuscript letters to Margaret Sweat. Allison-Shelley Collection, Rare Books and Manuscripts, Pennsylvania State Univ. Libraries.

———. *The Morgesons, and Other Writings, Published and Unpublished*. Ed. Lawrence Buell and Sandra A. Zagarell. Philadelphia: Univ. of Pennsylvania, 1984.

Sturgis, Caroline. "The Letters of Caroline Sturgis to Margaret Fuller." Ed. Francis B. Dedmond. In *Studies in the American Renaissance 1988*, ed. Joel Myerson, 201–51. Charlottesville: Univ. Press of Virginia, 1988.

Sweat, Margaret. *Ethel's Love-Life: A Novel*. New York: Rudd & Carleton, 1859.

———. "The Novels of George Sand." In *Antonia: A Novel*, by George Sand, trans. Virginia Vaughan, 1–23. Boston: Roberts Brothers, 1870.

Tappan, Caroline Sturgis. "Art and Artist." *Dial* 2 (October 1840): 232.

———. Correspondence and Manuscripts, Caroline Sturgis Tappan Papers. MH-H.

The Una: A Paper Devoted to the Elevation of Woman. Ed. Paulina Wright Davis and Caroline Healey Dall. Boston: Hewitt, 1853–55.

[Whitman, Sarah Helen]. "Emerson's Essays, by a Disciple." *United States Magazine and Democratic Review* 16 (June 1845): 589–602.

Woman's Era. Ed. Josephine St. P. Ruffin and Florida R. Ridley. Boston: Woman's Era Club, 1894–97.

The Woman's Journal. Ed. Lucy Stone, Mary Livermore, and Julia Ward Howe. Boston: American Woman's Suffrage Association, 1870–1917.

SECONDARY SOURCES

Adams, Katherine. *Owning Up: Privacy, Property, and Belonging in U.S. Women's Life Writing*. New York: Oxford Univ. Press, 2009.

Adams, Kimberly VanEsveld. *Our Lady of Victorian Feminism: The Madonna in the Work of Anna Jameson, Margaret Fuller, and George Eliot*. Athens: Ohio Univ. Press, 2001.

Adams, Stephen. "'That Tidiness We Always Look for in Woman': Fuller's *Summer on the Lakes* and Romantic Aesthetics." In *Studies in the American Renaissance 1987*, ed. Joel Myerson, 247–64. Charlottesville: Univ. Press of Virginia, 1987.

Albert, Judith Strong. "Currents of Influence: 'The Electrical, the Magnetic Element in Women?'" In Urbanski, *Margaret Fuller: Visionary*, 199–239.

———. *Minerva's Circle: Margaret Fuller's Women*. Novato, Calif.: Paper Mill Press, 2010.

———. "Refrains: Margaret Fuller's Presence between Centuries." In Fleischmann, *Margaret Fuller's Cultural Critique*, 55–71.

Allen, Margaret Vanderhaar. *The Achievement of Margaret Fuller*. Univ. Park: Pennsylvania State Univ. Press, 1979.

Amlong, Terri A. "'Universal Human Rights': The New Rhetoric of the Woman's Rights

Movement Conceptualized within the *Una* (1853–55)." *American Periodicals: A Journal of History, Criticism, and Bibliography* 23, no. 1 (2013): 22–42.

———. "Women of Reform: The Periodical Editing Careers of Margaret Fuller, Lydia Maria Child, Caroline Healey Dall, and Jane Grey Swisshelm." PhD diss., Univ. of South Carolina, 2006. DAI Sec. A (67:9).

Ard, Patricia M. "Transcendentalism for Children: Mary Peabody Mann's *The Flower People*." In Elbert, Hall, and Rodier, *Reinventing the Peabody Sisters*, 216–31.

Avallone, Charlene. "Catharine Sedgwick and the 'Art' of Conversation." In *Catharine Maria Sedgwick: Critical Perspectives*, ed. Lucinda Damon-Bach and Victoria Clements, 192–208. Boston: Northeastern Univ. Press, 2008.

———. "Circles around George Sand: Margaret Fuller and the Dynamics of Transnational Reception." In Bailey, Viens, and Wright, *Margaret Fuller and Her Circles*, 206–28.

———. "Elizabeth Palmer Peabody and the 'Art' of Conversation." In Elbert, Hall, and Rodier, *Reinventing the Peabody Sisters*, 23–44.

———. "The Red Roots of White Feminism in Margaret Fuller's Writings." In *Doing Feminism: Teaching and Research in the Academy*, ed. Mary Anderson et al., 135–64. Lansing, Mich.: Women's Studies Program, Michigan State Univ., 1997.

———. "What American Renaissance? The Gendered Genealogy of a Critical Discourse." *PMLA* 112 (1997): 1102–20.

Badaracco, Claire M. "Pitfalls and Rewards of the Solo Editor: Sophia Peabody Hawthorne." *Resources for American Literary Study* 11, no. 1 (Spring 1981): 91–100.

Bailey, Brigitte. "Fuller, Hawthorne, and Imagining Urban Spaces in Rome." In *Roman Holidays: American Writers and Artists in Nineteenth-Century Italy*, ed. Robert K. Martin and Leland S. Person, 175–90. Iowa City: Univ. of Iowa Press, 2002.

———. "Introduction: Fuller at Two Hundred." In Bailey, Viens, and Wright, *Margaret Fuller and Her Circles*, 1–10.

———. "Introduction: Transatlantic Studies and American Women Writers." In Lueck, Bailey, and Damon-Bach, *Transatlantic Women*, xiii–xxviii.

———. "Margaret Fuller's *New York Tribune* Dispatches from Great Britain: Modern Geography and the Print Culture of Reform." In Lueck, Bailey, and Damon-Bach, *Transatlantic Women*, 50–70.

———. "Representing Italy: Fuller, History Painting, and the Popular Press." In Fleischmann, *Margaret Fuller's Cultural Critique*, 229–48.

Bailey, Brigitte, Katheryn P. Viens, and Conrad Edick Wright, eds. *Margaret Fuller and Her Circles*. Durham: Univ. of New Hampshire Press, 2013.

Baker, Anne. "'A Commanding View': Vision and the Problem of Nationality in Fuller's *Summer on the Lakes*." *ESQ: A Journal of the American Renaissance* 44, nos. 1–2 (1998): 61–77.

Barton, Cynthia H. *Transcendental Wife: The Life of Abigail May Alcott*. Lanham, Md.: Univ. Press of America, 1996.

Bäumer, Konstanze. "Margaret Fuller (1810–1850) and Bettina von Arnim: An Encounter between American Transcendentalism and German Romanticism." *Internationales Jahrbuch der Bettina-von-Arnim-Gesellschaft* 4 (1990): 47–69.

Baym, Nina. *American Women Writers and the Work of History, 1790–1860*. New Brunswick, N.J.: Rutgers Univ. Press, 1995.

———. "The Ann Sisters: Elizabeth Peabody's Millennial Historicism." *American Literary History* 3 (1991): 27–45.

———. "Rewriting the Scribbling Women." *Legacy* 1, no. 2 (Fall 1985): 3–12.

———. *Woman's Fiction: A Guide to Novels by and about Women in America, 1820–1870*. Ithaca, N.Y.: Cornell Univ. Press, 1978.

Beam, Dorri. "Fuller, Feminism, Pantheism." In Bailey, Viens, and Wright, *Margaret Fuller and Her Circles*, 52–76.

———. *Style, Gender, and Fantasy in Nineteenth-Century American Women's Writing*. Cambridge: Cambridge Univ. Press, 2010.

Bean, Judith Mattson. "Conversation as Rhetoric in Margaret Fuller's *Woman in the Nineteenth Century*." In *In Her Own Voice: Nineteenth-Century American Women Essayists*, ed. Sherry Lee Linkon, 27–40. New York: Garland, 1997.

———. "Margaret Fuller and Julia Ward Howe: A Woman-to-Woman Influence." In Fleischmann, *Margaret Fuller's Cultural Critique*, 91–108.

———. "Margaret Fuller on the Early Poetry of Julia Ward Howe: An Uncollected Letter." *ANQ: A Quarterly Journal of Short Articles, Notes, and Reviews* 7, no. 2 (1994): 76–80.

———. "'A *Presence* among Us': Fuller's Place in Nineteenth-Century Oral Culture." *ESQ: A Journal of the American Renaissance* 44 (1998): 79–123.

———. "Texts from Conversation: Margaret Fuller's Influence on Emerson." In *Studies in the American Renaissance 1994*, ed. Joel Myerson, 227–44. Charlottesville: Univ. Press of Virginia, 1995.

Bedell, Madelon. *The Alcotts: Biography of a Family*. New York: Clarkson Potter, 1980.

Belasco, Susan. "The Animating Influences of Discord: Margaret Fuller in 1844." *Legacy* 20, nos. 1–2 (2003): 76–93.

Blair, Karen. *The Clubwoman as Feminist: True Womanhood Redefined, 1868–1914*. New York: Holmes & Meier, 1980.

Blanchard, Paula. "Corinne and the 'Yankee Corinna': Madame de Staël and Margaret Fuller." In *Woman as Mediatrix: Essays on Nineteenth-Century Women Writers*, ed. Avriel H. Goldberger, 39–46. Westport, Conn.: Greenwood, 1987.

———. *Margaret Fuller: From Transcendentalism to Revolution*. 1979; Reading, Mass.: Addison Wesley, 1987.

Borghi, Liana. "Margaret Fuller: Maps and Patterns of a Transgressive Journey." Universita di Roma, w3.uniroma1.it / dprs / sites / default / files / 333.html. Accessed 18 July 2013.

Boudreau, Kristin. *Sympathy in American Literature: American Sentiments from Jefferson to the Jameses*. Gainesville: Univ. Press of Florida, 2002.

Bowman, Nancy. "Caroline Healey Dall: Her Creation and Reform Career." In *Women of the Commonwealth*, ed. Susan Lynne Porter, 121–46. Amherst: Univ. of Massachusetts Press, 1996.

Boyd, Anne E. *Writing for Immortality: Women and the Emergence of High Literary Culture in America*. Baltimore: Johns Hopkins Univ. Press, 2004.

Brodie, Susan Lundvall. "Margaret Fuller and Charlotte Perkins Gilman: Rhetoric and the Shape of Learning." *Wisconsin English Journal* 28, no. 3 (1986): 2–4.

Buell, Lawrence. *Literary Transcendentalism: Style and Vision in the American Renaissance*. Ithaca, N.Y.: Cornell Univ. Press, 1973.

———. *New England Literary Culture from Revolution through Renaissance*. Cambridge: Cambridge Univ. Press, 1986.

Butchart, Ronald. "Edmonia G. and Caroline V. Highgate: Black Teachers, Freed Slaves, and the Betrayal of Black Hearts." In *Portraits of African American Life since 1865*, ed. Nina Mjagkij, 1–14. Wilmington, Del.: Scholarly Resources, 2003.

———. *Schooling the Freed People*. Chapel Hill: Univ. of North Carolina Press, 2010.

Capper, Charles. "Getting from Here to There: Margaret Fuller's American Transnational Odyssey." In Capper and Giorcelli, *Margaret Fuller: Transatlantic Crossings*, 3–26.

———. *Margaret Fuller: An American Romantic Life*. Vol. 1. *The Private Years*. New York: Oxford Univ. Press, 1992.

———. *Margaret Fuller: An American Romantic Life*. Vol. 2. *The Public Years*. New York: Oxford Univ. Press, 2007.

———. "Margaret Fuller as a Cultural Reformer: The Conversations in Boston." *American Quarterly* 39 (1987): 509–28.

Capper, Charles, and Conrad Edick Wright, eds. *Transient and Permanent: The Transcendentalist Movement and Its Contexts*. Boston: Massachusetts Historical Society, 1999.

Capper, Charles, and Cristina Giorcelli, eds. *Margaret Fuller: Transatlantic Crossings in a Revolutionary Age*. Madison: Univ. of Wisconsin Press, 2007.

Chapman, Mary. "Gender and Influence in Louisa May Alcott's *A Modern Mephistopheles*." *Legacy* 13, no. 1 (1996): 19–37.

Chevigny, Bell Gale. "'Cheat Me [On] by No Illusion': Margaret Fuller's Cultural Critique and Its Legacies." In Fleischmann, *Margaret Fuller's Cultural Critique*, 27–41.

———. "Growing Out of New England: The Emergence of Margaret Fuller's Radicalism." *Women's Studies: An Interdisciplinary Journal* 5 (1977): 65–100.

———. "The Long Arm of Censorship: Myth-Making in Margaret Fuller's Time and Our Own." *Signs* 2, no. 2 (1976): 450–60.

———. "Mutual Interpretation: Margaret Fuller's Journeys in Italy." In Capper and Giorcelli, *Margaret Fuller: Transatlantic Crossings*, 99–123.

———. "To the Edges of Ideology: Margaret Fuller's Centrifugal Evolution." *American Quarterly* 38 (1986): 173–201.

Clifford, Deborah Pickman. *Crusader for Freedom: A Life of Lydia Maria Child*. Boston: Beacon Press, 1992.

Cole, Phyllis. "The Advantage of Loneliness: Mary Moody Emerson's Almanacks, 1802–1855." In *Emerson: Prospect and Retrospect*, Harvard English Studies 10, ed. Joel Porte, 1–32. Cambridge, Mass.: Harvard Univ. Press, 1982.

———. "'Conversation That Makes the Soul': Writing the Biography of Mary Moody Emerson." In *Lives Out of Letters: Essays on American Literary Biography and Documentation, in Honor of Robert N. Hudspeth*, ed. Robert D. Habich, 205–24. Madison, N.J.: Fairleigh Dickinson Univ. Press, 2004.

———. "Fuller's Lawsuit and Feminist History." In Bailey, Viens, and Wright, *Margaret Fuller and Her Circles*, 11–31.

———. "The Literary Landscape of a Woman's Rights Periodical." In Von Frank and Argersinger, "Reexamining the American Renaissance," 81–94.

———. *Mary Moody Emerson and the Origins of Transcendentalism: A Family History*. New York: Oxford Univ. Press, 1998.

———. "Men and Women Conversing: The Emersons in 1837." In *Emersonian Circles: Essays in Honor of Joel Myerson*, ed. Robert E. Burkholder and Wesley T. Mott, 127–59. Rochester, N.Y.: Univ. of Rochester Press, 1997.

———. "The Nineteenth-Century Women's Rights Movement and the Canonization of Margaret Fuller." *ESQ: A Journal of the American Renaissance* 44 (1998): 1–33.

———. "Pain and Protest in the Emerson Family." In *The Emerson Dilemma: Essays on Emerson and Social Reform*, ed. T. Gregory Garvey, 67–92. Athens: Univ. of Georgia Press, 2001.

———. "Stanton, Fuller, and the Grammar of Romanticism." *New England Quarterly* 73 (2000): 533–59.

———. "Woman Questions: Emerson, Fuller, and New England Reform." In Capper and Wright, *Transient and Permanent*, 408–46.

Conrad, Susan Phinney. *Perish the Thought: Intellectual Women in Romantic America, 1830–60*. New York: Oxford Univ. Press, 1976.

Cooke, George Willis. *An Historical and Biographical Introduction to Accompany "The Dial."* 1902; New York: Russell & Russell, 1961.

Cooper, Michaela B. "Should Not These Things Be Known? Mary Mann's *Juanita* and the Limits of Domesticity." In Elbert, Hall, and Rodier, *Reinventing the Peabody Sisters*, 146–62.

———. "Textual Wandering and Anxiety in Margaret Fuller's *Summer on the Lakes*." In Fleischmann, *Margaret Fuller's Cultural Critique*, 171–89.

Crouse, Jamie S. "'If They Have a Moral Power': Margaret Fuller, Transcendentalism, and the Question of Women's Moral Nature." *American Transcendental Quarterly* 19, no. 4 (2005): 259–79.

Damon-Bach, Lucinda L., and Victoria Clemens, eds. *Catharine Maria Sedgwick: Critical Perspectives*. Boston: Northeastern Univ. Press, 1998.

Davis, Cynthia J. "Margaret Fuller, Body and Soul." *American Literature* 71, no. 1 (1999): 331–56.

———. "What 'Speaks in Us': Margaret Fuller, Women's Rights, and Human Nature." In Fleischmann, *Margaret Fuller's Cultural Critique*, 43–54.

Deery, Patricia. "Margaret Fuller and Dorothea Brooke." *Review of English Studies* 36, no. 143 (1985): 379–85.

Deese, Helen R. "Caroline Healey Dall and the American Women's Movement, 1848–75." *American Nineteenth Century History* 3 (2002): 1–28.

———. "Louisa May Alcott's *Moods*: A New Archival Discovery." *New England Quarterly* 76 (2003): 439–55.

———. "A New England Woman's Network: Elizabeth Palmer Peabody, Caroline Healey Dall, and Delia S. Bacon." *Legacy* 8 (1991): 77–91.

———. "Transcendentalism from the Margins: The Experience of Caroline Healey Dall." In Capper and Wright, *Transient and Permanent*, 527–47.

Delano, Sterling. *Brook Farm: The Dark Side of Utopia*. Cambridge, Mass.: Harvard Univ. Press, 2004.

Delano, Sterling, and Joel Myerson. "Letters from Brook Farm: A Comprehensive Checklist of Surviving Correspondence." *Resources for American Literary Study* 31 (2006): 95–123.

Delphendahl, Renate. "Margaret Fuller: Interpreter and Translator of German Literature." In Urbanski, *Margaret Fuller: Visionary*, 54–100.

Dimock, Wai Chee. "Literature for the Planet." *PMLA* 116 (2001): 173–88.

———. "The Planetary Dead: Margaret Fuller, Ancient Egypt, Italian Revolution." In "American Literary Globalism." Special issue, *ESQ: A Journal of the American Renaissance* 50 (2004): 23–57.

———. *Through Other Continents: American Literature across Deep Time*. Princeton: Princeton Univ. Press, 2006.

Dobson, Joanne. "Reclaiming Sentimental Literature." *American Literature* 69 (1997): 263–88.

Douglas, Ann. *The Feminization of American Culture*. New York: Alfred A. Knopf, 1977.

Doyle, Christine. *Louisa May Alcott and Charlotte Brontë: Transatlantic Translations*. Knoxville: Univ. of Tennessee Press, 2000.

———. "Singing Mignon's Song: German Literature and Culture in the March Trilogy." *Children's Literature* 31 (2003): 50–70.

Duran, Jane. "Margaret Fuller and Transcendental Feminism." *Pluralist* 5, no. 1 (2010): 65–72.

Dykeman, Therese Boos, ed. "Ednah Dow Cheney." In *American Women Philosophers 1650–1930: Six Exemplary Thinkers*, 263–327. Lewiston, Me.: Edwin Mellen, 1993.

———. "The Philosophy of Halfness and the Philosophy of Duality: Julia Ward Howe and Ednah Dow Cheney." *Hypatia* 19, no. 2 (2004): 17–34.

Dykstra, Natalie. *Clover Adams: A Gilded and Heartbreaking Life*. Boston: Houghton Mifflin, 2012.

Earhart, Amy. "Elizabeth Peabody on the 'Temperament of the Colored Classes': African Americans, Progressive History, and Education in a Democratic System." In Elbert, Hall, and Rodier, *Reinventing the Peabody Sisters,* 77–90.

Elbert, Monika M. "Elizabeth Palmer Peabody's Problematic Feminism and the Feminization of Transcendentalism." In Elbert, Hall, and Rodier, *Reinventing the Peabody Sisters,* 199–215.

Elbert, Monika M., ed. *Separate Spheres No More: Gender Convergence in American Literature*. Iowa City: Univ. of Iowa Press, 2000.

Elbert, Monika M., Julie E. Hall, and Katharine Rodier, eds. *Reinventing the Peabody Sisters*. Iowa City: Univ. of Iowa Press, 2006.

Ellison, Julie. *Delicate Subjects: Romanticism, Gender, and the Ethics of Understanding*. Ithaca, N.Y.: Cornell Univ. Press, 1990.

Elsden, Annamaria Formichella. "Watery Angels: Sophia Peabody Hawthorne's Artistic Argument in *Notes in England and Italy*." In Elbert, Hall, and Rodier, *Reinventing the Peabody Sisters,* 129–45.

Fergenson, Laraine R. "Margaret Fuller in the Classroom: The Providence Period." In *Studies in the American Renaissance 1987,* ed. Joel Myerson, 131–42. Charlottesville: Univ. Press of Virginia, 1987.

Finger, Anke. "Bettine in Boston: Margaret Fuller and the Reception of *Die Guenderode* in Transcendental America." Master's thesis, Brandeis Univ., 1995.

Fish, Cheryl. "Unconnected Intelligence and the Woman of Letters: Margaret Fuller's Darting Critique." In Fleischmann, *Margaret Fuller's Cultural Critique,* 153–67.

Fleischmann, Fritz. "Introduction: Cultural Translation as Cultural Critique." In *Margaret Fuller's Cultural Critique,* 1–24.

———, ed. *Margaret Fuller's Cultural Critique: Her Age and Legacy*. New York: Peter Lang, 2000.

Foreman, P. Gabrielle. *Activist Sentiments: Reading Black Women in the Nineteenth Century*. Chicago: Univ. of Illinois Press, 2009.

Foster, Travis. "Grotesque Sympathy: Lydia Maria Child, White Reform, and the Embodiment of Urban Space." *ESQ: A Journal of the American Renaissance* 56 (2010): 1–32.

Francis, Richard. *Fruitlands: The Alcott Family and Their Search for Utopia*. New Haven: Yale Univ. Press, 2010.

———. *Transcendental Utopias: Individual and Community at Brook Farm, Fruitlands, and Walden*. Ithaca, N.Y.: Cornell Univ. Press, 1997.

Fry, Ingrid. "Elective Androgyny: Bettine von Arnim and Margaret Fuller's Reception of Goethe." *Goethe Yearbook* 10 (2001): 246–62.

García, Ivonne M. "Transnational Crossings: Sophia Hawthorne's Authorial Persona from the 'Cuba Journal' to *Notes in England and Italy*." *Nathaniel Hawthorne Review* 37 (2011): 97–120.

Gardner, Eric. "Remembered (Black) Readers." *American Literary History* 23, no. 2 (2011): 229–59.

———. *Unexpected Places: Relocating Nineteenth-Century African American Literature*. Jackson: Univ. Press of Mississippi, 2009.

Gatta, John Paul. *American Madonna: Images of the Divine Woman in Literary Culture*. New York: Oxford Univ. Press, 1997.

Gaul, Theresa Strouth, and Sharon M. Harris, eds. *Letters and Cultural Transformations in the United States, 1760–1860*. Surrey, U.K.: Ashgate, 2009.

Gemme, Paola. *Domesticating Foreign Struggles: The Italian Risorgimento and Antebellum American Identity*. Athens: Univ. of Georgia Press, 2005.

Gilmore, Susan. "Margaret Fuller's 'Receiving' the 'Indians.'" In Fleischmann, *Margaret Fuller's Cultural Critique*, 191–227.

Giorcelli, Cristina. "A Humbug, a Bounder, and a Dabbler: Margaret Fuller, Cristina di Belgioioso, and Christina Casamassima." In Capper and Giorcelli, *Margaret Fuller: Transatlantic Crossings*, 195–220.

Glasser, Leah Blatt. *In a Closet Hidden: The Life and Works of Mary E. Wilkins Freeman*. Boston: Univ. of Massachusetts Press, 1996.

Gollin, Rita K. *Annie Adams Fields, Woman of Letters*. Boston: Univ. of Massachusetts Press, 2002.

Goodwin, Joan W. *The Remarkable Mrs. Ripley: The Life of Sarah Alden Bradford Ripley*. Boston: Northeastern Univ. Press, 1998.

Greven, David. "New Girls and Bandit Brides: Female Narcissism and Lesbian Desire in Margaret Fuller's *Summer on the Lakes*." *Legacy* 29, no. 1 (2012): 37–61.

Guida, Francesco. "Realism, Idealism, and Passion in Margaret Fuller's Response to Italy." In Capper and Giorcelli, *Margaret Fuller: Transatlantic Crossings*, 156–71.

Gura, Philip F. *American Transcendentalism: A History*. New York: Hill & Wang, 2007.

Gustafson, Sandra M. "Choosing a Medium: Margaret Fuller and the Forms of Sentiment." *American Quarterly* 47 (1995): 34–65.

Hall, Julie E. "At the Crisis of Our Fate: Sophia Peabody Hawthorne's Civil War Correspondence." In Elbert, Hall, and Rodier, *Reinventing the Peabody Sisters*, 61–76.

Haronian, Mary-Jo. "Margaret Fuller's Visions." *ESQ: A Journal of the American Renaissance* 44 (1998): 35–59.

Hendler, Glenn. *Public Sentiments: Structures of Feeling in Nineteenth-Century American Literature*. Chapel Hill: Univ. of North Carolina Press, 2001.

Holly, Carol. "Nineteenth-Century Autobiographies of Affiliation: The Case of Catharine Sedgwick and Lucy Larcom." In *American Autobiography: Retrospect and Prospect*, ed. Paul John Eakin, 216–34. Madison: Univ. of Wisconsin Press, 1991.

Hudspeth, Robert N. "Margaret Fuller and the Ideal of Heroism." In Capper and Giorcelli, *Margaret Fuller: Transatlantic Crossings*, 45–65.

———. "Margaret Fuller and Urban Life." In Bailey, Viens, and Wright, *Margaret Fuller and Her Circles*, 179–205.

Hurst, C. Michael. "Bodies in Transition: Transcendental Feminism in Margaret Fuller's *Woman in the Nineteenth Century*." *Arizona Quarterly* 66, no. 4 (2010): 1–32.

Innes, Sherrie A., and Diana Royer, eds. *Breaking Boundaries: New Perspectives on Women's Regional Writing*. Iowa City: Univ. of Iowa Press, 1997.

Irons, Susan H. "Channing's Influence on Peabody: Self-Culture and the Danger of Egoism." In *Studies in the American Renaissance 1992*, ed. Joel Myerson, 121–35. Charlottesville: Univ. Press of Virginia, 1992.

Jones, Diane Brown. "Elizabeth Palmer Peabody's Transcendental Manifesto." In *Studies in the American Renaissance 1992*, ed. Joel Myerson, 195–207. Charlottesville: Univ. Press of Virginia, 1992.

Kaledin, Eugenia. *The Education of Mrs. Henry Adams*. Philadelphia: Temple Univ. Press, 1981.

Karcher, Caroline L. *The First Woman in the Republic: A Cultural Biography of Lydia Maria Child*. Durham, N.C.: Duke Univ. Press, 1994.

———. "Margaret Fuller and Lydia Maria Child: Intersecting Careers, Reciprocal Influences." In Fleischmann, *Margaret Fuller's Cultural Critique*, 75–89.

Kearns, Francis E. "Margaret Fuller and the Abolition Movement." In Myerson, *Critical Essays*, 247–54.

Kelley, Mary. "Epilogue: 'The Measure of My Foot-Print': Margaret Fuller's Unfinished Revolution." In Bailey, Viens, and Wright, *Margaret Fuller and Her Circles*, 229–43.

———. *Learning to Stand and Speak: Women, Education, and Public Life in America's Republic*. Chapel Hill: Univ. of North Carolina Press, 2006.

Kete, Mary Louise. "Gender Valences of Transcendentalism: The Pursuit of Idealism in Elizabeth Oakes-Smith's 'The Sinless Child.'" In Elbert, *Separate Spheres*, 245–60.

Keyser, Elizabeth Lennox. *Whispers in the Dark: The Fiction of Louisa May Alcott*. Knoxville: Univ. of Tennessee Press, 1993.

Kolodny, Annette. "Inventing a Feminist Discourse: Rhetoric and Resistance in Margaret Fuller's *Woman in the Nineteenth Century*." *New Literary History* 25 (1994): 355–82.

———. *The Land before Her: Fantasy and Experience of the American Frontiers, 1630–1860*. Chapel Hill: Univ. of North Carolina Press, 1984.

———. "Margaret Fuller's First Depiction of Indians and the Limits on Social Protest: An Exercise in Women's Studies Pedagogy." *Legacy* 18, no. 1 (2001): 1–20.

Kopacz, Paula. "Feminist at the 'Tribune': Margaret Fuller as Professional Writer." In *Studies in the American Renaissance 1991*, ed. Joel Myerson, 119–39. Charlottesville: Univ. Press of Virginia, 1991.

LaPlante, Eve. *Marmee and Louisa: The Untold Story of Louisa May Alcott and Her Mother*. New York: Free Press, 2012.

Lawrence, Kathleen. "The 'Dry-Lighted Soul' Ignites: Emerson and His Soul-Mate Caroline Sturgis as Seen in Her Houghton Manuscripts." *Harvard Library Bulletin* 16 (2005): 37–67.

———. "Margaret Fuller's Aesthetic Transcendentalism and Its Legacy." In *The American Renaissance*, ed. Harold Bloom, 273–95. Philadelphia: Chelsea House Press, 2004.

Lazo, Rodrigo. "Against the Cuba Guide: The 'Cuba Journal,' *Juanita*, and Travel Writing." In Elbert, Hall, and Rodier, *Reinventing the Peabody Sisters*, 180–95.

Leach, William. *True Love and Perfect Union: The Feminist Reform of Sex and Society*. New York: Basic Books, 1980.

Lee, Pamela. "Queen of All I Surveyed: Sophia Peabody Hawthorne's 'Cuba Journal' and the Imperial Gaze." In Elbert, Hall, and Rodier, *Reinventing the Peabody* Sisters, 163–79.

Lewis, Linda M. *Germaine de Staël, George Sand, and the Victorian Woman Artist*. Columbia: Univ. of Missouri Press, 2003.

Livengood, Nicole C. "Resisting the Overplot: Intertextual Interventions and Generic Interplays in the Writings of Margaret Fuller, Elizabeth Stoddard, Lydia Maria Child, and Julia Ward Howe." PhD diss., Purdue Univ., 2007. DAI, Sec. A (68:12).

Loeffelholz, Mary. "Essential, Portable, Mythical Margaret Fuller." In *Challenging Boundaries: Gender and Periodization*, ed. Joyce W. Warren and Margaret Dickie, 159–84. Athens: Univ. of Georgia Press, 2000.

Lord, Susan Toth. "Extraordinary Women All: The Influence of Madame de Staël on Margaret Fuller and Lydia Maria Child." PhD diss., Kent State Univ., 2004. DAI, Sec. A (65:11).

Lott, Deshae E. "Like One Happy Family: Mary Peabody Mann's Method for Influencing Reform." In Elbert, Hall, and Rodier, *Reinventing the Peabody Sisters*, 91–107.

———. "On the Margins and in the Margins: Margaret Fuller and the Testaments." *Resources for American Literary Study* 28 (2003): 83–109.

Lueck, Beth L., Brigitte Bailey, and Lucinda L. Damon-Bach, eds. *Transatlantic Women: Nineteenth-Century American Women Writers and Great Britain*. Durham: Univ. of New Hampshire Press, 2012.

Lukens, Margaret A. "Columnist of Conscience: Margaret Fuller's New York Years." In Urbanski, *Margaret Fuller: Visionary*, 183–96.

Maas, Christel-Maria. *Margaret Fuller's transnationales Projekt*. Göttingen: Univ-drücke, 2006.

Machor, James L., ed. *Readers in History: Nineteenth-Century American Literature and the Contexts of Response*. Baltimore: Johns Hopkins Univ. Press, 1993.

Mailloux, Steven. "Misreading as a Historical Act: Cultural Rhetoric, Bible Politics, and Fuller's 1845 Review of Douglass's Narrative." In Machor, *Readers in History*, 3–31.

Marshall, Megan. "Elizabeth Palmer Peabody: The First Transcendentalist?" *Massachusetts Historical Review* 8 (2006): 1–15.

———. "Epilogue: The Peabody Sisters as Sisters." In Elbert, Hall, and Rodier, *Reinventing the Peabody Sisters*, 248–58.

———. *Margaret Fuller: A New American Life*. Boston: Houghton Mifflin, 2013.

———. "Margaret Fuller on Music's 'Everlasting Yes': A Romantic Critic in the Romantic Era." In Bailey, Viens, and Wright, *Margaret Fuller and Her Circles*, 148–60.

———. *The Peabody Sisters: Three Women Who Ignited American Romanticism*. Boston: Houghton Mifflin, 2005.

Matteson, John. *Eden's Outcasts: The Story of Louisa May Alcott and Her Father*. New York: Norton, 2007.

———. *The Lives of Margaret Fuller: A Biography*. New York: Norton, 2012.

———. "'Woes . . . of Which We Know Nothing': Fuller and the Problem of Feminine Virtue." In Bailey, Viens, and Wright, *Margaret Fuller and Her Circles*, 32–51.

McCabe, Tracy. "Avenging Angel: Tragedy and Womanhood in Julia Ward Howe's *The World's Own*." *Legacy* 12, no. 2 (1995): 98–111.

McFadden, Margaret H. "Boston Teenagers Debate the Woman Question, 1837–1838." *Signs* 15 (1990): 832–47.

———. *Golden Cables of Sympathy: The Transatlantic Sources of Nineteenth-Century Feminism*. Lexington: Univ. Press of Kentucky, 1999.

Mielke, Laura L. "Sentiment and Space in Lydia Maria Child's Native American Writings, 1824–1870." *Legacy* 21 (2004): 172–92.

Miller, Edward Haviland. "A Calendar of the Letters of Sophia Peabody Hawthorne." *Studies in the American Renaissance 1986*, ed. Joel Myerson, 199–281. Charlottesville: Univ. Press of Virginia, 1986.

Mills, Bruce. *Cultural Reformations: Lydia Maria Child and the Literature of Reform*. Athens: Univ. of Georgia Press, 1994.

Mitchell, Thomas R. *Hawthorne's Fuller Mystery*. Amherst: Univ. of Massachusetts Press, 1998.

Mott, Wesley T., ed. *Biographical Dictionary of Transcendentalism*. Westport, Conn.: Greenwood Press, 1996.

———. *Encyclopedia of Transcendentalism*. Westport, Conn.: Greenwood Press, 1996.

Mueller, Monika. *George Eliot U.S.: Transatlantic Literary and Cultural Perspectives*. Madison, N.J.: Fairleigh Dickinson Univ. Press, 2005.

Murray, Meg McGavran. *Margaret Fuller: Wandering Pilgrim*. Athens: Univ. of Georgia Press, 2008.

Myerson, Joel. "Caroline Dall's Reminiscences of Margaret Fuller." *Harvard Library Bulletin* 22 (October 1974): 414–28.

———, ed. *Critical Essays on Margaret Fuller*. Boston: G. K. Hall, 1980.

———, ed. *Fuller in Her Own Time: A Biographical Chronicle of Her Life, Drawn from Recollections, Interviews, and Memoirs by Family, Friends, and Associates*. Iowa City: Univ. of Iowa Press, 2008.

———. *Margaret Fuller: An Annotated Bibliography of Criticism, 1983–1995*. Westport, Conn.: Greenwood Press, 1998.

———. *Margaret Fuller: An Annotated Secondary Bibliography*. New York: Burt Franklin, 1977.

———. *Margaret Fuller: A Descriptive Bibliography*. Pittsburgh: Univ. of Pittsburgh Press, 1978.

———. "Mrs. Dall Edits Miss Fuller: The Story of Margaret and Her Friends." *Papers of the Bibliographic Society of America* 72 (1978): 187–200.

———. *The New England Transcendentalists and "The Dial": A History of the Magazine and Its Contributors*. Rutherford, N.J.: Fairleigh Dickinson Univ. Press, 1980.

———. "Sarah Clarke's Reminiscences of the Peabodys and Hawthorne." *Nathaniel Hawthorne Journal* (1973): 130–33.

———. "Supplement to 'Margaret Fuller: A Descriptive Bibliography.'" In *Studies in the American Renaissance 1996*, ed. Joel Myerson, 187–240. Charlottesville: Univ. Press of Virginia, 1996.

———. "Supplement to 'Margaret Fuller: An Annotated Secondary Bibliography.'" In *Studies in the American Renaissance 1984*, ed. Joel Myerson, 331–85. Charlottesville: Univ. Press of Virginia, 1984.

———. "'A True and High-Minded Person': Transcendentalist Sarah Clarke." *Southwest Review* (Spring 1974): 163–74.

Myerson, Joel, Sandra H. Petrulionis, and Laura Dassow Walls, eds. *The Oxford Handbook of Transcendentalism*. New York: Oxford Univ. Press, 2010.

Myerson, Joel, Daniel Shealy, and Madeleine B. Stern. "A Calendar of the Letters of Louisa May Alcott." In *Studies in the American Renaissance 1988*, ed. Joel Myerson, 361–99. Charlottesville: Univ. Press of Virginia, 1988.

Newman, Lance. "Margaret Fuller's *Summer on the Lakes, in 1843* and the Condition of America." *Romanticism on the Net* 38–39 (May 2005), http://id.erudit.org/iderudit/011668ar. Accessed December 1, 2013.

Packer, Barbara L. "Dangerous Acquaintances: The Correspondence of Margaret Fuller and James Freeman Clarke." *English Literary History* 67, no. 3 (2000): 801–18.

———. *The Transcendentalists*. 1995; Athens: Univ. of Georgia Press, 2007.

Petrulionis, Sandra Harbert. "By the Light of Her Mother's Lamp: Woman's Work versus Man's Philosophy in Louisa May Alcott's 'Transcendental Wild Oats.'" In *Studies in the American Renaissance 1995*, ed. Joel Myerson, 69–81. Charlottesville: Univ. Press of Virginia, 1995.

———. *To Set This World Right: The Antislavery Movement in Thoreau's Concord*. Ithaca, N.Y.: Cornell Univ. Press, 2006.

Pfaelzer, Jean. "The Sentimental Promise and the Utopian Myth: Rebecca Harding Davis's 'The Harmonists' and Louisa May Alcott's 'Transcendental Wild Oats.'" *American Transcendental Quarterly* 3 (1989): 85–100.

Putzi, Jennifer. "'Two Single Married Women': The Correspondence of Elizabeth Stoddard and Margaret Sweat, 1851–1854." In Gaul and Harrison, *Letters and Cultural Transformations*, 117–36.

Rankine-Galloway, Honoria. "Margaret Fuller: Transcendental Traveller." In *Engendering Identities*, ed. Susan Castillo, 93–106. Porto, Portugal: Universidade Fernando Pessoa, 1996.

Reichardt, Mary R. *A Web of Relationship: Women in the Short Fiction of Mary Wilkins Freeman*. Jackson: Univ. of Mississippi Press, 1992.

Reynolds, Larry J. *European Revolutions and the American Literary Renaissance*. New Haven: Yale Univ. Press, 1988.

———. "From *Dial* Essay to New York Book: The Making of *Woman in the Nineteenth Century*." In *Periodical Literature in Nineteenth-Century America*, ed. Kenneth M. Price and Susan Belasco Smith, 17–34. Charlottesville: Univ. Press of Virginia, 1995.

———. "Prospects for the Study of Margaret Fuller." *Resources for American Literary Study* 26, no. 2 (2000): 139–58.

———. *Righteous Violence: Revolution, Slavery, and the American Renaissance*. Athens: Univ. of Georgia Press, 2011.

Rigsby, Mary Bortnyk. "Margaret Fuller's Feminist Aesthetic: A Critique of Emersonian Idealism in the Works of Fuller, Alcott, Stowe, and Freeman." PhD diss., Temple Univ., 1992. DAI 52:9.

Ritchie, Amanda. "Margaret Fuller's First Conversation Series: A Discovery in the Archives." *Legacy* 18, no. 2 (2001): 216–31.

Robbins, Paula Ivaska. *The Royal Family of Concord: Samuel, Elizabeth, and Rockwood Hoar and Their Friendship*. N.p.: Xlibris, 2003.

Robbins, Sarah. *Managing Literacy, Mothering America: Women's Narratives on Reading and Writing in the Nineteenth Century*. Pittsburgh: Univ. of Pittsburgh Press, 2004.

Roberts, Heather. "'The Public Heart': Urban Life and the Politics of Sympathy in Lydia Maria Child's *Letters from New York*." *American Literature* 76 (2004): 749–75.

Robinson, David M. "Margaret Fuller and the Transcendental Ethos: *Woman in the Nineteenth Century*." *PMLA* 97 (1982): 83–98.

———. "Margaret Fuller, New York, and the Politics of Transcendentalism." *ESQ: A Journal of the American Renaissance* 52 (2006): 271–99.

———. "Margaret Fuller, Self-Culture, and Associationism." In Bailey, Viens, and Wright, *Margaret Fuller and Her Circles*, 77–99.

Rodier, Katharine. "Authorizing Sarah Winnemucca? Elizabeth Peabody and Mary Peabody Mann." In Elbert, Hall, and Rodier, *Reinventing the Peabody Sisters*, 108–25.

———. "Lucy Stone and the *Woman's Journal*." In *Blue Pencils and Hidden Hands: Women Editing Periodicals, 1830–1910*, ed. Sharon M. Harris, 99–122. Boston: Northeastern Univ. Press, 2004.

Ronda, Bruce A. *Elizabeth Palmer Peabody: A Reformer on Her Own Terms*. Cambridge, Mass.: Harvard Univ. Press, 1999.

———. "Elizabeth Peabody and the Fate of Transcendentalism." In Elbert, Hall, and Rodier, *Reinventing the Peabody Sisters*, 232–47.

———. "Print and Pedagogy: The Career of Elizabeth Peabody." In *A Living of Words: American Women in Print Culture*, ed. Susan Albertine, 35–48. Knoxville: Univ. of Tennessee Press, 1995.

Rose, Anne C. *Transcendentalism as a Social Movement, 1830–1850*. New Haven: Yale Univ. Press, 1981.

Rose, Jane E. "Expanding Woman's Sphere, Dismantling Class, and Building Community: The Feminism of Elizabeth Oakes Smith." *CLA Journal* 45, no. 2 (2001): 207–30.

Rosowski, Susan. "Margaret Fuller, an Engendered West, and *Summer on the Lakes*." *Western American Literature* 25, no. 2 (1990): 125–44.

Samuels, Shirley. *The Culture of Sentiment: Race, Gender, and Sentimentality in Nineteenth-Century America*. New York: Oxford Univ. Press, 1992.

Scacchi, Anna. "Margaret Fuller's Search for the Maternal." In Capper and Giorcelli, *Margaret Fuller: Transatlantic Crossings*, 66–96.

Scholl, Diane G. "Fallen Angels: Sophia Hawthorne's *Cuba Journal* as Pièce de Résistance." *Nathaniel Hawthorne Review* 35 (2009): 125–44.

Schöpp, Joseph C. "Playing the Eclectic: Margaret Fuller's Creative Appropriation of Goethe." In Capper and Giorcelli, *Margaret Fuller: Transatlantic Crossings*, 27–44.

Schweikart, Patrocinio. "Reading Ourselves: Toward a Feminist Theory of Reading." In *Gender and Reading*, ed. Elizabeth A. Flynn and Patrocinio P. Schweikart, 31–62. Baltimore: Johns Hopkins Univ. Press, 1986.

Shakir, Evelyn. "Ednah Dow Cheney: 'Jack at All trades.'" *ATQ* 47–48 (Summer–Fall 1980): 95–115.

Shealy, Daniel. *Alcott in Her Own Time: A Biographical Chronicle of Her Life, Drawn from Recollections, Interviews, and Memoirs*. Iowa City: Univ. of Iowa Press, 2005.

Showalter, Elaine. "Miranda and Cassandra: The Discourse of the Feminist Intellectual." In *Tradition and the Talents of Women*, ed. Florence Howe, 313–27. Urbana: Univ. of Illinois Press, 1991.

Sicherman, Barbara. *Well-Read Lives: How Books Inspired a Generation of American Women*. Chapel Hill: Univ. of North Carolina Press, 2010.

Simmons, Nancy Craig. "A Calendar of the Letters of Mary Moody Emerson." In *Studies in the American Renaissance 1993*, ed. Joel Myerson, 1–41. Charlottesville: Univ. Press of Virginia, 1993.

Smith, Susan Belasco. "*Summer on the Lakes*: Margaret Fuller and the British." *Resources for American Literary Study* 17, no. 2 (1991): 191–207.

Sotiropoulos, Carol Strauss. *Early Feminists and the Education Debates*. Madison, N.J.: Fairleigh Dickinson Univ. Press, 2007.

St. Armand, Barton Levi. "Veiled Ladies: Dickinson, Bettine, and Transcendental Mediumship." In *Studies in the American Renaissance 1987*, ed. Joel Myerson, 1–51. Charlottesville: Univ. Press of Virginia, 1987.

Steele, Jeffrey. "Editing Margaret Fuller's Poetry." In Fleishmann, *Margaret Fuller's Cultural Critique*, 265–74.

———. "Freeing the 'Prisoned Queen': The Development of Margaret Fuller's Poetry." In *Studies in the American Renaissance 1992*, ed. Joel Myerson, 137–75. Charlottesville: Univ. Press of Virginia, 1992.

———. "Keys to 'the Labyrinth of My Own Being': Margaret Fuller's Epistolary Invention of the Self." In Gaul and Harris, *Letters and Cultural Transformations*, 99–106.

———. "The Limits of Political Sympathy: Emerson, Margaret Fuller, and Woman's Rights." In Garvey, *Emerson Dilemma*, 115–35.

———. "The Lost Lady in the World of *Comus*: Catharine Maria Sedgwick and Margaret Fuller Read Milton." In Lueck, Bailey, and Damon-Bach, *Transatlantic Women*, 175–87.

———. *The Representation of the Self in the American Renaissance*. Chapel Hill: Univ. of North Carolina Press, 1987.

———. "Sympathy and Prophecy: The Two Faces of Social Justice in Fuller's New York Writing." In Bailey, Viens, and Wright, *Margaret Fuller and Her Circles*, 161–78.

———. "'A Tale of Mizraim': A Forgotten Story by Margaret Fuller." *New England Quarterly* 62, no. 1 (1989): 82–104.

———. *Transfiguring America: Myth, Ideology, and Mourning in Margaret Fuller's Writing*. Columbia: Univ. of Missouri Press, 2001.

Stefanelli, Maria Anita. "Margaret Fuller on the Stage." In Capper and Giorcelli, *Margaret Fuller: Transatlantic Crossings*, 221–37.

Stern, Julia. *The Plight of Feeling: Sympathy and Dissent in the Early American Novel*. Chicago: Univ. of Chicago Press, 1997.

Stern, Madeleine B. "Louisa Alcott's Feminist Letters." In *Studies in the American Renaissance 1978*, ed. Joel Myerson, 429–52. Boston: Twayne, 1978.

———. "Louisa Alcott's Self-Criticism." In *Studies in the American Renaissance 1985*, ed. Joel Myerson, 333–82. Charlottesville: Univ. Press of Virginia, 1985.

———. "Margaret Fuller and the Phrenologist-Publishers." In *Studies in the American Renaissance 1980*, ed. Joel Myerson, 229–37. Boston: Twayne, 1980.

Stern, Madeleine B., and Kent Bicknell. "Louisa May Alcott Had Her Head Examined." In *Studies in the American Renaissance 1995*, ed. Joel Myerson, 277–89. Charlottesville: Univ. Press of Virginia, 1995.

Stone, Susan M. "Transcendental Realism: Natural Environment and Social Reform from Ralph Waldo Emerson to Mary Wilkins Freeman." PhD diss., Univ. of South Carolina, 2001.

Tatlock, Lynne, and Matt Erlin. *German Culture in Nineteenth-Century America: Reception, Adaptation, Transformation*. Rochester, N.Y.: Camden House, 2005.

Thrailkill, Jane F. *Affecting Fictions: Mind, Body, and Emotion in American Literary Realism*. Cambridge, Mass.: Harvard Univ. Press, 2007.

Toegel, Edith. "Margaret Fuller, Bettina von Arnim, Karoline von Günderode: A Kinship of Souls." *Yearbook of German-American Studies* 23 (1988): 141–51.

Tompkins, Jane. *Sensational Designs: The Cultural Work of American Fiction, 1790–1860*. New York: Oxford Univ. Press, 1985.

Tonkovich, Nicole. *Domesticity with a Difference: The Nonfiction of Catharine Beecher, Sarah J. Hale, Fanny Fern, and Margaret Fuller*. Jackson: Univ. Press of Mississippi, 1997.

———. "Traveling in the West, Writing in the Library: Margaret Fuller's *Summer on the Lakes*." *Legacy* 10, no. 2 (1993): 79–102.

Tonn, Mari Boor. "*The Una*, 1853–1855: The Premiere of the Woman's Rights Press." In *A Voice of Their Own: The Woman Suffrage Press, 1840–1910*, ed. Martha Watson. Tuscaloosa: Univ. of Alabama Press, 1991.

Tuchinski, Adam-Max. "'More Anon': American Socialism and Margaret Fuller's 1848." In Bailey, Viens, and Wright, *Margaret Fuller and Her Circles*, 100–127.

Urbanski, Marie Mitchell Olesen. "The Genesis, Form, Tone, and Rhetorical Devices of *Woman in the Nineteenth Century*." In Myerson, *Critical Essays*, 268–80.

———, ed. *Margaret Fuller: Visionary of the New Age*. Orono, Me.: Northern Lights, 1994.

———. *Margaret Fuller's "Woman in the Nineteenth Century": A Literary Study of Form and Content, of Sources and Influence*. Westport, Conn.: Greenwood Press, 1980.

———. "The Seeress of Prevorst: The Central Jewel in *Summer on the Lakes*. In Urbanski, *Margaret Fuller: Visionary*, 142–58.

Valenti, Patricia Dunlavy. *Sophia Peabody Hawthorne: A Life*. Vol. 1, *1809–1847*. (Vol. 2 forthcoming.) Columbia: Univ. of Missouri Press, 2004.

———. "Sophia Peabody Hawthorne: A Study of Artistic Influence." In *Studies in the American Renaissance 1990*, ed. Joel Myerson, 1–21. Charlottesville: Univ. Press of Virginia, 1990.

Vasquez, Mark. "Declaration and Deference: Elizabeth Palmer Peabody, Mary Peabody Mann, and the Complex Rhetoric of Mediation." In Elbert, Hall, and Rodier, *Reinventing the Peabody Sisters*, 45–58.

Von Frank, Albert J. "Life as Art in America: The Case of Margaret Fuller." In *Studies in the American Renaissance 1981*, ed. Joel Myerson, 1–26. Boston: Twayne 1981.

———. "Margaret Fuller and Anti-Slavery: 'A Cause Identical.'" In Bailey, Viens, and Wright, *Margaret Fuller and Her Circles*, 128–47.

Von Frank, Albert J., and Jana Argersinger, eds. "Lydia Maria Child." Special issue, *ESQ: A Journal of the American Renaissance* 56 (2010).

———. "Reexamining the American Renaissance." Special issue, *ESQ: A Journal of the American Renaissance* 49 (2003).

Von Mehren, Joan. "Margaret Fuller: Woman of Letters." In Urbanski, *Margaret Fuller: Visionary*, 18–51.

———. "Margaret Fuller, the Marchese Giovanni Ossoli, and the Marriage Question." *Resources for American Literary Study* 30 (2005): 104–43.

———. *Minerva and the Muse: A Life of Margaret Fuller*. Amherst: Univ. of Massachusetts Press, 1995.

Warren, Joyce. *The American Narcissus: Individualism and Women in Nineteenth-Century American Fiction*. New Brunswick, N.J.: Rutgers Univ. Press, 1984.

Wayne, Tiffany K. *Encyclopedia of Transcendentalism: The Essential Guide to the Lives and Works of Transcendentalist Writers*. New York: Facts on File, 2006.

———. *Feminism and Transcendentalism in Nineteenth-Century America*. Lanham, Md.: Lexington Books, 2005.

Welter, Barbara. "The Cult of True Womanhood: 1820–1860." *American Quarterly* 18 (1966): 151–74.

Werner, Marta, and Nicholas Lawrence. "This Is His—This Is My Mystery: The Common Journal of Nathaniel and Sophia Hawthorne, 1842–43." In Elbert, Hall, and Rodier, *Reinventing the Peabody Sisters*, 3–22.

Wider, Sarah Ann. *Anna Tilden: Unitarian Culture and the Problem of Self-Representation*. Athens: Univ. of Georgia Press, 1997.

———. *The Critical Reception of Emerson: Unsettling All Things*. Rochester, N.Y.: Camden House, 2000.

Williams, David R. "The Wilderness Rapture of Mary Moody Emerson: One Calvinist Link to Transcendentalism." In *Studies in the American Renaissance 1986*, ed. Joel Myerson, 1–16. Charlottesville: Univ. Press of Virginia, 1986.

Williams, Gary. *Hungry Heart: The Literary Emergence of Julia Ward Howe*. Amherst: Univ. of Massachusetts Press, 1999.

Wilson, Leslie Perrin. "'No Worthless Books': Elizabeth Peabody's Foreign Library, 1840–52." *The Papers of the Bibliographical Society of America* 99 (2005): 113–52.

Wood, Mary E. "'With Ready Eye': Margaret Fuller and Lesbianism in Nineteenth-Century American Literature." *American Literature* 65, no. 1 (1993): 1–18.

Ziegler, Valarie H. *Diva Julia: The Public Romance and Private Agony of Julia Ward Howe*. New York: Continuum, 2003.

Zwarg, Christina. "Feminism in Translation: Margaret Fuller's Tasso." *Studies in Romanticism* 29, no. 3 (1990): 463–90.

———. *Feminist Conversations: Fuller, Emerson, and the Play of Reading*. Ithaca, N.Y.: Cornell Univ. Press, 1995.

———. "Footnoting the Sublime: Margaret Fuller on Black Hawk's Trail." *American Literary History* 5, no. 4 (1993): 616–42.

———. "Reading before Marx: Margaret Fuller and the *New York Daily Tribune*." In Machor, *Readers in History*, 228–58.

———. "Womanizing Margaret Fuller: Theorizing a Lover's Discourse." *Cultural Critique* 16 (1990): 161–91.

Contributors

KATHERINE ADAMS is Associate Professor of English at the University of South Carolina. She is the author of *Owning Up: Privacy, Property, and Belonging in U.S. Women's Life Writing* (Oxford Univ. Press, 2009) and editor of "U.S. Women Writing Race," a special issue of *Tulsa Studies in Women's Literature* (2010). Her current projects include a study of black racial formation and global cotton in the late nineteenth century and a coedited collection of essays on writer Alice Dunbar-Nelson.

JANA ARGERSINGER is an editor of *Poe Studies: History, Theory, Interpretation*, past president of the Council of Editors of Learned Journals, and coeditor of both *Hawthorne and Melville: Writing a Relationship* (Univ. of Georgia Press, 2008) and *Poe Writing/Writing Poe* (AMS, 2013). As an editor of *ESQ: A Journal of the American Renaissance*, she collaboratively developed thematic issues on such subjects as Margaret Fuller, the concept of the American Renaissance, and female transcendentalists—the latter of which grew into the present volume. She has published articles on nineteenth-century American literature, especially women writers, in such journals as *American Literature*, *Edgar Allan Poe Review*, *Documentary Editing*, and *Profession*. Her current work-in-progress explores relational aesthetics in the epistolary journals of the Peabody sisters.

NOELLE A. BAKER is editorial consultant for the Princeton edition of Henry D. Thoreau's *Writings*. Her publications have focused on transcendentalism; women's writing; and *The Almanacks of Mary Moody Emerson: A Scholarly Digital Edition*, which she is coediting with Sandra Harbert Petrulionis in collaboration with the Brown University Women Writers Project. Presently, she is at work on *Stanton in Her Own Time: A Biographical Chronicle of Her Life, Drawn from Recollections, Interviews, and Memoirs by Family, Friends, and Associates* (Univ. of Iowa Press, forthcoming).

DORRI BEAM is the author of *Style, Gender, and Fantasy in Nineteenth-Century American Women's Writing* (Cambridge Univ. Press, 2010), a literary archeology reconstructing the politics and aesthetics of "highly wrought" style in American romantic writing from the mid- to late nineteenth century. She has recently published essays in *American Literature's Aesthetic Dimensions* (Columbia Univ. Press, 2012), ed. Christopher Looby and Cindy Weinstein, and *Margaret Fuller and Her Circles*, ed. Brigitte Bailey and Conrad Wright (Univ. Press of New England, 2012). She is Associate Professor at Syracuse University.

PHYLLIS COLE is Professor of English, Women's Studies, and American Studies at Penn State Brandywine. As well as her book *Mary Moody Emerson and the Origins of Transcendentalism* (Oxford Univ. Press, 1998), she has published numerous essays on the crossings of nineteenth-century feminism and the transcendentalist movement. In the course of this work her productive conversations with Jana Argersinger led to the Exaltadas project, first as an *ESQ* special issue and now as a much larger essay collection, *Toward a Female Genealogy of Transcen-*

dentalism. She has served as president of the Ralph Waldo Emerson Society and in 2011 won its Distinguished Achievement Award; now she is first vice president of the Margaret Fuller Society. Her ongoing book project is titled *The Afterlife of Margaret Fuller*.

HELEN R. DEESE, Professor Emerita of English at Tennessee Tech University and Caroline Healey Dall editor for the Massachusetts Historical Society, is the author of numerous articles on the transcendentalist movement. She is the editor of *Jones Very: The Complete Poems* (Univ. of Georgia Press, 1993); *Daughter of Boston: The Extraordinary Diary of a Nineteenth-Century Woman, Caroline Healey Dall* (Beacon Press, 2005); and volumes 1 and 2 of *The Selected Journals of Caroline Healey Dall* (Massachusetts Historical Society, 2005, 2013). She lives in Ann Arbor, Michigan, where she is preparing volumes 3 and 4 of Dall's journals.

MARY DE JONG teaches English and Women's Studies at Penn State Altoona. Her research interests include Brook Farm, the correspondence of nineteenth-century women reformers, poet Frances Osgood (who published a lyric in *The Harbinger*), and nineteenth-century hymnody (the writing and performance of hymns). She is now exploring Caroline Healey Dall's relationship with Associationist and Christian Socialist Rebecca B. Spring, a friend of Margaret Fuller.

STERLING F. ("RICK") DELANO is Emeritus Professor of American Literature at Villanova University. He is the author of *Brook Farm: The Dark Side of Utopia* (Harvard Univ. Press, 2004); *The "Harbinger" and New England Transcendentalism* (Fairleigh Dickinson Univ. Press, 1984); and numerous articles about the transcendentalists and their world. From 2009 to 2013 he was director of the National Endowment for the Humanities–funded summer programs in Concord, Massachusetts, on "Transcendentalism and Social Action in the Age of Emerson, Thoreau, and Fuller."

MONIKA ELBERT is Professor of English and University Distinguished Scholar at Montclair State University, Montclair, New Jersey. She is editor of the *Nathaniel Hawthorne Review* and has published widely on nineteenth-century American literature and on gothic fiction. Her recent publications include several essays on Hawthorne; a coedited collection titled *Transnational Gothic: Literary and Social Exchanges in the Long Nineteenth Century* (Ashgate, 2013), which includes her essay on New England gothic women writers and Catholicism; and a coedited collection titled *Culinary Aesthetics and Practices in 19th-Century American Literature* (Palgrave Macmillan, 2009), which includes her essay on Hawthorne's food preferences and national loyalties in old and New England.

IVONNE M. GARCÍA is Associate Professor of English at Kenyon College in Ohio, where she teaches nineteenth-century American literature as well as Latino / a and postcolonial literatures. She has received the Board of Trustees Teaching Excellence Award and the one-year Whiting Teaching Fellowship for research. Most recently, Dr. García's essay "Transnational Crossings: Sophia Peabody Hawthorne's Authorial Persona from the 'Cuba Journal' to *Notes in England and Italy*" appeared in the *Nathaniel Hawthorne Review* and earned an award from that journal. Her book manuscript, titled "Haunted by Cuba: U.S. Imperialism, Slavery, and the American Colonial Gothic," is currently under consideration by a university press.

ERIC GARDNER is Professor of English and Associate Dean of Arts and Behavioral Sciences at Saginaw Valley State University. His *Unexpected Places: Relocating Nineteenth-Century African American Literature* (Univ. Press of Mississippi, 2009) won the Research Society for American Periodicals / EBSCOhost Book Prize and was a *Choice* "Outstanding Academic Title." With the support of a National Endowment for the Humanities Fellowship, he is completing a book on the *Christian Recorder*, official newspaper of the African Methodist Episcopal Church, during the Civil War era.

DANIEL S. MALACHUK, Associate Professor of English at Western Illinois University, is a recent fellow at the Notre Dame Institute for Advanced Study (2013) and a Fulbright Senior Lecturer at the University of Heidelberg (2014). Coeditor with Alan M. Levine of *A Political Companion to Ralph Waldo Emerson* (Univ. Press of Kentucky, 2011), he has lately published chapters in *The Blackwell Companion to George Eliot* (Blackwell, 2013) and *Emerson in Context* (Cambridge Univ. Press, 2013).

CAROL STRAUSS SOTIROPOULOS is Professor of German Studies in the Department of Modern Languages and Literatures at Northern Michigan University. She has written and presented widely on late-eighteenth- and early nineteenth-century documents pertaining to European women's education. Since the 2007 publication of her volume *Early Feminists and the Education Debates: England, France, Germany 1760–1810* (Fairleigh Dickinson Univ. Press), she has expanded her research to the American context and presented several papers on the impact of German romantic writers on women writers associated with the American transcendentalist movement.

JEFFREY STEELE is Professor of English at the University of Wisconsin–Madison. He is the author of *The Representation of the Self in the American Renaissance* (Univ. of North Carolina Press, 1987), *The Essential Margaret Fuller* (Rutgers Univ. Press, 1992), and *Transfiguring America: Myth, Ideology, and Mourning in Margaret Fuller's Writing* (Univ. of Missouri Press, 2001), as well as numerous essays on Margaret Fuller and other mid-nineteenth-century American writers. He is a past president and current executive officer of the Margaret Fuller Society. His current research considers the ways in which writers (including Fuller) in antebellum New York conceptualized a new American phenomenon—the metropolis.

SUSAN M. STONE is the Faculty Chairperson and an Associate Professor of English at Loras College in Dubuque, Iowa. A recipient of the Budde Award for excellence in teaching and the O'Connor Chair of Catholic Thought, she pursues research interests primarily in nineteenth-century American literature, feminism, and Native American studies. Selected publications include articles in *Studies in American Fiction*, the *Concord Saunterer*, and *The Dictionary of Literary Biography* as well as other reference texts.

LAURA DASSOW WALLS is the William P. and Hazel B. White Professor of English at the University of Notre Dame, where she teaches nineteenth century American literature. She has published widely on American transcendentalism, particularly Emerson and Thoreau. The research for her most recent book, *The Passage to Cosmos: Alexander von Humboldt and the Shaping of America* (Univ. of Chicago Press, 2009), led her to wonder about the German origins of Louisa May Alcott's character "Professor Bhaer."

SARAH ANN WIDER is Professor of English and Women's Studies at Colgate University, where she teaches courses in nineteenth-century American literature, women's biographical and autobiographical writings, and contemporary Native American literature. She is the author of *Anna Tilden, Unitarian Culture and the Problem of Self-Representation* (Univ. of Georgia Press, 1997) and *The Critical Reception of Emerson: Unsettling All Things* (Camden House, 2001). With Ronald A. Bosco, she is editing the extensive unpublished correspondence between Ralph Waldo Emerson and Caroline Sturgis. One of the founding members of the Emerson

Society, Wider served as its president from 2005 through 2006. Reflecting a long interest in a female genealogy of transcendentalism, her research addresses the multifaceted connections among the different generations of women who sparked this artistic, intellectual ferment.

GARY WILLIAMS is Professor of English at the University of Idaho. In the past two decades he has written extensively on Julia Ward Howe and is the editor of Howe's never-before-published novel titled *The Hermaphrodite* (Univ. of Nebraska Press, 2004), as well as coeditor of a recent collection of essays about this work, *Philosophies of Sex* (Ohio State Univ. Press, 2012). He was an inaugural College of Letters and Science Humanities Fellow at the University of Idaho and in 2007 was named the university's first Distinguished Humanities Professor.

Index